PERGAMON INTERNATIONAL LIBRARY
of Science, Technology, Engineering and Social Studies

The 1000-volume original paperback library in aid of education,
industrial training and the enjoyment of leisure

Publisher: Robert Maxwell, M.C.

P9-CSF-460

Human Aspects
of Urban Form

Towards a Man—Environment Approach
to Urban Form and Design

THE PERGAMON TEXTBOOK
INSPECTION COPY SERVICE

An inspection copy of any book published in the Pergamon International Library
will gladly be sent to academic staff without obligation for their consideration for
course adoption or recommendation. Copies may be retained for a period of 60 days
from receipt and returned if not suitable. When a particular title is adopted or
recommended for adoption for class use and the recommendation results in a sale
of 12 or more copies the inspection copy may be retained with our compliments.
The Publishers will be pleased to receive suggestions for revised editions and new
titles to be published in this important international Library.

THE URBAN AND REGIONAL PLANNING SERIES

For a complete list of titles and other titles of interest see the
end of this book.

Pergamon Urban and Regional Planning Advisory Committee

Human Aspects of Urban Form

Towards a Man—Environment Approach to Urban Form and Design

AMOS RAPOPORT

B.Arch., M.Arch., Dip.TRP, FRAIA, ARIBA

Professor of Architecture, and Anthropology
University of Wisconsin-Milwaukee

PERGAMON PRESS

Oxford . New York . Toronto . Sydney . Paris . Frankfurt

U.K.	Pergamon Press Ltd., Headington Hill Hall, Oxford OX3 0BW, England.
U.S.A.	Pergamon Press Inc., Maxwell House, Fairview Park, Elmsford, New York 10523, U.S.A.
CANADA	Pergamon of Canada Ltd., Suite 104, 150 Consumers Road, Willowdale, Ontario M2J 1P9, Canada.
AUSTRALIA	Pergamon Press (Aust.) Pty. Ltd., P.O. Box 544, Potts Point, N.S.W. 2011, Australia.
FRANCE	Pergamon Press SARL, 24 rue des Ecoles, 75240 Paris, Cedex 05, France.
FEDERAL REPUBLIC OF GERMANY	Pergamon Press GmbH, 6242 Kronberg/Taunus, Hammerweg 6, Federal Republic of Germany.

First Edition 1977
Reprinted 1980

Library of Congress Cataloging in Publication Data

Rapoport, Amos.

Human aspects of urban form.
(Urban and regional planning series; v. 15)
Bibliography: p.
1. Cities and towns — Planning — 1945 — I. Title.
II. Series.
HT166.R332   1977   309.2′62   76-26598

ISBN 0-08-017974-6 (Hard cover)
ISBN 0-08-024280-4 (Flexicover)

Printed in Great Britain by A. Wheaton & Co. Ltd, Exeter

Contents

Preface and Acknowledgements

I have been working continuously in the general area of Man—Environment Studies since 1967; it is, therefore, difficult to say when this book really began. Many of the themes here developed can be found in a different form in many of my articles. Some of the ideas which began to germinate in Berkeley were further developed in London, where I was helped by the stimulating milieu in which I found myself, and by small grants from the RIBA and the University of London.

Actual writing began and the early, and hence crucial, drafts were completed while I was at the University of Sydney. There I benefited from small, regular grants from the University between 1969 and 1972 and tested some of the developing ideas in courses.

On arrival at the University of Wisconsin-Milwaukee, where the final version was completed, I was also able to base several graduate seminars on the developing text, which helped greatly. I benefited from a summer grant from the Graduate School in 1973 and continued without support during 1974. The award of a three-year Research Professorship starting in 1974—75 enabled me to take off a semester, obtain typing assistance, and complete the manuscript by the end of 1975.

I am also grateful to my wife and son who had to put up with long periods when I was quite unapproachable.

Introduction

The city has been an object of curiosity for a very long time. Many ways of conceptualizing it have been proposed and it has been analyzed and described as a social system, an economic system, in political terms; it has been seen as a work of art, an instrument of communication, an historical artefact, and there have been correspondingly many approaches to its planning and design.

In recent years a new field of studies has emerged, most commonly called Man—Environment Studies, which is concerned with the systematic study of the mutual interaction of people and their built environment. This discipline differs from traditional design in stressing man, including his social and psychological environment and in being systematic. While basing its knowledge of people on the findings and approaches of a number of social and behavioural sciences, it differs from them by its stress on the physical environment which, by and large, these disciplines have neglected. In being concerned with what to design and why, with arriving at human criteria for design based on an understanding of man—environment interaction, one is dealing with some specific aspect of three general questions:

(1) How do people shape their environment — which characteristics of people, as individuals or groups of different sizes are relevant to the shaping of particular environments?
(2) How and to what extent does the physical environment affect people, i.e., how important is the designed environment and in which contexts?
(3) What are the mechanisms which link people and environments in this two-way interaction?

Several years ago it would have been necessary to go into a great deal of detail about the field generally. Now, however, a brief summary of the specific formulation of it adopted here should be sufficient.

Given that any specific question in the field can be seen as forming part of the above three basic questions, a discussion of some aspects of man—environment studies can, therefore, begin most usefully with a somewhat more detailed discussion of these questions.

1. The first question is concerned with the characteristics of people — as members of a species, as individuals and as members of various social groups — which affect (or, from the designers' point of view, *should* affect) the way in which built environments are shaped.

Ideally this should involve a consideration of constancy and variability, i.e., the existence and nature of species — specific behavior, tendencies and predispositions. In turn this raises questions about the potential importance of knowledge about the evolutionary background of man, both the physical and social environments within which

1

he evolved, in providing a baseline. This would provide ranges and set certain limits on the ways in which environments can best respond to human needs and ways in which certain activities or thought processes lead to specific environmental solutions.

In the case of individuals the primary concern is with people's sensory capacities, the ways in which they, as active users and explorers of the environment, perceive it through the senses and give it meaning. Since, however, the ways in which environments are used, the ways in which they are understood and interpreted, and even which sensory modalities are stressed, are all affected by membership in particular groups people must inevitably be considered as members of such groups with particular values, beliefs and ways of understanding the world.

In addition, of course, people's membership in small groups, families, large social groupings and institutions, subcultures and cultures affects their roles, the ways in which they communicate, the relative importance and ways of handling social networks, kinship systems, values and the many other group characteristics of humans. These influence the form of the environment — and might, in turn, be affected by it.

2. This last point forms the subject of the second major question. It is essential to know what are the effects of the built environment on human behavior, mood or well-being. If there are no effects, or if these effects are minor, then the importance of studying man—environment interaction is correspondingly diminished. It is also an extremely difficult question to answer since the evidence is often difficult to compare, is contradictory and there is no consensus or generally accepted theoretical position. What follows is a summary version of a particular theoretical formulation.

The question of what effect the physical environment has on people has received attention in cultural geography and in environmental design research. The experience in geography, even though it deals with a different set of variables at a different scale, offers a useful parallel to developments in the design field. Briefly, there seem to have been three attitudes in geography.

(a) *Environmental determinism* — the view that the physical environment determines human behaviour.

(b) *Possibilism* — the view that the physical environment provides possibilities and constraints within which people make choices based on other, mainly cultural, criteria.

(c) *Probabilism* — the current view that the physical environment does, in fact, provide possibilities for choice and is not determining, but that some choices are more probable than others in given physical settings.

In planning and design environmental determinism has been the traditional view — the belief that changes in the form of cities and buildings can lead to major change in behaviour, increased happiness, increased social interaction and so on. As a reaction, much as in geography, the view was put forward that the built environment has no major effects on people and that it is the social, economic and other similar environments which are of major importance.

The current view is that the built environment can be seen as a setting for human activities. Such settings may be inhibiting or facilitating and a particular setting may be facilitating to the extent of acting as a catalyst or releasing latent behavior but cannot, however, determine or *generate* activities. (While this distinction may be difficult to determine by observation, theoretically it seems very important). Similarly, inhibiting environments will generally make certain behaviors more difficult, but will not usually block them completely, although it is easier to block behavior than to generate it. Moreover, while it is generally (although not universally) accepted that the built environment has important, although not determining, effects the inhibiting effects may, under conditions of reduced competence or environmental docility (e.g., the elderly, the ill, children) become much more acute and may, in fact, become critical.

This reduced competence may be cultural as well as physical, so that groups undergoing very rapid change or groups whose culture is "marginal" may be affected critically by inappropriate forms of the built environment — those, for example, which prevent or destroy particular forms of family organization, prevent the formation of homogeneous groups for mutual help, disrupt social networks or certain institutions, prevent certain ritual or economic activities and so on. All cases of reduced competence or environmental docility, physical, mental or cultural, seem to have a common factor — reduced ability to cope with high levels of stress so that the *additional* stress of overcoming inhibiting environments may become too great. A complicating factor is that the effects of adaptation in terms of stress are frequently remote in space and time from the initial occurrence and hence difficult to trace. Under those conditions supportive or prosthetic environments may be necessary.

It should be stressed that environmental effects are mediated by "filters", i.e., they are part of the perceived environment and involve expectations, motivations, judgements and symbolic meanings. Notions of environmental quality, standards and the like are also variable so that the definition of a slum, the evaluation of a squatter settlement, the meaning of privacy or density are all fairly complex issues.

The fact that people act and behave differently in different settings suggests another important point, which is that people act appropriately in different settings because they make congruent their behavior with the norms for behavior appropriate to the setting as defined by the culture. This implies that the built environment provides *cues for behavior* and that the environment can, therefore, be seen as a form of *non-verbal communication*. Using the distinction between fixed feature space (walls, doors, etc.), semi-fixed feature space (furniture, furnishings, etc.) and non-fixed feature elements (Hall 1966) — people and their dress, gestures, facial expression, proxemic relationships, posture and so on (which are the traditional subject of non-verbal communication studies) it is possible to fit them all into a single model.

People then act according to their reading of the environmental cues and thus the "language" must be understood. If the design of the environment is seen as a process of encoding information, then the users can be seen as decoding it. If the code is not shared, not understood or inappropriate, the environment does not communicate.

Using this approach it is possible to distinguish between direct and indirect effects of the environment. The former are those where the environment directly affects behavior, mood, satisfaction, performance or interaction. The latter are those where the environment is used to draw conclusions about the social standing or status of its occupants and behavior modified accordingly.

In this discussion, as typically in most discussion on this topic, there is an implicit assumption that somehow people are placed in environments which then act on them. Yet in most cases people select their habitat, resulting in various forms of migration —

international, interregional, interurban, down to the selection of neighborhood, house and furniture. In effect people vote with their feet and a major effect of environment on people is a positive or negative attraction — *habitat selection*.

In some cases habitat selection is blocked by poverty, infirmity or discrimination and this becomes a major environmental problem. In cases of forced habitation (of which institutionalization is an extreme example) the environment becomes more critical and those are precisely the conditions of environmental docility already mentioned which also operate at the cultural level. In such cases the survival of cultures may be linked with the form of housing and settlements so that the built environment may become critical and almost negatively determining.

3. The third major question is, in a sense, a corollary question. If there is a mutual interaction between people and environments, then there must be some mechanisms which link them. Several have already been mentioned — the environment as a form of non-verbal communication, i.e., a code decoded by users; the environment as a symbol system; perception (through the various senses) and cognition (giving meaning to the environment by naming, classification and ordering) seem to be other important mechanisms. In the case of several of these the environment is, then, closely linked to culture and a number of aspects of man—environment interaction and design can be seen in terms of congruence, whereby people try to match their characteristics, values, expectations and norms, behaviors and so on to physical environments — through design or migration.

People in the city are a special case of people in the environment generally, hence this book is concerned with man—environment interaction in urban settings and will provide a broad conceptual framework using a range of disciplines. There is thus a need to bridge many arbitrarily defined boundaries separating fields which, at least potentially, can contribute to an understanding of the way cities are organized, how people see them and use them and how cities should be organized. Some of the disciplines involved, even when they have considered the environment have done so abstractly, in ways unrelated to the city as a setting for life, as experienced, known and evaluated by people. Very rarely have the social and behavioral disciplines been concerned with the actual three-dimensional space at the smaller scale at which people actually experience and use cities. This has been the concern of the design professions. They, however, have been action-oriented rather than academic and have therefore been less influenced by new insights from other fields and have not developed a theoretical base. When not normative, they have been descriptive rather than analytical. Finally, neither the social sciences nor the design professions have approached the subject using examples from different cultures.

I will try to apply findings about the way in which people perceive the city, structure it mentally, what effects given forms have on people, the role of images, how important cities are for human behavior or satisfaction, or how people actually experience the city to urban design. There are human characteristics which should be congruent with certain physical characteristics of the designed environment. These characteristics, of individuals and groups, are both universal — common to people as organisms and members of a species — and also culturally variable. Thus, while it is important to avoid over-generalizations (specially when based on *a priori* assumptions) and to deal with the variability of both physical and social environments, it is also important to remember that underlying this variability there may be much more invariant processual principles of the ways in which people interact with their urban environment.

In addition to being interested in the interplay of constant and variable factors and their expression in urban space, we are also concerned with the way given urban configurations fit psychological, cultural and social needs of people. Whatever the development of the city in the future, it is my contention that some principles based on the constancy of human characteristics will need to be considered since these constancies underly the cultural and subcultural variability which I will be stressing, so that evidence of certain long-standing patterns of human behavior may lead to the rejection of certain current theories about the future city, the variety of which is staggering. Many findings now exist from ethology, psychology, social psychology, sociology, anthropology, geography and man—environment studies which throw light on man—environment interaction generally and within the urban setting specifically. Nor do these findings exist in isolation — they interact mutually and begin to form a synthesis. These interconnections are not always apparent since the material is scattered in a wide variety of journals, books and symposia and are widely varied in nature, concepts, methodology and orientations. By relating them to one problem area, we might see to what extent they are mutually illuminating or contradictory and take a first step towards creating a conceptual framework for looking at the built environment at the urban scale.

This book does not report any original empirical findings. Rather, a wide range of man—environment data is considered, a number of major concepts selected and pulled together, applied to the urban setting and their relevance to an understanding of urban form considered. This relevance is of two kinds. The first is analytical, where the theory and data lead to a greater understanding of the form of cities, their parts and their congruence with people. The second are design applications where there may be specific suggestions about the planning and design of urban elements and systems. This book thus has three functions — to review the data, to synthesize the data, and to test the relevance of this data to the analysis and design of urban form.

Important questions to be tackled include how cities really are experienced and comprehended by their users, the effects of values, images and schemata — and human behavior — on the shaping of urban form; the link between the physical form of the environment and the way in which people live in, and use, cities, the insights to be gained by broadening the sample so as to include vernacular urban design as well as grand design and to consider traditions other than the Western, and to look at more than one country.

The goal is one often stated — to design a city for people, but the underlying notion is that there are a number of new organizing concepts starting to emerge from man—environment studies which can clarify problems such as the meaning of city centres and neighborhood, density, privacy, "slum", the relation of physical form and social interaction, location and use (or non-use) of facilities, standards and the meaning of environmental quality and the like. In urban design and planning, as in design at other scales, the need is for clear and explicit objectives based on real knowledge. These objectives are not only needed for design decisions to be made, but in order to evaluate the success of decisions made. In fact the absence of evaluation, and hence a cumulative body of knowledge about buildings and cities, has been a major weakness of the design endeavor. In this book we will be concerned with the kinds of data and approaches which are needed to lead to reasonable objectives for design. Although much of this data is not yet really operational, it seems most important for designers to become aware of this point of view and current state of the art. Such knowledge will inevitably change their perceptions and approach to cities and urban design.

It may also be useful to state what this book is not. It does not deal with social planning, with political process, with matters of policy, with economic matters or even with formal design. Yet in stressing socio-cultural, psychological and similar aspects of the city I do not deny any other criteria. This book is meant to supplement those others and be complementary to many other urban design and planning books.

Neither does this book attempt to evaluate the relative importance of various sets of criteria in the planning and design process — important though such an evaluation would be. It tries to provide a framework for understanding the city in terms of man—city interaction and is thus neither a review of the literature (in spite of the large number of references) nor a manual of urban design or site-planning.

My concern, then, is with urban form in terms of psychological, behavioral, socio-cultural and similar criteria. The stress is on urban design rather than planning — although the distinction has never been very clear. I will assume that this distinction is partly a matter of scale, planning being concerned with larger units, so that we are dealing with parts of cities. Secondly, I will assume that urban design deals with the nature of urban elements and their relationships as experienced and understood while planning deals more with locational and policy decisions. My purpose is to propose an approach giving the evidence available. It is not proposed to give simple answers, nor is it a finished or complete conceptual framework — it is a contribution towards a theory of the what and why of people in the city. I will stress the physical, experiential and design aspects of the material. While it is now accepted that one cannot design a *whole* city (although one can organize or structure it) it is arguably still possible to design areas within a city for specific groups of users.

We are interested in the human actors and will view the city from the perspective of individuals, of small and large groups, and will try to derive empirically and theoretically valid statements about them. We are interested in how people experience cities, give meaning to what they perceive, how they understand the city and organize it conceptually, how they give identity to environmental elements, how they classify elements and how they behave as a result of this, how designed environments reflect ideal images and how they affect behavior, how choices are made and on what basis.

The approach is thus ego-centered, dealing with the individual's and the group's experience of the physical and socio-cultural environment, the starting point being the experienced world of the individual and his interpretations, and groups seen as collections of individuals with common social, cultural and psychological characteristics and needs which should be reflected in, and should correspond to, appropriate elements in the physical environment. Such sub-areas of the city can then be related to those various characteristics and various unifying concepts can link these apparently different groups and places providing structuring elements for the city as a whole.

Chapter 1 introduces many of the concepts which are later elaborated and provides a framework for later chapters. After discussing urban design as the organization of space, time, meaning and communication, it considers the nature of the environment, cultural differences, role of values and the concept of environmental perception as it is currently used. Some difficulties with this current usage are raised and three different terms are proposed — these being evaluation, cognition and perception. The concept of image and schema is introduced as a broad, organizing concept linking many findings.

In the following three chapters the three meanings of "perception" are then discussed in turn — the notion of environmental quality and preference as a variable concept, and its constituent parts; various aspects of environmental cognition and its relation to design; finally, perception proper and various aspects of it. Hence, the sequence perception-cognition-evaluation (leading to action) is discussed in *reverse order*. We then turn to social, cultural and ethological concepts which complement those already discussed and clarify the nature of urban space organization, following which symbolism, in the broad sense, is discussed as a factor in the communicative function of the urban environment and the cross-cultural implications of this are evaluated.

Finally, the need for people's involvement in the environment and the relationship of activity and form is examined and notion of open-ended design introduced.

A large, yet still highly selective, bibliography (seen as a very important part of the book) follows. The literature in the field is growing rapidly. It was thus decided arbitrarily to make a cutoff point of approximately the end of 1972 for literature to be cited with some carefully selected exceptions. This is partly due to the fact that between the time the second draft of this book was completed (in July 1972) and subsequent work on drafts three and four (in 1973, 1974 and 1975) several hundred new items were consulted but did not alter any of the conclusions — rather they provided additional evidence for points already made.

CHAPTER 1

Urban Design as the Organization of Space, Time, Meaning and Communication

Since the urban environment is a special case of the environment generally it is useful to begin by considering this latter term. At its broadest the environment can be defined as any condition or influence outside the organism, group, or whatever system is being studied. While recent ecological thinking stresses the need to consider the organism *in* environment rather than organism *and* environment, it is customary to distinguish the surrounding environs in this way. Of a number of recent conceptualizations, several seem useful. One describes the environment as an ecological system with seven components (Ittelson 1960):

(1) *Perceptual* — the ways in which individuals experience the world, which is a principal mechanism linking people and environment.
(2) *Expressive* — which concerns the effect on people of shapes, colors, textures, smells, sounds and symbolic meanings.
(3) The domain of *aesthetic values* of culture and, I would add, the whole area of values.
(4) *Adaptive* — the extent to which the environment helps or hinders activities.
(5) *Integrative* — the kinds of social groupings which are facilitated or inhibited by the surroundings.
(6) *Instrumental* — which refers to the tools and facilities provided by the environment.
(7) The *general ecological interrelationship* of all these components.

A different formulation, Lawton (1970), describes the environment as an ecological system having five components:

(1) The *individual*.
(2) The *physical environment*, including all natural features of geography, climate, and man-made features which limit and facilitate behavior, and the "resources" of the environment.
(3) The *personal environment*, including individuals who are important sources of behavior control — family, friends, authority figures, peer-group members and so on.
(4) The *suprapersonal environment* which refers to the environmental characteristics resulting from the inhabitants' modal personal characteristics due to grouping by age, class, ethnic origin, lifestyle or other specific characteristics.
(5) The *social environment* consisting of social norms and institutions.

These, and other models proposed, have two things in common. Firstly, they suggest a multiplicity of environments — social, cultural and physical. Secondly, they imply a link between changes in the physical environment (which the designer manipulates) and which provides a setting for people and changes in other areas — psychological, social and the like.

The environment is a series of relationships among elements and people and these relationships are orderly — they have pattern. The environment has a structure and is not a random assemblage of things. It both reflects and facilitates relations and transactions between people and the physical elements of the world. These relationships in the physical environment are primarily *spatial* — basically objects and people are related through separation in and by space.

Even animal societies are non-randomly distributed in space due to an interaction between the physical and social environment (McBride 1964, 1970; Wynne-Edwards 1962). Among people psychological, social and cultural characteristics are often expressed in spatial terms as, for example, the separation of various homogeneous groups in cities. Among both people and animals grouping is a spatial as well as a social concept implying that members within a group are separated by smaller physical and social distances than they are from members of other groups.

Space is experienced as the three-dimensional extension of the world which is around us — the intervals, relationships and distances between people and people, people and things and things and things, and space is at the heart of the built environment. Spatial organization is, in fact, a more fundamental aspect of the designed environment than shape, materials and the like.

For example, consider a village with dwellings surrounding a central space (as in the Eastern highlands of New Guinea or thirteenth-century Germany. (Fig 1.1(a))). The shape and materials of the houses and even the shape of the central space might be changed without basically changing the nature of the organization (Fig 1.1(b)). However, by arranging the traditional houses along streets, a fundamentally different settlement results (Fig. 1.1(c)). Or consider a city based on courtyards or compounds — what I call

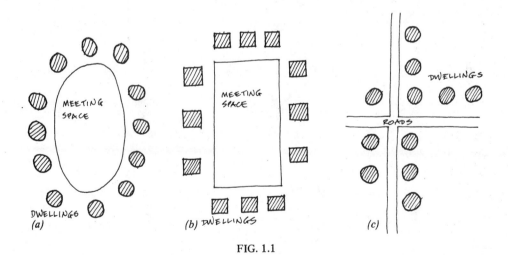

FIG. 1.1

the "inside-out city" (such as a Moslem, Yoruba, Latin American or Japanese city). This is ·fundamentally different to cities where houses face, and are related to, streets, whatever the materials or forms of the houses. (see Fig 1.2).

This difference reflects a division into domains of private and public which is my last example. Consider a clear division into private and public domains with a controlling

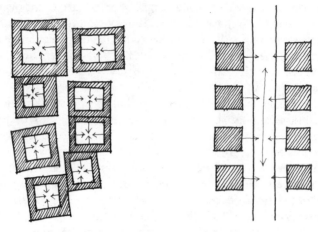

FIG. 1.2

"lock" of some sort (Fig 1.3(a)). Changes in the shape of the domains and the materials used to construct them is less fundamental than a change in the relationship into one with a permeable boundary and no lock (Fig 1.3(b)).

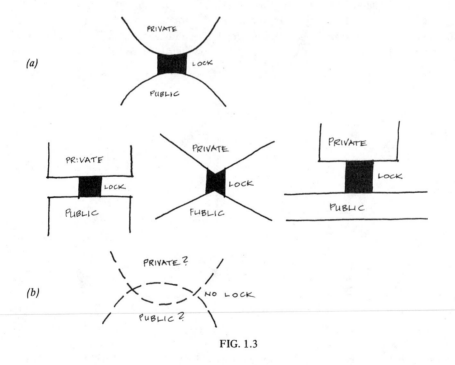

FIG. 1.3

One can, in fact, see design and planning, from the landscape of a region to the furniture arrangement of a room as the *organization of space* for different purposes and according to different rules which reflect the needs, values and desires of the groups or individuals designing the space and represent the congruence (or lack of it) between social and physical space. This is not to deny the importance of the shape, proportions and sensory quality of spaces and their enclosing elements, as well as their symbolic meaning, but these all occur within a spatial framework of the type I have just described and space organization is hence the key element and the most useful for comparing environments and studying the rules of their organization.

A good example of continuity in space organization at several scales which constitutes an essential characteristic of the place is San Cristobal las Casas, Mexico (Wood 1969). The dwelling consists of rooms divided along personal and functional grounds arranged around a rectangular, neutral courtyard. At the next level of the barrio (neighborhood) the same pattern is found — a number of elements (houses) divided along personal and functional lines arranged around a plaza. Finally, the town as a whole consists of a number of barrios, of differing character and personality, clustered around the main plaza. It is within this spatial framework that other environmental characteristics and all human activities occur.

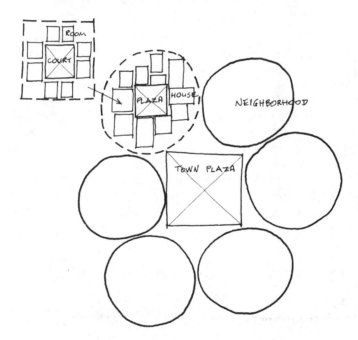

FIG. 1.4. Organization of San Cristobal Las Casas, Mexico (diagrammatic) (based on Wood 1969).

The built environment does, of course, have other properties. For example, it is also, and importantly, the *organization of meaning* and in this connection materials, forms and details become important. While space organization does express meaning and has communicative and symbolic properties, meaning is frequently expressed through signs, materials, colors, forms, landscaping and the like — i.e., through the eikonic aspects of the built environment. Thus meaning may coincide with space organization or may represent a separate, non-coinciding, symbolic system (Venturi *et al.* 1972) through which different settings become indicators of social position and a way of asserting social identity to oneself and others (Duncan 1973). This means, of course, that physical elements in the environment take on varying meanings and their influence and importance, and their effect on behavior, change accordingly (Royse 1969; Rapoport 1975(a)).

The environment is also temporal and it can be seen as the *organization of time* (or, at least, as reflecting and affecting the organization of time). This may be understood in two ways. The first refers to large-scale cognitive structuring of time such as linear flow vs. cyclic time, future orientation vs. past orientation, how time is valued and, hence, how it is subdivided into units and so on. The second refers to the tempos and rhythms of human activities and their congruence or incongruence with each other. Thus people may be separated in time as well as, or instead of, by space, so that groups with different rhythms occupying the same space may never meet. Clearly spatial and temporal aspects interact and influence one another (and one should probably speak of space-time).

The spatial characteristics of the built environment also greatly influence and reflect the *organization of communication*. Thus who communicates with whom, under what conditions, how, then, where and in which context is one important way in which the built environment and social organization are linked and related. In the case of urban environments this can also be understood in two ways — as being concerned with movement and communication systems or with human communication face to face. These are, of course, related and the built environment and its organization can be seen as a way of controlling interaction — its nature, direction, rate and so on.

There is a slight semantic problem here. The organization of meaning is an aspect of non-verbal communication and "communication" is thus used in two different ways — communication by the environment and among people in the environment — but so far I have not found any better terms.

Clearly these four aspects of the built environment interact so that, for example, communication among people is affected by the meanings which various parts of the environment have for them; space organization is related to time and communication and so on. This formulation, however, is useful for analyzing man-environment interaction.

The Meaning of Space

While space is a very important aspect of the environment, it is not a simple or unitary concept (Rapoport 1970(b)). Space is more than three-dimensional physical space. At different times and in different contexts one is, in effect, dealing with different "kinds" of space and their congruence is an important design issue. Even neglecting a whole set of spatial meanings which one might call ethological space (home range, core area, territory and so on which will be discussed later) it is easy, without trying to be exhaustive, to list many meanings of the term.

The most basic distinction is between human and non-human space (the womb or interior of an atomic pile). All space with which designers are concerned is basically human although there is a difference between an Athenian Plateia and a freeway at rush hour. We can then distinguish between designed and non-designed space — designed meaning ordered according to some rules, and reflecting some ideal environment (however dimly). Two alternative rule systems illustrate two other kinds of space — the abstract geometric space of the U.S. midwest, and sacred space which is made distinct from profane space, using some cosmic model or prototype to make it habitable (Eliade 1961; Littlejohn 1967; Rapoport 1969(a), (d), (f)). Many traditional settlements and houses can only be understood in these terms as can many cities in high cultures such as China, India, and others (Wheatley 1971; Rykwert, n.d.; Müller 1961).

Both the above spatial categories represent symbolic space. In fact, abstract geometric space is symbolic of nineteenth-century America in the same way that sacred space is of the ancient Chinese city. Space for Australian aborigines is symbolic without being physically demarcated (Rapoport 1972(e)) so that in order to understand spatial symbolism we must look at it in terms of the people concerned since, except for those who understand the symbolism, such space may be indistinguishable from other forms of space although its meaning or evaluation may be quite different. Currently symbolic space may be a high status urban area or a development with a wall or a lake (Rapoport 1969(f)). In a larger context symbolic space may be a category of meaningful space (Barthes 1970–71).

One can then speak of behavioral space or action space (Brown and Moore 1971) which is related to movement space (Hurst 1971) — space used by given individuals or groups. The behavioral spaces of different groups (age, sex, ethnic or racial) may be very different from the total urban space shown on a map (Haynes 1969; Tibbet 1971; Porteous 1971). This is equivalent to suggesting (Sonnenfeld in Saarinen 1969, p.6) that within the physical or geographical environment there is an operational environment within which people work and which affects them. Within that is the perceptual environment of which people are conscious directly and to which they give symbolic meaning and within that is the behavioral environment of which people are not only aware but which also elicits some behavioral response.

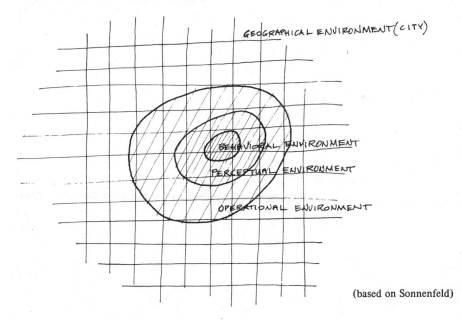

(based on Sonnenfeld)

FIG. 1.5.

This space, actually used by social groups and reflecting their behavior patterns and perceptions, can also be called social space, a concept prominent in French urban geography and sociology (de Lauwe 1965(a); Buttimer 1971, 1972; Murdie 1971). While social space occurs in physical space, it is distinct from it and the congruence between the two is important. Social space has often been studied in terms of what might be called abstract analytic space — that of urban ecology, area analysis and the like (Bourne 1971; Roggemans 1971; Timms 1971; Johnston 1971(a)) athough, once again, underlying this — and all others — is actual, three-dimensional space.

Behavior space is related to subjective space, which is distinct from "objective" space and is a special case of psychological space, another aspect of which is experiential or sensory space which may be visual, acoustic, olfactory, thermal or whatever and there may be cultural differences in the type of modality stressed (Wober 1966).

Behavioral and psychological spaces are also related to cultural space defined by various groups in terms of varying categories, taxonomies or domains (Rapoport 1972(b); Rapoport, 1976), one example of which is the difference in the way designers and non-designers define space, while another is imaginary space which is only imaginary to an observer from another culture because it affects the behavior of people who hold it (Watson 1969; K. Thompson 1969; Heathcote 1965, 1972; Burch 1971).

Other categorizations have been proposed (Gould 1972(a); Craik 1970; Norberg-Schultz 1971; Cox 1968, Skolimowski 1969; Ehrenzweig 1970) but the complexity of the concept should be clear. Different groups build up a perceived spatial environment which contains elements of many of these, their specific mix or flavor leading to specific cultural characteristics.

Rules of Organization

The rules which guide the organization of space, time, meaning and communication show regularity because they are linked systematically to culture. Without trying to define culture (Kroeber and Kluckhohn 1952) one can say that it is about a group of people who share a set of values, beliefs, a world view and symbol system which are learned and transmitted. These create a system of rules and habits which reflect ideals and create a lifestyle, guiding behavior, roles, manners, the food eaten — as well as built form. There tend to be greater similarities within cultures than among them*. The regularities within cultures relate lifestyle and built environment and also lead to continuity across scales.

In the case of the built environment these rules affect the separation of objects and people according to various criteria — age, sex, status, roles or whatever. What distinguishes one environment from another is the nature of the rules embodied or encoded in it. "Unplanned", organic or disorderly environments can be understood as resulting from a set of rules different to those of the planning/design subculture, as can the views of French observers that the American city lacks structure, or American views that Islamic cities have no form.

Similarly the view that the U.S. West had no plan (Doxiadis 1968(b), p. 224) means that the rule system is considered strange. Clearly the organization of the U.S. West had a set of rules and an underlying philosophy — stressing growth and process, open-endedness, infinite extendibility, easy transfer of land (viewed as a commodity) and a specific relationship between public and private. In effect one can suggest that the organization of

---

* At this point I will not discuss the extent to which cultural variability is limited by certain regularities and constancies of people as a species. From the designer's point of view the differences are precisely what is important (Rapoport 1969(a), 1973(e)).

the environment is a mental act before it is a physical one, as I have tried to show regarding Australian Aborigines (Rapoport 1972(e)).

Given that urban design is the organization of space, time, meaning and communication, one is then more concerned with the relationships among elements and the underlying rules than with the elements themselves (Rapoport 1969(e)). One can argue that the physical components of all cities are the same — houses, streets, gathering places, cult buildings, plants and so on. It is the nature of the meaning and underlying principles of their organization and relationships which differ, as well as the associated behaviors, and these need to be analyzed so that generalizations and comparisons may be made.

The Choice Model of Design

The organization of the environment is, therefore, the result of the application of sets of rules which reflect differing concepts of environmental quality. Design can hence be seen as an attempt to give form of expression to some image of an ideal environment, to make actual and ideal environments congruent. This involves ideas of environmental quality which are extremely complex and variable and cannot be assumed *a priori* but need to be discovered (Rapoport 1969(a), (c), 1970(b), 1971(b)). In other words depending on the meaning of "good" environment, the images which a people has about the good life and the appropriate setting for it, one would expect to find a variety of places designed always directed towards the making of better places through the application of sets of rules based on definitions of environmental quality.

Any artefact, whether environment or pot (Deetz 1968) is the result of a series of choices among various alternatives. All man-made environments are designed in the same sense that they embody human decisions and choices and specific ways of resolving the many conflicts implicit in all decision-making. Since there are few places left on earth which man has not altered in some way (Thomas 1956) we could say that much of the earth, and certainly all cities, are designed. This is a much broader definition of design than is common but essential if our concern is with all that has been built. Designed environments obviously include places where man has cleared or planted forests, diverted rivers or fenced fields in certain patterns, laid out roads and lined them with diners and second-hand car lots. The work of a tribesman laying out a camp or a village is as much an act of urban design as a new town or pedestrian mall. In fact, the many apparently mundane activities just described are the most important in their impact on the built environment since the way cities, regions and whole countries look depends on the decisions of many individuals and groups both in the past and at present.

What all this activity has in common is that it represents a choice among many alternatives. The specific nature of the choices made tend to be lawful, to reflect sets of rules, so that one way of looking at culture is in terms of the most common choices made. It is the lawfulness of choices which makes landscapes different, which enables us to tell whether a city is Italian, Peruvian, English or American — i.e., faced with the question of why environments are so different, a reasonable answer seems to be that since every group has many alternatives they tend to select different ones. This consistent system of choices also affects many aspects of human behavior and symbolic meaning — the way people interact, their proxemic distances, how they structure space, whether they use streets for interaction and so on.

In fact what is commonly called style can be defined as a system of consistent choices based on the rules and culture of a group (whether tribe or profession). Design can then be seen as *choice process*, or a process of elimination, from among a set of alternatives (however such alternatives are generated in the first place). Both the generation and elimination of alternatives is based on the application of certain criteria which may be explicit, but are commonly implicit and unstated, so that many alternatives are never considered at all being, as it were, eliminated through major cultural constraints; they never form part of the initial set, so that its shape and size are affected. This is more

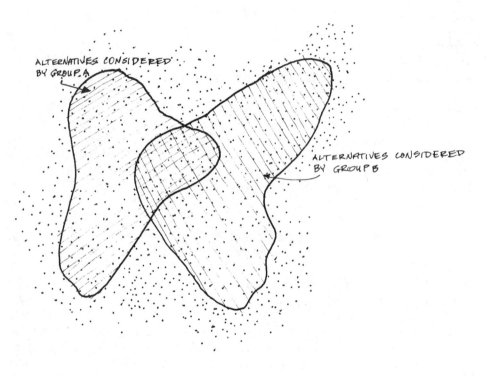

ALTERNATIVES CONSIDERED BY GROUP A

ALTERNATIVES CONSIDERED BY GROUP B

FIG. 1.6

obvious in primitive and vernacular situations, so that in a traditional Moslem city outward facing houses would never be considered; in a traditional Mexican city plazas would always be used. However, this also operates today. For example designers would never consider using a park for car-parking whereas city councillors or parking lot operators well might (Rapoport 1969(c)). In traditional situations, moreover, there are fewer choices due to both cultural and physical constraints (Rapoport 1969(a)) whereas today there is an excess of choice and the development of man—environment studies can be seen as an attempt to provide more valid and humane choice criteria. In either case, the successive application of certain criteria eliminates alternatives until one is left, so that this choice model of design can be represented diagrammatically as follows.

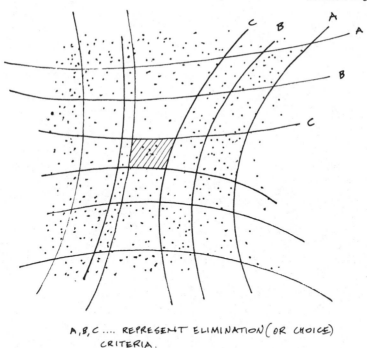

A,B,C .... REPRESENT ELIMINATION (OR CHOICE) CRITERIA.

FIG. 1.7

This model thus links all design in terms of *how* it takes place while allowing for, and stressing, the differences in the underlying choice criteria. The question then becomes how, and for what reasons, choices are made, and criteria based. An important reason is to achieve congruence with some ideal so as to maximize a set of ranked values and this also occurs in habitat selection (migration) which can be seen as a form of environmental response.

Different forms of design, e.g., high style and vernacular, can be distinguished by the criteria used (Rapoport 1969(a), 1973(a)) and also the degree of sharing of such beliefs, the congruence of designers' and users' criteria and values. In primitive and vernacular design the image is clear and shared, and the matching is relatively straightforward. Currently there is a multiplicity of relatively idiosyncratic images which are thus unshared, sometimes antagonistic and the matching process is much more difficult and mismatches rather frequent.

The types of criteria applied affect the outcome by eliminating different alternative i.e., making different choices and one function of man—environment research is to provide valid criteria, based on a knowledge of human characteristics to supplement economic, technological and others. (See Fig. 1.8).

The kinds of criteria developed by man—environment research are particularly important in the case of cities because they are used by a very wide range of people, have a large time and space scale and there is a great separation of designer and user. Some of these problems may be handled by open-ended design or user involvement but norms are still needed, because there are many things users cannot do at the urban scale, because

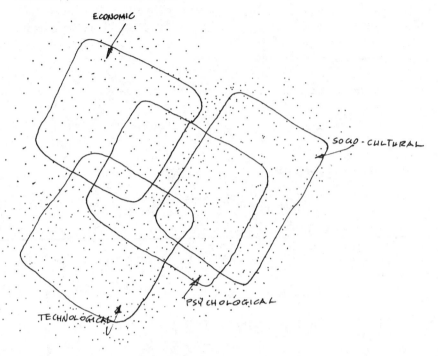

ECONOMIC

SOCIO-CULTURAL

PSYCHOLOGICAL

TECHNOLOGICAL

FIG. 1.8

designers need to deal with the joints between areas and organize the overall structure and, finally, because designers need to know the relative importance of elements to various groups.

Clearly these criteria embody the values and norms of different groups. Not only do various groups of users differ, but so do designers and users. In the case of the latter we find very different ways of seeing problems, very different definitions of space and what it means and very different preferences (Rapoport 1968; Lansing and Marans 1969; Michelson 1968; Eichler and Kaplan 1967; Hartman 1963).

As one example, in Elizabeth New Town (S.A.) (Australian Frontier 1971) a serious mismatch was found between teenagers' preferences for leisure activities and provision for them.

Activities	Preference	Provision	
Socializing (meeting informally, dances, parties, mass trips, coffee lounges, discotheques, etc.)	1	4	main mismatch
Semi-socializing activities (social but more formal and organized).	2	2	match
Sporting	3	1	major mismatch
Specialized (Hobbies, arts and crafts etc.)	4	3	mismatch

This has also been found in connection with children's play (Bishop, Peterson and Michaels 1972; Gold 1972; Rapoport 1969(b); D.O.E. 1973) and many other activities, and in our later discussion it will be found that these mismatches are not just due to values but also a matter of different images and cognitive styles so that people make sense of their surroundings by classifying them into certain categories with attached meanings and expected behaviors, and match these against schemata and expectations. This means that behavior and activities cannot be taken at face value (Rapoport 1969(c)).

Consider activities. These, and activity systems (in space and time) have been very important in planning and design yet even at the level of so-called basic needs they seem extremely variable. The following schema can be suggested:

Any activity can be analyzed into four components, which are:

(1) The activity proper – eating, shopping, drinking, walking.
(2) The specific way of doing it – shopping in a bazaar, drinking in a bar, walking in the street, sitting on the floor, eating with other men.
(3) Additional, adjacent or associated activities which become part of an activity system – exchanging gossip while shopping, courting while strolling.
(4) Symbolic aspects of the activity – shopping as conspicuous consumption, cooking as ritual, a way of establishing social identity.

Consider shopping which is the exchange of money (or goods) for goods; the specific way of shopping may vary, with major implications for the design of the setting – supermarket or bazaar – and its relationship to the city, as well as sensory interaction with both goods and people in the various sense modalities. The total activity system will be affected by the associated activities, if any, and whether it is talking, eating, socializing, getting messages to people, finding out about what goes on and so on (de Lauwe 1965(a), Jacobs 1961; Hoffman and Fishman 1971; Rapoport 1969(a); Rapoport 1965). Finally the symbolic function may be display, conspicuous consumption, shopping as recreation or a way for women to get out of the house. An understanding of this total system is then necessary in order properly to design and plan for it. Similar arguments could be made about drinking alcoholic beverages, cooking and many other activities.

It is the difference between these four aspects of apparently simple activities which lead to specific forms of settings, differences in their relative importance, the amount of time spent in them, who is involved and so on – in fact all the kinds of things which affect built form.

This schema goes beyond the distinction recently proposed between manifest and latent function in the built environment (Zeisel 1969; for a different view see Frankenberg 1967, pp. 255 ff) although, in effect, (1) and (2) above are mainly manifest while (3) and (4) fit into the latent category, but it is the variability of (2), (3) and (4) which leads to differences in form and the differential success of various designs. In fact, acceptability and choice (including habitat selection) would appear to be most related to (3) and (4) which are also the most variable and the most likely to be embodied in images.

The typology suggested above is related in an interesting way to the hierarchy of levels of meaning ranging from the concrete object through use object, value object to symbolic object (Gibson 1950, 1968; Rapoport and Hawkes 1970; Rapoport 1970(c)). There also the variability increases as one moves to the symbolic end of the scale – more people will agree about what they actually see than about how to use it, fewer will agree about its value and fewest about its symbolic aspects (although, in at least one case, more agreement was found about aesthetic quality than about use (Coughlin and Goldstein 1971)). The value and symbolic end of the scale seems most related to environmental choices, so that in both cases the latent and symbolic aspects seem the more important.

This is a reflection of culture, values, world view, etc. embodied in *lifestyle* which may be a key element in understanding how cities operate and how people make choices and behave in them (Michelson and Reed 1970; Michelson 1966; Feldman and Tilly 1960). Activities, as described above, may help in understanding lifestyle and through it more global concepts such as value, world view and culture — and how they interact with the built environment (Rapoport 1973(a), in press(a)).

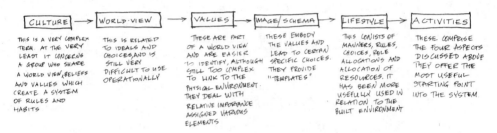

FIG. 1.9

Life style may prove to be one of the main variables influencing the organization of the city through specific ways in which areas are organized, in space, time, meaning and communication, by the clustering of people homogeneous along various characteristics — race, ethnic origin, religion, class, income or whatever variables have operated at specific times, so that the city is a collection of different groups, with different lifestyles reflecting different cultures and subcultures. We shall see that this is a long-standing (historically) and widespread (cross-culturally) pattern which may modify arbitrary arguments against clustering (Sennett 1970) or policies to achieve heterogeneity.

This means that places in the city, belonging to different groups, have meaning, they symbolize and indicate status and social identity — they are not a locus for manifest activity only. In architecture this leads to the distinction between a kitchen for cooking versus that same kitchen as a symbolic place and indicator of status, a living room as a place to "live" as opposed to that same room as a "sacred space", a window for light and air (and, in some cultures, view) as opposed to its use as a means of communicating with other people in the street and in other dwellings (Zeisel 1969). In an urban context it leads to the distinction between a lawn as open space and an indicator of status, a house as shelter and symbol of social identity, a street as space to be traversed or space in which to live (Rapoport 1969(a)).

For example urban parks provide for leisure activities. The specific activities will vary with culture but still represent manifest functions. If we then see parks not being used we may conclude that they are failing in their purpose (Gold 1972) yet they may have a latent function of indicating status and value of an area, or symbolically indicating that an area is not crowded and not deteriorating (Carson 1972). In that case the latent function of the park may, in fact, be valid even if the park does not seem to be "used" in the manifest sense of people walking in it, playing in it and so on.

Cultural Variability of Urban Environments

While all urban settings have organization — of space, time, meaning and communication — the principles of this organization differ so that while U.S. cities maximize movement and accessibility, traditional Moslem cities limit movement and control behavior by controlling mobility (Brown 1973). (see Fig. 1.10). Even whole land-

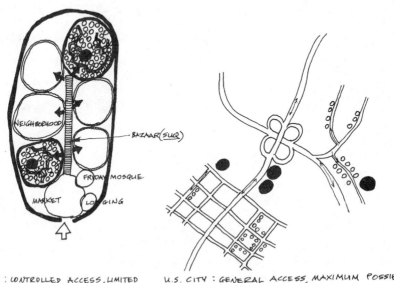

MOSLEM CITY : CONTROLLED ACCESS, LIMITED
   MOBILITY. ACCESSIBLE AREAS : MARKET, SUQ,
FRIDAY MOSQUE, LODGING.
(BASED ON BROWN 1973; DELAVAL 1974)

U.S. CITY : GENERAL ACCESS, MAXIMUM POSSIBLE
   MOBILITY. ACCESSIBLE AREAS : ALMOST
   EVERYTHING.

FIG. 1.10

scapes, resulting from the decisions of innumerable people, reflect certain organizational principles, some vision of reality (Jackson 1951; Rapoport 1969(a)). Migrants select areas similar to those from which they come and attempt to transform them further (Eidt 1971; Heathcote 1972; Stewart 1965; Shepard 1969). This is related to environmental perception and the role of schemata (Gombrich 1961; Smith 1960) but in any case, if the system is known one can often tell at a glance where a given landscape is, and why it is the way it is (Lowenthal 1968; Lowenthal and Prince 1964, 1965).

In the case of cities the difficulty of defining what *is* a city (Wheatley 1971; Krapf-Askari 1969) is related to the use of different schemata and it is easy to show differences in the way cities are structured (Larimore 1958; Stanislawski 1950; Caplow 1961(a), (b)).

These differences — in location, definition of domains (King 1970, 1974(a), (b)), the meanings given various elements (Duncan 1973; Royse 1969) are all due to varying perceptions, cognition and evaluation of environmental quality, images, values and many socio-cultural variables all of which need to be understood before differences in spatial organization can be fully understood.

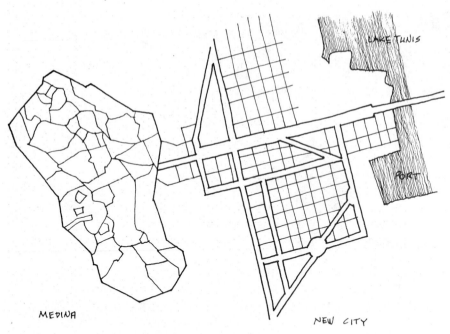

MEDINA   NEW CITY

THE COLONIAL CITY IN NORTH AFRICA (TUNIS)
    SHOWING CONTRAST BETWEEN INDIGENEOUS
    AND NEW CITIES.
    (DIAGRAMMATIC: ROAD PATTERNS APPROXIMATE ONLY)   (AFTER BROWN 1973)

FIG. 1.11. The Colonial City in North Africa (Tunis) showing contrast between indigenous and
new cities (diagrammatic: road patterns approximate only) (after Brown 1973).

It should be reiterated that this applies equally to the organization of meaning, communication and time. Regarding the latter, for example, the rhythms, time distributions and values attached to time vary greatly in different cultures (Fraser *et al.* 1972; Doob 1971; Yaker *et al.* 1971; Parkes 1972, 1973). Even the definition of obligatory vs. discretionary activities (Chapin 1968, 1971; Brail and Chapin 1973) may be variable, with many obligatory ones becoming discretionary and vice versa, as well as occupying very different amounts of time.

These differences are important because they have been neglected in most discussions of urban form and urban design, which have been based on the high style tradition only, and the Western city, along with a consequent tendency to overgeneralize "human needs". It seems important to redress the balance by considering other kinds of examples also.

Generalizations based on U.S. data may not apply elsewhere, Western theory may not apply in non-Western contexts. On the other hand very different expressions may have underlying regularities at a higher level of generalization. For example, the English townscape group (Cullen 1961; Nairn 1955, 1956; Worskett 1969, de Wofle 1971) make generalized statements about urban design which may not be universal with regard to users (Lansing and Marans 1969; Jackson 1964). Yet their arguments can be seen as a specific expression of a general principle, a liking for complexity, which may take on other expressions also. The use of a large and varied sample may show regularities which allow valid generalizations. These may be hypotheses of the form; for behavior A (U,W,V) environmental characteristics X, Y, Z are needed. This would be significant if found to occur widely over space and time and also means, of course, that both physical form and behaviors must be studied.

One example is the criticism of homogeneous clustering (e.g., Sennett 1970). Taking the above approach it is found that some form of such clustering is very prevalent (Michelson 1966, 1970; Murdie 1971; Epstein 1969; Timms 1971; Frolic 1971). Detailed examples and reasons for this will be discussed later. At this point it is enough to point out that there may be good reasons for it, and that it has implications for urban form and design. A similar argument applies to the separation of public and private domains (Sennett 1970, pp. 48, 53 ff). The argument against such separation is not based on a broad enough sample. But even for Chicago itself the analysis is not based on sufficiently fine distinctions, so that even a very small area there can be shown to be a complex organization of private and public domains as well as group clustering (Suttles 1968). Once the sample is extended to Moslem, Japanese, Latin American or African cities the argument becomes even more suspect.

In such cities (the "inside-out" city) there is a clear separation of public and private. In the case of the Japanese city very different behavior is expected in public and private areas and they are treated very differently (Meyerson 1963; Rapoport 1969(f)). At the same time the Japanese city is characterized by a lack of public open space so that shopping centers and amusement areas are used instead. This is very different to Western cities (Rapoport 1969(a); Maki 1973) and affects the city at both the micro-and macro-scale. It also contrasts with the ancient Greek city where the public domain was the most important. In a more contemporary situation consider the distinction between the definition and use of public and private by working class and middle class Americans (Hartman 1963; Fried 1973; Gans 1971) and, more generally, the different use of urban space by different groups, which introduces the concept of the house settlement system (to be discussed later). The use of urban space is a function of this system, of the way the house and parts of settlements are used together for various activities (Rapoport 1969(a), 1972(b)).

The ways in which whole cities are structured vary, as is the case with Japanese and Western cities. In the past cities have also used very different cosmic symbolism (Rykwert, n.d.; Wheatley 1969, 1971; Müller 1961; Lang 1952; Rapoport 1969(f); Tuan 1974). It also follows that very different hierarchies are found among urban elements in different cultures so that such hierarchies differ in U.S., European and Asian cities, and they have also varied over time.

Sub-urban units, with which we are mainly concerned, are likely to show more regularities transculturally than larger urban forms, since they are linked more intimately to some basic human characteristics. Thus the interplay of constancy and change is likely to vary with scale, and it is my hypothesis that there is more constancy at smaller than at larger scales — the metropolis is more variable than the neighborhood. Hence more can be learned by analyzing smaller-scale units historically and cross-culturally.

Human characteristics and activities themselves comprise constant and variable elements. Within future technologies present behavior will not change radically but will be modified in ways similar to current culturally variable expressions. The city can thus be seen as an expression of certain constant factors in variable terms.

The Role of Values in Design

It follows from the above that the values and rule systems of different groups help understand the urban forms which their choices produce. Values thus affect the definition of problems, the data used and the solutions proposed (Rapoport 1967(a), 1969(c), 1969(f)). In that sense planning and urban design reflect the values of the people involved — whether these be professionals or not. At the same time a caution is in order. The relationship between values and physical form is difficult to trace, particularly in modern cities where values are rarely consensual and it is difficult to use values predictively and "unrealistic to anticipate a one-to-one correspondence between values and behavior" (Timms 1971, p. 94; see also Tuan 1968(a)) which is similar to the difficulty of relating concepts such as culture or subculture, world view (W. Jones 1972) or lifestyle to environment. But such relationships exist (Jackson 1966(a)).

With regard to planning the pro- or anti-urban bias of particular peoples or professional groups would clearly make a major difference to approaches to urban problems — particularly if these biases were unarticulated and beyond awareness. In English and American planning the anti-urban motif has been pervasive (White and White 1962; Glass 1955; Howe 1971) and has affected specific attitudes to issues such as density. In India also this anti-urban and pro-village bias is very strong (Tagore 1928) and has had effects on planning, design and the nature of cities to this day (Sopher 1964).

After World War II cities in West Germany were reconstructed very differently than in other parts of Europe. This was due to a clear preference for retaining traditional forms and the presence of specific values regarding small shops, housing preferences, modes of transport and so on (Holzner 1970(a)).

It is important to bear in mind that planners/designers and the public represent very different value systems (Coing 1966; Fried 1963, 1973; de Lauwe 1965(a), (b); Pahl 1971). Similarly planners in different cultures have different values and major differences are found between English and American planning philosophy (Bunker 1971) and, in turn, a difference between Anglo-American and French planning and urban sociology (Rapoport 1969(c)). Within the profession itself the ideology changes with time so that a content analysis of an American planning journal from 1950 to 1965 at five-year intervals reveals major shifts in values with stress on communication, form, economics or social planning (Quick 1966). Finally, in Britain one finds three planning ideologies — the planner as umpire or judge, the planner as promoting a better life by improving the physical environment, and the planner aiding community life by designing cities which embody values such as small, low density communities, the preservation of picturesque streetscapes and tidy, orderly settings (Pahl 1971, pp. 129—130).

Turning to urban design, consider the differences between the visions of the city by Yona Friedman, Michael Ragon or Le Corbusier in France; the English townscape group (Cullen, Nairn, de Wofle, Thomas Sharpe) and so on. There are clearly aesthetic and social values operating, embodied in images which become particularly clear if we look at the recent Civilia proposals (de Wofle 1971) where the whole design of the city is in terms of images, which reflect a clear value system, and play a normative role.

Zoning and the spacing of buildings has been shown to reflect aesthetic bias (Crane 1960) and one could argue that the freestanding building, and destruction of the street in modern cities, are related to values and imagery, a refusal to accept the distinction between the important domains of "front" and "back".

The general point is that values embodied in the different image one holds of what a city should be will lead to different cities (e.g., Elmer and Sutherland 1971). The problem lies not in this, but in the fact that designers' values have not been made explicit and that the images and values of non-designers rarely considered. As a final example consider attitudes the very different evaluations of Los Angeles (Banham 1971) and the critics whom he cites (Von Hoffman 1965), the American landscape and roadside strip (Jackson 1964; Nairn 1965) or Las Vagas (Venturi *et al.* 1972) vs. almost any other designers.

The discussion in this section suggests that how things are seen is terribly important and introduces the notions of the perceived environment, filters and images to which we now turn.

Environmental Perception

If one accepts the choice model of design with its goal of achieving some ideal, and given the resulting cultural differences in environmental organization, it would follow that environmental quality most also be a variable concept. This leads to the notion that in design, action proceeds through the perception of environmental problems, opportunities and ideals to solutions (and their acceptance or rejection through matching against some ideal or schema) — i.e., one is led to the concept of *environmental perception*.

Avoiding the obvious philosophical problems, one is concerned with how the environment is apprehended and how this known environment relates to the "real" environment. An important question is whether situations are perceived in the same way by different groups. In terms of cognitive anthropology we are dealing with the distinction between *emic* aspects (how things look within a system) and *etic* ones — the way an outside observer evaluates the same events.

I suggested above that certain possible solutions are eliminated without being considered. In effect they are not part of the perceived environment of that particular decisionmaker. The criteria used also reflect perceived opportunities and costs. It is this which makes this concept of interest in planning, geography, social science and man—environment studies.

Much of this work initially came from geography because of its concern with how people make decisions affecting the earth. Thus the concept of the perception of opportunities, hazards and resources came to play an important role. Consider a band of Australian Aborigines camped on top of a seam of minerals. This seam — or even the concept of minerals as such — is not part of their perceived environment. Even in more technologically advanced societies the interpretation of natural resources is variable and dependent, at least in part, on attitudes and values. Resources are seen and evaluated differently, "resources are not; they become" (Hewitt and Hare 1973, p. 29; see also Spoehr 1956) and even visible urban elements may not form part of the perceived environment (Rapoport 1970(c)).

Various landscapes, such as mountains and wilderness were seen very differently at different times (Prince 1971; Nicolson 1959; Lucas 1970). These changes and the distinction between urban and rural (i.e., the definition of cities) are all aspects of the perceived environment seen most broadly. Assuming that leisure and recreation will become more important as design criteria, then it is clearly *perceived* leisure and recreation which become important in design (e.g., Christy 1971). Places will be very different if leisure is spent mostly in the dwelling and its immediate surroundings, in art, education or spectator sports, since this will affect the facilities needed, transportation, the meaning which elements have and so on.

From the psychological point of view we are discussing the definition of stimulus situations and their properties (Sherif and Sherif 1963, p. 82) and there is evidence that this definition applies to many environmental characteristics (Rapoport and Watson 1972). Given the various conceptualizations of the environment, the perceived environment will include perception of both people and their artefacts. The regularities in the environment are then due not just to their design but also the perception of the observers who impose order on the environment.

The physical environment in itself, particularly through meanings attached to it, may affect people's perception of environmental quality and the good life (Sherif and Sherif 1963, pp. 92—93) so that, in a way, this becomes a self-perpetuating system. People act in certain ways shaping their environment which then becomes a socializing medium giving children ideas about what are proper environments and affecting their perception of environments generally and the people with which they are associated; also important are the environmental elements seen and read about in mass media, books and advertising.

Given evidence for the relativism of absolute judgements with regard to satisfaction (Partucci 1968) it seems likely that if the context and other variables affect satisfaction, then the same environment may be evaluated quite differently depending on how it is perceived. This is indeed the case as when elderly and non-elderly residents of the same housing areas perceive them as too private and not private enough (D.O.E. 1972; Architectural Research Unit 1966), when different meanings are attached to the environment (Duncan 1973) and when changing perceptions change attitudes to slums and squatter settlements.

This approach also suggests that there are many factors which enter into the evaluation and definition of a situation as it is perceived (Blumer 1969(a)). This seems to apply to both people and events (Warr and Knapper 1968) suggesting that the perceptions of physical and social environments have common characteristics. Such perception is affected not only by culture and previous experience but by expectations which these generate and the consequent mental set which may affect how various specific objects (for example, money, food or front lawns) are perceived. For example, arctic workers starved for company perceive people very differently than if satiated (Warr and Knapper 1968, pp. 38—39) which is also the reason for the difference between the elderly and others cited above. An environmental example is the importance attached to greenery and water in Moslem cultures or front lawns in the U.S. or the different evaluation of places depending on background (Wohlwill and Kohn 1973) which is related to adaptation.

Thus the individual and the environment form a system and their mutual interaction is partly determined by the physical environment and other people or, more correctly, the individual's perception and interpretation of them and their significance. Environmental perception thus involves the present stimulus information, present context information as well as stored stimulus information; also acting are the perceiver's current and stable characteristics (Warr and Knapper 1968) and previous experience, as well as hopes, ambitions, fears, values and various other "real" and "imagined" elements.

The designer can obviously do more about current stimulus information than about stored information (although at the group level he can *allow* for it). He can also consider the perceiver's stable characteristics but not his current state which is much more variable, although it may be partly predictable given certain settings, roles and the like. In any case, to consider environmental perception means having to include these kinds of variables.

Environmental perception is important because it introduces variability (cultural and personal) and modifies the notion of a single environment with invariant properties. Once it is accepted that the user's perceived environment and its positive and negative qualities may be different to the planner's or designer's, and that different groups of users may have different perceived environments, then one's approach to understanding the city and the criteria used for design must be different. As we shall see, there is much evidence for this proposition, and the concept of environmental perception helps to relate all this evidence.

It is an approach which initially makes matters much more difficult since "separate personal worlds of experience, learning and imagination necessarily underlie any universe of discourse" (Lowenthal 1961, p. 248) but one which cannot be ignored or avoided. Thus a study of an Australian suburb points out that "it is daunting to see the variety of opinions that physically similar houses and surroundings stimulate; can these people really be speaking of the same place?" (Bryson and Thompson 1972, p. 130). Yet, clearly, to design effectively this must be taken into account. Consider our discussion of activities (or function) which showed that far from being simple or universal they are rather complex.

Given the notion of environmental perception, the distinction between manifest and latent functions is to be expected. Furthermore, the greater importance of the symbolic aspects of latent function also follows since it seems that we tend to symbolize environmental stimuli and react to the symbols (Dubos and others cited in Rapoport and Watson 1972). Consider shopping where the latent functions may be very different, and these specific latent functions may be very different in various cultures. For example where bargaining plays a major role an apparently "efficient" way of transacting business may not work — shopping as an activity or function is perceived very differently in the two cases, so that in Paris, for example, these non-manifest functions, such as socializing or information are the more important (de Lauwe 1965(a); Coing 1966) as they can be for Puerto Ricans in New York (Hoffman and Fishman 1971) or in the West End of Boston, which will greatly influence the character of the shops and their location relative to other activities (Brolin and Zeisel 1968). These considerations have often been neglected in planning as when the important role of the mobile shops was neglected in the designs of Chandigarh (Prakash 1972) although the social function of shops in India is quite crucial. Similarly in Mexico, travelling vendors at markets have an important function of passing essential information. When, in the interest of hygiene and prices, the market was replaced by permanent shops, the vendors no longer came and the social system was disrupted; a combination of shops and market met both goals*.

The prestige and symbolism of various areas and urban elements, their relative importance and how they are used are much more variable than the relatively limited and similar, although still variable, manifest activities and functions, these differences are a consequence of the perceived meanings of these functions and the perceived congruence with appropriate settings for them.

The concept of environmental perception helps explain how a few basic activities, or

* Personal communication from Mr. Michel A. Antochiw, of AURIS, State of Mexico, July 1973.

climatic types, can result in a large variety of responses and settings, since solutions are a consequence of perceptions. There may also be settings where latent functions are more significant than in others (Frankenberg 1967, p. 257). While environmental perception has been shown to be important in various fields, I would suggest that in design it is even more important because of its lower criticality (Rapoport 1969(a)), so that environments can be shaped with greater freedom than is the case with, say, economic decisions. In design, therefore, the environmental perception of various groups become even more important.

Thus people perceive problems and possible solutions in different ways; they define "basic needs" differently and give them different priorities; they define standards (space, "slum" or comfort) and also ideal environments differently; they give different meaning to concepts such as density or privacy, and also define domains such as front/back or neighborhood differently. The perceived environment and the schemata in which it is embodied are therefore at the heart of design decisions, since any designer perceives the environment, evaluates it and makes choices so that there is a link between environmental perception and behavior (e.g., R. King 1971(a)).

Any attempt to deal with the man—environment interaction must involve three areas — knowing something, feeling something about it and then doing something about it. We are thus concerned with three broad areas:

(1) Cognitive — involving perceiving, knowing and thinking, the basic processes whereby the individual knows his environment.
(2) Affective — involving feelings and emotions about this environment, motivations, desires and values (embodied in images).
(3) Conative — involving acting, doing, striving and thus having an effect on the environment in response to (1) and (2).

Learning also plays a role since all these change with experience.

Environmental perception thus seems central and can help clarify many aspects of man—environment interaction. For example, health has recently been defined not as a state of physical vigor and wellbeing, or even long life, but rather as the condition best suited to reach the goals which each individual formulates for himself (Boyden 1970, p. 134). This could be described, in our terms, as perceived good health and has obvious implications for planning standards many of which have attempted to provide a setting for a healthy life (Jackson 1966(b)).

Environmental perception includes the particular mix of attitudes, motivations and values of various groups which influence their perceptions of the environment and also affect their actions, which respond to perceptions of external stimuli (Downs 1968; English and Mayfield 1972; Linge 1971, pp. 31–32; Lowenthal 1961; Saarinen 1969; Wood 1970). These decisions may or may not be valid depending on the accuracy of the perceptions and there are real-world consequences which prevent the model being totally solipsistic. Also, in spite of variability there must be considerable correspondence between different people's, perceptions and reality — or humanity would not have survived (Sprout and Sprout 1956, p. 61).

The Perceived Environment

In the previous section the terms environmental perception and perceived environment were used interchangeably. However, the process of environmental perception seems distinct from the product — which is the perceived environment. While environmental perception is a property of the mind the environment as perceived is a construct which includes "the whole monistic surface on which decisions are based including natural and non-natural, visible and non-visible, geographical, political, economic and sociological elements" (Brookfield 1969, p. 53). Thus the common *process* of environmental perception, of selecting relevant "facts" from the real or behavioral environment and structuring them may lead to different constructs constituting the environment in which the organism operates.

Important here are possible implications of the proposed distinction. One important consequence is that decisions are made within the perceived environment and at least some of the conflicts and difficulties in urban planning and design can then be seen as being due to the different actors in the decision-making process operating within very different perceived environments. Another important thing about the perceived environment is that it can be conceived as a construct in people's minds based on what is known, expected, imagined or experienced and such constructs, often embodied in images and schemata, can be mistaken or "unreal" yet still affect behavior. This helps explain the action of "imaginary" environments (Watson 1969; Thompson 1969; Heathcote 1965; Burch 1971) as well as the differential use of recreational resources such as beaches (Mercer 1972) where, for example, it may be *perceived* pollution which affects use (M. Barker 1968).

The operational value of the concept has been questioned, given the difficulty of dealing with it (Brookfield 1969). There is also the dilemma that if designers and respondents to a survey have different perceived environments then the answers cannot provide anything relevant to design (Ravetz 1971). In spite of these criticisms the concept is heuristically useful because it helps to understand cultural differences in environments, particularly if one takes the view that the designed environment reflects some "ideal" or imagined environment (Langer 1953; Eliade 1961; Rapoport 1972(e)).

Later, we shall discuss how people structure the world conceptually. One view is that people construct systems for handling the world — they form hypotheses based on past experience, knowledge and expectations and predict the future accordingly. These constructs vary among people who do not react to stimuli but what they expect stimuli to be (Kelly 1955) and can be seen as part of the perceived environment as well as being given physical expression in built environments.

The perceived environment can also be linked to concepts such as Lewin's (1951) life space, von Uexküll's (1957) *Umwelt* and Tolman's (1948) behavior space. It clearly relates to our previous discussion about the definition of stimuli and their symbolization and subsumes concepts such as movement space, action space and the like. In effect we can say that the perceived environment constitutes people's action space since what is not known — or acknowledged — cannot provide opportunities for action. Hence the major gaps in people's perceived environments which are reflected in their mental maps.

For example, people may be unaware of problem areas so that when visiting Lima in 1964, it seemed that many inhabitants were not aware of the Barriadas, which did not form part of their perceived environment; in fact upper and middle class Limenos are largely unaware of soccer grounds which are most important to other groups (Doughty 1970, pp. 33, 38). This is because the whole area of which they form part is outside the perceived environment of the better established, more cosmopolitan inhabitants. It is also likely that now people have been made aware of the Barriadas which have become part of their environment — even if they have never actually been there, or do not know the details. More generally, as we shall see later, the perceived environment and behavioral space are a result of defining given areas as useable, safe and so on.

The Excessively Broad Meaning of "Perception" in the Literature

The term "perception" is used in the environmental design literature differently to the way in which it is used in psychology — it seems to be used in the sense of how things are "seen". For example, it is used to describe how social change is seen (H-B. Lee 1968, p. 434) or in the sense of the perception of possibilities, resources or hazards (Burton 1972; Burton and Kates 1972; Kates 1962; Saarinen 1966; Kates, Burton *et al.* ongoing). It has been used to describe the perception of the mutuality of interests among various groups of actors in the design process. In political science it has been used to study how people see the world and to trace the major differences between the views of the public and academics (Robinson and Hefner 1968). Yet classifying countries as similar or dissimilar, and evaluating them, is a cognitive and evaluative process and the result is not really a perceptual but a cognitive map or, more correctly, a display of evaluative rankings.

I suggested above that the perceived environment is a construct based on what is expected and known as well as what is experienced and that a perceived ideal environment is somehow involved in design. These are widely different uses. The experience of existing environments through the senses, comprehending them through what is known and expected, evaluating them in terms of values, ideals etc. and imagining and creating ideal environments are very different kinds of activities and processes. In fact there seem to be at least three distinct major uses of the term "perception" and to use it for three such different processes leads to confusion.

There is, firstly, the obvious and traditionally discussed way in which people perceive the environment through the senses. More recently people have also increasingly come to know the environment through information which is not experiential, so that there are changes in their knowledge due to messages provided by the media and other information systems. In the past also hearsay information was available, legends and myths proliferated and had behavioral consequences (e.g., Burch 1971), but today very much more is known about many more places than in the past. Finally, both experienced and indirectly known environments are evaluated as good or bad, desirable or undesirable.

The use of "perception" in the literature therefore seems too broad, and it would seem useful to make some distinctions between perception, cognition and evaluation. This all the more since one could argue, in spite of some evidence for cultural effects on perception as sensory experience, that these three processes lie along a scale of increasing variability based on factors of mental set, adaptation, culture and so on (not unlike the previous discussion about manifest and latent function and the use object — symbolic object typology).

Sensory experience of environment. Most people experience more or less the same things and can agree that there is a tree, building or open space in a given place. This is needed for the survival of the human race (Gibson 1968; Gregory 1969) although there is evidence for some differences based on culture (Segall, Campbell and Herskovits 1966; Price-Williams 1969; Wober 1966) as well as effects of education and experience in terms of the ability to discriminate among stimuli (Rapoport and Hawkes 1970).

Comprehension and Knowledge. Here there is more variability because this knowledge already involves more choice, schemata and values. Thus everyone will see a building as being in a given place but will not understand it as a pub unless pubs are known. Similarly everyone will see a linear space (which we call street) or non-linear space (which we call plaza) but knowing for what they are used, how one behaves in them and so on are more variable (Rapoport and Hawkes 1970; Rapoport 1970(c)).

Evaluation of existing environments and *imagining* "ideal" ones is the most variable of all since values and images are operating in strength (Rapoport 1970(c), 1973(a)).

Evaluation, Cognition and Perception

It seems, then, that perception has been used in the environmental context in the general sense of "seen", whereas three distinct meanings are really involved which may be clarified through this alternative formulation:

(1) Perception is used to describe the evaluation of the environment, i.e., the perception of environmental quality, and hence preference, migration (choice), behavior and decisions. A better term might be *ENVIRONMENTAL EVALUATION OR PREFERENCE.*
(2) The term has been used to describe the way in which people understand, structure and learn the environment and use mental maps to negotiate it. This might better be called *ENVIRONMENTAL COGNITION.*
(3) Finally, perception describes the direct sensory experience of the environment for those who are in it at a given time. This is the least abstract and is the process for which the term *ENVIRONMENTAL PERCEPTION* should be reserved.

For example, most cities have areas regarded as high status, i.e., evaluated highly. Their location and extent are known and defined in certain ways cognitively. One such area may be scruffy and treeless whereas the other is what one would expect a high status area to be — neat, green with many trees and views (Newcastle, NSW, Australia "The Hill" vs. New Lambton Heights). The one is *perceptually* high status; the other is not but is *known* to be so. (See Fig. 1.12, p. 32). A visitor would evaluate these very differently. Similarly, certain elements are perceived, they are then construed to signify high or low density and then evaluated as crowded or not (Rapoport 1975(b)).

It could be argued that a different order of discussion would be more logical since, in effect, perception deals with how information is gathered and obtained, cognition with how it is organized (although the two are closely related) and preference deals with how it is ranked and evaluated. Since, however, people's responses to the environment are often global and affective, there seem to be advantages to discussing them in the reverse order of preference, cognition and perception (the next three chapters).

These three aspects of constructing a perceived environment should be seen as phases of one process rather than separate processes but, for our purpose, it is useful to distinguish among them. A very useful distinction between perception and cognition is based on the role of indirect knowledge, messages and information from the media, in cognition. Through this non-experiential way people know and evaluate places which they have never seen (Gould and White 1968, 1974)*. Perception is more sensory, more

---

* In September 1972, after writing the second draft of this chapter, I came across Goodey's (1969) environmental, extra-environmental and preferential perception which correspond to my perception, cognition and evaluation. He has also called cognition the perception of far places and, like myself, stressed the effects of the mass media and popular culture. Downs and Stea (1973) have also since made a similar distinction.

New Lambton Heights, Newcastle, NSW, Australia.

"The Hill", Newcastle, NSW, Australia.

FIG. 1.12. A comparison of two high status areas in a single city. (*Photos by Dr. D. Parkes, Dept. of Geography, University of Newcastle, NSW, by permission*)

related to direct experience, and involves the individual in the specific environment. As experience becomes less immediate, and the amount of inference made increases, we can speak of cognition. For example, perceived distance is an interval between points seen simultaneously whereas cognitive distance is the distance estimate made in the absence of objects, relying more on memory, stored impressions and the like. Cognition is thus more intellectual than perception (Brown and Moore 1971, pp. 205–207) and cognitive rules may overcome perceptual reactions – "it looks as if . . . but I know . . . " (Bower 1971, p. 38). Cognition simplifies more than perception which has much greater perceptual richness, hence the difficulty of remembering adequately even that part of the city which one knows best.

This proposed distinction corresponds to that between direct and indirect person perceptions (Warr and Knapper 1968, pp. 26–28) where the former comes through face-to-face interaction while the latter comes from press, films and the like. The perceived environment seems to be the result of both direct and indirect perception of elements; their location, classification, categorization and arrangement, and finally their evaluation (e.g., Harrison and Howard 1972) against some ideal or standard which leads to action which affects the "real" environment.

In effect there are four processes involved:

(1) Processes which are largely perceptual although they involve some measure of cognition and memory.
(2) Encoding processes stressing memory, learning, taxonomies, imagery and some values – these are mainly cognitive and hence partly culturally variable.
(3) Affective processes of preference and evaluation based largely on values and images and hence culturally extremely variable and leading to
(4) Action.

I have already suggested the increasing variability of the processes. Perception is relatively stable, consistent, enduring – it works, and there is *relative* constancy across cultures. By and large, people see the same streets, buildings, trees or whatever when faced with them although there may be some cultural effects. There is less constancy at the cognitive level – people can get disoriented in strange kinds of cities where the structure is difficult to grasp and space is organized according to different rules and different hierarchies operate. Preference and evaluation are the most variable – the environment seen as good by one group can be seen as bad by another. Thus a landscape seen as polluted by one group, and hence aesthetically bad, may be seen as good by another because it is productive as described by the nineteenth century Yorkshire proverb "where there's muck there's brass" [money] . Similarly everyone would see the same buildings and streets but they might be evaluated as a slum by one group and as a reasonable or even good place to live a certain kind of life by another. Historical changes in attitudes and views about standards, scenery, vernacular architecture, various styles and so on are equivalent to different preferences at a single time. Whatever position one takes on the relation of language and perception (The Whorfian Hypothesis) (Whorf 1956; Lloyd 1972; Rapoport and Horowitz 1960) it appears that the apprehension of space (perception) is more constant than the *concept* of space (cognition). Since design is the making visible of conceptual space and preferences, not only are there major differences in spatial organization (Rapoport 1969(d)), but it follows that the Whorfian Hypothesis may be more relevant to environmental design (and cognition) than to perception (Lenneberg 1972; Rapoport, in press(a)).

The distinction between perceptual and cognitive aspects may also be a matter of scale. Perceptually all people inhabit a flat earth, although cognitively we know that the earth is round. At the small scale of the average person the flat earth of perception is, in fact, preferable to the curved one of knowledge. Our perception is of very small parts of cities while our cognition is of larger parts and wholes (Michelson 1970(a)), and generally the larger the unit, the smaller the perceptual component and the greater the cognitive. Scale distinctions also seem to apply to imageability (Lynch 1960) so that, for example, Venice has high imageability at the large scale, in the sense of being unique and memorable while at the small scale has low imageability — it is easy to get lost in it.

Most urban environments are too large to be seen at a glance. Memory and inference are essential. The user constructs cognitive schemata which not only link and give form to the various sequentially experienced elements (Pyron 1971, pp. 386–387) but have predictive value (Kelly 1955). This process occurs over time and cognitions are built up gradually, from direct and indirect experience, whereas perceptions are *more* instantaneous. Scale effects on preference and evaluation seem more ambiguous. On the one hand people may have very strong feelings about a distant country or alien religion or way of life, none of which they have experienced. On the other hand there may be stronger feelings about what is present than what is not present (Bartlett 1967, p. 84); the reaction to a freeway in one's street is different to that at the other end of town, one's neighborhood more involving than a remote one.

The Distinction Between Evaluation, Cognition and Perception in the Urban Environment — an Example

The three processes are different aspects of a single process and interact. The distinction proposed is thus for convenience in analyzing and studying man—environment interaction in the city. Consider three studies about driving, freeways and roads — *The View From the Road* (Appleyard *et al.* 1964), *The City as Trip* (Carr and Schissler 1969), and *Driving to Work* (Wallace 1965), which seem to show an increasing cognitive component and help clarify the distinctions proposed and theoretical issues involved.

The View From the Road. This study deals with the aesthetics of highways as experienced by the driver through *direct experience* in terms of the play and organization of space, views and motion, light and texture — with the highway as an enjoyable, dynamic experience mainly through vision, since the car acts as a filter for most, although not all, other sensory modalities. The stress is on factors such as the motion of the field, sense of space and spatial contrast, rhythm and kinesthetics. While it deals with locational images, orientation and comprehension of the city, its objectives are to design highways as a visual experience; to create a rich, coherent sequential form with continuity, rhythm, contrast and well joined transitions; to strengthen and help create a well structured, distinct urban image and to deepen the observer's grasp of the environment — its uses and symbolism. Thus, although there are some cognitive elements, the primary stress is on experiential, perceptual aspects.

The City as Trip. In this study we move from the aesthetic quality of the highway trip to a consideration of the way in which people organize and transform sequential sensory experiences into cognitive environmental representations. The stress is on people's expectations and on how they remember what they experience. It becomes clear that a process of coding is involved, that categorization helps memory which also seems to be a function of expectations. Categorization is partly cultural, involving images and schemata, so that differences were found between drivers and passengers, commuters and occasional travellers — not so much in terms of the relative importance of elements but the number of items remembered. However, different kinds of elements were also remembered differently with utilitarian elements poorly remembered — even when large and prominent against the background.

This suggests two things: Firstly, that memory, i.e., incorporation in cognitive schemata is *selective* and involves some preferences and, secondly, that symbolic aspects (and hence imagery) may be important. This study differs from the previous one by stressing cognitive and affective factors *vis-à-vis* perceptual and the structuring role of memory and categorization. This is important because it is possible to drive on urban freeways seeing very little of the actual physical environment yet knowing the city very well as a cognitive schema consisting of movement channels and names rather than real places.

Driving to Work. This study of a seventeen-mile drive to work where the author draws a map from memory differs from the other two both methodologically (being intro-spective) and in its starting point (psychological anthropology). The interest is in cognitive maps and how the individual creates a "behavioral environment". This is approached through the concept of "mazeway", which is the sum of all of a person's cognitive maps, valued experiences and states of being which attract or repel him; thus, in our terms, including evaluation and affect as well as cognitive factors. The resulting map has a number of characteristics. Firstly, any segment can be "blown up" to include more detail. Secondly, in addition to features of the physical environment (streets, buildings, traffic, signs, etc.) and the social (people and activities), the schema includes non-environmental components — another significant shift from perception to cognition. These elements include the rules and routinized behaviors used in driving and behaviors meant to increase comfort. These various activities, and both external conditions and external states, are monitored through the various senses. A cybernetic model of driver and car is proposed, establishing a link between the cognitive representation and behavior/activities, in other terms an action plan (Miller, Gallanter and Pribram 1960). There are thus five elements — a route plan including origin, destination and major decision points (a spatial or cognitive map), driving rules (general rules for making choices among alternative actions), control operations (minimal behavioral responses available to the actor), monitored information (the specification of the type of data relevant to the task at hand) and organization (the pattern of interpretation employed in relating data to action).

This analysis of how a regular urban activity — in this case driving to work — is turned into a cognitive schema is clearly rather remote from the perceptual experience, yet related to it. In fact, these three studies form a continuum and are relevant to each other and to design. For example, the evidence from *City as Trip* about what is remembered can be related to the decision points in *Driving to Work* and to noticeable differences in the experienced environment (*View From the Road*). The reminder about the use of different sense modalities is related to the other two studies in terms of what designers manipulate and the congruence of settings with people and activities (Steinitz 1968). Although preference and evaluation are implicit in some of these studies, they can be introduced more clearly by asking why, for example, one would drive seventeen miles to work daily. Clearly certain residential characteristics are valued more highly than time — or driving is seen as pleasurable. Whether driving or public transport are used involves preference and evaluation and affects both trip behavior and location of residence — near highways, public transport routes — or close enough to work to walk. There are also preferences in the choice of driving on freeways or on surface streets (which are used in the third example), in evaluating the aesthetics of the freeways (which is where the first study begins) but which can be treated very differently either in terms of safety (Tunnard and Pushkarev 1963, pp. 205—206) or by contrasting the very different aesthetic experience of driving on a freeway as opposed to experiencing the freeway as an object in the city.

Pros and Cons of Making These Distinctions

Without becoming embroiled in psychological arguments it seems useful briefly to consider the validity of the distinctions proposed. The current view in psychology, although there is some disagreement, is that it is difficult to separate cognitive and perceptual processes (e.g., Gibson 1968, pp. 206 ff, ch. 12 & 13; Arnheim 1969; Proshansky *et al.* 1970, pp. 101—102; Neisser 1967; Gregory 1969; Hochberg 1968) although one may speak of receptive and interpretative phases of perception. The view that perception is the passive reception of information and stimuli from the environment which is subsequently structured by the mind is no longer accepted. Rather than passively accepting the bombardment by sensory data people actively search the environment for meaningful information to help in hypotheses and action and hence even "ordinary" perception is seen as an active and creative process.

All the processes from perceiving to thinking are a search after meaning and significance, involving structuring and symbolization. But for analytical purposes it is possible to separate the two extreme ends of the process. This is particularly so in the environmental context which is rather different to the laboratory setting of most traditional psychological research.

While there is evidence that higher cognitive processes affect perception through mental set, available categories and coding (Bruner 1968) there is also evidence that infants perceive objects before they know what they are (Bower 1971) (i.e., have categories for them) so that while they register most of the information adults do, they are able to handle less of this information (Bower 1966) so that differences may be due to ways of handling information. Since there is more agreement about what is perceived than about how it is structured or evaluated, perception is more nearly specified by stimulus information from the environment than is cognition or, even more, evaluation. Stated differently, the degree of abstractness or concreteness varies, with perceptual processes being more concrete than cognitive and the evaluative being the most abstract.

Treating cognition separately allows concentration on structure as culturally different while allowing for the relative constancy of perception of the same buildings and streets, trees, light and shade, quiet and activity. It allows for different definitions of where activities take place, where parts of cities begin and end, how they are related to each other. It also helps explain the variations in architectural and urban form in response to few "basic needs" (Rapoport 1969(a)). Implicitly this distinction is frequently made even in psychology, if only a distinction of convenience, but in any case it helps to discuss differences in environmental evaluation and preference (perceived environmental quality) separately from lesser differences in urban structuring and the almost invariant perceptions of the physical environment.

It allows to separate primarily sensory processes from vicarious experience, and hence helps distinguish between how people learn the city, structure and organize it conceptually and how the city is experienced through the senses. Learning consists in knowing where to look, how to remember what one has seen through cognitive structuring rather than in changes in what one sees (Hochberg 1968), important in distinguishing large-scale from small-scale environments.

Perception, cognition and evaluation as used here are, in effect, ideal types. While they form a continuum, it seems possible to separate them so that a particular process belongs more or less in one of these categories.

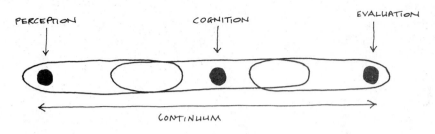

FIG. 1.13

It is not an absolute difference but one of degree which, if nothing else, helps clarify the extensive literature on "environmental perception" where the term is used interchangeably in these three ways.

The distinction proposed is not between innate and meaningless sensations and objects, but rather between the experience of urban elements, hence already structured and significant, and their relation to uses, the values and symbolic meanings which they have for various groups and their relation to urban structuring.

Consider some environmental examples. The actual perception of a stretch of desert, its colors, texture, hills, plants, light, heat and smells would be comparable, if not identical, for an Australian aborigine and a white, allowing for variations in acuity of perception due to experience and set. Much greater differences would occur in the cognitive organization into domains, places, campgrounds, and paths while the values attached to these, say as sacred or profane, and the rules for their use would vary even more (Rapoport 1972(e)). These latter differences would then also apply between traditional and detribalized aborigines. Similarly, both we and a Temne would perceive the same physical object and would move through the same physical space in a Temne house, but there would be no agreement about the cognitive categories — relating to sacred space and symbolism — and the values attached (Littlejohn 1967).

At the urban scale it is likely that if we could walk through an ancient Chinese city we would see it very much as the inhabitants did and move through the same spaces. We would not, however, understand it in the same way. In terms of the cognitive and evaluative criteria the city would be very different. In these as in other ancient cities the city was made habitable through an act of making it sacred. Urban form, and the way people understood it, was in terms of celestial archetypes, sacred chronograms — it was an aspect of "astrobiology" (Wheatley 1971, pp. 414—444 and last chapter; Eliade 1961). Similarly today people experience and perceive the same elements in cities but outsiders have problems in detecting the structure and hierarchy involved — hence the arguments in France that the U.S. city has no structure, the Western view that the Islamic city has no structure and the very different evaluations of cities such as Las Vegas and Los Angeles — or the roadside strip.

The usefulness of separating perceptual, cognitive and evaluative aspects seems to be supported by some recent empirical work on how people conceptualize the city, how they see, remember and evaluate it (Rozelle and Baxter 1972). With regard to "seen" (although the term is used more cognitively than in our discussion since recall rather than sensory experience is involved) structural landmarks, general visual impressions, and transport routes were most important while very different elements, social, economic and cultural, were important in evaluation. Remembering was a synthesis of the other two. Different physical and socio-cultural urban elements are thus involved in seeing, remembering and evaluating the city and all three processes are used in the total conceptualization which is the perceived, or cognized, environment.

The Filter Model

Models have been proposed for linking input variables with subjective reactions (Warr and Knapper 1968; Ekman 1972) which can be subsumed under the generic name of filter models. The perceived environment, different attitudes to and evaluations of landscapes, cities and buildings; people's propensity to define and symbolize stimuli and to react to the symbols, the ways in which people define stimuli and react to these definitions and symbols, led me previously to suggest a model of how the perceived environment might be imagined to result from perceptual inputs (Rapoport 1969(c), 1971(b)).

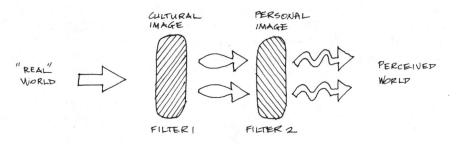

FIG. 1.14

This particular model ignores the effects of the non-perceptual material which, as we have seen, seem to be important in environmental cognition, and which could be classified as knowledge and expectations. In any case there are a number of such filters.

It has been suggested (Golledge, Brown and Williamson, n.d.) that the objective and perceived worlds are separated by an information filter (knowledge) and an attitude filter (goals). It has also been suggested that this model can be expressed as an electronic analogue*. In all these proposed models, however, the basic pattern is the same. The perceptual and other data are filtered — amplified, weakened, transformed, arranged and ranked, or eliminated until a construct results which is the perceived world within which people operate. Its distortions, although individually variable, are also consistent and regular for given groups of people.

The rules used in the selection, modification and structuring are part of the general system of cultural rules used in making the choices so that there are rules for constructing the perceived environment and also for acting within it. There are also rules embodied in the organization of the built environment.

The link between the mediating elements, the perceived world and the built environment is provided by images which occur in all, because values are embodied in images and also because images help simplify the complexity of the world by eliminating that which is seen as irrelevant, given the context — and hence expectations.

Thus, when going to Paris on a pleasure trip "the fringes of . . . consciousness would at once be crowded with half-remembered, floating images of bistros, streets, galleries, metro stations; but if it is a business trip, a different code enters into action and the matrix is cluttered with timetables, appointment books, galley proofs and dustcovers . . . " (Koestler 1964, p. 162). The city experienced in these two cases would be very different. Similarly, the city experienced by different people living in it, by different visitors and different planners and designers would also be very different — although in all cases there would the commonality of it being Paris rather than London or New York. In each of these cases different activity systems would follow from the different expectations and images. These activities, in turn, would lead to different behavioral spaces which would reinforce the initial action plans through what is seen and experienced.

One example of the action of such filters on the development of perceived urban environments is the West End of Boston. The average Bostonian hardly knew that area and thought it to be a slum (Gans 1971). Gans's view changed when he became a resident rather than a visitor and applied different criteria. "My perception of the area changed dramatically . . . I developed a kind of selective perception, in which my eye focussed only on those parts of the areas which were actually being used by people. Vacant buildings and boarded-up stores were no longer visible . . . " (Gans 1971, p. 305). Similar examples can be given of the effects of mental set on the "visibility" of mail boxes, restaurants or parking signs (Rapoport and Hawkes 1970).

Similarly the analysis of the perceptions, conceptions and decision processes of individual tripmakers in the study of travel behavior is, in fact, an attempt to discover the perceived environment and the "filters" of these travellers. Thus "movement space" defined as "a perceived part of the environment within which movement occurs" (Hurst 1971, pp. 250, 253) is clearly part of the perceived environment and constitutes a subjective environment "filtered through conscious and unconscious brain processes, programmed by needs, desires and abilities" (Hurst 1971, p. 254) and, one could add, all the other kinds of factors already discussed — and to be discussed.

I suggested earlier that in design some possibilities are eliminated without being

---

* By Dr. Ron Hawkes, School of Environmental Studies, University College London, in a personal communication.

considered so that it is possible to distinguish between a theoretical range of choice and more limited range of real choices, the difference being a result of the action of filters and the resulting perceived environment within which the decisionsmaker is operating. This suggests the possibility of combining the filter-model diagram and diagram of criteria used in reducing alternatives in design into one diagram.

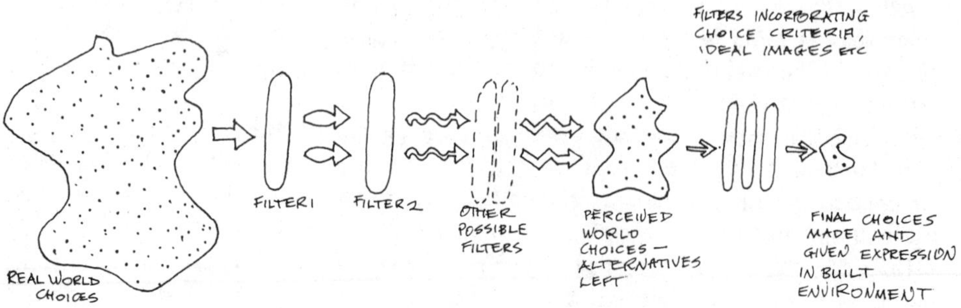

FIG. 1.15

This diagram suggests that filters and the resulting different perceived environments within which people act — the different perceived possibilities, criteria and choices — are intimately linked to images. An understanding of images may therefore be very important for an understanding of man—environment interaction. They are an efficient and effective way of embodying values and beliefs, they help simplify the complexity of the world and, as we have seen, designers always seem to match solutions against images whether it is an aboriginal making a spear (Gould 1969), an artist trying to represent a landscape, city or building (Gombrich 1961; Smith 1960) or an urban designer choosing among alternatives.

Furthermore, design can be seen as a process of making users' experiences more congruent with designers' intentions, of making some sets of reactions more likely than others, of eliciting more restricted sets of images from users, so that designers, by manipulating physical elements try to guide peoples' schemata.

The General Concept of Image and Schema

I have just suggested that the notion of "image" seems to offer possibilities of becoming an organizing concept in man—environment interaction as it seems to be in psychology (i.e., Antrobus 1970; Segal 1971). Most generally an image is an internalized representation and, regarding the environment, it is "an individual's mental representation of the parts of external reality known to him via any kind of experience" [including indirect experience] (Harrison and Sarre 1971). Although this concept is probably older, its original use in psychology can be traced to Bartlett (1932) and his concept of schemata, while the modern usage of the term comes from Boulding (1956) who elaborated and developed it, suggesting "eikonics" as the name for the study of images. It is from Bartlett and Boulding that these concepts have entered psychology and social psychology and through them politics, international studies, geography, man—environment studies, marketing and other fields — as well as ordinary speech (Willis 1968; *EDRA 3*, Section 7). In fact, like perception, the term is used almost too broadly and vaguely and it is the intention of this section to clarify this broad usage while leaving the discussion of specifically urban applications and meanings of this term to chapter 3.

The term stands for notion, stereotype, plan or map, plan of action, concept, self concept and so on. It is used to emphasize that the city has different meanings for different people — the slum dweller, commuter, geography teacher or planner (i.e., it is used interchangeably with perceived environment), sometimes it is used in a stylistic sense as when the question is posed of what is the appropriate image or expression of buildings in Islamabad in terms of traditional Moslem or international forms (M. Lee 1968) in the latter half of the twentieth century. This is close to the advertising and political usage of the term so that in advertising and marketing one can compare two stores in terms of images aimed at satisfying different expectations of women and projecting different personalities (e.g., a "quality store" vs. "happening and 'now' store"). The term has also been used to describe future trends or patterns of development in a rather "objective" sense without the mental component which most other uses of the concept imply (Gottmann *et al.* 1968). "Image" has also been used to describe conceptions of the city either in terms of images such as the city as an airport control tower, giant switchboard, clover-leaf intersection (Cox 1966, p. 64) or living organism (somewhat in the nature of analogues, similes, metaphors or figures of speech — rather literary in nature) or images describing ways in which people have reacted to the city and have recorded their impressions in literature (Strauss 1961).

Image also refers to memory and this has become dominant in planning and urban design (Lynch 1960; Carr and Schissler 1969). It has also been suggested that the image, or conception, that people have of their place in society results in the development of self-images which constitute a whole other use of this term.

Images have been described as the "point of contact between people and their environment" (Downs 1967) thus linking them to behavior. In this formulation they are used loosely — reference is made to "images, mental maps or space perceptions, call them what you will" which represent a form of "attitude to space" and are thus linked to feelings, prejudices or biases, preconceived notions, ideas, fears. This is related to the interest in social psychology on how images (in the sense of stereotypes) affect the perception of others and through shared social schemata, action and behavior, and more generally, an interest in how images affect action and behavior. It also fits the sociological notion of satisfaction as a feeling-state which arises from the perception of the match, or congruence, between expectations and attainments. In this sense it is clearly related to what I call environmental preference and evaluation, and is related to environmental cognition in the sense of creating categories and matching against them. In this connection the term is related to values since the latter tend to be embodied in images — whether of the good life, proper behavior or satisfactory and satisfying environments. All evaluation and design occurs through matching against such images and the consequent acceptance or non-acceptance of behavior or environments.

Socially shared images and schemata exert pressure for conformity. Experiments show that in a group with a group consensus established by the experimenter, the individual or subgroup tested will often report the "wrong" thing — i.e., the social schema is accepted against the judgement of one's own senses. The evidence to be reviewed later on different sensory modalities stressed by different cultures is also related to schemata. In preference — whether about environments, clothing, manners and the like, this is stronger still and shared images are reflected in the lifestyles of groups. It is in this sense that we can understand the effects of cultural schemata on art — where the matching process against images and schemata is fairly clear. The Castel san Angelo is drawn as a gothic fortress (Gombrich 1961), early topographic drawings of Australia use English type trees and colors (Smith 1960) and parts of Australia (and most of New Zealand) were actually transformed into a simulacrum of the old country's landscape (Heathcote 1972); Shepard 1969). As an architectural example, there is the way Egyptians avoided using the arch except where it could not be seen because it did not fit the concept (image/schema) of what a building should be (Gombrich 1961) and brief examples have already been given of the use of buildings and cities to express sacred and cosmological ideas. In all these cases, then, the image of an ideal is given physical expression in architectural or urban form (Wheatley 1971; Tuan 1974).

In this sense the concept of image and schema relates to view (Cassirer 1957) that people endeavor to form an idea of the world as an abstraction based both on sense and other data. The perceived environment can then be seen as a very large scale image. These constructs, or symbolic forms, vary with culture and are "ways of coming to grips with the world" — the image of the world being then a coherent and systematic construct (Cassirer 1957) which is also my general argument about the meaning of cognition (Rapoport 1976). If we accept the view that design is making visible an ethnic domain, i.e., an ideal symbolic form (Langer 1953) or an *imago mundi* (Eliade 1961), then we can speak of urban design as giving physical expression to an ideal environment embodied in images, and the great variety of built environments can be partly explained in terms of the great variety of images held by different people.

Generally, then, images seem to be structures or schemata incorporating (1) some notion of ideals and (2) ideas and knowledge of how the world is and how it works. In order to clarify the different uses of this term and to illustrate, in general terms only at this point, how the various uses proposed are of relevance to environmental and urban contexts, consider the development of the concept of image and schema.

The Development of the Concept of Image

The notion of schemata, important in Piaget's developmental psychology, was used very effectively in 1932 by Sir Frederic Bartlett to describe some aspects of memory (Bartlett 1967). He showed that schemata vary with culture and things are remembered not in order of presentation but how they are assembled into schemas. Thus a myth from another culture underwent systematic changes in the memories of English people since it did not fit the cognitive schemata which they had learned over a lifetime of being exposed to other values and other ways of telling and constructing stories. For similar reasons different aspects of a story are remembered by different groups. The schemata, then, are ways in which people organize past and present behavior and experience and anticipate future behavior by using these schemata predictively. Children's development is, then, partly the growth of schemata and acculturation the change in schemata.

Schemata and images are critical in culture and all mental life and allow people to combine memory with present situations to solve problems. Studying images is difficult because they vary individually and they are combined in very special and irregular ways (Bartlett 1967). Yet images are more than individual — they show regularities and systematic interrelationships so that groups of people are organized groups because they share images. These affect the way they organize their ideals, fashion, and the like — including environments — very much the way the choice model of design seems to work. In fact, one can argue that people use these different organizations as ways of establishing and stressing their identity. The image/schema of the group leads to specific ways of coping with the environment, selecting from it and organizing its elements, i.e., designing it. At the same time the social organization and the choice of environment help to transmit and develop particular images (Bartlett 1967, pp. 252–255).

There are both spatial and aspatial schemata, the latter related to the ways in which people structure and control information and behavior. Cognition is construction and this construction leaves traces behind (Neisser 1967, p. 287).

New information is related to old through the way it fits into schemata and this predisposes the organism to act in some ways rather than others so that schemata affect the known environment and *Umwelt*. Schemata are then "persistent, deep rooted and well organized classifications of ways of perceiving, thinking and behaving (Vernon 1955, p. 180) and they can also prevent things being noticed (Abercrombie 1969, pp. 31–32) corresponding to the notion of filters.

After a long hiatus the notion of schemata and images has recently reentered the social sciences generally, art history and environmental studies, a major stimulus having been Kenneth Boulding's (1956) *The Image*.

Boulding argues that all behavior depends on the image — on what we *believe* to be true — and the image is defined as subjective knowledge, all the accumulated, organized knowledge that an individual has about himself and the world. Images are very resistant to change and messages which are in conflict with it are first rejected (i.e., filtered out), but if contradictory messages continue the image is eventually changed. Parenthetically, this corresponds closely to the notion of paradigmatic shifts in science (organized knowledge) (Kuhn 1965) and the paradigm has major elements of image about it. It is thus also relevant to changes in professional ideology and concerns.

Images are composed of both facts and values (my twofold classification above into ideals and knowledge of the world). Values are concerned with rating the world and its parts on a scale of better or worse (evaluation) and these are the most important in determining what we see as truth and how we act. Even though images are subjective, people act as though they were shared. There are public images while other, more value oriented, aspects are more idiosyncratic so that there are widely shared images, those of smaller groups and private ones, although as I have argued above, in some cultures, particularly traditional ones, the degree of idiosyncrasy is less, and the area of agreement greater (Rapoport 1970(c), in press(a)). This seems to correspond to the idea of perception being more constant than cognition and much more than evaluation and the increasing variability of the concrete — symbolic object typology.

It is important to consider Boulding's concept of the ten dimensions of the image (Boulding 1956, pp. 47–48) and to elaborate and discuss this classification.

(1) *Spatial image.* The picture of the individual's location in space. This is not just local but world-wide since people know where they are in the world [although it depends on culture].
(2) *Temporal image.* A representation of the stream of time and man's place in it [it is important to point out that this in itself is an image since other cultures have other views of time — notably the cyclic concepts of many traditional people].

(3) *Relational image.* The picture of the universe around an individual as a system of regularities [once again this is variable with culture].

(4) *Personal image.* The picture of the individual in the midst of the universe of persons, roles and organizations around him. This is part of (3) the relational image at a social level and again culturally variable.

(5) *Value image.* The ordering on a scale of better or worse of the various parts of the whole image [and extremely variable culturally and individually].

(6) *Affectional image.* Emotional image by which various items in the rest of the image are imbued with feeling or affect.

(7) The division of the image into *conscious, subconscious* and *unconscious* areas.

(8) Dimensions of *certainty* or *uncertainty* of the image – its clarity or vagueness; some parts are certain and clear while others are vague and uncertain.

(9) The image of the correspondence of the image itself with some "outside" reality, i.e., a dimension of *reality–unreality*.

(10) Closely related to (9) but not identical with it, there is a scale of *public–private* according to whether the image is shared by others or peculiar to the individual. [One could add the size of the group sharing this image–humanity, culture, subculture, group, family, etc.].

Clearly, many images are non-spatial and, in addition to their characteristics as a class, they fall into two classes: (a) value images (Nos. 5 and 6) and (b) factual and knowledge images (Nos. 1, 2, 3, 4).

It is not particularly useful to ask whether each of these images has an urban equivalent, but it may be useful to give an example of potential insights into urban matters of each of these ten dimensions of images.

Nos. 1, 2 and 3 are clearly related to urban images (as the term is commonly used) and mental maps since space, time and relation are major aspects of urban organization and behavior. Time, as already pointed out, has been neglected in urban studies and only recently has there been work on this subject in psychology and anthropology (Doob 1971; Yaker *et al.* 1971; Fraser *et al.* 1972; Ornstein 1969; Cohen 1964, 1967; Holubař 1969; Lynch 1972). People have temporal as well as spatial images and the temporal images of various groups need to be coordinated since they need to mesh. Temporal rhythms and tempos in fact discriminate among groups (Parkes 1972, 1973). Thus an understanding of time, space and relation enter into an understanding of the city, how it is shaped and how it is used.

No. 4 affects the way people see themselves and also the structures of their society. This affects design through motivation and self-image and also through definition of roles and appropriate behavior and settings for them, groupings of people by perceived commonalities with major implications for the organization of space, time, meaning and communication.

Nos. 5 and 6 are the image of an ideal and play a major role in evaluation and preference influencing activities, lifestyle, migration and habitat selection as well as design. They may also influence subjective distance and time – important aspects of urban cognition. No. 7 influences the strength with which images are held, on the assumption that subconscious and unconscious images are more emotion laden and may be more resistant to change. (They are also more difficult to study). No. 8 has major consequences for the way in which mental maps are constructed and hence on how people learn to use and know environments which may need to be designed to facilitate environmental learning — and through it the use of urban areas. Through the confidence which groups have about the truth of their images, and hence the difficulty of changing them, there may be major implications for implementation of designs rather than for their form. No. 9 is related to 8, but its impact is in terms of the consequences of decisions which occur in the real world (preventing the model being solipsistic).

No. 10 is of great importance in relation to environmental desires, choices and standards, i.e., perceived environmental quality, particularly as it relates to the differences among groups — whether designers and users or different groups of users. This affects implementation once again, since large scale design decisions which reflect public (widely shared) images stand a much better chance of acceptance than private (idiosyncratic) images — and decisions at all scales have a better chance of working well if they reflect group images so that, in one case, a school plan and housing were not accepted because the wrong image was embodied (Turner and Fichter 1972, pp. 134, 156) while in the planning and design of the new town of Bhubaneswar (Orissa, India) mistakes were made as a result of ignoring people's images about density. A Western, low density Cantonment model (=image) was used which interfered with many social activities such as informal gathering of women. Similarly, too heterogeneous a mixture of people were housed together given a highly segregated and hierarchically grouped society with visible environmental symbols of status. Conflicts also arose with regard to privacy and distinctions of front and back (Grenell 1972, pp. 100—110), all of which relate to imagery.

Thus even before urban images and schemata proper are examined, these general concepts seem to be useful in helping to understand cities from a man—environment perspective. A central theme of this book is the importance of images and image systems as linking people and environment and affecting behavior. Such links between images and action are essential in considering planning and design. But, in the same way that it is difficult to get from concepts such as culture, values and world view to activities and design consequences, it is also difficult to link images and behavior to discover how action results from the images held.

In effect, the image model is still incomplete because there is a gap between image and action. While schemata intervene between stimulus and response, there is no indication how behavior results (Miller, Gallanter and Pribram 1960). The suggestion made is that there is another component — the *plan* — which leads from the image to behavior. This can be seen as a rough course of action, defined as a hierarchical process within the organism, strategic at the molar level and tactical at the molecular, which controls the order in which a sequence of operations is to be performed. It is also an incongruity testing mechanism activated by an incongruity which can be seen in terms of my notion of a matching action against some ideal embodied in an image. Crucial to this matching and testing is the fundamental building block of the nervous system — a feedback loop called a TOTE unit (test-operate-test-exit).

Values and intentions are both involved. While values refer to the image, intentions refer to the plan; values are important in deciding *which* plan to execute, not *why* plans are executed. The discovery that two plans are incompatible may completely revise the image, but generally, while images are very stable among members of similar cultures plans differ much more.

In some ways these plans, which seem to operate in most psychological processes, can be compared to the rule systems of particular cultures and they are used in solving problems by going through likely hypotheses (cf. the construct as hypothesis (Kelly 1955)) until a stop rule is applied after testing. Plans thus guide behavior using the image. This suggestion for bridging the gap between image and action makes the concept of image more useful operationally in dealing with environmental actions. Ideally, it would be possible to show how each of Boulding's ten dimensions of image is related to the corresponding plan, but images are so complex that this is hardly possible. In general terms, however, it does seem possible to go from image to action.

Some of the things we have already discussed illustrate the effects of images. For example, what I have called the elimination of alternatives without consideration (see also Whyte 1968, p. 229), the action of stereotypes (Berry 1969), the choice of goals in planning, the anti-urban bias in English and U.S. planning which has greatly affected many of the decisions taken (White and White 1962; Howe 1971; Glass 1955; World Federation of Mental Health 1957). Similarly, the way the city is defined, i.e., the criteria which distinguish it from non-city, is related to one's image of "city".

Many of the examples on the different ways in which environments are structured and how cities have been built reflect images, as when the Sudanese government rejected a plan for Aswan because it did not incorporate a riverside avenue — an essential image (Rapoport 1969(c)). Standards and codes often incorporate images (Crane 1960) as do specific characteristics of cities (Meyerson 1963) and people's evaluation of environments. In turn, people's images depend on their group membership, culture, education and other variables (de Lauwe 1965(b), p. 153).

The construct which I have called the perceived — or *KNOWN* — environment is, in effect, an image of the environment incorporating the ten categories discussed and corresponds to the *Umwelt* (von Uexküll 1957) a very early (1909) but extremely useful concept dealing with how organisms structure their environment in terms of their *Merkwelt* (perceived world) and *Wirkwelt* (world of action or effect). This seems related to image-plan-action and also the concept of people's action or behavior space.

For example, people's images about urban areas, characteristics of neighborhoods, and entire urban sectors (and of people living in them) have major effects on how people search for housing vacancies (Brown and Moore 1971, p. 206), whom they ask and trust, the newspapers they read and the visual cues on which they rely when they search in the real city are all also affected by images. The perceived environment which the household has is both spatially selective and differential with regard to the values attached to various aspects of the city. It will, therefore, affect both the awareness space and the action space within which the dwelling is sought as well as the evaluation of the dwellings and neighborhoods being considered.

The organization of the environment depends, at least in part, on people's images of ideals of what is good and bad, of what a city is for, as well as the more "factual" images they have about the possibilities, opportunities and resources. By studying images, their meanings, structures and their role in action, insights are possible into the differences among various groups of users (e.g., working class vs. middle class) various planning theories (French vs. English vs. American) various approaches to urban design (Corbusier vs. Hilbersheimer vs. Cullen) and the nature of cities (Western vs. non-Western; high style vs. vernacular) as well as the latent meaning of activities.

In a different context it has been suggested that all cultures differ in their cognitive organization in terms of a dominance hierarchy in the order of:

(a)   Subjective priorities (values, etc.).

(b)   affinity structure — pattern of relatedness.

(c)   intergroup similarity of themes, how things are clustered and seen as linked and related (Szalay and Bryson 1973; Szalay and Maday 1973).

This seems to relate well to the three categories into which I have grouped Boulding's ten aspects of image and seem to offer a general structure of image components.

(1) Ideals and preferences, affective ranking of values, etc. (5, 6).

(2) Factual knowledge and how this related grouping and arrangement of elements (1, 2, 3, 4).

(3) Grouping and similarity in terms of structure, properties and components (7, 8, 9, 10).

There are clearly other ways of studying images (Stea and Downs 1970; *EDRA 3*, Section 7) but I will structure the discussion by using the above schema, the concept of matching and congruence and of the known environment as resulting from the processes of preference and evaluation, cognition and perception.

CHAPTER 2

Perception of Environmental Quality — Environmental Evaluation and Preference

In ideal terms, cities are designed to meet people's environmental preferences and notions of environmental quality. If images incorporate ideals, then people test reality against these images and evaluate environmental quality against these ideals. More generally, people test a stimulus situation against some cognitive schemata which, of course, are variable.

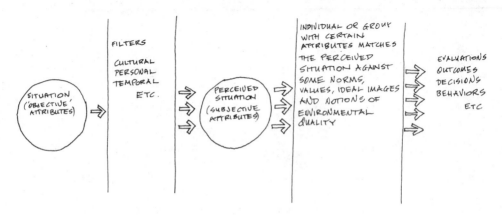

FIG. 2.1

These evaluative schemata are influenced by previous experience and adaptation levels, and by culture. They may also be influenced by deprivation, so that those lacking certain features — spaciousness, greenery, newness and single storey houses (i.e., the suburban image) may value them particularly highly (Flachsbart and Peterson 1973; Ladd 1972). Familiarity and aspirations also play a role, so that children in Sydney expressed realistic/conservative preferences, selecting places near where they lived — but slightly better. At the same time they had ideal environments — the Northern Beach Suburbs (Clarke 1971), a good example of our previous discussion of factual and ideal components of images.

Urban environments, therefore, must match environmental quality criteria and the imagery of their intended occupants and, more generally, the specific spatial and other organizations of cities are the result of the interaction between various constraints and possibilities and the cognitive processes of individuals and groups.

A good example is provided by the relationship between city center and social status. In most preindustrial cities high status individuals live near the center, which is highly valued — as in the Inca city, Baroque town, precontact Japan and many others (e.g.,

48

Timms 1971, pp. 220–221). This may still persist in some cities (e.g., Caplow 1961(a), (b), but see Rhodes 1969), to the extent that in Paris lower status groups ignore the center (Lamy 1967). In Italy the symbolic value of the center is still so high that first run movies, all theaters and all socially valuable activities take place there (Schnapper 1971), and this is even found in squatter settlements (e.g., MacEwen 1972).

In the U.S. city today the center is seen as a dense, lower class, dark area of low environmental quality and high crime rate (Cox, cited in Seamon 1972, pp. 7–1–3), i.e., the relationship of center and desirability is reversed. In terms of the congruence of social and physical space it is interesting to compare the U.S. situation with Michoacan, Mexico where Spanish towns show a positive relationship of center to high status while Indian towns show no relationship (Stanislawski 1950).

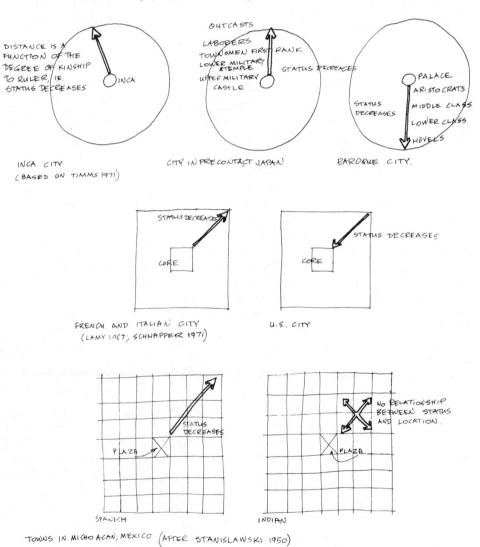

FIG. 2.2. Examples of relationships between location and status

In terms of the choice model people use different criteria in comparing alternatives. The matching of environments against ideal images suggests that people react to environments globally and affectively before they analyze them and evaluate them in more specific terms. Any material first arouses a feeling which provides a background for more specific images which are then fitted to the material (Bartlett 1967, pp. 35, 41), and in the case of environments affective images play the major role in decisions (Murphy and Golledge n.d.). For example, at a small scale, the overall satisfaction of students with residence halls is relatively independent of satisfaction with specific architectural features. Rather, the perception of the character and feel, the general image of the building and its positive or negative symbolism, the congruence of desires and images are the critical elements (Davis and Roizen 1970). This also seems to apply to classrooms (Artinian 1970).

Similarly, preferences for wilderness recreation seem to be mainly related to affective aspects (Shafer and Mietz 1972) and vary for different groups, which also vary in their landscape preferences generally (Vogt and Albert 1966). This influences the management of National Parks (Shafer 1969(a); Lucas 1970). It follows that other preferences vary greatly, whether for housing (e.g., Kuper 1970; Sanoff 1969) or large regions (Gould and White 1974) and the cities within them. Thus, in the U.S. South, Atlanta and New Orleans are preferred to Jackson, Miss. or Birmingham, Ala. (Doherty 1968). It therefore seems that in the large-scale environment also, the initial affective and global response governs the direction which subsequent interactions with the environment will take (Ittelson 1970; Acking and Küller 1973; Coing 1966).

Affect is thus of great importance, dominating much of our behavior and, although there are constancies as well as cultural differences (Osgood 1971, p. 37) people allocate resources differently, and the different preference structures and expenditures of various groups are of considerable importance in marketing.

The relative nature of priorities is of great importance in the environmental context (Rapoport 1969(f); Hoinville 1971) and involves the subjective evaluation of the relevance of various things for satisfaction as well as the costs involved. For example, the strong preference in the U.S. for single family dwellings affects the relative acceptability of various other forms which are evaluated against rural images of space and trees, and social images associated with different housing types, to the extent that political decisions are affected, independently of economic realities, the object being to maintain the desired community image (*N.J. County and Municipal Govt. Study Commission 1974*). Generally, then, designs which match images should be more successful than those which meet specific criteria but violate image expectations.

Different groups have differing images of environmental quality. At a general level people may have very different color and form preferences (e.g., Suchman 1966). Landscapes are evaluated differently so that in Bali traditionally the sea was regarded as bad and the mountains as good, whereas we regard the sea as ideal and this is where expensive tourist hotels are now being put. With regard to urban environments the majority in the U.S., when asked to draw their ideal environment (which they had no difficulty doing), indicated purely residential areas of single family dwellings. A smaller group indicated identical dwellings but with some very carefully selected services incorporated (Michelson 1966) but designers generally disapprove of such settings (Nairn 1955, 1956; Gans 1969; Timms 1971, pp. 106–107; de Wofle 1971; Ekambi-Schmidt 1972).

This creates obvious difficulties, since designers and users may both speak of "good environments" but have very different images of environmental quality (e.g., Stagner 1970) as may different groups of users (including visitors compared to residents). This is compounded by the fact that affective responses tend to be beyond awareness.

There seem to be similarities between the ways in which people and things (including those organizations of things we call environments) are perceived (Warr and Knapper 1968). In social psychology it is known that subliminal perception seems to play an important role in person perception and to be based on large numbers of cues in various sense modalities. The thresholds which make the stimuli subliminal when they are below awareness vary and it is not clear how the different cues are used (Mann 1969, pp. 96–97). It would appear possible that the affective, global reaction to environment may be of this type and the possibility of subliminal environmental perception has, in fact, been raised (Smith 1972). Another similarity is that person perception also involves images, although they tend to be called stereotypes (Mann 1969, pp. 92–100; Berry 1969) and seems to be similar to the way in which global, affective reactions are formed to environments.

I have already discussed historical and cultural variations in notions of environmental quality and the fact that different groups in cities select different dwellings and neighborhoods leading to differentiation in urban social space (e.g., Timms 1971; Johnston 1971). In the example of post World War II West German urban reconstruction already mentioned (Holzner 1970(a)) it seems clear that particular definitions of environmental quality, embodied in images of what cities should be like, led to a concern with preservation of old forms rather than remodelling, so that compactness and traditional appearance and layout were kept — unlike other parts of Europe. There was little interest in spacious living, and an interest in preserving street markets and small shops. In investigating environmental quality preferences of campuses there were also regional, student-faculty and male-female differences (Wheeler 1972) and the variability of definition of environmental quality of neighborhood and dwelling now seems very well established (Sanoff and Sawhney 1972), as does their close relationship to symbols and images (Davis 1972) and the consequent need to *discover* environmental quality rather than assume it.

Consider the preferences of upper, middle and lower class Americans for environments and also the differences in how environmental cues are "read" in terms of status, i.e., relative environmental quality. For example, upper class individuals rank natural vegetation very highly, whereas the middle class rank it low and prefer clipped, highly manicured vegetation. Similarly new suburban settings are ranked as the first choice by the lower class, as the second choice by the middle — but are disliked by the upper class. At the same time lowered density in this form of development is of very high importance to upper class people, increasing their liking for the area greatly, of moderate importance to the middle group — but of no importance to the lower status group; there are also major differences in relation to style, materials, fences and the evaluation of older areas (Royse 1969). Class differences in environmental preference were also found in France (Lamy 1967; Coing 1966) and they seem to be related to self image and to be relatively stable (McKechnie 1970).

It is also found that very different elements are used by two equally wealthy groups to establish the identity of their areas, resulting in two quite different urban landscapes and problems of non-verbal communication (Duncan 1973). There are also differences among various ethnic groups and educational levels in the U.S. in their preference for urban or suburban settings (Sklare 1972; Gans 1969) while there are sex differences in how suburbs are evaluated, men stressing peace, quiet and "puttering around", and women nice neighbors and friendliness (Gans 1969, p. 38).

Given these differences among different cultures and subcultures depending on cognitive styles, education, training and experience, one would expect that planners and designers constitute a group with very special values, abilities and ways of seeing the world and there should be major differences in the way they and the public evaluate environmental quality (Porteous 1971). This seems to be the case so that, for example, designers prefer higher levels of complexity and ambiguity than the public and people generally can make finer distinctions in environments which they know well (Rapoport and Kantor 1967; Rapoport and Hawkes 1970). There are differences between Swedish designers' and the public's evaluation of "pleasantness" – i.e., environmental quality (Acking and Küller 1973). In the U.S. planners and the public rated spatial organization very differently, the former preferring enclosed urban areas with clustered buildings while the latter preferred open, scattered developments; these differences were greater for members of the public without tertiary education (Lansing and Marans 1969) and architectural students, as they go through school, absorb the values of their subculture in their space preferences (White 1967). In England, also, similar distinctions seem to exist between designers' liking for enclosed, structured, joined-together dwellings and public preference for freestanding, separate, open arrangements (Cowburn 1966; Taylor 1973).

The public's preference for scattered development is related not only to distance from neighbors and rural imagery but also to a preference for private forms of recreation – it may be as much a recreation as a housing phenomenon (Mercer 1971(a); Young and Wilmott 1973). This would seem to relate such preferences to lifestyle (Michelson and Reed 1970), presence of children and so on. It has also been suggested that environmental preferences are affected by sensation seeking needs (Markman 1970; Mehrabian and Russell 1973, 1974), that these may differ between designers and non-designers (Markman 1970) and, as we have already seen, this also affects housing evaluation by different age groups (D.O.E. 1972; Reynolds *et al.* 1974). If the purpose of design and planning is improved environmental quality, it would follow that different meanings of this concept among designers and users will affect their evaluation of places and results.

We have already seen that this is the case with suburbs, scattered housing and the like and, more generally, if planning can be seen as the creation of an image (Werthman 1968; Eichler and Kaplan 1967, pp. 10, 50; Rapoport 1972(a)), then these groups have different images. Planners see planning as the creation of better environments based on an understanding of land-use requirements and certain ways of organizing space while users see it very differently. While they also see planning as leading to improved environmental quality, they give this concept very different meaning. Among other variables, they stress the "class image" of the community and for them the essence of planning is to prevent change and maintain this class and status image of the area. This image is expressed through symbolic attributes of physical elements so that while very few people (7–16%) in new developments expected to use recreational facilities, 90% wanted these facilities since they expressed the appropriate image (Eichler and Kaplan 1967, p. 114), what I would call the latent function of recreational facilities. This is due to the *meaning* which physical elements have for people (Coing 1966; Duncan 1973; Royse 1969; Rapoport 1975(a)) such as the great symbolic significance of front lawns (Sherif and Sherif 1963) the maintenance or appropriate treatment of which can generate conflict. For some people housing is shelter, for others a physical symbol of their position in society (Pahl 1971, p. 55). For the latter, planning is seen as maintaining and protecting an appropriate visual character, and hence also value, of an area (a social aesthetic) indicating status and a way of life. Such people expect to be judged by the condition of their houses and the area in which they live.

The quality of an area is also judged by the absence of industry, offices, and shops, and planning is seen as an attempt to keep out undesirable elements — whether people or uses, i.e., the maintenance of socially and physically homogeneous areas — a goal markedly different from planners' goals. There is also a conflict in the aesthetics involved, which for the users are mainly symbolic, and non-uniformity of houses is stressed (*Milwaukee Journal* 1973) as well as landscaping and outside maintenance which are so important that they are often done before they can be afforded (Werthman 1968) (very much like the purchase of elaborate front doors before roofs in the Barriadas of Lima (Turner 1967)).

The success of environments, therefore, depends on their congruence with appropriate images (e.g., Wilson 1962; Coing 1966; Cooper 1972; Marans and Rodgers 1973). The appropriate middle class image in the U.S. includes sporting facilities, bodies of water, interesting topography, absence of all non-domestic uses (including churches) and appropriate shopping (Werthman 1968; Eichler and Kaplan 1967). Similar arguments apply to new towns, if they are to attract middle- and upper-class residents (Rapoport 1972(a)) and also to the design of housing (Rapoport 1969(f)). This provides support for the variability of environmental preference and for the importance of affective and symbolic aspects which are embodied in social and physical images.

At a global level different groups may share a single preference and image system. Thus it appears that in the U.S. today the suburban ideal of the single-family dwelling and middle-class images are held by most young people regardless of race, family background or current place of residence. Suburbia symbolizes the attainment of freedom and identity, it reflects an ideal of a natural environment free of stress (e.g., Ladd 1972). There will, of course, be minority preferences, and this ideal may not apply elsewhere. More detailed analysis may also show more variability in front/back distinctions, the nature of social homogeneity, the symbols used or the preferred size of community and their centrality (Hinshaw and Allott 1972). In any case, though, environmental evaluation is influenced by expectations, values, cultural norms and previous experience which influences the standards for matching or the comparison level (Thibaut and Kelley 1959) through adaptation.

The effect of adaptation on judgement of urban quality is shown by the judgement of American travellers in Russia. Whether Moscow or Leningrad were judged as more drab or lively depended on the itinerary so that the city visited first was judged as more drab because the adaptation level based on American cities was used. A stay in Russia, however, modified the adaptation level, changed the standard of reference and different conclusions resulted (Campbell 1961, p. 34). Similarly, the same town in the U.S. was judged as quiet, clean and safe or noisy, dirty and dangerous depending on whether people came from a metropolis or a rural area (Wohlwill and Kohn 1973).

The psychological literature on adaptation (e.g., Helson 1964) and on the social effects on how things are seen and evaluated would lead us to expect such results so that a major factor in accounting for environmental preference may be the environmental background of the people concerned. This may be a function of familiarity, or of inflating the value of what is missing which was discussed above (Flachsbart and Peterson 1973) — provided that there are no more pressing needs and that adaptation to what is missing has not occurred (Sanoff 1973). An example of this process is the strong preference by Scottish students for detached houses, rare in Scotland, while Australian students preferred terrace houses — unusual in Australia but common in Scotland (Thorne and Canter 1970). Matching against a very low standard will give very different evaluations than matching against a very high standard. Thus while in France a limit of 170 sq. ft. per person in dwellings is regarded as necessary for mental health, and the U.S. Public Health Association, in 1950, set it at more than twice that figure, in Hong Kong 43 sq. ft. per person seems acceptable (Mitchell 1971). Clearly, judgements of density, crowding and stress would be very different (Stokols 1972; Rapoport 1975(b)). While no adaptation effects seem to exist for privacy preferences (Marshall 1970) they play an indirect role through cultural differences (Rapoport 1972(b)). In any case it appears that people from cities, suburbs and rural areas do evaluate various designs differently at least along certain dimensions, and one of the variables involved may be familiarity with certain ways of structuring urban space (Pyron 1972).

Generally, then, people have different evaluations and preferences. An example of this, not generally considered in relation to environmental preference, is the matter of taste and fashion. It has recently been pointed out that fashion is much more central and important than generally assumed and operates in many diverse areas — including architecture (although the urban environment was not mentioned). Fashion is seen as an attempt to be abreast of new tastes (Blumer 1969(b)) — i.e., an image matching and selection/choice process, a public standard offering a basis for acceptance or rejection and shaping objects and environments. Taste is culturally and subculturally variable, is an expression of lifestyle and is used to stress identity and status. While its effects on choices of food, clothing, furniture and houses have been shown (Allen 1968) there is little with regard to urban space organization. Yet there are such effects, so that in Britain there are urban differences between North and South matching other differences. For example, there are more pubs per capita in the South than in the North; there is more personalization, a clearer separation into specialized domains, more detached houses with back-gardens but no front garden in the South. There are differences in resources allocated to housing, in timing of activities, not only between North and South but among other regions of Britain. There are differences in shopping preferences, colors used and very striking differences in the form, arrangement and use of houses (Allen 1968). The different preferences of different groups are partly a function of taste, a preference for given attributes of objects and their arrangement, and these apply to environments also. For example, changes in taste in eighteenth century England led to marked changes in the physical environment of both cities and landscapes and the different tastes and preferences of Americans and English lead to very different environments (Lowenthal 1968; Lowenthal and Prince 1964, 1965).

Stylistic changes are a matter of taste and style is, after all, the result of a series of consistent choices, and changes from a grid to curved "suburban" streets can be attributed to changes in taste. The effect of residential and neighborhood amenities on urban growth and locational choice can be interpreted in terms of taste so that in a Latin American city a shift in taste from traditional courtyard houses towards Northern models, and the corresponding preference for greater space and peripheral rather than central location, have had major impact on urban form through "migration" (Amato 1969, 1970)*.

Geography offers interesting evidence on the role of environmental evaluation in migration. For example, the settlement of the North American prairies was delayed by the negative evaluation, in terms of familiar treed areas, given a treeless area which was considered to be a desert (Watson 1969). In Australia also the evaluation of given areas differed greatly among different groups with important consequences for settlement (Heathcote 1965). In this latter case, as in others, the preferences and images also led to design consequences as migrant groups to recreate landscapes which they valued highly (Heathcote 1972; Shepard 1969). Substantial areas of California, notably the central valley, were evaluated negatively because of the congruence of certain environmental characteristics with the then current image of disease origins (the miasmic theory of malaria) (K. Thompson 1969). It was only when new evaluative standards were used that the evaluation changed — and it is well known how California is seen now. Even today areas can be evaluated so negatively as to stop settlement (Gould and White 1974) and one of the problems in planning is the incongruence between the evaluations of planners and potential migrants.

There is less evidence on urban environments but in Sydney, Paddington and similar areas of terrace houses were evaluated negatively as slums to be cleared, the criterion being the suburban house as the ideal. The values and image of preferred environments of certain professional and other groups changed and Paddington (and other such areas) became fashionable, much sought after — and expensive. Occasionally there is a time lag in the change of such evaluation and conflict results as when slum clearance authorities (The Victorian Housing Commission) continued to evaluate Carlton (in Melbourne, Australia) negatively after a shift among certain groups, comparable to the Paddington example, had taken place.

Different elements of the environment may vary in two ways for different populations. Firstly, there are use differences (corresponding to the resource definition of which I spoke earlier). Secondly, given the perception of similar uses there may be differences in the value attached to them so that snow will be evaluated differently by a farmer, his children or a hydrologist. All may see it as interfering with travel but the importance of this will vary (Sonnenfeld 1969). All this leads to different environmental evaluation.

A useful paradigm for environmental evaluation is the work in geography on the perception of hazard, such as floods, drought or snow (*evaluation* of hazard in my terms) (e.g., Burton 1972; Burton and Kates 1972; Kates 1962; Saarinen 1966) which has been shown to vary with culture, values, experience, adaptation, to involve thresholds and to occur in the perceived environment with both opportunities and dangers evaluated. In urban contexts this seems to apply to pollution (Swan 1970) and hence to definitions of environmental quality and also to the recent publication of books on safe (i.e., hazard-free) communities in the U.S. where crime is low, air clean and taxes moderate (*Time* 1972(a)).

The evaluation of hazard seems to be affected by three sets of variables:

(1) The relative potential importance of the hazard which is affected by the dominant resource use.

* Amato's interpretation of his data is rather different.

(2) The frequency of the occurrence of the hazard with thresholds raised by familiarity.
(3) The degree of personal experience with the hazard, introducing adaptation effects on thresholds.

The implications for the evaluation of urban quality seem clear although because of its lower criticality (Rapoport 1969(a)) its evaluation may be more variable. Gans's (1971) reaction to the West End of Boston which we have already discussed shows clear effects of adaptation on evaluation (an example of (3) above) and has obvious implications for planners' evaluation of urban areas and "slums" and also methodological implications in terms of familiarity with areas before evaluation, and the variable evaluations of visitors and residents.

Typical professional criticism of suburbs and new towns is often in terms of lack of visual enclosure, compactness and urbanity (e.g., Whyte 1968, pp. 232–233) but we have seen that the public evaluates "urbanity" differently as do different publics (e.g., by educational level), but generally tend to prefer green, open, unstructured development. This can be seen as an example of (1) above — the dominant resource use being the individual house, garden and neighborhood in terms of lifestyle, private recreation, values and status indications. These different views about the purpose of a neighborhood and house are, in effect, different interpretations of environmental resources. Regarding (2) above, the frequency of occurrence may be related to the use of the city, the time spent in different areas, activity cycles and one's behavioral space, so that unfamiliar areas, for example, will tend to be evaluated as better (or worse) than familiar ones. A striking example is the hazard map of Manhattan for French tourists (*New York Times* 1972) which I will discuss in chapter 3. It is interesting that U.S. cities generally, and New York specifically, are seen as more dangerous by people overseas and other areas of the country than by residents, i.e., they show clear frequency and familiarity effects.

Intraurban migration (to be discussed later) clearly involves the evaluation of "perceived stress" (Brown and Moore 1971, pp. 201–202) and differs among different people depending on the kinds of "hazards", the thresholds and the image of the ideal.

We have already seen that accessibility to high status locations may explain the differences between different cities (and we shall see later that "accessibility" itself is a variable and subjective concept). One may use either latent and symbolic aspects of environmental preference, or the more traditional economic and job accessibility criteria, to explain residential choice. The evidence on the relative importance of these is contradictory. While some recent work (e.g., Brown 1975) suggests that work location, rather than tastes, preferences or changes in lifestyle determine residential location in the U.S., and also in France (Ekambi-Schmidt 1972, p. 47), there is much evidence that such considerations are relatively unimportant (Simmons 1968; Boyce 1969; Ward 1971; Johnston 1971(a), pp. 322–329). Beyond the quality of the dwelling itself the important elements are social and physical environments congruent with various criteria. Thus we shall need to consider what the desirable urban features are — compatible people (Moriarty 1974), schools (Weiss, Kenney and Steffens 1966), the center (Schnapper 1971), desirable topography or certain environmental features such as space, views or types of dwellings (Young and Wilmott 1973, pp. 43–58).

Latent, socio-cultural and symbolic aspects — the value attached to the Common, Public Gardens, historical buildings, and districts such as Beacon Hill — have affected the pattern of Boston to the extent that it became less efficient as a shopping center — and that in a culture which in gross terms stresses economic efficiency and success (Firey 1947, 1961). The moves of Norwegians in New York over a period of several generations were influenced by preferences, reflecting certain values and ideals, for relatively low density, trees, and proximity to and views of water and ships (Jonassen 1961) and other groups in New York had very different patterns.

Preference reveals the social valuation of environmental features, so that in Belfast topography (natural environmental quality) greatly influenced the urban pattern — but it was not altitude but the social valuation of altitude which explained the pattern (Jones 1960).

In considering European cities "illogical" aspects were found (Anderson and Ishwaran 1965, pp. 62–63) which I would interpret as the evaluation of environments against subjective, symbolic and cultural schemata — ideal or symbolic environments or landscapes (Stea 1967; Carr 1970). These can be understood in terms of two concepts which help explain the components of environmental quality. These are the related concepts of manifest and latent function and the scale of the concrete object to the symbolic object already introduced.

Recall that higher levels of meaning (value and symbolic, latent) are more culturally determined than the concrete and use end, so that attitudes and expectations play a larger role (Rapoport and Hawkes 1970; Rapoport 1970(c)). Thus an urban area would be perceived by all in the same way although the fineness of discrimination in that perception may well vary. At the use level a run-down area would be seen differently by a designer wanting to renew it, by people living in that area at low rent and with social ties in it and by a real-estate man. At the value level the differences would be even greater and the area might be evaluated as a slum or as a desirable neighborhood. At the symbolic level the variation might be even greater — the same area might be seen as symbolizing the architectural heritage of the past, the home of noble working-class people or as a cesspool of crime and danger, symbolizing the shiftless poor.

It is these kinds of facts which explain the historical Anglo-Saxon preference for the rural and picturesque rather than the regular (Taylor 1973) and this still persists so that in cities rural looking beaches are much preferred to urban looking ones (Neumann and Peterson 1970) and one needs to understand the specific elements which lead to these two classifications. Similarly, while complexity predicts preference in either rural or urban scenes, rural scenes are preferred no matter what the levels of complexity (Kaplan and Wendt 1972) i.e., the two types of settings are in distinct domains and the evaluation reflects culturally linked preferences based on the high positive values attached to rural settings and the anti-urban bias generally, in English speaking countries. One can suggest that in those countries the rural (natural) dominates imagery while in other countries (e.g., France or Italy) the urban (man-made) dominates.

Another example of the importance of latent and value/symbolic evaluative criteria is the variable use of urban open space which in one context is just for circulation, whereas in another the associated activities of eating, drinking, playing bocce, showing off, seeing and being seen are much more important (Rapoport 1969(a), (f)). For example in Greek urban open spaces seeing, being seen and interacting are much more important than circulation or even view so that the latter may be ignored (Thakudersai 1972). This affects not only the organization of the space but the implicit definition of environmental quality — i.e., what is a good space, or a good part of the space to be in, and hence habitat selection.

This also applies to shops. In planning Columbia, Maryland, the social role of shops has been considered and corner shops provided (Eichler and Kaplan 1967, p. 67). It is unlikely that they will work, given the middle-class images described above. It also suggests that while the concentration of shops and other facilities has been justified economically, it has also been a function of planners' values which had been strongly in favor of zoning and grouped facilities. These values, however, are not congruent with those of other groups so that a dispersed pattern may be preferable for Puerto Ricans in New York, Italians in the West End of Boston or in Paris as described in Chapter 1. For Britain it has been shown that corner shops and pubs help to foster and maintain acquaintances among people and are important in working class areas (Wilmott 1963, pp. 88–125).

These kinds of differences also help explain the morphology of the Japanese city where there is an inordinate amount of shopping space, which is intimately linked with entertainment and recreation and organized into an almost independent network of shopping lanes and arcades. Japanese cities never had public open space. One reason is that domains are separated, the public streets not only clearly distinguished from the houses, each house being a separate world behind whose walls each household does what it wishes (Taut 1958; Canter and Canter 1971; R. Smith 1971) but also treated differently. The result is "public squalor and private beauty" (Meyerson 1963). Community life, therefore, occurred in other places, starting with pleasure resorts and amusement centers with which shops became associated. (Ishikawa 1953; Nagashima 1970). This pattern of social interaction worked because shopping is an amusement and social pastime.

It follows, firstly, that very different public elements are valued in different cities and, secondly, that "recreation" can have very different meanings and consequently require very different settings for its satisfaction. Unlike Japan, most cities in history were, defined in terms of their public elements, although these varied in different places so that the status of "city" was denied settlements if the appropriate public facilities were missing. Thus the Greeks insisted on an Agora, Gymnasium and theater, and the Moslems on a Friday Mosque, permanent market, public bath, and so on. How the public elements were used, and how they were related to the urban system, is important since each set of elements and the associated uses implies a different view of urban form and life.

While recreation will be discussed later, the variability of that concept will be considered briefly. Given some amount of leisure time, people will use it differently. Some will spend most of their leisure around the dwelling and its immediate surroundings; others will go to concerts, opera, theater, art exhibitions or the like, or become actively involved in the arts; others yet will go back to school, or travel — to beaches, rivers or hills, to national parks, interstate or overseas; another alternative is sport, either active as participants, or spectators. In different places and at different times these will be selected by different percentages of people leading to different facilities. Recreation, because it is discretionary, most clearly shows the operation of the choice model, of latent and value considerations, and seems more closely related to personality and lifestyle than to age, sex or social class (Havinghurst 1957) so that the form of recreation selected reflects images of self and the good life (Christy 1971) as well as sensation seeking (Csikszentmihalyi and Bennett 1971). Recreation choice has important implications for planning, particularly if the latent functions are considered. For example, there are many people in cities who need to "kill time". In the provision of public libraries one might need to consider not only the manifest function of reading and lending books (which is one form of recreation) but also the latent function, possibly the most important from an urban viewpoint, of providing a place for such people to congregate in comfort and dignity (Howland 1972). This is also an important function of certain all-night movies in the U.S. and when, in July 1973, Grand Central Station, New York was closed at night for the first time a large number of people who had used it to sit and sleep were displaced. The evaluation of places would clearly be affected by such considerations. Different groups of users would evaluate such uses very differently (Becker 1973) and planning and design would be affected.

The variability of evaluation which follows from the dominance of symbolic and latent factors suggests the existence of what one might call a *preference space* defined by world views, value systems, lifestyles and the like within which certain environments — urban and natural — may, or may not, fall.

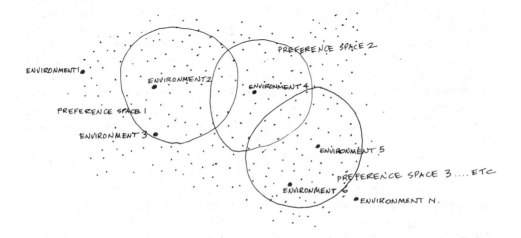

FIG. 2.3

Much recent urban and housing project design has been characterized by free-standing buildings which, I have already suggested, reflects aesthetic preferences. This makes it very difficult to differentiate between *front* and *back*. In manifest terms there may be no need for this — garbage is rarely that messy, increasingly there are garbage shutes or disposal units. Yet there is much evidence that people very clearly differentiate between front and back areas since very different symbolic values are attached to them, they are treated very differently and given very different physical expression. The front is where display occurs, where status is communicated through good maintenance, planting, fences, gnomes, birdbaths and their various equivalents. The back is where one works, dries laundry, strips bicycles, stores things or grows vegetables (Madge 1950; Shankland, Cox *et al.* 1967; Raymond *et al.* 1966; Pettonnet 1972(a)). At the same time back areas allow one to be oneself corresponding to a backstage region (Goffman 1957, 1963). This back area does not have to be "scruffy" — it may be a place for swimming pool or barbecue in middle class areas but it is private, not public, and *different* to the front. Areas may be classed as "slums" partly because of incongruent front and back behavior — people sitting and eating in the street or using inappropriate symbols relative to some norm. For example, the fronts may not be elegant and the most striking things may be stripped cars. In terms of middle class evaluation these belong in back areas but to the occupants the car and working on it may replace smooth lawns and gardening as display symbols and, in any case, symbols are used differently with consequent problems of meaning.

An important reason for prefering single family dwellings is because they provide the possibility of clearly differentiating between front and back and expressing this difference through appropriate symbols. Other reasons are also symbolic and latent, so that people see no incongruity in claiming that detached houses provide fresh and clean air while complaining that laundry in the back yard gets black because of dust and smoke (Raymond *et al.* 1966). Because the preference for detached houses has such major effects on urban form, these findings and the importance of rural imagery generally suggest that if physical equivalence of such concerns could be derived it might prove possible to satisfy them without using the forms themselves (Rapoport 1969(c)). This would seem more useful than the long and futile struggle by designers against suburbs: by understanding the meaning of forms, new ones might be devised which match the underlying preferences.

It has been pointed out that the distance walked from a parking lot to an office may be greater than the walk from public transport (Gruen 1964, p. 35), yet door to door convenience is a major justification for using cars. People have also often said in polls that they would not use public transport even if it were free. Clearly, value/symbolic and latent aspects are involved. Cars may be preferred because they represent a territory, provide privacy, prevent the intrusion of others, act as status and power symbols or help unload aggressions through driving. In fact all of these hypotheses have been put forward, but the important point at this stage is that only through an understanding of these meanings of the preference for the car can transportation problems validly be analyzed.

We have already seen that particular forms of recreation are selected to reflect images (Christy 1971) and that recreational facilities are often more for status and class image than for use, and they become central in designing high status areas. Similarly, where one lives in the city, one's address is for many people also a matter of status, using environmental characteristics to indicate appropriate environmental quality. This becomes particularly important in large modern cities where there are few other ways of demonstrating one's position, particularly as clothes and cars become more standardized and generally available (Johnston 1971(a); Lofland 1973) and people are not known the way they are in smaller settlements, or where social hierarchies are clearer and environmental ways of establishing social identity are much less important (Rapoport 1975(a); Duncan, in press).

Components of Environmental Quality

Environmental evaluation, then, is more a matter of overall affective response than of a detailed analysis of specific aspects, it is more a matter of latent than of manifest function, and it is largely affected by images and ideals. It can, however, be clarified by identifying some of its constituent elements.

For example, in Britain it has been accepted that the main variable in satisfaction with the housing estate (i.e., urban subarea) is appearance (D.O.E. 1972; Reynolds *et al.* 1974) but it has been suggested that this is less important in the U.S. where "practical" considerations are said to be more dominant (Voorhees 1968, p. 336; Cooper 1965). Yet it appears from the discussion above that appearance is equally important in the U.S. although its components, and their meaning, may be different and may differ further among various subgroups. It is thus necessary to discover the specific components, the specific mix of which will define environmental quality in any particular case and will specify the preference space. There are two obvious interpretations of the concept of environmental quality:

(1) the simpler one is related to aspects such as air and water pollution, the consequences of overpopulation, depletion of resources, radiation, thermal pollution and the like. These we could call the material and biochemical aspects of the physical environment and we have already seen that these are also partly subjectively evaluated (e.g., Sewell 1971; Swan 1970; Rapoport 1971(b)).

(2) The more complex interpretation is related to the less easily definable, and more variable, qualities of the natural and manmade environment which give satisfaction to people, its sensory quality in all modalities; the positive and negative effects on human feelings, behavior or performance and its meaning. These could be called the psychological and socio-cultural aspects of the environment and these are the ones which concern us here.

Some of the components of this aspect of environmental quality have already been mentioned; for example, the preference for natural over manmade in Anglo-American culture. There seems to be a general aesthetic factor which, in the case of natural landscapes, seems the most important and comprises terms such as colorful, beautiful, natural or primitive; also important are concepts such as rugged and complex at one extreme and hushed, delicate and simple at the other — with both linked (Calvin *et al.* 1972; Shafer 1969(a); Shafer and Burke 1965). In the case of urban neighborhoods, likely factors in global preference are density, trees and greenery, social quality and status of the area, safety and crime, quality of recreational and educational facilities, proximity of services, microclimate and suitability for gardens, freedom from pollution or noise, views and topography. One might thus create a composite index of *amenity value* which might be applicable in all cases but the specific mix of which would vary.

Individual components also vary. Consider topography. Generally, higher elevations are preferred (Toon 1966; Petonnet 1972(b), p. 62) and so are hilly locations, so that one frequently finds a relation between altitude and status or income (Jones 1960; Young and Wilmott 1973, pp. 51—60) and in Lincoln, Nebraska income correlates well with elevation and hilliness*, while in London it correlates with elevation, views, open space, historically significant buildings and water which is not used for industry (Young and Wilmott 1973). In Rio de Janeiro, however, the strong preference for water and beaches resulted in the hillside becoming the locale for squatter settlements whereas in Italy when the upper class leave the traditional center they move into the hills and there is a persistent model where, in all cities at the foot of hills, the desired places are the center or the hills and the undesirable the plain or the periphery (Schnapper 1971, pp. 93, 127). Recall also the relation of desirability to center or periphery in other cases. It is also interesting to note that positively and negatively evaluated aspects of environmental quality can often be quite different — i.e., different factors are mentioned in criticisms and in praise (Bryson and Thompson 1972, pp. 132 ff).

* Personal communication from M. Hill, 1975.

Preference and evaluation can be studied in many ways — through questionnaires, semantic differentials and so on, through observation, through studies of migration, understanding the culture of given groups and correlating this with the form of their environment. It can also be studied by analyzing books, songs, paintings and advertisements (Rapoport 1969(g), 1973(b)). There is some indication that the methodology used may affect the preferences discovered, so that real environments are judged differently than environments presented verbally (Lowenthal and Riel 1972). Different environments also produce different specific components, although much of the imagery people use in evaluating environments is related to mass media and advertising so that their analysis can reveal much about such images.

For example, looking at advertisements of housing developments over time reveals certain differences in the things stressed. It may be vegetation, views, location, features of the house or the site, the environmental atmosphere of the area, recreational facilities or status (the people who will live there). Differences can also be found in advertisements for houses versus apartments (Michelson 1971, pp. 144–145), in different price ranges and in newspapers aimed at different groups. Consider, for example the names given to subdivisions — they tend to include terms such as hill, crest, heights, cliffs, dales, manours, estates, park, lake, view and the like indicating clearly the kinds of images which are highly valued. The following examples are from actual advertisements collected from Sydney, Australia newspapers during April, 1972. (See Fig. 2.4).

Similar insights can be obtained by analysing more typical real estate advertisements and real estate pages in newspapers, and it might be useful for planners and designers to analyse real estate advertisements in their area aimed at the group for which they are planning. The types of things found (in Sydney, Australia papers April, 1972) stress seclusion, location among trees, lovely views, sweeping lawns, quiet streets, quality shopping, sports and recreational facilities. They stress that particular areas are desirable because they have beautiful beaches, splendid views, exclusive atmosphere and provide recreational facilities and scenic walks; they stress the price of the land and the high quality of houses and consequently the high status and income of the inhabitants, or the presence of small exclusive shops in the area with larger shopping only a few miles away in a less exclusive area.

Regarding "the richest . . . choicest . . and most desirable residential site in Victoria . . . " the criteria are that the area is part of the most exclusive suburb of Melbourne (Toorak), where millionaires live, houses are status mansions and people own exclusive breeds of dogs and makes of cars; the fact that the land is high with glorious views, that the river is near and the general atmosphere is safeguarded by the fact that the land is sold only to individuals — never developers (Auld 1972). The combination of social and physical factors is familiar from one previous discussion.

The role of trees in creating a positive image of environmental quality is clear. Most desirable residential areas are well treed. News stories dealing with the spread of the Dutch Elm Disease use before and after photographs to make this point implicitly (*Time* 1972(b)). (See Fig. 2.5).

Similarly, positive evaluations of a 110 acre middle-income housing project in the U.S. were mainly related to the preservation of "natural systems" (Wolffe 1972).

It thus appears that, at least in the U.S., Britain, Australia and Canada (and probably more generally) trees, outdoor space and freedom of choice (with its attendant expression and individuality) are very important components of environmental quality. Regarding

DOWNS
PLEASANT VIEWS OF GREEN, WOODED HILLS ... SMALL BUSH RESERVES ... NATURAL BEAUTY .... TREE FRAMED ESTATE .... LEVEL BLOCKS, KERBS AND GUTTERS, WATER .... ONLY 3 MILES FROM —— SHOPPING CENTRE AND CLOSE TO —— STATION ....

PARK.
PEACEFUL, RELAXING, SERENE ..... —— BASIN SURROUNDS THE ESTATE ... SWIMMING, SAILING, FISHING, PRAWNING AND BOATING ...... GOLF-COURSE AND BOWLING CLUB ..... KANGAROOS AND OTHER WILDLIFE .... LAND FOR SALE IS APPROXIMATELY 300 YDS. FROM WATER AND HANDY TO THE GOLF-COURSE ....

LAKE
WATER VIEWS .... LANDSCAPED .... ONLY A STROLL FROM WATER, PARK AND BEACH .....

EXCLUSIVE .... 5 ACRE HOMESITES.
—— PARK.

PRESTIGE... SOUGHT AFTER DISTRICT .... UNIQUE POSITION... LEAVES NOTHING TO BE DESIRED .... GREEN ROLLING HILLS ... VIEWS EXTENDING RIGHT ACCROSS TO THE —— MOUNTAINS... OVER MILES OF LUSH COUNTRYSIDE, YET ONLY 30 MILES FROM THE CITY .. WATER .... ROADS FULLY SEALED .... SPECIAL COVENANTS PROVIDE PROTECTION AGAINST ANY UNDESIRABLE DEVELOPMENT AND ENSURE A HIGH STANDARD OF HOMES THROUGHOUT THE ESTATE... RARE OPPORTUNITY .... SPACIOUS COUNTRY ATMOSPHERE .... CLOSE TO THE CITY.

FIG. 2.4. Environmental quality in housing advertisements. Five examples (Sydney, Australia, during April 1972).

this latter point, there is a law in Glendale, Wis. prohibiting houses too similar to neighbors', and legal suits have in fact been instituted (*Milwaukee Journal* 1973). Generally, then, the house on a suburban lot is the ideal: it reflects the rural image of maximum outdoor space and trees, provides separation from neighbors and hence privacy (defined as control of unwanted interaction (Rapoport 1972(b), 1975(b), in press (a)) as

FIG. 2.5. Two Midwest streets — before and after Dutch elm
disease.

well as compatible neighbors and appropriate community status reflected in the value,
appearance and maintenance of houses and landscaping.

This is confirmed by recent studies where neighborhood ratings (the most important
aspect of community satisfaction) are related to social aspects of the area (its reputation,
friendliness and similarity of people), its upkeep, attractiveness, safety, privacy, convenience and openness in that order (Burby 1974). In all these cases the evaluative
schemata and images are those of the Anglo-American middle class — but variable even
within it.

"Good images" mean higher land values in cities and they affect development not only
in residential areas but also of central business districts, so that the recent development of
Manhattan has been influenced by image factors such as Wall Street or Rockefeller Center
and amenities such as parks, rivers, good shops and restaurants (*Regional Plan Association*
1969). In order to describe in more detail some of the principal components of positively
evaluated urban environments, I will summarize a selection of major findings from the
literature (mainly on residential environments) so that quick comparisons can be made,
differences and similarities traced and generalizations become possible.

Several things are clear. There is such a thing as environmental preference and

TABLE 2.1 Summary of important components of environmental quality from selected studies
(Note: each study provides many more specific details; environmental preferences of planners and designers have not been included; in cases of disagreement the majority view is generally given).

Reference	Setting	Group Agreement	Scale	Components	
				Physical	Social
USA Wiggins (1973)	Urban spaces	differences between design students and others in evaluative criteria and receptivity	—	• degree of enclosure • size of space • character of space • nature of enclosing elements • amount of greenery	• activity • function/uses
UCLA (1972)	small town in a recreational area	disagreement among various groups except first 3 components (over-all 11 issues identified)	—	• scenic beauty • small town atmosphere • visual quality – signs distinct districts orientation • air quality and weather • transportation	• variety and quality of goods and services
Marans and Rodgers (1973)	residential area	some group and individual differences	• micro-neighborhood (5–6 houses around) more important for satisfaction than macro-neighborhood or community	*Macro-neighborhood* • housing maintenance *Micro-neighborhood* • maintenance • density – noise • adequate outdoor space • privacy in yard • low traffic level • many trees • clean air	*Macro-neighborhood* • neighbors • safety • convenience *Micro-neighborhood* • type of neighbors • safety

Reference	Setting	Group Agreement	Scale	Components	
				Physical	Social
Cooper (1972)	multi-family housing	—	—	• generally environment congruent with image • non-institutional environment, hence individual houses • personalization • landscaping and trees • semi-private outdoor space • distinction front/back • maintenance and upkeep	• social status • nature of people • crime and safety • presence of "community" • services and amenities
Wilson (1962)	city and neighborhood	—	Neighborhood more important than city	Generally congruence with image *Whole city* • climate • ocean, beauty • rural • accessibility *Neighborhood* • spaciousness • beauty • countrylike character • low density • privacy • front and back yards • greenery – large shade trees • quiet • newness and cleanliness	*Whole city* • status • nature of people *Neighborhood* • good for children • exclusiveness • friendliness • services and facilities

Reference	Setting	Group Agreement	Scale	Components Physical	Social
Appleyard and Lintell (1972)	City blocks and streets	some people adapt, others move away [habitat selection]	—	• traffic hazard • noise, vibration, pollution, trash • maintenance • privacy • greenery • complexity, variety	• friendliness • feeling of community activity
Brigham (1971)	residential area	—	—	• spaciousness • clean air • microclimate • topography and view	• accessibility • nature of people • value of houses • prestige • good place for children
Lowenthal (1967)	parts of town	some individual differences	—	• natural preferred to artificial • variety and contrast	
Michelson (1966)	neighborhood	—	neighborhood far more important than city	• single family dwellings • wide spacing • purely residential	• facilities accessible but distant
Hinshaw and Allott (1972)	residential areas	there are differences among ethnic groups	—	• location (suburb or small town) • single family detached dwelling with private outdoor space • attractiveness • access to parks	• no closeness to relatives • homogeneity • safety • proximity to good schools • proximity to public transport significant • proximity to shops, work and entertainment not important

Reference	Setting	Group Agreement	Scale	Components Physical	Components Social
Lynch and Rivkin (1970)	urban streets, downtown	—	—	• spatial quality (interest, contrast greenery liked, – dirt, constriction disliked) • intrinsic interest of features • specific buildings • nature of traffic and parking	
Zehner (1970)	residential areas	—	—	• maintenance level • for low density area – quietness • for high density area – open space for family activities	• compatibility of neighbors
Jonassen (1961)	migration pattern of one group	groups differ greatly	—	• views of water and ships • low density • greenery • rural character • congruence with home milieu (W. Norway)	• homogeneity *implicit*
Boyce (1971)	residential areas	—	house and neighborhood most important	• traffic and noise	• nature of people • accessibility to work not impor- tant • distance from rental property

Reference	Setting	Group Agreement	Scale	Components: Physical	Components: Social
Brown and Moore (1971)	residential area	relative weighting of variables varies	–	● upkeep of area, streets ● maintenance of houses and property ● spaciousness ● beauty ● quietness	● accessibility to various facilities ● services and facilities ● prestige and status of area ● nature of people ● value of properties
Peterson (1967(a), (b), 1969)	residential areas	–	–	● physical quality – age –expensiveness –maintenance –order ● harmony with nature –openness –greenery –naturalness –privacy ● variety and richness rather than uniformity and monotony	● status of area *implicit*
Kasl and Harburg (1972)	neighborhood	differences elderly – non-elderly	house more important than neighborhood except for elderly	● maintenance level	● social characteristics ● crime and safety
Royse (1969)	residential areas	major group (class) differences	–	● nature of vegetation ● level of maintenance and cleanliness ● density level ● materials and style of dwelling	● social and racial composition

Reference	Setting	Group Agreement	Scale	Components — Physical	Components — Social
				Congruence with image from media	
Ladd (1972)	residential areas	teenagers	neighborhood very important (this only summarizes neighborhood elements)	• suburban image-detached houses, large back yards, natural surroundings and trees	• proximity to school • privacy
				Congruence with values	
Rossi (1955)	migration in city	—	space in house more important, then neighborhood	• maintenance level • physical structure of neighborhood	• status • social composition of area • access – to employment, services, friends
Sanoff and Sawhney (1972)	residential areas	—	this only summarizes neighborhood and site aspects	• traditional appearance • trees	• friendliness of neighbors • homogeneity of neighbors • services – fire police schools garbage, etc.
Van der Ryn and Boie (1963)	part of city	—	—	• natural character • views without obstructions • special dislike – utility poles	

Reference	Setting	Group Agreement	Scale	Components — Physical	Social
Van der Ryn and Alexander (1964)	part of city	—	—	Congruence with images • maintenance level • low pollution • noise at night • traffic disliked • ownership and identity of house • detached houses • low density • openness, spaciousness • greenery • hilliness and views	• nature and status of the area • nature of people • homogeneity • proximity to some services • stability of area
Eichler and Kaplan (1967) Werthman (1968)	new planned residential areas	major differences between planners and public	—	Congruence with image • maintenance level • detached houses • low density, openness • recreational facilities • climate • topography • landscaping • quietness • distinct front and back • no overhead wires	• location relative to city • class and social status • stability • security
Kaiser and Weiss (1969)	residential area	—	House and neighborhood most important	• maintenance • quietness • physical nature of area	• proximity to schools services and facilities • nature of people • reputation and prestige of area

Reference	Setting	Group Agreement	Scale	Components Physical	Components Social
Lansing and Marans (1969)	residential area	differences between planners and users	—	• openness • interest and pleasantness • varied topography • landscaping and planting • maintenance level • variation in architecture	• nature of neighbors • prestige
Lansing, Marans and Zehner (1970)	planned residential areas	differences among groups by income and education	differences in components for large scale and neighborhood	For neighborhood • maintenance • low density as expressed in privacy in yard • low noise level • adequate yard space • hills, lakes, etc. • lots of space • trees	• compatibility and homogeneity of neighbors • neighborliness • safety, low crime • prestige and status • accessibility
Kaplan and Wendt (1972)	general visual character of scenes	—	—	• natural greatly preferred to urban • within any class-complexity legibility identifiability coherence interestingness "mystery"	social factors not considered

Reference	Setting	Group Assessment	Scale	Components Physical	Components Social
Neumann and Peterson (1970)	urban beaches	some group differences	—	• rural appearance preferred — greenery, few people • for urban beaches — sand texture and surrounding building quality	
Wheeler (1972)	university campuses	differences by region and group (students/faculty)	If campuses are considered analogous to urban areas the similarities are striking.	• high level of visual and spatial variety • varied architectural styles • rural character much preferred to urban • spaciousness, openness, greenery • landscape very important • minimize but do not exclude traffic	• proximity of related uses
Winkel, Malek and Thiel (1969)	roadside environments	—	—	• elimination of utility poles and overhead wires more important than elimination of billboards	Social factors not considered
Carr (1973)	urban streets	some age differences	—	• signs recognized hence important — not seen as problem • legibility and orientation	Social factors not considered

Reference	Setting	Group Agreement	Scale	Components		
				Physical	Social	
CONTINENTAL EUROPE Acking and Küller (1973) (Sweden)	general landscape scenes	–	–	● pleasantness ● complexity, originality, interest, surprisingness ● unity ● enclosure ● affection related to the old and genuine	● social status	
de Lauwe (1965(a)). (pp. 116–144) (France)	city	–	–	● lively, exciting city – shops, street life ● those elements furthest from rural life ● symbolic aspects – cultural symbols		
Coing (1966) (France)	slum compared with renewal area	differences working class and others	dwelling very important. Summary deals with neighborhood (*quartier*) scale	● street life – activity, excitement, shops, cafes ● complexity and richness	● attachment to area ● most facilities within area ● stability of population and social links – feeling of "community" ● meaning attached to places, partly as image of lifestyle ● proximity to local work	

Reference	Setting	Group Agreement	Scale	Components	
				Physical	Social
Raymond *et al.* (1966) (France)	residential areas	major differences planners and public	dwelling and garden very important	• detached houses • identity of house, personalization • garden and back-yard • distinction front/back	• status and its symbolism • clear separation public/private
ISRAEL Elon and Tzamir (1971)	public housing	differences architects and public	—	• aesthetic satis-faction, pleas-antness, interest, attractiveness • spatial enclosure • mixture high and low buildings • repetition (monotony) disliked	(deliberately ignores non-physical elements)
AUSTRALIA Browne (1970)	apartments in suburban areas	great differences among groups	—	• planting and land-scaping most impor-tant • visual and spatial complexity • bright color dis-liked • identity of indi-vidual units • topography	social factors not considered

Reference	Setting	Group Agreement	Scale	Physical	Social
				Components	
Barrett (1971)	urban areas	—	—	● *High status areas* good scenery and topography hills and views good soil for gardening no industry proximity to beaches ● *Low status area* opposite characteristics – flat, bad soil, no views, industry	● social status (which persists over time)
Troy (1970)	residential areas	differences between planners and public	—	● maintenance and cleanliness ● no mixture of land-uses ● aesthetics ● pollution ● no traffic or noise ● trees and landscaping ● private outdoor space ● low density	● social environment ● location – various proximity levels
King (1971)	various urban areas in large city	—	—	Congruence with image ● general appearance of area ● elevation or apparent elevation ● extensive views of water or trees but no industry ● detached houses ● newness ● greenery ● spaciousness ● individuality	● status and prestige ● respectability ● privacy ● friendliness ● accessibility not important

Reference	Setting	Group Agreement	Scale	Components Physical	Components Social
Toon (1966)	housing areas in a large city	—	—	• spaciousness • private garden and good soil • water views • topography • microclimate • general aesthetics • access to water and recreation	• privacy • status • social aspects
Daly (1968)	residential areas in a smaller industrial city	—	—	• freedom from industrial nuisance • country setting • good views	• accessibility unimportant • services (e.g. sewers) • good for children
Bryson and Thompson (1972)	outer suburban working class area	major group and individual differences	houses most important	• garden and backyard • openness • country-like character • microclimate • recreation	• accessibility to shops, schools and transport • social image of the area • nature of the people
GREAT BRITAIN Jones (1960)	industrial city	—	—	• topography – the higher the land the more desirable	• status
Buttimer (1972)	neighborhoods	Groups have different ranking of similar variables	neighborhood more important than house	• cleanliness • views from living room • greenery • general appearance • noise	• neighborly contact • accessibility to shops • safety • privacy

Reference	Setting	Group Agreement	Scale	Components — Physical	Components — Social
D.O.E. (1972) Reynolds *et al.* (1974); *Architects Journal* (1973)	various large housing estates	some group differences —designers/public —elderly/non-elderly —with children/without children	deal with estate, not dwelling	● overall appearance of buildings, open space, etc. ● children's play spaces ● gardens, trees, flowers, greenery, private gardens and access to dwellings ● maintenance and cleanliness ● spaciousness liked, tight over-shadowed spaces disliked ● low density ● closeness to country ● views from living room of open space, trees; dislike views of other buildings or car parks ● monotony disliked – dislike drab, dull, grey, boxlike, bleak buildings; like light, bright buildings variety and complexity	● privacy ● age separation ● nearness to friends and relatives ● accessibility and convenience not very important ● status of area ● friendliness
Cook (1969)	gardens	different groups vary	—	● gardens not for cultivation but for family activities ● size of garden important	● privacy

Reference	Setting	Group Agreement	Scale	Components	
				Physical	Social
				Congruence with image	
Cowburn (1966)	housing	differences designers/public	—	● freestanding house no clustering	
Young and Wilmott (1973)	city and parts of city	some group differences	—	● spaciousness – the more space the better ● detached houses with gardens ● views – specially over large commons ● rural character or desirable older central areas (historical snobbery) ● topography – height and hills preferred to flatness ● proximity to water if no industry along it	● prestige and status ● social homogeneity
Wilmott (1963)	new residential area	differences working class and middle class	—	● variety of houses – monotony disliked ● culs-de-sac ● corner shops and pubs	● facilities and services ● community, identity ("place") ● neighborliness ● privacy

Reference	Setting	Group Agreement	Scale	Components	
				Physical	Social
COMPARATIVE Johnston (1971) (variety of countries)	urban areas	—	—	• proximity to recreation, water etc. • views • microclimate • proximity to open country • low density and space • greenery	• status, prestige of area (good address) • proximity to high status areas • accessibility to work, etc. not important • nature of people
Bracey (1964) (US/Gr. Britain)	residential areas in two small cities	significant differences US/Gr. Britain	—	*Agree* — *Disagree* • purely residential in US, some mixture in Gr. Britain • sidewalks and street lights highly desired in Gr. Britain, not wanted in US • near freeway desired in US, not in Gr. Britain • closeness to country more important Gr. Britain than US • country character desired in both but more in Gr. Britain than US.	*Agree* • social status and prestige *Disagree* • proximity to shops important in Gr. Britain, not in US

perceived environmental quality. It is composed of a number of discriminable components relating to dwelling, neighborhood, the larger setting and social characteristics. There are cultural and subcultural differences and also some striking regularities.

The similarities and differences seem due to different ranking of similar components. The detailed analysis of the summaries given and of the literature cited will be left to the reader; it will prove most useful.

Habitat Selection and Migration in Response to Environmental Preference

The various preference spaces and the components which make them up inevitably affect behavior, although the match is never perfect (e.g., Tuan 1968(a); Neumann and Peterson 1970). Decisions are influenced by preference systems, and before people act they match environments and images and other cognitive schemata. The specific organization of the city, and behavior in it, are the result of the interaction of environmental characteristics, the choice processes of individuals and groups, and various constraints. In any ideal situation each group of people would move to match their preferences and the city would consist of a set of areas expressing the social identity, status and preferences of various groups. That this process actually occurs is supported by the fact that, at least in the U.S., the distribution of population remains remarkably stable. In given areas the characteristics of in- and out-migrants are similar and people tend to move to areas of similar character (Simmons 1968) and this seems also to happen in Great Britain (Young and Wilmott 1973).

The selection process, occurring in ways already described, involves positive (pull) and negative (push) criteria: certain alternatives are seen as being available (within an awareness space) and, on the basis of direct and indirect information affected by filters, the relative attractiveness of various social and physical characteristics are evaluated.

For example, at the large scale, Islamic cities have been located either inland or on the coast at different times depending on changed attitudes (Issawi 1970); Japanese cities were never located on mountain tops (even though land was in short supply) whereas in the Mediterranean area they often were, with differences between Spain and Portugal (Meyerson 1963) and differences in site selection can be found among most cultures (Rapoport 1969(d)). Urbanization also expresses preferences, so that in South Africa the English and other European groups settled in the city whereas the Boers and Bantu remained rural. There are both pull factors — preference — and push factors — economics and discrimination — involved. One reason for believing that there is a major element of preference involved, even in the case of the Bantu, is that even those living in cities give up few of their traditional habits (Holzner 1970(b)). Similar differences in urban/ rural preferences distinguish Chinese and Malays in Malaysia (Gould and White 1974, pp. 167–170).

Environmental decisions are made in planning and design as well as in migration which is an overt expression of preferences — an example of the most fundamental effect of environment on behaviour, *habitat selection*. Given an opportunity people (and animals) will select the habitat which best matches their needs, preferences, lifestyle and images, whether these be suburbs, old areas, or urban villages; large metropolitan areas or small towns. Thus in Barrow, England different groups settled in different parts of town, had different occupations and even used different types of housing (Pahl 1971, p. 21). Clearly, there are various constraints on free choice but it operates as far as is possible.

The choice, whether of physical or social environments (which I will discuss) or for economic and other reasons, only operates when people have options so that there are economic, prejudice and other constraints which, in fact, often represent the environmental problem of the group in question — further stressing the importance of habitat selection (e.g., Timms 1971, pp. 96—98).

People have always been concerned with the physical and social properties of places where they choose to live and work. In the past, however, there have been economic and technological constraints which, while still operating, have become weaker — at least for some groups and some industries and different criteria can then operate (e.g., Gould and White 1974; Rapoport 1972(a); Stea 1967) and these apply to cities as they do to larger systems.

Aspirations and behavior rarely coincide fully. People's choice may not result in action because locational opportunities, desired environments or resources are lacking; the incongruence may also result from lack of information (Timms 1971, pp. 110—111; Tuan 1968) so that comparisons of preferred locations with actual growth patterns reveal major differences depending on what is possible. In addition to these long-term choices there are also shorter range and more frequent ones, for example, travel routes which are also affected by preferences and habit, and influence other activity systems. Habitat selection also operates in the choice of transportation means (public or private), the routes taken, and the willingness of people to *be* pedestrians. There has been very little work on the role of environmental preference and habitat selection in transportation planning (but see Hurst 1971) although the implications seem clear.

Thus urbanization itself, the organization of cities and behavior in them depends in part on preference and, given the importance of affective, symbolic and latent factors, the study of preference offers a most important way of dealing with urban problems (Rapoport 1972(a), 1973(d)). The concept of urban habitat selection is old: Aristotle pointed out that people stay in the city to live the good life. The problem is to understand the meaning of "good life" and its environmental correlates. Decisions about location seem related to dwelling characteristics, status, prestige and social homogeneity, greenery, topography and views, safety, good schools, and ideas about mixtures of uses and proximity which are embodied in environmental images and which are used in matching.

From the previous section it is clear that we seek an understanding of the most important factors and images and their ranking. If it is accessibility, is it to work, shops, or recreation (and of what type), to the center of the city or open country, to friends or relations, to coethnics or whatever; and how are "close" and "far" judged and hence what land use mixture and activities sought; is it price range and value; is it size, style, type of dwelling and its location; is it the amount, variety and quality of open space; is it the physical environment — microclimate, topography, gardens, trees, traffic and noise levels, views, spaciousness, variety and complexity; is it safety, good schools or social aspects of the environment — its status, population, character and homogeneity, maintenance levels, appearance and appropriate symbols of social identity.

People pick settings with characteristics which they value highly (pull factors) and avoid (or leave) environments which they regard negatively (push factors). We have already seen this regarding migrants and landscapes; recall that in many cases people have not only settled in areas reminiscent of their homes, even when the soils and climates were better elsewhere, but they have tried to recreate their own landscape eradicating the native vegetation. They also recreate dwelling and settlement forms, examples of which can be found in Australia, Latin America and elsewhere (Stewart 1965; Eidt 1971; Rapoport 1969(a)). Various groups thus use environmental symbols to express belonging and preferences. Colonial cities, already mentioned, show this clearly so that many cities in Africa show the national origins of the designers and in Dar-es-Salaam "the air of Bavaria still dominates much of its architecture" (Epstein 1969, p. 249).

In the case of migrants to existing cities similar processes operate, so that in Australia Southern Europeans tend to congregate in inner city areas while Dutch migrants are attracted to "certain outer zones bordering on the rural belt of the metropolitan area" (Zubrzycki 1960). While economic factors play a role, culturally based preferences are crucial. Inner city areas seem to reflect a Mediterranean urban image of intense street life while a Dutch image of the rural life is made possible by Australian conditions. This is the more likely explanation since this pattern is found consistently in very different places (Johnston 1971(a), pp. 274–282). As a result Australian cities, like others before them, are developing ethnic enclaves. This affects house styles (whether new houses are built or old houses altered), colors used, the services such as stores, restaurants and clubs, street life, temporal rhythms and so on. It is often possible, merely by inspection, to distinguish the presence of different groups in Australian cities by social, visual and activity differences. Different groups tend to cluster to differing degrees. The English cluster least, then other Northern Europeans and Southern Europeans most. The locational differences of these concentrations are clear enough in both Melbourne and Sydney for them to be mapped and described, with Southern Europeans in central city areas and Northern Europeans either on the periphery (Dutch) or specific suburban areas (Germans, Jews, etc.) (Burnley 1972).

There is, by and large, no discussion of *preferences* in these studies. However, in the case of Greek migrants the selection seems to be based on social aspects (compatriots, coffee shops, clubs, groceries) and changes with acculturation (Mavros 1971). Furthermore, comparing six migrant groups in Sydney — three Mediterranean (Armenians, Turks and Lebanese) and three Northern European (German, Finns and English), one finds that not only do the different groups select different kinds of dwelling but they attach varying importance to the presence of relatives and friends, schools, to the dwelling or neighborhood, to gardens and space; they also handled gardens and front and back differently. Moreover, these differences were traceable to the culture, history and experience of the group and were reflected in drawings and descriptions of ideal houses (Stanley 1972).

People's decisions to move depend on matching desires and images with environments, while actual moves depend on differences between present and perceived opportunities (e.g., Abler, Adams and Gould 1971, p. 197) and various constraints. Thus habitat selection through environmental preference involves the characteristics of people and environments. When preferred environments cannot be selected, people's lives are affected by having to adapt, having to reduce incongruencies and having to give up certain activities which become too difficult.

Choice is shown most clearly where the constraints are weakest, e.g., in the case of tourism and recreation which have already been mentioned. It seems clear that tourism depends on an evaluation of the relative attractiveness of places generally, and the images which tourists use in the evaluation (Williams and Zelinski 1971). In Asia choices reflecting values and cultural patterns are pre-eminent, so that different people evaluate environments very differently and use similar environments (e.g., beaches) very differently (Robinson 1973; see also Mercer 1972; M. Barker 1968) and one cannot generalize for "recreation" any more than for anything else, with clear implications for planning and design. Within specific recreational areas people go to considerable trouble to find places which match their expectations (Lime 1972), i.e., match their images. I have already discussed the importance of recreation in planning new towns and residential areas. Since the location of industry has become freer. it may be related to the preference of a few people for the image of an area so that more and more it is climate, scenic, cultural, intellectual and recreational resources of an area which attract executives who make locational decisions (Gould 1972(b)). The evaluation of hazard also related to habitat selection because the "inhabitants of hazard area are a self selected sample" (Burton 1972). Within cities certain hazards, such as heavy traffic, will gradually lead to those who cannot tolerate it leaving, while those who stay either are not bothered or adapt, so that migration can be seen as a response to perceived stress (Wolpert 1966; Appleyard and Lintell 1972, pp. 96–98). It is those who wish to leave but cannot who suffer the most — in effect their selection of habitat is being blocked. Thus stress may be due to undesirable effects of the environment or non-achievement of another, preferred environment even though the present one is "adequate" — i.e., stress is also a subjective and variable concept dependent on congruence with norms. Similarly, the evaluation of hazards such as crime and deteriorating neighborhoods, lead people to move (Kasl and Harburg 1972). It follows that factors involved in habitat selection may be represented as follows:

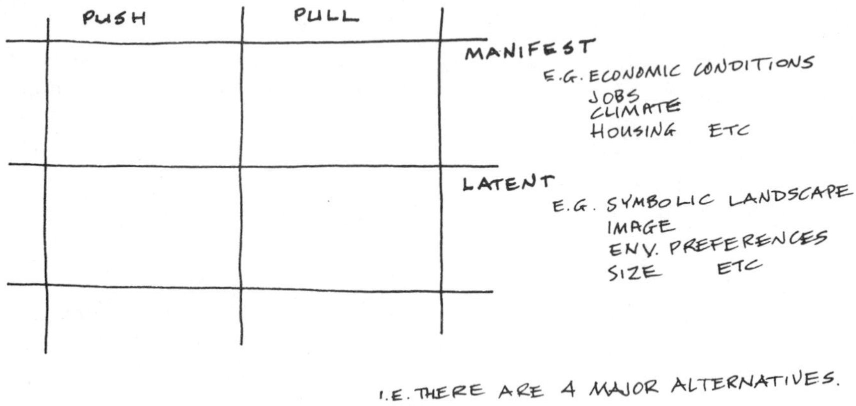

FIG. 2.6

Both push and pull factors involve an image of what is a good environment and this is used to evaluate both existing and new environments — a "personal preference function" (Rushton 1969) is used to evaluate alternatives.

Behavior is based on various components of the preference function, ranked and evaluated differently and resulting in different characteristics among those who stay and those who leave. For example, people may move to the suburbs from central cities because of push factors such as crime, deterioration, bad schools, or low status but also because of pull factors such as an image of lifestyle or ideal rural environment. This helps explain why different groups in the U.S. differ in the extent to which they leave the central city because they evaluate differently village life of which the suburb is an image (e.g., the symbolism of unmade roads and lack of street lighting often preferred) (Bracey 1964, p. 89) and also the differing housing types (Sklare 1972). Different populations are attracted to planned and unplanned new communities, i.e., there is habitat selection, with different reasons given for moving to different communities. Thus planned communities generally attract more educated people, more interested in planning, proximity to nature and recreation (Lansing, Marans and Zehner 1970, pp. 23, 38–40). It is also found that while certain locations affect social interation these locations are selected by people seeking appropriate sociability (Strodbeck and Hook 1961; Whyte 1956; Boudon 1969). Areas are left for various reasons and eventually, within new towns, one finds increasing segregation (Bryson and Thompson 1972, pp. 128–149, 162–163, 166), and one also finds different populations in regions, such as Northern and Southern California, reflecting two lifestyles and sets of preferences (Wilson 1967).

Since the upper classes can move most easily, it is of interest to consider them. Such groups move because of the obsolescence of style and quality of dwellings, or locational obolescence — i.e., undesirable physical or social changes generally (Johnson 1971(a), pp. 96–99, 103 ff., 143). The interpretation of these is variable and may involve aspirations based on lifestyle and fashion, as well as "objective" deterioration or changes in stage of life cycle. In the example of Bogota, Colombia already mentioned the moves of upper class residents can be interpreted in terms of "function" or fashion and I would argue that the change from the inward turning house (which makes central location feasible because of the way it solves locationally induced problems) to the outward facing house a matter of fashion with connotations of status and modernity (Amato 1969, 1970 disagrees). Voluntary moves have different effects to involuntary ones. Thus most moves to suburbs do not cause changes in lifestyle because they result from a certain lifestyle and search for certain ideals (Johnston 1971(a), pp. 236–237; Gans 1969, pp. 434–444; Donaldson 1969; Anderson 1971; Wilmott 1963, pp. 123 ff.; Michelson 1971(b), pp. 301 ff.; Greer 1960) so that those moving there had different attitudes and preferences to those remaining in the city (Lundberg 1934, p. 42; Whyte 1956; Berger 1960; Keats 1956). People select environments to suit their preferences. Other groups, however, may be greatly affected by a move from dense inner city areas to suburbs because the new lifestyle is very different from the traditional, and the new environment not of their choosing. In such cases, and in developing countries, many social and family patterns may be disrupted with serious consequences. Similarly a group forced to live in an inner city area will be affected differently to a group which selects an "urban village".

It can be suggested, by analogy with other related decision processes, that habitat selection does not aim for optimal but for satisfactory levels in terms of reasonable aspiration levels, willingness to move or change, level of knowledge of possibilities and economic and other constraints (e.g., Wolpert 1964). People also reduce the cognitive incongruity or inconsistency whether in terms of a dissonance model (Festinger 1957) or some other model (Rosenberg 1970). In addition to self-selection, people may assess an area favorably to justify the fact that they live there. If moving is impossible, then staying may be rationalized and stress, in effect, reduced. Finally the environment, the lifestyle or the image may be changed for the same purpose. Thus people tend to judge the beaches they use favorably, independently of overall preference (Neumann and Peterson 1970).

Habitat selection also occurs in terms of levels of complexity, stimulus and challenge so that recreational choices may represent desired levels of complexity; travel, fast driving and holidays are all examples of preferences for appropriate levels of stimulation. Different urban and housing areas, reflecting lifestyles, may also be related to arousal-seeking and desired interaction levels leading to a self-selection process.

The various choices are based on the kinds of lifestyle criteria described which offer a better explanation than income. People want to separate themselves from others and income is merely a way of achieving this objective (Feldman and Tilly 1960). Of the three possible reasons for racial segregation in the U.S. — poverty, choice and discrimination — the latter (i.e., the choice of the majority — a push rather than pull) is by far the strongest (Taeuber 1963) and this is related to perceived threat (Rose 1970) or hazard. Although difficult to evaluate because of limited choice there is even an element of voluntary clustering among blacks (Adjei-Barwuah and Rose 1972) based on some differences in values between blacks and whites (although no major cultural differences) (Rokeach and Parker 1970), and greater differences in lifestyle and use of the environment (Ellis 1972; Hall 1971). The elements of discrimination and choice may be difficult to distinguish but many groups — ethnic, cultural, age, religious or migrant together to support their status position, lifestyle, symbols, social institutions, environmental characteristics and various specialized services at least partly because of preferences and choice. Generally these choices are seen most clearly for higher status areas, since higher status people have more options so that, as we have seen, it is possible to correlate status and various environmental characteristics. But even other groups have environmental preferences so that the most disadvantaged groups are concerned primarily with shelter from human and non-human threats, the traditional working class with personalization while the more prosperous modern working class are interested primarily in the middle class image of status (Rainwater 1966). This needs to be qualified in two ways. Firstly, as we have seen, the ideal image for the lower class seems increasingly to resemble the majority image — at least in the U.S. (Ladd 1972). Secondly, even for the prosperous working class and middle class there may be a major element of fear and threat involved (Eichler and Kaplan 1967; Werthman 1968). However, there are clearly differences in preference leading, as we have seen, to a resegregation process in new towns (Bryson and Thompson 1972).

Thus the clustering found in cities, especially among recent migrants (Ward 1971, p. 295) is due to habitat selection — especially regarding the social environment. For example, in Cairo migrants to the city select a "village" setting and people of like origin. These migrants tend to settle on the side of the city nearest their origin (Abu-Lughod 1969) and this happens in other African cities (Epstein 1969, pp. 254–255), in Aboriginal camps in Australia (Rapoport 1972(e)) and even in London (Young and Wilmott 1973, pp. 58–59). These different preferences lead to different requirements and if these are not met designs may not succeed (Yancey 1971; Rothblatt 1971) and it is important to make designs for specific groups congruent with their characteristics.

In this connection the concept of lifestyle seems most useful, corresponding to the notion of *genre de vie* in French cultural geography (Rapoport 1969(a)). Lifestyle is related to values and distinguishes among different groups: it has been defined as the configuration of roles which individuals choose to emphasize from a larger number of possibilities open to those of similar "basic" characteristics (Michelson and Reed 1970, p. 18). It thus affects the allocation of resources, time and space, social activities, leisure and recreation, definition of privacy, degree of interaction desired, the importance of the dwelling and various facts of the city. People sharing given lifestyles are more comfortable living together than those who have different lifestyles and thus tend to cluster together and also select different environments which provide appropriate settings.

This concept has become important in marketing where it sometimes replaces variables such as sex, age, stage in life-cycle or occupation, etc. because demographically similar groups can differ profoundly in lifestyle. One group might stress records, art, concerts, overseas travel, liquor and so on (experience oriented) while another might stress outboard motors, television sets, engage in outdoor barbecues and wall-to-wall carpeting (material or home oriented) (Layton 1972(a), (b)). Lifestyle thus explains better people's interests, involvement in various activities, their resource allocation and what products they use. Thus the kinds of artefacts people use (their consumption system) springs from their lifestyle and included are environmental artefacts and products, so that the element of choice involved in lifestyle has environmental consequences.

In fact four generalized lifestyles which affect environmental preferences have been proposed (E. Moore 1972)

consumption oriented (Central apartment locations)

social prestige oriented — related to job and position in community; location in certain suburban areas of prestige value.

family oriented — right environment for children; maximize size of dwelling, yard and other family oriented facilities.

community oriented — interaction with others of like values. This may be hippie commune or retirement village [but also urban village, ethnic enclaves or other homogeneous areas].

Another useful distinction is between localites and urbanites (Buttimer 1972, pp. 291—293) which will be illustrated below and fits the distinction in the literature between spacebound and non-spacebound groups. For example, in Toronto people at comparable life-cycle positions, and having comparable choice, were studied, the hypothesis being that lifestyle would lead to different preferences and hence allocation of time and other resources. It appears that those in suburban single-family houses will stress family-centered roles while those in central locations will stress extra-residential activities; those in houses should participate more in physically active pursuits since these are considered to be almost impossible in high-rises as usually built (Michelson and Reed 1970). These expectations reflect images rather than reality but this is to be expected, since lifestyle implies *an image of an ideal life.*

Another very good example comes from Sydney where two extremely high-status areas of the city (Wahroonga and Vaucluse) were compared, the residents of both having virtually no economic constraints on their choice (Borroughs and Sim 1971). The two environments were quite different and the evaluation of residents was obtained to their own *and the other area.* Wahroonga residents chose it because of trees and gardens, spaciousness, privacy and homogeneity of the area. Trees were valued because they were seen as being responsible for privacy and the peaceful semi-rural character [latent function]. Any move would be to similar areas and Vaucluse was evaluated very negatively because of its high density with people on top of each other, lack of trees and proximity to the center of the city. Wahroonga residents actually see their distance to the city (about 15 miles) as an advantage and the distance from water as not being a problem. Their preferences are clearly based on lifestyle and images because they illustrated the difference between the areas in terms of a barbecue in both.

Vaucluse residents evaluated their environment in the same way but the opposite sense. Any moves would be to another similar area; proximity to water, water sports and to the central city are valued as are views (unimportant in Wahroonga) and the animation, shops and restaurants. The area fitted their image of how they wished to live and they also knew the other area and disliked it. The two sets of choices were, therefore, quite conscious, and related to lifestyle and images of an ideal life. Some specific components of these can be listed:

Vaucluse	*Wahroonga*
watersport — sailing and swimming	watersport unimportant — backyard
attend lunches and dinners	barbecue and gardening
more travel overseas and interstate	more home entertainment
more out of home activities	less travel
covering a larger area	home more central and a smaller
the image of sweeping views,	area of out of home use
yachts and cocktail parties	the image is of sweeping lawns,
	shade trees, dogs and horses,
	and outdoor tea parties

(See Fig. 2.7, p. 89).

These could be generalized for the Eastern suburbs versus the Northshore of Sydney reflecting an urban versus a rural image — which is reflected in real estate advertisements for such areas (e.g., Michelson 1970 on Toronto). This is also similar to the distinction between Lake Shore Drive in Chicago versus the Northern suburbs (Evanston and the like), so that much discussion about high or low density is thus not very meaningful unless environmental preferences, images and habitat selection are considered.

These two examples of Toronto and Sydney well illustrate habitat selection as do different preferences for urban versus rural beaches (Neumann and Peterson 1970), areas displaying wealth and status through environmental symbols (Duncan 1973) or not (Duncan, in press 1976).

Clearly lifestyle and images of ideal environments play a role, and cultural differences in habitat selection are also found in Paris where central areas attract high status people while the suburbs house the working and lower class. This choice and preference are based on images — "visions of the core" which differ among different groups. The less favored group sees the core as belonging to an alien urban world while for the upper classes the situation is reversed (Lamy 1967).

People's decisions, including habitat selection, are made within their awareness space, that set of places which they know because of their activities — direct contact reflecting their behavior space and home range, and indirect contact reflecting their social networks and the information sources on which they rely, all of which incorporate biases and "filters". Within this awareness space is a more limited domain, the search space, where people's aspirations are most likely to be met so that some alternatives are eliminated

Wahroongah Rd., Wahroongah (north shore of Sydney).

Darling Point from Rushcutter's Bay (eastern suburbs of Sydney).

FIG. 2.7. Two images of environmental quality in Sydney.

(Photographs by author)

without being considered (as I have already suggested on other grounds) and the remaining choice criteria are highly variable (Brown and Holmes 1971).

Whether people actually move depends on constraints and another set of choices – in addition to choosing environments people also choose whether to move. This may depend partly on their culture or subculture (and their attachment to a place or to people) and also on age, personality, lifestyle, lifecycle and other variables so that one would expect those who move to differ from those who do not. This is, in fact, the case (Carrington 1970).

It is clear from the literature on intra-urban migration that most moves are short, they are related to environmental quality (Clark 1971) and the choice process involved is the main mechanism for improving congruence between preference and the perceived environment (E. Moore 1972). While this literature deals with migration, the process applies to *all environmental decisions* and, in addition to migration, people may change their values, expectations and preferences; change their evaluation of the existing environment, or alter the environment but, in all cases, the attempt is to improve the congruence with certain images.

Real estate people manipulate images to match lifestyle aspirations of particular groups. One can similarly argue that manipulating images may be the best way of handling urban design problems for the aged, so that it might be possible both to meet the aspirations of the elderly and also to indicate to the larger community improved status, thus helping solve the principal social problem of the elderly in the U.S. (Rapoport 1973(d)). Similarly in designing new towns environmental preference should be a major variable considered, and one important way of attracting middle class and high status groups to new towns (always a problem) might be through the manipulation of the appropriate images and achievement of appropriate preferences at the neighborhood scale (Rapoport 1972(a)). Once again recreation offers an instructive analogue. The study of investment in resort land – of where people *want* to live as opposed to where they *have* to live – shows clearly the values and images at any particular time. These attractions vary with culture and over time – but at any one time it is instructive to study the climate, location, atmosphere and design elements of successful resorts.

Similarly, one can argue that the only way of dealing with over-rapid urbanization in developing countries is to consider the function of imagery in preference and to stress the positive nature of traditional settings (Rapoport 1973(c)). One needs to consider the characteristics of declining places which people leave as well as those of places they like (push and pull) so that unbalanced growth and chances of reversing such imbalance seem to hinge on an understanding of environmental preferences. Overall satisfaction with places is related to three major characteristics – the ability to identify with a home area, accessibility to desired places, people and services and a physical setting corresponding to an image of an ideal environment (e.g., Buttimer 1972, pp. 289–290) all of which, in fact, are embodied in an image of a preferred lifestyle.

Consider "mobile homes". Social and physical environmental preferences can clearly be expressed, and mobile home dwellers, as a group, are a self-selected population of people who tend to be neighborly and sociable so that trailer parks resemble small urban villages. Safety, and the site as private enclave, are important so that in spite of their "mobility" such places resemble other areas of similar socio-economic groups. Extreme social homogeneity is also important so that appropriate behavior, moral and social standards, cleanliness, and symbols such as lawns and suitable patio furniture are all accepted and used to maintain status. These are communities voluntarily created by choice and they attract some groups but not others of similar age and income (S. Johnson 1971).

The stress on homogeneity of areas which keeps reappearing and will be discussed later is *perceived* homogeneity, i.e., *social preference* so that demographic and socio-economic homogeneity may be unimportant (Zehner 1970). The major satisfaction variable which we have seen over and over again is maintenance level, which is also related to the presence of compatible neighbors who share the same standards, expectations and meanings of environmental elements.

The implications of the concept of habitat selection for planning and design seem obvious. Thus the assumption, in urban renewal, that expensive housing in central cities in the U.S. would attract high income people back to the city is probably incorrect since the majority of the affluent *select* suburban living for its low density, individual houses and extra land (Alonso 1971). Accessibility may not only be unimportant but it may be a disadvantage. What seems critical is to discover what percentage of this group are likely to select center city environments.

We have already seen that in Paris, Bologna, and other cities there is no tendency for the well-off to abandon the center. Neither is there in India but there the reasons are different and will affect planning. There the population lives in enclaves based on caste, occupation, religion and kin rather than income. Each area has specific cultural values, related to lifestyle (cf. Duncan, in press, 1976); Mukerjee 1961; Fonseca 1969(a), (b)), and the spatial arrangements reflect meanings and communication patterns with Brahmans near the main temple and tank finishing with the untouchables at the periphery. This gradient is very resistant to change since the enclaves retain stability as long as the culture is intact (Anderson and Ishwaran 1965, pp. 64–65).

Such clustering makes it easier to maintain the appropriate symbolic character and identity of areas. Cities become clustering systems based on physical and social environmental preferences expressing the relative importance of various components of environmental quality – density, housing type, maintenance, landscaping and open space, social compatibility, schools, non-residential uses, unwritten rules about street use and so on (Buttimer 1969, 1971; Feldman and Tilly 1960; Wheeler 1971; Rent 1968; Duncan and Duncan 1955; Johnston 1971(a); Timms 1971).

It has been suggested that the various urban ecology models (multiple nucleus, concentric and sectorial) in fact apply to different social characteristics – ethnic status, family status and economic status respectively (Murdie 1971) and their interaction creates urban social space. Using lifestyle and environmental preference and relating them to physical and social characteristics of areas helps understand cities. While the specific choices differ, there is a common underlying process of choice and selection based on preferences, reflecting different priorities, standards, ideals and images.

The Variability of Standards

The usefulness of a single set of planning and design standards seems doubtful in view of our discussion – variable standards seem much more likely. The definition of comfort and the value attached to it vary and this affects architectural standards of lighting, acoustic separation, heating, storage and so on (Rapoport and Watson 1972). The importance of privacy, view and sunlight also varies as does the relative importance of space versus equipment in dwellings in France and the U.S, (deLauwe 1967, pp. 77, 80–81; Mitchell 1971, p. 19) and the distribution of space within the dwelling (Rapoport 1968). In the case of cities, the validity of rigidly applying standards and of defining substandard housing has been questioned (Abrams 1969) as has the concept of absolute standards generally. The suggestion is that they must be seen in context, leading to the concept of "relative habitability" (Fraser 1969). This general conclusion, that generalized absolute standards may not be very useful is at odds with much planning theory and practice. This is a difficult, complex subject and becomes more complex as one moves from designers' standards to cross-cultural samples and users' standards. Yet it should be possible to deal with variable standards within a generalized theory through an analysis of man–environment relations.

One suggestion, already made, is that rather than dealing with highly generalized "basic needs" one should consider the *specifics* of a situation, the context, the images involved, and the latent and symbolic aspects of function. This specificity applies even in relation to climate and site so that the use of English standards in Beersheba (Israel) and other new towns there, in India, and elsewhere led to severe problems which the use of standards based on traditional settlements of the areas and inhabitants' lifestyle could help alleviate.

We have already seen that the very meaning of "planning" varies greatly (Eichler and Kaplan 1967; Werthman 1968) and that zoning is often arbitrary being based on aesthetic biases and ideals (Crane 1960), so that they are biased in favor of free-standing buildings influenced by images such as Le Corbusier's Ville Radieuse (Rapoport 1969(e)) and neglect important distinctions between front and back or public and private. Similarly, with regard to streets the view that they are for moving traffic dominates to the exclusion of all other uses. Yet there are two views of urban space.

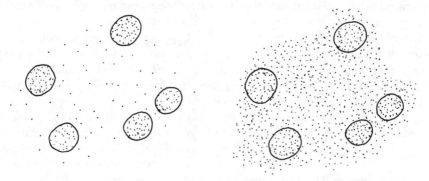

BUILDINGS PROVIDE ALMOST THE WHOLE SETTING FOR LIFE; STREETS, AND THE REST OF THE SETTLEMENT, FORM CONNECTIVE OR 'WASTE' SPACE. THIS IS TYPICAL OF ANGLOAMERICAN AND HIGH DESIGN TRADITION SETTLEMENTS.

BUILDINGS ARE A MORE ENCLOSED AND PRIVATE PART OF THE SETTLEMENT, THE WHOLE OF WHICH, AND PARTICULARLY THE STREETS, FORM AN IMPORTANT SETTING FOR LIFE. THIS IS TYPICAL OF LATIN, MEDITERRANEAN AND VERNACULAR SETTLEMENTS.

FIG. 2.8

In one, the street is a locus for life and activity, in the other this is denied which not only has major implications for the design of streets and urban areas, but also affects shopping by eliminating street markets. Similarly parks, playgrounds and greenery are seen as the only open spaces and the role of streets and plazas as open space is not considered. Yet children often prefer to play in the street (Rapoport 1966; 1969(b); Brolin and Zeisel 1968; D.O.E. 1973) although even here there are some cultural variations (Coates and Sanoff 1972). When urban spaces are designed for such activities there is often opposition because these two views make space sharing difficult due to their very different standards and preferences. This happened in the Sacremento Mall (Becker 1973) and in Portland, Oregon some outdoor spaces and fountains attracted different populations (Love 1973) and also generated opposition from residents. This is also implied by the finding in Britain that the noise of children's play is more disturbing than traffic noise (D.O.E. 1972).

In many cases this view may correctly reflect the values of the group, embodied in unwritten rules (Goffman 1963) which may sometimes find expression in legislation as when a new police commissioner in Tasmania (Australia) ruled that even two people window-shopping together be regarded as loitering (*The Australian* 1972) to prevent streets being used. But in situations where different views prevail, the application of inappropriate standards will lead to undesirable consequences. For example, in France the introduction of non-use type spaces in housing and urban areas has led to major dissatisfaction (Kaës 1963; Rapoport 1966, 1969(b)) as could have been predicted from a knowledge of French life and the preference for animated streets already discussed. Where the street is used as a major social milieu and communication setting, as is the case in Greece (Thakudersai 1972) or if, as in Italy, the promenade (or *passagiata*) is a central social urban function (Allen 1969), then the provision of the wrong kind of urban space may be destructive to the culture. (See Fig. 2.9, p. 94).

Let us examine the related question of mixed uses and proximity of services to housing in more detail. On the one hand zoning into areas of specific uses, and the concept of non-conforming uses, has been common, while on the other designers have argued for mixed uses the avoidance of purely residential areas (e.g., Jacobs 1961; Nairn 1955, 1956; de Wofle 1971; Rudofsky 1969). Each of these standards reflects the environmental preferences of particular groups and both are correct in the appropriate context, although designers' standards in, say, a middle class U.S. milieu are at odds with users' preferences. For example, when a sample of students was asked to design ideal towns they placed different elements centrally as their importance varied with different assumed roles. The grouping of facilities showed some regularities reflecting desired proximities. In the role of homeowner a core element of home and school was placed at one end of town, bordered by a small area containing shopping, theater and museum and which acted as a buffer to other services such as town-hall, fire-station and police; furthest from the dwelling were factories, offices and transport (Baird *et al.* 1972).

In another study a majority preferred purely residential areas with all services distant; a sizeable group wanted church and elementary school close, with drug store, food and clothing stores, post office and medical care not too far away (a minority actually wanted these within the residential neighborhood). Restaurants, movies and high school tended to be wanted further away with offices and factories most remote. There were also some people who opted for areas of mixed use (Michelson 1966), indicating that even in the small sample used there were preference differences best solved through the provision of a variety of environments with groups clustering through habitat selection.

In yet another American study (Peterson and Worall 1969) it was found that accessibility to neighborhood and community services was not highly valued. There

Street as setting (Venice, Southern France).
(*Photograph by author*)

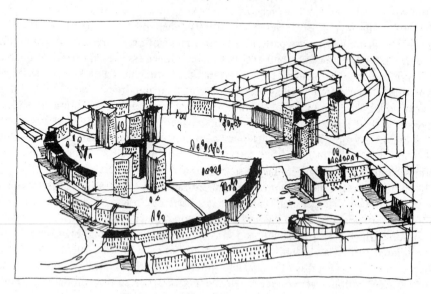

Forbach Wiesberg (Moselle) New Town.

FIG. 2.9. The spaces make the use of "streets" as settings most unlikely.

seemed to be two conflicting objectives — the need to use services and thus have accessibility and the desire to avoid irritation and hence undue proximity. The services studied included local community services (e.g., worship, shopping, park), informal activity centers (close friends' houses), access points (freeway or public transport) and local distribution centers for services (fire-station, hospital). These elicited different accessibility preferences. The emergency hospital, church, shopping, public transport, fire-station and children's park were closest; friends came next and the freeway ramp was furthest, so that accessibility in terms of time results in very different spatial arrangements depending on the transport mode; neighborhood preferences therefore differ for car and pedestrian oriented people while others are indifferent to the location of all services.

The details are less important than the fact that there are clear differences in the preference for accessibility of different urban elements (E. Moore 1972, pp. 6–8). Generally, though, in the U.S. people want purely residential areas without local shops or even churches although convenient to various services located at the edge of the area not its center and maximally separated from industry and offices, even when these are of the "campus" type (Eichler and Kaplan 1967; Werthman 1968).

In England results are rather different. Most food shopping is done in local centers and most housewives walk to them, a major reason being their "nearness". Most of the sample studied had at least one local center within 0.8 km. and most could reach one in under 10 minutes' walk. A large majority wanted the following shops (in decreasing order) as part of the local center — chemist, sub-post office, grocer, baker, butcher, green-grocer and newsagent-tobacconist. Then came a series of shops of medium desirability and least wanted were fish-and-chips shops, liquor stores and cafes [probably for social reasons]. Many regarded the possibility of buying locally as essential and there were variations with lifestyle (Daws and Bruce 1971). While this is not comparable to the U.S. studies, it suggests a greater desire for local facilities, which is supported by the finding that mixed land uses are more accepted (and even preferred) in England than in the U.S., shops are regarded as a more important aspect of environmental quality, going to shops is seen as more of a social occasion and the preferred distance to shops in England was 5 minutes' walk compared to 20 minutes' drive in the U.S. (Bracey 1964) — a spatial difference between 1/3 mile and 10–15 miles. The differences are not due merely to car ownership, so that among car-owners working class people prefer shops closer than middle class. The effect on behavior of these proximities would be significant (e.g., Willis 1969). Convenience is clearly subjective, and it is this subjective definition which will affect the meaning of specific elements and their impact on behavior. The definition of environmental quality will determine the relative weight given to the convenience of shops close-by, purely residential areas or open space and, as we shall see, distance itself (i.e., proximity) is subjectively evaluated.

In France we find much greater satisfaction with shopping in old areas than new. Since the former are typically of mixed use, with many shops and other facilities intermingled with dwellings this tells us much about preferences, and it seems clear that shops and the like are wanted very close (Coing 1966; deLauwe 1965(a), pp. 116–144; Metton 1969). Other facilities are grouped as follows in order of increasing distance:

(1) children's playground, public park
(2) library, pool, sports ground and "youth house" (*maison de jeunesse*)

(3) various clubrooms, meeting hall, cinema, theater
(4) stadium
(5) museums, cafes, dance-halls

Although it appears that cafes and dance-halls would really be preferred closer but the preference is affected by present planning (de Lauwe 1965(a), p. 136; 1965(b), p. 20) which is supported by our discussion before (see also Gardiner 1973).

This discussion, and much of the discussion of preference and variable standards, applies to density (as it can to many important planning concepts). We will discuss density later but it is clearly more than the number of people per unit area. It involves the perception of various characteristics leading to *perceived density* and its evaluation against preferred levels of stimulation and the controls available. We are dealing with the subjective evaluation of places as dense, or not, depending on a large number of physical characteristics, e.g., the degree of enclosure, the nature of space, activities and uses, certain temporal rhythms, the presence of people and their traces, light, noise, vegetation and so on and a varying preference for such levels by different groups (Rapoport 1975(b)).

We have seen that the context and use of spaces influence perceived density and its evaluation, so that in areas where the whole area is used and rather high levels of inter-action preferred a high number of people per unit area does not result in excessively high densities. The nature of both physical and social boundaries and the availability of appropriate social and physical defences leads to similar numbers of people per unit area being evaluated very differently (Rapoport 1975(b)). This is because specific layouts are evaluated in terms of privacy and are thus related to the facts above as well as the characteristics of people (D.O.E. 1972). In Britain, quite apart from the usual preference for low densities, gardens and space are valued for their privacy effects so that an area in Stevenage was judged as denser than another one of similar physical density because it looked more built up (Wilmott 1962; MacCormack and Wilmott 1964) and were also evaluated differently by the inhabitants. Density, therefore, like other standards, is related to latent functions, images, traditional cultural schemata and aspirations for new forms, i.e., standards, for example of proximity, form part of the perceived environment, are variable and depend on preference and evaluation.

Other spatial arrangements may also be evaluated quite differently – on the basis of attitudes to friendliness. Assuming that certain street forms affect friendliness or reserve, they may still be evaluated differently by those who value friendliness or those who value reserve (Wilmott 1963, pp. 65, 74), i.e. different standards apply. Similarly the openness of the typical American middle class house with its picture window and lack of fences, where the whole outdoor space is open to children, is at odds with the lower class dwelling seen as a refuge from a hostile world. Finally, even under the harshest conditions some groups may resent planning "improvements" (Porteous 1971).

The Problem of "Slums"

One consequence of the discussion so far is that the definition of substandard housing and "slums" is rather more complicated than traditionally assumed and, in fact, it appears that slums are not always what they seem. Like environmental quality, of which it is a specific expression, the definition of "slum" reflects values and images. There are many cases where the definition depends on aesthetic preferences so that areas with specific cladding materials on houses may be defined as slums (Sauer 1972) and so may untidy areas and those with old refrigerators, stripped cars or garbage cans in the street or front yard (Royse 1969). Given the importance which is attributed to maintenance level in defining environmental quality this is to be expected. It is also an example of the distinction, and the use of symbolic status indicators to evaluate areas where buildings and yards do not have this communicative function. Similar problems arise with the use of different symbols, such as lawns versus "country gardens" of bare earth and flowers (Sherif and Sherif 1963).

With experience and deeper knowledge of the area such evaluation may change considerably (Gans 1971). At the same time there are more objective criteria which need to be applied. For example the presence of rats and cockroaches and damp would, in most areas, be *prima facie* evidence for the presence of a problem which could, however, be rectified without necessarily eliminating the area or changing other aspects of it.

An interesting comparison is between the "slums of hope" of Latin America and the "slums of despair" of the U.S. (Peattie 1969). Although the former are much worse *physically* than the latter, they have quite different social effects because "slums" must be seen in the total social context, and a dwelling or neighborhood is more than a place to live; it is a base of operations for preserving certain values or entering a new life. Under those conditions physical standards are less important than location, preservation of mutual support, acquisition of skills and the saving of money. The imposition of unrealistically high standards — often designed to eliminate eyesores — can create problems. Thus slum clearance in Lagos brought more hardships than benefits and the preservation of kinship structures (e.g., for the security of the old), the value of traditional forms and the importance of marginal trades and crafts outweighed the untidiness (Marris 1967).

Similarly in Puerto Rico the destruction of extended family links which could exist in the "slum" but not in new housing had undesirable social consequences compounded by the impossibility of keeping pets, raising pigs and chickens or engaging in trades and crafts. (Laporte 1969). This can be generalized for other places (Rapoport 1972(d)) and it also appears that the effects of such changes differ, depending on whether the change is voluntary or not. Similar conclusions were reached about London working class communities, where the retention of social networks was more important than higher physical standards — and, in any case, the new physical environment was not necessarily evaluated as better (Young and Wilmott 1962; Wilmott 1963).

The residents of the West End of Boston, which has been studied in some detail, regarded that area, defined as a slum, as being of great quality and they liked living there. Many had money and a choice but lived there out of preference (Hartman 1963; Fried 1973) and those relocated from there (and from East Harlem (cf. Lurie 1963)) grieved for a long time (Fried 1963). They liked living there not only because apartments were larger and cheaper than the new housing, but also because of social links and a strong sense of identity with the local place — local urban space and its use were much more important than in other areas, and the design of new areas was unsatisfactory with no shops, services or streets for use (Fried and Gleicher 1961; Brolin and Zeisel 1968). This distinction, which we have already discussed, meant that the whole area was seen as a use domain and the surrounding neighborhood was an important component of the lifespace which not only affected satisfaction but had implications for density. Because the whole area was used – the stoops, street corners, windows, shops, other apartments and hallways, more space was available than planners thought (Hartman 1963).

This suggests the importance of considering the *context* of an area, the preferred levels, intensities and patterns of interaction and their effects on standards and environmental preference. Thus in Vienna slum families had no wish to move to better housing in the suburbs – the area, its streets and facilities formed a neighborhood and were liked (Anderson and Ishwaran 1965, p. 63) while in a number of cases people relocated have actually moved back to their old areas (Brolin and Zeisel 1968). In other cases relocation led to substantial rises in crime rates as in Stuyvesant Village, N. Y. (reported as early as 1940) (Agron 1972) and similar examples have been reported (in personal communications) about rehoused American Indians and Australian Aborigines.

This suggests the need to develop standards based on the aspirations of urban dwellers (Stagner 1970)* – i.e., on what I have called perceived environmental quality and which affects the definition of "slums". The criteria used in such definitions show some interesting instances of culturally determined criteria. For example in the 1953 Milwaukee screening survey (cited in E. Pryor 1971, p. 70) a number of the variables are arbitrary and reflect preconceptions – e.g., age of dwellings, low rental, density over 30 persons per net acre, and renter occupancy. In the Louisville screening survey (cited in E. Pryor 1971, p. 71) 3 of the 5 criteria are of this type – age of structure, density and mixed land uses. In the case of Hong Kong the most complex mixture of uses in a given area is also regarded as a criterion although it has always been typical of Asian cities and may, in fact, have advantages.

I am less concerned here with the actual development of the rating scale than with the indications that some very arbitrary criteria are used. For example 30 people per net acre is very low; older buildings may be better to live in than new and may be preferred, there may be people for whom renting is most desirable and low rents essential, a mixture of land uses may not, in some cases, be undesirable and may be preferred. Clearly "slum" is an evaluative not an empirical term (Gans 1968) and that evaluation is based on the social image of an area and its physical condition – although as we have seen, the physical condition is often evaluated in terms of appearance – which, in turn, is an indicator of social character. The appearance, maintenance, front/back relationship and the like are used to evaluate the desirability or undesirability of the inhabitants (in terms of compatibility with the evaluator) so that, in effect, areas are defined as slums by being tested against images of desirable places.

It also seems clear that the concern with many such areas comes from those living outside, so that in Africa (even more than in the West) (e.g., Suttles 1968) slums do not necessarily coincide with areas of social pathology and disorganization and such areas, which are really urban villages, provide a particularly integrated and satisfying life for their inhabitants (Mabogunje 1968, p. 235).

Thus any one area may be evaluated differently by different groups: outsiders may see it negatively while residents see it positively, outsiders' views may change with experience (Gans 1971; Fellman and Brandt 1970) and the residents themselves may comprise two groups – those tied to the area socially and emotionally and those who are socially mobile and not attached to the area – and these two groups then evaluate the area differently according to their images and standards (Fellman and Brandt 1970).

* I do not accept Stagner's reliance on Maslow's hierarchy. The relative importance of "higher" and "lower" ones also partly depends on preference (e.g., Rapoport 1969(a)).

This is partly related to habitat selection, since people of like character, including those with problems, tend to group together and how people perceive and evaluate the situation may be more important than the "reality" (Wilson 1963, pp. 5–8). For example new housing with gardens may be evaluated as less satisfactory than one's so-called slum (Wilson 1963, p. 12) and since some groups have such very different attitudes to the physical environment and what it signifies it may be essential to accept areas which are not appealing if they are not harmful (Wilson 1963, pp. 14–18). Only that area can be defined as a slum which is harmful to residents or the larger social milieu (Gans 1968) which is rather a different matter. The notion of habitat selection, variable preference and standards helps understand slums and their nature (e.g., Schorr 1966), and helps with their definition. Through an understanding of the relation of lifestyle and places it should also help predict which groups would benefit from specific types of rehousing or would adapt best to middle class forms of housing (Ashton 1972), why and at what rate.

A caution is in order. There is a need to guard against an overly romanticized image of the slum (Pred 1964). In adopting a more objective and balanced view one need not claim that the slums are better than upper class areas or that middle class life is terrible. Rather the aim should be of a variety of environments, some of which one may not oneself like, which suit various groups and which provide habitat selection opportunities.

To illustrate some of the points made several examples will be discussed in a little more detail. They will be from England, (based on newspaper reports), India, France and the U.S.

England. A controversy about Tower Hamlets, Stepney clearly shows different preferences and evaluations. The first article criticizes the redevelopment and speaks with nostalgia of the old Stepney — its charming streets, interest, vitality, mixed land uses and liveliness. Among other criticisms are being told where to live [lack of habitat selection], institutional blocks, identical front doors, bare and unused grass and so on (Downing 1968(a)). In a reply (Longstaff 1968) the point is made that the East End of vitality and charm only existed in the imagination of romantic novelists and upper-class do-gooders: it was an area of filth, vermin, poverty and discomfort whereas the redevelopment is airy, neat, healthy and so on. The reply (Downing 1968(b)) was that eliminating deficiencies is not synonymous with redevelopment, that there *was* much of quality in Stepney which a more detailed and specific analysis would have revealed, leading to very different solutions. The existing redevelopment is traced to a suburban image (a point which is implicit in Longstaff's argument). A similar conflict is found between planners and inhabitants of North-West England who argue that much can be learned by planners and designers from so-called slums in that part of the country — from the pubs, shops, street life, social networks and the like (Chartres 1968).

India. I have already referred to the difference between colonial and native cities. This example (Fonseca 1969(a), (b)) demonstrates the conflict of views between outsiders and inhabitants regarding Old Delhi and re-evaluates that place using criteria different to those used by planners and architects. The lack of structure criticized by architects is shown to be a different kind of structure — what I call an inside-out city using courtyards — which well suits the particular lifestyle of the population. The narrow, winding streets disliked by planners have many advantages and the analysis forcefully justifies many of the characteristics of the city with suggestions for specific improvements.

France. An analysis of the renovation of an area of the 13th Arrondissement of Paris (Coing 1966) makes it clear that the old area had a very specific way of life, special rhythms and rituals and places for them which were localized in the *quartier*, with great importance attached to the streets and their facilities and to neighboring. This way of life was appreciated by the inhabitants and was destroyed by renewal. As a result people are isolated, the neighborhood has been destroyed and life is different — although not better. There is a sense of loss for the past — the *ambiance*, neighborhood and social links, personalized relationships in shops, social and even government services. The changes are approved by one group and condemned by another — two reactions which we have already encountered, distinguished by very different standards, preceptions and preferences.

These two groups are distinguished by their attitudes to urban space (as I have described it above). One group spends its time in the *quartier* and that whole space is inhabited; the other group uses the whole city and, as a result, the neighborhood is used much less although the streets are, of course, used for generalized activities in Paris as they are not in English countries. The way of life of the first group is more closely linked to the destroyed setting, the types of dwelling, their relation to the street and its activities, the density of interaction and the quality and scale of urban spaces than is that of the second group.

USA. In this most thorough study of a slum area in Chicago (Suttles 1968) it is clearly shown that the area has a complex social structure which has spatial implications, both at the scale of the city of which it is a constituent neighborhood, and locally in terms of the microspatial arrangements. These arrangements are very complex, of four distinct ethnic groups with different lifestyles and unwritten, but clear, rules about how places are used so that, once again, one needs to be far more specific than is usual.

Squatter Settlements

Squatter settlements, known variously as favelas, barriadas, colonias or bidonvilles are "recent slums" and represent urban areas of great importance in many places — including some Western countries. Attitudes to squatter settlements have changed from wholesale condemnation to a more sophisticated view, very similarly to those on slums. As in that case, a caution is in order against over-romanticizing squatter settlements (e.g., Juppenlatz 1970) while accepting their positive qualities, which will be stressed here. In many cases, for example, inhabitants of these areas come from the city rather than the bush and have deliberately chosen lower physical standards in order to re-allocate resources (Peattie 1969, 1972) to build equity through their own efforts, through sharing tasks and expenses, raising animals, running shops and workshops. The prevailing view now seems to be that squatter settlements are of value, may provide a better social environment than other areas and that even physical standards gradually improve, so that imposing unrealistic absolute standards is undesirable (Mangin 1967, 1970; Turner 1967; Turner and Fichter 1972; Oram 1966, 1970; Peattie 1969, 1972).

Squatter settlements have advantages because they express culture and the latent and symbolic aspects of activities; allow culturally valid homogeneous groupings, locating people in physical and social space; provide appropriate symbols of social identity and appropriate social structures (Petonnet 1972(a), (b)) as well as allowing appropriate priorities in resource allocation. They also allow for mutual help and the support of familiar social networks, religion or place of origin (e.g., Abu-Lughod 1969). This not only helps mitigate stress, but helps the transition to urban life while helping cultures to survive — in effect these are prosthetic environments for people in a state of reduced competence and environmental docility (White 1959; Lawton 1970(a); Rapoport 1972(d)). Such settlements are often preferable to designed areas not only for all these reasons but because they offer choice and a possibility of habitat selection. They also allow for upgrading and change as lifestyle and priorities change since they are flexible and open-ended, and they also offer more variety and express preferences better than do designed areas.

For example, in the case of Greece, changes and additions, reflecting kinship, social relationships, clustering of extended families and other groups, the need for dowries and for unmarried sons to remain in the parental home, and other cultural imperatives, were achieved in spite of the difficulties due to the designed housing because controls were weak (Hirschon and Thakudersai 1970). In squatter settlements such changes become easier, houses can grow and change and shops and workshops are easily provided (Romanos 1969, 1970).

An example of some of the advantages of squatter settlements comes from Barranquilla, Colombia where the hypothesis of the primacy of socio-cultural factors (Rapoport 1969(a), 1969(d), 1972(c)) was investigated in squatter settlements. Major determinants of house form were the prestige of new materials, and the separation of formal and informal, public and private zones so that an "intimacy gradient" is set up, and the houses incorporate a penetration gradient with various barriers from the street to the most intimate spaces. Security is another major determinant of spatial organization, the use of perimeter walls providing both security and privacy. The open patios provide for many activities, for animals and for relief (Foster 1972). The spatial organization of this squatter housing is more useful than planned housing where excessive street setbacks meant inadequate patio space. The defenses and barriers are very similar to those lacking in public housing in Western countries where similar gradients exist (Harrington 1965). While there is no analysis of the settlement in Barranquilla the perimeter walls, patios, use of front *terrazas* and street for sociability all have major implications for settlement form.

An interesting example of priorities in terms of latent and symbolic functions is the situation where elaborate front doors take priority over roofs (Mangin 1970, pp. 51–52) because they symbolize house and provide status (and security). Similar are the prestige value of new materials and forms and the practice of enclosing houses within expensive masonry walls, and even finishing the street facade, before building a permanent room. Although that is cheaper and would appear more important there is logic to it because it protects the site, it provides privacy and security and it helps create an urban street early which is a great stimulus to those who live there and use it (Turner and Fichter 1972, p. 146) and it also symbolized "house".

In any case the priorities are very different to those of planners and architects and it is this variability of standards and preferences which needs stressing and also their relationship to images (Turner and Fichter 1972, pp. 134–135, 148–169). The layout of areas has received much less attention than dwellings, although house layouts affect the settlement and they are also affected by the large number of shops, workshops and markets as well as the use of streets for social activity, all of which are very different to planned settings although a few designers have tried to investigate these matters (e.g., Alexander *et al.* 1969). In the Aplichau area of Hong Kong the multiple use of streets is important because hawking is economically advantageous, so that hawkers, who are mobile, can set up at points of highest demand while small industries can also more easily be accommodated (Wong 1971).

. In squatter settlements (as in other urban areas (Rapoport 1969(e)) spaces may be more important than buildings. In India, for example, squatters have capitalized on this most effectively and related these spaces to their culture and social relationships, allowing clustering and the retention of the traditional joint family. There is a major movement space, the houses along it having private courtyards allowing space for water-buffalos and summer sleeping. Houses at the end of culs-de-sac share communal open spaces, providing a balance between privacy and community lacking in designed housing laid out in straight arrows. As in traditional villages narrow lanes lead to open spaces with trees which act as a social focus for adjoining houses (20–30 families) (Payne 1971; Rapoport 1969(a); *Architectural Review* 1971, pp. 339–343; Vickery 1972). The result is much more satisfactory than most newly designed areas (e.g. Grenell 1972).

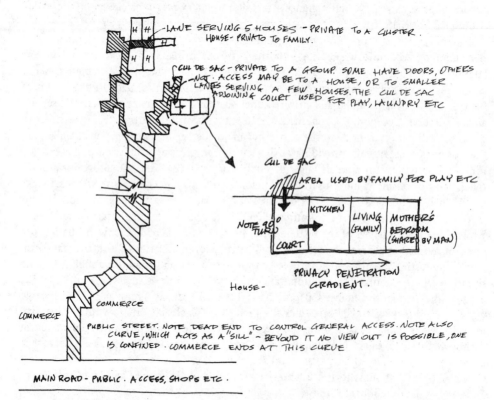

FIG. 2.10. Diagram of spatial organization of Indian squatter settlements (based on Payne 1971, 1973). Note its close resemblance to traditional Indian villages (Vickery 1972).

Very similarly a North African squatter settlement in Nanterre, France also reflects cultural preferences within economic constraints, the result being a traditional road pattern with limited access and a hierarchy of spaces of public street, semi-public street, private street and dwelling (Herpin and Santelli 1970–1971) using walls to separate domains.

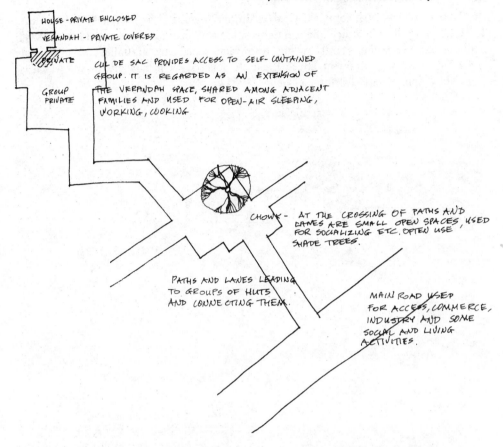

FIG. 2.11. North African squatter settlement in France (after Herpin and Santelli 1970–71). The structure is similar to the Indian squatter settlement in Fig. 2.10, but clearer and more hierarchical, reflecting North African traditions of building. (*Note*: streets are men's domain, houses women's.)

Habitat selection is clear from the fact that in many cases people have returned to squatter settlements after being rehoused (Brolin and Zeisel 1968). This choice is often conscious and related to factors such as spacing, access to outside, privacy and social relationships. This was the case with Aboriginal squatter settlements compared to government housing in adjoining towns (Savarton and George 1971). For Aborigines, possessions and houses are less important than kinship and social interdependence; dwellings are shelters with most living done outdoors. There is thus need for easy access between inside and outside which government housing does not provide. Aboriginal settlements have a spatial organization reflecting social, kinship and tribal patterns, which is very different to Western models. The area around the houses (which are adaptations of traditional forms) are for sleeping, sitting and working and houses are clustered by kinship. Linking paths reflect social relationships and come together at dwellings of "leaders". Houses are widely spaced reflecting privacy and other mechanisms which are of great subtlety and could be destroyed by greater proximity or even outdoor lighting (e.g., Hamilton 1972). Spacing is used in lieu of walls in the Indian and Moslem examples, and the layout reflects the complexity of traditional camps (Hamilton 1972; Rapoport 1972(e), 1974). The presence of a hierarchy of use and meeting spaces and a low density, scattered layout are importantly related to privacy, socializing, grouping and movement and is violated by government housing, closely spaced and in straight rows — which is rejected by Aborigines (Savarton and George 1971).

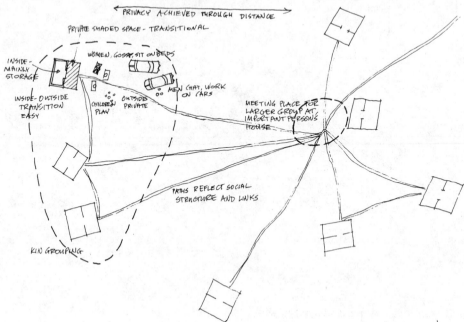

DIAGRAM OF PART OF ABORIGINAL SQUATTER SETTLEMENT (BASED ON SAVARTON & GEORGE 1971). THE STRUCTURE OF THE SETTLEMENT AND DWELLINGS SIMILAR IN ESSENCE TO TRADITIONAL SETTLEMENT (RAPOPORT 1972(e), 1974; HAMILTON 1972)

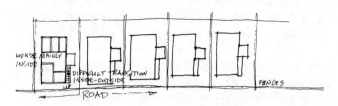

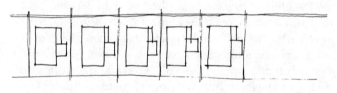

FIG. 2.12

Very similar differences can be found between Indian squatter settlements in Quebec and government housing. Here the contrast is also between a free arrangement based on kinship and focused on a series of village stores as meeting places versus a linear arrangement along streets.*

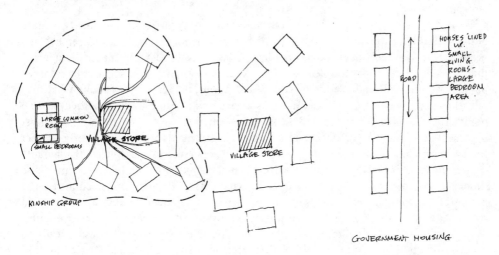

FIG. 2.13. Diagrammatic arrangement of Quebec Indian squatter settlement.

Studies of residents' problems reveal that in Lima, for example, the main dissatisfactions were with medical services, property titles, services — such as sewers, water, light, street paving, post offices and police protection and there were some complaints about food and clothing shops. Education, except kindergarten, was given low priority, there were few complaints about houses and no desire for credit — people preferred to build up equity gradually (Andrews and Phillips 1970). Residents see the squatter settlement as an area which is gradually upgrading and dissatisfactions are with detail (and comparable with other, more "normal" areas) rather than global — hardly a place which is terrible and should be torn down.

Settlements differ greatly in different countries and within countries. Their size and organization differ, some have links with villages while others do not, some have many small shops and businesses which others lack (Ray 1969, pp. 23–39)). In all cases, however, they reflect the specifics and express choice and preference in layout, public spaces, social and kinship relationships, privacy and the like. Therein lies their importance. While spatial arrangements facilitate social relationships the latter are most important. Associations based on common origin, or any other criteria selected, help people to organize their lives meaningfully (Abu-Lughod 1969; Doughty 1970). By selecting places in the city closest to their area of origin and by constructing physical environments basically similar to what they have known, their adjustment to urban life is aided since these areas act as "half-way houses" allowing a pacing of the adjustment to urban life (Rapoport and Kantor 1967; Meier 1966).

Among physical characteristics stressed by migrants to Cairo are houses with courtyards, interior streets and alleyways free of wheeled traffic duplicating the rural

* This is my interpretation of material which I was shown by Mlle. Lefebvre at the School of Architecture, University of Montreal, February 1971.

function of the street as playground, meeting place or place for animals. Squatter settlements allow laundry as a communal activity, and social networks can be stressed and localized by clustering and the use of coffee houses and the like for particular groups as meeting and information centers (AbuLughod 1969). Most of these are missing in designed areas.

As in the case of slums, in spite of outsiders' reactions, environmental quality is often better than in the tidier planned areas which bear much less relation to preference and needs. As we have seen these may be met in existing areas through habitat selection but in that case the physical environment itself is fixed. In large cities even changes in colors or planting are difficult and the use of streets and stoops, the kinds of shops and what they sell, the social networks, clubs and pubs as a social place can only be modified up to a point. The spatial organization and location of activities cannot be changed, not least because of codes and regulations, and in squatter settlements there is frequently a direct spatial expression of lifestyle and preferences for example, in the Nucleo Bandeirante settlement near Brasilia, where the traditional Brazilian urban form of plazas and dense shopping has been recreated, satisfaction is higher than in the new planned areas. The nature of the spontaneous area also helps women's employment because of density and grouping; even very bad housing is correlated with satisfaction because, in relative terms, it is an improvement. In Brasilia, on the other hand, much "better" housing leads to lower satisfaction because of social isolation, breaking of social links and longer travel. In fact, in Brasilia generally, social interaction and access to schools and services were most important so that for the inhabitants, unlike the planners, housing standards are not the most important thing. The Bandeirante area (like other similar ones) provide many leisure activities and are preferred to planned sectors (Smith *et al.* 1971).

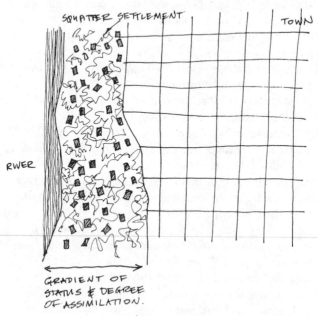

FIG. 2.14. Argentine squatter settlement and town, diagrammatic (inferred from verbal description in MacEwen 1972).

Preference and habitat selection are also found in an Argentine squatter settlement which is very different to the orderly city, with houses randomly scattered along the river with a profusion of natural vegetation, many children and animals. This area is rural in character and seen as a distinct place (housing an out group) by urbanites. Within the fairly small squatter settlement people cluster by degree of assimilation, forming a gradient from the more assimilated near the town to the less assimilated on the outskirts. There is thus a series of clearly distinguishable status areas, differentiated by proximity to town (MacEwen 1972) — the result of habitat selection, different values, lifestyles and standards and the use of appropriate symbols of social identity. (See Fig. 2.14, p. 106).

CHAPTER 3

Environmental Cognition

There are two meanings of the term environmental cognition which, while related, are conceptually different. These two meanings might broadly be called the psychological and the anthropological. The former has been influential in recent work on environmental cognition and can be traced to the ideas of Bartlett (1967), Lewin (1936, 1951) and Tolman (1948) as well as the more recent work of Piaget and other developmental psychologists (Piaget 1954, 1963; Piaget and Inhelder 1962). The anthropological approach, derived mainly from cognitive anthropology (Tyler 1969, Spradley 1972) has been used hardly at all in environmental cognition, yet it is important in its study. There are various conceptual differences between these two approaches to the subject but generally speaking the psychological approach can be seen as a special case of a more general and larger concept of environmental cognition which can be derived from cognitive anthropology.

While both approaches agree about the importance of cognition as a mediating mechanism between the individual and the environment, the psychological view tends to stress *knowledge* of the environment while the anthropological takes the position that cognitive processes are concerned with making the world *meaningful* and that there are different ways in which meaning can be given to the world. This view of environmental cognition is that it is mostly about giving meaning to the world rather than knowing about it. One consequence is that one needs to take a comparative view — cross-cultural at a moment in time and also through time, because the meanings which people give to the world are more variable than the ways in which the world is known or even used (the distinction between the concrete, use, value and symbolic object).

The "Anthropological" perspective, then, suggests the importance of the schemata, classifications, taxonomies, and cognitive splits used to structure the world and behavior in it. It is thus necessary to consider cultural cognitive habits (if one might call them that) in order to understand the way in which the environment is conceived and structured by the individual. People, as active, adaptive, goal-seeking organisms structure the world as a result of three major factors, organismic, environmental and cultural, which interact to form cognitive representations. In this chapter I will be discussing and relating both approaches but since most work is of the psychological type I will begin by discussing briefly the main aspects of the anthropological approach (see also Rapoport, 1976).

There are several points which characterize cognitive anthropology — at least as it relates to the environment. Cognition is a taxonomic process, the world being made meaningful by naming, classifying and ordering through some conceptual system. Different cultures do this differently, based on meanings and relative importance although there are species-specific regularities. It then follows that there are two major considerations: which material phenomena are significant to people in a culture and how they organize these phenomena (Tyler 1969) — what people value highly, how and what they select and how they organize it.

I have already suggested that while there may be some theoretical difficulties in separating cognition and perception, since both involve information processing (Ittelson 1973) and perception is an active process (Antrobus 1970) it is useful to do so on various grounds related to the directness of the experience. Thus location in the city only becomes really familiar after *direct* experience and even names mean more once a place is known and experienced.

Cognition, from the Latin word for "getting to know" refers both to the process of knowing and understanding and the product — the thing known. Our interest is with the way people give meaning to the physical world, how they know it, the schemata they use to structure the environment in the mind and how these affect behavior and design.

In terms of our discussion it is clear that before we can evaluate we must *know*, i.e., the elements evaluated must be part of our awareness and must fit into some schema. Cognition is then a search for order and a process of imposing an order — the type of order varying with the "cognitive style" of particular groups. This ordering involves the process of abstracting and creating concepts and schemata which even animals seem to have (Von Uexküll 1957; Peters 1973). For example, civet cats seem to be able to distinguish "bent" from "straight" which implies a matching against some schema (Hass 1970, pp. 56–57). Organisms thus impose spatial, social and temporal orders which are different but related, since all organisms manage to coexist in a spatio-temporal frame-work in the same world and since all the orders rely on the same processes of learning, memory, identity, location and orientation.

The basic cognitive act is the placing of the individual in his physical and social milieu. This involves the definitions of various places and social groups, which imply the idea of being here rather than there physically, of being us rather than them socially with consequent distinctions among them and attitudes towards them. This search for co-ordinated spatio-temporal and social frameworks is basic, and this structuring is important not only because it enables people to understand the environment and make it meaningful but also because design itself is the physical expression and making visible of cognitive schemata. One such schema which will come up several times is safe/unsafe or usable/unusable (e.g., Gould and White 1974, pp. 30–34). More generally in the case of the built environment it can be suggested that the following process occurs:

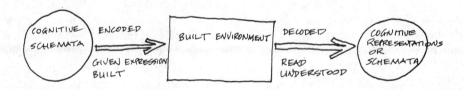

FIG. 3.1

The physical environment is then an expression of cultural cognitive categories such as wilderness, garden, city (Tuan 1971) public, private and so on (Rapoport 1972(b)) which, if the environment is meaningful, produce the appropriate and intended cognitive schemata. The priority of conceptual organization is illustrated by the case of the Australian Aborigines where a complex cognitive spatial, social and temporal organization exists without the corresponding use of physical devices such as wall, fences and the like (Rapoport 1972(e)). More generally the built environment can be seen as the making visible of an "ethnic domain" (Langer 1953, pp. 92–100), a non-spatial concept linked to culture, values, symbols, status, lifestyle and the like. In many cases, therefore, cognitive categories and domains can be given direct environmental equivalents. Considering the previous example of the difference between the colonial and native indigenous city, it has recently been shown that this distinction in India can be well related to the classification system used and that the spatial environment corresponds to ethnosemantic terms (King 1974(a), (b); Rapoport 1972(e); in press(a)). In many of the examples of categorization naming is important. Ordering the environment into meaningful categories is often done through naming things and identifying places and domains with particular groups, uses or activities.

In cosmologies chaos is frequently ordered through naming – (The Word) – which is equivalent to creating cognitive categories. Thus an analysis of Genesis points out that the world was not really finished until man had named the components and through this incorporated them in his life (Cox 1966, pp. 86, 89–90, 252). Naming is also important in defining place and how things are classified and named also affects evaluation and preference – positive and negative meanings attach to named categories of things.

Names incorporate memories and meanings of particular groups. Whether language affects perception is still an open question (Whorf 1956; Rapoport and Horowitz 1960; Berlin and Kay 1969; Stea and Carson n.d.; Lenneberg 1972; Lloyd 1972). However, the relation of naming and language to cognitive categories and classifications is clearer. Classification seems to be an essential process in human existence in spite of some arguments to the contrary. It seems even clearer in relation to the built environment, since that gives physical expression to cognitive domains which are always named. This affects the very definition of city (Wheatley 1971; Krapf-Askari 1969) and the structuring of cities and other environments as cosmic symbols (Wheatley 1971; Müller 1961; Eliade 1961; Rapoport 1969(a); Fraser 1968; Rykwert n.d.). More specifically, in Southern Italy, the environment is classified into country and town. The country is seen as "outside" even though most town inhabitants are peasants; town is positive, country – negative. This conceptual division is one of the social controls which influences other institutions, behavior and the settlement pattern. Residence is concentrated, social controls and family are in towns while work is outside. Land is subdivisible, town houses are not: since they are given to daughters, the neighborhoods and towns become women-centered (Davis 1969). Naming is also important in making people feel at home in another sense than making the world meaningful. Considering migrants, we find that not only do they select familiar landscapes as far as possible and alter them further but they also tend to name things in terms of where they come from to make the unfamiliar familiar. Thus in the New World we find names for streets, rivers, mountains, plains and cities, as well as plants and animals, based on the country of origin. In countries of varied migration naming reflects the origins of settlers (as do forms and urban patterns) and these names and forms can, in fact, be used to determine origins. Naming places in this way may be a form of "linguistic landscaping" (Lowenthal 1971, p. 242). We have already seen the importance of names in suggesting certain qualities and images of housing estates.

A small example is the continued use of Sixth Avenue in New York 30 years after renaming. A more striking instance is the resistance to name changes of areas in cities. In Sydney, Australia, in mid 1972, the Geographical Names Board was trying to change the names of urban areas. There was tremendous resistance, much political activity, letters and petitions. The general feeling was that name change would lead to "loss of identity" and was a very serious matter. Aldermen of high-status areas argued that they were different to other, lower-status areas and that the distinct individuality and identity would disappear with renaming. There was fear of negative connotations, loss of status and value and a wish to preserve long established names (*Sydney Morning Herald* 1972). There was also resistance to boundary changes, but name changes seemed to generate more passions – they seemed more related to identity. I suspect that in both cases higher status areas resisted being merged with lower status ones more than vice versa.

Thus the importance of names, representing cognitive schemata, may persist when the original physical equivalents have disappeared (Cox 1968) although when names and cognitive schemata coincide with physical equivalents, the environment becomes particularly clear and forceful.

Identification by self or others is at the heart of the attachment to names and this process is also the essence of cognitive classification whether of places or social groups. In each case categories are constructed which are distinguishable from other categories (Barth 1969) and humans classify in order to impose order and organization on the physical and social worlds. This is done in accordance with cultural rules producing the distinctive cognitive categories and styles whereby groups understand and shape the environment.

The process of constructing spatial, temporal or social cognitive schemata seems to involve decisions about whether things are alike or different. Discrimination among elements, and deciding whether they are alike or unlike, can be done either through identity categorization (seeing stimuli as forms of the same thing) or equivalence categorization (seeing a set of discriminate stimuli as belonging together). This latter categorization can be done through three broad classes of equivalence categories – affective, functional or formal (Bruner *et al.* 1956) or, in another formulation, using five major modes (Olver and Hornsby 1972):

Perceptible. On the basis of color, shape, size or position, i.e., what I call noticeable differences.

Functional. On the basis of use or function – what elements can do or what can be done to them.

Affective. In terms of evaluation, emotion aroused or preference.

Nominal. By attaching ready made names from the language.

Fiat equivalence. Arbitrary definition of equivalence.

The mode stressed, and the specifics of each mode, probably vary with culture, and both linguistic and symbolic/image schemata are important in this process. In any case it follows that different features of the environment are emphasized in establishing likeness and grouping and these would tend also to be organized in different ways (Rapoport 1976). There are, for example, cultural differences in the sense modalities stressed, so that Western culture taboos smells and taste because they are related to pleasures of the body and hence there are no schemata for assimilating or recalling olfactory information (Neisser 1968; Hall 1966; Wober 1966) and there are also differences in sensitivity to kinesthetics, texture, wind-movement, sound and so on. Similarly categories of use and function, such as work and play, or streets for sitting in or for passing through, are variable and affect evaluation and the design of the environment. Thus the way in which space and people in space are organized reflects spatial, temporal and social cognitive categories reflecting equivalence and identity groupings. For example, in a Maya village the relative lack of distinction between cognitive categories such as nature and house, house and house, and person and person is reflected in the absence of sharp boundaries between landscape and village, inside and outside and so on (Gutmann 1969) very differently to the sharp and strong boundaries of an Indian village or Moslem or Yoruba city. These different cognitive domains are reflected in the environment and the "cognitive domains of a culture may correspond to the concrete spatial divisions of everyday life" (D. Rose 1968). For example the categorization of space and domains related to:

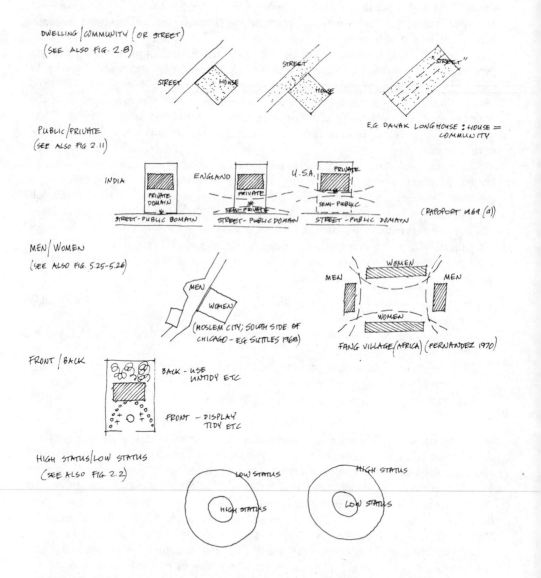

FIG. 3.2. When reversals in domain definition are found, different location of boundaries or different ways of marking domains, problems of decoding and understanding may occur.

Consider the distinction between street and dwelling. But the definition of "street" is also a matter of categorization. Is the morphological definition of street as "space between buildings" useful or would a definition in terms of a place where certain activities take place be more useful in which case a court or compound may become its equivalent. Other analogous functions may take place in restaurants, pubs, coffee shops, teahouses or dwellings (see Chapter 5) and any such discussion would have to include the cultural rule system for public behavior and the space splits corresponding to the cognitive domains. It is this problem of what could be called functional non-equivalence, and the failure to relate environmental form to cultural norms, which weakens otherwise insightful studies of the street by various designers (e.g., Rudofsky 1969). Related to this is how people understand the street system once it is in place, how they orient themselves in it and hence how they use it.

Time, like space, meaning (symbols) and communication is also organized conceptually — there are temporal categories. There are clear cultural differences in large-scale (almost philosophical) temporal orientations, taxonomies in terms of past vs. future, linearity vs. cyclicity (Doob 1971; Yaker *et al.* 1971; Green 1972; Panoff 1969; Ortiz 1972, pp. 136—137) and all languages allow for temporal distinctions. Temporal images thus affect the environment, so that habitability is related to culturally experienced time and temporal orientations are a good indicator of values, so that in the West there is a linear concept of time whereas in India there is a cyclic view of time (Pande 1970) as there is in most traditional cultures. In the case of India this has affected the landscape by preserving elements which otherwise would have disappeared and also shaped the character of cities (Sopher 1964). Temporal orientations even vary between the U.S. and Great Britain and their future and past orientations respectively have led to very different cultural landscapes (Lowenthal 1968; Lowenthal and Prince 1964, 1965). Such differences also lead to very different behavior in terms of smaller-scale time patterning (H. B. Lee 1968).

Time is, in fact, also structured differently in more immediate and smaller-scale ways. Based on how valuable and important time is, it will be spent in different ways and with differing accuracy. Because the allocation of available time, the rhythms and tempos of activities and their synchronization will affect how frequently different parts of the city are seen, whether they are seen during the day or night, during working hours or weekends (in themselves an example of a cognitive taxonomy!), at leisure or in a hurry, such cognitive temporal splits will affect the development of cognitive urban schemata. The tempos or rhythms of different groups in the city need to be considered and synchronized — time is closely related to activity systems and people can be separated or joined in time as well as in space (e.g., MacMurray 1971, pp. 202—203), i.e, there is social time as well as social space (Yaker *et al.* 1971, p. 75). The wrong rhythms or tempos and their inappropriate synchronization will influence the use of the environment and lead to lack of contact among groups, or contact with the wrong groups, and hence to stress.

Cognition in this anthropological sense is thus related to the making of places — physical or social — by defining what is done where and when, who is here or there and when, how here differs from there. This could be greatly elaborated (e.g., Rapoport 1976), but the main point has been made and I will now turn to a brief introductory discussion of psychological aspects of environmental cognition (e.g., Neisser 1967; Moore and Hart 1971; Ittelson 1973; Moore and Golledge 1976).

Most of this research deals with how people come to understand their everyday world.

Given an environment which they did not design, how do they understand it and use it. This process may also involve categorization (Craik 1968) relating it to the broader view discussed above. Environmental cognition is, therefore, concerned with the elements into which the environment is classified, the relationships (distances and directional systems) among them which constitute an overall cognitive representation of a portion of the world, the schemata, images and cognitive maps whereby people orient themselves and use the environment.

There is evidence that there is an important location processing system in the human brain affecting mental maps. This system is primitive (since it exists in simple animals also) and may consequently be unconscious and flexible; it relies on experience of space, locomotion and location in it (orientation) (Kaplan 1970). The important point is that there seems to be a mapping process, that people identify spatial domains, define their place in them, orient themselves in space and move through it.

It is clearly important for all organisms to know where they are and what is likely to happen next before they can know whether things are good or bad and act accordingly (Kaplan 1971). The latter two are evaluation and action (discussed in Chapter 2), the first two are aspects of environmental cognition. Put differently, since the self must be prepared for action in a spatio-temporal frame of reference it is essential to have spatial and temporal orientation. While animals have to find their way in space, define places and remember paths (e.g., Von Euxküll 1957; Tolman 1948; Peters 1973) they do not use as elaborate schemata with culturally constituted reference points. People have a heightened awareness of their location in space and time. Being lost or spatially disoriented is distressing to any organism. The ability to move freely and intelligently, to visualize one's spatial location and to have conceptual maps of getting to destinations and back is commonplace — yet an achievement. Place names are important ways of creating focal points, as are spatial and temporal orientational systems. Identification with place is also related to uses, perceptual differences, affect, social identity and status (e.g., Hallowell 1955). In all this the subjective, cognized environment clearly corresponds in some way to the real since without this correspondence people would not have survived (Sprout and Sprout 1956).

One of the important functions of all these cognitive processes is to reduce information and to make a basically chaotic environment predictable, orderly and manageable. Cognitive categorization is then similar to cultural rules which help to simplify life by making behavior habitual (culture as habit). In the same way as people know how to eat, dress, use their voice and body, and what manners to employ they also know how to use the environment effectively. These cognitive processes are clearly ways of reducing information through imposing a structure on the environment. The known environment and its cognitive representations are a *simplified* environment. By setting up routines, using only part of the available environment and even avoiding knowledge of parts of it information is reduced and fewer conscious decisions and less conscious monitoring are necessary.

Urban Images

Images are modality specific and often beyond awareness; they include both concrete and abstract stimulus information, the former involving parallel processing whereas the latter is processed sequentially. All images, however, are schematic and hence formed by integrating many separate elements (Segal 1971). They control the assimilation of perceptual events, i.e., only those which fit the image tend to be accepted (e.g., Boulding 1956) but since images are checked against the real world (e.g., Miller, Gallanter and Pribram 1960) they eventually change if there is incompatible information.

Images and schemata clearly play a major role in environmental cognition and are occasionally used interchangeably. Images are then seen as mental representations of those parts of reality known through direct or indirect experience, grouping various environmental attributes and combining them according to certain rules (Harrison and Sarre 1971). Yet it seems more useful to consider images as influencing cognitive schemata, such as mental maps, in the same way that they influence environmental evaluation. An important type of images which have been used in the sense of schemata are urban images (lynch 1960; de Jonge 1962; Gulick 1963) the interest in which played an important role in the development of environmental cognition.

Lynch (1960) was interested in how people understand the structure of cities and how they use them. There were two basic questions — do people know and mentally structure the physical environment and, secondly, which features do they notice and to what extent is the structuring due to people and to what extent does it depend on the environment, i.e., are there any regularities? This concern was almost exclusively with imageability — the clarity and ease with which people form urban images and how memorable these are.

He concluded that people noticed the physical environment, were able to talk about it, describe it and draw maps of it and that in spite of subjective differences there were some regularities in the things noticed — the well known 5 categories: districts, edges, paths, nodes and landmarks. It was also apparent that people had different images of different cities, that the ease with which they were generated also varied in different places as did the elements used.

In Holland these findings were confirmed and enriched. Map images seem easiest to form where the street pattern is regular with a single dominant path and where there are characteristic nodes and unique landmarks. Where overall structure and pattern were difficult to grasp and unclear, isolated landmarks, single buildings and individual paths became more important as did visual details. Comparing new and old neighborhoods it was found that difficulties in orientation and low imageability could also arise where the structure is quite clear but the elements too uniform to be distinguished (de Jonge 1962), i.e., not noticeably different.

In a different culture (Lebanon) there was general agreement once again but also greater differences, particularly the greater importance of socio-cultural associations relative to visual cues, i.e., both visual form and social significance were important in the construction of urban images (Gulick 1963).

In terms of the five modes of equivalence one might suggest that while American and Dutch subjects relied on the perceptible mode, Lebanese subjects added a combination of functional and affective criteria. This finding that more than the perceptual mode is used seems more general. Thus among children in Berlin visible signs of human activity and involvement in the urban landscape seemed critical for the clarity of the image and memory of the city, so that small details with these characteristics were often more important and memorable than historical monuments or major buildings (Sieverts 1967, 1969). In Birmingham, also, elements at the human scale seemed more important than major features and these latter were singled out only when they were noticeably different from the urban fabric at a small, meaningful scale (Goodey *et al.* 1971). In Boston memorable areas were those with congruence of form and activity (and it also seemed that the mode of travel played a role so that motorists and pedestrians had different images) (Steinitz 1968).

In a recent study of Houston it was found that different aspects of the city were used depending on whether it was a matter of seeing it (its visual image), remembering it or attaching importance to it [meaning, value or preference]. For visual imagery structural (man-made) features seemed most important, for evaluation and preference (importance) social features were critical, while for remembering a combination of mostly structural and some social. Natural features were least mentioned (Rozelle and Baxter 1972) although this might well be different in different cities.

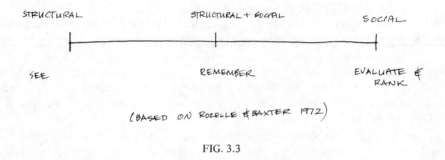

FIG. 3.3

This would tend to confirm the view that while Lynch (1960) suggested that there were three components of urban images — identity, structure and meaning, he neglected the latter (Crane 1971). In a recent study of Englewood, Colorado it was found that uniqueness of design (i.e., noticeable differences) helps imageability. Meaning helps make things noticeable and can be shared by groups or be personal (when they become associations) (Rapoport 1970(c) and Chapter 6). In this particular case associations were generally unimportant while meaning was used for nodes, landmarks and, mainly, districts. The location of physical elements was more important than their appearance and paths were the most important element (unlike in the Houston study where they were third after buildings and the general structure and skyline). Meanings were related to economics and there was little attachment to, or involvement with, the city. For most people the meaning was one of function — of how it served their purposes (Harrison and Howard 1972). The specifics would probably change in different cities and cultures but it reinforces the general tenor of many studies of a rather more complicated notion of urban images and their elements, variations due to age, sex, education, and ethnicity, idiosyncratic variations due to differences in use and movement patterns and cultural differences such as the importance of the Central Plaza in Latin America (Wood 1969), all of which strengthens the importance of relating urban images to the broader aspects of environmental cognition.

For most urban designers the term "urban image" corresponds to Lynch's use of the term and most of the new developments in environmental cognition from man–environment studies have not become part of their conceptual tools. That usage has several problems in addition to the neglect of meaning. One is the stress on legibility at the expense of complexity (see Chapter 4). The other concerns some inherent weaknesses and difficulties with the basic categories of node, landmark, edge, path and district — which might be clarified by applying the broader notions of cognition introduced earlier.

The major problem is that these categories have been defined by the researcher and ignore the inherent variability of definitions and classifications — the users' cognitive schemata are ignored. Yet, when considered cross-culturally, major differences in such classifications are found. For example in the West valleys are considered as regions bounded by hills, but the Yurok Indians reversed this, thinking of hills as regions bounded by valleys (Waterman 1920) — a reversal very difficult to conceive. Landmarks thus depend partly on socio-cultural variables — uses, meanings, names, associations and preference rankings as well as perceptual and locational prominence. Their definition may well vary — as has already been implied (e.g., Gulick 1963; Sieverts 1967, 1969; Goodey *et al.* 1971).

Subjectively, the same physical element could be classified as either an edge or a path, depending partly on people's roles — for motorists it may be a path, for residents an edge. Age, health or income would affect people's mobility and transport available so that a major road seen as a path by commuters could be seen as an edge by the old, very young, handicapped or some locality bound group. The mode of travel (whether approached on foot or by car) and the direction from which it is approached may also play a role.

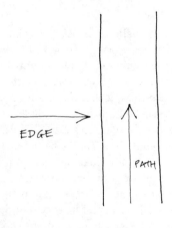

FIG. 3.4

Roads are, in fact, often treated as edges and tend to be major edge elements. In the case of the West End of Boston the peripheral highways or train lines were classified as paths by travellers and as edges by those living there. Widening Cambridge Road in the 1920's made it a better path for motorists while turning it into a boundary for the inhabitants and led to a symbolic as well as physical separation of the area (Gans 1971, pp. 300, 302). A similar distinction was found in some unpublished student work in Sydney, where non-residents classified a major road as a path whereas to residents it was the one clear edge. Even in Los Angeles roads are often seen as boundaries by residents (Everitt and Cadwallader 1972). This means that the classifications used by various groups need to be discovered rather than one classification imposed. Thus districts are defined as large areas into which one enters and which are distinguishable from the surrounding area — but this definition can be subjective and variable. Nodes are roughly equivalent to small districts, and are distinguished by their importance, so that their definition involves many variables. Different elements may be used at different scales and the different categories brought together into cognitive wholes, so that a market square is not just a distinct area but also a node, a meeting point of paths defined by edges and landmarks (Porteous 1971) and may also itself become a landmark or a district characterized by certain uses (e.g., the old Les Halles, Paris or Covent Garden, London).

Thus these elements are likely to vary for different groups so that associations, unimportant in Englewood, Colorado (Harrison and Sarre 1972) may be important elsewhere (Porteous 1971). Also, it appears that landmarks are selected differently by various people. The elderly often use landmarks no longer existing while the young use new projects ignored by older groups rather than well established urban elements (Porteous 1971; Rapoport 1973(d)). The activity patterns will also affect which elements are encountered, and when, so that people with widely varying activity systems will use different urban elements (see Chapter 5).

In effect, due to people's variable cognitive systems there is an inherent ambiguity in all such elements (e.g., Barthes 1970–71). For example, a feature such as the Bull Ring in Birmingham can be a landmark, node or district and a tall building may be a node, a focus of paths or a landmark. More generally, a node can be a landmark, an edge can be a path, a node can be a district (Goodey *et al.* 1971, pp. 41–42) and the definition of districts is also variable.

Urban images are not only visual: all senses enter into their formation, they are affected by non-experiential factors, which increase in importance with increase in scale and by age, education, skills, socio-cultural variables, symbolic and associational values of individuals and groups, and variations in their activity patterns and extent of behavioral space so that if, due to cognitive rules, a street is classified as a place in which to sit, eat and talk the urban mental map, and behavior, will be very different than if it is categorized differently – as merely a space to traverse. Thus, although Lynch's proposed elements are a useful starting point they cannot be defined by designers or analysts – their subjective definition by various individuals and groups needs to be discovered.

Such definitions will depend on cognitive categorization and criteria of similarity and dissimilarity, on familiarity, the mode of travel and nature of traffic, the temporal rhythms, tempos and sequence of movement. The extent of people's behavioral space also affects their experience, since places which are used are known much better than those which are not and knowledge is also affected by preference and evaluation – by the means attached. As people move through the environment they divide it into "regions", "paths" and "barriers" (e.g., Lewin 1936, 1951) because "space", in a philosophical sense, is empty and needs bounding and identification by people: this is the cognitive process of giving meaning which we have been discussing. It is apparent that we should be dealing with fundamental cognitive processes and constructs rather than just urban images.

Cognitive Schemata and Mental Maps

One major characteristic of cognitive schemata is that they include areas and places never experienced but known indirectly. The accuracy of such knowledge depends on education, the accuracy of the data, skill at interpreting it, and so on. Direct experience, particularly over time, leads to clearer and more accurate schemata. This, of course, corresponds to the view that specific places which people know fit into an image of the whole world (Boulding 1956).

Schemata are affected by roles. Thus urban areas might be given administrative, tourist, residents' or planning definitions with corresponding schemata. The distinction between say, administrators' and other people's schemata may have major effects on decision making (e.g., Linge 1971; Heathcote 1965; Gould and White 1974) as discussed in Chapter 2. Cognitive schemata and mapping seem to be fundamental since children seem to have it at a very early age (Blaut *et al.* 1970; Blaut and Stea 1971) and "primitive" people not only have complex maps but also seem to be able to read aerial photographs (Hallowell 1955, p. 194). Animals also have schemata of their lifespace, its territories, barriers and paths as related to hierarchy and status (e.g., Wynne-Edwards 1962; Peters 1973).

The idea of an organism's schema of its environment corresponds to the notion of *Umwelt* (Uexküll 1957) which includes concepts such as the perceived environment and the effects of knowledge and behavioral space on the construction of a subjective spatial realm. It considers the effect of different sensory spaces — visual, tactile, olfactory and deals with coordinate systems. Finally, and most importantly, it distinguishes between the *Merkwelt* — the perceptual image and the *Umwelt* which is a construct (or schema) based on the *Merwelt* and related to the *Wirkwelt* (or action space). Animals' *Umwelten* differ, depending on how they use and structure their environment and generate spatial maps, and the information used is affected by search images which may block perceptual images (what I have called filters).

It is quite remarkable that we have here, in 1910, almost a complete description of the elements and processes which operate in the area of environmental cognition and lead to cognitive schemata and there are some equally useful insights in Bartlett's work in 1932 (Bartlett 1967).

If we accept that schemata represent the subjective knowledge structure of an individual — a sum of his knowledge, values and meanings organized according to certain rules and affecting behavior, then *mental maps are those specific* **spatial** *images which people have of the physical environment* and which primarily affect spatial behavior.

The term "mental maps" has been used in several quite different ways and some clarification is needed. One important usage describes geographers' mapping of, say, people's environmental preferences which *in themselves are not spatial or map-like* (Gould 1972(b); Gould and White 1974). I would argue that these are not mental maps — since the mapping is not done by the people concerned. It is rather a preference scale given spatial form by a geographer and there are many examples of such geographers' mappings of desirability, utility, value, opportunity and the like — they are rather spatial inferences of non-spatial preferences. Such preferences may be for parts of countries which people have never seen or experienced except vicariously (Gould and White 1968; 1974).

These are not really mental maps because the mapping was done by the geographer. This becomes even more important when we realize that geographers and non-geographers tend to have different mental maps of the same area, for example, the New England States (Stea 1969). I would reserve the term *mental map* to spatial schemata or representations held by the individuals themselves, and reflecting affective, symbolic, meaning, preference and other factors — even though it is often stressed in the literature that there is no evidence for mental maps being in any way map-like.

Mental maps are a series of psychological transformations through which people acquire, code, store, recall and decode information about their spatial environment — its elements, relative locations, distances and directions and overall structure (e.g., Downs and Stea 1973); they can also be called cognitive maps (Tolman 1948; cf. also Trowbridge 1913).

Mental maps, like geographers' maps, help the individual who only knows what is nearby and has trouble knowing what is distant. In both cases various spatial attributes such as distance, direction, or area are transformed into simplified symbolic forms which are easily grasped in their relationships. These help the individual comprehend and use the environment. Geographers' maps, maps of "primitive" people and cognitive maps are structurally similar and the differences are of degree not of kind (e.g., Hallowell 1955).

For example, maps can be seen as a physical expression of mental maps just as built environments can be seen as physical embodiments of conceptual space. Such maps are frequently distorted as a function of values and mythical variables so that we find the well known New Yorker's view of the U.S., medieval maps with Jerusalem in the center, and many others involving some central place, *omphalos, axis mundi* or whatever (e.g., Adler 1911) reflecting judgements about importance, sacredness, centrality, relatedness and so on.

Other early maps were guides for itineraries and showed straight line routes with stages and features of the country on both sides (Crone 1962). They tended to ignore directions and were based on roads, their junctions and turns (very much as people's mental maps are frequently based on paths). Maps of large areas were often distorted because of certain assumptions. One such was the ancient Greeks' assumption of straightness and symmetry (Craik 1970, p. 80) which reflected a deeply felt and strongly held value judgement. Advertising maps today also show the relative importance of places, what is centrally located and relations and paths. (See Fig. 3.5, p. 121).

All maps, mental and other, are, of course, about identity, location and orientation and there are cultural differences in what is named, and stressed, how these elements are related and what coordinate system is used — which follows from our discussion on cognition generally (e.g., Sapir 1958). Maps among "primitive" people generally clearly contain a non-pragmatic component, which is usually sacred and ritual so that there are maps locating the land of the dead, paradise or hell (Hallowell 1955; Ohnuki-Tierney 1972). The differences between such maps and modern ones is not only increased knowledge in the latter, but different cognitive styles (of which the increased knowledge itself is a part) and different motivations, attitudes and expectations as well as different activities, all requiring different types of maps. Primitive maps generally link important points by known paths and show barriers. Such points may be waterholes, sacred sites, rivers, portages — and time indications may replace distances.

Thus while some Aboriginal maps serve as ways of finding hunting grounds or waterholes, most tend to show only ritually important features. One similarity between Aboriginal maps and mental maps of cities is that both are assemblages of elements in the mind coinciding with important features in the environment — natural features in the case of Aborigines, urban elements in the case of cities (Rapoport 1972(e)).

The importance of mental maps, their distortions and gaps is that human behavior depends on them (e.g., Jackson and Johnston 1974). For example, the most important social activities of certain lower class groups in Lima, playing soccer, takes place on vacant sites which are named in ways reflecting the origins of the players using them.

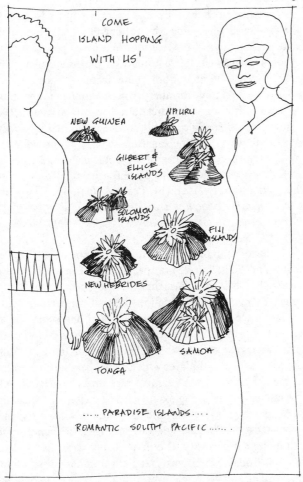

FIG. 3.5. Example of "mental map" based on tourist criteria, reputation and romantic image rather than geographic size or relationships (based on *Air Pacific* advertisement, *The Australian*, Jan 13, 1972).

These are unknown to middle- and upper-class Lima residents, yet are so important for those using them that "if one has not trod the dust [of these grounds] he does not know the Lima of today" (Doughty 1970, pp. 37–38). The mental maps of these two groups would be very different, so would their behavior spaces affecting the parts of the city used and, in turn, the further growth and development of mental maps. Also, ignorance or neglect of this system of spaces and their use would invalidate planning for recreation, travel, patterns, neighborhoods, social networks and the like. The differential lacunae in urban mental maps of different groups have major implications for planning generally, as do differences in the elements regarded as important and hence used. Thus, in Ciudad Guyana planners stressed topography which was absent in people's mental maps, and there were also major differences in the importance of the city center (Lynch 1972, pp. 20–21). The mental maps of whole countries and regions which people have also affect their travel behavior (Peattie 1972).

One cannot demonstrate unequivocally that mental maps exist in any given case, but clearly people act in accord with some form of cognitive schemata. For example, there have been alternate explanations of the sectoral behavior of people in cities — that people of similar socio-economic class cluster sectorially or that their mental maps of cities are sectoral. It was then suggested that both these factors — socio-economic status and mental maps — might be operating together, so that various groups employ certain basic status symbols — style of houses and address and live among their peers and as close to their social superiors as possible. Since their knowledge of cities is sectoral (Adams 1969) they also settle in that way. This explanation seemed to be valid, and residents in Christchurch (N.Z.) seemed to have sectoral mental maps and agree about the social desirability of areas, their knowledge being spatially constrained by the sector of the city in which they live (Johnston 1971(a), (b); Lee 1971(b)). The most interesting point is that *preference and habitat selection are constrained and affected by the cognitive schemata and mental maps which people have of cities* — thus linking these two broad topics.

The fact that behavior is more closely related to cognitive than to physical maps (MacKay, Olshavsky and Sentell 1975), a special case of people acting in the perceived environment, means that the gaps, inaccuracies and specifics of the mental maps of various groups must be known. The variations in such maps are related to the physical structure of the city, place of residence, socio-cultural and other characteristics of the group, means of travel and so on. Such gaps are often in terms of unpopular or unacceptable areas, as in the case of Lima. Similarly, in the San Francisco Bay Area people only seem aware of pleasant places which symbolize the area. In Sydney also there is a blank in the mental maps of many people regarding the Western suburbs which are only known as an unpleasant area, the extent and character of which are unknown. Yet half of Sydney's population live there and it contains some very pleasant areas. In Milwaukee also knowledge of the East side and South side are almost mutually exclusive.

This is partly a matter of necessity. People probably never had a clear mental map of the *whole* of any city. Today, when most people live in connurbations and urban fields, the city cannot be visualized as a whole even using maps and can only be experienced in limited segments. Since one of the functions of mental maps is precisely to simplify the environment, the gaps and omissions become essential. This is supported by the fact that, in the case of children, there is a negative correlation between community size and extent and detail of their cognitive maps (Gump 1972; Wright 1969, 1970).

People only use parts of the city — by ignoring much of it they make it into a set of small places. People generally remember whole cities through small symbolic parts. "New York" suggests the lower- and mid-Manhattan skylines, the Statue of Liberty — yet these form a very small part of that city. There would be differences between visitors and residents to be sure; for the latter there are well known elements in Mid-town Manhattan so that Times Square, Rockefeller Center and the Fifth Avenue department stores comprise over half the places mentioned by residents. I suspect that the skyline was known but, in any case, vast areas of Queens, Brooklyn and the Bronx were *terra incognita* (Milgram 1970, p. 1468; Milgram *et al.* 1972).

Similarly Rio de Janeiro means Copacabana Beach and Sugarloaf, Paris — the Eiffel Tower, the Seine, Notre Dame, the Boulevards and Montmartre, i.e., cities are identified by symbols and symbolic views and remembered by these. Even in Ipswich, not a large city, it was the medieval core, and even particular parts of it, that symbolized the town, and the preference for it (as having "country town" atmosphere) was related to that core (Wilmott 1967, p. 393). It is very useful to look at travel posters and world maps at airports to identify such elements (e.g., the recent addition of an Opera House to symbolize Sydney on such maps). Such elements help remember places and are important in environmental preference — they constitute an important part of the symbolic landscape. When such features are missing, cities become indistinct — they have low imageability (Lynch 1960) or legibility (Barthes 1970–71).

Mental maps thus consist of two kinds of elements: those known by outsiders and by most inhabitants except possibly the most deprived and immobile, and local elements used by inhabitants of specific areas, having special associations and values for smaller groups or individuals depending on the specific variables involved. There is thus a hierarchy of memorable elements of differing significance and attraction for various groups. These elements may be areas (Left Bank, Soho, Beacon Hill, Greenwich Village), topographic features (Sydney Harbor, Berkeley Hills, Sugarloaf), buildings or structures (Golden Gate Bridge, Parliament House and Big Ben, Eiffel Tower, Sydney Harbor Bridge and Opera House) a group of buildings (San Giminiano, Manhattan Skyline) or paths (Freeways in Los Angeles, the Boulevards) yet such shared elements are limited (e.g., Taylor 1973, p. 301) and, at the local scale, there is even more variability with ever smaller groups sharing elements, although these may become more important since the neighborhood is a most important place for satisfaction (Wilson 1962; Lansing *et al.* 1970; Marans and Rodgers 1973). Thus the cognitive maps of these smaller areas provide a link between the dwelling and the city and, in designing, the whole hierarchy of elements should be identified and considered.

One thus finds simplification of the city at the overall level and different forms of elaboration at the local level. The city center and major elements although known to all may be differentially symbolized (Prokop 1967) leading to marked differences in use, so that in Paris certain working class groups regard the center as outside their orbit while the suburbs are ignored by the upper- and middle class (Lamy 1967). The difference is that the local elements are only known and valued by residents. Behavior, such as recreation, results from an interaction and particular preferences and knowledge of opportunities (Mercer 1971(a)) which is embodied in people's mental maps. Such discretionary behavior is then affected by place of residence, travel routes and so on (Mercer 1971(b)) while preferences for specific activities and places are related to lifestyle.

Much more than merely physical elements are involved in the creation of mental maps. Clearly symbolism, meaning, elements no longer physically present, socio-cultural aspects, congruence of activity and form, context, and activity stereotypes (latent as well as manifest) cleanliness, safety, the types of people all play a role. Thus New York may be seen as frenetic, dirty, dangerous with unfriendly people and such stereotypes can even exist for whole states, including personality types and lifestyles — as has been shown for Australia (Berry 1969). For example, I would predict that Les Halles in Paris (before they were pulled down) were structured in terms of activities and unique time-cycles (e.g., after theater dinners), smells, food, flowers, prostitutes and the hotels serving them as well as architectural and urban elements. Harley Street in London is incorporated into maps in terms of knowledge and name rather than physical elements. For other areas such as Soho or the garment district, activities, and people, sometimes reinforced by form and other sensory cues, would also play a part (as in an oriental bazaar).

The construction of cognitive maps, then, incorporates a large variety of cues.

Following the example (in Chapter 1) of how a driver constructs a cognitive map (Wallace 1965) I will describe, introspectively, the cues used in constructing a cognitive map while commuting on a train on the North Shore line between Gordon and Redfern Stations in Sydney. I took this trip three days a week during term for three years starting as a new arrival. I tended to read and tried to keep track of the trip so as to know when I had reached my destination.

* Initially one relies on vision — mainly written material — railway station signs, signs on shops, churches, halls and banks which mention place names and also other physical elements such as buildings, TV towers, views of water by the harbor and the harbor itself, downtown skyline, the bridge, parks, certain residential areas.
* Gradually spatial cues become known: at Chatswood and North Sydney there is a wide space with many platforms compared to the more typical narrow space with two platforms. The spatial location of stations also varies — North Sydney in a deep cutting, Milson's Point and Central Station raised high above the surroundings.
* There are temporal cues such as the length of different halts: those at North Sydney, Chatswood, Wynyard and Central Station tend to be much longer, marking important places (in each case reinforced by other cues as described).
* While the number of stops is not actually counted one is aware of their rhythm, particularly since North of Downtown they occur at one-mile intervals with an unusually large gap between Chatswood and St. Leonards.
* Changes in light quality play a part. The major ones occur at several tunnels — a major one north of North Sydney and the underground stretch Downtown. The two ends of the latter are very different — in one case one emerges onto the Harbor Bridge with extensive views in all directions of water, ships and so on as well as a very special light quality, while at the other end one emerges under a large parking structure with a gradual increase in light level, and industry all around. More subtle light quality changes are gradually picked up. Light quality differs near water, on the bridge and away from water; it changes due to buildings and vegetation, the amount of sky exposed, proximity of walls, whether one is in a cutting or on a crest and in many other ways.
* Kinesthetic cues are also present. There are several major climbs and descents involving curves and spirals, acceleration or slowing down.
* These latter also lead to changes in noise level. On curves there is much squealing of wheels, on slopes greater engine noise. There are very different sounds in tunnels, underground, on the bridge, in cuttings, on crests. At North Shore Stations one is struck by the relative quiet, the sound of birds and rustle of leaves although at certain times this is masked by the almost deafening sound of cicadas as one goes north. There are many schools in the area and, at the times when I travelled, many children entered at certain stations on their way home. The noise they made became a very important cue.
* The density of people on the train changes and the crowding and emptying stresses major stops. These take longer because of the greater number of people getting on and off (Chatswood, North Sydney, Wynyard, Central). There are also changes in the noise level within the carriage — a bustle as people collect their parcels, get up and leave while others come in. There are also changes in the type of people who come in at different places — women shoppers, workmen, businessmen, students, school children — which identify these places.

* Smells provide strong cues. There is a strong smell of frying at St. Leonards (where there is a potato chip factory) and the smell of a brewery just north of Central Station, the tarry smell as one goes underground, sea smells near the harbor and on the bridge, a strong smell of vegetation and flowers as one gets onto the North Shore where the air quality generally improves due to altitude, greenery and distance from industry so that smog and fumes generally weaken and disappear by Roseville, and the smell of burning Eucalyptus leaves all year but becoming stronger in the autumn. South of Central industrial smells become stronger.
* Temperatures also change — it cools off markedly as one climbs up and reaches the more open and vegetated areas of the North Shore.

These cues include visual, acoustic, olfactory and kinesthetic, the built and natural environments, social cues and so on. They are additive in many cases, so that the congruence between the number of people getting on and off, the length of stop, the smell, noise, light, going underground or emerging from underground, getting near water and onto a bridge at one place makes it particularly important.

There are undoubtedly other cues that people use, and those described may well not be noticeable to many people since cues must be noticed before they can be understood or used. This list does, however, provide a repertoire from which specific cues are most likely selected, although there is no information on their relative importance. This introspective exercise suggests many possibilities and goes beyond the kinds of variables usually considered in design. It also relates to orientation and learning since at first I looked up anxiously at every station not even knowing what followed, while towards the end I was able to read without worry and be ready to get off at the right time.

The rather detailed schema of this route contrasts with the big gaps in one's schema of Sydney as a whole, reinforcing the notion of a hierarchy of schemata at different scales. For children in the Western suburbs the most important elements were, in order of importance, the Sydney Harbor Bridge, Opera House, Circular Quay, Botanical Garden and Luna Park (an amusement park). More generally there tends to be an emphasis on the harbor and certain beaches and, for people living elsewhere, a gap for the Western suburbs. There would also be specific gaps related to place of residence and activity systems (Riley 1971). Local areas would be known in detail in ways different, but comparable to my example. Most people had a mental map of their own very small area and a name "Sydney" for which they had no map or schematic equivalent (King 1971(b)).

A study of 7 Indonesian visitors to Central Sydney is suggestive (Bunker 1970). Even in this small group there were differences, architects having more generalized impressions of views, skylines, areal associations, while engineers recalled specific buildings and projects — i.e., they had different cognitive styles. The visitors had a fairly clear idea of the area and its major elements. Chief overall impressions were of intensity of activity, movement, busyness and vitality, tall buildings, lack of open space and spaciousness, and cramped and confined feelings. Topography and ease and comfort of walking were important and the harbor and views of it were most exciting. Important points and areas were located — the Harbor Bridge, Opera House, Botanical Gardens, Hyde Park, Town Hall, Australia Square and other notable buildings. Between these fixed points, the relationships among which were fairly accurate, and an idealized and simplified street pattern was used to incorporate other points, the accuracy of which may go up with time. Street patterns and widths were used to contrast Sydney with Melbourne.

The importance of the street pattern is confirmed in a comparison of areas in Holland (de Jonge 1962). In a grid layout with uniform buildings people tended to get lost and often relied on detail — even curtains in windows: in such areas residents' associational values become particularly important. In a more articulated area the identity of each part, and architectural and spatial variety, helped orientation and mental maps were clear. A third area, with curved streets, made orientation almost impossible. Thus mental maps are clearest when there is a regular street pattern, a single dominant path, many noticeable differences in areas and buildings. When the pattern is not clear more attention is given to individual details of various kinds. Patterns which are almost regular are made fully so — circles, semi-circles and right angles are easy, minor bends and quarter circles difficult. Major difficulties occur either where streets are irregular, specially curved, or where the structure is clear but the elements not distinct enough.

This may be different in other cultures, since cognitive maps are a product of the physical setting, cognitive styles and socio-cultural associations. In Lebanon distinctive areas or quarters of the city are stressed rather than individual elements or paths (Gulick 1963). This reflects the nature of the traditional Moslem city which is a cluster of special districts — ethnic, religious, trade or use, and even those elements which are buildings in other cultures become small districts (e.g., the Souks and Mosques) (Brown 1973; Weulersse 1934). The distinctiveness of districts, perceptually, morphologically, in terms of uses, activities and social values (i.e., noticeable differences among them) become important.

Rather than structuring urban schemata in terms of paths and point as in the West, it is done more in terms of areas (as is even more the case in Japan) — an example of a different cognitive style, although the difference may also be due to different urban environments (Rapoport, 1976). In the case of Mexico also, the neighborhood is of extreme importance in the life and morphology of the city. The persistence of this pattern is striking when one compares Aztec cities, with their *calputlin*, with contemporary Mexican cities. The structure of a small town like Tlayacapan with its central plaza with town church, the city divided into four quarters and 26 neighborhoods, each with its own chapel, each neighborhood representing agnatic groups and reflecting the complex social and cognitive spatial and temporal categories is very similar to the structure of Tenochtitlan (e.g., Ingham 1971).

Not only does this urban structure reflect cognitive categories but it is dominant in the mental map of San Cristobal (Wood 1969). There the central plaza is most important, being the symbolic center of the town, and the route structure and various uses and hierarchies are related to it. There is extreme cognitive consistency with a complex system of rules relating the house (rooms around a patio), the neighborhood (houses around a local plaza) and the city (neighborhoods around the main plaza) stressing the link with the Meso-American tradition described above and reinforced by religion — house altar, neighborhood church, city cathedral. Each neighborhood is distinct, with a different character and personality, street names, specific functions or crafts, and they also vary in color, sound, smell and morphology.

The relationship to the Arab example is instructive, as is the schema of the city as a set of small places, the effects of culture (and subcultures *within* the city which I have not discussed but which show a variety and non-overlap of cognitive maps), the importance of the congruence of many different cues using different sense modalities, and a consistent system.

The effects of morphology and scale can be seen by comparing the mental maps of San Cristobal with those of other cities in Mexico (Stea and Wood 1971). These differences also occur at different scales within cities so that mental maps differ at the macro, meso and micro-scale in England (Porteous 1971). Urban cognitive schemata also contain very important verbal and other material which has effects on whether subways and overpasses inhibit movement on psychological rather than physical grounds, as was the case in Birmingham (Goodey and Lee, n.d.; Goodey *et al.* 1971). There also cognitive maps of the central area differed according to whether they were from "within" (where eye level elements were important) or from "without" where the skyline became of great importance (Goodey *et al.* 1971, pp. 44, 50).

Thus people's knowledge of a city is partly the result of their experience of it so that social position, roles, activities, friendship patterns, location and travel affect the extent and nature of cognitive schemata. Different populations, therefore, have different mental maps varying from very large to very small. In the case of Los Angeles, people with the most extensive social contacts had a generalized map of the entire area while others had schemata of only a few blocks although all had large gaps and lacunae (Orleans 1971).

Men and women may also have different cognitions of the same environment (a neighborhood)* because of their different activity patterns and degree of involvement, and time spent, in the local area — women have a more extensive local area. Men tended to use an abstract coordinate system whereas women tended to use the dwelling as a basic reference point: men had a more comprehensive schema than women who relied more on point details (Orleans and Schmidt 1972). These differences may be due partly to cognitive style and partly to activity patterns, so that I would expect men to have a more extensive knowledge of the whole urban area.

In the case of the new town of Ciudad Guyana, Venezuela, the importance of buildings (landmarks) in mental maps seems related to their relative prominence, form, visibility and significance. Of importance to form were movement, how buildings stand out, size, shape, surface, quality and context. Of importance to visibility were location and hence viewpoint intensity (i.e., how many people see it). Regarding viewpoint significance — the location, mainly at decision points, immediacy (relation to route and cone of vision); of importance to significance were use intensity, use singularity and symbolism (in most cases these are aspects of noticeable differences). Congruence of physical use and significance patterns were important in cognitive schemata as was naming. The schema consists of an "owned", a use, a visible and a hearsay zones, and there are major differences among various groups which have different cognitive styles stressing different elements and sensory modalities and organizing them differently. The lack of a common schema is striking — due to a non-homogeneous population which is also modernizing rapidly with disruption of cognitive rules. Interestingly, in Ciudad Guyana, unlike elsewhere, lower class individuals had the more extensive schemata, a result of their wider movement through the city in seeking work. Upper-class people had more limited orbits because they tended to confine themselves to their own areas (Appleyard 1969, 1970(a), n.d.).

This very difference follows, therefore, from a common model based on use, activities and social links and supports much of the argument thus far. Cognitive schemata exist and they vary among different groups. These schemata are based on experience and

---

* Note that Lynch (1960) dealt with the differential effects of the *physical* environment.

knowledge and on names and categories which reflect cognitive styles. Physical and non-physical factors are involved — the nature of the environment, cues in all sense modalities, meaning, values, culture, symbolism, preference as well as activities, ways of travelling and social links so that one can find tourist, recreational, use and other schemata (Wood 1969; Stea and Wood 1971). In the case of cities, schemata have clear spatial expression in the form of mental maps. These have certain characteristics of content and organization which are dynamic, changing with time and familiarity. One suggestion is that they consist of a number of points hierarchically arranged in space, divided by distance and related by bearings. Maps are bounded in some way and divided into other bounded areas. Points and domains are connected so that one can get from one to another, the degree of connection, and the strength of separation, being variable (Stea 1969(a), (b)).

Spatial schemata not only locate people in space and control behavior, they also organize and order incoming information (Cox and Zannaras 1970; Von Uexküll 1957) acting as filters and resisting change. Inconsistencies are ignored or the map distorted to allow for them, but shifts occur when the weight of inconsistent information is too great.* Schemata depend on a classification process and hence on naming, and are related to preference and evaluation of particular places, groups and symbols, so that behavior is related both to preference structures and spatial schemata. Mental maps thus contain both locational and non-locational attributes, hierarchically organized, and exist at all scales from the largest to the smallest — ranging from hearsay to "ownership". When cognitive maps are inadequate, and in large scale environments and new places, physical maps are used. Information from these is gradually incorporated into cognitive maps — but only if the area becomes familiar. Mental maps are at different scales which do not merge but are kept separate and used as needed.

There is a relation between the knowledge of a place, its evaluation and how it is placed in a mental map. Cognitive maps are combined with values, preferences and other knowledge into major images which are used in matching ideals and reality and affect behavior. In the case of a shopping center the image was found to consist of 8 categories in two broad groups, one relating to the shops — service, quality, price, shopping hours and choice; the other relating to spatial design, concerned with structure, pedestrian movement, visual appearance and traffic conditions (Downs 1970). Other aspects are also probably involved so that urban cognition is complex and multidimensional, some elements are more easily impressed on the mind than others and knowledge and evaluation are also linked to indirect forms of communication so that information tends to be biased towards the home area (Goodey 1969). Indirect as well as direct information is used and in the case of the latter all the senses are involved.

The various elements incorporated into mental maps are selected on various grounds and fitted into categories and schemata which vary with culture, the environment and personal characteristics related to education, place of residence, familiarity, activity systems and means of travel. Mental maps are thus learned and take time to construct. There is a spillover from known places to surrounding areas so that as places become better known so do their surroundings. The most significant places act as primary nodes anchoring cognitive representations at these specific points (Rapoport 1972(e)). It has been suggested that there are primary, secondary, tertiary and minor order nodes linked

---

* The analogy to the change in schemata known as "paradigm shifts" in science is striking (e.g., Kuhn 1965) as is the resemblance to Boulding's (1956) argument about images generally.

by paths (Briggs 1972). A skeletal framework of places and paths is modified as new information comes in, and this is related to specific activity systems. In each city there are major places common to most people to which individuals add more idiosyncratic elements, but in each culture or place there will be more agreement than in different ones. Mental maps thus include areal, linear and point locations and elements of agreement and overlap as well as variation.

Mental maps can be classified as sequential or spatial, with differing degrees of elaboration within each class (Appleyard 1970(a)). Generally maps fell into three major classes — *associational* depending on differentiation, association and patterning of functional, social or physical characteristics; *topological* depending on continuity and juncture of movement and character and *positional* emphasizing spatial placement, direction and distance (Appleyard 1970(a), pp. 114–116). There are developmental differences with a sequence from undifferentiated concrete egocentric, through differentiated and partially coordinated to abstractly coordinated and hierarchically integrated (G. Moore 1972, 1973). These differences may also be in terms of spatial relationships (topological, projective and Euclidean), modes of representation, systems of reference (egocentric, fixed and coordinated) and types of topographic representations (route and survey) (Hart and Moore 1971). There are also differences based on social role, formal education and environmental experience leading to appositional maps (with relative placement by points which themselves may be incorrect) or propositional maps (with geographically correct placement) (Stea and Taphanel, n.d.).

The close correspondence between characteristics of mental maps and images and schemata strengthens the suggestion that the former are a special case of the latter. In terms of the categories of images discussed in Chapter 1 (Boulding 1956) one can say that mental maps, although primarily spatial, involve temporal, relational, self-image, value, emotional/affective, conscious, unconscious and subconscious, real and unreal and public/private dimensions and it is the interaction of all of these which results in the particular map. Like images and schemata generally mental maps are simplified, since one of their functions is to help with information processing (see Chapter 4). They help people cope with the physical environment, act as mnemonic devices and lead to routinized behavior.

The city is thus construed as a series of defined places organized and linked to give some structure. In the study of spatial schemata one is, therefore, interested in the nature of the elements, relationships among them, whether they form domains and how these are bounded, linked or separated. One is also concerned with the stability and persistence of such schemata, the nature of hierarchies involved and their relation to social, cultural, psychological and other similar factors as well as the overall manner of structuring the map.

The Construction of Mental Maps

Much of the preceding discussion suggests that learning plays a role in the construction of mental maps. This process needs to be understood and the mutual relation between it and design considered.

Experience and learning affect how information is structured and simplified. Learning through exploration, or through trial and error, gradually leads to the development of stereotyped behavior or habits which then slow further learning. Like people, animals seem to have both long and short term memories, to learn by experience, trial and error and even by imitation and to know their territories and paths. In such learning animals require the identification of various and numerous landmarks, thus wasps circle to fix the neighborhood in memory, bumble-bees do one circuit when landmarks are conspicuous 'and learning easy but do several circuits if the landmarks are inconspicuous (Eibl-Eibesfeld 1970, pp. 220, 363–380).

Such learning seems to be based on association with some distinguishing features, and the innate recognition of key stimuli which becomes more effective through learning. In addition animals know their *Umwelt* and are also able to deal with abstractions such as "straight" and "bent" and the resemblance of known areas, paths and activity spaces between people and animals is striking (Leyhausen 1970, pp. 185–186). In children, Piaget and his associates have identified four major stages in the development of spatial concepts – sensorimotor, based on action where initial relationships are established; the preoperational period with elementary transformations and gradually internalized actions; a concrete operational period where reversibility becomes possible and finally a period of formal operations where abstract systems develop. These lead to development of topological properties first, followed by projective and finally Euclidean properties with a metric, and related to a coordinate system (Piaget 1954; Piaget and Inhelder 1962; G. Moore 1972, 1973; Hart and Moore 1971).

It has also been suggested that people generally behave like "scientists", testing hypotheses against the environment (Kelly 1955). Mental maps can then be seen as hypotheses, the testing of which clearly involves learning so that while incongruent data may at first be rejected, they eventually are fitted into the schemata which are elaborated and modified. Which attributes are coupled to others and how is important, and learning changes not what people see but where they look and how they remember what they have seen (Hochberg 1968) – i.e., *schemata are partly mnemonic devices* so that differences among groups may be related to learning (Seagrim 1967–68; Rapoport 1972(e)). There are probably underlying regularities in the way people construct schemata, with specific cultural variations. These regularities may be in the psychological processes of logic and inference, similarity, use or relational structures of the simplification processes of closure and "good gestalt" (e.g., de Jonge 1962, p. 276).

Schemata are constructed over time and related to the individual's experience in the city and hence to variables such as class, culture, location, activity patterns and travel behavior. It appears to be simultaneously a process of simplification and elaboration (e.g., Wallace 1965).

Different learning models have been discussed with relation to environmental learning – concept identification models (in which cues are identified to locate in space and act as focal points in mental maps), stimulus ranking models related to preference and urban hierarchies (e.g., Golledge 1969) and personal construct theory (schemata as hypotheses) (Kelly 1955). They can be generalized diagrammatically to include the real environment, and the process whereby a perceived environment is created, tested and amended. (See Fig. 3.6).

Cognitively the process of constructing schemata and, spatially, mental maps is a way of reducing alternatives and narrowing choice (Craik 1970). Fresh information is matched against existing schemata – although these are gradually modified (Neisser 1967), and learning occurs in the development of both cognitive structures and processes (Neisser 1968). Areas of frequent use, high value and affect will be vivid, and have frequently

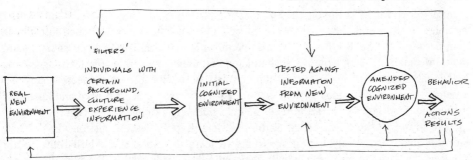

FIG. 3.6. One model of environmental learning.

updated images and mental maps. Other areas will be grouped into much broader and vaguer categories. Urban mental maps thus have areas which are very clear, detailed and accurate and those which are vague, general and inaccurate. Since large cities provide vast amounts of information with only a limited increase in people's ability to process it, such maps help in handling information. Since infants can register most of the information that adults can, but cannot handle it (Bower 1966), it appears that processing ability is learned — and this involves constructing schemata.

Part of the learning is vicarious, through indirect information (e.g., the media, formal education or enculturation) which not only helps construct mental maps but also evaluative schemata and rules for behavior. These processes also exert a unifying influence by presenting similar images and information to individuals whose direct experience may be very different, allowing them to coordinate their behavior, some of their preferences and helping them to handle situations for which they have no direct experience (Abrahamson 1966, pp. 19–20).

People can thus have clear preferences for places not personally experienced which are based on gradually accumulated information. For example, among Swedish school children, information about local places is more detailed than about remote areas but there are peaks of information based on prominence in the news (Gould 1972(a)). This information space grows and develops as children mature, and influences, and is influenced by, their mental maps. This process is partly developmental, partly cultural and partly environmental. Cognitive maps of large areas are learned and provide a schema into which new experiences and actions can be fitted and integrated. In urban areas similar processes occur so that children can draw maps of their route to school and gradually are able to model ever larger areas (Stea and Blaut 1971).

Cognitive maps as constructs can be distinguished from the process of cognitive mapping. The process is one of gradual construction involving various sense modalities, and active movement through the environment increases the dimensionality of schemata created through indirect experience (Stea and Blaut 1970). The importance of active movement helps explain why images and mental maps of known and experienced areas are so much more vivid and accurate than those derived entirely from vicarious data.

The construction of mental maps goes hand in hand with other learning — of attitudes, values and goals — all of which affect spatial behavior. In the case of shopping, recent migrants to urban areas seem to undergo a process of "funneling" — with learning spatial variability is reduced. New arrivals try many shops but gradually the number of options is reduced (Rogers 1970). This process may well be generalized for urban behavior, the specifics varying among individuals and groups. Initial schemata affect behavior and are themselves continually modified by location, lifestyle, activity patterns and other variables (Horton and Reynolds 1971). Since commuters have more detailed knowledge than occasional travellers, it seems that some information is gathered during each trip and that information is gradually accumulated although the rate of learning slows. Individuals begin with a provisional mental map, possibly based on objective maps and other information. This map is then elaborated starting at those areas used and inhabited (hence the importance of location) and the map gradually extended from there.

With regard to the effect of travel routes several hypotheses are possible. In the first, the new arrival is actively exploring, trying to learn the city and the best route to use between the major nodes with which he is initially concerned. As the best routes are found their number is gradually reduced. This would correspond to funneling behavior in shopping discussed above. An alternative hypothesis is that initially the simplest and most obvious routes based on road maps would be used — relying on arterials. Gradually various short-cuts would be learned, the best route for various days and times (in terms of traffic or weather conditions) and routes to various specific places, so that over time more routes would be used so that exploratory behavior occurs in later, rather than initial stages. In the third hypothesis both these processes are combined — and this can occur in two ways. In the first one would begin by increasing routes and then eliminating bad routes; in the other reduction would occur after exploration and then new ones would be added. Diagramatically:

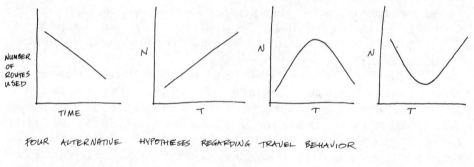

FOUR ALTERNATIVE HYPOTHESES REGARDING TRAVEL BEHAVIOR

FIG. 3.7

Exploratory behavior might also be a permanent factor — people varying their routes occasionally just for a change but this would depend on a time factor (i.e., criticality) as well as values and attitudes.

I am not aware of studies which have investigated these alternatives. There is some evidence, however, that route selection, specially in connection with work travel is learned, and routinized, quickly so that the first alternative applies (Golledge, Brown and Williamson n.d.). In the case of recreation and other discretionary travel, both destination oriented and diffuse travel routes may occur (Mercer 1971(a), pp. 267–269; 1971(b), pp. 140–141). It is also likely that routes are selected according to different criteria, depending on context and general attitudes, so that time, convenience, distance, views, complexity, noise level, speed and microclimate may all play a role. The distinction between work and recreation travel behavior, and the general likelihood of criticality (Rapoport 1969(a), pp. 58–60) affecting learning, is confirmed by comparing shopping and recreation (Murphy 1969).

Attitudes generally affect discretionary activities more than they do shopping, so that distance is more a factor for necessary than for discretionary activities. The certainty of information is also important, so that the distance and time which people are prepared to travel will depend on the certainty of their mental maps. When a stimulus is seen as attractive, distance becomes less of a problem, so that attitude affects spatial behavior and spatial learning which reduces alternatives through routines and habits while, at the same time, attitudes and preference structures themselves may be modified. The latent function of shopping may play a role so that funneling with learning (Rogers 1970) would be affected by these symbolic factors. Those for whom eating and cooking are recreational may visit many more, and more widely scattered, shops and attitudes would then play a larger role. Such people would have many more shops in their information space, a different search pattern and different criteria for evaluating distance and attractiveness. Learning which shops are available would still play a role and the search for special food sources would affect their mental maps of the city — their knowledge of areas and routes.

Learning generally tends to stabilize spatial behavior by establishing habits. Habits affect behavior and mental maps since spatial knowledge is encoded in such maps as a result of behavior. Expectations based on prior knowledge affect initial behavior so that the desire to use something comes first, then knowledge of its spatial location, the ability to find it and then action. Such action becomes more or less habitual and, in turn, affects mental maps which, in turn, affect further behavior, through the information encoded in them, the values attached to them (strength of attraction or repulsion), the evaluation of barriers or paths and the like. Habit formation itself is related to rules, lifestyle, cognitive styles — i.e., to culture. Culture plays a role in how and where people live, what they do and the extent of their networks, homeranges, and activity systems (Chapter 5). The interaction of these with the specific environment and the areas they use or reject (e.g., Lamy 1967; Doughty 1970, Prokop 1967) influence the construction of mental maps.

FIG. 3.8. Learning as the gradual construction of schemata related to loci of activity, routes used, travel modes, extent of behavioral space, etc. Differences are due to differences in those and location, habits, activity patterns, etc.

Environmental learning involves learning the location of places and the paths which connect them (Tolman 1948) and active interaction with the environment is crucial (Held and Heim 1968; Piaget 1954; Stea and Blaut 1970). Cognitive representations are built up over time, they become more complex and accurate and they consist of places, distances and relations. Once many places and ways of getting there are known they are ordered hierarchically, based on their significance and frequency of interaction with them. Such places and paths can be primary, secondary, tertiary and minor (Briggs 1972). Highly valued places will be well known and located in well known areas — there is a spillover from higher order places to secondary ones. Places are related and coordinated in various variable ways involving proximity, separation, dispersion or clustering and orientation. Initially a skeletal place and path network is built related to important living, working and recreational places and activities and this is modified by continually adding bits of information, and adjusting locations and relationships until a relatively veridical, or at least operationally adequate, schema is achieved which then remains relatively stable. In rapidly changing cities such schemata may again become inadequate and this presents a particular problem for people in developing countries (Rapoport 1974) or for the elderly (Rapoport 1973(d)) for whom the restructuring of schemata may prove difficult.

The process of positioning elements is one of an identification of elements linked loosely at first and gradually becoming more firmly interconnected. Areas of greatest familiarity and importance are used as reference points, these are related to bounded known areas. The areas known, their extent and the choice of reference points depends partly on culture, age, sex, lifestyle, class, activity patterns and partly on the physical environment, and within these areas other points and places are located and related through distance, bearing, paths and barriers (physical, social or conceptual). Various reference points and areas are related to each other — either through an abstract coordinate system or the road pattern. New places are related to these and to the closest reference point in similar ways. Some sections are accurate and detailed, others are much less so: areas used frequently are much clearer and more strongly differentiated than distant ones which are unclear and relatively uniform (Eyles 1969; Abler, Adams and Gould 1971, p. 218). The coordinate system (whether abstract or not) is also more accurate in known areas than others, and this further distorts the relationships and location of reference points although closure and continuity must be achieved in order to allow people to behave adequately. This means that some parts of the cognitive map are more veridical than others and in unfamiliar parts of the city people use remarkably little information to make inferences (Appleyard 1970(b), p. 99). (See Fig. 3.9, p. 135).

As we shall see there are cultural and environmental differences in coordinate systems. Also, discontinuities or shifts in the grid (as in San Francisco at Market Street where it is assumed, being in the Western U.S., that there is a uniform grid), affect mental maps which may become inaccurate and disorient people. Similarly the Boston common, although within an irregular grid, is assumed to be rectangular rather than five-sided with resulting confusion.

Given the likely link, at least in Western cultures, between the coordinate system and the road pattern it is likely that known areas and reference points are frequently related to each other through paths, so that the coordinate system is based on the path system as simplified and made regular cognitively, and a gradual network is built up. (See Fig. 3.10, p. 135).

While the coordinate and paths systems have been suggested, at least implicitly, as alternatives they are very similar and both are actually used. The role of paths and the early learning of areas along paths seems clear, as does the imposition of a conceptual coordinate system on the road system, although this latter depends on cultural factors such as the use of grids and block numbering in the Western U.S. but not East of the U.S. and also environmental variables.

In comparing experienced and novice taxi-drivers in Paris, it was found that primary

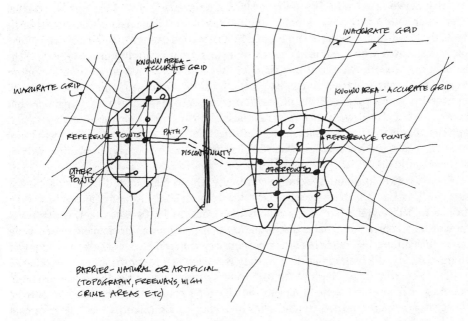

BARRIER- NATURAL OR ARTIFICIAL
(TOPOGRAPHY, FREEWAYS, HIGH
CRIME AREAS ETC)

FIG. 3.9

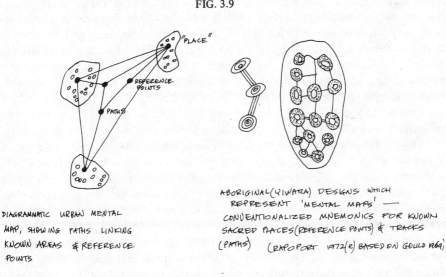

DIAGRAMMATIC URBAN MENTAL
MAP, SHOWING PATHS LINKING
KNOWN AREAS & REFERENCE
POINTS

ABORIGINAL(YIWARA) DESIGNS WHICH
REPRESENT 'MENTAL MAPS' —
CONVENTIONALIZED MNEMONICS FOR KNOWN
SACRED PLACES(REFERENCE POINTS) & TRACKS
(PATHS)   (RAPOPORT 1972(e) BASED ON GOULD 1969)

FIG. 3.10

road networks were used by all, and were veridical and metrically correct. This network map can be constructed in two ways: using directions, angles and triangulation or by relating to an overall coordinate framework. Both seem to be used with the coordinate system probably dominant. Secondary networks were used little and inefficiently, and mental maps of them were not veridical and discontinuous. The major difference with experienced drivers was that they were able to get back more quickly to the primary network. Learning effects also existed in the mental maps so that the primary networks of experienced drivers were more extensive and denser than those of novices. In the primary networks cross-roads were important and, in travel, a plan was followed so that every such cross-road (decision point) that direction was taken making the smallest angle with the destination in the mental map. In the secondary network tactics rather than plans were used with intermediate goals so as to get back to the primary network. The secondary network was not *remembered* but could be *recognized* and important buildings, details, colors and the like were used. In the construction of the primary network there was some evidence of *gestalt* principles, so that angles were straightened but curves, rare in Paris, were retained (Pailhous 1970). In such simplification generally, it appears that gradual curves and changes of direction are less noticeable, and less useful, than clear and sudden changes which help in the difficult process of obtaining closure (Lynch and Rivkin 1970) and continuity.

There are two possibilities regarding continuity. One is that minor discontinuities, such as a small park in a residential neighborhood, are most likely to be forgotten since they are "absorbed" by the larger, continuous use (Golledge 1970). The other, which I will develop in Chapter 4, is that a discontinuity, being a variation in character, becomes a noticeable difference and hence an important element in the cognitive map. These two alternatives could be tested but there already is some evidence for the latter view. Thus in Berlin "anomalies" in the overall grid, empty sites and little "wildernesses" had importance far beyond their proportion in the total context and the other important elements — monuments, activity and signs of human action (Sieverts 1967, 1969) are all discontinuities in the overall pattern, and hence noticeable differences important in cognitive maps. Similarly in Boston it was found that while the creation of a sense of order or continuity was a major goal, discontinuities of various sorts were used as important elements in schemata (Lynch and Rivkin 1970). In more general terms any change in a uniform or uniformly varying attribute, such as rate, direction, slope, curvature, use, grid or whatever becomes an event, hence memorable and used in cognitive mapping (Gibson 1968; Thiel 1970, p. 596).

Location, relation to work, environmental characteristics and the direction of symbolic centers all play a role as do socio-economic and socio-cultural characteristics such as age, sex, education, lifestyle, stage in life cycle, occupation, social networks, and these act through cognitive style, mobility, behavior spaces and activity systems. People's movement space (Hurst 1971) is the starting point from which the map is constructed and this depends on the *meaning* which places have for people, the role they play in people's lives (Jackson and Johnston 1974; Harrison and Sarre 1971; Lamy 1967) so that meaning is central in cognition.

Within the movement space there is a core area which is most familiar, a median area traversed occasionally and an extensive movement space only known indirectly. The extent and nature of these obviously affects the nature of the known city, the mental map and hence further movement and use. The fact that children in small towns have larger and more detailed cognitive maps than children in large cities (Gump 1972; Wright 1968, 1970) is related to their greater mobility in small towns (Parr 1969(a)) (and partly to undermanning (R. Barker 1968; Bechtel 1970)).

Since the journey to work is routinized first, the link between residence and work is likely to be learned first, followed by shopping, recreation and friendship and social links. Thus people with intensive (space bound) and extensive (non space bound) networks construct different mental maps, so that in Cedar Rapids, Iowa schemata were affected by socio-economic attributes, location, travel preferences, length of residence at a given place, the objective nature of the urban environment and the actual activities pursued as well as the coordinate system used (Horton and Reynolds 1971). Thus on a base of the objective structure and form, differences based on subgroup membership were important. The location of dwelling and work, major roads and shopping centers are all very important in the learning process.

As the individual moves about the city he learns and elaborates a more or less unique, although generalizable, spatial pattern and, in combination with some preference and hierarchy ranking, constructs a cognitive map. This includes symbolic and meaning dimensions, so that some areas are not only unknown but actively avoided and since different populations use and avoid different areas they have different sizes of cognitive maps (E. Moore 1972, pp. 15 ff.) and also different lacunae and different mental maps (Lamy 1967; Strauss 1961). These not only influence the individual's behavior but are communicated to others, either through enculturation or in other ways. Thus, while in housing search information comes from newspapers, real estate agents and display boards, personal contact is the second most frequently used but the most effective (Brown and Holmes 1971).

The spatial range of activities seems to be a critical factor, so that generally deprived groups tend to have restricted mental maps of the city although, as we have seen in the case of Ciudad Guyana, this may vary. Thus the limited mobility of Aboriginal children meant that they knew their core area well but had hardly any concept of "Sydney" as a city. Learning occurred, so that the mental maps of kindergarten children contained a few elements significant for the child — home, school, corner shop and park — which were linked in a sensorimotor way and once they left their habitual path such children got easily lost.

Gradually the number of elements and the extent of the known area grows and seems to last for the rest of their primary school days. In this particular case it is bounded by large railway yards and an industrial area — i.e., barriers to mobility. Since Aborigines maintained a close-knit social network entirely within this area the child's knowledge of this limited area is reinforced, as is the lack of knowledge outside it (Riley 1971). A white child's mental map would be more extensive because of greater family mobility, more extensive social networks and more dispersed recreational patterns. On the other hand the home area is known in more detail by Aboriginal children.

This view is supported by the fact that the only places outside the immediate area known is the Foundation for Aboriginal Affairs which children visit. This forms another node which, since it is at the edge of downtown, leads to some knowledge of that district with its different activities, movies, noise, lights and big buildings, although this knowledge is indistinct and vague while that of the home area is clear and detailed. The role of learning, activity space and the meaning of elements is supported by the sex differences found. As boys start to play rugby, they travel to parks which might be outside their intimate area; they sometimes also travel as spectators to various sports grounds about one mile East of their home area and also learn the names of teams (which are named after geographical areas of Sydney, although they have no clear idea where these places are located). Due to rugby they develop a symbolic notion of their home area as South Sydney (the name of the local team) rather than specific names of areas such as Redfern, Waterloo or Alexandria, and the home area is placed in a larger context (Riley 1971).*

* The importance of football grounds is interestingly reminiscent of the importance of soccer grounds in the Barriadas of Lima (Doughty 1970) discussed before.

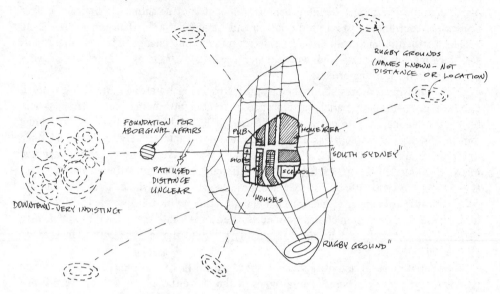

FIG. 3.11. Typical mental map of aboriginal children (based on verbal descriptions in Riley, 1971).

This confirms the view that elements in the city become known (and incorporated in maps) because of operational, responsive and inferential aspects. Operational aspects are like the ones just described — related to activities such as school, family, social networks, recreation — or work and other activity systems. Responsive aspects are more perceptual and also related to meanings, while inferential aspects relate to the building up of a generalized system, linking the various elements and making them predictable.

I have already suggested several times that, in spite of the role of indirect data, movement through the environment is most important in environmental cognition. Thus one may know the names of places without knowing their location or their relative position may be known without having experiential equivalents. The points and routes may then be clear but the boundaries and the nature of the elements may be vague and distorted. For example freeway drivers in Los Angeles may know the channels, routes, and names without being aware what these names represent. People driving on surface streets would have a very different mental map with different detail and information.

Active movement both in animals and children is most important so that they cannot learn an environment by being taken through it passively. In the case of children the separation of home and school is much more severe, both emotionally and in terms of non-connectivity of schemata, when children are taken to school by bus than when they walk — i.e., more actively (Lee 1971(b)). In the former case there is a break in cognition due partly to the lack of control but also to the means of travel.

This then suggests that the method and means of travel may greatly influence the construction of cognitive maps. By making certain parts accessible and others inaccessible, transportation may not only alter familiarity through use but also preference, relative hierarchy and so on. The kinds of barriers, the kind of route and the means of getting there, the distance traversed and what is seen, the degree of active involvement, will all interact with the nature of the environment, cognitive styles and ability leading to different schemata.

Whether one drives on the right or the left may affect what one sees by altering points of view and turns, producing different experiences and different maps. A city designed for one type of travel may become difficult to understand when that changes. Traffic rules and characteristics — such as the slowing down or speeding up of traffic or the introduction of one-way streets — may have similar effects. In this latter case the movement or behavioral space actually available is greatly reduced (Haynes 1969). One might thus hypothesize that the replacement of a uniform grid of streets by arteries, and then freeways, will have a channeling effect and reduce the detailed knowledge of the city while possibly increasing its extent.

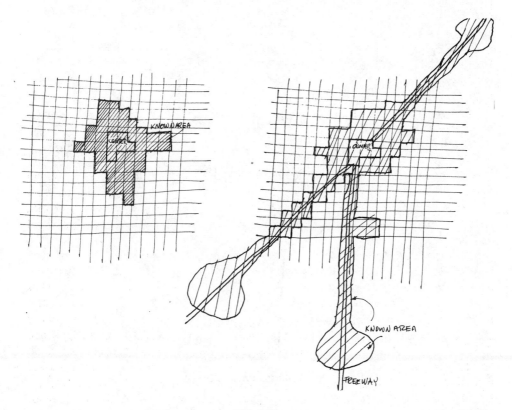

FIG. 3.12

One could also hypothesize that with more potential routes there would be less channeling than when routes are limited. (See Fig. 3.13, p. 140).

This is supported by the sectoral bias which has been found to exist and seems to be related to major transport routes. Thus a resident at point X will know the areas shown in the shaded sector but will not know about Y (Adams 1969). (See Fig. 3.14, p. 140).

Thus people in cities have mental maps which are partly limited by their location and partly by their transport routes and this directionally biased map affects spatial behavior. It is of interest to note that our discussion is generalized from theoretical, recreational

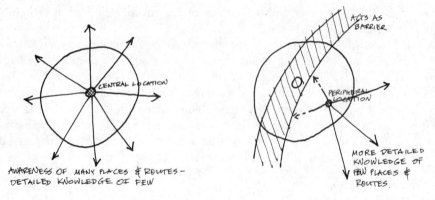

FIG. 3.13

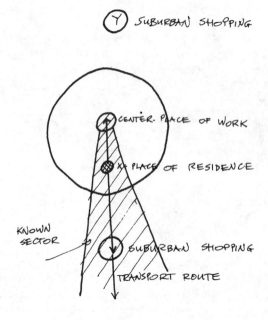

FIG. 3.14. (from Adams 1969).

and shopping considerations and that similar directional biases also affect mental maps of social status (Johnston 1971(b)).

Among the movement variables affecting the construction of mental maps are not only location and route, but also the mode of transport and whether travel is intermittent, frequent or infrequent. The difference between regular and intermittent travel would be expected from the discussion so far on the role of learning and the gradual development of schemata. It would follow that frequent repetition of routes has an effect on correlating the many variables needed for learning, while the variety of routes taken affects the extent known and the connectivity — the understanding of the overall structure. This has been demonstrated (Carr and Schissler 1969; Craik 1970) and is confirmed by the variation in knowledge and evaluation of places by residents and visitors (e.g., Jackson 1957). This is due to the frequency and routinization of travel, and the context (work or tourism) and even pedestrians behave differently during the morning and evening rush, i.e., going to or from work (Stilitz 1969). It also tends to be confirmed by the effect on mental maps of cities which, unlike ours, tend to restrict mobility — as is the case with the classical Islamic city (e.g., Brown 1973). The direction of entry into areas also affects cognitive maps so that entering the Chicago Loop by car or train leads to different maps (Saarinen 1969).

The means of travel — train, bus, subway, car, bicycle or pedestrian — affects not only the route but also influences what is seen. Thus in Birmingham, pedestrians and drivers, bus travellers and bus drivers, had different urban schemata (Goodey *et al.* 1971). In Sydney the general environmental awareness of bus passengers was rather low. While noticeable differences were the important factor they tended to be confined to breaks in the journey (stops or traffic light stops — where, possibly, people look up) and affected by traffic conditions. Associational elements were important and the correct location elements improved with frequency of trip (Bartlett 1971). In Ciudad Guyana people travelling by private car have different, and more complete, mental maps of the city than those who only use buses (Appleyard 1970(a)) which is probably related to the ability to change routes and also to direct experience, involvement and control, and this was also the case with children in Houston (Maurer and Baxter 1972). On the other hand driving a car forces concentration on traffic so that passengers and drivers see very different things and hence build different schemata (Carr and Schissler 1969) with drivers using different cues, more related to driving and traffic safety, than passengers.

Thus drivers' mental maps are likely to be clearer in terms of routes, but less rich in environmental content and detail, so that pedestrians have much richer and more complete schemata of areas than drivers (Steinitz 1968) (although they would know more limited areas). Traffic conditions and speed of travel also have an effect, so that people in quiet streets had much richer cognitive maps than in busy streets, due to traffic blocking environmental awareness (Appleyard and Lintell 1972, pp. 95–96). Also more concentration on traffic is required on freeways than on slower surface streets which also provide more, and different, experiential cues.

One can then suggest that walking, bicycling, driving on surface streets of freeways and public transport — bus, train and subway — will each provide different amounts of information depending on the ability to vary the sequence, to stop and look, to absorb information outside the task of moving, the ability not to look at all and how much of the urban environment is actually displayed — with very different resulting mental maps. It is possible that the bicycle provides the optimum combination of extent and detail. Different cultural groups may also need different emphases — some on the pedestrian network within the neighborhood, others on extensive movement systems to the center (Coing 1966, pp. 178–181).

Particular groups may have difficulty reading maps and schedules which makes it more difficult for them to use the city (Davis 1972). There is thus a need to make route maps, information systems, transport routes and urban form congruent with each other and with the way in which people construct mental maps (their cognitive styles). For example stations may need to be consistent on given routes but individually variable, routes should relate to urban areas, landmarks and directions and so on (Appleyard and Okamoto 1968). Highways should be related to urban form (Appleyard, Lynch and Meyer 1964), and transportation generally should be designed so as to help people learn the city and structure it cognitively — by making increased exposure to various places easier, by stressing noticeable differences and those urban elements which have widely shared significance (e.g., Carr 1970). Thus not only is the direction of entry important but also what is seen so that different entry points, particularly if used by different groups, may need to display different information and cues (e.g., Porteous 1970, pp. 138–139).

Urban form, transport routes and speed of movement should be related so that, in terms of design, one should consider how cities might be designed for easy learning and construction of cognitive schemata while, at the same time, retaining perceptual richness and variety — i.e., cities should be designed both *for cognitive clarity and perceptual opulence.*

Orientation

Since mental maps consist of places, space and time distances among them, and the overall relational system, these three topics — the definition of places (place implying a knowledge that one is "here" rather than "there"), subjective distance and orientation — need to be discussed, beginning with orientation.

Orientation is extremely important and basic to the behavior of all motile organisms — animals and people. It is linked to survival and sanity (Lynch 1960; Hall 1966). While it is basic it is also culturally variable. It involves the codification and classification of "whatness" and "thereness" (Lee 1969) and is the directional relationship of places and distances organized into a system whereby navigation through the environment becomes possible.

Orientation concerns three questions — where one is, how to get where one is going, how one knows that one has arrived. For this one needs to know one's location relative to the larger environment, and the nature of that environment (relationship among elements, distances, directions, paths, obstacles and barriers). Involved in this process are recognition and noticeable differences, informational systems (Carr 1973), perceptual accessibility, spatial configuration and cognitive style, preferences and classification into desirable and undesirable; the meaning, significance and salience of elements, distances or barriers and their symbolic importance and pathtaking — the paths taken given a choice (Porter 1964; Garbrecht 1971).

Both physical and mental maps involve orientational systems and are aids to orientation. They are made, and used, in order to orient in space and use the environment — they improve predictability in the environment. At the simplest level this is clear from the way directions are given — in terms of distance or time; city blocks may be used or landmarks. Different cognitive styles are involved and, if incongruent, misinterpretation may result. From the designer's point of view similar questions are involved — what directions does the environment provide and how congruent is this information with the particular cognitive style.

Just as there are cultural differences in cognitive styles and taxonomies there are also differences in orientational systems (Lynch 1960, Appendix A; Hallowell 1955; Lowenthal 1961; Rapoport, 1976). The coordinate systems vary — for example Eskimos use the number and shapes of turns but are uninterested in linear distance, being concerned mainly with temporal distance, the duration of travel (very much like Los Angelenos). Tikopians use landward and seaward as the main coordinates even in daily life. In the Tuamoutus compass directions refer to winds but places are located in terms of their relation to principal settlements. Westerners are more spatially egocentric than the Chinese or Balinese. Whereas we tend to locate in terms of ego, the Chinese used cardinal directions, both indoors and out, which often have religious or magic significance (cities in N. China, the Feng Shuei system in the South).

In Bali compass points are used to an extraordinary extent and disorientation is very serious. North is the direction of the sacred volcano — Agong Agung — so that North shifts as one moves around the island. In Iceland two orientational systems are used — one local, one island-wide (Haugen 1969). Spatial and temporal systems vary greatly — and we find, for example, the Andamese calendar of scents (Lowenthal 1961, p. 220), the temporal sound and smell orientation in Las Casas (Wood 1969), the time divisions of the Maenge (Panoff 1969) or the Pueblo Indians (Ortiz 1972). There are many complex orientational systems which differ greatly with culture. All, however, have in common the recognition of certain features and a schematic notion of how they relate to the larger context. People get lost in a desert or arctic waste because they fail to recognize features. The same desert enables Aborigines to navigate well, because they can notice cues and relate them to the environment (Rapoport 1972(e)) and Eskimos can use wind, snow and smell cues (Carpenter *et al.* 1959; Carpenter 1973) none of which are noticeable to others. The noticeable differences and the kinds of cues used are, of course, an aspect of cognition as are the reference systems used to link them and may be geographical features, cosmological systems (e.g., Ohnuki-Tierney 1972; Wheatley 1969, 1971), social systems (Ingham 1971), pilgrimage sites and rules (Sopher 1969; Vogt 1968) and others.

Cognitive systems may change. This may happen because of culture change, as among the Fang in Africa who traditionally used a river based system as a framework for mental maps (and direction giving). Among younger men, however, this has changed to a road-based system; as a result the cognitive schema of village/fields/bush/river has changed to road/town with very different importance, preference and organization — and, very likely, different mental maps and orientational systems (Fernandez 1970). The change may also follow from a change in the environment. Since the names of streets in Rabat were changed to Arabic, Europeans no longer use them — space has become "savage" and they use a modified Moroccan system relying on landmarks and relating routes among them (Petonnet 1972(b)).

Moroccans generally do not use abstract spatial schemata but rely on *known* areas. Once such areas are left, people zero-in places by asking. A sense of East (a sacred direction) is always kept but there are many paths to any place so that, in giving directions, only the major direction is indicated and indirect routes are preferred to straight ones, which seems to be related to different notions of time — i.e., space and time are related (Petonnet 1972(b)).

A comparable example is the different organization of Western and Japanese cities. The Western system is one of lines and points, to the extent that it has been held as universal (Cherry 1957). To find a house one follows lines and locates sequentially organized points. However, the Japanese city is organized as a series of areas of even smaller size with information sought at each boundary crossing. Within areas numbered in temporal order of construction so that several houses may have the same number and a small police box provides that information. (See Fig. 3.15, p. 144).

The line and point system was introduced from China in 800 A.D. (Kyoto) and attempts were made to reintroduce it during the U.S. occupation and before the

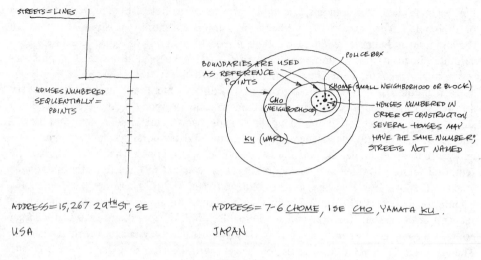

STREETS = LINES

HOUSES NUMBERED SEQUENTIALLY = POINTS

BOUNDARIES ARE USED AS REFERENCE POINTS

POLICE BOX

CHOME (SMALL NEIGHBORHOOD OR BLOCK)

CHO (NEIGHBORHOOD)

HOUSES NUMBERED IN ORDER OF CONSTRUCTION SEVERAL HOUSES MAY HAVE THE SAME NUMBER; STREETS NOT NAMED

KU (WARD)

ADDRESS = 15,267 29th ST, SE

USA

ADDRESS = 7-6 <u>CHOME</u>, 15E <u>CHO</u>, YAMATA <u>KU</u>.

JAPAN

FIG. 3.15

Olympics, yet the areal system has persisted and seems related to cognitive styles expressed in the importance in Japanese design of the *Mu* or interval.

A similar distinction in orientational systems seems to differentiate younger and older people in our own culture and, in that case, there are also sensory differences (DeLong 1967). The wrong systems and inability to use the cues provided leads to disorientation among those accustomed to others. Such systems are also differentially sensitive to certain planning decisions. The Moroccan or Japanese system (and that of the elderly) is more sensitive to change, and the disappearance, or drastic alteration, of important points and areas is much more critical than it is in a more generalized line and point system where specific elements are *less* important. The difference may be that between a static, traditional system based on *knowing* and one based on change and process (e.g., Kouwenhoeven 1961; Jackson 1966(a), 1972) — and people who are essentially strangers.

All such systems are extremely ethnocentric. Americans assume that their system is much clearer and more logical than the Japanese — or even the English where houses are often named rather than numbered. Yet, in France the American system is seen as confusing mainly because it lacks a clear hierarchy — the result is a lack of perceived order (Michel 1965).

Such differences may be due either to features of the environment (and the activities and experience of individuals) or to spatial habits (developed or innate). An example of the former is the difference in orientational systems used in Milwaukee, Wis. and Charlotte, N.C. (which are typical of the Midwest and the East Coast). In Milwaukee the grid, numbered blocks and cardinal directions are used. The latter are so prevalent that they are used even inside buildings. Instructions would be to go west X blocks or miles, turn left and go south Y blocks, turn right and go west 2 blocks. The address is 1234 W such a street. In Charlotte, due to topography and the curved street pattern, directions are to named areas, then to landmarks (such as shopping centers or churches) within these areas, then street intersections and very few blocks (Rapoport, 1976). (See Fig. 3.16).

Similarly in Lincoln, Nebraska the Capitol tower does not seem to be used as a landmark and there are only 3 or 4 named areas of spatial character which were engulfed

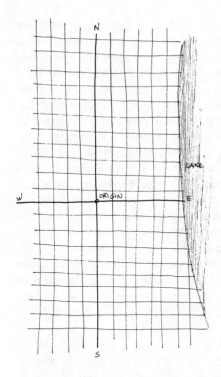

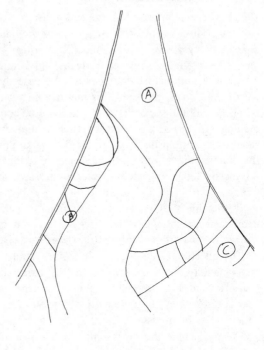

MILWAUKEE, WIS. — TYPICALLY GRID NUMBERING FROM POINT OF ORIGIN, FEW NAMED DISTRICTS.

CHARLOTTE, N.C. — TYPICALLY FREE ROAD PATTERN, VERY MANY NAMED AREAS (EG Ⓐ, Ⓑ, Ⓒ).

FIG. 3.16

by the city. The main division is into north or south of O, street, with the south desirable and north undesirable. O, street is thus the main orienting element and there is 99% agreement on O, street and 10th/11th street as the center of the city.*

In a very different context it has been suggested that ego-centered spatial relationships are related to orientation, while more abstract spatial relationships are related to visualization. There is thus a distinction between orientation and visualization, and spatial ability has three factors — spatial relationships and orientation, visualization and kinesthetic imagery (Guildford *et al.* 1957; Stringer 1971). In some cases, then, ego-centered locational and orientational system, affected by kinesthetic imagery seems more important while in others spatial visualization is more important. Orientation relates to individual places, directions and positions within some system and is essentially subjective so that in New York, although compass directions are easily known, a system of uptown, downtown and cross-town is used. While it is variable even in directly experienced environments, orientation becomes even more so, and more dependent on cognitive schemata, in larger environments which are not seen or apprehended at once (Trowbridge

* Personal communication from Mr. Michael Hill, Dept. of Geography, University of Nebraska, and Professor R. Mittelstaedt, Dept. of Marketing, University of Nebraska.

1913) where more abstract systems must be used (e.g., Ryan and Ryan 1940). More generally these two systems — egocentric and abstract — have been described as characterizing all living organisms (Trowbridge 1913) and, for example, distinguish men and women in Los Angeles (Orleans and Schmidt 1972) and shopping centers (Baers 1966). Orientation becomes possible because the environment, and people's interaction with it, are predictable and this predictability and order are imposed cognitively. Underlying the cultural variability there seem to be constancies and regularities of the inference making and cognitive processes (much as underlying the great number of languages there seem to be certain linguistic rules). This possibility is strengthened by the suggestion that the human brain may have a special locational mechanism using an analogue system relying on locus, movement, size, texture and number and operating beyond awareness (Kaplan 1970).

Predictability is related to redundancy, i.e., the congruence of meaning, location, prominence, symbolic value, salience, use, activity and so on, and effective cues for urban orientation may reduce information overloads (Deutch 1971, pp. 225–226).

The question is always which features and what coordinate systems are used. There has, generally, been little work on this, particularly at the geographical and urban scale (e.g., Howard and Templeton 1966). It seems clear, however, that cues are multisensory, that coordinate systems are culturally variable and that mental maps are constructed over time as already discussed.

Clearly people use environmental features in orientation — even at small scales. In crossing St. Mark's Square, Venice people do not take the shortest route (diagonally) which one would expect from pathtaking behavior, but move between lampposts — i.e., use navigational landmarks (Hass 1970, p. 81). Similarly people navigate in buildings by using a series of decision points at which they expect relevant information (Best 1970, pp. 72–75) which may be signs, or environmental and socio-cultural cues. In uniform environments pedestrians also use a series of decision points but additionally tend to walk along boundaries rather than enter bounded areas. This affects orientation and relates to the definition of areas since we are dealing with *perceived* boundaries. Once inside areas, destinations and grids are used (Garbrecht 1971) approximating to the perceived shortest distance (Porter 1964). Since movement, mental maps and orientation are related, pathtaking principles such as perceived shortest distance, least effort, visibility of destination, the meaning and attraction of various elements, the interest of the path, perceived obstruction or difficulty will all affect orientation and environments should not be uniform.

In discussing Manhattan it has been suggested that the disappearance of contrasts between clustered tall buildings at points of highest accessibility, and lower buildings in between, reduced identity and made orientation more difficult. Similarly the loss of small buildings, specialty shops and restaurants reduced the variety of areas, confusing orientation at the smaller scale (*Regional Plan Ass'n* 1969). This can be derived from the principles being discussed, as can the requirement that movement paths be linked and not disjointed. The prediction that a distinct pattern of buildings and spaces, of nodes and routes, would help orientation needs to be tested, although it is likely that it would reinforce location and orientation by street names and personal schemata, the development of which can also be helped by design (e.g., Burnette 1972). Also to be considered is temporal orientation — a clear awareness of time of day and seasonal variation and activity cycles.

It is also clear that different orientational systems and cues are needed for different transport modes. Freeways may create problems in that exit directions are often unrelated to perceived destinations, so that one turns left to go right. A conflict is set up between the sign and percept and *the latter must be ignored.* Yet in order to create a coherent schema of the city transport routes and channels should be laid out so as to clarify the structure of the city, and graphic and other information should relate to route layout and urban form. All these, in turn, need to be congruent with people's orientational systems and cognitive processes – which may become difficult in a pluralistic city (Appleyard 1968; Appleyard and Okamoto 1968; Davis 1972).

Orientation can also be disturbed by certain planning decisions such as a change to one way systems of traffic (*New Yorker* 1969, p. 18) which requires restructuring schemata. Similar effects can be expected when driving is changed from left hand to the right. The disappearance of widely used landmarks can also lead to disorientation, as can the reliance on subways which give no cues as to location between stations and where station exits suddenly deposit people in the middle of an area. People using freeways may be able to orient in the metropolitan area but be lost in local areas which remain unknown. In a city like Los Angeles freeway structures and signs become important cues. In finding one's way onto a freeway cues used were (in descending order) signs, grade changes, freeway structures, typical freeway furniture, ramps, traffic intensity, traffic direction, traffic signals, narrowing of street and street design while buildings and open spaces were unimportant (Jones 1972). Once a frame of reference and system of rules are adopted, environmental information will be fitted into it and if there is a lack of congruence then problems may arise which will be compounded by misreading the hierarchy of elements, their meaning and also sensory and social cues.

Activities are also important. People orient themselves to activity centers – plazas in Latin American cities, particular areas in an Arab city, shopping and amusement streets in Japan, temples in South India – and use paths which lead to them. These activities are reinforced by temporal orientational cues indicating periodicity and rhythms. The importance and visibility of elements is not only reinforced by the congruence of location, importance and symbolism, but also congruence with cultural rules about use and cognitive schemata (Rapoport, 1976), the appropriate sensory cues and redundancy.

Orientation is thus a matter of both physical elements and socio-cultural rules. Lostness may result from inadequate or wrong information or because a given element is new and has not been fitted into a schema – or because it is at odds with existing schemata. An example is the difficulty people had finding the Hayward Gallery in London when it was first built. This was attributed to the location of the gallery on the South Bank (where no important buildings had previously existed), faults in the signing system, the complexity of the path and the inappropriate symbolism of the building (Sharply 1969).

Orientation may take place in three ways – (1) topologically by recognizing continuity, (2) through patterning – identifying elements and placing them in a frame of reference and (3) through positioning – using directional clarity and spacing. Generally some combination of all three is used, the specific mix depending on the environment concerned and the personal and group characteristics of the individual; all involve the construction of schemata. In forming a schema of the Seattle World's Fair the major orientation activity seemed to be one of locating entrances and exits and identifying the route system. Having oriented in the larger environment, using views from entry points, secondary schemata were constructed for sub-areas and the same process followed. Strong visual elements were used as landmarks and only those areas visited which were on the routes and included in the schema (Weiss and Boutourline 1962). In both cities and buildings orientation is based on previous experience and habit, and if reality is incongruent with that, disorientation results (e.g., Bonnett 1965). Thus in shopping centers orientation was related to the physical environment, e.g., entrances, particularly if they reveal the overall layout, to the individual identity of shops and other elements, signs, their location and characteristics. Shoppers, goals and attitudes also affected orientation which differed for destination oriented, comparison of browsing shoppers, depending partly on temporal orientation.

Given these variations there were four main methods of orientation used (Baers 1966):

(1)   signs and verbal aids (asking) were the most important although sign systems are often ignored by designers (e.g., Best 1970; Appleyard 1968; Carr 1973); their location at decision points, placement relative to eyelevel, clarity and information provided were important.

(2)   recognition of a pattern of location was not used much in shopping centers – possibly because it is deliberately confused to encourage impulse buying.

(3)   habitual patterns of behavior are commonly used both in terms of the order of shopping, the type of shopping and the use of a limited area of the center – very much as in the city.

(4)   landmarks were also important although their definition is partly subjective and then significant only to the individual (i.e., associational). Their effectiveness in being more than just associational depends on:

    (a)   their contrast in function, which makes them stand out from the background (i.e., functional importance) or perceptually noticeable differences such as color, form, size, special features and the like.

    (b)   prominence of location and relation to activity nodes.

    (c)   relation to a unifying path system.

There were sex differences – men using physical landmarks while women relied more on merchandise and associations. This is partly due to familiarity since, in the U.S., women do most shopping but also to the fact that men tend to use more conceptual, abstract systems. Thus physical elements, signs, activity and merchandise are used differentially by different groups.

Generalizing, these relate to noticeable differences of the elements, their location, congruence with activities, relative salience and relation to path system and are very similar to the characteristics described for cities (e.g., Appleyard 1969, 1970, n.d.).

Orientation was most difficult in the simplest rather than the most complex shopping centers, because of their sameness in all directions, so that many noticeable differences and clear organizational principles, easily grasped, help orientation.

Orientation can then be restated to be a process whereby individuals locate in space and time and are able to predict and use the environment. Elements based on noticeable differences (subjectively defined to an extent), and related to prominence, symbolism, meaning, use and so on are filled into some frame of reference. This latter is based on physical, verbal, cultural and cognitive criteria, on some plan of action and pattern of activities related to a path system which has connectivity and which is related to barriers and other impediments.

The Subjective Definition of Areas

Among the places which form a crucial part of mental maps, areas are most important in the urban context. If place implies knowing that one is "here" rather than "there", then place definition and the definition of areas concerns identity. Countries are clearly not uniform and consist of identifiable regions and cities. Similarly cities consist of areas — neighborhoods, downtowns, theatei or restaurant districts, commercial or industrial zones, named areas of all kinds, such as the Left Bank, Soho, Nob Hill, West End, East Side or North Shore.

The definition of such areas is important in understanding urban morphology, selecting units for analysis or design — and in the formation of cognitive schemata. Yet the meaning of such units is not obvious — their definition is part of the cognitive taxonomic process discussed before and subjectively defined areas are an important part of mental maps. The meaning of city center or neighborhood needs to be discovered (and, as we have seen, the very definition of "city" is variable) (e.g., Davis 1969; Lapidus 1969; Wheatley 1971; Lewis 1965). In the past, most such definitions have either been arbitrary (e.g., the neighborhood unit) or based on "objective" criteria. The innovation in man— environment research is the stress on the subjective definition. Of primary interest are three questions: how are areas defined subjectively, how do such definitions relate to "objective" or arbitrary definitions and, finally, how do such definitions relate to physical, social and cultural characteristics of cities and people.

I will not review the vast literature on objective definitions. Briefly, such definitions depend on the selection of certain measurable characteristics and their use to determine where areas change their nature. For example, in Europe central districts have been defined using retail trade, land values, daytime populations, kinds of businesses, number of offices, number of telephone lines and so on (*Urban Core and Inner City* 1967). Similarly there is a vast literature on what I call arbitrary definitions, primarily of neighborhoods, with long arguments about population size and various other criteria *implicitly* based on some theory (e.g., Timms 1971; Johnston 1971).

An alternative approach is to discover how people cognitively define areas and places and what criteria they use. The question is how and when do people conclude that they have gone from one place to another — from urban to non-urban, from downtown to non-downtown, from an area which is "theirs" to one which is not. For example individuals differ in judging transitions from urban to non-urban, but each individual is usually quite consistent (Clayton 1968). From our previous discussion it would follow that there is likely to be more variability among groups than within them, so that generalizations become possible with design implications for different contexts, particularly as one relates subjective and other definitions.

In order validly to compare such different definitions one would need studies of the same places using different approaches. However, some conclusions can be drawn from an overall comparison. My stress, however, will be on the subjective definition since it is far less known and also because behavior is primarily related to cognitive schemata.

Cognitive styles affect the cues which are noticed, how they are categorized and then used to define areas subjectively. If a set of elements, which is categorized as being similar, begins to change the question is at what point it becomes noticeably different, i.e., when are the elements categorized as having become fully dissimilar and a boundary defined.

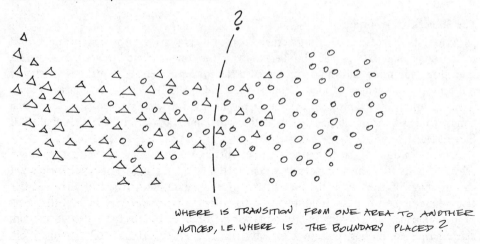

WHERE IS TRANSITION FROM ONE AREA TO ANOTHER
NOTICED, I.E. WHERE IS THE BOUNDARY PLACED?

FIG. 3.17

We have discussed the five main modes for distinguishing equivalence: perceptible, functional, affective, nominal and by fiat (Olver and Hornsby 1972). In the definition of areas perceptual qualities (noticeable differences) would be first, then affective (preference, evaluation and judgement of social identity (Sanoff 1973; Duncan 1973). Various rules and categories would then be used to draw boundaries, i.e., establish discontinuities, where two or more subjectively different areas come together. The meaning of cues also plays a role. Cues must not only be noticed but also understood and then, in some cases, obeyed. Thus a residential area with curved streets in a grid city will not only constitute a definable area through noticeable differences (*if* they are noticed) and proclaim a certain character. It will also provide safety not only by discouraging cars physically, but also saying "keep out", by making orientation and the construction of mental maps more difficult so that people become lost. At the same time some people may deliberately disregard all these cues — to annoy the inhabitants.

While we will be discussing the concept of noticeable differences in more detail in Chapter 4, it may be useful to list some among them which probably play a role in the subjective definition of areas:

Levels of complexity
Urban grain and texture
Scale and size, building height and density (e.g., Rapoport 1975(b))
Colors, materials, details
People — language, dress, behavior, social changes
Signs
Activity levels
Uses — shops, buildings; rules about front/back and streets
Noise levels
Light levels
Man-made or natural; nature of plants, gardens, fences
Smells
Maintenance and cleanliness

Generally the distinctions add up to the concept of cultural landscapes (see Chapter 6), and the subjective definition is helped by clear transitions and the congruence of social and perceptual cues — in addition to drawing physical boundaries social boundaries are also being defined (e.g., Barth 1969).

Consider some examples. Regarding urban grain, it is clearly a matter of solids and voids, the relationships of buildings and spaces, the patterning of streets. It has been suggested that one distinction is among ribbing, studding and clumping (Smailes 1955). These are clearly judgemental and whether they are noticeable for a given population, and used to distinguish among areas, is a researchable question.

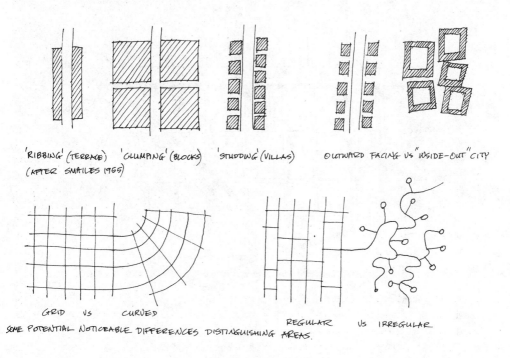

'RIBBING' (TERRACE)   'CLUMPING' (BLOCKS)   'STUDDING' (VILLAS)   OUTWARD FACING VS "INSIDE-OUT" CITY
(AFTER SMAILES 1955)

GRID   VS   CURVED   REGULAR   VS   IRREGULAR
SOME POTENTIAL NOTICEABLE DIFFERENCES DISTINGUISHING AREAS.

FIG. 3.18

It has also been suggested that people are concerned with several urban elements — panorama, skyline or profile, urban space or place, and experience of motion (Smailes 1955, pp. 108–109). Whether people are actually aware of these is, once again, researchable and it is likely that different elements will be used in internal cognition, i.e. within the city and its areas, and external cognition — the city in the landscape (Papageorgiou 1971; Goodey *et al.* 1971).

Consider some examples of the informal definitions of areas in cities which may gain general acceptance. In Mexico City, since 1963, there has gradually developed a shopping-entertainment area called the Zona Rosa. As far as I have been able to determine this began informally among the merchants of the area, and is now used in advertising and is mapped in guides and tourist literature. It is described as the principal shopping and art exhibition district in the city with approximately 600 establishments (excluding hotels). It covers twenty blocks and is bounded by Insurgentes Sur,

Chapultapec Avenue, the Paseo de la Reforma while the fourth side is variously described as Varsovia, Florencia or others depending on the particular tourist publication.* This is interesting because the first three are large avenues and very different to those *within* the district, and on these three sides the character of the areas outside is very different, socially and physically, while the fourth is, in size and character, part of the district and hence more ambiguous. The definition of the area is also helped by naming — all the streets within the Zona Rosa being named after European cities and changing outside it — except on the fourth side. Thus we find that some subjective boundaries are clearer and less ambiguous than others — and boundaries may be clear, fuzzy or may form gradients.

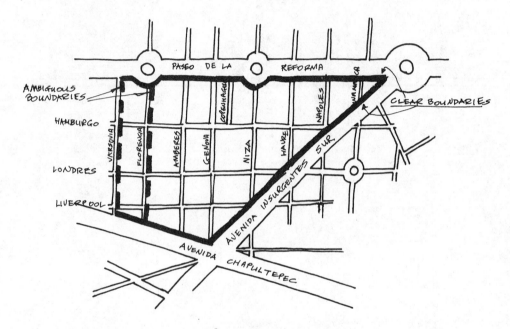

FIG. 3.19. "Zona Rosa," Mexico City.

The variability of definitions is also partly a matter of scale so that in the case of campus, in spite of some individual differences, there was much agreement while for the Chicago Loop the variability was greater and partly related to the degree of familiarity and use and on how it was entered. Workers within the Loop gave a tighter definition with more detail while outsiders gave a more extensive definition with more emphasis on external landmarks (Saarinen 1969, pp. 15–18) (an example of internal vs. external cognition). Variability is thus partly due to those social, cultural and personal characteristics which influence cognitive schemata generally, related to social networks, home ranges and activity systems, and types of activities (e.g., Lucas 1972) and familiarity (Downs 1970).

In Miami, the Cuban area (Habana Chica) is also described in tourist publications. Its location is not as precisely described but the characteristics which distinguish it are

* Using Varsovia — *Donde* (where to go/what to do in Mexico) June 1973, p. 25; using Florencia — *The Gazer* (El Miron) No. 1206, June 29-July 3, 1973, map p. 47.

significant (Levine 1974). They include music, men conversing around coffee stands and the coffee served, the language used, aromas of spices, general atmosphere, foods in shops and restaurants, shops generally and their signs.

In New York a new "Bohemian" quarter (Soho), comparable to the Left Bank, Chelsea, North Beach, or Ramblas (each of which presents a definitional problem) is also included in tourist magazines. In this case the criteria used are not clear but the boundaries are mapped and the name is reputedly descriptive of its location — *So*uth of *Ho*uston Street (Marks 1973) although I suspect that there are echoes of the other Soho implied.

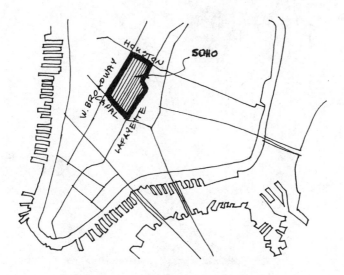

FIG. 3.20. The "Soho" area in Lower Manhattan.

There are implicit conflicts between planners' definitions and others. Consider a small, street-size urban district — Manhattan's 42nd Street — which has been described as a single unit, four blocks wide and fourteen long, from River to River (*Regional Plan Ass'n* 1969, pp. 86–89). It is defined in terms of continuity of movement and activities and its popular impression as a unit. It is questionable whether it is actually seen as a single unit since, on the basis of activities, and character it can equally validly be divided into three or four units — for example East River to Madison, Madison to Fifth Avenue, Fifth Avenue to Times Square (or Sixth?), Times Square to 8th and then on to the Hudson River. Whether it is understood as a linear strip or a series of areas needs to be discovered.

Crime boundaries are not clearly drawn but are known by inhabitants affecting their behavior (Goodey 1969, p. 41). Such cognitive maps of perceived crime should affect behavior more than any objective data since they represent behavioral space and its barriers. Thus in Philadelphia people's behavior is greatly influenced by their awareness of areas of high and low crime so that in moving North-South very roundabout routes will be taken to avoid the "peaks" and use the "valleys" (Gould 1972(a)). Even more striking is a map published by *L'Aurore* for intending visitors to New York, showing areas unsafe at all times, areas unsafe at night and relatively safe areas (*New York Times* 1971).

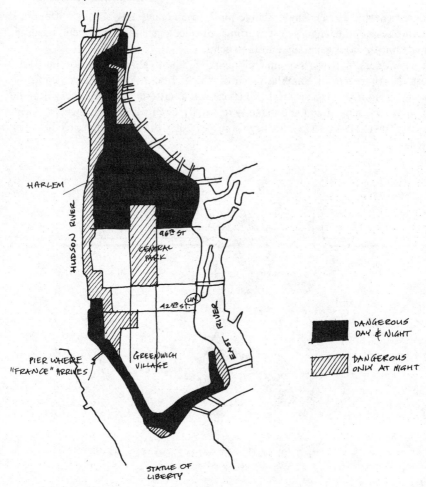

FIG. 3.21. "Safety" map of Manhattan from *L'Aurore* (*New York Times*, 1971).
Note also the landmarks used.)

While the *New York Times* reciprocated with a comparable map of Paris, a more interesting comparison is with Alaskan Eskimos and the areas which they avoid because of evil spirits (Burch 1971). Although different categories and cues are used, both represent definitions of profane, dangerous, undesirable and unsafe — in a word *uninhabitable* — areas as opposed to sacred, safe, desirable safe and *usable* (Rapoport, 1976). At a small-scale this helps explain the differences in front/back behavior (Brower and Williamson 1974) but, more generally, such maps, whether published or unpublished, affect behavior. The Manhattan map surely affected the distribution of French visitors there in 1971 in the same way that Eskimos avoided areas in Alaska. An area like the Zona Rosa attracts tourists and possibly repels poor Mexicans although, in this case, the barriers would tend to be weak and permeable. Also, once areas become unknown due to such definitions they are less used, hence less known in a cycle of positive feedback.

I now turn to the literature on the subjective definition of two important types of areas: city centers and neighborhoods.

City Centers. Among "objective" criteria used in defining city centers have been their diversity and complexity from the air (Vance 1971), the percentage of frontage used for retail shops (DeBlij 1968), floor-space use intensity, concentration of certain employment, bank and administration, telecommunications data, commuter and visitor flows, residential densities in people per room and so on. Even here cultural differences can be found: in Europe the urban core is generally defined more broadly than the Central Business District in the U.S.; in France the definition of the core is little developed (*Urban Core and Inner City* 1967). Many of these criteria would clearly not constitute noticeable differences for residents (quite apart from the different cognitions of experts).

Among subjective criteria, apart from the types of noticeable differences already listed, would be the meaning of elements, their symbolic values, the intensity of use, in some cultures the role of the center in sociability and interaction (*Urban Core and Inner City* 1967). The larger the city, and the further from the center that people live, the larger the extent of the center as subjectively defined (Heinemeyer 1967; Saarinen 1969) and, more generally, the closer one lives to *any* area the smaller is that area defined subjectively (King 1971(b)) and areas tend to be stretched towards the direction where one lives (Eyles 1969; Klein 1967).

In general, subjective definitions seem to be a function of meaning and symbolic value reflecting preferences and hierarchies, so that elements important for particular groups tend to be included by them. These coincide with certain noticeable physical characteristics congruent with activities. The definition becomes clearer and is helped by the presence of multisensory cues, changing clearly, and the presence of strong physical and social barriers which act as boundaries. These are modified by place and length of residence and cognitive style. Some elements are agreed upon by all, the elderly may use historically important elements even when these no longer exist, the young may use the most recent elements and other groups select others yet, depending on culture, lifestyle activities and so on. The physical environment also plays an important role so that whereas in Tokyo, where there is no single city center, there is little agreement with places on opposite sides of the geographical center, as far as three miles apart being named (Canter and Canter 1971, p. 61), in Karlsruhe some places elicited 95% agreement (Klein 1967) and in Lincoln, Nebraska 99% of the population agreed about the center.* Subjective definitions are frequently different to "objective", which is important for planning and design generally and especially in relation to new towns and work in other cultures.

In the case of Amsterdam (Heinemeyer 1967), the city center is defined in both physical and social terms, so that it has differential attraction for different groups with different "core mindedness" (as was the case in Paris (cf. Lamy 1967)), the stress being on symbolic aspects (cf. Schnapper 1971). The core is a social and symbolic fact as well as a material one. Monuments play a part and so does a feeling of being at the center of things. Generally, the center of Amsterdam was rather limited and its definition was influenced by activities such as shopping for women, and a wider variety of activities for men. While there was agreement about the heart of the central area (as in most other

---

* Prof. Robert Mittelstaedt, Dept. of Marketing at Seminar, University of Nebraska.

studies) the extent varied, some boundaries being clear and others diffuse. Preference was most important with diversity and complexity the most preferred characteristics (Heinemeyer 1967).

In Bologna and other North Italian cities, the social status of the center is the most important factor. The center has the highest value, to the extent that other upper class areas (e.g., on the hills) are socially integrated with the center (in social, not geographic space). The cultural center is particularly limited and clearly defined. All first-run cinemas, art galleries and museums, important theaters and clubs are there, and the higher the status the closer to the center. All important commercial activities in Bologna, Turin and Milan occur in an area of less than 50 ha. (125 acres). Such activities are not accepted when outside this center so that "the museum" means the one in the center, the other not being considered a museum. The basic taxonomy is bipolar—center/non-center (like sacred/profane), reflecting the bipolarity of the social world — there is spatial and social congruence, concentricity being reflected in art, religion and all culture; the center is good, the periphery bad (Schnapper 1971, pp. 44, 95–100, 122–124).

In London the public's perception of the location and extent of Piccadilly is very different to planners'. Only 27% saw Piccadilly as the immediate circus area — 29% saw it as the wider West End and another 44% as the whole "bright lights" area extending to Leicester Square between Coventry St., Shaftesbury Ave. and Charing Cross Road. This was more than ignorance, although some people put Selfridge's and Carnaby St. there; it was because Piccadilly is seen, positively, as the center of London, a place of crowds, tourists, cinemas, young people, neon lights (and, by fewer people, negatively as a place of drug addicts, pornographic bookshops, criminals and dirt) (Harrison 1972) and areas matching these criteria are included.

In Birmingham it appears that areas are included in the central city on the basis of historical, aesthetic or economic criteria, and where all three coincide there is most agreement and greatest importance. The extent of the center varied greatly: at a minimum it includes New and Corporation Streets; at the next level it is that area located within the Inner Ring Road while some include new developments at Five Ways. New Street is always the core and gradients vary in steepness on different sides, with the clearest boundaries where impenetrable barriers such as railway yards, industrial areas or extremely undesirable areas exist (Goodey *et al.* 1971) (cf. Philadelphia and Manhattan). Place of residence (cf. Prokop 1967) and age (in terms of *new* development (cf. Porteous 1971)) also played a role.

In the case of Berlin (Sieverts 1967, 1969) children relied on activity and its congruence with physical elements, as well as "anomalies" in defining the center; again the size and extent varied although there was agreement on the heart which had sharp boundaries.

The most thorough study of the subjective definition of a city center is of Karlsruhe, Germany (Klein 1967). Two elements were included by over 95% of the people, three more by over 80% and nine others by over 66%. There were sex differences, women knowing the center better than men and stressing cultural and shopping areas, whereas men stressed arterial roads and administrative areas. Age, length of residence, class and education had effects but mobility only had minor ones. Location of residence was important so that the direction of approach was significant (cf. Saarinen 1969).

It might, therefore, be predicted that boundaries of areas will depend on where one lives. Learning is clearly involved, and all the factors already discussed are significant —

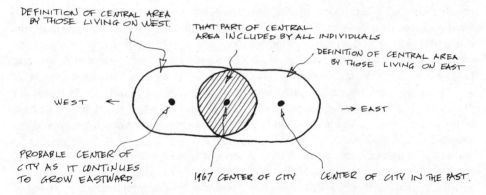

FIG. 3.22. Subjective definition of central area of Karlsruhe (W. Germany) (from Klein 1967).

such as means of travel, relative attraction, familiarity, activities and the role of the schema in affecting the reception of new information. Meaning, noticeable differences and urban structure are important and the congruence of several sets of factors leads to particularly strong schemata; there is much agreement about some strong boundaries and less about others which are more variable and vague (Klein 1967).

Neighborhood. Judging by the extent of the literature, the residential area — neighborhood, *quartier* or whatever, is of the greatest importance, reflecting its importance as a life space closely linked with the social group and the dwelling. Even Australian Aborigines structure their environment into regions of greater or less "ownership" and significance (sacred in that case), with corresponding strength of boundary separating strangers from related people (Meggitt 1965). People and places are identified through environmental symbols and while the relationships between people and their immediate environment vary with culture, this example suggests the fundamental nature of such definitions of living space (Rapoport 1972(e)). These definitions reflect the fact that environments are not a uniform field for human activity, but consist of areas of greater or lesser importance to people. In cities these areas are of relatively limited size and have some congruence with activity patterns and population characteristics.

Historically cities have tended to be divided into neighborhoods along clearly understood lines, i.e., the city consists of discrete elements with certain physical and social characteristics. For example the smallest unit in Tokyo is the *chome*. One district, Dazawa has 10 chomes; Satagaya prefecture has 30 districts the size of Dazawa and Tokyo has 23 prefectures (Canter and Canter 1971) so that at the very least Tokyo has close to 7000 such areas which have subtle but clear environmental distinctions in urban texture — street pattern, house size, wall height, details or even color (Lenclos 1972; Canter and Canter 1971; Smith 1971). They also vary socially forming coherent communities sharing services, shrines and the like.

Researchers' definitions of neighborhood are extensive (e.g., Johnston 1971(a), Sawicky 1971; Goheen 1971; E. Pryor 1971; Nelson 1971; Meenegan 1972). In planning theory it has been defined *a priori* on the basis of service functions (shopping or schools) or population size (typically ranging between 5000–10,000). The subjective definition concerns what neighborhood means to residents, and the effects of mobility, the relative attraction of other places, the effects of social links and the propensity of people to cluster on the basis of certain characteristics. While such work goes back over fifty years

(McKenzie 1921–22), most of the work in man–environment research is recent. Generally, people define small areas within the immediate vicinity of their dwelling, the limits of which depend on the physical and social characteristics, the extent of movement and regular contacts. Such neighborhoods can be mapped and they vary with age, sex, occupation, mobility, social networks and the physical nature of the city; they change with time, stage in life cycle and other characteristics. Thus neighborhoods are important places which differ for different people but also overlap (Wilmott 1962) and, as we have seen in the case of Aboriginal children, social networks and visiting patterns affect neighborhood definition.

It is very unlikely that people have a schema of megalopolis or even the entire city. Most likely people's cognitive definition only extends to intermediate areas and it is significant that neighborhood is uniformly shown to be the most important aspect of satisfaction (Chapter 2).

Subjectively, neighborhood could mean:

(a)   just the dwelling, the area around it being merely a matter of convenience which might be the view of people without children or with extensive networks based on community of interests.

(b)   the area immediately around the dwelling symbolizing status.

(c)   a set of people, either liked or disliked, but forming the immediate social environment.

(d)   some ideal, such as a village-like community, with face-to-face associations and intimate relationships or related to an idea, such as Bloomsbury, Chelsea or Greenwich Village.

(e)   an area based on services and the people who run them (e.g., Wilson 1963, pp. 19–20).

(f)   a distinctive physical area separated from other areas by clear physical or conceptual boundaries.

(g)   an area of people subjectively homogeneous by race, ethnicity, religion, lifestyle, ideology and the like, and reinforced by activity patterns and social networks.

These fall into two major classes – physical and social – and neighborhoods are most clearly defined when social and physical space coincide, i.e., when physical boundaries, social networks, local facilities and special symbolic and emotional connotations are congruent in people's minds. This subjective definition varies for individuals but can be generalized for certain groups. Both physical and social criteria are used to define neighborhood and preference and habitat selection play a role, since similar people pick similar areas and reinforce their social and physical character so that environmental quality characteristics are also used in defining discontinuities among areas. We have seen that greenery, good maintenance and other characteristics are used to define high class areas (Chapter 2) and when these disappear the area changes – i.e., status is used to define neighborhood (Mills 1972). Homogeneity of status is an important criterion (Bryson and Thompson 1972, p. 23) so that in Canberra in 1971–72 attempts were being made to give identity to the new area of O'Malley by differentiating it from others around it through the price of dwellings and land (which would need to be expressed by noticeable differences in the quality of houses and gardens).

While neighborhoods tend to be fairly small, they fit into larger areas which are also ranked by outsiders who conceptually divide the city into areas of varying character and status. Thus in Brisbane, Australia such areas are identified by social and physical characteristics and have widely known associated images and preferences (Timms 1971, pp. 111–117). Such status differences are often embodied in names and people will go to great lengths conceptually to alter boundaries so as to "live" in areas of higher status. Thus taxi drivers in Sydney often complain about being misled by passengers using high status addresses when they actually live in adjoining areas of lower status (for such rankings see Congalton 1969, part 1) and we have already discussed the controversy about renaming areas and redrawing suburban boundaries (e.g., Miller 1971). This process is supported by a literary reference to North and South Kensington (London) – both areas which have changed. But while "South Kensington isn't what it was, but it can hardly be said to have gone down in the world; it has merely changed. North Kensington is a different story, a dirty story, a squalid story . . . a part of London . . . not entirely suitable for the fastidious . . . . The district, of course, has its periphery. Notting Hill claims to be a cut above the rest of the area, and along the edges of Notting Hill there are some decent addresses – but mostly they profess to belong either to Bayswater, to the East, or Holland Park, towards the West" (Culpan 1968, pp. 121–123).

Such status considerations may distort the more general principle that, as in the case of central areas, the closer to an area that people live the smaller their definition of it. More generally, outsiders and residents define areas differently (MacEwen 1972; Golledge and Zannaras n.d., p. 33). This is partly due to the fact that for outsiders it is a matter of generalized schemata while for residents it is a matter of much concern, and the latter also have more data and information – and more categories to perceive noticeable differences, make distinctions and draw boundaries. Thus in Sydney residents subdivided their areas into subareas not acknowledged by the council (Pallier 1971) and length of residence (possibly another aspect of familiarity) also helped restrict the size of areas. The size of the areas defined is also affected by friendship patterns (Sanoff 1970), ethnicity (Suttles 1968), location, lifestyle and activity patterns and varies with climate, becoming smaller in the winter and larger in the summer (Michelson 1971(a)) as the activity space varies. Generally, though, people tend to draw boundaries as close to their dwelling as possible (Barwick 1971). While boundaries are often fuzzy (Wilson 1962) people do identify with compact home areas which are much smaller than official areas.

In Raleigh, N. C., such areas were quite small and areas considered as a unit by outsiders were subdivided by residents (Sanoff 1970); this was also the case in Chicago (Suttles 1968). In London, also, many areas are subdivided conceptually so that Lewisham had at least 6 areas and Bethnal Green consisted of 6 distinct, subjectively defined areas (which were indistinguishable to outsiders) (Taylor 1973). In many cases, though, such divisions are based on generally noticeable differences, such as major barriers or general character. Thus Bow is clearly marked by being on the East of the Regent's Canal with well kept houses, gleaming windows, shining doorknobs and whitened doorsteps while on the West side was a "black spot" with dilapidated houses, casual employment and so on; to the North of that a respectable area with middle-class pretensions (Taylor 1973).

People throughout England, in fact, identify with and can conceptualize small home areas on the basis of social attachment, local affairs, local employment or conviviality (pubs, clubs and so on) reinforced by physical characteristics and boundaries (parks, streets, bus routes and the like). Very rarely do official political subdivisions coincide with such neighborhoods and the city is never so defined. Such areas must be distinguishable from others, boundaries must have meaning and they must have a characteristic common life and the larger the city, the smaller the area defined. Most typically such areas tended only to include several streets around the dwelling and typical descriptions mention streets, churches, pubs, betting shops, topography and named areas (*Royal Commission on Local Govt.* 1969; Hampton 1970).

Thus both official political units (*Royal Commission on Local Govt.* 1969) and standard planning neighborhood units (Feldt *et al.* n.d.) are too large and, in addition to social characteristics, friendship and activity systems areas, in order to be defined, need clear boundaries (major streets, large open spaces, industry, etc.) and readily perceptible characteristics, i.e., definition is clearest when various cues are congruent and when cognitive schemata can coincide with major features of the physical environment as is the case with Australian Aborigines (Rapoport 1972(e)).

The definition of areas implies the definition of boundaries, which depend on perceived discontinuities in physical and social cues. The variability of definitions depends on judgements about where one place ends and another begins, where "ownership" and belonging change. Thus topography, i.e., clear natural physical discontinuities, may reinforce ethnic clustering (as in Cincinatti) and other discontinuities and barriers, such as industry, freeways or railways also produce clearer boundaries than do places with more ambiguous transitions. Boundaries are clearest and strongest, and the distinctions among areas clearest, when all physical and social cues coincide.

Subjective boundaries are important because they restrict movement and guide behavior and, ideally, planned and subjective boundaries would be congruent. When boundaries are closely intertwined with cultural patterns, as in traditional societies, the imposition of inappropriate administrative boundaries can be most unsatisfactory (Adams 1973, p. 266), although in most modern cities the effects are not as great.

All cities have their East sides, lower East sides and North Shores. They exist in people's minds and influence where they live, which areas they avoid, how they move through the city. Understanding this subjective morphology of the city and its relation to the physical environment is critical for design. Consider the North Shore of Sydney. It is "a region that had no definition only a cachet; it had nothing to do with any shore and, by rough estimate and depending on where one lived, began some five or six miles from the shores of the harbor" (Cleary 1970, p. 85). It is clear from the novel that someone who lived there made it "sound like another country".

I asked about a dozen people to define the extent of the North Shore. Here are six examples of replies:

(1) Male, academic, psychologist, native of Sydney, lives in a part of the North Shore. Roseville to Pymble between Pacific Highway and Archbold St. Some vague extension to Wahroonga.

(2) Male, architect, native of Sydney living at an inner city area on the West — everything North of the harbor — an example of the rule that the further one lives from an area the larger the area defined.

(3) Female, secretary, native of Sydney, living on the North shore along the railway line — only those suburbs between Roseville and Wahroonga and, if on the West of Pacific Highway only those areas forming part of these suburbs. St. Ives is not included because it is too recent, i.e., she only includes old suburbs and works by names. She was looking for a house for her son in the area and was influenced by the real estate

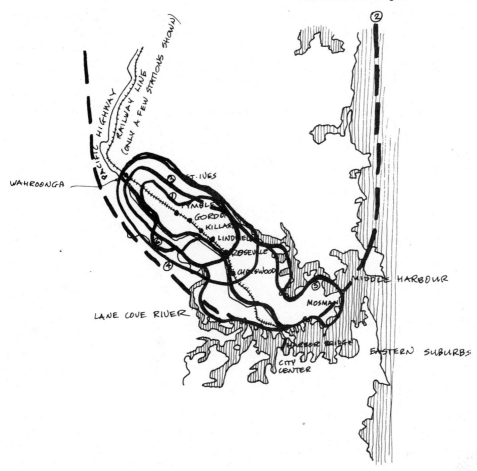

FIG. 3.23. Six subjective definitions of "North Shore", Sydney, Australia.

columns, which, incidentally, had just changed the map and taxonomy of the areas of Sydney from three (West, East and North) to six, as shown in Fig. 3.24.

(4) Male, town planner, immigrant but in Sydney many years, resident of North Shore — professionally uses strip between Lane Cove River and Middle Harbour starting at Harbour and excluding Northern Beaches. Informally, however, he thinks that it only includes the municipality of Ku-ring-gai and that it is related to the North Shore railway.

(5) Male, architect, native of Sydney and North Shore resident — defines it in terms of what he leaves out rather than what he includes. Leaves out everything up to Chatswood but includes Mosman [which is very high status] up to Hornsby (vague at that point but tends to exclude it [it is low status]). East to Middle Harbour, West to Lane Cove River. Fullers Bridge and Gordon West included, Northern beaches excluded. Related to railway but quality aspects decide what is in or out.

(6) 3rd year architecture student, native of Sydney. Includes area between Chatswood and Wahroonga, excludes Hornsby and area West of Pacific highway although

Gordon and Pymble are included as far as the Lane Cove River. Includes Mosman, Northbridge, Castle Cove [again status] and excludes Northern beaches.

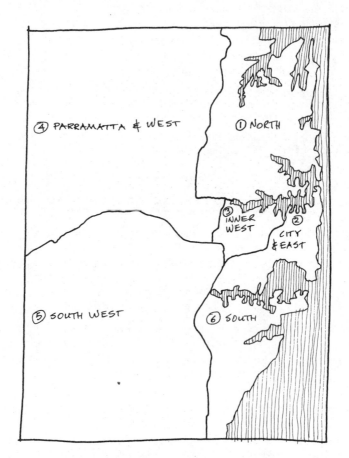

FIG. 3.24. Sydney metropolitan regions used in real estate advertising. (Formerly three divisions were used: North, West and East-South, each much larger.)

While I claim no general validity for this very informal survey, it seems to confirm the relationship of size and distance, the role of status in including or excluding areas, and effects of various population characteristics. While some places are universally excluded, there is much variation in defining this area and some of the places of change actually show different physical characteristics. In any case people know when North Sydney gives way to Chatswood and Chatswood to Roseville: the question is, how do they know and how can designers influence this apparently universal process.

Some tentative answers to this question have already been given. The perception of differences may depend on meaning (Duncan 1973, in press 1976; Werthman 1968) and on the definition of the stimulus properties and situations which tends to be variable, and both material and non-material items of culture are used to differentiate neighborhoods by social rank (Sherif and Sherif 1963; Royse 1969). In the case of San Antonio the most striking visible difference between low rank and middle and high rank areas is the decreased importance of well kept lawns and the appearance of "old country" gardens of flowers and bare dirt in the former (Sherif and Sherif 1963). Such differences are also most important in shaping the individuals' conception of standards and hence future evaluations. Gardens and plants can, in fact, be used to distinguish among different culture areas (Kimber 1966, 1971, 1973; Duncan 1973) and cultural landscapes.

Motivation and preference thus affect the definition of areas (as it does distance), so that where areas are both well known and highly valued they are emphasized in some way (either enlarged or *reduced* — to increase the value and rarity) and others are distorted — as smaller, larger, as blanks or as dangerous. In the case of conceptual maps of larger areas, familiar, important and valued areas are exaggerated (Stea 1969(b)), and even when people share activities their mental maps will differ because of the different importance attached to the activity (e.g., Tuan 1974, p. 62).

Generally the definition of neighborhood is part of the category "subjective space" and is based on an act of categorization involving a group defining itself as such, and having some boundary outside which are "others". The idea of perceived homogeneity is part of this (Chapter 5) and boundaries may be used to preserve some form of cohesion and identity (Barth 1969; Siegel 1970; Rapoport, in press(b)). Similarly, clustering and like people are needed to support specialized institutions, and boundaries are then defined through rules, conventions or physical attack and physical elements are used mainly to indicate a clear demarcation point (Rapoport 1972(e); Suttles 1968) reinforcing social boundaries.

In Belgium it is suggested that there is a difference between a *"Unité de voisinage"* which is a group of people living close together and having individualized social relations (e.g., friendship), and the *"quartier"* which is a neighborhood based on social distinctions — on professions or socio-economic status (Roggemans 1971, pp. 47 ff.). If one added to this social homogeneity, lifestyle and the like, the distinction proposed would then seem to depend on a subjective definition of criteria of similarity, and by implications dissimilarity, as well as the distinction between neighboring and friendship (Keller 1968). The division into neighborhoods affects those living in them and there is both spatial and cultural integration in the city — spatial being defined as objective, and cultural as subjective structuring — although subjective urban morphology must be based on some objective structures (Roggemans 1971, pp. 50—52), i.e., noticeable differences and in clear boundaries. Thus La Laja is the most clearly defined neighborhood in Ciudad Guayana because of the presence of industry, the river and a river flood plane (Peattie 1972, pp. 8—9, 54).

The maintenance on such boundaries depends on whether cues are noticed and understood by outsiders, and whether they are prepared to obey the messages of these boundaries regarding the degree of control and belonging. If that happens, interaction *within* such boundaries is more intense and meaningful than outside. The areas of space-bound groups can be divided into three zones — the core, where they form a majority and there is homogeneity, sharing and understanding of rules, intense interaction, specialized schools, churches, shops, bars and so on; the domain, where the group is dominant but less fully in control and the sphere, or outer zone, where they are a minority (Meining 1965). We have seen that the environment generally can be conceptualized as the separation between people and people, people and things and things and things. The urban environment can also be understood in such terms — and this separation may be spatial, temporal, social or symbolic.

As a result of habitat selection areas come to be seen as the home of various groups and take on certain meaning and identity (the *core* of a group) so that neighborhood becomes the most meaningful concept in the city (e.g., Michelson 1966). The neighborhood reflects people's lifespace (Lewin 1936, 1951) and, like it, has regions, paths and barriers: since different individuals and groups have differing life spaces they have different neighborhoods. When private lifespace dominates, neighborhood is unimportant whereas when group lifespace is important, "urban villages" are found, and there is a link between lifespace, activity space or orbit and the physical space subjectively defined as one's neighborhood (Paulsson 1952). Objective and subjective definitions seem to interact and cannot always be neatly separated. If neighborhoods are usefully defined in terms of socio-cultural, economic, or organizational characteristics, communication networks and physical character, then each of these can be used "objectively" by planners and scholars on the one hand or subjectively by the people concerned. Thus, although the major difference is in who makes judgements, the types of criteria used also vary depending on cognitive styles and noticeable differences. The perception of physical characteristics and their meanings, knowledge of kinship and other social networks and social barriers, the use of local facilities, activity systems and temporal rhythms, symbolic and affective aspects, perception of homogeneity, the history of the area and the names used informally are all likely to be different for different individuals (although generalizable for groups) and thus used differently by them.

The *process* of defining a neighborhood subjectively is universal, since people must make sense of a world by relating to some area smaller than the city, but the variables and classifications used vary. Thus even when cities, as in North India, consist of areas (Mohallas) their subjective definition is much smaller. It is confined to an alley or portion of an alley and is defined partly in terms of social networks (knowing "everyone") so that people within a neighborhood are "closer", because of social and psychological barriers, than people physically closer but in another neighborhood. Each individual thus has a subjective, egocentric neighborhood the boundaries of which, while unclear, are related to physical features but are mainly socially determined which, in the Indian context, means shared rules and norms based on *caste* (and class) (Vatuk 1972, pp. 149 ff.). Swahili towns were also organized by neighborhoods (*Mitaa*) which, although difficult to isolate on a map, are known to inhabitants who identify their position in town by citing them and see the city as an assemblage of *Mitaa*. The inhabitants of each are related and thus have the same status and responsibilities reinforced by religious ties (Ghaidan 1972, p. 88).

In Australia also, people define and name bounded areas so that the city becomes a series of named places with variable and well understood status related to job and social position (Congalton 1969) as well as the noticeable social and physical characteristics already discussed above (and in Chapter 2). Places are thus defined by noticeable changes in character producing an edge or boundary. All these cues also have temporal element indicating change, either for the better or the worse, so that areas can be differentiated as stable, upgrading or deteriorating.

It may well be that in the U.S. and other countries where other status differences tend to be unclear, address and house become the principal indicators (Johnston 1971; Timms 1971; Gans 1968; Lofland 1973) so that planning is seen as being mainly to keep out lower status people (Eichler and Kaplan 1967; Werthman 1968). In such cases the social distance between areas, and hence their precise definition, is greater than where status is more clearly and rigidly fixed in other ways.

In general there thus seem to be three major elements in the definition of neighborhood: socio-cultural characteristics and criteria, the location and use of various services, facilities and activities and, thirdly, the physical environment and its symbolic meaning. Socio-cultural characteristics affect the importance attached to the local area and its services (e.g., Stone 1954), and hence to neighborhood, so that the meaning of a social area depends on them, as does the definition of the permeability of barriers. The time spent within an area also affects the importance given it and hence its definition *vis-à-vis* other areas. Thus women frequently define neighborhood differently than do men, and the length of the journey to work affects the time spent in an area and hence its definition (de Lauwe 1965(b), Vol. 2, p. 57, 1960). The tempos and rhythms of various groups also influence the definition of areas in which they live, so that there is social time as well as social space (Yaker *et al.* 1971, p. 75).

The formal modern study of the subjective definition of neighborhood began with Lee (1968), and has proved extremely influential. Beginning with the relative lack of congruence between spatial and behavioral aspects of the concept, he adopted a phenomenological approach. Neighborhood is defined in both cognitive and social terms, being intermediate between the individual and the city and resulting in the concept of the *socio-spatial schema*, which is meaningful for most people who are aware of its boundaries. Such boundaries are often based on roads and may be clear, vague and blurred, or form gradients. The schema — its buildings, spaces and people — stands out as a rather clear figure on the rather formless urban background.

While schemata varied individually in size and shape, based on unique experiences, they could be generalized for various groups. The size and makeup of subjective neighborhood is a function of the physical environment, name, symbolic elements and group behavior and characteristics (Lee 1971(a)). An important role is played by the neighborhood quotient which describes the use of local facilities (the importance of local neighborhood) and the degree of involvement. These varied with class, age, length of residence and type of housing. Among important social variables were friendship networks within the locality and local club membership; the use of local shops was positively, but not significantly, related to neighborhood definition due to the wide use of such shops generally in the English context. Among important physical variables were the number of houses, shops and amenity buildings included in the area (Lee 1968, 1971(a)). Neighborhood is not defined in terms of population but in terms of area — about 75 acres (Lee 1968) amended, in later work, to between 75–100 acres (Lee 1971(a)). In either case higher densities within the area would lead to greater populations, hence more nearby facilities with consequently greater use and a greater stress on neighborhood. The influence of social networks could be reinforced through congruence with noticeable elements, group homogeneity and the other variables which we have discussed.

Size and importance vary with the neighborhood quotient and this is related to particular groups as well as individuals. Lower income groups tend to have smaller neighborhoods so that, in Britain, middle class people have neighborhoods larger than 100 acres* which may be related to mobility, lifestyle and extensive social networks. In the U.S. working class areas also seem more important and smaller than middle class areas (Hartman 1963; Fried and Gleicher 1961; Fried 1973; Fellman and Brandt 1970; Yancey

* Personal communication, in 1969, from Dr. David Harvey, then at the University of Bristol.

1971; Hall 1971) although some researchers question the highly localized nature of working class areas (e.g., Bleiker 1972). However, most of the evidence suggests that there are class- and lifestyle-related differences in neighborhood size, so that in Los Angeles the mental maps of four groups reflected neighborhoods varying from a few blocks to much larger areas (Orleans 1971) although for any one group there is agreement and consistency with roads used as boundaries (Everitt and Cadwallader 1972). The argument that neighborhood is unimportant today since people live in a "non-place realm" seems at odds with the evidence, although the importance of neighborhood as the *exclusive* locus for life seems to be reducing for most people (Timms 1971, pp. 250–251). Thus in Ipswich, England all people were able to indicate their neighborhood and felt that they belong to it (Wilmott 1962). A likely model is of a set of overlapping neighborhoods which vary culturally, with some people only having local neighborhoods while others have additional ones and more extensive networks. These differences reflect localized versus cosmopolitan lifestyles and networks and the extent of home-ranges (Chapter 5).

In addition to socio-cultural differences within countries there are also variations among countries so that, compared to Europe, in the U.S. neighborhood generally is less salient and people more aspatial — identifying less with a particular area (Sawicky 1971, pp. 64–66). Comparing people in Bristol and Columbus, Ohio it was found that Americans were more mobile, cared less about their local area, which led to more rapid deterioration, and that for middle class groups the neighborhood in the U.S. is more extensive and less spatially restricted than in Britain. There shops are desired within 5 minutes' walk whereas in the U.S. a 20 minutes' drive is acceptable (Bracey 1964, pp. 22–23) — a difference between 1/3 of a mile and 20 miles and similar differences apply to other facilities.

On the other hand there is evidence for the continued importance of neighborhood in the U.S. (e.g., Suttles 1968), that neighborhoods are defined and that their size is larger than in England. Thus in Columbus, Ohio 80% of a sample population designated 0.45 sq. miles for their physical neighborhood (Golledge and Zannaras n.d., p. 41), i.e., double Lee's amended figure of 100 acres (Lee 1971(a)). There are differences among men and women and, in Los Angeles, their size, for middle class groups, was significantly larger than in Britain (1.3 sq. miles for women and 0.7 for men) (Everitt and Cadwallader 1972). This sex difference might be related to the different orientational systems used by men and women (Orleans and Schmidt 1972) and variations in home range behavior which also affects mental maps generally (Anderson and Tindall 1972).

In the case of black teenagers in the Eastern U.S. the area varied from less than one block (0.0008 sq. mile) (as for Aboriginal children in Sydney) to an unusually large 0.75 sq. mile, from part of one street to 25 streets (Ladd 1970). As in other cases, names seemed to have some effect.

In Boulogne Billancourt, France, neighborhoods were also intermediate between the individual and the city — an area well known and used — and all people understood it as that part of the city which "belonged" to them. Subjectively defined neighborhoods were of three types — linear (along one street), areal — polygon bounded by streets, and compound — an area with an extension along a shopping street or to a school. While there were individual differences, there was group agreement among those living in the same areas. Two sets of variables were important in neighborhood definition: *physical elements* — shops and markets, activities, dead areas, cinemas, cafes and schools; main traffic arteries are used as boundaries and there are clear effects of distance from the dwelling so that even areas used on a weekly basis are excluded if located too far from home. Then there are *population characteristics* — socio-professional status (workers having *larger* neighborhoods than higher class people)* age (younger people having larger neighborhoods) length of residence (growing in size with it) and degree of integration into the *quartier* (larger than if do not belong). Less than 10% mentioned a large area of the city; over 56% identified an area of 30 ha. (75 acres) and 75% one of up to 60 ha. (150 acres) (Metton 1969), which seems to agree with other figures.

In Britain 1/3 of people in an area of Stevenage gave the *name* of the neighborhood in which they lived, the rest the name of the housing estate, of which there were 5—6 in each neighborhood. For most people the neighborhood was much smaller than planned, so that over 75% showed a 1/4 mile radius, i.e., 184 acres — within the range already discussed and one-fifth the size of planned neighborhoods which were *not* important (Wilmott 1962).

In Newcastle, Australia the neighborhood core was even smaller, being only 4—5 acres, although there was a familiar area of between 60—70 acres which constituted an action space. Higher status neighborhoods tended to be larger than lower status, and physical characteristics played a major role so that land uses, major roads, railway lines, water edges, limited points of entry and exit, grid vs. curved streets and so on affected the size as did length of residence (cf. Spencer 1971; Metton 1969), social networks, size of family and so on.†

All this confirms the suggestion already made that the neighborhood unit used in planning may not only be unrelated to subjectively defined neighborhoods, but is inherently too large. In Cumbernauld there are recognized, named, local areas which people use and to which they give names regardless of whether planners do (Wilmott 1967). Thus, often the neighborhoods in which planners expect people to live are not identified by residents (Henry and Cox 1970), i.e., subjective and "objective" definitions do not usually agree.

From designers' point of view it is significant that all studies seem to agree that clarity and noticeable differences in the physical environment are most important in the subjective definition of areas, particularly if they are congruent with social networks, activity and service links, extent of home range, salience, meaning and symbolism and other socio-cultural variables. It follows that different cultural groups, the very young and very old, the handicapped, will have different definitions of neighborhood. The designer's role is then to reinforce and help such subjective definition or even to help modify it, and the incongruence between planners' and users' definitions have greatly affected the success of planning and design (Timms 1971; pp. 8, 31—34; Keller 1968). Still needed is information on how different groups define neighborhood and on the effect of specific physical variables and design features, services and densities which will help such definitions to take place in desired ways.

Clearly, the cognitive definition of areas generally, and neighborhood specifically, is not a single, unitary concept. It involves the many elements already described (cognitive style, social boundaries providing a minimum population needed to support social institutions, maintain group cohesion and, through meanings, act as symbols of social

---

* Although all studies agree that neighborhood is more salient for working class people there is disagreement about size (e.g., deLauwe 1960, 1965(a); Coing 1966; Lamy 1967).

† Personal communication, November 1971, from Mr. P. C. Sharma, Department of Geography, University of Newcastle. At that time the figures had not yet been fully analyzed.

identity; elements of territoriality and home range, social and service networks, the nature of the physical environment). The critical factor is the congruence among them — between physical and social space, between cognitive style and particular physical features of the environment; congruence among all subjective criteria and between subjective and objective (e.g., Tilly 1971; Buttimer 1972).

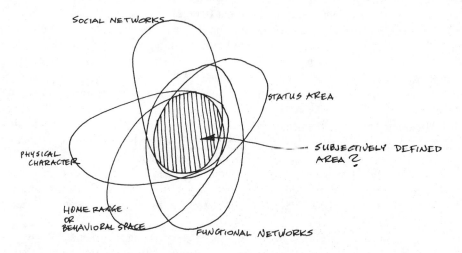

FIG. 3.25. Subjective definition as result of congruence among various criteria.

Knowledge, behavior and noticeable differences are linked in the mind of the individual, producing the socio-spatial schema of the neighborhood, i.e., a physical area corresponding to a social, conceptual, behavioral and territorial space, and this over-lapping and congruence helps explain why even small areas are further broken up into sub-areas. Where neighborhood exists physical and social space are congruent.

Variability is due not only to differences in social space but also to selective choice of physical cues and different cognitive categories, so that neighborhood depends on the *meaning* given both to physical and social elements and their relative significance and evaluation which, in turn, depend partly on the image held (Barthes 1970–71), i.e., congruence between the physical environment and aspirations and values. For example, the striking differences among working and upper classes in Paris is partly due to such factors. Not only are higher status jobs in the center and lower status ones on the outskirts, leading to different activity patterns, but social networks are different for such individuals so that workers have all their social relationships in their own district, or within limited distance, while higher class individuals have theirs over a large part of Paris. These groups also hold very different images — the center being attractive to upper class individuals and avoided by lower class (Lamy 1967).

Thus the definition of neighborhood and other areas is partly *image based* and, since physical and social images are both variable, not only do areas and sizes vary but so does the degree of coincidence of social and physical space. One can postulate a continuum of neighborhood cognition and use, which ranges from a polar case of absolute congruence between social and physical space, with absolutely clear neighborhood boundaries to the other, equally unlikely, polar extreme where there is no congruence and no neighborhood at all (Buttimer 1971, 1972).

The example of Paris above implies a notion of subjective distance and it has already been suggested (in Chapter 2 and elsewhere) that the variability of neighborhood definition (and effect of mental maps on behavior) may be related to subjective distance estimates — a topic to which we now turn.

Subjective Distance — Space and Time

Cognitive maps consist of places, relationship and distances. Having considered the subjective definition of areas and their orientational coordinating systems we need to turn to the distances separating elements. Subjective space implies, once again, *subjective* distance which is different to objective or Euclidean distance (e.g., Haynes 1969). If urban areas are defined subjectively, the distances which separate them should also be subjectively defined and, since distance is frequently experienced and estimated in terms of time, it is also likely that there is a subjective experience of time involved. While these matters have been discussed in geography, psychology and man—environment studies, in planning and design map, measured or Euclidean distances continue to be used. This in spite of the fact that there is evidence for the role of subjective distance, even if only anecdotal and experiental knowledge that trips through pleasant and interesting places seem shorter than through dull areas (see Chapter 4) as a function of complexity so that people go faster or monotonous roads (Tunnard and Pushkarev 1963).

Distance between places clearly greatly affects use, but it is subjective distance (and mental maps generally) which influences decisions and choices. Clearly where movement is difficult, whether due to age, health, lack of transport or lack of perceived control, distances are effectively greater (Wright 1969, 1970; Gump 1972; Parr 1969(a); Lee 1971(b)) and similar effects may be due to climate, e.g., cold and snow (Michelson 1971(a)) or heat, density of traffic, traffic lights — or one way streets (Haynes 1969). There may also be cognitive category effects so that, if places are placed in *different* categories, they may appear further than if they are placed in the *same* category.

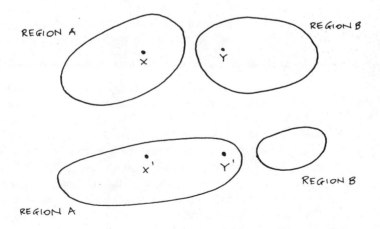

FIG. 3.26. Hypothesis: Subjective distance XY is greater than X′Y′.

The concept of subjective distance goes back to the 1950's. Thus in discussing the effects of site planning and propinquity on social interaction, the distinction between physical and functional distance proved useful (Festinger *et al.* 1950; Whyte 1956) and it seems clear that functional distance is, at least partly, a function of subjective experience as well as of the nature of the environment. This is further reinforced by the fact that social interaction is greatly affected by social variables such as social distance. A similar difference between physical and functional distance is due to the effects of traffic on interaction across a street, so that a heavily trafficked street is effectively wider, and people across it further from each other, than on a lightly trafficked street (Appleyard and Lintell 1972).

One cannot, therefore, judge the effects of subjective distance by measuring geographic distance or, which is even worse, using straight line or as-the-crow-flies distance. One cannot assume that two places equidistant in measured distance will be seen as equidistant conceptually and subjectively — and hence behaviorally. There is some argument as to whether cognized distance is generally greater or smaller than geographical distance. One suggestion is that while it is generally related to actual distance and time, it is generally overestimated (Mittelstaedt *et al.* 1974). Other work suggests that short distances are overestimated while long distances are reduced, that there are directional differences (North-South vs. East-West) as well as other specific distortions based on location, knowledge and so on (Rivizzigno and Golledge 1974). Subjective distance affects behavior also in terms of the degree of certainty of the information (Mittlestaedt *et al.* 1974) as well as the relative attraction of places, so that the cognized distance from a place is a combination of actual distance from, and attitude to, that place.

This latter point is quite critical. For example, in the case of shops in San Francisco which were equidistant objectively in road distance and driving time those seen as undesirable (discount stores) were estimated as further in both distance and driving time than department stores (which were seen as more attractive) (D. Thompson 1969). Thus the image of environmental quality affects subjective distance, so that if distance is the separation of people from people, people from things and things from things, then the distance of undesirable elements will be judged as greater, reflecting avoidance. Considering the crime map discussed before one can assume that very high perceived crime areas may never be visited which is equivalent to infinite distance while, on the contrary, highly desirable places and people will be seen as close and visited. The subjective distances in cities and the desired and cognized proximities among elements form a system — as discussed in Chapter 2.

In connection with shopping it has also been suggested that distances *towards* the center of the city are seen as shorter than those away from it, so that shops in the former direction are seen as closer than in the latter (Lee 1962). More generally it has been suggested that non-Euclidean space may have a downtown axis bias for both shops and housing (Haynes 1969). This focus towards downtown may be based on the satisfactions of the center which cause the foreshortening of subjective distance in that desirable direction. Thus in Dundee distances were overestimated in both directions, but the degree of overestimation was much less towards the center than away from it. Women seemed more affected than men which, given their greater interest in shopping, would again imply greater attraction and positive valence as the factors involved. This seems likely since uses ranked high in the subjects' value system were judged closer than those ranked lower — stimuli judged favourably are seen as closer than those judged unfavourably (Lee 1970, 1971(b)).

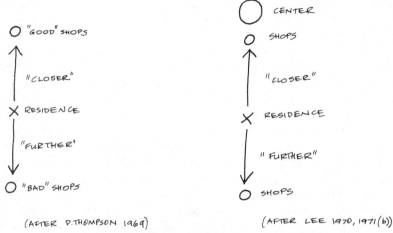

FIG. 3.27. Relationship between subjective distance and attractiveness and location of shops.

Valence seems to be a major element factor influencing subjective distance, so that a small commuting distance may be seen as a greater obstacle than an extra 30 km. while on vacation (Abler, Adams and Gould 1971, pp. 218, 230–231) and similar factors of attractiveness and positive valence may operate in migration.

It seems clear from the literature that psychological distance is a factor of actual distance, time and preference; there is also some evidence that subjective time may be more affected by the evaluative and attitude component (e.g. Mittelstaedt *et al.* 1974). The effects of valence are shown not only by a large number of studies in psychology and social psychology (e.g., review in Lee 1971(b)). At the geographical scale there is an inverse square law relation between subjective distance and emotional involvement for cities at large distances, which is a function of the importance attributed to the cities, the interest in them and the degree of knowledge about them (Ekman and Bratfisch 1965; Dornic 1967; Bratfisch 1969) all of which are subjective. The important thing in this very different context seems to be the relationship between emotional involvement and subjective distance.

This relationship is also implied by studies which have found an increased subjective distance towards the city center, so that in Columbus, Ohio, distances towards the center were consistently overestimated (Golledge, Briggs and Demko 1969; Golledge and Zannaras n.d.). This might be due to experimental factors, to driving conditions, i.e., congestion, number of stop signs and traffic lights, and difficulty of parking which make travel towards the center less pleasant and more difficult (another aspect of valence), or to cultural differences in the valence of the city center – positive in some places (e.g., Europe and Britain) and negative in others (e.g., the U.S.) (as discussed in Chapter 2). What all these studies have in common is that attraction, preference and positive valence lead to shorter subjective distance and vice versa. If the attraction is toward the center, then it is seen as closer; if away – then the converse is true. This had been my conclusion on the basis of the data discussed so far and received confirmation from Australian studies of recreational behavior where distances generally were also seen as shorter in the direction away from the central business district (Mercer 1971(b), p. 268). Thus beach use is related to lifestyle, status and proximity, but beaches in the direction away from the city center are much more attractive and used more than those located towards the center for *identical objective distance* (Mercer 1972). In effect these beaches are seen subjectively as closer than others and movement away from the center is preferred to movement towards the center.

This was predictable from the valence hypothesis given the outdoor image of Australia, the meaning of "beach", the weekend escape from cities, the preference for suburban living in detached houses with gardens, and the Australian image of environmental quality. One can thus suggest cultural differences between Australia and the U.S. on the one hand and England (and probably continental Europe) on the other. There thus seems to be a link between preference and cognition, so that the specifics of outskirts or center, quality of shops and merchandise, ease of driving and parking all fit into a single model. Thus the use of Paris is affected by subjective distance related to preference and hence selective in its impact (Lamy 1967).

The results of studies specifically designed to test this hypothesis were negative (Cadwallader 1973; Canter and Tagg 1975) but all other evidence seems to point in this direction. For both shopping and recreation favorable attitudes mean greater travel times (Murphy 1969) (i.e., greater distances travelled) which implicitly suggests smaller distance estimates, since it becomes less of an obstacle to those attracted by the stimulus. This is supported by a cross-cultural study of the shopping behavior of old order Mennonites and other Canadians in the same area of Ontario, where major differences were found. Mennonites used more local facilities and effects were greater for "traditional" than for "modern" goods (Murdie 1965). These cultural differences in behavior may be interpreted in terms of differential attraction leading to different subjective distances and evaluation of barriers to movement.

In the case of cities, such barriers may be lack of bridges or difficult topography so that unknown places difficult of access are seen as further than well known places easy of access (Canter and Tagg 1975). Even the evaluation of topography, however, may be affected by preference and positive valence, so that in Bologna houses in the hills are cognitively closer to the center than are equidistant houses elsewhere — 2000 meters towards the hills is a much shorter distance than 2000 meters towards the plain. Similarly certain activities, when located outside the center, become "too far" and a move of 250 meters on the same street (from No. 34 to 59) may be equivalent to kilometers in social space and greatly reduce use. The positive valence of the center is so great that an Italian mother whose daughter lived in Paris tried to suggest the quality of the area by saying that she lived in the center of Paris — although that area, Auteuil, is very far from the center (Schnapper 1971, pp. 44, 97–99, 122–124).

So far I have been arguing for the importance of positive and negative valence in affecting subjective distance. Other suggestions of factors involved in this process have been made, such as the interest of the route and number of turns (Lee 1970, 1971(b)), traffic conditions (Gollege, Briggs and Demko 1969; Golledge and Zannaras n.d.), or the introduction of one way streets (Haynes 1969) — some of which, in turn, may be related to valence. Another possible variable is familiarity which would relate to the observation that trips appear shorter with learning and experience. This may be due to the reduced need to process information as the route is organized into schemata and behavior routinized. Continuity may also be a factor and there is some suggestion that trips made up of different segments may appear longer than when they are all the same, although the contrary view is also proposed (see Chapter 4).

It is likely that many variables other than those already discussed play a role — the energy used, estimation of time and velocity, direct perception of distance, use of some regular pattern or repetitive elements and maps and roadsigns (Briggs 1973) or, alternatively, the relative attractiveness of places and paths, estimated strength of barriers familiarity and actual distance (Stea 1969(b)). The degree of control over the trip may also play a role so that the effects of going to school and maternal separation on small children was greater for those going by bus than for those walking. This is because subjective accessibility is related to a sense of control and also the ability to construct a complete and reversible schema (Lee 1970). In effect, the school is effectively "closer" in the one case than the other.

Regarding complexity and continuity the question of the effect of turns and changes in direction needs to be considered. In the case of buildings the number of changes of direction alone had less effect than the number of decision points which affected lostness (Best 1970) suggesting that the route was subjectively longer. The opposite prediction was also made — that the more turns the shorter the route will seem (Stea 1969(b)). There is some evidence that turns lengthen subjective distance, which increases fairly steadily with the number of corners and curves the effect of the latter varying with their acuteness and their shape (whether S or U curves) (Lee 1971(b)).

This evidence came from a laboratory study and thus dealt with the estimation of length. In real life people tend to estimate distance in terms of context, accessibility or time which need to be considered. Context includes the attractiveness of the stimuli, already discussed and also whether one is going to it or from it — which affects the speed of travel (Mercer 1972) and hence probably also the subjective distance. Studies of pathtaking suggest that paths with turns which seem to head for the desired destination seem subjectively shorter than a straight path which apparently leads away from the goal, and the former is used more (Porter 1964).*

Time also seems to play a role in subjective distance (which is, however, always related to geographic distance) (e.g., Lowry 1970). Distance is often expressed in terms of time — a five minute drive, a ten minute walk — and we, therefore, need to consider the time component at least briefly. It has been suggested that while psychophysical factors (the physical environment) tends to dominate cognized distance, the evaluative and attitude components are more dominant in time estimation (Mittelstaedt *et al.* 1974). Since the value attached to time, and hence the fineness of the units into which it is divided, vary with culture, time allocation is related to lifestyle and behavior. This influences both leisure, and time/distance estimation generally, because an hour's (or even day's) trip in one culture may be subjectively less than in another.

Time experience is thus variable in terms of the subjective evaluation of accessibility and distance and plays an important role in environmental cognition. This is, once again, affected by culture, age and sex (Holubař 1969) and by context. Thus an architectural student in Montreal who also drove a taxi told me that, because of the way taxi fares are calculated, he thinks of distance in terms of money which involves both space and time. Subjective time perception which is influenced by the mode of travel, actual time taken, comfort and so on, affects distance perception and hence location — whether people live close to A or far from B (Peterson and Worrall 1969).

It is clear that people and animals live in space—time (Von Uexküll 1957; Orme 1969; Doob 1971; Yaker *et al.* 1971; Fraser *et al.* 1972; Holubař 1969; Ornstein 1969; Cohen

---

* I have also confirmed this in a large number of student exercises on pathtaking.

1964, 1967). People, therefore, locate in space and time rather than space alone, and time use, tempos and rhythms can be used to distinguish among people (Yaker *et al.* 1971; Parkes 1972, 1973). Judgements of time and distance are interdependent and mutually influence one another (Orme 1969). The longer it takes to traverse a given distance the greater it is judged to be; the faster one travels for a given time the more is distance underestimated while slower speeds lead to overestimation (Tau and Kappa effects) and such judgements are partly influenced by visual and other sensory cues (Cohen 1967). This implies that the amount of stimulation received affects subjective time and distance estimation — a supposition supported by the fact that distances seem subjectively shorter when familiar: once a route is known less attention needs to be paid (Fraser *et al.* 1972, p. 295).

Similarly spatial environments can affect the sensation of time so that routes with very little interest seem longer (Yaker *et al.* 1971) and people frequently speed up in them (Tunnard and Pushkarev 1963). This will be discussed in Chapter 4, but subjective space and time are also affected by internal states (happiness, health, boredom) and there are basic, particular and idiosyncratic effects. Thus the metric of mental maps involves a time component which also affects the form of the city (Choay 1970—71, p. 10) although the study of subjective time in the city (and time generally) has been neglected; while there is a recent *realization* that people live in space time, there is little knowledge — and most of that restricted to time budgets (e.g., Anderson 1971; Chapin 1968, 1971; Chapin and Hightower 1966). All we can say is that if mental maps consist of places related by connection, direction and distance then time plays a major role in distance and some in connection.

Both space and time aspects of subjective distance seem to be related primarily to positive or negative valence, so that social distance always plays a role. The distance in space—time between areas of widely different social character will be subjectively greater than between socially similar areas. Regarding Sydney a novel says: "Waterloo . . . was only a few miles from Double Bay but a geological age away in social strata" (Cleary 1970, p. 120) — the relative subjective distances between a high-class and low-class area or vice versa and the distances among socially similar areas would seem to be eminently researchable questions.

Subjective Urban Morphology

We have seen that people have images, schemata and mental maps which are learned and constructed. These involve internal components, the people, their socio-cultural and personal characteristics and external — the information and cues from the environments. Places and areas, relations and orientational systems, distances and barriers, are all subjective to a degree and are also evaluated differently and given different relative importance. It seems likely, therefore, that subjective urban morphology — the city as experienced and understood — may be quite different for different groups — one can speak of a phenomenology of the city (e.g., Carr 1970). This subjective urban morphology may also be very different to the plan form — as we have already seen for the grid in terms of the social significance of location or symbolic meaning (Chapter 1).

Although there is evidence for a subjective morphology of the city there is little evidence on its specifics or how the physical design of the city can affect it. For design one would need to know how cognitive structuring based on socio-cultural characteristics and cognitive style, travel modes, extent of behavioral space, and all the other variables discussed coincides with urban form. It seems unlikely that people have clear metropolis-wide schemata although there is a hierarchy of spatial schemata ranging from the world to very local ones. Hierarchies themselves may be variable, however, and little is known about relative urban hierarchies.

Taking an information processing approach and considering human limitations on information processing (see Chapter 4) it could be suggested that the clarity of different schemata is related not only to the frequency of use and familiarity, but also to the size of the areas, so that the amount of information is constant:

$$size \times detail = constant$$

so that schemata of large areas, while shared, are unclear and generalized while those of local areas are specific to groups but very detailed.

Subjective morphology will also differ due to differences in the elements selected and their organization. We have already seen that there seem to be well known urban symbolic elements which are known by all and more variable local ones — an example of the difference between shared and idiosyncratic symbols (Rapoport 1970(c)). There are thus widely shared elements signifying particular cities to all and more local associational ones shared more strongly by smaller groups. Possibly:

$$degree\ of\ sharing \times strength = constant$$

Thus most Parisians (and even foreigners) would know the Eiffel Tower but fewer will know the local cafe, the *boules* ground, the Algerian quarter. In the case of New York Manhattan is more widely shared than the rest of the city (Milgram 1970, 1972). In Manhattan itself, the skyline and other elements will be widely known but fewer will know the local quarters, and even Manhattan is still a city of local quarters such as Little Italy, lower East Side, upper East Side, Harlem, Spanish Harlem — or Yorkville (e.g., Franks 1974).

In Athens one could predict that most people will know of the Acropolis, Constitution Square, Omonia Square or Lycobetos but most people live in local, distinct quarters and their morphology of the city probably coincides at the major landmarks and does not at the local level. There may also be people whose mental maps are so restricted that they do not know the major landmarks at all — they only have a localized morphology. Athenians have always lived in local townships and even after the centralization by Theseus these habits prevailed; people still comment that Athens is a collection of small towns and villages. These places

"are all separate worlds with their own shops and taverns for whose inhabitants life centers around their own *plateia*, quite uninfluenced by that of the next-door community and only slightly affected by that of central Athens. So firmly do these various districts retain their individuality, so worthily do they maintain the tradition of the city-states of antiquity that it is no unusual thing to find oneself at the distance of one bus stop from a notoriously Red center in a neighborhood where every other house displays the slogans and symbols of uncompromising Royalism" (Lancaster, cited in Kriesis 1963, p. 59, fn. 1)

It is likely that not only will the subjective urban morphology of inhabitants of these areas be rather different at the local level but that they will have distortions and gaps at the overall level due to location, travel direction, home range and so on.

We have discussed similar factors in London, Paris and other cities, and also seen that even in Sydney and Los Angeles there are people with extremely localized mental maps of the order of a few city blocks, i.e., with highly idiosyncratic morphologies. The very numerous and varied cues of the urban environment can be organized in very many different ways although the cues set certain limits *given certain agreed upon conventions*. For example in our culture a low density, open area will rarely be seen as an urban center or CBD and the name itself is indicative — central *BUSINESS* district. Yet in Japan one major center of the multicentered city of Tokyo is such a "void" — the Imperial Palace. The centers of other traditional cities were also such palace "voids" (Wheatley 1971; Krapf-Askari 1969) and very different elements were used to define the center in ancient China, North and South India, Islam and other places. Thus the meaning and significance of elements, which are defined culturally, are important in subjective urban morphology.

Thus the definition of the neighborhood by white, Mexican and black children involved the same number of categories, but different preferences for natural or man-made elements, for animals, plants or people. There were major ethnic differences in the size of neighborhoods, degree of home-centeredness, elements noticed, the sensory modalities stressed and the degree to which larger, city-scale schemata, existed (Maurer and Baxter 1972).

Subjective urban morphology is clearly a result of cognition, of knowing and giving meaning to the environment by selecting direct and indirect information from it, with variable stress on different sensory modalities and the noticeable differences used and through the coding and taxonomic conventions specific to the cognitive style. In contrasting subjective urban morphology with "objective", there is no question of relative validity but rather a question of how the designed elements can best be made to coincide with the specific cognitive structuring, so that the objective and subjective morphologies can be made congruent. This is best done by creating significant places at which the cognitive and physical landscapes can coincide, overlap and be congruent as is most clearly shown by Australian Aborigines (Rapoport 1972(e)). In the same way as cognitive maps are built around frameworks of first, second, third and lower order places and paths, the design of the city should be in terms of elements which can anchor lower order information.

To use a rather simple example, the location of tall buildings in cities has been considered from economic, aesthetic, perceptual, symbolic and other aspects (Rapoport 1971(e), 1975(b); Heath 1971). They should also be considered from a communicative perspective — indicating hierarchy as they have done in some traditional cities (e.g., Bangkok, medieval cities) and as they still can do, locally or for the city as a whole. From the point of view of urban cognition, they can act as orienting elements, helping to structure schemata if they are clearly related to the direction of roads and other movement systems, leading to hierarchically important places (which they do *not* do in Cumbernauld). This would be helped by the consistent use of colors (as in ancient Peking where color was reserved for hierarchically important elements) and other cues, as well as congruence with activities (e.g., Steinitz 1968).

From the point of view of cognition, urban design involves helping the largest number of people to achieve certain types of cognitive organizations, influencing use and behavior. Since different groups differ, there are difficult problems of avoiding contradictory organizations. Subjective urban morphology seems related to the concept of place — the city as a cognitive construct is a series of places of varying degree of size, importance and significance defined through various cues and having clear or fuzzy boundaries or gradients of transition. These places are linked by paths and separated by barriers and related to some orientational framework involving directions and space/time distances. Each place has values and emotions attached to it, each route and barrier is evaluated as to ease or difficulty, positive or negative valence. These constructs are shared by smaller and larger groups and behavior, depending on noticing, understanding and obeying cues, depends on these schemata rather than on objective morphologies. It is the subjective environment which affects behavior.

CHAPTER 4

The Importance and Nature of Environmental Perception

Before elements can be organized into schemata and evaluated, they must be perceived. Perception is thus the most fundamental mechanism linking people and environments — the all-pervasive process involved in all man—environment interaction. People experience environments through the senses and all data comes to us through perception — our's and someone else's. Before cues can be understood and obeyed they must be noticed; before the social significance of elements can be assessed they must be perceived; before messages — whether signs, buildings, areas or locations — can be evaluated they must be discriminated from "noise".

The term comes from the Latin "Percipere" — to take hold of, to feel, to comprehend. Among the many dictionary definitions the most useful seems to involve awareness through the senses, since it stresses the proposed distinction between evaluation, cognition and perception. Without reverting to the early psychological distinction between sensations and perceptions it is useful to stress the difference between a scene as experienced and as described, remembered or schematized: what is experienced and what is remembered differ profoundly.

It is possible to distinguish between perceptual cognition, or knowledge *of* the environment, and symbolic cognition or knowledge *about* the environment (Gibson 1968, p. 91). The former is perception, the direct sensory response to things and places, while in the latter, cognition, the information is precoded and may come from indirect sources. While all people see the world more or less the same way (Gibson 1968, p. 321) they structure it and evaluate it quite differently.

Perception is a process involving the interaction of the perceiver and the environment and has always raised complex philosophical issues such as the mind—body problem, the nature of objective reality and the value of introspection. The current position stresses the continuum between sensation, memory and perception, applies information processing and relates perception and cognition (Haber 1968). It follows that perception is affected by the nature of the stimuli, the physiology of perception and the state of the organism — expectation, attention, motivation, selectivity or adaptation. Most current theories of perception stress this interactional aspect, and argue that it must link sensory, cognitive and conative aspects so that the perceptual properties of an object are a function of the way in which the stimuli coming from that object will affect the existing state of the organism (Werner and Wapner 1952). This involves notions of homeostasis, meaningful information, changes in schemata and noticeable differences. If both environment and observer are important, then the various personal and cultural characteristics of the perceiver — for example his past history and experience, adaptation level, and cultural schemata — must be considered (e.g., Gregory 1969; Arnheim 1960). When trying to mail a letter, mail boxes will become very apparent, when hungry — restaurants, when driving — parking places, and as cognitive and emotive states change so will perception. There is also some evidence that culture affects perception (Segall *et al.* 1966; Stacey 1969; Wober 1966) although these effects are less than for cognition or evaluation.

Those theories which include the effects of set, knowledge and learning see perception as a man—environment mechanism. For example, perceptual learning consists of changes in where one looks and remembers what one saw, rather than changes in what is seen in any momentary glance (Hochberg 1968). This also corresponds to the distinction between the visual field and the visual world. The visual field shifts with eye movement, is oval in shape and clearer in the center, while the visual world is extended in distance, modelled in depth, oriented upright, stable and constant, without boundaries, without a center, colored, shadowed, illuminated, textured, made of surfaces, edges, shapes and interspaces and filled with things having meaning — i.e., the world we know (Gibson 1952, 1968) and this can be generalized to the perceptual world.

Environmental perception is then the most direct and immediate, sensory experience of the environment while actually in it, and although affected by set, memory, cognitive schemata and culture, as independent of these as it can be.

Perception is always related to action and hence it is involving, participant, related to meaning and motivation. It is multimodal and involves the environment all around, not just small central parts of it. Environmental perception differs from object perception because of scale; there are greater effects of motion, texture changes and sequential and additive views; there is ambience or atmosphere which is difficult to define but very important and consists of social as well as physical elements, people as well as things (Ittelson 1970, 1973). There is always more information present than can be processed.

One result is that subliminal perception may be important in overall responses to the environment. Most data is not consciously received and there may be two neural systems operating — the subliminal, more primitive system, which receives all input and the conscious, which deals with selected data, so that filters seem to operate (cf. Broadbent 1958). That information which is not selected is still received and classified and affects people beyond awareness. This means that while the consciously handled data become manageable, the larger environment has an impact on attitude and strategy: while subliminal perception sets the scene the focus is on specifics. Subliminal perception is the ground against which prominent or important elements, hazards or inconsistencies stand out (Dixon 1971; Smith 1972) — these become noticeable differences (Rapoport and Hawkes 1970; Rapoport 1971(a)) or changes in any state (Gibson 1968). This follows from the fact that subliminal perception is related to homeostasis, and equilibrium and adaptation play a role (Walker 1972; Wohlwill 1971; Wohlwill and Kohn 1973). Generally schemata are used which stabilize perception so that with time there is a tendency towards totally homeostatic, subliminal perception. The environment may need to disturb homeostasis through strong and unique stimuli, i.e., noticeable differences: new information leads to arousal and alertness. Environmental perception should be a combination of homeostasis and tension, with certain levels of novelty preferred.

Some of the characteristics of stimuli which lead to arousal have already been discussed in Chapter 3 — the strength of a stimulus, its size, location, prominence, contrast against background, use, symbolic significance and the like (Rapoport and Kantor 1967; Rapoport and Hawkes 1970; Rapoport 1971(a); Gibson 1968; Appleyard 1969). Unconscious or subliminal perception is also important in helping to explain the richness of direct experience. Through such perception we perceive mainly things which, do not fit into patterns or schemata (Ehrenzweig 1970, pp. 44—45) which accounts for the richness of the experienced environment as compared to any representation of it.

Selectivity in environmental perception is due not only to set, motivation, experience and adaptation levels, but also to cognitive needs, such as connectedness, identity, scale and orientation. For example, identity demands that we recognize elements from different positions and approaches. The need for connectedness and relationship means that perceptual information which cannot be fitted into a schema may be rejected — although one still reacts to it subliminally. Thus while a roadside strip may be too chaotic to organize, and the two sides unconnected, we still react to the elements in terms of chaos, stimulation, light, color, texture, traffic, noise, smell and the like.

The perceiver also plays a role in another way. Perception involves judgements and, in making judgements, two elements play a role — nature of the stimuli and observer sensitivity and the person's willingness to make discriminations (his criterion state) and both of these vary. Signal detection theory (e.g., Murch 1973; Daniel *et al.* (n.d.)) suggests that there is always some uncertainty about real environments and hence the criterion state becomes important — the willingness to decide whether a certain state exists given minimal cues, and hence willingness to act. In classical psychophysics there are absolute thresholds (what sense organs are capable of perceiving) and differential or relative thresholds (the just noticeable difference which depends on background, context, and various perceiver characteristics). In signal detection theory there are no thresholds but it is possible to separate observer sensitivity and bias. One can ask whether two or more stimuli really differ in their impact on the perceiver, whether two or more perceivers really differ in their sensitivity to stimuli and, finally, whether such perceivers differ in their bias (or criterion states) so that they will act differently for the same stimulus.

Any stimulus consists of signal and noise. There are different probabilities that signals can be detected and that people are prepared to act (Daniel *et al.* (n.d.)). This clearly assigns a more active role to the perceiver but also implies a hypothesis-making process (e.g., Kelly 1955) — i.e., people differ in the amount of evidence they need to support a hypothesis. Perception, the awareness of here and now, involves discrimination and it is a three-stage process. There is expectancy and set — people do not see and hear, they look and listen. Perception occurs in a "tuned" organism and any given hypothesis results in an arousal of cognitive and motivational processes. In the second stage information from the environment is received and, finally, it is tested (Sandström 1972). Also, in terms of our previous discussion, perceptual information is tested against cognitive schemata and evaluative criteria.

It would not be helpful to review the vast literature on perception generally (one of the largest in psychology). For one thing, much laboratory research may not prove immediately useful for designers and is available in any recent standard text on perception. There is also much disagreement in the literature, so that the topic "perception" takes over 50 pages in the International Encyclopedia of Social Science. It is more useful to discuss *environmental perception* using a few selected concepts and data from the psychological literature and providing an approach to understanding and evaluating much of the literature on urban design.

With regard to environmental perception, there is no unified single theory which links urban perception and cognition but one can distinguish three dominant types of urban perception — operational, responsive and inferential (Appleyard 1970(b)) — and the perception of urban elements to cognitive needs. Operational perception depends on use and is related to purposeful action. Since people's actions and behavior systems differ, operational perception is variable and is partly *associational* rather than perceptual

(Rapoport 1970(c)). Responsive perception is more passive and related to the physical environment — to noticeable elements of all kinds. Inferential perception is probabilistic in nature and people match new stimuli against schemata. In urban perception congruence between the various modes is important so that they reinforce each other and produce the requisite levels of redundancy. Thus congruence of activity, form, intensity, location, hierarchy, symbolic meaning among others will tend to reinforce both perception and cognition but, due to the impact of individual and group perceiver characteristics, are difficult fully to predict and design.

The importance of perception is implicit in the very notion of urban design — from Camillo Sitté to the English Townscape group. It is the difference between planning and design, between the colored map and the experience of urban environment. It is far from certain that an area colored pink and one colored green will, in fact, be perceived as being different, so that in Chandigarh, bazaar streets and green strips often seem identical — at least to visitors. Environmental perception involves an interplay between the perceiver and the environment and urban designers have suggested that for spatial perception the latter include the size of the enclosure, the degree of enclosure and its shape (e.g., Goldfinger 1941(a), (b); 1942). There is an alternative view that the perception of openness-enclosure is determined by the relation of boundary height to boundary distance and is independent of actual size (Spreiregen 1965). This latter view has received some support (Hayward and Franklin 1974) but does not consider kinesthetics and other sensory data. However, such statements, and much of the urban design literature generally can be seen as a set of hypotheses which need to be evaluated in the light of data from man—environment studies.

Another example is the argument about the skyline which some designers have regarded as very important (e.g., Worskett 1969), while others have argued that most people do not look above eye level and only notice the first ten feet except for very distant views (e.g., Sinclair n.d.). In Chapter 3 the distinction was made between internal and external perception which may help resolve the disagreement — different elements are perceived in different contexts.

The human field of view normally has a 180° angle of peripheral vision horizontally and 150° vertically with a clear field of vision 27° high and 45° wide, although these angles decrease as speed increases (Lynch 1962; Tunnard and Pushkarev 1963; Pollock 1972). Figures can be derived for what can be seen and recognized at various distances, although these also change with speed. For pedestrians with 20/20 vision and under normal lighting conditions an angle of at least 1 minute must be subtended. Thus one can see 3.5" at 1000 ft., while at 465 ft. an object 1/2" can be seen, i.e., facial features. Thus at approximately 4000 ft. a human figure can be detected, at 400—500 ft. one can tell whether it is a man or woman and discern gestures, at 75—80 ft. a person can be recognized, his face becomes clear at 45 ft. and one can feel in direct social contact within the proxemic range (3—10 ft.). Thus outdoor spaces are intolerably close at 3—10 ft., intimate at 40 ft. and still at "human scale" at 80 ft. Most successful urban squares of the past rarely exceed 450 ft. (Lynch 1962; Hosken 1968). These figures give some indications of how design influences whether tall buildings are seen as landmarks or small parts and details used. These depend on the relationship between distance and height, or degree of enclosure. Thus an object the major dimension of which is the same as its distance from the eye cannot really be seen as a whole and details dominate; when it is twice as far it is seen clearly as a whole; when three times as far it is still dominant but seen in relation to other objects whereas when its distance exceeds that distance it becomes part of the general scene (Lynch 1962). Such data underly rules such as that enclosure is most comfortable when the enclosing elements are 1/2–1/3 as high as the width of the space, that below 1/4 there is no enclosure whereas over 1/2 the space becomes a trench or pit (e.g., Sitté 1965). All these rules, however, ignore the nature of the elements, the role of kinesthetics and other sense modalities, the dynamic nature of perception, and observer characteristics. Another complicating factor, usually ignored, is that both height and distance are subjectively estimated (Kittler 1968) and depend partly on the size of the space itself, the lighting conditions and are also related to the various ways in which depth and spatial extension are estimated – relative size, overlapping of objects, parallax of stereoscopic vision, motion parallax, height above horizon, textural gradient, shading, linear perspective (which involves estimates of absolute size) and atmospherics (Gibson 1952).

The view that perception is indeed important in studying man–environment interaction and urban design is not universally accepted. Its central role may be accepted while questioning whether it can be measured accurately and whether there are not too many variables involved (e.g., Murphy and Golledge (n.d.), p. 3; but cf. Golledge, Brown and Williamson (n.d.), p. 36). Another, more extreme view, argues that "perception as the mediating variable between environmental design and its human consequences is ... of limited help" (Perin 1970, pp. 39–41).

It is true that subliminal effects make measurement difficult. It is also difficult to recreate the sensory experience through other, non-direct, means because of the enveloping nature of environmental perception which makes design applications difficult. Since the total experience involving peripheral and, indeed, spherical vision is so different to any simulation, the difference between the vividness of perception and simulation, memory or cognition tends to be frustrating. This is compounded by the fact that perception is not purely visual but multisensory, so that people are subliminally aware of a great range of different environmental stimuli of extraordinary richness, and by the fact that perception is dynamic, not passive. Yet a consideration of perception provides very useful insights into urban form.

One reason why I have had to justify the separation of perception and cognition is that perception is active rather than passive. The perceiver extracts information from the environment and the kinds of information extracted, the resulting analysis and redirection of search develop as a function of experience, i.e., repeated interactions, so that cultural differences are partly due to cognitive styles and partly to shared experience. There is much evidence to suggest that people search the environment for significant information rather than merely being bombarded passively by data (e.g., Gibson 1968; Arnheim 1969; Murch 1973). Thus perception is a dynamic process whereby the perceiver turns potential stimuli into effective stimuli (Gibson 1952, 1968) and sensory messages interact with the characteristics of the perceiver, his motivation, knowledge and hypotheses. Direct sensory messages play a greater role in perception than in cognition and, while there is hypothesis testing in both, they are different types of hypotheses.

In any case people are involved in the environment – they are participants rather than observers. People are immersed in the environment and act in it and on it – they almost never look at the environment as though it were a perspective, photograph or slide. The environment is not something "out there" to be perceived or known. It is an essential part of people who are always in it and of it. The environment and people are in an active, dynamic and systemic interrelationship. While for purposes of discussion it is possible to consider the environment as though it were "out there", and that is the way it is designed, in reality people not only interact with it and act on it, they are goal-seeking in it, search for or avoid stimuli and thus select the cues which they use in ways already discussed. At any given time it is man in environment not man and environment, and people can hardly be imagined outside an environment which includes other people, images, values and symbols.

This last point is important because people have a tendency to symbolize everything and to treat the symbols as though they were the environmental stimuli (Dubos 1966; Lee 1966; Rapoport and Watson 1972). While this process is much more dominant at the evaluative and cognitive levels, it also operates at the perceptual level if only in terms of cultural differences in the selection of cues and the structuring process. After all, if people are behaving in an environment they have to evaluate it and continuously create preference and cognitive structures.

The dynamic and active nature of perception is shown by illusions and distortions. For example, vertical elements such as buildings and hills tend to be exaggerated and to look much smaller when photographed (Lynch 1962; Kittler 1968). Similar distortions are introduced by interest and high value and are a special case of the social effects on perception. This means that the context plays a role in environmental perception although these effects are greater in evaluation and cognition, i.e., the non-sensory influences on perception are less than on cognition and evaluation.

Consider attention, which is a system of selectivity meant to cope with the limited information handling capacity of people. This means that we eliminate many things and concentrate on others (Triesman 1966), relating to our discussion of filters. Since people's interest varies so does their attention so that, in addition to cultural and other relatively invariant filters, there are rapid changes in what is eliminated and stressed in the environment. Generally new signals, those which provide new information, are noticed and there is thus an element of novelty which involves changes in the environment as well as characteristics related to culture, and to sensation seeking (Markman 1970; Mahrabian and Russell 1973, 1974). This is supported by linguistic evidence, the fact that left has negative connotation in most languages. On the other hand, the difficulty of imagining a graph with positive values on the left of the origin seems to be a cultural convention as does the rise of preferred directions in art (Giedion 1962, 1964). Similarly it has been suggested that a line rising from left to right would be interpreted as uphill by a culture reading from left to right but downhill by a culture reading the opposite way (Baker 1961). This argument has not been resolved but the significant thing is the presence of scanning – an active, dynamic part of perception reinforcing the human need for sensory stimulation.

Eye-movement is essential in visual perception. The human eye is always actively scanning, gradually building up a percept even in the case of small scale objects. If the image is stabilized on the retina the object disappears (Noton and Stark 1971). At the urban scale also, perception is built up of a series of short scans with images lasting between 1/50 and 1/25 sec. (Hosken 1968). It has been argued that this denies the holistic, gestalt conception of perception but it appears that the percept thus built up often conforms to the well-known simplifications described by the gestalt psychologists such as levelling (strengthening by suppressing certain features), sharpening (accentuating certain characteristics) and normalizing (bringing it closer to some well-known form or structure) (e.g., Wülf 1938).

The fact that active scanning, and the building up of the percept, occur raises the question of which elements and cues are selected and how they are organized. The elements selected tend to be those regarded as important and this is affected by culture, personal experience, attention and motivation. Also, features of high information content tend to be selected. Generally (and most work has been done at smaller scales than cities) people tend to concentrate on unusual, unpredictable contours (sharp curves and corners, unusual or novel elements, changes in states — any noticeable differences). The order of fixation tells something about the interconnections of features into overall perceptual representations. Eye movements for small settings (e.g., paintings) are cyclic and complicated (Noton and Stark 1971).

In urban contexts eye movements through space, searching for cues, differ both among groups and between streets and squares. In the case of streets, due to the nature of the space, the movement is directed, centered on the middle distance scanning left and right. Recognition patterns are thus balanced, and attention drops smoothly with evenly decreasing amounts of information. Squares, on the other hand, with their more ambiguous spatial quality, result in a focus of attention on a narrow band which oscillates about the center, with primary attention on foreground and middle ground. Recognition patterns are nebulous and attention goes up and down: unlike the smooth profile in streets, those of squares tend to be composed of a series of S-curves, probably reflecting the need for supplementary information due to the greater ambiguity of the space (Vigier 1965). The sequential and dynamic nature of perception thus leads to differences in scanning.

Another contextual element influencing perception is the speed and mode of travel which influence perception as well as cognition. This is partly related to time perception, so that space and time can be substituted for one another. Since there is equivalence of temporal and non-temporal information, the perception of time which is a succession of events, and the perception of the environment which is likewise a succession of events, are interrelated and time can be evaluated by the number and nature of events in a given time or space segment (e.g., Fraser *et al.* 1972; Ornstein 1969; Cohen 1967). Temporal criteria also help distinguish between perception and cognition. Cognition is effectively static (changing very slowly), while perception varies continually, is active as a process and the organism seeks variation in stimulation while trying to maintain cognitive schemata constant. Thus such schemata need stability and clarity while perceptual experience needs to be active, dynamic and complex. While all perception is active and dynamic, environmental perception, the perception of large-scale environments, is particularly so since it involves exploration and movement through it. It also involves much inference, experience and memory — due to the variety and ambiguity of the stimuli. The physical environment demands exploration because of this variety and ambiguity of potential percepts and their arrangements.

The Multisensory Nature of Perception

There is another reason why the environment cannot be treated like a perspective, slide or even film — too much stress on vision results, with a corresponding neglect of the multisensory nature of perception. Designers have been particularly prone to stress vision to the exclusion of the other senses — partly because of their own prejudices and values, partly because visual criteria are more easily controlled and partly because it is much easier to deal with it in drawings and models. Psychology also has tended to concentrate on vision to the extent that frequently "perception" has meant *visual perception* although there is a body of work on hearing. One reason is that it is far more difficult to study the other senses.

The different senses are different means of communication between the world and the perceiver. One can distinguish between two basic modes of perception — subject centered or *autocentric* and object centered or *allocentric* (Schachtel 1959, specially pp. 81–115).* The former concerns how people feel, and is a combination of sensory quality and pleasure whereas the latter is concerned with objectification and understanding, and involves attention and directionality. This differentiates among senses, taste, olfaction, tactile, thermal and proprioceptive being mainly autocentric while vision and, to a lesser extent, hearing are allocentric. The distinction generally is relative not absolute: hearing shares characteristics of both — being allocentric with regard to speech and autocentric with regard to tone, music and sound generally, and even in vision we find more autocentricity with regard to colors and light than form.

Objectification does not tend to occur in the more primitive, autocentric senses and only occurs among the higher animals and man; it also increases with maturation only reaching full expression among adults. The autocentric senses are more physical, with a strong link to pleasure and comfort and, through them, behavior tends to be more controlled by the environment itself and less by knowledge. The allocentric senses are more intellectual and "spiritual" and, in Western culture, they have become dominant with an atrophy of the autocentric senses.

Allocentric perceptions lend themselves much more readily to voluntary recall through schemata which stress principal features with a loss of richness, while autocentric senses transcend schemata. They are also much more difficult to communicate so that olfactory, gustatory, thermal, kinesthetic and even acoustic experiences are much more difficult to share than those of words or forms. The development of aesthetic appreciation leads to the development of secondary autocentricity of allocentric perceptions (Schachtel 1959) and different cultures also tend to value different modalities (e.g., Wober 1966) so that until recently tactile and other perceptions and sensitivity was highly prized in China and Japan, smells in Oceania, sound and kinesthetics in Africa and so on. Other senses are also important among children before they become acculturated and one can speak of visual, tactile, olfactory, and acoustic spaces (Hall 1966; Frank 1966(a)).

This description of the autocentric senses suggests why they have not been studied — it is clearly much more difficult to deal with them in the experimental (or the design) mode. Most research in psychology has, therefore, been on vision and hearing and it has been accepted that smell and taste are the most primitive senses and the most difficult to explain. For example there is no single characteristic, and no clear environmental properties, which correlate with olfactory, gustatory, tactile or proprioceptive experiences, although it appears that there are four basic tastes — sweet, salty, bitter and sour and seven basic odors — camphoraceous, musky, floral, pepperminty, ethereal, pungent and putrid (Held and Richards 1972, pp. 40–43).

With the exception of taste, however, the use of these other senses in design may be emotionally extremely important and satisfying, because the precise smell, sound, texture involves attention and directionality. This differentiates among senses — taste, olfaction,

---

* I am grateful to Dr. Joachim Wohlwill for bringing this and several other references on non-visual senses, to my attention.

or bodily movement is experienced *de novo* each time rather than remembered or schematized, and because they operate beyond awareness, always playing a role. At the same time it is clear that vision is the dominant sense in our own culture — and possibly for humans generally, providing most information and being of greatest help in acting in the world. However, being a *major* sense does not mean being the *only* sense and, in design, vision has been treated pictorially and the environment consequently treated as a picture.

Any environment is experienced in all modalities (e.g., Chapter 3) and it can be understood in terms of the individual's total perception of, and response to, the external physical and social milieu and the concurrent monitoring of his internal environment (motivation, attention, health, alertness or hunger) which affects the perception of the external environment. The body is immersed in the environment and responds to its meaning, sound, smell, feel, texture, temperature and so on as well as vision.

Vision. This is the dominant sense in humans, and that most studied in psychology and design, although its relative dominance may vary in different cultures and for different individuals. It provides far more information, and enables places to be recognized and used much more effectively, than the other senses. When vision is put in conflict with other senses experimentally, it is dominant, although the degree of dominance and the specific conditions are in question (Rock and Harris 1967; Fisher 1968). Vision is not pictorial but active and searching, involving peripheral vision and an awareness of behind and above. Orientation is largely visual although in some cases (e.g., Eskimos) it may involve olfactory, tactile and acoustic information (e.g., Carpenter 1959, 1973). Visual environmental perception relies among others on space, distance, textural gradients, light quality, color, shape and contrast gradients (Gibson 1952). It varies as a function of culture and individual experience and even the acuity of vision varies, with corresponding changes in noticeable differences (Rapoport and Hawkes 1970; Rapoport 1972(e)).

Olfaction. Smell is a primitive and immediately emotionally involving sense although, being ambiguous, it is not very accurate. It may play a major role in evoking powerful memories of places and certainly can greatly enrich the sense of place. Smells also receive socially assigned meanings and are used to confer moral and social olfactory identity (e.g., Largey and Watson 1972). Olfaction has been greatly suppressed in most English speaking countries, particularly the United States, even when compared to France and Italy (Hall 1966) and there are also sex and age linked, as well as personal, variations. Compared to such more smell-oriented cultures, Anglo-Saxon countries are sensorily impoverished. Elsewhere cities and places can become memorable through smell — port cities, places where particular foods are made or sold — whole urban areas like the green-tea city of Uji in Japan which becomes a unique olfactory experience; a chocolate factory or brewery in a city; butchers shops or bakeries in traditional cities; Middle-Eastern bazaars (as compared to supermarkets). Design could help reinforce olfactory aspects of the environment (within cultural norms) rather than weakening them through ubiquitous gas fumes and loss of contact with the richness of the olfactory environment through packaging or air-conditioning. Literary descriptions — from Proust to detective novels — often stress the importance of smells in the environment better than professional writing: " . . . There was a smell of strong coffee coming from a small sidewalk bar across the street and some other spicy odor that tingled the nostrils. The Greek seemed to read Brad's unspoken question. "Sesame", he said. "It is the fresh baked sesame rolls that you smell, Mr. Smith. The scent of Athens. Blindfold me anywhere on earth and take me to Athens. Still blindfolded I will know where I am by the scents in the air. Welcome to Athenai, Mr. Smith"." (Nielsen 1971, p. 26). Anyone who has travelled at all will be able to think of many comparable examples.

Sound. This has been the only sense other than vision studied to any extent, and also extensively described in literary sources. Acoustic space is non-locational, spherical and all surrounding and has no boundaries: it emphasizes space rather than objects (as vision does) (Carpenter 1973; Carpenter and McLuhan 1960). Thus it is transitory and unfocussed, context tends to be lacking, it is fluid compared to the permanence of vision and it lacks the precision of visual localization and orientation (Fisher 1968). It is also more passive — vision can much more easily be blocked off than hearing: it is thus ubiquitous. It is also the source of verbal information and human communication. It is extremely important in other cultures: in Africa, where descriptions exist of people listening with interest and pleasure to two-stroke motors (Wober 1966). For Eskimos sound may be said to be more important than vision (Carpenter 1973, pp. 32—37). At the very least everyone can distinguish silent from noisy places, reverberant from dead ones. Environments are full of different sounds which, in modern cities, are masked by ubiquitous traffic noise which also has the effect of decreasing hearing acuity (which is dropping among industrial people as compared to tribal societies) and which makes it increasingly difficult to experience the acoustic environment. Such acuity can be developed as shown by hunting and gathering people and the blind. Yet even with low acuity designers could manipulate acoustic environments more than they do — contrasting noise from silence so that one moves from a noisy space into a hushed precinct suddenly becoming aware of trees, birds, a breeze, water murmuring. This occurs in an Iranian Mosque, an English cathedral precinct, a Moslem or Latin American courtyard generally and of greatest importance is the awareness of a contrast — that a transition has occurred.

Tactile. In addition to visual texture which is important in the perception of depth and space, there is also texture experienced through touch. Since to experience it through our fingers takes a deliberate effort, the major experience of texture is underfoot. One can distinguish between soft and hard, smooth and rough; among grass, moss, stone, concrete, cobbles, pebbles, sand, mud or boarding. In modern cities the ubiquitous use of asphalt (and in buildings of smooth, easily maintained surfaces) has almost eliminated such experiences. Older cities often provide almost the whole range described and, once again, this is more important in other cultures where textures are consciously manipulated. In Japan, for example, inside buildings, because no shoes are worn, there is very sophisticated manipulation of soft mats, polished wood, wood with raised grain and so on, and similar manipulation in gardens. Tactile texture is reinforced by vision, through sound (no sound on soft surfaces, clicking of shoes on hard ones) and kinesthetics where one may slide on slippery surfaces while sinking into soft ones. Recently there have been attempts to use tactile cues in traffic control — warning grooves on freeways or cobbles on slow speed streets, but the potential remains unexplored.

Kinesthetics. This operates through the proprioceptive senses, being the experience of the body's displacement and movement through space and is related to the sharpness of angles and curves (cf. Chapter 3) (Gibson 1968, p. 67), the speed of movement and its rate of change, the rate of change of direction, slipperiness of pavements, movement up or down slopes and stairs, changes in bodily orientation and whether such movement is active or passive. This works mainly at small-scales, i.e., it is experiential (Howard and

Templeton 1966, pp. 256–261). Once again some cultures are much more conscious of this than ours, so that American cars are much less involving kinesthetically (as well as regarding sound, breezes and smells) than European (Hall 1966). At a smaller scale there are many examples of the conscious use of kinesthetic experience. Thus in Japanese gardens one finds stepping stones over water, grass, or moss which force one to watch and feel as one moves in a non-straight pattern, becoming extremely conscious of one's body and its kinesthetics. This is reinforced by the views exposed at each change of direction. At Katsura there is also a manipulation of kinesthetics at entrances and transitions, stressing noticeable differences but this is even clearer in Iran. For example, the design of entries to Mosques in Isphahan use some very sudden changes of direction and high sills which heighten kinesthetic experience of up and down and changes in direction, and reinforce the transition experience of other senses — sound, light, smell and temperature (Rapoport 1964–65) which will be described later.

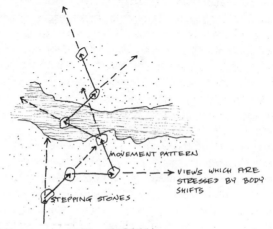

DIAGRAM OF KINESTHETICS IN JAPANESE GARDEN.

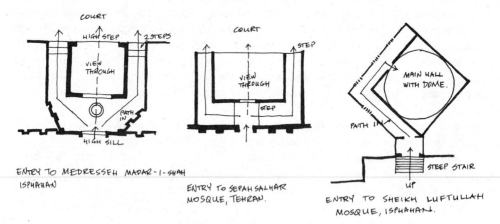

ENTRY TO MEDRESSEH MADAR-I-SHAH ISPHAHAN

ENTRY TO SEPAH SALHAR MOSQUE, TEHRAN.

ENTRY TO SHEIKH LUFTULLAH MOSQUE, ISPHAHAN.

(FROM RAPOPORT 1964-65)

KINESTHETICS IN IRANIAN MOSQUE ENTRANCES

FIG. 4.1

Air Movement and Temperature. People can become quite sensitive to air movement —
the blind can distinguish 12 air speeds (Berenson 1967–68) and Eskimos can distinguish
at least as many types of wind and their sensitivity to wind can hardly be exaggerated
(Carpenter 1973, pp. 22–23). There is some general sensitivity to this: a sudden warm
damp breeze or one from water (with its special smell), changes of temperature as one
goes from a sunny to a shady area (light quality also changes), radiation of heat both
from the sun and off surfaces, the warmth of stone at night after a hot day or the damp
coolness of grass, the coolness of a courtyard and the breeze in it (reinforced by its
soughing through tree branches) as against the hot stillness of a narrow street, the
difference between a shaded bazaar street and a large sunny plaza in terms of air
movement, temperature and light. In certain cities near tall buildings there are windy
street corners (e.g., downtown New York or San Francisco). This can be manipulated in
design by allowing a breeze to blow across a path or by providing still areas. For example,
a sudden opening in a long built up "wall" will stress a breeze; getting out of a cold wind
into a sheltered area will strengthen both experiences. This can also operate at the urban
district scale as when one approaches the sea or moves from a built up areas to a
green-planted area or large park where there is a sudden change in temperature and breeze
(and also smell, vision, sound and kinesthetics as the road becomes sinuous). Thus, in
Sydney as one enters Soldiers' Memorial Park going along Archbold Street or the
differences during the train trip described in Chapter 3. (See Fig. 4.2).

Generally in literature — novels, poetry, even travel books — one finds places,
markets, cities, streets and so on, described in terms of sound, smells, textures,
temperature changes — many places have been described in multisensory, and even non-
visual, terms. This is partly because affective reactions are being elicited and vision is
more abstract than the other senses. I will not analyze such literary sources here but will
use another introspective example — of some of the sounds and other sensory elements of
which I became aware during a recent brief business trip to Mexico City — probably the
least multisensory of Mexican cities. For example: *Sounds*: Craftsmen, music of
orchestras and mariachi bands, street musicians, organ grinders, street singers, toy flute
sellers, guitar strummers, traffic, fountains, trees in the wind, the silence of courtyards,
church bells, birds, school children chattering. *Smells*: food shops, restaurants, street food
vendors, flower sellers, trees and flowers in parks and courts, bakeries, butchers, incense
from churches, gasoline which smells different from U.S. gasoline. *Textures*: walls,
underfoot. *Kinesthetics*: sharp turns, changes of level, ramps and stairs. *Uses*: clustering
of trades, shops, groups of people, different clothing, lifestyles, foods, rich and poor
areas, tourist and resident areas. *Vision*: great spatial contrast from narrow alleys to large
plazas, textures, colors, window and door details, different people, historical monuments
from many periods, markets, parks, squatter settlements. This partial description suggests
that traditional cities have a range of sensory cues which are not present in most modern
cities (Rapoport 1973(c)).

They have also tended to be neglected by designers: both by not being consciously
manipulated and by not allowing them to happen — which they usually do if not blocked.
It is also significant that most redevelopment and new designs have tended to eliminate
multisensory experiences and contrasts — as places have been tidied up, "sanitized" and
their variety reduced: for example the removal of Covent Garden Market or Les Halles in
Paris; the elimination of street markets, local bakeries, butcher shops, fishmongers,
fruiterers and other uses which contributed, mainly through smell, to the variety of sense

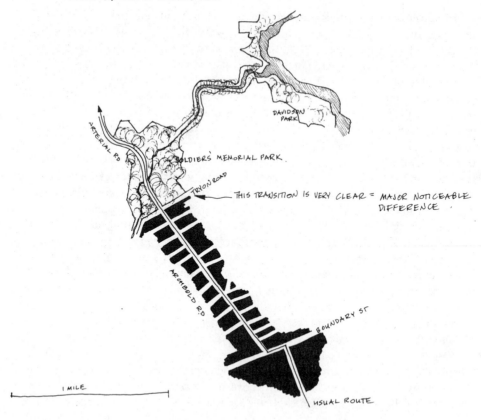

FIG. 4.2. Noticeable difference along travel route, Sydney, Australia.

experiences in the city. Similarly sounds are masked by traffic and textures eliminated in favor of traffic. The common complaint that all cities are becoming more alike is due to the lesser role of these other senses as well as changes in visual environments.

Clearly the full range is a matter of culture — in English speaking countries such richness may not be desired. Oriental bazaars — the combination of people, sights, sounds, smells, colors, contrasts, textures and feeling merchandise give an idea of the palette available; their contrast to the very different quality of residential areas and courtyards increases the range of perceptual experiences possible. From that range, different cultures may select and use different vocabularies. Such preferences may vary over time. For example, there is currently an increased desire for sensory involvement — for touching, smelling, feeling and hearing — a desire for increased sensuality manifest in many fields, which may permit urban design with greater multisensory information if only designers can take advantage. The popular press again seems ahead of designers: as early as 1968 in London, a newspaper story commented on the importance of smell in Covent Garden, and its evocative power (echoing Proust), decried the probable loss of this in the redevelopment, the lack of multisensory experience of food and the environment generally. Yet this seems at odds with the desire of people in Britain to use all their senses to the full (Raison 1968).

Although the more primitive, but more involving, senses tend gradually to be replaced by more abstract and intellectual ones as children in our culture mature, they persist longer in other cultures (e.g., Suchman 1966): they tend to be suppressed in Western industrial societies, particularly the U.S. (Neisser 1968). It is likely that this need persists — after all man evolved using all his senses and all perception, including spatial, is multisensory (Jeanpierre 1968). It is also clear that the perception of natural environments is equally multisensory and while vision is the most important the other senses play a role. The odor of pine needles, skunks, a swamp; the taste of food, specially if one cooks fish one has caught; the sting of a cold wind, of rain, the warmth of a campfire; sounds — birds, frogs, surf and wind are all crucial components of perception (Shafer 1969(b)). Texture underfoot and the kinesthetics of movement are also most important. The similarity of this example to urban and architectural examples suggests the fundamental role of all senses in perception: the visual information on which people mainly rely is correlated with sound, smell, touch, kinesthetics, air movement and others — and these may either reinforce or weaken the visual cues and thus help or hinder information processing. In any case they contribute to the greater richness of the experienced environment compared to its cognitive representations or memory. Also, given the nature of the other senses, they play a major role in affective responses (disregarding, for the moment, symbolic meaning and associational aspects).

Generally, however, urban perception and design still tend to be discussed in purely visual terms. Thus in criticizing the monotony and poverty of urban environments for the pedestrian the elements mentioned are color, texture and pattern, occasionally paving is mentioned although even it tends to be treated visually (Chermayeff and Tzonis 1971, p. 95; cf. Sitté 1965; de Wofle 1971; Spreiregen 1965, etc.). Similarly most perceptual notation languages, and hence the cues and elements stressed, are purely visual (e.g., Thiel 1961, 1970; Cullen 1968). Sometimes the non-visual senses are ignored on the ground that they are not susceptible to design unless they reach nuisance levels (Scott-Brown 1965). The difficulty of controlling them does not mean that one should not try — particularly given the examples where they have been used successfully. They can only be reintroduced as a conscious act of design.

Social and activity aspects also play a role in defining the importance of elements and thus whether they are selected as cues and perceived. Not only are there social influences on thresholds (and on the symbolic and associational value of elements). If the view is accepted that high meaning information, cues and elements are selected then things related to people and their activities should become important, and form a major part of environmental perception which must of necessity be selective. Such elements are very important to children (Sieverts 1967, 1969; Maurer and Baxter 1972). In some cases activities were not very important to adults (Lynch and Rivkin 1970) but in others, in the same city, they seemed to be and, moreover, it was important that they be congruent with form (Steinitz 1968). Many of the examples I have used in this section have been activity related and much environmental complexity is also related to activity variables.

Activity also plays a most important role in distinguishing between perceptual and associational elements and distinguishing between operational and other types of perception. Thus meaning may be more important than physical elements as such, but these must still be perceived through the senses.

It is important to know the role which the different senses really play in environmental perception. The evidence is not unequivocal, but tends to support the existence of cultural and age variations. Thus in the U.S., smells, sounds and visual aspects such as colors and activities generally seem to elicit few remarks (e.g., Lynch and Rivkin 1970) (although recall that they operate beyond awareness). Yet, for children in the U.S. olfactory characteristics — pollution, factories, grass, horses, food and flowers — and auditory ones, such as thunder, children, dogs, bugs, horses, squirrels, crickets, frogs, and traffic generally, were important, with ethnic (i.e., cultural) differences (Maurer and Baxter 1972). In San Cristobal, Mexico, however, non-visual senses were important and olfactory and acoustic cues were noticed and used to distinguish areas of the city although not as clearly as visual cues; smells particularly proved difficult to study (Wood 1969; Stea and Wood 1971) as predicted above. Moreover, this study concentrated on memory and cognition rather than perception, so that the difficulty of bringing non-visual memories to attention consciously, and communicating them verbally, played a role. Studying non-visual experience and perception rather than memory and cognition, while difficult, would be useful.

If all senses play a role in environmental perception and effective responses and even play a role in memory, then the obvious and critical question from the designer's point of view is how the different senses work together — when they reinforce and when they weaken each other, whether their interaction is linear or non-linear, additive or multi-plicative, which senses best work together and so on. Yet there is remarkably little work on this important question in traditional psychology, and even less in environmental perception, so that reviews on perceptual integration and intermodal transfer agree that the topic is important but that little is known (e.g., Pick *et al.* 1967; Loveless *et al.* 1970; Freides 1974). This is not only because of the difficulties involved, but also because of the approach and methodology so that much perception research has been experimental, hence in the laboratory rather than the real world, and single variable or, at best, bisensory — never multisensory. While it is clear that the visual, tactile, olfactory, acoustic and kinesthetic sense modalities combine to give an integrated representation of the environment — the invariant stable world in which we live — it is not clear how this happens. While there is disagreement about specifics, due to lack of knowledge, there is some agreement on general principles — much of it too general to be *directly* useful to designers.

(1) The different senses interact and affect each other, but it is not clear how, when and to what extent although it appears that the different sensory spaces are organized in a similar way (Fisher 1968). There is clear evidence for the effects of one modality on another under carefully specified conditions, and also that the different senses have the ability both to differentiate and integrate information. There seem to be specific sensory connections between modalities and some use of common information processing and encoding methods for all modalities. It is also possible that the senses process information in parallel, not serially, so that one can only "tune in" on one channel at a time but one can switch channels so that each of the multiple, parallel processing systems analyzes an input to detect the presence or absence of trigger features (Held and Richards 1972, p. 61).

Thus images in a given modality interfere with the detection of signals in that modality: people orient themselves within a specific sensory modality and then that channel is tuned towards both internal and external information. Yet images in other modalities also block visual images, so that there is some general influence of central attention, and also of familiarity (Segal and Fusella 1971). Thus threshold changes induced across modalities (Hardy and Legge 1968) and experiments show both increased and reduced visual acuity with other forms of sensory stimulation (Pick *et al.* 1967; Loveless *et al.* 1970, Freides 1974).

(2) Vision is dominant and visual images are easiest to retrieve and communicate.

(3) There is increasing differentiation of senses with maturation so that it becomes easier to concentrate on a single modality in the presence of another. The different senses mature at different rates and different modalities handle different information and have different tasks. At the same time there is also the development of coordination among modalities; this integration is cognitive and involves information processing.

(4) In general, visual information is the most accurate, followed by auditory, proprioceptive and olfactory — this is the order in large-scale spatial orientation. For some small-scale laboratory situations, however, the order may be visual, tactile — kinesthetic and auditory (Fisher 1968).

(5) There are clear intermodal and cross-modal effects and these are non-symmetrical: they may be stronger in one direction than another depending on the senses involved and the context. Thus if one sense is lost, other senses can substitute allowing the organism to operate in the environment, i.e., different senses may have equivalent effects depending on the state of the organism (Werner and Wapner 1952). The degree of separation of the cues also plays a role (Fisher 1968).

Two views are possible. Either each modality has a distinct pattern, is unique and processes information separately or there is a single, non-modal information processing mechanism so that cross-modal integration occurs through coding. Both these views have received supporting evidence and two recent reviews differ about which operates in the case of simple and of complex stimuli (Pick *et al.* 1967; Freides 1974). Since the structured messages from the senses add up to a *single* total experience rather than different sensory worlds, it is likely that some central coding occurs and is made consistent so that all the senses give the same message and it has been suggested that we need to learn to "break the code" (Leach 1970).

(6) In theory the different modalities working together should yield a gain in information through increased redundancy. This gain depends on the information available and the strategy used in integrating and also on the type of information so that if the different channels convey relevant information this is more advantageous. Meaningful stimuli thus give more veridical results than abstract ones — which tend to be used in the laboratory (Fisher 1968). Also if the information is congruent there is a gain, if it is not — a loss. Different modalities may increase the amount of information which can be handled per unit time or, when stimuli are difficult to detect, may possibly improve detection but this does not seem universal nor is there general agreement, although the consensus seems to be that detectability is additive

Intersensory summation may occur in two ways. If probability summation occurs, independent judgements are made in each modality with some transfer to a central decision point. Different strategies are used by different people and at different times resulting in variations due to culture, experience or genetic endowment. If physiological summation occurs, the response is due to the joint occurrence of stimuli which alone may not produce a response but which together increase the probability of detecting a stimulus. An analogy is offered by the fact that non-verbal messages are intensified through redundancy due to different forms of information (Mehrabian 1972).

The critical question is thus still not answered. To do this a great deal more information is needed about how the various senses work together in an environmental context, both consciously and subliminally (Kaplan 1970; Hass 1970, pp. 70–71). The importance of all senses in environmental perception seems clear. The environment provides an array of stimuli available to the various senses which differ in their reliability and availability and in the type and amount of information they can process (Stea and Blaut 1972). What is not clear is the *specific* way in which the senses interact in an environmental context, when they reinforce or cancel each other, or operate "synergistically" as is the case with stress (e.g., Wilkinson 1969; Rapoport, in press(c)). It is clear that many of the factors discussed in this book so far play a role, so that in the case of space perception it appears that conflicts among different modalities are resolved differently depending on the context and while vision tends to dominate, kinesthetics and touch play a role and all the senses are involved (Jeanpierre 1968) as are socio-cultural aspects related to significance and meaning. One of the ways in which the various sensory modalities are integrated is through movement, which increases the dimensionality of information being provided through the senses. Motion helps integrate the various senses over time. For example, the amount of information which remains more or less constant while one is at rest begins to increase as movement begins and more senses become involved. Movement helps people to take up information from the array presented by the environment and organize it, so that people's perception of the world is not a matter of adding different kinds of perceptions — visual, tactile, olfactory, acoustic or kinesthetic space — but an organizing process leading to a single field.

Studies of more than one sense modality in urban contexts are few and those are bisensory. Consider, for example, the interaction of sound and vision in urban perception (Southworth 1969). Auditory perception improves when accompanied by related visual cues and vice versa. Sounds provide an important link to reality, are enriching and protective — for example we often hear cars before we see them. Without sound, visual perception is less contrastful and less informative. People who only hear notice more sounds; those who only see — see more (i.e., compensation occurs). Sounds in cities have perceived character and variety and can be distinguished by their uniqueness or singularity in a particular setting *vis-à-vis* other settings; their informativeness — the extent to which activity and spatial form is communicated by sounds; their affective quality (whether liked or disliked) which depends on the frequency of the sounds, their novelty and culturally defined values. The most prevalent sounds, traffic and people, demand most attention but communicate least information, and contrast is important — novel or unexpected sounds (i.e., those providing new information) are noticed as are those distinguishable above the background or, when moving, sounds before and after —i.e., noticeable differences (Rapoport 1964–65; 1969(e)). Both the identity of, and preference for, the sonic environment gains as it becomes congruent with visual data; areas where this happens are richer, more intense and more informative but also less attention-demanding (which would follow from their increased redundancy).

In Montreal a pilot study with architectural students (who may be expected to be particularly sensitive to the environment) found that the order of importance of the senses in urban settings was vision, hearing, touch and smell. Spaces vary in interest: the curves for general interest coincide with hearing and smell, while vision and thermal curves vary quite differently. The senses interact so that when there is nothing interesting to see other senses are brought into play; whereas when the visual environment is interesting the other senses seem to play a smaller role [at least consciously]. Even people with neither vision nor hearing were able to give astonishingly accurate representations of the areas traversed (Passini 1971) clearly based on other senses which came into operation. The stress in this study was on cognition but there is support for the conclusion that non-visual senses are used in environmental perception and that they have a hierarchical order.

There thus seem to be a number of suggestive indications about how the various senses operate in general and in urban environments specifically. If it is accepted that vision is dominant not just in our culture but in an evolutionary perspective (Kaplan 1971) then the other senses must reinforce vision and this should be the function of design. In fact from an evolutionary perspective it would seem that the total, integrated and instantaneous awareness through all senses played an essential part in the survival of man as hunter. The development of built environments, tourism, mechanical travel modes and various habits of modern man have greatly affected this ability of which a stay in a wilderness area can give a pale reflection (Coulter 1972). Yet this evolutionary perspective offers a baseline and indication of what design should aim for – the greatest possibility of multisensory perception.

Information Approaches – Sensory Deprivation and Overload

Information theory was developed by communication engineers to deal with the performance of communication equipment, but has since become a major theoretical construct in modern physical science. It has also been used in psychology and, by extension, in environmental psychology. While intuitively reasonable, this presents problems. One is, of course, that in classical information theory the receiver is basically passive while people are extremely active perceivers, they select information according to certain rules and synthesize it in various ways. Theoretically the message with most information is indistinguishable from noise, i.e., it is meaningless, and only becomes interesting when people know how to organize it hierarchically into ever larger elements (e.g., Moles 1966). Active perception also means that the receiver defines messages, i.e., information is not the result of the stimulus itself but is phenomenologically defined (Rapoport and Hawkes 1970; Heckhausen 1964).* The world of signs and signals has to be transformed into one of messages which have symbolic meaning (Frank 1966), i.e., provide information which involves learning, culture and mental set, so that units of information become difficult to define and measure. Yet, in spite of all these difficulties, the concept is a useful one because it has explanatory and heuristic power if not taken too far or applied too directly.

The concept of information in the urban environment is at the heart of urban perception, cognition and evaluation. Signals become messages, i.e., meaningful information distinguishable from "noise" and received, when they are organized – in fact if it isn't meaningful, it isn't information. The organizing structures which turn signals into messages are related to cognitive categories, images, schemata, mental maps and preference structures. Images and meanings turn physical stimuli into phenomenal ones and channel capacity relates to significant or meaningful information only. Messages are

* I only discovered Heckhausen (1964) in April 1971 after completing draft 2 of this book.

ordered sets of elements, defined and coded by the receiver in ways already discussed —
this is where information theory, symbolism and the study of cognition come together.

Once information is received it is encoded into schemata and cognition is more static
than perception. Evaluation is then the matching of incoming information against
schemata, particularly ideal schemata, so that urban migration occurs on the basis of
information received and evaluated by people (Brown and Moore 1971, p. 207). Thus
information theory concepts, with adequate safeguards and modifications, apply to the
perception, cognitive structuring and evaluation of the environment.

When applied to human perception the most important concepts from information
theory are amount of information, channel capacity and redundancy. Information is
defined as that which removes previous uncertainty and is composed of "bits". One bit of
information is that amount needed to make a decision between two equally likely
alternatives and every time the number of alternatives is doubled one bit of information is
added. The number of choices, i.e., the amount of information, leads to different reaction
times so that a driver and pedestrian are coping with different amounts of information
per unit time and different reaction times are demanded. Since their informational
environments are very different this has major effects on the preferred rates of movement
and the design of the environment — as we shall discuss below. The central idea of this is
that there are limits on people's ability to process information so that there must be ways
of coping and reducing levels to manageable proportions (avoiding overload) while
avoiding the other extreme of deprivation and boredom; both lead to the idea of
preferred levels of information and complexity.

This also leads to the notion of channel capacity — that there is an upper theoretical
limit to the rate of information processing in any system including people. This is partly
because acquiring information takes time so that it is impossible to acquire unlimited
amounts of information. When that limit is approached the organism takes action to
protect itself by maintaining its equilibrium. This apparently useful notion has been
questioned (e.g., Kaplan 1970) but is widely used. For example it has been argued that in
large cities this absolute threshold, in terms of the amount of time available to obtain
and process information, is being approached and that people are busy eliminating and
avoiding information by reducing numbers of contacts, of roles, of friends and using
other strategies (Milgram 1967), by developing habits and routines, and relying on
environmental redundancy.

Redundancy makes it more likely that information will get through and messages will
be understood. As a result most human systems have built-in redundancy which, in the
case of language, is 50%, i.e., half the letters can be left out and a message still understood. The purpose of redundancy is to increase the amount of transmitted information
and get it as close as possible to limits set by the channel capacity (Miller 1956).

For example people can handle about 2—3 bits of information, i.e., 3—15 categories in
the case of uni-dimensional judgements. If more dimensions are used more information
can be handled, so that the more independently variable attributes of stimuli there are the
more information can be processed (although accuracy of judgements falls). The
implications for the use of multisensory information and adequate levels of redundancy
in the environment seem clear.

At the perceptual level inadequate information can be equated with deprivation while
excessive information is equivalent to overload. The literature on the former is much
greater than on the latter (but see Wohlwill 1970; Milgram 1970; Glass and Singer 1972).

Although there are still problems with knowing what adequate information is above the level of clear deprivation, I shall concentrate on overload and coping strategies, leaving deprivation until we discuss complexity.

The concept of overload and ways of coping with it have most important and interesting consequences for the understanding and design of the urban environment and even has implication for complexity which can be seen as the antithesis of chaos, i.e., overload. Overload can exist both at the perceptual and the cognitive levels, and is equally applicable to the physical and social environments so that we can speak of overload due to excessive physical and social information (Rapoport 1975(b), in press(b)) since the physical environment expresses and structures human activity and has social meaning.

At large scales the whole city can be seen as a communication system with potential problems of overload (e.g., Meier 1962; Deutsch 1971). These may be due to size since, when numbers of people are large, the number of interactions is proportional to the square of this number (Hardin 1969, p. 86). Some of the problems of large cities may, in fact, result from attempts to reduce this overload – anomie, anonymity or role separation – or violence and aggression when it cannot be reduced (e.g., Milgram 1970). The nature of the information is also important. In our culture the large amount of attractive information presents a particular problem – affective surfeit (e.g., Lipowski 1971) and the most highly dominant and structured message system in cities is advertising (e.g., Carr 1973). Overload is also compounded by the nature of people – when they are strangers more information must be processed than when they are known and understood (Rapoport 1975(b), in press(c); Lofland 1973).*

Given the concept of information processing and overload one can examine the effect of the physical environment in terms of potential stressors. People function best at certain levels of stimulation, with both too high and too low levels undesirable (Rapoport and Kantor 1967). Between deprivation and overload (physical or social) there is a preferred range in which five variables play a role – level (i.e., noticeable differences), diversity (variety is stimulation), patterning, instability (with the consequent importance of movement since dynamic elements are difficult to ignore and one also needs to react quickly) and meaningfulness (Wohlwill 1971).

It must be stressed that in all this adaptation plays a role so that the same environment may be evaluated as overcomplex or not, depending on previous experience (e.g., Wohlwill and Kohn 1973). Adaptation is different to adjustment, which is a change in the behavior, modifying the stimulus conditions rather than a process of neutralization which changes *preference*.

To reduce overload people use filters – they tune out much of the physical and social environment although there are costs involved in doing this, as there are in adapting. Thus while people adapt to overload there are costs which may express themselves in frustration and in other ways which are not directly measurable, and may also be distant in time. The effects of information overload seem to depend not only on adaptation but also on context, for example the extent to which it interferes with tasks or blocks action. The same setting may be interesting to a tourist but overloading to someone trying to work there. Thus information overload is also affected by cognitive factors, expectations and feelings of control (Glass and Singer 1972, 1973) so that one can also distinguish between the effects of passive and active adaptation (Rapoport 1968) (See also Chapter 6).

---

* I discovered Lofland (1973) in 1975 after developing these ideas independently. I am grateful to Dr. Harold Proshansky for bringing this book to my attention.

City life can be seen as a constant encounter with potential overload and people must cope with that. They, therefore, set priorities and make choices about various inputs stressing some and ignoring others (Milgram 1970), i.e., they use filters. It is clear that coping strategies must be used because people are able to cope with the vast increase of information which a city like New York represents when compared with the environment of a !Kung Bushman or a New Guinea native.

Some of these coping strategies depend on filtering out information, allocating less time to each input and ignoring low-priority inputs — low priority being, of course, subjectively defined. Physical devices also play a similar role as do areas of homogeneous people and mental maps which reduce the area known and used. Other strategies depend on arranging information into ever-larger structures — chunks (Miller 1956) symbols and super-symbols (Moles 1966) so that people organize perception through hierarchies of units within units (Gibson 1968). This hierarchical organization reduces the amount of information to be handled, because only one chunk or symbol needs to be handled instead of many bits. Thus overload becomes a theoretical concept unifying psychological, sociological and physical aspects of the city and, since deprivation is also a useful concept, the unifying concept is really information processing.

It may be useful to review some of the strategies used.

(1) Relative rather than absolute judgements are made. The number of dimensions along which stimuli can differ is increased. This latter means that more channels are used to process information increasing the amount which can be processed.* Tasks are arranged so as to allow a sequence of judgements to be made (Miller 1956). This also makes it easier to make behavior habitual.

(2) People make simple processes unconscious and develop habits and routines. These may be personal and cultural; in fact one can speak of culture as habit. Simple motor or non-random tasks can be made unconscious, taken for granted, so that they do not require attention or awareness and this is also the function of manners and etiquette. The quick habit formation in commuter travel, simple shopping behavior and home range behavior are examples. Known environments require less attention.

(3) People recode information into larger units — bits into chunks (Miller 1956) and then symbols (Moles 1966); this aids memory since that works on the number of items not the amount of information per item and larger chunks are then more efficient. Clearly learning is also involved.

(4) There are cognitive strategies — mental maps, schemata and mnemonic devices of various sorts which, with selective attention and limited home-range behavior, help filter data while reinforcing important elements. Cognitive styles do this at the cultural level. Perceptual "defenses" and constancies also play a role as does the use of *gestalten.*

(5) People give less attention to each element perceived (Milgram 1970).

(6) Habitat selection and changing activities to ones less stressful and with less information content are used to reduce overload.

(7) Social overload can be reduced through various social defenses such as ignoring people in specific roles, avoiding involvement, depersonalization, anonimity (Milgram 1970) and clustering with like people who share customs, lifestyle and symbols; this

---

* Dr. J. Metcalfe at the University of Sydney suggested that one channel can handle 2.1 bits, two — 3.4 bits while three channels — 4.6 bits which is reaching the upper limit.

requires less attention because of increased redundancy (Rapoport 1975(b), in press(c)). Privacy can be increased, reducing the flow of information about people and activities.

(8) Various physical design elements and defenses can be used — barriers, wall, fences, compounds, courtyard and other housing forms, physical distance and planting.

These can be generalized into three major categories: (a) cognitive — learning, recoding and organizing information, using simplifying schemata and so on; (b) behavioral — changing habitats and activities, habits and the like: this is related both to cognition and learning and (c) defenses of various sorts — perceptual, physical and social.

The first two are primarily a function of the individual and his group, although they are affected by the environment which influences activities and experiences; if understood they will affect design. The third, while partly related to the individual and his culture is mainly a function of the physical and social environments and their design: it relates to design as the organization of communication (using the organization of space, time and meaning). All these forms of organization and devices — buildings, courtyards and walls, separation by lifestyle, symbols and shared rules (clustering), space and spatial separation, separation through time and time allocation have a similar objective: to control the need to absorb and process information.

For example, given that both monotony and overload are disliked and undesirable, one finds that people in chaotic environments either "turn off" or recode information as described above. This latter process may explain why one needs more complex environments with time: since learning and recoding occur, environments must retain information. Design, from this perspective, is a matter of sufficient redundancy for habituation and sufficient new information for interest, and temporal changes play an important role. An interesting question which, to my knowledge, has not been studied, is whether in very simple environments people break chunks back into smaller units. This may be the process of finding complexity in detail which occurs with expertise and also in descriptions of apparently simple environments like deserts, prairies and prisons which report increased awareness of apparently insignificant details.

If this is so, then we might say that the recoding process is always one of relating noticeable differences to an order which may be physical, cognitive or social, and the result of coding is to produce complexity from either monotony or chaos — although clearly some environments produce desirable information levels more easily than others. In the case of overload the reduction achieved by recoding is not reduction *of* complexity but reduction *to* complexity. It is, of course, possible that the extreme amount of chunking required in very chaotic environments is in itself too difficult and also leads to an excessive loss of information. This, as well as the major other defense against overload — ignoring environments and people — results in a dulling of the urban environment as a sensory medium so that it fades into background — which it also tends to do as a result of subliminal perception. The role of changes over time, which can be aided by design, help to defeat these processes as does design for appropriate informations levels initially.

Consider an example of defenses and how they operate in Japanese cities. These are large, have high information content and operate at very high densities. They work because they are divided into many small areas each being a small place which is homogeneous by choice (Maki 1973; Smith 1971) with few "strangers". Each such place is different and their number is remarkable, thus avoiding monotony (Canter and Canter

1971). There are also many eating, drinking and entertainment places for meeting on more neutral ground which also act as mechanisms for dissipating stress (Rapoport 1969(a), p. 81). Houses are designed for extreme privacy from outside, there are agreed rules about noise and smells, the only information which could penetrate the traditional house, and privacy is for the group, not the individual. Very similar processes and devices are used in traditional Moslem and other cities.

My discussion has been predicated on the notion that both deprivation and overload are undesirable. While the former view seems general the latter is not universally accepted. It has thus been argued that the tension and unease resulting from overload and excessive sensory and social information is desirable, and that an "anarchic" urban environment is useful (Sennett 1970). This seems to be a romantic view which ignores the evidence of the undesirable effects of overload and human channel capacity, as well as the clear preference of human beings and can thus be questioned on both ethical and factual grounds. For example, it would appear that overload will result either in withdrawal, aggression, escape through increasing territorialization or increased and more rigid hierarchies (e.g., Esser 1971(a); Leyhausen 1970; Altman 1970; Altman and Haythorne 1970).* My argument is that design and planning should reduce information loads to levels which given groups of people prefer and hence reduce conflict and maintain stability, allowing people excess capacity for the things which they wish to do. People should be able to choose the levels they wish, the forms of the physical environment and other people in their immediate neighborhood. People, in fact, choose defenses whenever they can. They move to suburbs, they have unlisted telephone numbers, they insulate

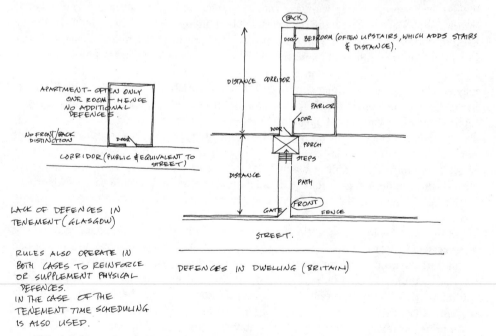

FIG. 4.3 (From Rapoport (1973) based on verbal description and analysis in Harrington (1965)).

---

* There is a large literature in ethology and man–environment studies bearing on these matters which cannot be reviewed here.

themselves in all ways possible. In fact the organization of space, time, meaning and communication can be seen as ways of reaching appropriate levels of information (e.g., Rapoport 1972(b)). The choices people make among different habitats can also be understood in these terms — for example the preference for single-family dwellings as opposed to tenements (e.g., Harrington 1965) and even apartments can be understood in terms of the defenses available. (See Fig. 4.3, p. 200).

In fact the notion of social overload and its obvious relation to density and crowding, make it possible to discuss density and privacy in sensory and information terms — i.e., in terms of perception — and in this chapter rather than in Chapter 5 (see also Rapoport 1975(b)).

Density and Privacy in Sensory Terms

It seems clear that density and crowding (the negative perception of density) are related to the experience of other people (and their environmental products) while privacy can be understood as the ability to exclude such experiences at will in the various sensory modalities (Rapoport 1972(b); 1975(b)). Thus we can see crowding as unwanted interaction leading to overload, and privacy as the ability to control interaction, i.e., to avoid unwanted interaction. Perceived density can then be seen as an aspect of environmental quality in terms of interaction and sensory information through all sense modalities, and relationships become more important than elements (Rapoport 1969(e)).

Density and crowding are both related to information, thus both Turkeys and Yagua Indians solve privacy problems by facing outwards and avoiding information and interaction (McBride 1970, p. 141; Rapoport 1967(b)). More generally, both among animals and people, density in terms of individuals per unit area is not sufficient and perceived density is a function of relationships. It is possible to list some of the characteristics of the environment which should lead to high and low perceived densities (Rapoport 1975(b)). These characteristics may be perceptual: tight and intricate spaces, large building height to space, many signs, many lights and high artificial light levels, many people (or their signs) visible, most man-made, high noise levels, many cars, high traffic density and much parking lead to high perceived density while the opposite characteristics lead to low perceived density: these are sensory stimuli indicating the presence of people. They may be associational and symbolic — tall buildings may indicate high density even when spaces and other perceptual cues indicate low density, as may the absence of private gardens and entrances in residential areas. There are temporal aspects such as fast tempos and rhythms, and activities extending over the whole 24 hours indicating high density, their opposites — low. There may be physical/socio-cultural characteristics such as the absence of defenses, high levels of "attractive stimuli" (Lipowski 1971), absence of other places, presence of non-residential uses in residential areas and mixed land-uses generally indicating high perceived densities, their opposites — low. There may, finally, be socio-cultural characteristics related to social interaction levels, feelings of lack or presence of control or choice, social heterogeneity or homogeneity and hence culturally shared rules, defenses and so on resulting in high and low perceived densities respectively (Rapoport 1975(b)).

Clearly most of these are related to information rates so that physical characteristics lead to perceived densities which, after matching and evaluation lead to affective densities (which may include feelings of crowding and isolation) (Rapoport 1975(b)). This would seem to be the reason why housing which is satisfactory in terms of information rates for young people with children have rates which are too low for the elderly who lack stimulation (D.O.E. 1972) and much of the literature on stress supports this view (Rapoport, in press(b)). Perceived density is tested against certain norms, expectations and adaptation levels and evaluated as either too high (crowding), too low (isolation) or just right. Thus crowding is equivalent to the inability to handle certain levels of information (Esser 1973; Rapoport 1975(b), in press(c)).

It is also significant that there is a difference between spatial and social density: at a given space per capita an increase in group size, or reduction in space have different effects (Loo 1973) and so does the nature and meaning of the group. With large groups and strangers present there would be more information overload since a major defense mechanism is keeping groups homogeneous. Thus in China, the same space per capita is less stressful when the group is related than when it is not (Mitchell 1971; Anderson 1972). Generally, when the number of people in a space goes up this increases cognitive complexity and uncertainty so that behavior is more difficult to organize; when the amount of space per person is reduced other people become more salient as stimuli and, once again, behavior is more difficult to organize. Acting together they lead to maximum information overload (Saegert 1973). Whether site crowding is worse than room crowding (Schmidt 1966) or not, it is always a matter of the presence of other people (Plant 1930; Schorr 1966) and undesired clustering is likely to be worse than heterogeneity.

In urban environments high perceived density leads to feelings of threat or stress, and major environmental components are the presence of different people who generate more information per capita because of uncertainty. Other aspects are various people surrogates, among them changes in the physical environment such as reduced large green spaces, increased traffic congestion, nose and industrial and commercial development in residential areas (Carson 1972, pp. 165–166). All of these lead to increased information and are the perceptual qualities of urban environments in all sensory modalities (e.g., Rapoport 1975(b)). Any social or physical environmental element or change which adds information may lead to overload and stress. To reduce it, the situation itself can be changed – or its symbolic equivalents: in the example above green space, in others other open spaces (Harris and Paluck 1971) although such spaces as a symbol of reduced information may be more noticeable in the city than suburbs or small towns and adaptation effects probably play a role (e.g., Pyron 1970).

These symbols, as well as coping mechanisms and levels desired will, within the limits of human capacity, be culturally variable. Density, crowding and privacy can be understood in terms of actual interaction among people or an awareness of potential interaction via their artefacts perceived through the senses. Design can help control the levels of actual interaction and information levels for any given number of people per unit area (e.g., Wilmott 1962) by providing physical barriers, space, considering rules and manners, time control, psychological withdrawal, role separation and so on – all of which control and reduce information flows. It can also do it by manipulating the sensory cues which indicate potential interaction levels (Rapoport 1975(b)). In all these cases more space, larger gardens, more trees, less noise, fewer smells and so on reduce information (and hence increase privacy) and lead to lower perceived density (and less crowding).

Any act of communication involves participants – senders and receivers; channels for sending and receiving; various shared codes – linguistic, paralinguistic, or kinesic; the form of the messages, their topics and meanings; and the setting (where are messages permitted, prohibited or encouraged, which may include locale (time and place) and situation). This linguistic model (Hymes 1964) has clear applicability to the environmental situation. Not only do people have different control systems such as the defenses already listed; among the codes are environmental ones (the environment as non-verbal communication). Hence the importance of homogeneity which makes codes easier to read and which then require less information processing.

Information flows among people are two-way: there is awareness of others and also knowing that others are aware of oneself. This latter leads to behavioral constraints and may be the major problem in housing and urban situations (Bitter *et al.* 1967). This information flows through all sensory channels: one can see and be seen, hear and be heard, smell and be smelt, touch and be touched, feel other people's heat and know they can feel yours; one knows that places are shared and that strangers may walk in, that paths may be changed to avoid contact. All of these play a role in the awareness of others in social situations, directly, or through environmental surrogates, and hence in information processing. If privacy is the ability to control unwanted interaction at will (Rapoport 1972(b), in press(a)) then this also involves environmental information flows, i.e., privacy involves controlling all information about people and requires a set of defenses — physical, spatial, temporal, social and psychological. Ideal and preferred environments seem to provide the possibility of controlling such information flows in all sense modalities while allowing sociability, and sensory information, when desired.

This awareness of others through the senses as a form of unwanted interaction is the major element in high perceived density as described above. It consists of human artefacts — sensory inputs due to lights, sounds and movement, smells, small amounts of open space and a wide range of sensory cues from the environment itself — quite apart from the presence of people or actual face to face interaction with them. If, in addition, these people and their environmental symbols are strange, the load is increased since they need constantly to be read to reduce uncertainty. Hence the desire for homogeneity in terms of lifestyle, manners and environmental symbols by some, the preference for heterogeneity by others. In any case desired levels are controlled by selecting contacts and relationships (Cox 1966, p. 54).

The critical factor in all this is *choice* — it is *unwanted* interaction which is the problem, and there is actually more socializing when choice is available, i.e., when one can withdraw at will — when one has fully private space (Ittelson 1960; Ittelson and Proshansky n.d.; Michelson 1969). Thus the ability to withdraw at will may enhance collective life, since the more an individual can protect his own life and reduce information flows at will the more he will enter into social relations with others and the more intense the interaction at such times. If there are limits on information processing and social interaction, then gregariousness should follow from the availability of environments into which one can withdraw — i.e., environments with low information content — which is supported by ethological data (Eckman *et al.* 1969). Thus for gregariousness and use of the environment one should design safe, familiar environments with clear and strong barriers, homogeneous populations and requisite levels of redundancy with levels of stimulation neither too high nor too low and also the ability to choose and vary these levels. This is to be expected if we consider that interaction and withdrawal form a system and cannot be understood separately (Schwartz 1968). For example, in large-scale French housing projects the main problem lay not in meeting people in buildings and grounds but rather the inability to be unaware of people in the dwelling itself (the place of withdrawal *par excellence*), i.e., the unwanted perception of others which interfered with personal and family independence (Ledrut 1968, pp. 100–101, 352).

The non-acceptance of apartments also hinges on a multisensory definition of privacy with one "modality" being merely the awareness of the physical sharing of an area or facility and knowing that someone might be there (Melser 1969). Similarly excessive openess of site layout and the absence of vegetation can inhibit use – people feel on display (Daish and Melser 1969). Once vegetation grows and separates various areas, use increases, so that privacy seems to be an element in the use of spaces and can be understood in terms of the sensory awareness of people (since one *knows* they are around even when there is vegetation). The role of space organization and barriers in such cases seems general (Baum *et al.* 1974; Desor 1972). In all these cases we are dealing with the organization of communication through the organization of space, time and meaning – as well as behavior itself.

The distinction between perceived and "objective" density is important in planning and design. Thus the New York–Washington megapolis contains 43 million people in 67,690 sq. miles and developed to Dutch standards it would hold 3 times as many. At the same time the perceived density of Holland is lower (Whyte 1968, pp. 9, 12) because of access to open country, noticeable differences among towns and behavioral, social and cultural rules. For example the Randstadt (the West of Holland) includes all the major cities and the population density is 6 times higher than the country as a whole. Yet the separation of towns and accessibility to open space helps lower perceived density. Among cultural defenses are a liking for small things, walking and using bicycles to reduce speed (and hence rate of information), reduction of information processing by *"reducing"* privacy: large, uncurtained windows put life on display so that one need not worry about what is happening, uncertainty is controlled and information load reduced. This is clearly a highly culture-specific system, yet information overload is still present and there are stress symptoms as a result of the need to control life and constantly being exposed to noise of others. Among psychological defenses are internal withdrawal, the separation of the country into homogeneous religious communities (reducing contact, information overload and friction) and high levels of conformity (Bailey 1970).

Urban grain, i.e., the number of elements per unit length or urban fabric may play a role in perceived density. Thus the clumping (Smailes 1955) which occurs when 25 or 50 small units are replaced by one large unit (because only plot ratios are used, neglecting plot area) changes the character and scale (*Architectural Review* 1972). (See Fig. 4.4).

Yet desired levels of perceived density cannot be created through visual design alone since the game will be "given away" through the other senses; nor can the social environment be ignored. It is also important to consider the organization of the system – the presence of open space, the use of streets and the organization of the environment into behavior settings with the requisite degrees of over- and under-manning (Barker 1968; Wicker 1973). It might even be suggested that the undermanning of small towns (Bechtel 1970; Bechtel *et al.* 1970) is a device to increase information levels while the overmanning of large city settings is a device to reduce such levels, i.e., different population numbers and densities lead to different behavior settings with the requisite information levels (see also Chapter 5).

The evaluation of given perceived density as crowding, i.e, subjective stimulus overload (Esser 1970(b), 1971(b), 1972, 1973; Stokols 1972) depends on the information levels

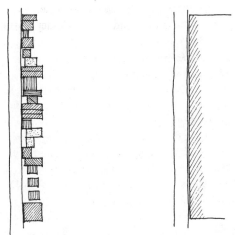

FIG. 4.4. Change in urban grain.

desired — and hence on the definition of "unwanted" interaction as well as the modalities involved. It should be remembered that sensory information means stimuli and stimuli themselves are defined — people symbolize stimuli and then react to the symbols as though they were the stimuli (Rapoport and Watson 1972). Preference levels are partly a function of sensation seeking, and partly of adaptation levels, and are likely to be variable within certain limits. Not only do some individuals and groups desire different levels of information, but they may also use different methods of coping, i.e., privacy mechanisms, all of which are, however, ways of controlling unwanted interaction and information. There may also be situations where, instead of individuals screening out the group, there is increased interaction within the group and reduction outside it. Hence there are different cultural enclaves in cities with different densities, different methods of screening, different time rhythms and time use, different environmental symbols and levels of sensory input. The hypothesis has been proposed (unchecked as far as I know) that there is a link between levels of social interaction and culture — that there are open cultures with high interaction, open facial expressions and open houses and closed cultures with contrary characteristics (Hass 1970, pp. 117 ff.).

If crowding is social overload, then it should be affected by the defenses and the context (which affects desired levels). We have seen that defenses do play a role. Moreover they must be socially acceptable. Given such acceptability minimal elements may help people filter out information (although there are costs of adapting to those stimuli which get through) (e.g., Dubos 1966, 1972). Social acceptability and strength of barrier will also vary with context. Screening out is then more important in the dwelling, and residential areas, as opposed to shopping areas or public entertainment areas — where it may, in fact, be undesirable. Thus, as a general rule, different levels of information and perceptual cues are necessary in different areas, with lower levels in residential areas than in certain other areas, although there will still be both individual and group differences.

A common defense against overload is to ignore the physical and social environments. With large numbers of people per unit area the number of people known by name drops, as does social interaction — i.e., anonymity increases as a defense (Lansing, Marans and

Zehner 1970, pp. 109—110). At very high densities, then, people tend to complain of isolation which would seem to be the result of avoidance as a result of overload. At lower numbers per unit area (mainly "medium densities") there are more complaints about lack of privacy with greatest satisfaction at lowest densities — with different reactions of elderly and non-elderly residents (Reynolds *et al.* 1974).

There seem to be three themes: (1) the great complexity of concepts such as density, crowding and privacy compared to the simple concept of people per unit area (2) the central role of perception in transmitting sensory data and information and of information processing levels, and (3) the possibility of variation due to culture, context, personality and adaptation level in the desire and tolerance for various information levels and hence crowding. This latter point is more important in considering the effects of given urban and residential physical densities. For example in Hong Kong such physical densities may exceed 4000 people per acre. This means that the median area per person is 43 sq. ft. Yet European figures suggest 170 sq. ft. as the lower limit for mental health and U.S. figures set 340 sq. ft. as a minimum (Mitchell 1971). It may well be that in order validly to compare densities it is perceived densities or levels at which problems occur which need to be compared rather than people per unit area. It is significant that in China the number of households is more important than the number of people in a room (Mitchell 1971; Anderson 1972) (an example of homogeneity) and the family also becomes more important in Holland (Bailey 1970).

Other defenses used in China, not all of which are applicable to the extreme Hong Kong conditions, are the clear separation of public and private domains, loose and flexible time use, preference for high noise levels and many people, and there is a clear status hierarchy and clear rules and hence low interaction rates (Anderson 1972). All these mechanisms are operating together and help explain the absence of behavioral sinks in Hong Kong. At the same time high flats create many more problems than equally dense areas of different configuration. This may be because it is harder to get away and hence there tends to be more interaction. Also since the street plays a most important role in China as a living space, the effective removal of that living space is equivalent to an additional increase in effective density (e.g., Hartman 1963; Harrington 1965; Suttles 1968; Rapoport 1975(b)) (see also Chapter 5). In high flats it is the parent—child relations which mainly suffer and there is also a discouragement of social interaction and friendship (as was also the case with the British army in Germany (Rosenberg 1968)). These effects are, therefore, due to social control in the neighborhood and control over the street. Part of the effect on children (mainly juvenile delinquency) is because in Chinese culture the whole social group is responsible for the control and socialization of children which is not the case in, say, white middle-class U.S. or Britain — a process analogous to that prevailing in certain Black communities in the U.S. (Hall 1971).

Isolation seems to result from high physical density and living on higher floors, but lack of stimulation can also occur in suburbs. Both can be seen in terms of information loads — in one case of overload, the other of social deprivation which are both subjectively similar, as is the case with environmental complexity, suggesting a similar process of perception and information processing. This view is supported by the distinction made between short and long term crowding since time plays a role. While this may be valid in some situations (a crowded dwelling may be worse than a subway ride) there is a complicating factor in the city. This is the possibility that while each situation and experience is short in itself, the individual moves from one short term overload situation to another — crowded lift; crowded, noisy, glary subway; crowded restaurant; noisy, smelly, overstimulating street so that the temporal durations may be additive. If the dwelling and neighborhood do not provide the type of retreat needed the situation is aggravated. Thus while the various resources and settings of the environment may help alleviate the problem, they do so by providing the ability to control information input.

Rather than using unitary and generalized density figures of people per unit area it may be necessary to define desired levels of interaction and information, the sensory modalities involved, how such levels are obtained and controlled. Culture plays a role in many of these (Rapoport in press(b)) and so does criticality (Rapoport 1969(a)) so that individuals and groups undergoing rapid change, and hence already dealing with much information, may not be able to cope with high-information environments, since they would lead to overload. Similar effects may follow from the need to restructure cognitive schemata (Rapoport 1972(d), 1973(d), 1974).

Central to this argument is the notion that people are aware of others through perception and that there is an interplay of withdrawal and interaction, privacy and community, various defenses and various ways of interacting, with preferred levels in each. There is a single information processing model which underlies environmental perception, density, privacy and crowding.

Environmental Complexity

I have just suggested that underlying the perception of both the social and physical environment is information flow and that between deprivation and overload there are desired levels of information. These constitute complexity.

An interest in complexity, richness and perceptual opulence follows from the proposed distinction between perception and cognition. The purpose of cognition is to clarify the environment by simplifying it to schemata and concentrating on limited parts of it. On the other hand perceptual experience through the senses is one of richness and complexity. No matter how much of the environment one tunes out, the direct experience is always much richer than any memory or schema. Except under the most extreme conditions the environment is incredibly rich. Furthermore this perceptual experience is desired and greatly influences the evaluation of environments. While people want to be oriented and understand the city cognitively, they also wish to experience its richness. In fact it is the interplay of a comprehended order and departures from it which constitute complexity. From this perspective, then, there is no conflict between a stress on clarity and legibility in the city (e.g., Lynch 1960) and the desire for complexity (e.g., Rapoport and Kantor 1967). Not only are they not mutually exclusive — they are complementary: one is a matter of cognition, the other of perception; at larger scale clarity is needed, at smaller — complexity.

Perception may, in fact, be dependent on orientation. Without being oriented and located in space and time, the organism cannot perceive — make hypotheses, collect information from the environment and test these hypotheses (Bruner 1951; Sandström 1972); neither can it enjoy the environment. While not wanting to become lost, people want complexity and richness. Being oriented is thus more important but at the same time no urban setting is exciting or interesting unless it offers some opportunities for mistakes in orientation by providing new information (and preventing complete adaptation, homeostasis and totally subliminal perception). At a small scale some degree of lostness may be desired which at a larger scale would be most undesirable. Thus complexity not only links cognitive maps and perception, but also suggests appropriate levels, the *pacer*, which challenges without exceeding capacity (Rapoport and Kantor 1967). Such levels of complexity provide moderate motivation and an absence of unnecessary frustration (Tolman 1948; Nahemow and Lawton 1973).

At this point I am ignoring associational and symbolic differences among places which contribute to complexity, and am concentrating on perceptual aspects. Rich and varied environments are preferred partly because they can induce a greater number and range of perceptions and also because such environments have greater uniqueness. It also seems clear that complexity is necessary for human wellbeing, that people need changing and complex environments. Animals also need such environments (e.g., Willems and Rausch 1969) and even organisms as primitive as planarians seem to prefer complexity (Best 1963).

Perception itself is dynamic, there is spontaneous activity throughout the central nervous system (Cooper 1968) so that constant change of stimulation is essential for perception to occur. With exposure to the same environment "stimulus satiation", and eventually stimulus aversion, occur so that the environment comes to be disliked, avoided and other environments sought. This is habitat selection and, in fact, complexity is a special case of environmental preference. People seek some uncertainty and novelty, i.e., information, both in the physical and social environments. Variety-seeking behavior may be of two types — diversive, seeking change as an alternative to familiar stimuli, and epistemic — seeking new information augmenting knowledge of the world (Jones 1966) so that both cognition and perception may need some variety and novelty, but in different amounts. Complexity is a pacer level between chaos and monotony which are subjectively similar; for example, people can be hypnotized both through monotony and overload (Miller, Gallanter and Pribram 1960, p. 106). The many environments in different areas, eras and cultures which are liked and preferred have one thing in common: they all seem to be perceptually interesting, complex and rich. My initial interest in complexity stems from this realization.

Starting in 1967, I and several colleagues have dealt with the issue of environmental complexity. Since then others have approached this topic from various points of view and most of these support the suggestions and hypotheses proposed, although some raise questions. At this point I will attempt briefly to restate the principal arguments (Rapoport and Kantor 1967; Rapoport and Hawkes 1970; Rapoport 1971(a), 1969(e), 1967(a), 1970(b), 1971(a), 1968, 1969(b)).

Complexity was initially discussed in terms of 4 main propositions (Rapoport and Kantor 1967):

(1) Recent psychological and ethological research shows that animals and humans (including infants) prefer complex patterns in their visual field.

(2) There is an optimum preferred range of perceptual input, with both too simple and chaotically complex visual fields disliked.

(3) There are two ways of achieving complexity: through ambiguity (in the sense of multiplicity of meanings rather than uncertainty of meaning) and hence using allusive and open-ended design, or through the use of varied and rich environments and environments which are not visible from one view, i.e., which unfold and reveal themselves and thus have an element of mystery.

(4) Much modern design has aimed at simplicity and total control of the environment which is unsatisfactory.

The ideas developed were applied in a preliminary way to writings of designers and critics on urban design whose position seemed to be explainable in these terms. Some problems with this approach soon became clear. The stress was too exclusively on vision neglecting other senses. The effects of learning, experience and adaptation were neglected. There was a neglect of social aspects and meaning. There were problems with using some of these concepts in design.

The main difficulty in this latter connection was with ambiguity. While it is one way of achieving "complexity in the mind", it is difficult to handle since the meanings which people attach to environments are related to symbols and associations.

Complexity	*Ambiguity*
Multisensory	May be non-sensory
perceptual	associational
number and organization of elements	symbolic and related to the meaning attached to elements and their relationships

In fact ambiguity itself has two meanings. One is uncertainty which is a perceptual quality and can still be handled. Thus a space or form which cannot be seen at one time and is thus uncertain is more complex than a simple one (e.g., Venturi 1966) but this can be understood as complexity, serial vision, unfolding and mystery. The other meaning — multiplicity of meanings — is a literary, and hence associational, quality. One can then show that the same environmental elements can have very different meanings and also that, while associations and symbols were shared and predictable in the past, particularly in traditional societies, they are highly idiosyncratic today, unpredictable and hence difficult for the designer to manipulate. In effect such past environments communicated; they do not do so today (Rapoport 1970(b), (c), 1972(e), in press(a)) and designers, at least currently, can only manipulate the perceptual elements (complexity) and not associational (ambiguity). Thus it is possible to distinguish between the perceptual and associational realms. In any given situation it may be possible to discover the most widely shared associations (and there may even be archetypal associations, i.e., certain common responses to certain stimuli (e.g., McCully 1971; Jung 1964)). Also, by the consistent use of associations such as form/activities, form/location, hierarchy/location or form and so on, they may be learned so that, in the long run, they may become usable.

The distinction between associational and perceptual is immediately useful in explaining certain anomalies in the preference for complexity which arise when one compares natural and man-made environments (e.g., Kaplan and Wendt 1972). The preference for natural elements is partly associational; complexity is just one dimension of preference — which is multidimensional. However, for design purposes ambiguity and the associational realm are less useful. They were hence put aside and those perceptual elements in the urban environment were stressed which the designer can manipulate. In the perceptual realm a major change was to replace the *optimal perceptual rate* by a *maximum rate of meaningful information* (Rapoport and Hawkes 1970).

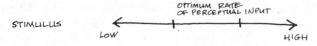

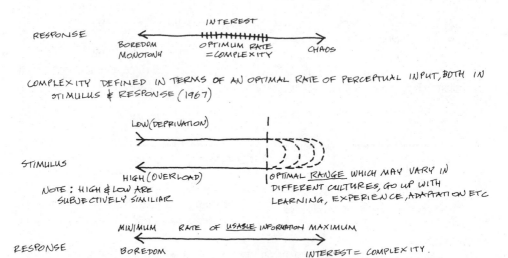

FIG. 4.5. Change in definition of complexity (from Rapoport (1971(a))).

This involves an active rather than passive receiver, the turning of signals into messages (which can be spatial or temporal since urban complexity can be in time as well as space) i.e., ordered sets of elements defined by the receiver. There is thus an associational and cognitive component which complicates the issue but allows for personality, learning and culture. The change in defining complexity as meaningful information — and hence phenomenal — makes its operational definition and use more difficult initially. But it is truer to reality and with more work it is potentially a more useful and powerful concept.

One result is that the effects of overload and deprivation become subjectively similar. In the same way that animals cease to respond to repeated stimuli (response saturation) people under chaotic stimuli cease to respond (which is also a defense against overload). One result is tunnel vision which impairs peripheral matching (Mackworth 1968), makes the environment poorer and the result is equivalent to monotony. The organization of stimuli into the various hierarchies already discussed is equivalent to coding in order to increase or reduce information to the *maximum usable rate* sought. There is, for example, a reduction of information *to* complexity not a reduction *of* complexity. Rather than dealing with the rate of perceptual input we are dealing with the rate of usable information, i.e., information received and processed, its quantity and pattern.

Usable information is related to stimuli which are detectable variations within an established system of expectations (which is equivalent to style). Expectations are built up and departures from them constitute variety. Complexity is thus also related to variations within an order, which are equivalent to noticeable differences which are important in perception generally: it is changes in stimuli rather than the stimuli themselves which are significant (e.g., Gibson 1968; Rapoport 1971(d)) and these occur in all sensory modalities. While the notion of noticeable differences will be discussed in the next section, it is clear that an environment can thus have low usable information for four reasons: (1) the elements are unambiguous, (2) there is little variety among the elements, (3) the elements, though varied, can be predicted in advance and there is no

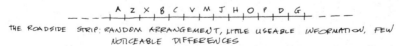

THE ROADSIDE STRIP: RANDOM ARRANGEMENT, LITTLE USEABLE INFORMATION, FEW NOTICEABLE DIFFERENCES

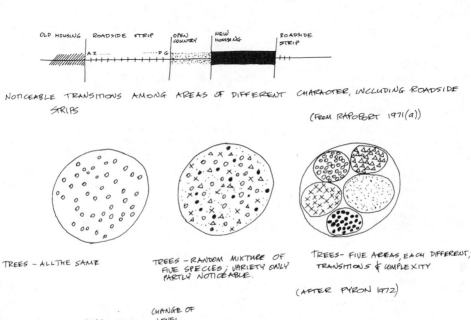

NOTICEABLE TRANSITIONS AMONG AREAS OF DIFFERENT CHARACTER, INCLUDING ROADSIDE STRIPS

(FROM RAPOPORT 1971(a))

TREES – ALL THE SAME

TREES – RANDOM MIXTURE OF FIVE SPECIES; VARIETY ONLY PARTLY NOTICEABLE.

TREES – FIVE AREAS, EACH DIFFERENT; TRANSITIONS & COMPLEXITY

(AFTER PYRON 1972)

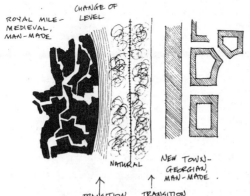

DIAGRAM SHOWING CLEAR TRANSITIONS IN EDINBURGH

(RAPOPORT 1971(a)).

FIG. 4.6

surprise, novelty — and hence no information, and (4) the elements are so numerous, varied and unrelated that there is no order, the perceptual system is overloaded and no usable information results. This position then avoids the problem which occurs when the term complexity is used as a descriptor and findings stated which are claimed to contradict the need or preference for complexity, yet clearly are an aspect of it. Thus in a study of housing preference it was claimed that complexity was disliked, but at the same time high levels of enclosure and tall and low buildings were liked and repetition disliked (Elon and Tzamir 1971) — yet all these characteristics are aspects of complexity as here defined.

Similarly, in a natural area a single species of trees, or a random mixture, will both be less complex than the presence of small areas of different trees with perceived transitions among them (Pyron 1972). The analogy to areas in the city is clear — as the example of Edinburgh shows. (See Fig. 4.6).

Complexity results from such interactions between the environment and people which lead to variety and change. In addition to the state of the perceiver the environment depends more on the relationships among the elements than the elements themselves since the order is relational, and it is variation within an order which must be grasped (Valentine 1962). Learning and experience increase the ability to grasp the order so that training leads to more emphasis on relationships rather than elements. For example, the public, in both urban and building environments, stress elements whereas designers emphasize order.* However, a sense of order is essential in all perception and design should help produce a clear sense of order. There is also a difference between *interest* (time of exploration) and *liking* (pleasingness) so that while the former increases monotonically with complexity the latter tends to be an inverted U-function (Wohlwill 1971; Smets 1971). Thus neither very complex nor very simple environments are liked (e.g., Acking 1973) although the nature of the stimulus may play a role (Walker 1970, p. 638).

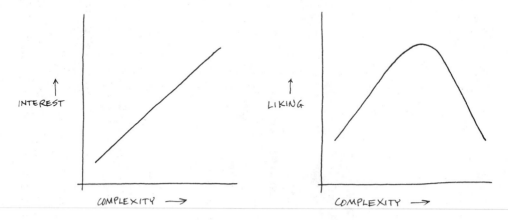

FIG. 4.7

Just as there are differences in preferred interaction rates there are also differences in complexity preferences among individuals and populations (since there is at least a possibility that personality and culture are related (e.g., LeVine 1973)). In addition to the

* This may be a problem with my argument about the primacy of relationships in Rapoport 1969(e).

effects of learning and experience there may be sensation seeking as opposed to non-sensation seeking people who have different requirements for complexity (Markman 1970; Hall 1966; Mehrabian and Russell 1973, 1974). Some people, who give structural descriptions of environments, get bored with them more rapidly than those who give experiential descriptions (Nahemow 1971) which supports my basic argument about cognitive order vs. sensory experience and may possibly also relate to the distinction between a scientific and aesthetic experience of cities (Gittins 1969). One might predict that the latter would retain their interest longer and perceive higher levels of complexity, although in all these cases objectively more complex environments would still be perceived as more complex by all. For example, differences among individuals are far smaller than the differences among environments and rich, vivid and complex environments tend to be liked while uniform, monotonous and chaotic ones are disliked (Lowenthal 1967).

The activity and context also play a role in desired levels of complexity. For example, for purposes of short-term exploratory activity (vacationing and recreation) people may prefer novel stimuli, different to those to which they are adapted, but for permanent activities (such as the choice of residential environments) they may be more dependent on adaptation levels (e.g., Wohlwill 1971). There may be areas where sensation seeking is not the goal and higher redundancy is necessary for more purposeful and routinized behavior. There may also be groups in the city — the elderly, those undergoing rapid culture change and so on — who require low-information environments (Rapoport 1973(d), 1974). This would also follow from the discussion above of the dwelling and neighborhood as a place of withdrawal from overload, and would also explain the differences in environmental evaluation of residents and visitors.

This has important design implications suggesting complexity levels for different areas. Thus entertainment, downtown, shopping and children's play areas should probably be extremely complex, and change over time to maintain novelty (while preserving continuity for orientation), whereas residential areas should be at middle levels of complexity (although there are ranges of variation in both). This will also lead to higher overall complexity since, paradoxically, if all places are complex, the total experience is more monotonous than if simpler areas contrast with more complex (Rapoport and Hawkes 1970; Rapoport 1971(a)).

Play is also indicative since it tends to be at the pacer level, being neither boring with too few requirements for ability or desires, nor anxiety provoking with too many (Csikszentmihalyi and Bennett 1971). One important way of creating complex environments for children is to provide natural areas in cities where children can explore, get "lost" and find wildlife which adds greatly to total complexity by contrast with the city around it (e.g., *The Sun* 1971). The fact that children often do not play in places provided is partly a function of such lack of complexity (Rapoport 1969(b); D.O.E. 1973; Whyte 1968; Friedberg 1970; Cooper 1970(a)). The kinds of places which children pick for play in urban areas always tend to be complex (e.g., Brolin and Zeisel 1968).

Those play spaces which are designed with complexity and are open-ended enough to allow for complexity over time, do tend to be used (Moore 1966; M. Ellis 1972). It is clear that in cases like these complexity is related to multiple uses, choice and diversity of activities at one time and over time, spatial variety, many physical elements, varied surfaces, shapes, textures, heights, colors, light and shade, smells, sounds, and materials. Such environments offer interesting analogues for urban design and their effects on children's behavior may well be replicated, if to a lesser extent, in the behavior of adults in the city who are less play oriented and more constrained in their behavior by culture. Yet even children's play is a function of both culture and spaces: streets, to be used, must be seen as appropriate settings (e.g., Schak 1972).

Much work on complexity also comes from visual art and music; it seems relevant to urban design. For example in music there are conscious articulating elements of scale, rhythm and harmony and anything falling outside these is excluded from normal attention, cannot be noted and is left to the performer. Yet these variations greatly contribute to the emotional impact of music and constitute the difference between good and bad music (or painting) (Ehrenzweig 1970). There are interesting analogies here with the cognitive structure of cities, the perception of them and the element of open-endedness (see Chapter 6).

The largest structures of music seem to be beyond the grasp of even well known conductors, while at the same time the microelements described above also defy conscious articulation (Ehrenzweig 1970). The analogy with people's inability to have mental maps of whole cities and their difficulty in describing the full richness and flavor of cities as experienced is striking. It would then seem to be a reasonable conclusion that the perceptual richness of the various microstructures and microareas of the city is very great and beyond awareness, and very different in kind to the clarity and organizing function of the larger scale cognitive structures which yet cannot encompass the whole city.

In fact this richness may be partly due to subliminal perception which receives all input while conscious perception, and even more cognition, only deal with selected stimuli. The effects of subliminal perception are also probably strongest in the non-visual, autocentric senses. The normal state is one of homeostasis between cognitive schemata and perception, and stimuli become consciously noticed when they change that state, i.e., when they are novel or unique. We have seen that with habituation and age, schemata become more important and there are variations in the strength of stimuli needed for reaction and hence in the pacer levels.

Complexity thus has beyond awareness components and involves, among other things, the number of elements, their intensity against the background, their novelty, super-singness, incongruity, mystery, temporal variations and meaning and symbolic aspects. In effect variety depends on the number and character of the elements (which is partly subjective) and the number of interpretations possible (which is ambiguity). The problems tend to be of a nature already discussed — the effects of observer characteristics which are difficult to deal with, adaptation (familiar stimuli are less complex than novel ones), associational values, and context (background), so that overall complexity seems to be different when two levels of complexity coexist and different again when three such levels are present (Phelan 1970). This has already been mentioned and has clear and interesting implications for urban design in terms, for example, of the number of areas traversed, their relative complexity, the manner and speed of travel and the like.

It also appears that if environments are complex along different visual dimensions (e.g., space and form) the process of perception of complexity is additive (e.g., Pyron 1971, 1972) and this process is strengthened when all sense modalities are involved. Also, if the diversity of a scene is related to the number of different elements, the categories into which they are classified, and their organization, then these are related to cognitive styles and are culturally variable. Thus variety has been defined as *the number of distinguishable elements* (Beer 1966). In terms of bits of information, for x elements the information is $\log_2 x$. More precisely, information is $\log_2 w$, where w is the

$$\frac{\text{number of states}}{\text{total number of possible states}}$$

and information is also related to time (Moles 1966).

Changes in perceived complexity with experience and adaptation are an important problem. The result of exposure is satiation and while there is some recovery, there seems to be a continuous long-term progression to preference for more and more complex stimuli. The result is that while at first exposure relatively simple stimuli may be preferred, more complex ones will be preferred later and stimuli which at first appear chaotic become acceptable with time, which is clearly a serious problem for the designer.* On the other hand learning leads to discovery of higher levels of complexity and hierarchy, and affects noticeable differences, so that with experience ever finer differences, cues and details are discovered in the environment. Thus what is dull to an outsider may be rich to the native — the desert to the Aborigine, the arctic to the Eskimo, the prairie to its resident. A forest is more complex to a botanist than a layman — a city to a designer. However, objectively more complex environments more easily provide greater amounts of potential information.

Complexity is also the result of movement through the city. People do not spend their time in environments closest to "optimal complexity" (cf. Walker 1972) (although they may select them in their residential areas); they move through the whole range of environments — from the simplest to the most chaotic — and this maximizes transitions and overall complexity. In this context design can help prevent satiation and adaptation. There is a difference between novelty and complexity, so that novelty is a short term phenomenon while complexity lasts over time and is related to uses, activities and so on. This also relates to the notion of "operational complexity" (Appleyard 1970) — that resulting from varied uses to which an environment can be put. Here also complexity is not a result solely of differences, changes and variety in physical characteristics but also *over time*. Thus in terms of areas traversed and routes taken sets of events are never quite identical: routes change, the environment itself changes over time, with seasons, weather, rebuilding and so on (and this can be encouraged through open-ended design) and so does the state of the observer and the context. Thus the psychologically expected results of habituation and adaptation seem less severe in real environments than in the laboratory. The urban environment is also large, so that one does not see it all at once and sees it in different sequences. Neither are large portions of it seen regularly so that one has time to forget its full richness and resensitize to it.

At the same time the memory of an environment is always much poorer than reality, especially in non-visual senses and they also allow shifts from channel to channel over time. We remember relatively little, even after repeated exposures, so that every time an environment is experienced it will be complex in comparison and will always provide new information. One remembers generalized schemata, the order and form of things not the detail (Bartlett 1967, p. 195). Memory is greatly simplified and affected by filters, expectations and mental set. There is always some loss of memory and hence always some

* Personal communication from Dr. E. L. Walker, Psychology Laboratory, University of Michigan.

surprise (and complexity is due to surprises — to departures from an expected order). New information is always present in the experienced environment. Also both subliminal perception and non-visual senses add to the richness of the experienced scene.

The amount of information in the urban environment always exceeds channel capacity so that different sets of cues are selected at different times and hence different parts of the potential information are used at different times. While familiar scenes tend to be seen as simpler than unfamiliar, novel ones and complexity is reduced somewhat over time (Bartlett 1967; Walker 1972) enough information remains for further notice. Even when we know what to expect after just one trip, and certainly after many, the perceptual experience is still there and has an impact — even if reduced.

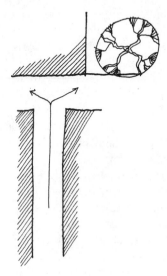

FIG. 4.8. The space and tree are not seen until the end of the street. Although known after one trip, the perceptual impact remains (from Rapoport and Hawkes, 1970)

Consider three examples from Sydney — all other cities provide comparable ones. (See Fig. 4.9).

Urban memory itself is affected by complexity. Thus perception of change and personalization (which are significantly related to complexity) leads to clearer memory of the city in German children than do simpler elements (Sieverts 1967, 1969). U.S. children also remembered areas with many apparently minor elements (Maurer and Baxter 1972) which, however, can be interpreted in terms of multisensory complexity. Australian children also seem to remember socially and physically complex urban areas more clearly and vividly than monotonous ones (King 1973, p. 74).

The designer can manipulate movement path options, the relationship of various areas, the location mix and changes of activities, opt for open-ended design and influence the nature of the physical environment. These seem sufficient to overcome habituation and adaptation effects. Thus vernacular environments tend to be more complex than high style design, and to remain richer, since there is a greater mixture of activities in space, a

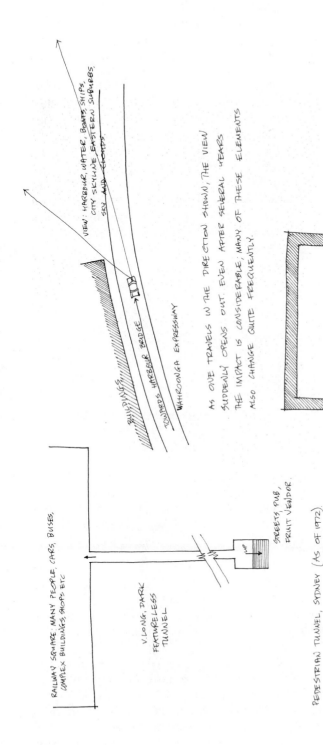

RAILWAY SQUARE. MANY PEOPLE, CARS, BUSES, COMPLEX BUILDINGS, SHOPS ETC

V. LONG, DARK FEATURELESS TUNNEL

BUILDINGS

VIEW: HARBOUR, WATER, BOATS, SHIPS, CITY SKYLINE, EASTERN SUBURBS, SKY AND CLOUDS.

TOWARDS HARBOUR BRIDGE

WAHROONGA EXPRESSWAY

AS ONE TRAVELS IN THE DIRECTION SHOWN, THE VIEW SUDDENLY OPENS OUT. EVEN AFTER SEVERAL YEARS THE IMPACT IS CONSIDERABLE; MANY OF THESE ELEMENTS ALSO CHANGE QUITE FREQUENTLY.

STREETS, PUB, FRUIT VENDOR.

PEDESTRIAN TUNNEL, SYDNEY (AS OF 1972) EMERGING AT EITHER END THERE IS A NOTICEABLE TRANSITION EACH TIME - EVEN AFTER YEARS. THE TRAFFIC CONDITIONS, WEATHER, PEOPLE, SIGNS - EVEN BUILDINGS - CHANGE

JACARANDAH TREE

MAIN QUADRANGLE, SYDNEY UNIVERSITY. EVEN AFTER YEARS, KNOWING EXACTLY WHAT TO EXPECT, THE IMPACT REMAINS:- THE CHANGE IN SCALE, ENCLOSURE, LIGHT, COLOR, MOOD, SOUND QUALITY; THE LAWN AND TREE. THE WEATHER & TIME OF DAY CHANGE, THE TREE SHOWS CHANGES IN SEASONS.

FIG. 4.9

greater number of activities in streets and hence more multisensory experience of these, changes in activities over time and also changes and additions to spaces and buildings (because of open-endedness) so that both in the space and time dimension the results are much richer. This is also helped by the very strong order which is easily "read" and understood, so that very minor variations from it become noticeable and contribute to information. Similarly, at a larger scale, cities which grow "naturally" show regional and individual differences, as well as area differences internally, and tend to be much richer, more complex and varied than those using uniform standards, layout and building types which tend to be identical, with little contrast, very uniform and drab.

In addition to the nature of the spaces themselves an urban area may encourage exploration depending on the number of possible paths. These not only lead to some uncertainty about where one will finish and how one would get there, and are an example of lostness at the small scale (within a clear orientational context), but can also be varied over time, leading to greatly increased complexity, allowing memory to fade before any one is seen again and allowing many possible combinations and permutations.

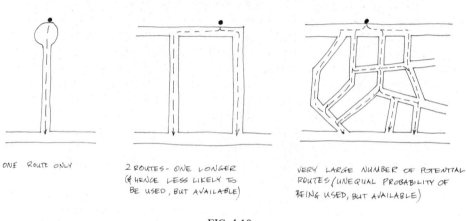

ONE ROUTE ONLY

2 ROUTES - ONE LONGER
(& HENCE LESS LIKELY TO
BE USED, BUT AVAILABLE)

VERY LARGE NUMBER OF POTENTIAL
ROUTES (UNEQUAL PROBABILITY OF
BEING USED, BUT AVAILABLE)

FIG. 4.10

It is interesting to compare a grid to apparently more complex path systems. A grid actually allows large numbers of alternative paths but has higher redundancy, hence less information and is simpler. It is made more complex by slopes (e.g., compare San Francisco with Midwestern cities) and variety of eye level elements and vegetation. It is significant that the grid tends to disappear when strong central authority and power are weakened (Stanislawski 1961) and to tend to a complex pattern as, for example, in Damascus with the decline of Roman rule (Elisséeff 1970). (See Fig. 4.11).

It is also interesting that this does not happen in the U.S., possibly due to the lack of major pedestrian use, since pedestrians always prefer more complex environments (Rapoport 1957; Wheeler 1972).

The effects of turns and changes of direction in paths on increased perceived complexity is partly due to the fact that each such change increases uncertainty, and hence information content — particularly if there is a decision point involved. Such paths also change subjective distance. We saw in Chapter 3 that the evidence of the effect of turns, bends and route segmentation on subjective distance is equivocal — there is evidence both for an increase and decrease in subjective distance. In terms of complexity

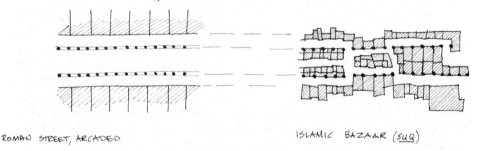

ROMAN STREET, ARCADED   ISLAMIC BAZAAR (SUQ)

FIG. 4.11. Transformation of Roman street into Islamic Bazaar, Damascus (after Elisséeff, 1970).

both views can be deduced. One would be that the more information per unit of route the longer the route should seem, given that we estimate route length by some measure of information per unit time. The other view is that the more information, the more interest and the shorter do distance and time appear. Experientially high information environments seem shorter to transverse than low information ones, but this is reversed in memory: complex routes are experienced as short and remembered as long and vice versa (Cohen 1967). Thus in complex, rich urban environments one can walk for long periods without becoming tired while the same distance through an open parking lot would seem endless because of inadequate rates of information (Parr 1969(b)). Varied environments provide much information with some always left over and they seem shorter to traverse because of interest — yet longer in memory (cf. Steinberg 1969).

Urban complexity is enhanced by expressing areal differences in uses and activities requiring different levels of complexity, areas of homogeneity and heterogeneity as well as all the changes over time possible. All these should be preserved, encouraged and stressed rather than evened out. Distinctive areas, whether regional or within cities, should be the aim. In fact diversity cannot be left to chance but must be planned and designed — with chance designed in. Contrast, diversity and dissimilarity in the environment must be nurtured. Within cities this means preserving the local character of areas and building new areas of diverse character in terms of uses, people, and physical character in all sense modalities. In fact most urban design writing which deals with the experience of urban environments in effect deals with complexity (but only in terms of vision) (e.g., Sitté 1965; Cullen 1961; Worskett 1969; Nairn 1955, 1956, 1965; Spreiregen 1965). Consider the recent proposal for *Civilia* (de Wofle 1971). It is clearly a plea for complexity so that design should be intricate, puzzling, pleasantly uncertain in all its eccentricities and permutations, too intricate to be fully brought into consciousness. While this is rather too sweeping, and the whole book rather extreme and neglects many important aspects such as meaning and symbolism, environmental preferences, group, cultural and individual variability, the need for cognitive clarity and simple, high redundancy areas contrasting with complex ones, it does suggest something about what might be needed in certain microareas. What is needed, of course, is design with levels of complexity so that one finds cognitive clarity at the largest scale, increasing levels of complexity as one goes down the scale with extreme levels in some types of areas (distinguished by use) and at small scales. Designing at the uniformly high complexity rates of *Civilia* throughout would actually result in a simpler environment. More importantly, considering complexity and information rates our approach not only allows the perception of the physical and social environment to be part of one model but also allows specific examples to be generalized.

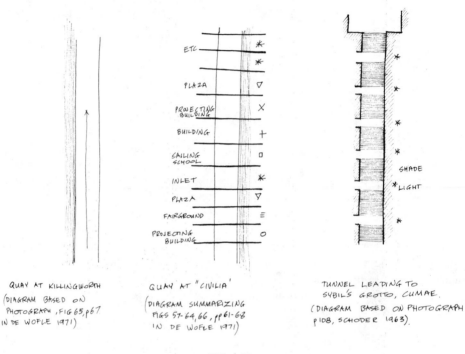

QUAY AT KILLINGWORTH
(DIAGRAM BASED ON PHOTOGRAPH, FIG 65, p67 IN DE WOLFE 1971)

QUAY AT "CIVILIA"
(DIAGRAM SUMMARIZING FIGS 57-64, 66, pp 61-68 IN DE WOLFE 1971)

TUNNEL LEADING TO SYBIL'S GROTTO, CUMAE.
(DIAGRAM BASED ON PHOTOGRAPH p 108, SCHODER 1963).

FIG. 4.12

Such generalizations can become useful in terms of urban streets. Thus, for example, in Berkeley, California, University Avenue was refurbished. Poles and wires were removed, small trees planted, brick pavements introduced and strong, closely spaced light fittings line the street. This has unified the street sufficiently so that the restaurants, shops and signs "fade" and become less obtrusive and the street becomes more interesting rather than chaotic (specially at night). While cold light was used on University Avenue, warm light was used on Telegraph Avenue. Whatever the reason, this has produced another noticeable difference at night. Also, in the case of University Avenue, it appears that the simplified rhythm at driving speed is contrasted with a more complex pattern at the pedestrian scale along the sidewalks which is even more strongly stressed in arcaded streets. (See Fig. 4.13).

These examples of complexity lead to the topics of the next two sections — noticeable differences and the effects of speed.

The Notion of Noticeable Differences

Much of the discussion in this chapter can be integrated through the concept of noticeable differences. Overload or deprivation depend on how many elements are perceived, and complexity is also closely related to the number of distinct elements which can be perceived; it is these elements which constitute variations from a perceived order.

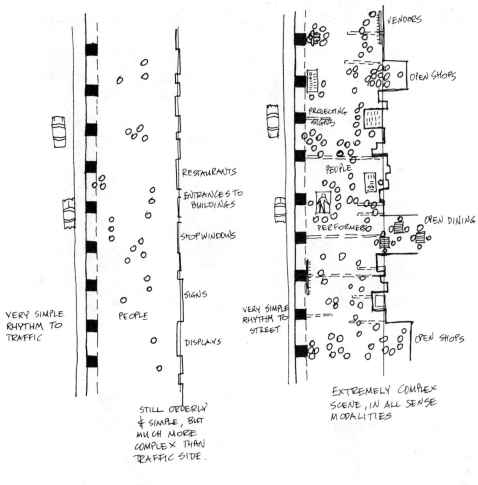

FIG. 4.13. Two examples of arcaded streets (many others exist in many parts of the world).

This helps explain the peculiar richness of vernacular design: because the order and the rules are so strong and consistent, very small variations are noticed and become important. In addition to limiting the vocabulary in this way vernacular design varies from area to area but is consistent within any given area. In high style design the rules are much more idiosyncratic and variations become more difficult because it is not as open-ended as vernacular while in a roadside strip very large variations are needed — if, indeed, any variations will be noticed. (See Fig 4.14).

Similarly a small church among tall buildings or an old building among new constitute noticeable differences — for example an old, ornate club among glass towers. (See Fig. 4.15).

Almost by definition such differences must be noticed by the perceiver. If one accepts Signal Detection Theory (e.g., Murch 1973; Daniel *et al.* (n.d.)) the idea of thresholds becomes suspect, because of the extremely important role of the readiness of the

Saorge (S. France)

Right bank of Seine (Paris)

FIG. 4.14. Vernacular: variety within an order.

(*Photographs by author*)

High Style: order, no variety
Rue de Rivoli, Paris.

Roadside strip: variety, no order
El Camino Real, Bay Area, California.

(Photographs by author)

Chifley Square, Sydney, Australia (1972).

(Photograph by author)

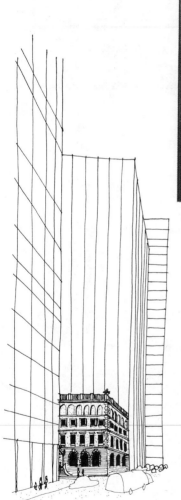

Composite drawing contrasting ornate building with glass towers (cf. Racquet Club and Lever House, New York and corner of Peachtree Avenue and Harris Street in Atlanta, Ga).

FIG. 4.15. Noticeable differences, with small elements dominant.

perceiver to make judgements on the basis of minimal or uncertain cues. That is, however, a personal variable and totally beyond the control of the designer. While taking into account group variables, adaptation and learning, all the designer can do is to try and control thresholds and the strength of signals — to provide requisite levels of noticeable differences for various groups along various dimensions and in various sense modalities. Thus data on visual thresholds at the urban scale can be given (e.g., Lynch 1962) although the criterion state would play a role mainly in the willingness to make, or act on, judgements.

Noticeable differences are seen in terms of the background, in effect as figure—ground relations*, or as a change of state or borders of the stimulus (Gibson 1968). This reinforces the notion that relationships among elements are more important than the elements themselves (Rapoport 1969(e)) since it is the juxtaposition of elements which leads to noticeable differences. Thus in Times Square the most striking element might be a dark shop and, in fact, at one point a small cinema which went out of business suddenly became a major noticeable difference; in the countryside it may be bright lights and the level of brightness needed will depend on the background.

Consider some urban examples. A tree in a forest is not usually seen as such unless it is very special, i.e., different (and it takes surprisingly few trees to make a forest) (Moles 1966, p. 73) while, in an urban setting, a single tree can be most noticeable and perceptually important — often more so than many trees. (See Fig. 4.16).

Similarly shape and color become important in an area where they are sparingly used — as in the red and blue domes of churches in Mykonos or the color and shape of the "Forbidden City" in traditional Peking where the rest of the city had to be rather monochrome and lower by law. One plaza in a corridor street becomes a major event — many of them a new kind of space in which the corridor street itself becomes the noticeable event. (See Fig. 4.17).

Along New South Head Road, Sydney, there are a series of small parks opening up onto bays, offering views of water, boats and so on. These become noticeable differences reinforced by smell, temperature change, sounds of seagulls and so on; along this street one also hears foreign languages in certain areas. (See Fig. 4.18).

More generally cities have ethnic areas with their various noticeable differences, variations in building height and density, views, traffic, noise, vegetation and the like — all are potential noticeable differences and cities can be analyzed in these terms at various levels of scale and detail.

Noticeable differences are critical to design. Many cities have clear structure, morphology and character when seen in plan or from the air. These are not perceived on the ground and the question is how to make this structure clear and perceptible, in addition to stressing clarity and contrast — the greenness of green areas contrasting with the busyness of busy areas and those, in turn, with the quietness of quiet areas — the perception of intended differences, by using the appropriate sensory, affective and symbolic cues. Both perception and use of cues are related to mode and speed of travel, extent of activity patterns and many other variables.

Cues also become noticeable as they become more meaningful and salient to the perceiver, i.e., as they become messages rather than "noise". For example in North Italy

---

* This idea of figure—ground relations and their application to complexity was further developed recently by Professor John Wade, School of Architecture and Urban Planning, University of Wisconsin-Milwaukee.

Single tree, Plaka, Athens.

Many trees, Evanstown, Illinois.

FIG. 4.16.

(Photographs by author.)

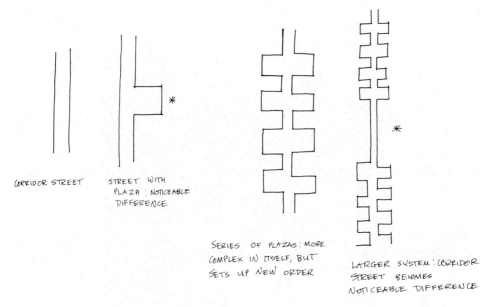

CORRIDOR STREET

STREET WITH PLAZA : NOTICEABLE DIFFERENCE

SERIES OF PLAZAS : MORE COMPLEX IN ITSELF, BUT SETS UP NEW ORDER

LARGER SYSTEM : CORRIDOR STREET BECOMES NOTICEABLE DIFFERENCE

FIG. 4.17

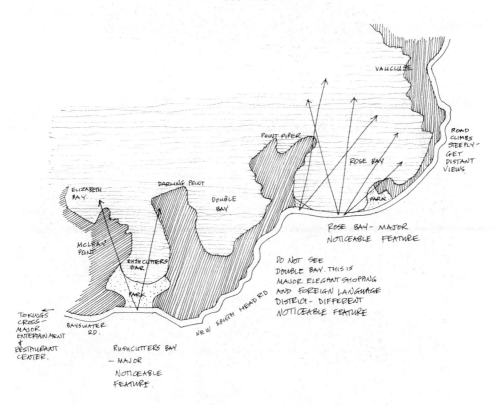

FIG. 4.18. Noticeable features along New South Head Road, Sydney, Australia. Australia.

status is related to centre city location and old houses (Schnapper 1971, p. 91). Address and the nature of the dwelling become highly noticeable. In a case where landscape features are used for such purposes of establishing social identity (Duncan 1973; Royse 1969) the people involved will develop high sensitivity to such elements. In a culture where colors, sounds and smells are important they will be used more to distinguish urban areas than in cases where they are unimportant. Thus in San Cristobal (Mexico) various quarters are distinguished by colors and these were widely known. Sounds and even smells were noticed and used — although they were studied in terms of temporal rather than spatial distinctions (Wood 1969; Stea and Wood 1971).

As another example recall the argument, in Chapter 3, that small parks in a residential area would be noticed and would not merge into the larger, predominant use pattern because they provide breaks in the urban fabric, edges and also changes in the thermal, olfactory and acoustic cues. Informal observations over time suggest that elements such as small parks, water views and open spaces in built up areas become noticeable differences and landmarks for orientation. This is then reinforced by salience and meaning. Planting and greenery are particularly important since they are used to judge the quality of places and to establish social identity of such spaces.

In cases where such variations are not perceived they do not produce complexity. A road through various areas (such as Pacific Highway in Sydney) will be perceived as complex if these areas are noticeably different and as monotonous if these distinctions are not noticed. The clearer, stronger and more salient the contrast the greater the likelihood that they will be noticed (even if these cues are not understood or, if that is intended, obeyed).

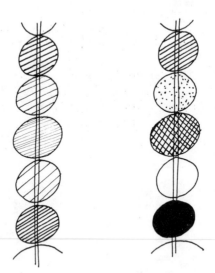

SUBTLE DIFFERENCES MAY NOT BE NOTICED.

STRONG DIFFERENCES ARE MUCH MORE LIKELY TO BE NOTICED

FIG. 4.19

Cities and areas of cities *are* different and sensitive observers are aware of these differences. There are two major questions, however: do non-designers notice such differences and to what are these differences due. Consider the latter question. An area such as Santa Monica is described as the most distinctive area in Los Angeles "though I'd be hard put to define it" (Banham 1971, p. 46). How, in fact, are places distinguished? How do we know a place is in London rather than Athens? How do we know that a particular street or square, which might be described identically (e.g., Thiel 1961, 1970) is in London, Paris, Safed, Rhodes, Tokyo or Kathmandu? These are important questions — and not only regarding perception. Clearly places and elements must be distinguishably different before they can be used in orientation, in the subjective definition of areas, in subjective distance (in terms of the perception of turns and curves) or incorporated into mental maps. These are also difficult questions with few answers. It is, however, possible, to suggest a list of cues among which people choose (not unlike my example in Chapter 3).*

Physical Differences
  Vision
    Objects — shape, size, height, color, materials, texture, details.
    Space quality — size, shape; barriers and links — merging, transitions, etc.
    Light and shade, light levels and light quality, temporal changes in light.
    Greenery, man-made vs. natural, type of planting.
    Visual aspects of perceived density.
    New vs. old.
    Order vs. variety.
    Well maintained vs. badly maintained or neglected.
    Scale and urban grain.
    Road pattern.
    Topography — natural or man-made.†
    Location — prominence, at decision points, on hills, etc.

  Kinesthetics
    Changes of level, curves, speed of movement, etc.

  Sound
    Noisy vs. quiet.
    Man-made sounds (industry, traffic, music, talk and laughter) vs. natural — wind, trees, birds, water, etc.
    Dead vs. reverberant.
    Temporal changes in sound.

  Smells
    Man-made vs. natural; plants, flowers, sea, etc.; foods, etc.

  Air Movement

---

* Some of these were explored by students in a Graduate Seminar based on this book in Spring 1974 at the School of Architecture and Urban Planning, University of Wisconsin-Milwaukee. B. J. Wentworth "What are noticeable differences in the environment" and D. Moses "An exploratory study of change in the environment", both unpublished and both in the library of the School.
† Note that artificial lakes and mountains go back to ancient times.

Temperature

Tactile
   Mainly texture underfoot.

Social Differences

People — languages spoken, behavior, dress, physical types.

Activities — type and intensity; clubs, restaurants, churches, fairs, markets, etc.

Uses — shopping, residential, industrial, etc.; uniform vs. mixed. Cars vs. pedestrians, other means of travel; movement vs. quietude.

Objects — signs, advertisements, foods, objects used, fences, plants and gardens, decorations, etc.

How the city is used — street use vs. non-use; front/back distinctions; private/public distinctions etc., introverted vs. extroverted. These are all related to cultural barriers and rules for behavior (the cues for which have to be understood and obeyed as well as noticed).

Hierarchy and symbolism, meaning, signs of social identity and status.

Temporal Differences

Long term: Changes over time from state A to state B: changes in people, in maintenance, in uses, etc. This is a whole set of cues indicating change vs. continuity and stability, and this change may be seen as positive or negative. Many of the potential noticeable differences listed can be read and interpreted as social indicators of good or bad, deteriorating or upgrading areas. They are culture specific.

Short term: Type of uses day and night, days of week, week ends, intensity of use over time.

Tempos and rhythms of activities.

Noticeable differences are used to distinguish among different environments — urban or rural (e.g., Swedner 1960), different social settings and so on. Among the many cues used are architectural distinctiveness — for example public housing which is often criticized as being all alike and, at the same time, criticized as being so different to its surroundings that it is known for what it is and constitutes a social stigma. Numbers of noticeable differences, i.e., complexity, also influence preference for particular streets (e.g., Appleyard and Lintell 1972) or natural environments (e.g., Shafer 1969(a)). The process can be conceptualized as shown in Fig. 4.20.

It is likely that noticeable differences become clearer and stronger as more cues in more different dimensions become congruent (e.g., Pyron 1971, 1972; Southworth 1969; Steinitz 1968). In addition to the strength of the figure — ground relation, their cultural or personal significance and salience, the congruence of cues and of sensory modalities, it seems clear that movement and living things generally tend to be the most interesting and noticeable (Bartlett 1967; Sieverts 1967, 1969; Maurer and Baxter 1972; Steinitz 1968; Gulick 1963; Weiss and Boutourline 1962). All these noticeable differences can occur at various scales — from landscapes, regions and whole cities, through areas within cities all the way down to parts of buildings.

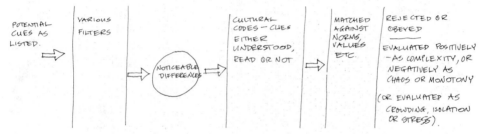

FIG. 4.20. (Compare with 2.1; Rapoport 1975(b), in press (b)).

Thus whole countries and regions differ along many dimensions — the geographers' concept of the cultural landscape and these result from certain values and ideals which influence the decisions of many people.

In large-scale urban areas there are the possible contrast of built-up and open as in the Randstadt in Holland and the proposed town of Alcan (Cullen 1964). The various finger plans and separation of connurbations only work if the contrasts are *experienced*. Other examples are an oasis in the desert, a well-treated Midwestern town in the prairies; the difference already described between colonial and indigenous cities in many areas such as India, North Africa, Indonesia and so on. It seems that Buckland Hill and the country around it was the only stretch of open landscape on the Stirling Highway between Perth and Fremantle (Western Australia) so that "it functions as a visual and psychological punctuation between the two connurbations" (Seddon 1970, p. 43). It is thus a noticeable difference separating two areas at the metropolitan scale.

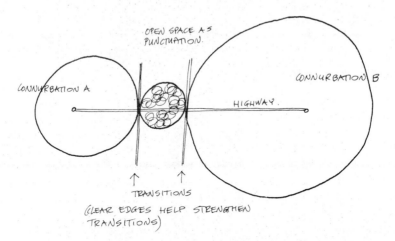

FIG. 4.21. Noticeable difference at metropolitan scale (based on verbal description in Seddon 1970, p. 43).

While this particular punctuation is in danger, and noticeable differences between places generally neglected today, in the 2nd century the Emperor Hadrian built the new town of Athens to the East of Classical Athens and erected an Arch clearly to mark the boundary between the two (Papageorgiou 1971, p. 38) i.e., stressing the difference and making it more noticeable.

Considering areas within cities a good example is provided by Edinburgh (see Fig. 4.6). London provides several good examples. Consider a few. Color distinguishes various areas: the area around Pall Mall, Buckingham Palace, Eaton Square, etc. is white. At King's Road (and including Sloane Street and Square, Cadogan Gardens, Clifford Gardens, etc.) the color turns to a warm red (different to the blue-red of other areas). At that point this change in color coincides with a transition from the City of Westminster to the Borough of Kensington and Chelsea. West Kensington is grey and brown', Kentish Town is black and so on. This is similar to San Cristobal and also Tokyo (Lenclos 1972) and a researchable question is whether Londoners use these differences the way Mexicans do.

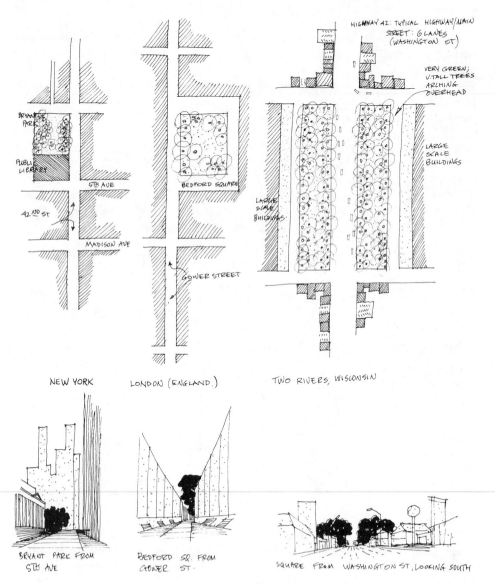

FIG. 4.22. Trees as major noticeable differences.

Activities also clearly distinguish places: on Saturday afternoons the West End is a scene of activity, people, color, noise, food smells and fast tempos whereas the city is quiet and dead. Finally the residential squares can be understood as noticeable differences in the street pattern, striking examples being Russell Square and, particularly, Bedford Square from Gower Street. A comparable example in the U.S. is the widening of Washington Street in Two Rivers, Wisconsin. (See Fig. 4.22).

Nineteenth-century New York, in spite of the uniform grid of streets, levelling of all hills, uniform house fronts, was very diverse because of the presence of many specialized areas — some just a block in extent, others the size of a small town each with different religious life, language, newspapers, restaurants, holidays and street life: to visit all was almost like a trip to Europe (Jackson 1972, pp. 205—206).

Another example is provided by Stone Town vs. Ngambo in Zanzibar. The former of tall, stone houses with narrow streets and alleys, is separated by an old creek from the latter with free-standing coral houses arranged randomly under a screen of coconut palms. The grain is different and one is inward turning, the other outward facing. The two areas are also inhibited by different populations and have very different street lives and activities, reinforced by sounds, smells, light and shade, temperature, air movement and so on (Nilsson (n.d.); Nimtz 1971; Ommaney 1955.).

FIG. 4.23. Diagrammatic representation of the character of two parts of Zanzibar after Nilsson (n.d.) and other information.

In fact a city like Zanzibar consists of areas homogeneous by race and religion with separate lives. These areas are very different visually and spatially, in terms of trades, smells, music, populations — in all modalities — and the transitions are clear.

In this example a number of cues are working together to reinforce noticeable differences — variations in houses; street pattern and urban grain, ethnicity, lifestyle, activities and the accompanying multi-sensory cues. The result is great richness and is one of the reasons for encouraging the presence of different neighborhoods in cities.

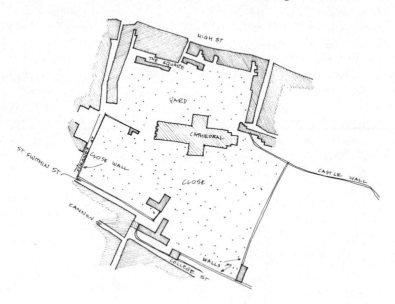

DIAGRAMMATIC PLAN OF WINCHESTER CATHEDRAL CLOSE (MANY BUILDINGS IN CLOSE LEFT OUT)
(CF. SALISBURY, EXETER ETC; CF. ALSO INNS OF COURT ETC)

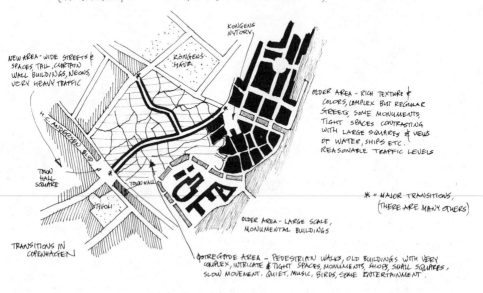

FIG. 4.24

Many examples at the scale of urban sub-areas can be found and they offer possibly the best opportunities for design since they tend to coincide with social and cultural factors (see before and Chapter 5). One rather specialized example is provided by English Cathedral closes where there is a very clear transition from markets, shops, traffic and densely built up urban fabric to openness, greenery, quiet, birds and the Cathedral itself, with all its associations. Copenhagen provides a more general example where there is a special scale, complexity and age of the old part, then a clear transition provided by the pedestrian area of the Østregade — which is 33 feet wide with different uses and shops, use of pavement, music groups, flowers, sauntering and hence tempo — and then another clear change to the Town Hall and area beyond with its wide streets, tall buildings, heavy traffic, noise, neons and bustle — a modern city like all others. (See Fig 4.24).

Such urban enclaves — whether the Binnenhof in The Hague, Bazaar districts in Middle Eastern cities, old areas in new cities or new areas in old — all lead to a plurality of townscapes within a single morphology. For complexity there must be morphological unity; without it there is chaos and disorientation. We are still dealing with variety within an order. This order may be through road networks and alignments, visual density, meaning systems, major urban spaces and the like (Papageorgiou 1971; Bacon 1967; Carr 1973).

Noticeable differences, however, may themselves be useful in establishing an order and helping orientation. Pacific Highway North in Sydney (see Fig. 4.19) becomes leafy and residential North of Chatswood. From then on there is a shopping node every mile coinciding with railway stations. These are very useful because they are noticeable and regular and one knows the rhythm of miles as one proceeds down the highway (as one does by train — see Chapter 3). Design could reinforce and stress these.

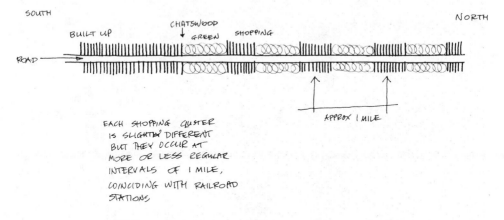

FIG. 4.25. Diagram of part of Pacific Highway, Sydney, Australia.

In movement generally, and in driving specifically, clear noticeable differences in road layout, surface and other environmental characteristics can help signs to orient the driver, warn him of traffic conditions and changes in them. Changes in road width can suggest faster speeds as can changes from built-up areas to open country, from sharp angles to gentler curves.

At the scale of the street there are, once again, different sets of noticeable differences and cues. Lights and signs can be organized so that private and public information systems can be distinguished; there can be special and general information districts, different areas can have different light levels, signs and lights can use figure/ground relations; different forms of information can control and guide movement, identify places, give advertising information and change seasonally and at shorter temporal scales. Signs themselves, often ignored by designers, are often the most noticed and used elements in the city (Carr 1973). This can be interpreted in terms of noticeable differences as can most studies of what people notice and remember (e.g., Lynch and Rivkin 1970).

One can also use architectural elements such as variations in form and shape, age, color, materials, texture and the use of walls, gates and courts which mark one of the clearest noticeable differences — the inside-out city. One example is Isphahan, another the High Street in Oxford.

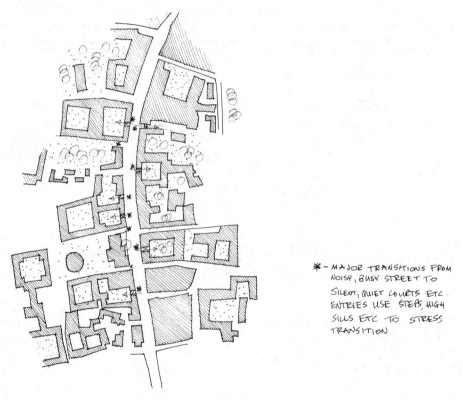

* — MAJOR TRANSITIONS FROM NOISY, BUSY STREET TO SILENT, QUIET COURTS ETC. ENTRIES USE STEPS, HIGH SILLS ETC TO STRESS TRANSITION

FIG. 4.26. Simplified, diagrammatic plan of High Street, Oxford.

Such elements are reinforced by the other sensory cues already described. Uses and "general character" can also be made congruent to stress noticeable differences. For example, in Mexico City the Ave. Cuahtemoc changes suddenly at Obrero Mundial. On the South of that intersection there is a plantation, trees, changes in buildings and uses, from second-hand cars and car parts to "nicer" shops, restaurants and hotels; at the end of this part there is a large fountain in a park. There is a corresponding change in maintenance levels of sidewalks and buildings and all these changes reinforce the transition.

Generally, then, there is a hierarchy of possible noticeable differences at all scales and of all kinds, using all sensory modalities. If used, these emphasize differences among places, increase complexity, help the definition of areas, construction of mental maps and orientation. In fact as cities become larger, and become clusters of places linked by networks (a common projection), the differences between these elements, and transitions among them, must become clearer and stronger, and are more important than in a small town, surrounded by countryside with a few very distinctive villages nearby.

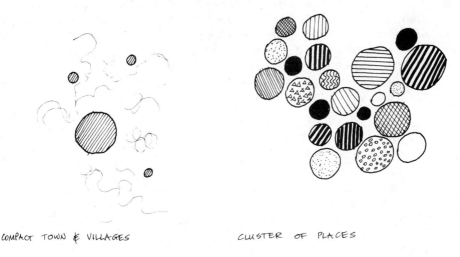

COMPACT TOWN & VILLAGES   CLUSTER OF PLACES

FIG. 4.27

This applies to all other cues so that the same noticeable differences that define areas also generate complexity and help control activities. Distinctions such as front/back, private/public, signs of change or uses can only be appropriately used if they are read and, ultimately, noticed. For example in Chandigarh, the green strips as opposed to bazaar strips are not noticeably different when compared to a traditional Indian city — e.g., the Chadni Chowk in Delhi compared to Moghul gardens, and there is no clear distinction in use either: the city lacks the clear transitions and richness of a traditional Indian city.

If differences are built-in but not noticed, they have no effect and are effectively absent: to become noticeable they must become psychological events, i.e., meaningful messages — although always ultimately related to elements in the environment. For example, at Park Hill, Sheffield, the "streets in the air" were only perceived as such by 4% of the residents and hence not used for talking or standing (Pawley 1971, p. 94). They were thus neither noticed, nor understood nor obeyed and one problem was the non-congruence between a cognitive category (street) and a form (corridor). This partly depends, then, on the cognitive categories used to define "like" and "unlike", since, after all, it is only that which is defined as different which becomes a noticeable difference. The perception of sameness and difference is a basic element of perception and is related to the number and kinds of dimensions and categories used (Kelly 1955; Olver and ·Hornsby 1972) (see also Chapter 3).

An apparently puzzling finding (in view of the importance of personalization generally, and for this purpose specifically, (e.g., Wilmott 1963, p. 4)) that form diversity does not affect accuracy of part location (Pyron 1971, 1972) can possibly be explained in terms of noticeable differences. Plan and elevation form differences were used, and it was assumed that people would be able to discriminate equally between changes in form and space. In fact form was more important than space — space variation tended to be less noticeable. Subtle space variations were particularly little noticed so that the use of simple or complex courts, of grouping buildings or not grouping them — the kind of variables designers tend to use — were not noticed. In the detailing of houses the roof shape, texture, color, openings and geometrical alignments were kept constant. Yet these may be precisely the elements which constitute noticeable differences; at the same time trees, grass and topography were not indicated to experimental subjects and we have seen that they are extremely important in preference and social identity — and hence probably noticed. I am suggesting that the wrong variables might have been used and, given current knowledge, they cannot be assumed *a priori* but must be discovered.

In one housing project 13 ways of introducing variety (all visual) were used (Cooper 1965, pp. 100–106):

(1) varying the number of units per row
(2) staggering facades of buildings
(3) using different materials and combinations of materials
(4) varying colors of adjacent buildings and roofs
(5) varying the sizes of units and combinations of sizes
(6) varying the height of buildings
(7) varying the position of front doors
(8) varying window spacing
(9) varying the design of front porches
(10) varying the design of some stairs
(11) varying roof vents with some enclosed and some not
(12) altering roof pitch, ranging from flat to steep
(13) varying the distance of units from the sidewalk and varying the orientation of units *vis-à-vis* traffic streets.

While the residents agreed that diversity was an important objective they hardly noticed most of these elements. Over half of them thought the houses looked the same. Of the 40% who noticed differences the principal was color, followed by variations in building height and size of units (which, in turn, influenced several other variables). Most were mentioned by very few (and highly idiosyncratically) — for example roof variations were not noticed at all. It is interesting that those features of an object which are mainly used in experimental situations, color and size (Bower 1971), are precisely those used in this case, since height is an element of size. In this case noticeable differences are clearly critical in achieving designers' objectives.

As usual there is hardly any research on non-visual noticeable differences. All that can be said is that it appears that in our culture this operates subliminally and as an enriching, although critical, addition to vision, reinforcing it and increasing redundancy; that these are more important in other cultures, and can be developed by experience and by active involvement with the environment through particular sense modalities.

The examples of the use of kinesthetics in Japan and Iran used before are, of course, understandable in terms of noticeable differences and, in the case of Iran, as a way of stressing transitions and making sure that noticeable differences are clear and strong. Also the introduction of stimuli in different modalities strengthens the noticeable differences since they reinforce each other. Thus in the case of the Isphahan mosque entrances (see Fig. 4.1) the changes in direction and level as one goes through are reinforced by changes in sound level from noisy street to quiet court, from haggling and traffic to the rustle of trees, gurgling of water, singing of birds and murmur of study and prayer; a change in color from the dun-colored street to the blue-green of tiles and green of trees; from heat to coolness, from dust to clean air, from market and bargaining to prayer — the vision is deliberately paradaisical (Rapoport 1964–65). The same set of reinforcing stimuli, although weaker and fewer, are used in the other examples given — the English Cathedral close, the Oxford Street and College courtyards and all kinds of urban enclaves generally,

In Safed, (Israel) I came across a court with ruins all around it where the wind was soughing through some trees — a wind I had not noticed before. There were shady spots in the clear sunny atmosphere and suddenly I became aware of the smell of pines and cedars, the singing of birds, the tinkling of bells on the necks of goats, of children playing — things not noticed before and noticeable because of the hubbub of the town itself before and after — it is the *transition* which is significant. Similarly the view of the valley and mountains from this court makes one aware of the setting which one had forgotten while in town. This heightened awareness also occurs in time, due to the Sabbath in Israel. Then the same town becomes quite a different place where everything is closed and there is no traffic and then comes back to life in a more striking way after dark on Saturday. In Safed this becomes a most noticeable difference over time, where the silence and holiness of the Sabbath are suddenly replaced, as chains come off the streets to allow traffic, by cars, noise, lights coming on, children start running and playing, demeanor changes, people's clothes are changed, smells as food starts to be cooked and sold. All this multisensory activity replaces silence, darkness and the sound of praying and singing in the Synagogues — a most striking example of a noticeable difference in time which is extremely powerful and helps temporal orientation. This is a symbolic and religious manner of stressing noticeable differences and transitions between sacred and profane in a temporal sense, in the same way that the Isphahan mosques (or English Cathedrals) do it physically.

It is significant that Aborigines who define places largely symbolically do it much more clearly and distinctly where there are noticeable differences in the landscape — water, rocks or major trees — and that the ritually most important places (which are the most important places generally) are distinct from their surroundings (Rapoport 1972(e)). In other places also, sacred places tend to be noticeably different although this difference tends to be reinforced through design and construction (e.g., Scully 1962). Designers can increase the likelihood of noticeable differences, complexity and the identity of places by stressing such cultural patterns and using multiple cues in all sensory modalities as well as the differences in lifestyles, symbols and activity patterns of various groups clustered in the city.

Recall our discussion of the subjective definition of areas which is related to noticeable differences. This definition depends on noticeable transitions among places and states (see Fig. 3.17). Through design, stimuli can be provided which are likely to become noticeable differences and used to construct schemata. Since no one set of elements is used by all, the more possible elements are provided, the more chance that some at least will be so used. On the other hand those elements which are widely used tend to have some characteristics in common (e.g., Grey *et al.* 1970) and these can be interpreted as noticeable differences. Thus the more potential noticeably different elements and environments exist, the greater the chances of more people perceiving them, experiencing complexity and orienting themselves. The manipulation of noticeable differences seems to provide an understanding of much of the urban design literature, a key to the objectives described in Chapters 2, 3 and 4 and to be discussed below. It seems a very useful, general and unifying concept.

Effects of Scale and Speed of Movement

The discussion on information processing, channel capacity and overload, complexity and noticeable differences all suggest that the *rate* of information is involved, i.e., the number of noticeable differences per unit time, and that speed plays a part in the perception of noticeable differences and complexity. For example it can be predicted that pedestrians and motorists will differ greatly in the way they perceive the city (Rapoport 1957). Perception of the city is sequential and the city is experienced in time. Perception is dynamic and sequential. It is made up of short scans, involving the integration of successive partial views, but these are only meaningful if there are noticeable changes in successive views and some uncertainty as to the next view (Rapoport and Kantor 1967; Rapoport and Hawkes 1970; Rapoport 1971(a); Pyron 1971; Thiel 1970; Johnson 1965). This integration of partial views is affected by speed and, more generally, by the rate of noticeable differences.

Speed affects both time and distance estimates (see Chapter 3) and is itself judged in terms of the rate of information flow: low information trips seem slower than high information ones. Speed influences how often noticeable differences occur, how long they are seen and hence whether they are noticed. Subtle cues need slow pace; driving is not only fast but it also demands concentration, leaving no time or channel capacity to appreciate the environment. Thus pedestrians have a much better awareness of places and clearer ideas of the significance, meaning and activities in the city than either drivers or users of public transport. Because of the lower speed and lower criticality of their movement, pedestrians can perceive many more differences in form and activity. Pedestrians are also less insulated from multisensory information and the active nature of walking increases the dimensionality of information. Thus the relative effects of different transport modes on the knowledge of the city (Chapter 3) can be partly interpreted in terms of the perception of noticeable differences.

This suggests that for different speeds, different cues and different levels of complexity should be designed. We have already discussed streets where two different rhythms of complexity can be provided for motorists and pedestrians. Long pedestrian underpasses, with white, shiny tiled walls are much too long and featureless at pedestrian speeds; the apparent rate of progress is reduced by the lack of noticeable differences and adequate levels of information. The roadside strip, at driving speeds, is too complex and chaotic, while residential streets seen at slower driving speeds or at pedestrian speeds are too monotonous: there is a reversal of needed levels of complexity related to speed. That some roadside strip which is full of parking lots and large elements is extremely open spatially and provides inadequate information to pedestrians (Rapoport and Hawkes 1970; Rapoport 1971, 1971(a)). Because of the lack of visible changes in cues and distance to goals at slow speeds there is a low rate of meaningful information, few noticeable differences and the environment is boring.

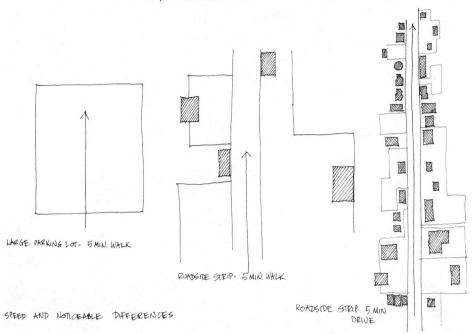

LARGE PARKING LOT - 5 MIN. WALK

ROADSIDE STRIP - 5 MIN. WALK

SPEED AND NOTICEABLE DIFFERENCES

ROADSIDE STRIP - 5 MIN. DRIVE

FIG. 4.28

The perception of complexity is thus related to the number of noticeable differences per unit time and hence to speed. Speed also influences the way people organize discrete stimuli into groups. At high speeds elements are grouped into simple chunks, while at slow speed more discrete elements are perceived. High speed makes a complex environment too chaotic; a simple environment, interesting at high speed becomes monotonous at slow speeds. Complexity in a traffic tunnel and simplicity in a prison are both undesirable (Chang 1956, p. 20). All these effects depend on the amount of information and hence the number of noticeable differences per unit time.

There are also effects of peripheral vision at high speeds. Central vision is essential for fine detail and small differences in contrast and color, while peripheral vision detects movement. Hence the presence of elements close to a rapidly moving observer, particularly if these elements are complex, can be most distressing by greatly exaggerating apparent speed.

Movement itself as it affects perception and creates sequences can be understood in terms of noticeable differences. Movement through an environment can be described in terms of transitions, "emergence from behind", sequences, and transformations (Gibson 1968, pp. 206–208). This can only happen when there are noticeable differences so that on a featureless plain or a completely featureless tunnel, and in a vehicle with no kinesthetic cues to speed and movement, the apparent rate of movement would be much lower than through an environment rich in transitions and noticeable differences. In other words, complexity depends on the number of changes or noticeable differences per unit time — changes of any uniform, or uniformly varying, attribute — whether rate, direction, slope, curvature, color, enclosure, smell, sound, light or whatever. An analysis of an urban environment in terms of transitions and sequences (e.g., Kepes 1961), while easily interpreted in terms of noticeable differences, must include a consideration of how fast they occur. Given a certain number of noticeable differences per unit length it is clear that at lower speeds that environment would tend to be simplified and tend towards monotony and sensory deprivation while at higher speeds it would tend towards chaos — and overload.

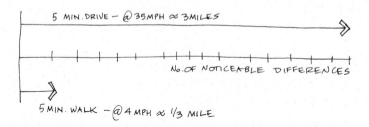

FIG. 4.29

There is the additional factor that at pedestrian speeds the perceiver is free to explore the environment and use all sensory modalities, which leads to some increase in complexity *if the environment provides it.* But, in any case, settings for high and low speed, for motorists and pedestrians, should be perceptually quite different. It would be impossible to appreciate the subtleties of Katsura Imperial Villa, Fahterpur Sikri or any of the traditional high style or vernacular architectural or urban design sequences at high speed and also impossible to appreciate a freeway at walking speed.

At car speeds there is not only the development of many car-oriented, and hence large scale, elements but the time available to read information is greatly reduced. This information may be verbal, heraldic, spatial or human — or a combination of these. Integrating these into patterns and making sense of them at high speeds demands large, infrequent, broad and smooth rhythms to give time for all this to happen and to avoid satiation effects. The pedestrian receives very different input — it is fine grain, he can vary the rate, he can look around and stop to observe detail, he is aware of environment all around him in all sense modalities. Urban light and sign systems are greatly affected by speed as anyone who has travelled along a highway strip at night at high speed knows. The notions of sequence in the design of highways have also been discussed (Appleyard, Lynch and Meyer 1964, Carr and Schissler 1969) but the effects of speed and perception of noticeable differences on the design of all spaces — pedestrian and motorist — have not received nearly as much attention (e.g., Ritter 1964; Venturi *et al.* 1972). The important conclusion is that, quite apart from the needs of safety and pollution, and hence *physical* separation, pedestrian and high speed environments are *perceptually* incompatible, i.e., the conflict is not between cars and pedestrians, but between fast and slow speeds, and also types of movement — smooth or jerky, straight or irregular.

To repeat, an environment comfortably stimulating from a car becomes monotonously boring on foot while what is interesting on foot becomes chaotic in a car. The Shambles at York are a good pedestrian environment while the Pyramids are ideal at car speeds (Parr 1969(c)). More generally the medieval city is pedestrian, Ville Radieuse and its progeny — for motorists. The two environments need to be quite different in terms of noticeable differences and perceptual organization: at high speeds one needs distant views, simplicity and large-scale while at slow speeds one needs small-scale, intricacy and complexity.

As speed increases, the task becomes more demanding, and concentration increases. Several other things also happen (Tunnard and Pushkarev 1963, pp. 172–174):

(1) *The point of concentration (or focus) recedes* from 600 ft. at 25 mph to 2000 ft at 65 mph. As a result elements must become larger. Also while objects perpendicular to the road become prominent those parallel to it lose prominence.

(2) *Peripheral vision diminishes* so that while at 25 mph the horizontal angle is 100° it reduces to less than 40° at 60 mph. One result is "tunnel vision" which may induce hypnosis and sleep. Side elements need to be quiet and subdued and perceived semi-consciously in the blurred field of peripheral vision, with the main features on the axis of vision and the point of concentration periodically moved laterally to maintain attention.

(3) *Foreground detail begins to fade*, due to the rapid movement of close objects. The earliest point of clear view recedes from 30 ft. at 40 mph to 110 ft. at 60 mph. At the same time detail beyond 1400 ft. cannot be seen as it is too small, so that the range is between 110–1400 ft. – and that is traversed in 15 seconds. Elaborate detail is thus both useless and undesirable.

(4) *Space perception becomes impaired* so that near objects are seen, get close and disappear very quickly. They thus tend to "loom", which is extremely stressful (Coss 1973) and elements too close to the edge or overhead, and sudden curves, should be avoided.

Motorists' perception is affected by the length of time each element is in view and also the criticality of the task. The pedestrian has each element in view as long as he wishes and can satisfy his interest in it because of the low criticality of this task. When pedestrians are harassed by traffic their task becomes critical and they cannot perceive the environment in the way appropriate to their speed – this is a common design problem.

The nature of the environment structures motorists' perceptions within the limits of their task, speed and car characteristics. It is generally used for orientation, destination location and curiosity, and certain environments help or hinder these. Given the changes in the visual field with speed described, it would appear that for motorists building setbacks should be greater than for slow speeds, and should not be uniform. Uniform and consistent surrounds confound orientation, confuse destination location and reduce curiosity, since they do not provide noticeable differences. The shapes of the visual fields on either side of the road should be similar, i.e., symmetrical, although one side is always dominant – the visual field never expands equally on both sides. Distances between peripherally and foveally viewed elements should be reduced, buildings should be regular in height and rhythms should be large-scale and simple (Pollock 1972).

These are clearly all complexity/speed factors. Elements along the road should provide information at an intermediate rate with gradual transitions – sudden contrasts between high and low information environments should be avoided; although areas of differing complexity are still needed the transitions among them should be gradual. There should be a smooth continuous succession of such areas with their intensity decreasing as speed increases. Generally, then, as speed increases the number of noticeable differences in the environment should reduce and the setbacks should also increase; as traffic intensity increases the perceptual complexity of the environment should be reduced (Pollock 1972; cf. Rapoport 1957; Rapoport and Kantor 1967; Rapoport and Hawkes 1971(a)).

Pedestrians can use, and desire, much more acute and abrupt transitions — spatial, kinesthetic, in light levels, sounds and all other sense modalities. Only they can notice, react to and respond to the variety of stimuli which can be used in a rich, opulent environment. The characteristics of pedestrian spaces, which also follow from the discussion generally, and those of high-speed spaces can be illustrated and combined as follows.

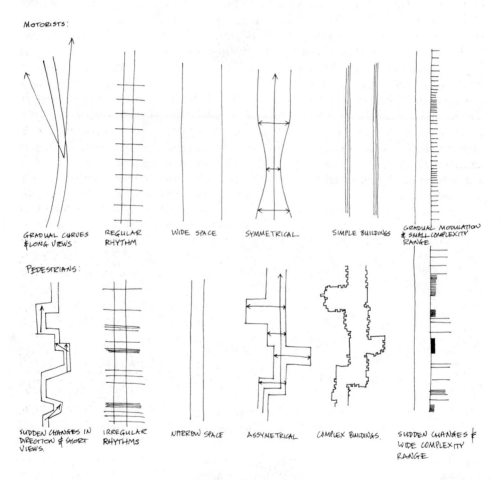

MOTORISTS:

GRADUAL CURVES & LONG VIEWS · REGULAR RHYTHM · WIDE SPACE · SYMMETRICAL · SIMPLE BUILDINGS · GRADUAL MODULATION & SMALL COMPLEXITY RANGE

PEDESTRIANS:

SUDDEN CHANGES IN DIRECTION & SHORT VIEWS · IRREGULAR RHYTHMS · NARROW SPACE · ASSYMETRICAL · COMPLEX BUILDINGS · SUDDEN CHANGES & WIDE COMPLEXITY RANGE

FIG. 4.30

Thus without ignoring the need for physical separation for safety and amenity, a major task of urban design is to consider perceptual differences per unit space and time. Areas used at slow speed, on foot or in slow vehicles, should be designed very differently to those designed for high speeds. While a residential neighborhood should be rich, full of detail, complex, with clear transitions and small-scale, irregular elements, a highway should be simple with large-scale, more widely spaced elements. Yet frequently the exact opposite is the case — residential areas are simple, dull and monotonous while roadside strips are complex and chaotic and at a scale which does not suit the pedestrian either. There are clearly differences between scenic road and a freeway and, generally, the higher the speed the less information is needed in the environment.

Because the effects of speed and scale have been neglected, many planning and design decisions are at the wrong levels of complexity with either excessive or inadequate levels for various purposes. The net result is that people are forced increasingly to ignore the environment which leads to less concern with its design, and so on in a vicious circle (Langer 1966). Similarly the neglect of the full range of noticeable differences and various senses in the city leads to greatly impoverished environments and a further loss of sensitivity. Activity will also modify these relationships since play and exploratory as opposed to grimly purposeful behavior will need very different levels of complexity at given speeds. Walking for pleasure or to a job are very different as is driving. People may thus select different environments for apparently similar activities depending on context but the difference between slow and high speed environments will persist.

At the scale of the city it is the existence of many levels of complexity which is important, and their appropriate relationship to the context. At that scale, for example, designers could modulate complexity levels to reflect the nature of areas and their activities, their importance in the urban hierarchy and the speed at which they will be perceived.

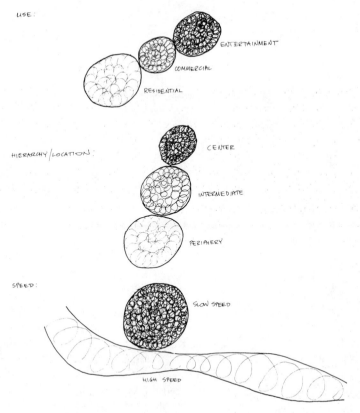

FIG. 4.31. Complexity and context.

We have already noted that pedestrians rarely look above eye level in enclosed urban spaces where perception of detail is almost inevitable. Given the needs of drivers as described their movement channels should be simple and it is freestanding elements and tops against the sky and clusters of tall buildings which become important (Heath 1971; Worskett 1969, p. 98).

RAISED SIDEWALK, BLVD. SAINT MARTIN, PARIS : ONE OF SEVERAL

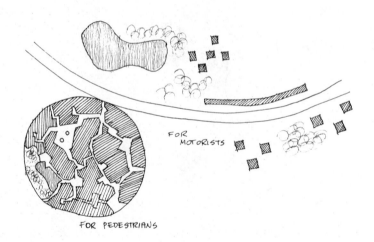

PEDESTRIANS & MOTORISTS - SEPARATION BY PERCEPTUAL NEEDS

FIG. 4.32

Pedestrian spaces themselves can be separated into movement and rest spaces. Movement spaces are dynamic for walking and moving, albeit slowly, whereas rest spaces are static — for sitting, eating, talking and gazing. This is an example of the need for specificity so that to say "pedestrian spaces" is not really enough. These two forms of pedestrian spaces may require different perceptual characteristics: movement spaces are linear, narrow and winding so that they entice with hidden views and encourage sauntering, while rest spaces are more static and wider. Such spaces, whether squares or avenues, encourage visual exploration from one place and act as a stage for people who become objects of interest and increase complexity levels. Thus wide streets like the Champs Elysées in Paris, or Dizengof Street in Tel Aviv, provide human interest in their outdoor cafes. By narrowing the pavement movement spaces are created and pedestrians and seated people see and are seen. In many cities one finds the contrast, as in the Plaka, Athens, of narrow shopping and pedestrian streets with wider rest spaces where cafes, taverns, tables, and markets are found, although these spaces can still be remarkably small.

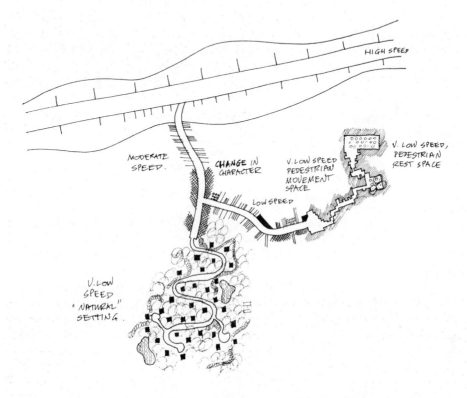

FIG. 4.33

There is, in effect, a continuum and hierarchy of movement and rest, related to noticeable differences. In urban design the high speed systems recently introduced (freeways or others) should be rethought in perceptual and cognitive terms. To redress the balance much thought needs to be given to pedestrian and residential areas in such terms and these, in turn, need to be differentiated with regard to complexity and noticeable differences depending on activities and location, comprising movement and rest spaces, with cities composed of areas of great variety reflecting the many socio-cultural characteristics to be discussed in the next chapter; the totality would be a new order of richness, complexity and noticeable transitions at various scales and in all sense modalities which would provide choice and perceptually satisfying cities.

CHAPTER 5

The City in Terms of Social, Cultural and Territorial Variables

The spatial, social and temporal systems of the city, which provide the perceptual inputs, the material for cognitive schemata and affective responses, are the result of a wide range of social and cultural factors. These include the organization of meaning and communication, the nature of social relationships and links, the character and spatial juxtaposition of various groups, and the systems of places in which activities occur. Such factors complement the psychological variables considered and will be discussed in the next two chapters.

The interrelationships among such variables are extremely complex and it is extremely difficult to separate them even for analytical purposes. In this chapter the city will be considered in terms of social, cultural and territorial variables while in the next the stress will be on symbolic and communicative aspects — the environment as the organization of meaning.

The following general points will be covered:

(a) The process of clustering of like people in cities resulting from habitat selection and choice of particular environmental quality, so that the city becomes a set of areas of different groups which tend to define themselves in terms of "us" and "them". There is a process of inclusion and exclusion, of establishing boundaries and stressing social identity by the use of cues and symbols, i.e., the organization of communication and meaning.

(b) This process is partly the establishing of group behavior settings which affect behavior through various cues. Such cues must be legible and obeyed (as well as being noticed); such settings are used and related differently. There must hence be some cultural homogeneity and sharing of unwritten rules, symbols and behavior, or conflicts arise. These may be due to incongruences in the organization of meaning and communication, space or time — conflicts in tempo and rhythm and their synchronization. Homogeneity and clustering are also important with regard to mutual support and the maintenance of specific services and activities; they are also ways of coping with density and crowding, excessive interaction and overload by increasing predictability and making the environment communicate effectively.

(c) Group homogeneity is defined subjectively with different criteria used at various times and in different places: all distinguish between us and them and try to make the physical environment congruent with the conceptual environment.

(d) Behavior settings and activity systems are related to certain spatial entities — home range, core areas, territories, and so on — derived from ethology. These, in turn, affect behavior space and the various distortions in cognitive schemata.

In effect, there are four major sets of variables which interact: the clustering of people on the basis of preference and other factors, leading to specific social networks and activity systems. These result in culture-specific behavior setting systems which are expressed in terms of meanings, symbols and various domains. These affect home range and behavior space — how much of the city is used and known — and hence cognitive schemata. The material being discussed is thus intimately related to previous chapters.

Clustering and Urban Enclaves

We have already briefly seen that, when there is no interference, a clustering process tends to occur in cities based on perceived homogeneity, differing interpretations of environmental quality, lifestyles, symbol systems and defenses against overload and stress. Although this tendency of people to cluster with others like themselves is often denied and suppressed, it has been suggested that it still occurs, but is then artificial rather than natural (e.g., Petonnet 1972(a)), i.e., based on imposed and arbitrary, rather than subjectively defined, criteria.

Neighborhoods are one particular type of homogeneous area. They tend to be small, and are an enclave of people providing a social and physical element intermediate between the individual and his family and the larger, heterogeneous group. Context may influence the desire for clustering. It may be that when overall homogeneity is high local homogeneity may be unimportant and low, and vice-versa (e.g., Johnston 1971(a)). This clustering may be partly voluntary even when it appears forced (e.g., Adjei-Barwuah and Rose 1972) and is related to shared images and a desire to preserve a lifestyle, religion or culture.

There may also be a distinction, large or small, between the appreciation of group identity (a cognitive criterion) and overt behavior. The latter may be constrained or distorted by other factors, however, and if and when people are able to cluster they will frequently do so. One can thus predict good agreement between cognitive and behavioral aspects within the constraints of habitat selection — which is confirmed (e.g., Cohen 1974, pp. 1–36). The critical factor is the apperception of homogeneity, which is clearly a matter of subjective definition of like and unlike, and hence an example of a cognitive taxonomy.

The group identifies itself and is identified by others as constituting a category distinguishable from other categories (Barth 1969). One of the purposes of culture is precisely to define groups and stress their differences *vis-à-vis* others; it serves both to integrate and to separate. These two functions can be seen as essentially the same — integrating groups by distinguishing them from "others", and this can be a form of defense against stress (Siegel 1970; Rapoport, in press(b)). In this process the use of physical environmental symbols to establish and affirm social identity is important, so that groups not only select different habitats but *create* them. An important part of such clustering are address and environmental symbols as a way of locating people in social space under conditions of mobility; less differentiated cars, clothing, houses and other artefacts; and as classes and other groupings become less clear. It offers a way of locating people in social space through their location in physical space: generally status and habitat are related among both people and animals. Although there is some disagreement with this view (e.g., Rent 1968), it seems fairly generally accepted that in all cities there is clustering and some form of social and spatial hierarchy.*

* After writing this chapter, and developing the argument on homogeneity, symbolism and coding, my attention was drawn to Lofland (1973) who develops some of these themes in more detail — and also somewhat differently.

The element of habitat selection is also seen in the case when groups move out because others, who are *too* different, move in. This is not just the case with Negroes in the U.S. but also Southern Europeans in Australia and other groups, and the difference seems to be related to lifestyle and values which are incompatible. If one accepts that lifestyles can be classified as consumption, social prestige, family or community oriented (E. Moore 1972), it is likely that in the case of family orientation, child rearing may be the most important variable, in the case of community orientation compatible neighbors, while in prestige orientation it may be appropriate environmental symbols.

Each group may share a public image — unconsciously (Boulding 1956, p. 133). Each group has an internal structure, a specific set of behaviors and values, tends to be a more or less organized whole and has a *boundary* to the outside environment. Boundaries can have several meanings. One is behavioral, the extent of space used influencing density and crowding (Rapoport 1975(b)); there are physical boundaries (defenses) controlling and filtering interation and information flows with different permeabilities in various directions. Finally, there are social boundaries (Barth 1969) separating group members from non-members, us from them. Since boundaries distinguish group members from non-members, they must be noticeable before they can be effective.

In this process the nature of the various groups plays a role as does the scale; the size which homogeneous areas should be is an important question on which there is very little work. It appears that the block should be homogeneous (Wilmott 1963, pp. 112 f.; Gans 1972, pp. 250–255) and also that an area of, say, 20,000 similar people is too big.

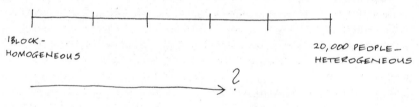

FIG. 5.1.

We have seen that neighborhoods may be defined subjectively as 75–150 acres, but, since their population may vary, that may be too big for social homogeneity, which depends more on social criteria. There seems to be some evidence that the division is of very fine grain, so that even relatively small areas, e.g., on the South side of Chicago, seen as homogeneous by outsiders are, in fact, made up of a number of small, and highly differentiated units (Suttles 1968). In North India also, the subjectively defined neighborhood is composed of a number of smaller areas — an alley or part of an alley — which are partly defined by physical features but mainly by social contacts and in terms of people like oneself who share feelings about customs and values, and do things in a certain way; areas are divided by religion, origin, class or being "nice" or "rough" (Vatuk 1972, pp. 149–153).

In the U.S., in a small village like Harrisburg, Texas, there is clear and distinct ethnic separation by streets (Maurer and Baxter 1972). In Scandinavia, a relatively homogeneous area, there is increasing segregation whenever choice exists (Michelson 1970(b)) and even in Israel, where there is an overriding homogeneity based on religion, history and recent nationhood, there is much voluntary clustering in new towns and housing projects by blocks, on the basis of place of origin. Such homogeneity, in fact, helps absorption, neighborly relations and is important for satisfaction, although planners argue that heterogeneity leads to mutual acceptance and official policy is to prevent such clustering. Many "low status" groups want to be near high status groups, although separate (Soen 1970). These different groups also have different environmental preferences, different family size and lifestyles, so that a good case can be made out for separation into subunits by ethnic community, family size and age, and recommendations made about which groups should be together, close or well separated (Marans 1969).

If we consider that culture influences personal space, territorial behavior and the reading of cues as threatening; that different groups evaluate the uses of front and back regions quite differently and have different norms for behavior in "public" places; that there are different norms regarding the roles of sexes, childrearing and so on, then it should be quite clear that grouping becomes understandable. When we add to this landscaping codes, maintenance of houses and planting, colors used, uniformity vs. variety in colors and forms, noise and light levels, and time rhythms, then the advantages of homogeneity become fairly evident.

In the West there seems to be a tension between the desire of many people to cluster and the values of politicians and planners which are opposed to such enclaves. The goal is heterogeneity: subpopulations and their areas are ignored and generalizations made for "urban man". There is a different tradition which has been called the levantine (Gordon 1962), although it is much more broadly prevalent, where it is widely accepted that the city is composed of distinct communities side by side and which has existed since the 3rd millenium BCE. In contrasting a city like Constantinople, Beirut or Alexandria with an American city such as Boston or New York, it is often argued that in the American case there is much less separation. In reality the clustering is ignored: American cities have great ethnic variety and one can speak of Harlem, Spanish Harlem, the Germans of Yorkville, the Jewish Lower East Side, Chinatown and so on — the names themselves suggest the reality and the perception. Yet the traditional and Middle East city is qualitatively different. In those cities groups maintain their identity, religion, language and peoplehood for centuries and even millenia, while in the U.S. such areas tend to lose population and often disappear when migration ceases — there is more assimilation, intermarriage and the like.

In the U.S., Australia, Canada and similar countries the situation is complicated because there is an interplay of assimilation and group survival. If plural cultures are to be maintained, there must be subsocieties which provide frameworks for communal existence with their own networks of cliques, institutions, organizations and informal friendships — and clustering remains important. In the U.S. group membership seems to be based on ethnicity, race and religion and, to a lesser extent, national origin, cross-cut by social class stratification. There are also some non spatial groups such as intellectuals. Each of these groups is an abstraction, although people feel that they belong to them, and their primary relationships occur within the group and its locale while secondary ones occur within the group but in non-group specific locales (Gordon 1964, pp. 158–161). This combination of ethnicity and class is also found in Canada (Marston 1969). In traditional cities the individual was related to the larger unit through the group and these groups were spatially separated, so that they could more easily maintain their identity, religious practices, language, food habits and lifestyle.

The separation into such areas was very strong in most Moslem cities which had . quarters within which people bound together by ties of language, religion, occupation, family, or common origin lived together (Von Gruenebaum 1958; Lapidus 1969; Hourani and Stern 1970) so that the classical Moslem city could be visualized thus:

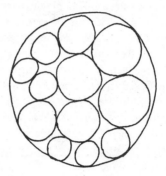

FIG. 5.2. The Moslem city as a collection of homogeneous areas.

In a traditional Moslem city such as Antioch, as recently as 1934, there were many specialized areas. There were 25 *souks* (bazaars) subdivided along three dimensions — technical (by crafts), topographic (with all artisans of one corporation side by side) and ethnic (grouping artisans of one corporation and bazaar). The souks were thus subdivided into very small and complex quarters. There were also many ethnic and religious residential quarters — 45 for 30,000 people. While this averages 6–700 people per quarter, some had only 20–25 residents. All these quarters were extremely significant, independent, self-contained and exogamous. Within the quarter one knew everyone and felt safe. Twenty-seven of the 45 quarters were Turkish and grouped in one area of 18,000 people [i.e., there was a hierarchy of grouping]; Christian and Arab quarters were even more differentiated, subdivided and varied and, in the case of Arab areas, even more introverted. The three large groupings expressed a status hierarchy, with Turks dominant (Weulersse 1934).

Damascus, also was divided into Souk areas and other quarters along ethnic, religious and other lines, subdivided into microquarters; each was a miniature city with all services — mosque, baths, bake oven and market — the same elements and organization as the whole city (Elisséeff 1970, pp. 172–173) very much as in San Cristobal where the same schema applied at all scales (Wood 1969). These areas were limited to members, i.e., the movement of strangers was limited and few paths available to them. In fact the separate and distinct areas which composed such a city controlled movement and communication — only those who belonged entered. This replaced our reliance on police and other institutions (e.g., Brown 1973; Delaval 1974) and also reflected a different value system — mobility was not seen as the ultimate good.

During the Ottoman period this was formalized into the *Millet* system, officially recognizing the existence of large numbers of separate and distinct communities. Even today many Moslem cities retain this characteristic, although the pattern is not as clear spatially it is indicated by trades and other cues (Awad 1970, p. 115) so that in North

Africa there are entire districts of particular crafts dominated by people from one or two villages (English and Mayfield 1972, p. 203). In North Afghanistan, in a town like Akapruk, even today each ethnic group and Moslem sect has separate quarters, although it should be stressed that this pattern is not universal in all Moslem towns (e.g., English 1973).

In traditional African cities there is a similar pattern. Thus in Nigeria there are regional tribal divisions, while cities are divided into quarters of the different groups and the heterogeneous population is grouped by ethnicity, religion, occupation and social status (e.g., Mabogunje 1968, p. 64). Yoruba cities are divided into areas of extended families comprising hundreds of nuclear families. All people within a neighborhood are closely related and adjoining areas are also related, although less closely. The city is thus a hierarchical system of houses, compounds, neighborhoods and clusters of neighborhoods of related people: these are closely built and larger spaces separate less closely related groups (Ojo 1969). This is important since it provides help to the elderly and poor, replacing social services, and leads to specific symbolism of place (with burial in the compound) and general identification with place (Onibokun 1970).

In Africa generally cities "belong" to different ethnic groups, and there is a long tradition of identifying territory with ethnic groups. Traditional cities thus often had quarters for aliens, whether visitors or permanent residents. Each enclave had a chief or headman responsible to higher level authority. In more heterogeneous cities, such as Jos in Nigeria, there tended to be more riots (Plotnicov 1972). The traditional system was preserved in colonial times and even today ethnic, tribe and kinship areas are extremely important in African cities, even if cross-cut by other forms of association (e.g. Epstein 1969).

Indian cities also preserve the traditional pattern, partly because people cling to old residential areas which are based not on income but on caste, occupation, religion, kinship and ethnic origin. Each area is often identified with definite cultural factors and a specific system for regulating the life of the area (Anderson and Ishwaran 1965, p. 65). This even happens in traditional villages, which also consist of wards with their own headman, and shrine, segregated by caste, occupation or whatever, and separated by streets. The wards cooperate at the village level, the villages at the regional level, and the religious symbolism of urban form and house form are a reflection of the religious symbolism of castes (Mukerjee 1961). There is a clear hierarchy — Brahmins occupy the apex of the social pyramid and are near the main temple and tank, whereas the untouchables are on the outskirts expressing spatially their social distance. In each ward residence is denied the outsider and Parsees, Christians and Moslems live in different areas. This pattern still persists in large cities like Delhi where, for example, Moslems have great difficulty renting accommodation in Hindu areas because they cook and eat beef (Sud 1973). This clear hierarchy is changing but it is a mistake to ignore this pattern in planning (e.g., Mukerjee 1961; Fonseca 1969(a), (b)) and even Calcutta is composed of areas clearly distinguishable by culture, tradition and history, language, caste, occupation, and place of origin (Bose 1965).

Most U.S. cities are clearly different in the extent and significance of clustering, but have areas of clearly distinct character. In many of them lifestyle (and, of course, race) seems more important than income in explaining clustering: income is the primary *means* (not reason) of achieving separation from others, desired location and environmental quality (Feldman and Tilly 1960; Eichler and Kaplan 1967; Werthman 1968). Money makes it possible to live in a desirable area which is defined subjectively, both in environmental and social terms. For immigrants in 19th c. U.S. cities, for example, social factors outweighed physical environmental quality; homogeneous areas were preferred even when others were available and when housing conditions were poor (Ward 1971).

At the same time, more in some U.S. cities than others, there is low group identity and relatively few distinct neighborhoods. Such cities, Los Angeles being one example, stress the individual and extreme mobility. There is a clear distinction between the private dwelling and the public city and a major commitment to the individual house. In the 30's, while East Coast cities were marked by feelings of territory, Los Angeles was marked by a feeling for property. The low density, lack of public transport and use of cars, and relative absence of ethnic neighborhoods prevented street corner gangs and there was no "turf". While teenagers did hang out, they did so at drive-ins, beaches and other widely scattered locations. This pattern was more marked in Los Angeles than elsewhere in the West and habitat selection operated, for example, between Los Angeles and San Francisco so that this pattern was gradually reinforced (Wilson 1967, pp. 39—41).

In Australia, majority culture and official policy are very strongly opposed to enclaves but there has been a large and rapid post World War II migration which has led to migrants clustering for mutual help, language, foods and social interaction. This has led to distinctive ethnic areas in Australian cities, recognized by novelists who can say that "the greater majority of German speaking migrants to Sydney tended to congregate in the area along the Southern shores of the harbor: the map of Europe with its national boundaries was being re-drawn ten thousand miles away" (Clearey 1970, p. 79) and in all cities different groups cluster in different areas. In Sydney, for example, Southern Europeans cluster in inner city areas and the inner Eastern suburbs, the Dutch and Germans are concentrated in the outer suburban periphery, Eastern Europeans in Western industrial suburbs together with Maltese and Italians, Jews in higher status Eastern suburbs. Greeks have the highest segregation and English the lowest (Dept. of Social Work (n.d.); Burnley 1972). This is probably because their "conceptual distance" (Rapoport 1974) from the majority culture was least. Groups having things in common will interact more than those who have little in common, i.e., the functional, subjective distance among homogeneous people is smaller than among heterogeneous ones. Unlike groups have larger socio-cultural distances, human spatial organizations are hierarchically ordered, and the hierarchies and ways of structuring and permeability of boundaries are rather different in different cultures (Soja 1971, pp. 3—10; Rapoport 1972(e)). In addition to clustering through chain migration and mutual help (so that one finds subdivisions among groups by cities, villages or islands of origin), there is also an element of preference and habitat selection involved, and these patterns are also found in Melbourne and other Australian cities.

This clustering, moreover, applies not only to migrants. Thus in Melbourne there is a clear grouping of people along different social dimensions — ethnicity, occupation, skills, stage of family cycle, social class and lifestyle. Where people live reflects not only income but also values and preferences. Since residential proximity in cities both constrains and provides opportunities for social interaction, people with similar values, expectations and social positions tend to cluster so as to maximize group interaction and maintain group norms by being with like and away from unlike (Jones 1968). The degree of separation depends on the extent to which their requirements and modes of life are incompatible, e.g., in terms of socialization of children or environmental symbols. Thus for individuals of some groups social interaction is more important than status, which is more important for others; when visual symbols are used for the latter, heterogeneity may lead to conflict. There is some evidence that clustering helps interaction with others (e.g., Johnston 1971) which has important policy implications.

Urban ethnic villages have often persisted in spite of some diffusion until their destruction by urban renewal and, in many cases, ethnic groups do not choose to join the dominant social system even when they are economically eligible to do so (e.g., Johnston 1971). This process is found in numerous countries, so that in Britain, in spite of some dispersal, immigrant areas are growing and segregation is increasing and likely to continue to do so (Jones 1970). There are areas in London which are exclusively Indian, where women are not seen in pubs, Indian music plays on juke-boxes, and the different culture is reflected in restaurants and food shops. Such clustering on the basis of a subjective definition of like/unlike, linked to the variability of environmental quality, symbolic meanings, values and lifestyles is important in making environments more congruent with specific groups and in making cities richer and more varied. Encouraging this process would help counteract what could be called increasing social and environmental entropy by stressing differences.

This is not an apologia for Ghettoes based on discrimination but rather a plea for the possibility of choice on the possibility for voluntary associations. Even U.S. sociologists committed to total mixing often stress the difference between "empowering" and "stigmatizing" segregation, although the topic has not been investigated. The subjective definition of commonality and the services needed vary. For example in Sydney, the Seventh Day Adventists built a sanatorium and hospital in Wahroonga: as a result members are now clustering in the vicinity. With the growing importance of the *Marae* (meeting grounds) to Maori culture and the consequent need for urban Marae, there is likely to be a growing clustering of Maoris in New Zealand cities which would also coincide with their rather different housing needs (Austin 1973, in press; Austin and Rosenberg 1971). Another example might be a group of Orthodox Jews, who must not drive on Saturday and need special food and services (such as synagogues and ritual baths) clustering in close proximity, as has happened in the Williamsburg section of Brooklyn and elsewhere. One reason for clustering is to reach "critical mass" so that services can be provided which will, in turn, attract others. Thus the Dutch in Kalamazoo, Michigan, were dispersed when they were few but clustered as soon as their numbers increased; there was even subdivision, with Fresians on the North and Zeelanders on the South with separate service facilities (Jakle and Wheeler 1969), another example of the fine grain of clustering.

Thus, while the process of clustering seems constant, the criteria for clustering change. Since such clustering depends on culture, the reason for clustering will also change with culture so that, for example, in Singapore ethnic homogeneity is changing to economic* while in the U.S. South, after the Civil War, class was the main criterion for separation, later race became the criterion — a process helped by the Black churches (Jackson 1972, pp. 146–147). More generally, since group cohesiveness has major effects on behaviour and family life, the subjective definition of its advantages and disadvantages greatly depends on images, values and beliefs. With change, group allegiance does not disappear but shifts to other criteria, and in all cases groups depend on the subjective definition of in-group and out-group characteristics (Guttentag 1970).

* Personal communication from Dr. Riaz Hassan, University of Singapore.

Some groups clearly desire homogeneity, others may seem to desire heterogeneity along such traditional dimensions as race and socio-economic characteristics. This may be because they have other values in common and such environments meet their ideals and are a result of habitat selection as, for example, the inhabitants of St. Francis Square in San Francisco (Cooper 1970, 1972). Such groups are, in fact, homogeneous. For example those attracted by specific environments, such as Laclede in St. Louis, argue that they wanted heterogeneity. Yet it is clear that this community attracted a very special group (e.g., Reed 1973) which is extremely homogeneous along dimensions such as liberalism, creativity and idealism. Generally cases like these still fit into the schema proposed, as do groups who desire suburban areas (Gans 1969; Eichler and Kaplan 1967; Werthman 1968) and select out within that class of environments (e.g., Berger 1960, 1966; Lansing *et al.*, 1970) or who select to remain in "slums" (e.g., Fried and Gleicher 1961; Hartman 1963).

People like to live with others who belong to the same culture; share values, ideas and norms; understand and respond to the same symbols, agree about child rearing, interaction, density and lifestyle — and hence leisure, food, clothing style, manners and rules. As Confucius taught in the Analects one cannot have friends who are not equals (cited in Duncan 1972, pp. 56—57).

Clustering is thus a general phenomenon with subjectively defined criteria which are variable over time and from place to place. They may be a religion, race, caste, kinship, occupation, class, lifestyle, community of interests, education, stage in life-cycle, place of origin or whatever. In all these cases the key process is habitat selection based on values and environmental preferences. The result is group identity reinforced by clustering, manifested by environmental symbols and contained by boundaries.

A model proposed for a larger scale seems applicable to the city, so that one can speak of the core, domain and sphere of a group (Meining 1965). The *core* is the area of greatest concentration and density of occupation, intensity of organization and strength and homogeneity of culture traits. It may also be the area of closest congruence with the specific environmental image and needs of the group and also contain the special services needed — shrines, institutions, schools, bars and restaurants, hangouts, special shops, clubs and so on. The *domain* are areas where the culture may still be dominant but with markedly less intensity than in the core, fewer bonds of connection and fewer of the specialized services and lower environmental congruence. Finally the *sphere* is that area where the group is in a minority, only certain elements are present and the environment may be non-congruent. This model seems to be applicable to various groups based on religion, ethnicity, age or whatever — for example the elderly in urban areas (Rapoport 1973(d)). Thus, while the traditional city was, in effect, a series of clear cores, the city today is a series of vague cores with major overlaps of domains, with most of the city consisting of a sphere for all groups.

The process of clustering helps cultures survive, provides the appropriate settings for behavior with cues which can be understood, appropriate organizations of meaning and communication, and sharing of symbols and unwritten rules, and congruent activity systems and temporal organizations. Thus people, homogeneous along certain important dimensions, having similar values, behavior patterns, non-verbal communication systems (in fixed, semi-fixed and non-fixed feature space), the same domain definition, and sex and age roles, can more easily take others for granted and need to process less information. By having clear, fixed and recognized areas, boundaries, rules, relationships, social hierarchies, physical devices, space organization, appropriate cues, symbols and markers, there are fewer problems and stress is reduced – one can use informal vs. formalized controls (Rapoport 1974, in press(b)). The result is that predictability is increased, (or unpredictability reduced), with clear effects on perceived density, crowding, overload and stress (Rapoport 1975(b), in press(b)). The environment is made more congruent with the socio-cultural and cognitive environments; its organization of space, time, meaning and communication is clear, easily decoded and social identity expressed.

It should follow that symbolic, lifestyle and other comparable factors should be more important than income. This seems to be the case. For example, new towns in the U.S. and Britain, and working class areas in Australia, all tend to undergo increasing segregation into smaller areas of homogeneity at the neighborhood level based on agreement about education, child rearing, standards and the like. There is habitat selection, and even in an area as homogeneous as Levittown there has been gradual clustering based on occupation, education, religion and ethnicity (Bryson and Thompson 1972; Gans 1969).

It is significant that in Soviet cities also, there is a very strong tendency for people of like status and other social characteristics to interact without dealing with other people. Since housing is assigned, this is not reflected in residential clustering but is reflected in networks, behavioral patterns and behavioral space. The higher the rank of people, the more exclusive their social relations. Even within the limitations of lack of free choice there seems a clear trend towards being with like. Soviet planning is greatly concerned with preventing clustering, for greater control of population, yet there are clear signs of various types of homogeneity developing and some very striking examples, such as at Akademgorodok, a scientific town (in itself homogeneous), where homogeneity which depends on academic status is reflected in housing allocation and leads to very rigid divisions (Frolic 1971).

Homogeneity based on the subjective definition of like and unlike is important because homogeneity seems to be associated with increased neighboring, although the evidence is not unequivocal. While there is evidence that interaction may be independent of homogeneity (e.g., Knapp 1969) there is more evidence to the contrary (e.g., Gans 1961(a), (b); Gutman 1966; Barnlund and Harland 1963; Keller 1968). There is also evidence that when people are able to withdraw to areas where they feel at home and confident, they interact more at other times and places (e.g., Ittelson 1960; Michelson 1969). Generally, then, the effects of homogeneity or neighboring are accepted (Feldt *et al.* (n.d.)). The key seems to be the distinction between subjectively and "objectively" defined homogeneity, with the former being significant. This may help explain apparently anomalous findings – that while racial heterogeneity increases crime, socio-economic heterogeneity does not (Sawicky 1971, p. 194).

In addition to the greater satisfaction and lesser conflicts of homogeneous areas they are also better able to govern themselves since it is easier to agree on decisions and have "pervasive consensus" when there is homogeneity (Gans 1972, pp. 120 ff., 176), when there is a clear image of what a suitable environment and behavior are (e.g., Eichler and Kaplan 1967; Werthman 1968); one person who is greatly at odds can wreck the system (e.g., Vernon 1962). Through clustering a consensus can emerge permitting areas to have some direction and self government which is extremely difficult in heterogeneous areas (Bryson and Thompson 1972). Thus where neighboring is important, (and the more homogeneity the more neighboring), different forms of cooperation may emerge than in areas where membership in formal organizations is a substitute. Since these two forms are often incompatible, cooperation becomes difficult. At the same time each form separately works better than the population is homogeneous.

For example, mobile home parks are village-like enclaves in the city and are the result of habitat selection; income alone is not a sufficient explanation since Blacks, for example, do not buy trailers for retirement. They are voluntary enclaves, private and based on high sociability and neighborliness, and defined by fences and gates which symbolize control and safety. Because of this intense sociability, people are expected to conform closely to moral and social standards, rules and regulations relating to cleanliness, pets and maintenance of trailers and lawns; gardens and patio furniture indicate status. These informal rules and controls, which depend on homogeneity and which are expressed in lifestyle, leisure activities and the like, ensure decorum; the separation of public and private enables community and sociability to develop by knowing who belongs (S. Johnson 1971). An important aspect may be what is done where, such as rules regarding street use. For example, Japanese living in Australia found the sight of people eating as they walk down streets, even an ice cream cone, "nauseating" (*The Australian* 1972(b)). Another reason may be to desired interaction levels (e.g., Feldt *et al.* (n.d.)) so that the elderly frequently do not want younger people around (e.g., Hochschild 1973).

Once cities acquire such homogeneous areas they affect behavior: they constrain peoples' lifespace and movement space, make some areas attractive to visit and others to be avoided at all costs. Their presence, distribution and relative attractiveness will then affect peoples' knowledge and mental maps of the city and further use. The use or non-use of facilities not only reflects preference and affects use space, but also influences social networks. Different communities differ in their networks and hence in their need for clustering, nature of settings, behavioral rules and symbols. It must be stressed again that the homogeneity may not be the one expected *a priori*. For example, some studies deny that working class areas are homogeneous (Bleiker 1972). However, people in one such area studied disliked transients, i.e. they were homogeneous in temporal terms, and also in terms of standards of behavior regarding noise, tidiness and so on. For example, new *owners* who conformed to these standards were accepted. There was thus homogeneity although not that defined in sociological terms. It also appears that there were three even more homogeneous subgroups in the area (an example of the fine grain of clustering) using different symbols such as curtains, clothing and cars respectively (Bleiker 1972).

The "visibility" of cues identified with groups is important in the perception of clustering and hence the behavior of other groups. Thus in Omaha, Nebraska there was a good deal of residential dispersion, even among immigrants, and no national group ever formed a majority in an area larger than one half mile square. But neighborhoods did acquire an ethnic identity due more to the visibility of concentrations of businesses and institutions associated with particular ethnic groups than from residential clustering (Chudacoff 1971). Three points can be made. Firstly, it is subjectively defined homogeneity which is important and affects behavior. Secondly, in order for such businesses and institutions to survive some minimum degree of clustering is needed. Thirdly, businesses and institutions were possibly used in these judgements because they are more clearly identifiable than houses — although the latter can be identified, often through landscaping, as in the case of Japanese and Mexican houses in Los Angeles (Rapoport 1969(a), p. 131, fn. 15) (see also Chapter 6). Such businesses and institutions also tend to be along major roads which are more widely travelled than residential streets, contributing to their greater visibility; they also play a larger role in people's construction of mental maps. This suggests how the appearance of differences among areas can be created without excessive segregation, and how their existence can be stressed perceptually.

Clustering also occurs in squatter settlements (Butterworth 1970; Mangin 1970). There also the criteria are subjective and the grain is very fine. Thus in Argentina townspeople grouped all squatters as an outgroup, while the squatters themselves used different criteria leading to much internal differentiation (MacEwen 1972), i.e., the grouping into like and unlike varies inside and outside the area, as does the fineness of the distinctions. These areas within the squatters settlement are identified with the social characteristics of their inhabitants and, when physical demarcations also exist, they come to symbolize the socio-economic position of the inhabitants. The settlement thus has many fine gradations in status from high to low, and urban to rural, and the closer to town the higher the status; the subjective perception of variation is also much greater than the objective. In the case of a fairly small squatter settlement in Rabat, there was also a division into quite distinct and separate areas by place or origin, age, occupation, house ownership, recency of arrival and tribal origin (Pettonnet 1972).

The reasons for clustering in such cases are similar to others, but even more acute in terms of mutual help, assimilation and urbanization, and the preservation of certain institutions. Clustering helps maintain and recreate networks, use familiar controls and cultural patterns. Generally residence in homogeneous or heterogeneous areas seems to have very different effects. In Canada, for example, the former lead to more confidence, more assimilation into the majority culture while preserving ethnic identity; because of less prejudice, people are freer to accept the outer culture while their cultural breakdown is inhibited. Homogeneous areas lose members slowly and will remain a fact for a long time. The major factor in cultural breakdown is education (Borhek 1970) but this is not inevitable: biculturalism can develop, as among Puerto Ricans in New York (Hoffman and Fishman 1971) particularly since in homogeneous areas specialized schools and other institutions can easily develop.

In order to survive such groups must stress certain cultural characteristics, be able to communicate easily, exercise control over socialization and marriage and be able to use appropriate symbols. The greater the stress the more important this "defensive structuring" becomes (Siegel 1970), but in all cases clustering helps and is thus important for the preservation of culture. For example, even in the U.S., most marriages occur among people who live close (75% within 20 blocks, 35% within 5 blocks) (World Federation of Mental Health 1957). In Wales, the loss of Welsh language and culture seems at least partly due to the inability to cluster, and hence lack of critical mass for chapels, schools — or even enough Welsh-speaking children (Rosser and Harris 1965, p. 133). In the case of the Caribbean, the same ethnic group (East Indians) survived culturally where they were able to cluster and did not survive where they were scattered (Ehrlich 1971).

One of the facts involved is clearly criticality. People who are already under great stress need the support of familiar and even "prosthetic" environments, so that groups who have lowered competence, or are in a state of cultural environmental docility, are more vulnerable (Rapoport 1972(d), 1974). There is empirical evidence from gerontology that when docility is lowered, homogeneity effects (among other environmental effects) are heightened (e.g., Gubrium 1970; Howell 1972). This, of course, explains the greater clustering of immigrant, squatter and urbanizing groups. Thus a town like Lae (New Guinea) is divided into areas of people of similar ethnic and linguistic background (*wantoks*). Networks are maintained with others of like kind in and out of town and all associations — voluntary, occupational or religious — are ethnically exclusive; people see themselves, and are organized, primarily in these terms (Lucas 1972). Ethnicity does not have to be the criterion, however; in Philippine cities it does not seem to be (e.g., Doeppers 1974), although ethnic and religious segregation seems to occur at the regional and village level. The Toba Batak, in Sumatra, organize in ethnic groups which did not exist before they moved to the city, but which preserve the structural principles of descent, territory and alliance; traditional patterns are applied in cities as ethnic clustering with networks maintained even to distant clusters and to "back home" (Bruner 1972). The planning importance of homogeneity in such migrant contexts is clear from the fact that the success of settlements established in Argentina seems related to it (since mixed colonies did not work): this is helped by the ability to choose the setting and reproduce certain environmental features in terms of space organization, house forms, services and family structure (Eidt 1971). Generally the success of rural migrants to cities depends on the ability to maintain urban villages, as has been so successfully done in Mexico City (Lewis 1965) and we have already noted the variety of areas in 19th c. U.S. cities during a period of rapid migration (Jackson 1972, pp. 205–206; Ward 1971) as well as the example of Australia today. In the case of Mexico City the assumption that immigrants adopt the traits of the majority seems wrong. they tend to settle with their own kind, preserve their lifestyle and culture, maintain network links within their areas and with home areas as well as preserving the patio-complex type of dwelling as long as possible. Wherever possible relatives and compadres live around the patio and sex separation while eating, and other customs, are retained.

In Cairo, also, immigrants form villages in the city which are related to the direction from which they come and thus their "port of entry" (cf. Australian Aborigine camps) (Rapoport 1972(e) and the Irish in London (Young and Wilmott 1973)). Not only is there clustering but the physical environment is so structured that it allows some patterns to survive, slowing transition, helping assimilation and reducing stress (Abu-Lughod 1969). This is also happening in Piraeus (Hirschon and Thakudersai 1970) and elsewhere, and seems to be a general phenomenon. If outside pressures were reduced, this would be even more prevalent. It would seem to be a most desirable strategy in developing and developed cities alike.

For example, the preservation of traditional patterns may be important not only for the survival of cultures but for the successful integration of villages into growing cities. A city which consists of homogeneous areas can more successfully incorporate a village, without destroying it, than can an undifferentiated city. Thus a city composed of a series of villages, such as the Kampongs of a traditional Indonesian city or quarters of a Moslem city, could easily engulf a village without destroying it, and grow differently than a more uniform city where such a village would have little chance of survival. (See Fig. 5.3).

The prevalence and desire for homogeneity is in conflict with planning ideology which is often based on forced heterogeneity which may be as bad as forced segregation. Voluntary association may be best. Planners both in developed and developing countries aim for heterogeneity (e.g., Chermayeff and Tzonis 1971) yet it is difficult to see why, except in the case where it is a deliberate device radically to "change" society (e.g.,

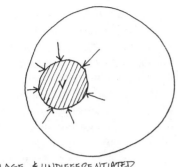
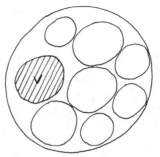

VILLAGE & UNDIFFERENTIATED
CITY

VILLAGE IN CITY OF "VILLAGES"

FIG. 5.3.

Sennett 1970). One argument is that heterogeneity reduces prejudice. Yet there is serious doubt that forced mixing would reduce prejudice — it may, in fact, increase it. When people select their habitat they evaluate others better than when they are forced to live with others, when there may be increased negative feelings (Festinger and Kelly 1951). If areas are homogeneous, with the security of a home base, people accept the proximity of strangers and those unlike themselves better than when there is heterogeneity. We have already seen that homogeneity seems to increase neighboring; in animals also the availability of a secure and familiar territory will increase gregariousness (Eckman *et al.* 1969).

Generally, a major influence on the evaluation of neighborhood quality is keeping out strangers: the main use of open space is as a barrier for this purpose (others are recreation and aesthetics) (James and Brogan 1974). The satisfaction with neighborhood depends on the perception of good neighbors which depends, at least partly, on homogeneity with respect to various characteristics — such as age, socio-economic level, values (mainly child rearing), and leisure interests (Sanoff and Sawhney 1972). Environmental quality is also importantly related to maintenance and aesthetics, i.e., shared environmental characteristics. Forced heterogeneity thus often leads to the deterioration of neighborhoods, and an important factor is the different allocation of resources and hence different treatment and maintenance of houses.

Thus clustering in towns is due partly to the symbolism of the environment expressing and communicating attitudes and values (Eichler and Kaplan 1967; Werthman 1968). In Colombia, for example, two subcultural groups at the same economic level responded very differently to the environment into which they were moved. The Mestizos stressed raising their income, home improvement, the house as the center of social life and symbol of social position and use of urban institutions; the Negroes had no interest in the house and its improvement and the stress on extended kinship led to economic levelling. The former wished to become urban working class, the latter better-off rural proletariat. The physical results were that Mestizos improved the front area of the house, sidewalks and the yard, enclosed and elaborated the front wall and windows and improved house interiors, while the Negroes made no improvements; Mestizos pen animals, Negroes let them run free (Ashton 1972). The potential for conflict if these two groups are mixed is quite clear and the design of homogeneous areas would seem to be strongly indicated, possibly with areas close enough for learning by one group from the other.

Small homogeneous areas with clear boundaries may, in fact, help integration. Studies in England following Asian immigration have shown that the relationship of proximity, contact and attitudes are complex, and that it is difficult to predict which areas will be "tolerant" or intolerant but prejudice seems highest where physical integration is highest and vice-versa. Proximity and shared pubs lead to greater prejudice than housing segration; on the other hand work integration leads to more liberal views, and there are also differences related to the particular Asian group and the congruence of their values and norms with those of the majority population [i.e., the conceptual distance between them and definition of like/unlike (cf. Rapoport 1974)]. Also, in some cases the identity is based on the family whereas other groups stress group identity; anything which erodes that is seen as a threat so that in one place neighborhood proximity relieves anxiety, in others – produces it. When the physical form of an area and its structure are clear, there is certainty and confidence and less feeling of threat than when the area is vague and there are fears of further erosion. Thus stable, well defined areas can tolerate more outsiders than vague ones (Marsh 1973). This would follow from the fact that if one can avoid confrontation by using smaller reference groups with more limited versions of success, then each socially homogeneous group can develop its own pride and respect; the more people are heterogeneous the more clash of norms and stress (e.g., Pahl 1971, pp. 27–28, 91). The importance of clarity and security suggests that areas of homogeneity would be important in *reducing* prejudice, particularly if groups can meet on neutral ground (such as workplaces).

Thus a defended neighborhood needs three elements: (1) distinct boundaries, unified ownership and design, agreed-upon use of streets and other facilities, and comprehensible cues and symbols, (2) some name, image or identity which people can accept and with which they can identify, and (3) some form of subjectively defined homogeneity (e.g., Suttles 1972).* The importance of such clearly marked residential areas can be seen in New York where the elimination of clear boundaries has led to clashes.† It seems clear that proximity is more acceptable and works better when there is homogeneity at the residential level with clear and unambiguous boundaries, and the attempts of planners to break the homogeneity of areas leads to major conflict unrelated to prejudice. Given interaction on "neutral" ground, the heterogeneity of Upper Broadway (Starr 1972) may be partly due to the use of private schools and also to residential clustering near it: people meet on the neutral street and retreat to homogeneous areas. (See Fig. 5.4).

The provision of special places for interaction does not always work, partly because of the subjective evaluation of their adequacy and desirability; i.e., the "neutrality" of places and services is a matter of subjective definition, will vary for different groups, and is a subject for research rather than *a priori* assumptions. Thus while the provision of services does lead to the identification with local community (e.g., Feldt *et al.* (n.d.)) it is not the actual use of facilities which affects individuals' sense of community but their perception of the supply (Sawicki 1971, p. 24); these perceptions are likely to be variable, and the role and the effect of facilities is rather complex.

In cases of extreme threat such as Northern Ireland even relatively neutral uses such as shopping become segregated [an example of "defensive structuring" (Siegel 1970;

---

* I came across Suttles (1972) after finishing the third draft of this book. Much of his argument reinforces the conclusions which I reached independently.
† Dr. Albert E. Scheflen in lecture, August 1973.

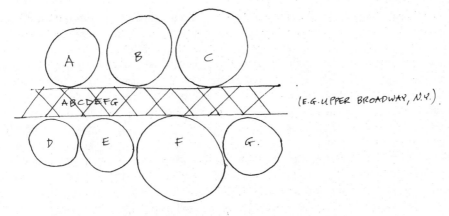

FIG. 5.4. Interaction of homogeneous groups on adjoining "neutral" ground.

Rapoport, in press(c)] , and attempts to build new towns which are heterogeneous do not succeed. In fact, there is increasing separation by religion and proximity to existing settlements of the same type. Once an area takes on a particular image it is perpetuated — a process helped by the design of the new town which consists of areas of 50—400 houses of unique design and color separated by space (Reid 1973). We have already seen that this process seems general in new towns so that scattering single executive houses in order to attract middle and upper classes will not work. Such houses must be grouped but with provision for interaction on a neutral ground. In effect, then, clustering is a form of symbol and image manipulation which cannot be ignored if new towns are to work (Knittel 1973); clustering must be given physical expression, i.e., made noticeable (Rapoport 1972(a)).

The relationship between homogeneity, heterogeneity and prejudice is thus far from clear or simple and, if anything, suggests that homogeneous areas may reduce prejudice. It also seems clear that homogeneous areas have lower delinquency and crime rates than heterogeneous ones regardless of poverty. If homogeneity and cohesiveness can be maintained, then low delinquency and crime rates are possible even during industrialization and the upheaval of rapidly developing areas (e.g., Guttentag, p. 114). In addition, the preservation and creation of homogeneous areas provides a greater range of physical and social environments and services, and hence habitat selection opportunities. It also leads to much higher levels of urban complexity.

The importance of clustering for migrants and other populations under stress relates to the concept of the pacer. From them one can derive the idea of the "half-way house" where the environment is graduated so as to allow people slowly to adjust to particular conditions. This has been used at the architectural scale for the handicapped; at the urban scale it has been developed in the suggestion for Asian cities where the individual might gradually be able to move from an area much like his rural village to a completely urban, highly sophisticated setting (Meier 1966).

Even suburban dispersal has partly perpetuated group clustering. Suburbs are not uniform; they have great cultural variety, combining class, ethnic origin, religion and lifestyle. They often represent symbolically enclosed residential communities, and are successful when they provide an appropriate setting for people and their institutions; a variety of settings for various groups as a pluralist alternative seems important (Berger 1966), particularly since pluralism seems to be increasing in the U.S. (Isaacs 1972) and as people move out of the old ethnic areas they form new ones (DeVise 1973).

It would, therefore, appear that whatever the merit of any specific form of clustering in a given context, on balance the advantages of the process greatly outweigh the disadvantages — in spite of current social, political and planning dogma. Recall that such clustering can be distinguished from forced segregation and reflects the desire that the socio-cultural and environmental characteristics of groups dominate the residential environment (Rose 1969).

The rather complex case Negro areas in the U.S. can be seen in the framework of the identification of a group with a particular area. Any attempt to alter that assignment results in both covert and overt group conflict (Rose 1970). It seems clear that while in the case of Negroes in the U.S. there is an element of choice, there is also a major element of coercion, and it does appear that unlike the case of other groups coercion is dominant (Taeuber 1965). An interesting and important question is what degree of self-segregation might occur by race or by other criteria — (such as lifestyle) given a free choice situation.

There are several advantages to clustering — greater congruence of environment and lifestyle, reduction of stress and conflict and, possibly, less prejudice and crime; lesser deterioration of housing and urban areas; greater complexity and richness of the urban environment. This general principle seems applicable to all cities — developing and developed: in all there should be homogeneous areas (although their definition will vary as will the criteria of homogeneity) with common meeting grounds. Adjoining groups should not be too far separated in terms of norms, values, lifestyles and symbols, unwritten rules, privacy, non-verbal communication and so on — i.e., the environment should communicate. The scale of such areas should be fairly small. Although their size has not been investigated, it will clearly need to vary with the nature of the group and its use of the environment, the "critical mass" needed to maintain them and other variables. Some groups seek heterogeneity; for some the setting is unimportant, for others it needs to be prosthetic (Lawton 1970(a); Rapoport 1972(d)).

This notion can be applied to urban environments in two ways: — what is needed compared to what is available, leading to the design of the supplement; or in terms of complementarity regarding various psychological, social and cultural variables. For example, if people tend to work in noisy, depersonalizing settings, environments may need to be quiet and involving. Given a certain level of stimulus, the environment may need to provide the opposite, i.e., the environmental needs and stimulus levels of various groups (age, lifestyle, occupational, cultural or whatever) differ and the design of areas depends on their homogeneity.

The urban environment should be composed of many varied settings, the specificity of which reflects that of the various more or less homogeneous groups which compose them (although the dynamic nature of urban systems demands a considerable level of open-endedness (see Chapter 6)). Portions of this variety of settings would be accessible so that it could be experienced, if desired, in a given period of time and via a variety of routes. This would lead to greater complexity not only by increasing noticeable differences through uniqueness and specificity, but also because the areas of different groups will have different complexity levels.

The isolation of such settings is unlikely, since interaction often increases under such conditions and is helped by the provision of potential interaction and meeting places, which are carefully related to relevant activity systems, include relatively similar groups, carefully related to temporal rhythms and house-settlement systems — so that they are truly neutral.

Cities need areas of common significance. Such areas of greatest common significance, symbolic, use or cognitive, should be most easily accessible to most people and, as areas become more specific, they should become less accessible. Both the commonality and consistency of general elements, and the uniqueness and specificity of specialized settings, needs to be emphasized. Thus zoning (assuming it is valid in the first case) must be congruent with the characteristics of the various groups and may vary in different areas. For example, in some areas strict single-family zoning is desirable, necessary and appropriate, in other situations people may surround themselves with kin and will exchange houses to do so, as well as changing the dwellings themselves (Hirschon and Thakudersai 1970) or will manipulate the system to achieve kin clustering (Young and Wilmott 1962). Single family zoning then becomes undesirable and prevents the formation of kin-clusters which are highly desired and desirable (e.g., Wilmott 1963). Also, as areas and elements become more specific and local, their open-endedness should also go up, to increase the impact and influence of groups of ever greater homogeneity, and thus better able to cooperate; if it is desired that areas be self-governing as much as possible there must be some minimal levels of homogeneity. The dwelling responds to the individual and the family; the block, neighborhood and district respond to various groups.

Socio-Cultural Aspects of the City

It should now be clear that socio-cultural variables play a major role in urban environments. Yet the design literature has stressed a unitary urban environment, while the urban sociology and ecology literature has neglected the design implications of urban differentiation. In order to be able to incorporate such material in design it needs to be investigated in more detail. I will discuss the communicative aspects of this in more detail in Chapter 6. At this point, some of these, as well as some concepts coming from sociology, anthropology and ethology, need to be reviewed as they relate to the form of the city and how it might better be organiz(d.

Rather than review the voluminous literature on urban sociology, ecology, geography and the like, it is more useful to see different groups as dividing their conceptual, social and behavioral spaces differently, maintaining different social networks and using different environmental cues and symbols. There are situations where rigid hierarchies exist, relying on mutual knowledge, clearly defined public and private domains, where physical space is highly congruent with social and conceptual structure. There are other cases where groups who maintain extended networks based on community of interest do not rely on spatial contiguity either for control, satisfaction and friendship.

These lead to different forms of residential areas. The different choices of perceptual and accessible distance from one another will be reflected in various environmental characteristics of house form, lot size, density, landscaping, proximity of facilities, use of streets and the house settlement system. Homogeneous areas, therefore, reflect the complementary notions of a number of people with subjectively perceived similar characteristics. A major explanatory variable is lifestyle (Michelson 1966; Michelson and Reed 1970). It is also related to the choice model presented earlier: the allocations and choices made among alternatives reflect some hierarchy of values. The environment of such groups incorporates what they value most in terms of spaces, things, landscapes, symbols, time allocations, behaviors, relationships, activities and the like, rather than their value systems *per se*.

In fact lifestyle and the nature, location and timing of activities may be the most useful way of understanding the socio-cultural aspects of the city and integrating approaches such as social networks, activity systems, time allocations, and behavior settings.

If, as I have argued, the shaping of the built environment is related to images, values and symbols, and if the environment acts on people through the way it communicates (i.e., if cognitive schemata operate at both ends of the process) it follows that traditional and vernacular environments provide a better fit between the organization of space, time, meaning and communication, and culture, i.e., there is better congruence between physical and conceptual space. Since schemata are shared they communicate and provide appropriate behavior settings. The closest comparable example today may be a homogeneous area — a setting for people of like lifestyle which communicates in fixed feature, semi-fixed feature and non-fixed feature space. People cluster together because they share unwritten rules and non-verbal communicative devices, environmental and behavioral, which make it easier to maintain the particular lifestyle and also reduces stress. In large cities people are constantly exposed to other people and their artefacts; an area of people with similar behavioral, spatial and artifactual codes provides a retreat, reduces stress and eliminates conflict. In areas of unlike codes people easily misread behavioral, territorial and object cues and overload may result.

We have already seen that one of the elements of variable environmental quality is the different proximity of various services and facilitates. If this is combined with the pacer frequency of the complexity of leisure activities, and hence those activities considered to be recreational, clustering will again be advantageous, whether it be the use of corner taverns (as on the South side of Milwaukee), the use of streets and stoops in many working class areas, the presence of poolrooms or whatever. It is thus frequently possible to "read" the makeup of an area from such facilities so that in Golders Green, London, there are no betting shops or pubs but many food and cake shops while in Kentish Town, with its very different population, there are no fine food and cake shops but an amazing number of betting shops and pubs.

Other characteristics which lead to clustering may be family type, friendship patterns, the importance of status, extent of home range, distinction in domains of public/private or front/back, the nature of the house-settlement system and so on. Many of these have been said to be related to "culture". This is a concept which is far from easy to define (e.g., Kroeber and Kluckhohn 1952) but all definitions accept that, in some way, it involves a group of people who have a set of values and beliefs which are learned and transmitted, which create a system of rules and habits, and lead to a lifestyle. This is partly a matter of choice in resource and time allocation, housing, leisure preferences and so on, reflecting an ideal and embodying images and schemata. These choices apply to manners, behavior, food, rules, gestures, kinship and built form, and are all related, show regularities and form a system which, if understood, can be highly illuminating. The habitual choices made, how they are organized and their regularities are what is called style — whether of the built environment or of life — and they are related to images.

Yet we saw in Chapter 1 that culture is too broad a term to be useful in design and that it is useful to try and begin with activities (Rapoport, in press(a) and see Fig. 1.9.). Lifestyles tend to persist and there is no inevitability that they will disappear. In fact, design for them will help them survive (Burns 1968; Rapoport 1972(d)) and clustering helps.

In any group, members interact more with each other than with others; they do so to achieve certain aims and this becomes possible through the sharing of norms, roles, status of members (cf. next section parallel animals), and agreement about role, status, hierarchies and unwritten rules. These structure behavior which requires appropriate settings. Some groups are extremely dependent on settings and cannot function without a specific locus; others are less so dependent. No groups however are totally independent of some locus, and behavioral space is structured into sets of places, barriers and paths generated by groups. The variations among these may be due to differences in culture and in definitions of life-space equivalents (e.g., Paulsson 1952; Lewin 1951).

The urban groupings discussed are complemented by primary social groups — family, special interest groups or loyalty groups. These differ: e.g., among upper classes neighboring is less important and private life-space dominates neighborhood relations, whereas there are very different relations in working class areas. For some groups their areas are status related; status is subjectively defined using different criteria and for such groups the physical environment reflects the symbols used to affirm status *vis-à-vis* other groups. Such differences may even exist at the housing project scale, where groups differing in social status show major differences in home range with lower status groups having restricted ones; use different symbols in dwellings, so that color, materials, styles, and barriers are used to distinguish these groups. They also have different time schedules which may generate conflicts. Mixing with unlike is resisted and, when it occurs, does so on neutral ground (Boeschenstein 1971). For lower-class people the dwelling is a retreat, whereas for middle and upper groups, who tend to have wider home ranges and greater use of social facilities, it is a way of indicating status (Rainwater 1966) and there are differences in the definition of public and private domains. Thus at this scale the paradigm of the larger scale applies — proximity with separation, withdrawal and interaction on neutral ground.

This difference in the extent of home range, dwelling and residential area as a retreat, or extensive use of facilities, relates to the notion of networks. Each individual in the city has a network of relationships with various people and places which vary, but are more similar for members of any group than among groups. The organization of space and how places are related is, therefore, important since they reflect and reinforce orbits and networks. Such social spaces consist of places and paths rather than surfaces.

Networks tend to be different in rural and urban settings. Networks link roles and a number of major types of role categories have been proposed: kinship, ethnic, economic, political, ritual and religious, and recreational. In urban areas such roles are sometimes more separated than in rural although there are major variations in the city among various groups in the extent of overlap or separation (Frankenberg 1967, pp. 248–251) and, in some cases, the urban-rural distinction is not useful (e.g., Lapidus 1969). There is also evidence that the distincting proposed between the friendship in rural, and isolation in urban, areas is invalid (e.g., Sutcliffe and Crabbe 1963). Thus it is the form and kind of networks which are important. Yet the physical and social environment affects such networks — they depend on culture, values, attitudes to neighboring, status aspirations, lifestyle, age, stage in lifecycle, activity systems and many other characteristics. They also depend on the nature of settings — activity spaces, house-settlement systems, distance — physical and functional — barriers, climate, temporal rhythms, density and so on.

For example, in Bethnal Green the friendship pattern is in small areas and takes place among kin on the street while in Dagenham it is more widespread and takes place more formally (Young and Wilmott 1962; Wilmott 1963). In the former group loyalty to small areas is reinforced by specific symbols — a particular plant in the front window, a particular breed of dog, curtains of particular color (Townsend 1957, pp. 12—13). Close networks tend to occur in homogeneous groups because propinquity tends to lead to marriage, and marrying within the group is still most important: residential location affects whom one marries (Timms 1971, pp. 12—13). There are also influences on child rearing, with whom children play, and what they learn from their peer group.

Living in a particular place with like people affects networks. The connections between an individual, his family, peer-groups, voluntary associations and many other groups tend to be facilitated (although not determined), even among the least space bound, by proximity and face-to-face contact, since non-verbal communication can then operate and it seems clear that such non-verbal aspects are the major element of communication (e.g., Mehrabian 1972; Buehler *et al.* 1966); homogeneity is essential, however, for these to be understood.

Networks have recently been studied by urban anthropologists, although their spatial aspects have been neglected (Mitchell 1971; Wolfe 1970; Epstein 1969). The number, strength and nature of the links between an individual and his various contacts have been studied but not their extent or shape, except at an abstract level of primary zone structure, second order star structure, second order zone structure and the like (Barnes 1971).* Even in specifically urban studies spatial factors tend to be neglected (e.g., Heiskannen 1969) although they would be most useful. For example, among Samoans in the U.S., the retention of social units and affective links helps integration and urbanization without loss of culture, and is aided by proximity, yet these spatial aspects tend to be neglected (e.g., Ablon 1971). Yet in addition to real shape and extent, which can be related to home range, one could also consider areas where most network links occur (best known and most used areas) and the differences in networks among various groups, as well as for specific purposes — social, shopping, medical and the like. Networks are, therefore, potentially extremely useful.

Networks could potentially also help to distinguish among various groups. We have already seen that women in the U.S. have different home ranges and hence also networks (Everitt and Cadwallader 1972; Orleans and Schmidt 1972; Orleans 1971). In Africa also neighborhood is more important for women since they are housebound (which is expressed in their networks). Thus networks are related to home areas, home ranges, and a number of important planning concepts such as activity systems in space and time (e.g., MacMurray 1971; Chapin 1968, 1971; Chapin and Hightower 1966; Brail and Chapin 1973). This could then help in the definition of groups, and their areas (by locating discontinuities in network links), location of neutral zones, placement of routes with least interference with important networks and activities. We have seen that the congruence between social, conceptual and physical space may vary (at least in theory) between 0% and 100%; the use of networks could help determine precisely the type of overlap existing, and hence best provided. The temporal distribution of activities could also be

---

* Some attempt has recently been made by a student of mine, Patrick J. Meehan in an M.Arch thesis (An approach to the use of social network analysis as an urban design and planning tool), School of Architecture and Urban Planning, University of Wisconsin-Milwaukee, May 1975.

studied through networks; knowing networks in space and time may help with the design of appropriate spatial structures for various groups (e.g., Anderson 1971) and for specific sets of activities.

For example, different groups, with different tempos and rhythms have potential conflicts in synchronization. By the temporal distribution of interactions of various groups, meeting can either be encouraged or discouraged through juxtaposition and the placing of facilities (Parkes 1972, 1973; Lynch 1972). For example, in the case of the elderly, it is likely that their changed day and night schedule affects which groups in the city they encounter or miss. (Rapoport 1973(d)). The effects are more critical for the elderly, young and women than active men (e.g., Gubrium 1970; Athanasiou and Yoshioka 1973) and for groups with certain specific characteristics. Differing schedules may also affect the shared use of facilities and generate conflict as when upper class groups, who start work late and have flexible schedules, make noise in facilities close to working class areas where people have early work and rigid schedules (e.g., Boeschenstein 1971). The locus of such activities and networks is also important and may generate conflict as in cases where the primary socializing place may be the street much to the disapproval of other groups for whom the street is not a meeting place.

Among problems with using network analysis in planning and design are the lack of data and the difficulty of obtaining them: large amounts of information must be processed, there are difficulties in sampling and in communicating data to designers. Another problem is the importance of specifics, so that for particular populations neighboring may be as important as kin networks in other situations. For example in the case of some French working-class people, neighboring networks were of extraordinary strength, and neighbors were critically involved in raising children which in the middle class is the function of the family alone. In this case, therefore, proximity was more important than kinship and an understanding of the spatial dimension of networks becomes a critical factor in appropriate design of a setting for leisure and social life, its relation to the control of delinquency and crime, and the importance of shared customs and values on which all agree (Vielle 1970).

Such design decisions have major effects on child rearing and these are often important considerations in clustering regarding speech patterns, schools and peer group influences (Pahl 1971, p. 111). Inappropriate design affects different groups differently. Thus in the U.S. problems occur with black families where the whole closely linked group (the block) is responsible for controlling children, and designs which make this impossible can have serious consequences (Hall 1971). Similarly in China, child rearing has traditionally been the responsibility of the group, and kin networks are most important so that the wrong form of design at given densities (e.g., high rise, or mixing kin and non-kin) can lead to undesirable social consequences (Mitchell 1971; Anderson 1972).

Design, therefore, should consider the shape, nature and extent of networks and avoid disrupting them and altering social relations. This is clearly related to the definition of neighborhood as a socio-spatial schema. Urban neighborhoods can then be related to lifestyle, so that in Minneapolis-St. Paul five groups — young footloose cosmopolites, blue collar working class, rising young families, mature established households and aged households were distributed and located in the city very differently (Abler, Adams and Gould 1971, pp. 176–178): their networks and neighborhoods were very different — given that such different locational preferences and choices are associated with differences in environmental quality, proxemic and network aspects, use of streets, public/private and front/back domain definition, non-verbal communication and coding, the value of the city as a series of environments of very different character rather than a unitary environment seems clear.

The role of preference and evaluation is very important in all this. One can contrast the anti-urban nature of Anglo-American culture with the pro-urban outlook of continental Europe and the Mediterranean world, but greater specificity is needed as usual. In the U.S. itself there have been marked differences so that, for example, Jews have been described as the most enthusiastic city dwellers with the strongest positive views about the urban environment, very unlike other groups — whether "ethnics" or "White Anglo Saxon Protestants" who tended to dislike the city and idealize the village. This is still reflected in environmental quality preferences today but has also had important implications for urban structure. Generally, in response to these differing ideal images of environments — landscape, housing and lifestyle — WASPS tended to flee the city, ethnic formed urban villages and Jews became city dwellers *par excellence* (Sklare 1972).

The relation of social and spatial structure is mediated by norms, shared rules and expectations not only about what is to be done but even more frequently on what is not to be done (cf. Rapoport 1969(a)). Spatial structure not only reflects but also influences social structure (e.g., Pahl 1968, p. 9). While there are limits to their variability, the differences among places and groups cannot be ignored and overgeneralization about "urban environment" must be avoided.

It can be suggested that the differing approaches of anthropology and sociology are precisely that the latter stresses averages while the former tends to be more aware of differences. The anthropological approach to cities seems important for this reason (e.g., Tilly 1971). There may well be methodological problems with traditional anthropological approaches due precisely to the variety of subcultures which must be tackled with more sociological techniques (e.g., Axelrad 1969).

The different networks and communication flows of different groups have implications for design. The organization of space, time, meaning and communication; barriers, environmental quality and activities affect people's behavioral space and mental maps. All these reflect the different criteria may be to distinguish people from one another. In the traditional Indian city, for example, networks are very complex. People belong to nuclear families, extended families and caste group rather than to the village or city. There are thus links to these groups in other communities both permanent and periodic (e.g., pilgrimages). But the use of networks and information flows allows consideration of non space-bound groups (e.g., Sopher 1969; Anderson and Ishwaran 1965, p. 29—30; Doshi 1969).

The relationship among networks, neighborhood and urban use is also clear from examples already discussed. Thus in Paris the use of the city and extent of networks, and hence importance of neighborhood, are related not only to class and income but also to lifestyle and preferences. The more limited networks of working class people are reflected in the greater importance of the neighborhood — where most relationships take place, very differently to the middle class and greatly influences the use and knowledge of the central city (Lamy 1967). Similarly, differential use of urban areas in Lima by different groups (Doughty 1970) is related to the activities and networks of such groups, their settings and different values, lifestyle, environmental preference and leisure activities — all socio-cultural variables. So are the different preferences for mixing or separation of certain facilities or uses in the city (Chapter 2) which result in specific urban organizations and activity systems.

Values expressed in lifestyle thus also affect activities and consequently particular network types. Thus in the case of the Batak in Sumatra we have already seen that they preserve, in a totally new climatic, social and physical environment their kinship ties. In the changing, ethnically diverse, heterogeneous and dense city they retain a wide variety of ties with other Batak kin based on descent and marriage. In the village these are known but in the city they have to be learned and are established before any interaction. The networks developed are new but designed to preserve the group in a new milieu. In this case it is the nuclear family rather than the individual which joins the urban clan association: the family may become more important due to residence patterns. In the village, while each family has its own house it is located in a patrilinear lineage context; a man's immediate neighbors are kin; a cluster of households form a hamlet, a series of hamlets separated by rice fields constitute a village community. In the city residence is neolocal, the family is physically isolated from lineage mates and relatives and the links, while retained and strengthened, are not spatially expressed (Bruner 1972). An interesting question is what type of physical setting might encourage and help this process.

The change from patrilocal to other forms of residence in the city is fairly general (e.g., Vatuk 1971, 1972) although the rate of change varies; it may be affected by urban form and design for clustering would probably affect such changes. This is likely, given the survival of traditional links in many cities rather than inevitable change to Western patterns (Bruner 1972), not only in spite of lack of design and planning concern for them but in the face of destructive planning. It seems clear that *with* such concern the survival and creative, rather than destructive, adaptation would be far more common.

Samoans, as we have seen, have also adapted to city life as a result of the retention of a traditional social system, with traditional units and affective ties modified for the city. In this case the main social units are extended families and churches. The overlapping bonds deriving from kinship, church and ethnic-linked occupations are so pervasive as to constitute a little community within the city with close social links and a specific lifestyle in terms of language, habits, clothing and food. Samoans live as close together as is practicable (several minutes apart by car), interact little with non-Samoans in the several working class neighborhoods where they live — most contacts are with family, church members and work mates; they get jobs for each other and there is much mutual help generally (Ablon 1971). It would be most interesting to discover the environmental preferences, residential patterns and degree of clustering, although the experience of other Polynesian groups (e.g., in New Zealand) suggests that both clustering and specific design features would be desired; to design appropriate environments, and to investigate the effects of such a clustered and culture-specific milieu (although this has already been predicted in general terms, e.g., in terms of coping with information overload and stress).

One can interpret the flight to the suburbs in such terms. People fled from strangers with different lifestyles and cultures, who were no longer able to elicit anticipated responses: there was thus increased stress, a loss of feeling of group identity and loss of a protected and protective environment. People no longer used, or responded to, appropriate cues and neighbors could no longer be assumed to honor traditional rights and obligations — or abstain from proscribed activities. The flight to the suburb was then a search for a place where all those things still operated and hence for a reduction of stress. At the same time there was a search for an environment more congruent with ideal images. Thus, as in the case of traditional cities and migrant areas, when able to, people selected to live with others like themselves in environments compatible with their tastes and ideals. This is quite different to, and at odds with, the rather romanticized heterogeneous environments often advocated (e.g., Sennett 1970; Chermayeff and Tzonnis 1971). Membership in a group can act as a stress reducing device for the individual and even being surrounded by a legible and predictable social and physical environment will greatly reduce stress and enable greater openness: ethnic groups which were minorities where they lived had higher incidence of disease and various social maladjustments (Holmes 1956; Dunham 1961; Miscler and Scotch 1963); thus, as density and other overload factors increase, clustering of like groups becomes more important (Rapoport 1975(b); in press(b)). Since a major stress factor in residential settings is fear of change, then exposure to different people — changes in the types of people encountered, their noises, smells, gestures, clothing and environmental symbols — can be highly stressful and threatening.

The search for stress reduction may lead to selection of habitats very different from suburbs. For example, working class neighborhoods and urban villages (space bound and linked to a place) or others relying on the protection of design, doormen and summer houses (i.e., non-space bound). Other individuals and groups may seek higher levels of information and hence heterogeneous areas.

The separation of the city into a series of social worlds then depends on the variety of environmental preferences and the social distance among groups, as well as the evaluation of their separateness. Actual physical distance is not always a good indicator of social distance — it is a matter of subjective distance or separation in social urban space and such boundaries can be more powerful than international boundaries. Thus in El Paso, Texas the social and ethnic barriers are a more effective and important obstacle to human interaction than the international boundary between Mexico and the U.S. (Abler, Adams and Gould 1971, pp. 232–233). That boundary in itself, of course, has led to totally different cultural landscapes in the short space of just over a century (Jackson 1951, 1966(c)) reflecting different environmental preferences, symbolic associations, use of streets and shops, definition of inside and outside, private and public domains and so on (see Chapter 6).

There are several concepts involved in neighboring, including friendship, the various role behaviors appropriate and desired among those living in proximity, and the area itself (Keller 1968). Before people can develop meaningful relationships they must agree about what one can expect of others. The differences among various forms of neighboring and neighborhood are related to different expectations and specific forms and differing importance of the spatial locale. But central to all is the importance of agreement on many subtle matters, often beyond awareness, which homogeneity makes possible.

For social relationships to exist people, individuals or groups, must be aware of each other and their behavior to each other must exhibit regularities; the overall pattern of relationships can be called social structure (Beshers 1962, pp. 19–20). Social organization is related to the physical environment and the cultural system — the knowledge people have of values, beliefs, norms and unwritten rules — and the objects symbolizing these. This is important since, in the city, personal close relationships with most people cannot be established and information is needed on which to base decisions and choices; this information is based on symbols, using criteria which vary from culture to culture. In any one case, areas of the city act as such symbolic markers which help the cohesion of the group made possible by clustering. Often such inconspicuous cues are used in ways which those not in the know may miss, misinterpret or use wrongly.

In many situations there is a persistence of various social and kinship forms for which special urban forms are needed and which planning and design prevent. It is the function of design to enable the various groups to find and create their appropriate settings with resultant greater complexity and more choice. Under such conditions other groups, with similar lifestyle and values, may decide to join the initial groups so that traditional forms of clustering may change and new groupings and forms develop.

For example there is no reason to assume that extended kinship is incompatible with African (or any other) urban society. The question is rather what aspects of traditional social organization are both useful and adaptable to new conditions (e.g., Gutkind 1969). For designers the question is what kinds of urban forms are suitable for these purposes. In Adelaide and other Australian cities kinship ties are still important although they vary with class. It is clear that geographical distance affects kin relationships among the working class more than in middle class areas, and that physical designs affect such relationships. In the inner city of Adelaide, for example, there were kin networks, dropping in, drinking together, and mutual help while in newer areas there were no such links, contacts are by car and telephone, and the differential availability of these has different effects on various groups. People also miss the friendly familiarity, busy atmosphere, local shops and relatives. Life is also more organized and the lifestyle different – relationships more formal and more scheduling necessary (Martin 1967). All these are very similar to London (Young and Wilmott 1962; Wilmott 1963). Generally contact with distant kin is less frequent than with those living near-by, but may still carry great weight so that people see each other at critical times and for longer periods. If there are groups which wish to preserve traditional kinship ties they would be able to do so and design should allow people to remain together whatever the basis of the desired association. It also means that a move to physically similar areas may have totally different results on different groups – both a result of their lifestyle and values and as a function of whether they desire the move or not, which is again related to its congruence with their values.

Thus the location of people in the city, and the nature of their networks and activity patterns (which are related to location of areas) affects their knowledge of the city and hence how they use it. For example, lower class or squatters' children living on the periphery will have very different exposure to, and knowledge of, the city and different access to the rest of it than children from equally poor areas located in the center. Since in U.S. cities the poor live in the center, in Latin America on the periphery and in India in little clusters throughout the city, and also considering the nature of their networks, very different results are to be expected. Given certain purposes, one can then decide where, ideally, particular groups should be located and what environmental characteristics their areas should have.

If cities can be analyzed in terms of communication and information flows (e.g., Meier 1962; Deutsch 1971), then one can argue that different groups have different levels of information and different forms of communication, different sets of people with whom they communicate, different places for communication to occur, and different means are acceptable. The environment can be conceptualized as a set of settings for different forms and levels of communication. Considering the different forms of communication, their channels and levels, may then be another way of understanding the environmental needs of different groups. At the same time the physical environment itself is a message symbol and communicative system with its proper levels of complexity, and can be designed and anticulated for different groups.

Designers have been very keen to generate "connectedness" and interaction, but various groups desire particular levels of interaction, i.e., it is perceived connectedness and continuity which is important. In this connection the argument for the non-place urban realm (Webber 1963) is partly correct although overstated. There *can* be interaction without physical connectedness but it depends on the group and the context. Different groups have different levels of interaction, different forms of networks, different loci for interaction, different territorial needs — telephones and cars may suit some but not others. Social links may be expressed physically (as in the Moslem city) or not (as among the Pomo Indians (Rapoport 1969(a)). Connectedness varies between the public and designers (Lansing and Marans 1969) and between two cultures such as the Navajo and the Pueblo (Rapoport 1969(d)). Contact can be achieved through physical clustering with permanent networks (as in the Eastern Highlands of New Guinea) or through periodic rituals and feasts of scattered populations, as in the Western Highlands. It may thus be possible to study the degree of connectedness and its nature — spatial or temporal — in terms of communication, desired levels, and who is excluded or included (cf. our discussion of density and crowding); the idea of the good life in terms of social interaction is reflected in space, time, use, meaning and communication.

In traditional forms of kinship, social relationships are often simplified by reducing people to a few categories. If this is disrupted by planning and design policy so that families have to be separated, as in Africa, then people next door may be strangers who cannot even speak one's language. Industrial towns and other new areas thus disrupt kinship which is replaced by tribalism (Mitchell 1970). There are two questions here. Firstly, should traditional forms be preserved through design and, secondly, how can the new tribal forms be developed through design.

In a number of countries similar processes seem to be developing — there are signs of an interest in extended families, three generation households and the like. Frequently both public and private housing does not allow such forms to exist. The development of extended kinship forms also has implications for urban design.

Communication involves the separation of some groups and individuals from each other by various devices and the facilitation of communication among others. Families and kin groups are then ways of defining some specially important groups. Different kinds of families have major consequences for housing in cities. For example, as the number of nuclear families increases, more space and more facilities are needed so that the size of cities goes up and their physical density goes down. Smaller households demand more land because more dwellings are needed and each dwelling needs certain service facilities (kitchens, bathrooms and so on); transport and road areas also go up (HUD 1969, p. 16–17). Also as the elderly, for example, move out new building types and social services are needed; similar changes occur for the young. The implications for land use policy, housing, social policy and the house-settlement system are significant (Rapoport 1972(d)).

While this is more directly related to housing it has implications for cities. The clustering process and habitat selection occur partly on the basis of certain types of family structures, sex roles and child rearing. Urban activity systems are related to households (Brown 1970), so that different forms of households will have different activity systems and need different urban settings. For example, an extended family in its compound in a Yoruba city will have different relationships to the rest of the city than a nuclear family, e.g., the extent and degree of localization of networks affects urban form. A less extreme example is provided by the degree of use of the small neighborhood *vis-à-vis* the whole city (e.g., Lamy 1967; deLauwe 1965(a), p. 124). The difference in the extent of the links with other areas of the city is marked, is related to the residence patterns of kin (and their importance), and has clear implications on the provision of services with the area and transport needs to other areas of the city, and is also influenced by the very different use of streets in such different areas.

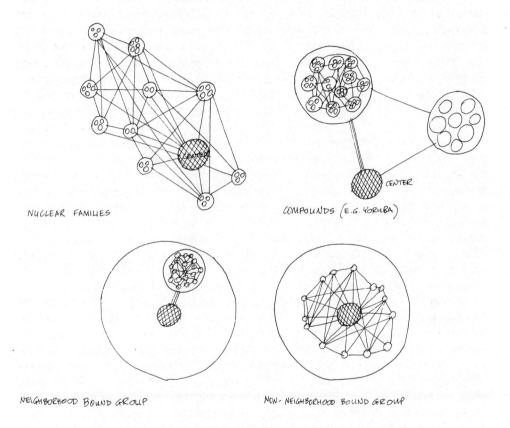

NUCLEAR FAMILIES

COMPOUNDS (E.G. YORUBA)

NEIGHBORHOOD BOUND GROUP

NON-NEIGHBORHOOD BOUND GROUP

FIG. 5.5. Diagrammatic representations of different networks.

Contact with kin also seems to vary with stage in life-cycle and different class groups may have different patterns of "life cycle of kinship" (Martin 1967, p. 54 ff.) and this would vary even more among more varied groups than social classes in Adelaide. One aspect of the relation of life-cycle to environment, the change of home range with age, will be discussed later. Preference for the small house is a deeply engrained cultural value in many countries which relates not only to play space for children, and basic attitudes to nature and privacy, but also to the meaning of family. Shifts in housing preference, with major impact on urban form, often follow changes in family cycle (Alonso 1971, pp. 440–441). There may also be corresponding shifts in preferences for location, the nature of environments, types and proximity of facilities and other urban design variables; intra-urban migration is thus also partly related to stage in life cycle (e.g., Rossi 1952) as are neighboring patterns, the importance of local areas and so on.

More generally the function of the neighborhood in mediating between the individual and the metropolis varies for different groups because of different networks, types and rates of social interaction, environmental needs and need for homogeneity and space boundedness. There are major differences among areas of different social status in terms of sociability, friendship, involvement in various associations and activities and these often depend on family and population structure. Their activities also differ greatly in both manifest and, even more, latent aspects and so do the settings for them. These settings and their relationships form part of the house-settlement system and will be discussed later in more detail. But clearly, differences in the manifest and latent aspects of activities and their settings play a role. For example, Puerto Ricans in New York have very different behavior patterns than Anglos. There are closely knit families, ethnically organized activities, more use of the neighborhood and a very different lifestyle. In fact there are two lifestyles (life is bicultural and one cannot say that acculturation is occurring): a Puerto Rican lifestyle for common everyday activities – eating, shopping, church, dancing and so on, and a more American lifestyle related to work the use of media and the like. Shopping is central to the Puerto-Rican lifestyle – not only do the shops (*bodegas*) carry traditional food but they are also important socially for the maintenance of Puerto Rican life. Within the *bodega* there is an atmosphere not available in a supermarket – all people are Puerto Rican, speak Spanish, and there is a leisurely pace. A man may meet friends for conversation or a game of dominoes inside the shop in the winter, and just outside in the summer (hence the importance of the street). In this setting, among friends and relatives, Puerto Ricans can engage in activities appropriate to their social structure (Hoffman and Fishman 1971). The implications for the physical environment are clear although unexplored. There is some minimum population size and concentration needed to support such stores and make them accessible. They need to be designed to allow for both latent and manifest functions of shopping, the relationship to the street and its use, and so on.

Social interaction and activities in settings also depend on appropriate cues and their relation to unwritten rules. The built environment represents these cues in fixed feature space; signs, landscaping, shops, foods and other object and "furniture" are semi-fixed feature space, while people, their behavior, rules and norms represent non-fixed feature space. All these differ for different groups, communicate differently to them and may also be incongruent with rules and norms (as in the two types of street use).

We have already seen that the wrong spatial organization negatively affects child rearing. Moreover the same spatial arrangements may have different effects on different groups. For example, informal neighboring, the strength and intensity of informal networks, is more important in some areas than others. In such cases the neighborhood may be more important than the dwelling; the proximity of kin and friends critical. Informal networks are then most important in handling conflict, mutual aid and coping with life generally. These informal networks are, at least partly, dependent on the presence of semi-public spaces and facilities present in many such neighborhoods. When such spaces are not provided the system may break down (Yancey 1971; Hall 1971). Without such semi-public spaces, or spaces which can be controlled, the environment affects people differentially – what works for some groups may not work for others and the specific cultural patterns must be known. For example, the lifestyle changes in moving to suburbs differ for different groups and have different effects.

Of course, more than spatial factors are involved. There must be some form of shared norms, views about child rearing and control of children, appropriate and inappropriate behavior and the ability to read non-verbal cues — e.g., the extent of responsibility for certain ambiguous areas, such as hallways and courts (Yancey 1971; Raymond *et al.* 1966). There must also be appropriate defenses; when these are absent, or there is no tradition of how to use them, unwritten rules may become more important. In either case agreement about appropriate behavior and respect for cues must exist. Since changes in social relationships, kinship structure and lifestyle are not due to "urbanization" *per se* but to change in norms and values, and hence pressures towards conformity (Heiskannen 1969), particular changes are not inevitable and depend on value change. There seem to be many cases where such changes are not desired, and clustering becomes important. The provision of a variety of appropriate environments would link habitat selection, environmental preference, social interaction, clustering, lifestyle, activities and appropriate symbols.

Thus the importance of such areas grows in conditions of rapid culture change, and as cities get bigger there is then greater need for intermediate organizations between the individual and the city which can be at various scales — the block, defended neighborhood, community of limited liability and so on (Suttles 1972). Various fixed-feature, semi-fixed feature and non-fixed feature elements indicate with whom it is safe and desirable to interact, and the larger the city the more important do these become. Also many groups have survived for long periods under difficult conditions and have developed ways of coping which could be helped by proper environments. When the cohesiveness of such groups is destroyed, results are bad. We have seen that under conditions of stress defensive structuring leads to an intensification of homogeneity and use of symbols (e.g., Siegel 1970). Also, as social dramas and rituals weaken or disappear, the environment becomes a more important shared symbol and hence more culture specific (e.g., Duncan 1972, p. 60; Lofland 1973).

The Relevance of Ethological Concepts in the City

Ethology has influenced man—environment studies in terms of methodology; in terms of conceptualizations of density, crowding, behavioral sinks, and the role of social organization, hierarchy and ritualized behavior; and, in terms of the effects of social overload, of a set of spatial concepts — which are partly related to crowding and density through spacing. These spatial concepts are extremely useful in understanding man—environment interaction generally and specifically understanding the city as a behavioral system. Regardless of the many disagreements about the relevance of ethological data to humans, ethological thinking has forced a reexamination of human behavior generally. For example, it has re-opened the argument about the continuity of human and animal behavior, the limits on human ways of acting, and thus constancy as opposed to the change, and indefinite flexibility and modifiability of human behavior; the role and importance of phylogenic adaptation and hence maladaptation (e.g., Eisenberg, and Dillon 1971; Esser 1971; Tiger 1969; Tiger and Fox 1966, 1971; Fox 1970; Boyden 1970, 1974 among others). The remarkable complexity in animal spatial, temporal and ritual behavior, which brings it much closer to human symbolic behavior, is also striking.

In their application to man—environment interaction a great deal of over-simplification has occurred. This has happened in relation to density and crowding and spatial concepts. In this section I will be dealing mainly with the latter although they are not really separable, space being a major mechanism for regulating social interaction (Wynne-Edwards 1962; McBride 1964; Kummer 1971). Used with care these concepts can be most enlightening. For animals, as for people, social and spatial organization and structure are closely related and one can often be read from the other. The distance among individuals and groups emerges as a compromise between attraction and repulsion although ecological factors play a role and, clearly, in the case of people various complicating factors of cultural and physical defenses and modifications play a role. Among both animals and people distance and communication are related: fixed and recognized relationships in space make behavior mutually predictable and reduce the need for constant communication. Among people it has also the important consequence that many informal and almost "automatic" controls can operate with less need for formal controls (such as police or written regulations) and also better maintenance and less vandalism, conflict and stress. Once boundaries are fixed, formalized and predictable movement follows — and hence reduced conflict. Among both animals and people physical hiding is a substitute for distance and rules, and generally devices are used to reduce communication and unwanted interaction; it is the latter and the presence of strangers which are stressful, not density *per se* and the more certain group membership the less stress (Kummer 1971; Rapoport 1975(b); in press(b)).

The major oversimplification with regard to spatial concepts has consisted in using the term territoriality or territory too broadly. Whether territoriality, as the propensity of people to define certain areas and defend them, is basic to people or not it does seem clear that some types of territorial behavior is common among people. In order to use such concepts to deal with urban problems, however, a more sophisticated model is needed.

A number of different conceptual schemes based on ethological concepts have been proposed but will not be reviewed. I will discuss one particular model which is composed of five elements (Rapoport 1972(b), (d)):

(1) *Home range*. The usual limit of *regular* movements and activities which can be defined as a set of settings or locales and their linking paths. Each individual has a typical shape and extent of home range (which differs for daily, weekly or monthly movement — a spatial signature). Members of particular groups will tend to have home ranges more alike than those of other groups — i.e., the individual variability can be generalized and there are cultural, age, sex and class differences. This concept of home range partly corresponds to behavioral space, life space, activity space and similar concepts, and is also related to the spatial nature of networks.

(2) *Core area*(s). These are those areas within the home range which are the most commonly inhabited and used — possibly daily — and best known. They can be conceived as a limited number of places in the city, the areas around the dwelling, local shops, employment or regular recreation; core areas also vary with culture, sex and age and change over time.

(3) *Territory*. This is a particular area or areas which are owned and defended — whether physically or through rules and symbols — which identify an area as belonging to an individual or group, and one important way in which people territorialize is through

personalization. Symbols used may include walls, fences, posts, changes in texture, changes in colour or landscape treatment — i.e., noticeable differences; cues must thus be noticed, understood or read, and obeyed. Generally symbols and rules are the most important ways of defining territory in humans although rights do exist for physical defenses (such as one's house in Common Law). This has been much more studied in buildings than cities (but cf. Greenbie 1973).

(4) *Jurisdiction*. This can be defined as "ownership" or control of a territory for a limited time and by some agreed-upon rules. The examples in the original formulation were sailors swabbing decks on a ship or cleaners in an executive's office after hours (Roos 1968). Urban examples would be an area which a particular group may use when certain circumstances exist but which they may not when these circumstances cease — e.g., passing over a turf when a supermarket is open or a sports event is in progress but not at other times (Suttles 1968).

(5) *Personal distance or personal space*. This is the spacing among individuals in face-to-face interaction, the bubble of space surrounding individuals which has been studied. In urban contexts it affects crowding in public areas, pedestrian movement and pavement use and, possibly, acceptability of public transport; generally, however, it is a micro-scale rather than meso-scale phenomenon. It is also *portable*, whereas the others, specially (2) and (3) are expressed in the built environment.

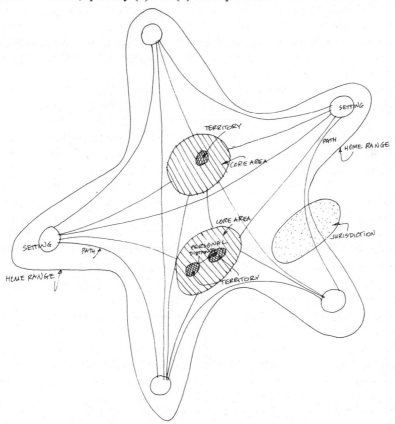

FIG. 5.6. The five-element ethological space model (from Rapoport 1972(b), (d)).

All of these have animal analogues. It is well-known that personal distance and space were first applied from animal studies. Home range, core area and territory are concepts fully derived from ethology and offer good analogues with people in cities. For example, among animals one can speak of home ranges consisting of first, second, third and lower order places connected by paths (Leyhausen 1970, p. 104), very much as among people (Briggs 1972). Similarly to people, among animals there is separation in time, and space is used differentially; some areas are avoided, animals orient to places they know and have good memory for places and spatial relationships. They also identify conspecifics with where they were met. As among different groups, animals of any one species have minimum and maximum sizes of territories and homeranges, and the latter overlap. Among animals as among people, if there is too much interaction and too many strangers, i.e., neither territory nor homogeneity, the result is continuous conflict, withdrawal, pathologies and the replacement of relative by absolute hierarchies (Leyhausen 1971).

The concept of jurisdiction was initially derived for humans, but animal analogues are found among many animals such as cats (Leyhausen 1971), monkeys and apes who tend to avoid each other in time and use paths according to rules which is equivalent to jurisdiction. Similarly the fact that people tend to meet and interact in neutral areas also has animal analogies (Eibl-Eibesfeld 1970, p. 229) and both animals and people in strange territories tend to be less aggressive and more submissive than in their own, and to explore and interact less. While man has greatly elaborated the spatial system used by animals, even though there is continuity (Hall 1963), the complexity of animal spatial and temporal behavior is quite remarkable with a complex of owned and neutral places, boundaries, paths, and temporal and rule systems (Wynne-Edwards 1962; Leyhausen 1970, 1971; Van Lawyck Goodall 1971).

These five components all change with place, context, culture, class, age, sex and other variables. Thus home range is very different for a working class person than a top academic or jet-setter. Thus the lifetime radius of movement in the 1950's for lower class Americans was 145 miles while for higher strata it was 1100 miles (Broom and Selznick 1957, pp. 202–203). While this is not strictly speaking home range it can be seen as a lifetime range of movement. Similar differences can be found in cities among various groups, as we have seen for Aboriginal and White children in Sydney, and men and women, and different ethnic and age groups, in Los Angeles. In the U.S. generally home range is bigger for boys than girls and for suburban children than inner city children (Anderson and Tindall 1972).* While generally lower class individuals have smaller home ranges, there are exceptions as we have seen for Ciudad Guyana.

Home range also changes over time, growing as the child grows and shrinking again for an older person: it increases from a bassinet to the room, house, block, neighborhood, city, region, country and, possibly, world and then shrinks again with age as the home range becomes restricted for a variety of reasons. It is also restricted differently in different cultures. For example, children are allowed into many more places in the U.S. than in England and thus have a more extensive home range (Barker and Barker 1961; Barker and Schoggen 1973) and children in small towns may have larger home ranges than in larger cities, and in traditional cities than modern ones. Home range also varies with caste, as in India, with sex — as in Moslem countries, with race — as for Negroes in

---

* Many of the areas called "home range" in Anderson and Tindall (1972) and others in *EDRA3* were really home setting or *core areas*.

South Africa or with religion — as in the case of the Jewish Ghetto. This concept thus relates to behavioral space and, as we saw in Chapter 3, has implications for the knowledge of the city, mental maps — and further use.

There are similarities between the way people use the city and the way animals use their environment, and human home range is very similar to photographs of animal home ranges (Wynne-Edwards 1962). In both cases the behavioral space or home range is a rather small proportion of the total space, and this even applies to large buildings. Thus the patient domain in a hospital is rather small and increases for other groups, with doctors having the largest (Willems 1972; LeCompte, p. 72) although the total space is never used by any one group. Generally it would be interesting and useful to find out the home ranges of different groups in the city. Informal exercises with students in Milwaukee suggest that for a group as relatively "homogeneous" the weekly home range varied from a few blocks around the university to a vast area including Madison, Wisconsin and Chicago, Illinois; there were also striking differences in the daily and monthly ranges.

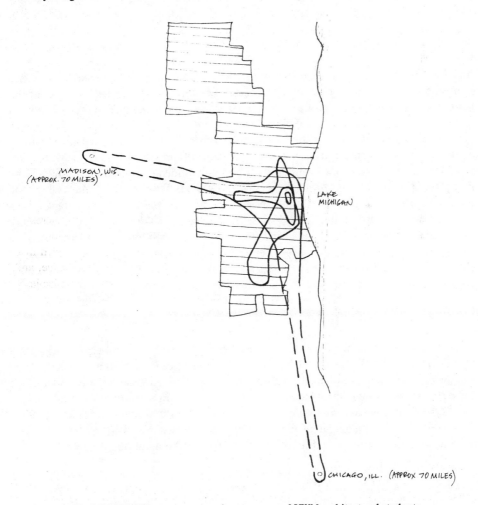

FIG. 5.7. Variability among some home ranges of UWM architectural students.

The major point is that all the elements of the model are important and must be included* and that the territorial model is rather more complex than generally accepted, and that it should be viewed "primarily as a behavioral system which is expressed in a spatial-temporal frame of reference" (Carpenter 1958). This model can usefully be applied to Australian Aborigines (Rapoport 1972(e)) as well as to student use of space in an American community. In fact, the latter can only be understood in these terms and is related to the house-settlement system, i.e., the use of the environment can only be understood if the whole system is considered. The use of dormitories at Berkeley cannot be understood without also considering the use of coffee shops, the campus, friends' houses, recreational areas and so on (Van der Ryn and Silverstein 1967) and this model fits well. As used, it is over-simplified since subcultural and sex differences which also exist are neglected.

One advantage of the model is that it links situations at various scales and provides insights into larger scale problems by looking at smaller scale phenomena. For example, in small groups there is a congruence between leadership (i.e., status), location and territorial rank (e.g., DeLong 1971(a); Strodbeck and Hook 1961). This is exhibited in the city by clustering and habitat selection, whereby upper status groups have the more desirable areas so that address and the physical environment have symbolic status, as does the exclusive nature of the domain. Similarly areas and objects are used to distinguish status and other differences as, for example, among "roughs" and "respectable" residents in both old people's homes and in housing estates (Wilson 1963; Lipman 1968). Similarly there are people in small groups, as in cities, who are hierarchically stable and not territorial while others are territorially stable.

Thus at various scales one finds that highest status individuals need no territorial markers since they can use the whole environment; high status individuals have the best and most desirable territories while the lowest status individuals have none and try and find places (Sundstrom and Altman 1972; Esser 1970(a)). Without taking the analogy too far, a hypothesis is possible for urban groups, so that there may be a range from extremely high status, mobile individuals with no need to be space bound, various groups with desirable and strong territories and finally low status groups without any areas they can call their own. If true, this may offer one way of distinguishing among groups in the city in terms of territories, home ranges and so on. Also the discussion in the previous two sections could be interpreted to mean that territorial behavior for groups greatly reduces conflict, as does the use of distinct core areas, jurisdictions separated in time, agreed upon and understood personal distances, home ranges overlapping at neutral points, and the use of appropriate physical and social defenses and markers.

In fact, given the importance of ritualized behavior even among animals (e.g., Wynne-Edwards 1962; Hediger 1955) it might be suggested that the applicability of ethological concepts to urban design lies not only in its analytical value as described above, but also in the understanding which it might provide of the importance of establishing group areas although most work has been on individual territoriality. While the territory in the building is of the individual, in the city it is rather of the group and there is a relation between perceived homogeneity and the definition of group territory.

---

* A student of mine, Bernhardt R. Kiessling, in a term paper in Dec. 1974, in fact suggested that a case could be made for another element – territorial jurisdiction – between territory and jurisdiction.

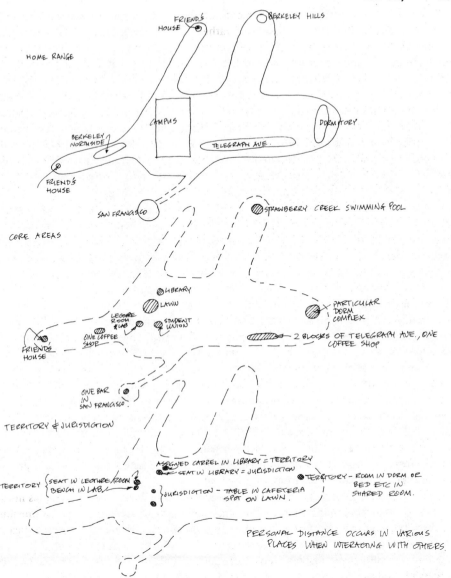

FIG. 5.8. Five-element model applied to Berkeley students (as described in Van der Ryn & Silverstein, 1967). Simplified diagram neglecting certain activities, sex and subcultural differences etc., etc. (from Rapoport 1972(b)).

Thus while it is possible that where there are high levels of individual territoriality (as in suburbs) group territoriality may be more difficult to establish, but if levels of homogeneity, sharing of norms and symbols are adequate both can, and do, coexist.

A critical question is how symbols are used by human groups to establish boundaries which, for them as for animals, reduce conflict and stress. Various animal species use very different markings for boundaries which are understood by conspecifics – sound (songs of birds, howler monkeys) smell — special glands in rabbits, urine in dogs and cats, feces in the hippopotamus; visible markings — scratches by bears; and others — including various displays such as genital displays which, it is claimed, have been duplicated in certain human boundary markers (Morris 1967). There is, therefore, no reason why different human groups after defining boundaries and places conceptually and cognitively, should not use very different markers and symbols which are understood by others in the group. In modern cities problems arise because there are many different groups who do not share symbol systems and may, therefore, either not be aware of the cues, not be able to read them or refuse to obey them (Rapoport 1970(c), 1973(a)).

It thus seems likely that apart from individual territories, group territories exist (e.g., Ucko *et al.* 1972) and influence the organization of space into clearly demarcated areas, or zones of influence, made distinctive and considered at least partly exclusive by their occupants. Essentially, the various mechanisms used to define boundaries and barriers introduce discontinuities in population distribution — inhabited space is non-uniform; boundaries lead to environmental differences (e.g., Jackson 1951, 1966(c)) and also greatly affect communication (Goodey 1969). An individual lives in an extremely complex set of spatial units — personal space, individual territory, territories of various groups, complex sets of core areas, jurisdictions and overlapping home ranges. These are reflected in the built environment and its use. At all scales, from the country (Soja 1971) to the room (Altman and Haythorn 1970) three characteristics are present — a sense of spatial identity, a sense of exclusiveness and the control of communication in space and time.

Note that this is equivalent to the separation of socially integrated groups — animal or human — through various boundary creating devices, barriers, defenses, acceptance of certain rights, expectations and obligations, sharing language and non-verbal communication, customs, norms, and rules, and environmental symbols. The boundaries and spatial domains are thus an expression of conceptual and social barriers and domains. The various forms of group clustering discussed above, urban discontinuities and boundaries and the different symbolic landscapes to be discussed in Chapter 6, are all ways of establishing group territories.

The nature and importance of these depend on people's behavioral space and are a function of their home ranges, core areas; their time rhythms are partly related to their jurisdictions: the same street may have totally different populations at different times of the day (Duncan 1976). It may also be used for different purposes at various times as in the case with street markets, and fairs, children's play in the summer or the turning of streets in Singapore (such as Albert Street) into dining streets at night or the case of Safed discussed above where the jurisdiction of sacred and profane use is very clear.

"Territory" in an urban context is far more than the ownership of private property. It is rather related to identifying individuals and groups through their home ranges, core areas, jurisdictional systems and group territories. The boundaries marking the latter may be visible or invisible but known (i.e., rules). In the case of a city visible boundaries are more useful since they have more chance to prevent *unintended* transgressions and here an understanding of the spatial and temporal arrangements, symbols used and noticeable differences becomes important, and will aid the designer to help establish adequate boundaries and reconcile conflicts among groups. At one level his task is similar to the ethologist's since both need to understand the devices used by a particular "species". At another level his task is different because of the greater number of potential mechanisms among people and the number of groups in the modern city, all using different systems (unlike traditional cities). The misunderstandings can be drastic. For example, among Australian Aborigines boundaries were weak for economically important areas and strong for ritual areas — a reversal of Western practice. The arriving whites therefore concluded that Aborigines did not "own" land since they did not value it as an economic resource. An even greater source of misunderstanding was the fact that boundaries were known rather than marked and that they were "fuzzy" except in the case of natural features. European settlers, however, did not consider such natural features as being equivalent to territorial markers nor did they conceive of periodic possession established through ritual (Rapoport 1972(e)), i.e., these cues were not noticeable to them. Almost any *noticeable* difference can be used to define an area as being different from another, and hence the transition as marking a boundary, and the discussion in Chapter 4 becomes extremely relevant in this context.

We have already seen that social stratification and symbols are related in the city. One possible reason for this very strong tendency to symbolize may in fact come from ethology (Rapoport 1970(c)), which suggests that animals show the essential characteristics of a society, that of providing conventionalized competition: conventions and conventionalized behavior are in the nature of artifacts which become symbols with arbitrarily defined meaning (Wynne-Edwards 1962). Threats are often made through purely formalized acts or postures showing off a signal harmless in itself but made formidable purely through associations — e.g., antlers seen as symbols (Hediger 1955) or genital displays (Morris 1967). Animals seem to accept decisions reached through purely symbolic methods (Wynne-Edwards 1962). Ritualized behavior can thus be seen as of great importance in both animal and human societies; domesticated animals are described as those which have lost their ceremonial, spatial and temporal systems and this can be regarded as a pathological condition (Hediger 1952). Generally, animals in abnormal conditions, in zoos and laboratories, develop abnormal behavior — notably ritual behavior (Huxley 1966) not unlike people in stress situations (Siegel 1970).

In normal situations people and animals seem to share patterns of ritualized behavior. Animals have organized characteristic patterns of behavior which may be the origin of human cultural behavior. In fact most animal behavior is ritualized and territorial ownership is advertized through such means. Ritualized behavior in humans is analogous: although there are radical differences between biological and cultural transmission of such behavior there is also some evidence of proto-tradition in animals. A society can be seen as set of concepts rather than an aggregate of people and the abstraction "society" is made perceptible through symbolic interaction (Blumer 1969(a)) or ritual (Huxley 1966). An important function of ritual is to overcome ambiguity and make behavior predictable: again the parallels with animals under normal conditions are striking.

Cultural behavior can thus be seen in terms of symbolic and ritual behavior. Even those everyday rituals which we call manners and which seem unimportant have several functions — communication, control of aggression, bond-formation (Huxley 1966) as well as simplifying life and reducing the amount of information processing. Settings such as schools can be analyzed in terms of ritual and have been, in Britain (Bernstein *et al*. 1966) and the U.S. In the case of an American high school not only is ceremony and ritual most important and is central for an understanding of how the system operates, it also appears that the idea that modernity and urbanization are incompatible with ritual is incorrect (Burnett 1969).

Ritual is, in fact, important in urban contexts. It played a central role in the operation of dispersed Mayan settlements which were unified through ritual (e.g., Vogt 1968). In the case of a polyethnic city in the Dominican Republic, the ritual activity of pre-Lenten Carnival reinforces class and ethnic boundaries while, at the same time, assisting in maintaining and integrating the whole system. Group identity is maintained by, among others, some measure of endogamy (and we have already discussed the relationship of clustering and marriage), a religious sanction of boundaries reinforced by periodic ritual, and certain symbols by which each group is known and its members recognized. Some groups are spatially isolated while others are not and they are also organized in a hierarchy (Gonzales 1970). Ritual may also be considered as a mechanism of urban adaptation as among certain Javanese groups in New Caledonia, where it enables the group to survive the forces of urbanization. The ritual is fairly complex, but it appears to be effective (Dewey 1970) and would probably work better if some clustering were possible.

A final point about ritual which will be developed in the next chapter is that some form of environmental symbols are often essential in such rituals such as these related to defensive structuring (Siegel 1970; Rapoport, in press(b)). For example, in the case of the Mayo Indians of Sonora, Mexico, the house cross is the element which helps maintain ethnic identity (Crumrine 1964). It thus seems clear that ritual behavior is important, is common to people and animals and, in the case of people, often involves environmental symbols as well as clustering. The purpose of such rituals and symbols, as of the other mechanisms is to assert group identity and make urban life less stressful.

Clearly, much of this discussion about human territoriality relates to our discussion of density and crowding. The mechanisms which I have described, and the notion of crowding as unwanted interaction, are closely related to comparable ethological concepts and have, in fact, in many cases received their inspiration from them. In both cases strangers are kept out and members are closer to each other than to other groups (McBride 1964, 1970), space is used discontinuously and individuals move through a framework of highly patterned space; an element of defense is clearly involved, even if sometimes overemphasized (e.g., Newman 1971).

Group and individual affective identification with an area, the use of symbols and norms to define it, i.e., a home ground (territory or core area) and to give it appropriate physical and social character, means having areas where one is dominant, and others where one has jurisdiction at appropriate times and where one can return after being in the larger sphere and domain. There also needs to be the ability to move through the city in ways which correspond to the desired activity orbits or systems, i.e., to develop the appropriate home range. The ethological model is thus congruent with many of the ideas discussed above.

The various elements vary for groups in any given place and time and also in different places and times. They have often been institutionalized and we have already seen the existence of such institutionalized areas in many cities. For example in England the Inns of Court, the colleges of Oxbridge, residential squares and Cathedral precincts all formalized areas for specific groups. In traditional Chinese cities there were also walled wards for various groups — market wards, high status wards near the centre and low status ones against the city wall (Tuan 1968, 1969). In fact, the city itself was a defended and sanctified group territory very different from the profane space around (e.g., Wheatley 1971). Different groups, therefore, had some territorial locus which helped preserve their identity and norms. In addition to environmental symbols, a whole armoury of non-verbal, institutional and social devices were used to assert and maintain group identity, although some groups were less spatially identified than others. Within such spaces, however, the group can enforce its norms and assume intelligibility of non-verbal communication and unwritten rules, and these spaces need to be related to the other elements of the system. From the design point of view, therefore, the need is to achieve congruence between that system and its physical and behavioral expression — between the different home ranges of various groups within the total potential space of the city, the exclusive or shared core areas of groups and group and individual territories of a higher degree of exclusivity and stricter control. The danger is in oversimplifying, e.g., relating home range to neighborhood; but even then behavior of teenage gangs in Victoria, B.C. Canada became clearer since the places of residence, school, employment, hanging out and deviant behavior were all clustered within a relatively small area with a diameter of 1½ and 2½ miles (Porteous 1971) which is clearly the home range.

By plotting the home ranges, core areas and territories for many groups in the city one could clarify the system. It would relate to people's subjective morphology of the city. Such an identification of the "urban mosaic" in terms of turfs, territories, home ranges and core areas, related to physical elements and environmental character, would be most useful and would well complement other studies based on social criteria, networks and cognitive schemata.

The relationship with the latter is immediately obvious. The core areas, territories and home ranges, and the time changes in jurisdiction, would specify behavior and the way in which the city is used (i.e., activity systems and behavioral space (e.g., Craik 1970; Pastalan and Carson 1970)) and experienced and should enable predictions to be made about the nature of mental maps and the nature of the environment suitable for particular groups or sets of groups, their transport needs and so on (e.g., Wolforth 1971).

Since people live in different areas, value different things and hence go to different places along different paths, and avoid different places, their networks, home ranges and behavioral spaces also vary and coincide with what has been called movement space — that limited part of the city through which people habitually move (Hurst 1971). In fact within this space it is possible to identify areas which are most frequently travelled, and regularly visited and hence familiar, and known, corresponding to core areas. The very different use by working and middle-upper class people of central Paris (Lamy 1967) already discussed several times, can be understood in terms of this model. The social links, leisure activities and shopping of working class people are all within their neighborhood, they spend more time in their core areas and territories and, in effect, they have a limited home range. On the other hand professional groups tend to use the whole of Paris, i.e., have a much more extended home range. There is also a third, younger, group who are particularly leisure oriented (a function of values, lifestyle and images) and hence have an even more extensive home range. In all cases these movements are also related to place of residence and work, i.e., core areas.

Clearly individuals in the city, like animals, follow different activity patterns which become regular for members of groups. This leads to areas dominated by various groups and to hierarchical arrangements, balance of power, socio-cultural rules about aggression and so on reflected in complex, but regular and comprehensible, spatial, social, temporal, meaning and communication organizations, rule and non-verbal communication systems and so on; these vary with time, age, sex, class and culture. The relative evaluation of different parts of the city, particularly in terms of their being "open" for given individuals or groups is partly related to the evaluation of physical cues which, as we have seen, can be institutionalized. In the modern American city, developments such as walled housing estates, and those with moats, bridges and guards can be understood not only in terms of crime and *physical* safety but also in terms of a clear and unmistakable definition of group territories and status at a time when the American city is experiencing both a polarization of groups needing clearer boundaries and assertion of group identity, and a diffusion, among a wide range of groups, of the traditional symbols used for defining status and group identity.

This interpretation becomes more likely when we recall some of the findings about the meaning of planning and the differing interpretation of the environment by different groups (cf. Eichler and Kaplan 1967; Werthman 1968). In middle class areas appearance is important and suburban settings have an important role in maintaining the traditional distinctions among groups. The appearance of areas is then interpreted in terms of the status and character of the group living there — an attempt to establish group territoriality through design character, using cues very different to those of groups regarded as undesirable. I am suggesting that in some way this is a universal process among animals and people, and only the definition of "undesirable", and the devices and symbols used to exclude them, vary. The process can be seen as one of establishing group territories within which are then defined family and, finally, individual territories in a hierarchy and, at higher levels, domains of like groups sharing core areas and home ranges.

In the same way that different animals define different territories (or none) and use different means, people do too. For some it may mean having a clearly defined private territory within an area maintaining certain visible standards, whereas for others it may mean defining an area all of which is identified with the group and its life. The distinction is really about where the boundaries are placed and what domains of private and public are defined, rather than of different types of territorial space. It does, however, have major implications for the relation of dwelling to street, use of street, provision of recreational and leisure facilities, location and relative proximity of various services, the amount of interaction with people and the nature and degree of privacy defenses.

The urban spatial system is an expression of a behavioral system and the purpose of all spatial divisions, clustering and the like is to improve communication, understanding, predictability and the legibility of and obedience to cues. Through this life is simplified, conflict and information processing reduced. The rules underlying these cues and the way in which they define places have to be learned, i.e., culturally shared. Different rule systems have been identified: I will briefly review three of the proposed typologies.

One proposes a fourfold division between *personal occupancy* (e.g., the dwelling) which impose the strongest restrictions on behavior and admission; *community occupancy* (a private club) where restrictions are accepted as long as they fall within the defined limits; *society occupancy* (e.g., a street) where access is available to all members of society [although here often misunderstandings occur due to the processes I have been discussing]; and *free occupancy* (a deserted beach) where there are, effectively, no controls (Brower 1965).

Another, related, typology proposes a six-fold division:

(1) Urban public — open to all (e.g., roads).
(2) Urban semi-public places for public use but with some limitations of purpose, special use etc. (e.g., post offices).

(3) Group public — the meeting ground between the public and private realms managed by the community.

(4) Group private — community gardens or storage areas managed by some group.

(5) Family private — the dwelling and garden under control of the family.

(6) Individual private — the innermost sanctum of the individual (Chermayeff and Alexander 1965).

An important point is that whereas in the first typology the specifics, the cues used and the context vary with culture and time, in the second the categories themselves seem to be culturally variable, they may change or not apply in various cultures.

Finally, a typology has been proposed of four elements — *public territories* where any citizen may enter although there is no complete freedom of action. i.e., one must observe the norms of the society; *Home territories* which are areas claimed by groups — e.g., homosexuals or a teenage gang; [our houses are clearly in that category as may be the neighborhoods of specific groups] ; *Interactional territories* which are really jurisdictional and are found when a small group interacts socially, but could be extended to cover any permanent social interaction although even then it would probably be partly jurisdictional; and *body territories* which correspond to personal space and are related to the individual and his body (Lyman and Scott 1970).

The rules built into such systems may be violated — e.g., sleeping in parks or eating in streets, territories may be invaded, i.e., entered against the rules; or contaminated, i.e., claimed by a particular group which makes it unusable by others. Three reactions are possible: turf defenses typical of teenagers and very like animal reaction only affecting conspecifics (other teenage gangs); linguistic collusion — developing codes and languages incomprehensible to outsiders (these may be physical and non-verbal) or insulation — putting up barriers which cannot be crossed. These various rules of occupancy, combined with the ethological spatial model and the discussion of socio-cultural variables and clustering provide a useful base for understanding urban space and people's distribution in it: it allows us to move to a discussion of private and public domains, behavior setting systems, the house settlement system and, in chapter 6, the symbolic nature of the physical environment through which these rules are expressed.

Public and Private Domains

We have seen that urban space generally is divided into domains distinguished by various rules and symbols. Their purpose basically is to establish boundaries between us and them, and public and private, thus ensuring the desired levels of interaction, inclusion or exclusion and providing the appropriate defences. All these differ among various groups so that if privacy is defined very broadly as the control of unwanted interaction, then "unwanted", "interaction" and "control" are all variable and matters of definitions, so that there are differences in the tolerance and, indeed, preference of various interaction levels. With whom one interacts, when and under what conditions; what constitutes withdrawal, where both interaction and withdrawal occur all vary. The nature, placement and permeability of barriers also vary accordingly, as does the cycle of withdrawal and interaction which form a system; neither is comprehensible by itself (e.g., Schwartz 1968).

The operational definition of privacy as the avoidance of unwanted interaction with other people involves information flow from person to person. How one avoids interaction, once defined is also variable, and there are at least five or six major mechanisms possible. Unwanted interaction can be controlled through *rules* (manners, avoidance, hierarchies, etc), through *psychological means* (internal withdrawal, dreaming, drugs, depersonalization etc.), through *behavioral cues*, through structuring activities in *time* (so that particular individuals and groups do not meet), through *spatial separation*, through *physical devices* (walls, courts, doors, curtains, locks — architectural mechanisms which selectively control or filter information). In most cases, of course, multiple mechanisms are used but particular ones are stressed and they are combined in different ways.

Each of these mechanisms and forms of interaction are related to different sense modalities which operate in two directions — one does not want to be seen or see, to smell or be smelt and so on. They are also related to context, so that the same amount of aural information, for example, may be acceptable in one situation but not in another in the same culture (Rapoport 1972(b), 1975(b); in press(a), (b)).

Without developing the argument further, the model could be summarized as follows:

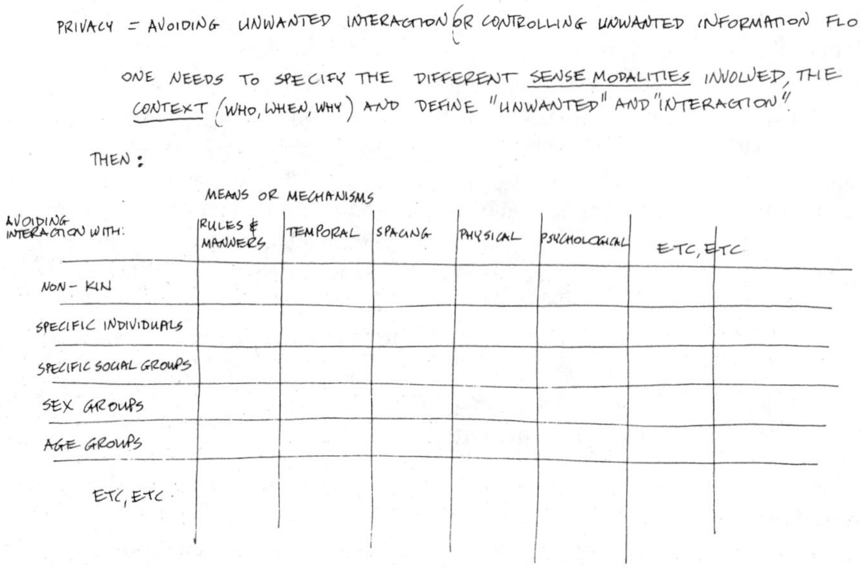

PRIVACY = AVOIDING UNWANTED INTERACTION (OR CONTROLLING UNWANTED INFORMATION FLOWS).

ONE NEEDS TO SPECIFY THE DIFFERENT SENSE MODALITIES INVOLVED, THE CONTEXT (WHO, WHEN, WHY) AND DEFINE "UNWANTED" AND "INTERACTION".

THEN:

AVOIDING INTERACTION WITH:	MEANS OR MECHANISMS					
	RULES & MANNERS	TEMPORAL	SPACING	PHYSICAL	PSYCHOLOGICAL	ETC, ETC
NON - KIN						
SPECIFIC INDIVIDUALS						
SPECIFIC SOCIAL GROUPS						
SEX GROUPS						
AGE GROUPS						
ETC, ETC.						

FIG. 5.9. (from Rapoport, in press(b)).

Each of the categories in this diagram can be greatly elaborated so that, for any situation, the location of any particular group may be plotted, related to the social structure and the organization of the built environment, how it is used and so on. Consider the idea of privacy gradients — the penetration of different classes of outsiders into a dwelling: in two Latin American situations one finds gradients which separate private and public, and front and back regions (Alexander *et al.* 1969 and Foster 1972).

These penetration or privacy gradients clearly separate individuals and groups and determine where one interacts with whom — as in the case of Moslem cities (English 1973; Brown 1973; Delaval 1974). Different mechanisms can also be used. Thus, in the case of the Colombian housing (see Fig. 5.10), some of the separation is achieved

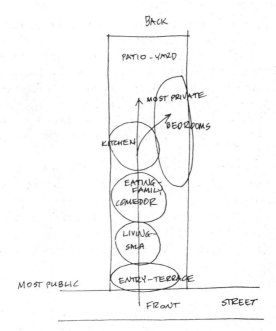

FIG. 5.10. Penetration gradients, Latin America
(Colombia and Peru) (Foster, 1972; Alexander
et al. 1969).

symbolically through open net or bead curtains which do the job because the rules are shared and accepted. This is even more striking in the case of the Yagua Indian house where the absolute rule relates to turning away from the center of the dwelling as indicating that one is "no longer present" (Rapoport 1967(b)). This way of avoiding unwanted interaction by facing outwards is also found among Australian Bush Turkeys (McBride 1970) showing the continuity of mechanisms. Separation can also be achieved through physical devices or space as is clearly the case in the traditional and colonial parts of Indian cities already described where the courts and inward turning dwellings of the native part can be contrasted with the spatial separation of the English cantonment with bungalows in large grounds. In the latter case there is still a wall around the compound, but the major protective element is space and the verandah acts as a transitional space, i.e., there are many more defenses and transitions than in the case of the courtyard dwelling which is much more abrupt. (See Fig. 5.11).

In addition, the bungalow was part of the cultural space of English people — i.e., a homogeneous group — contrasting with the native space of the traditional city (King 1970, 1974(a) (b)). Also, within the colonial city there were native parts, for servants and the like, which were at the back and, in fact, the whole idea of private vs. public domains can be related to the distinction between front and back areas: the former for display, presenting a formal face to the world and communicating a public image, the latter for private and service activities and "messy" behavior with corresponding control of penetration.

This concept was used in environmental analysis quite early (e.g., Madge 1950) but only picked up recently. It is related to images, to display, to the communication of

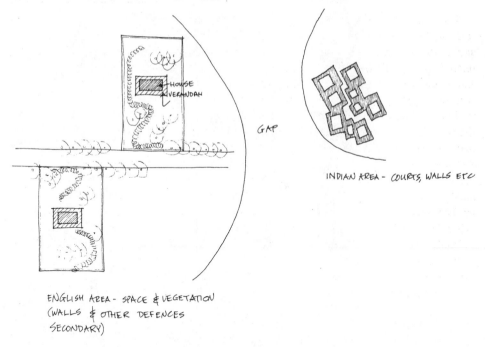

ENGLISH AREA - SPACE & VEGETATION
(WALLS & OTHER DEFENCES
SECONDARY)

FIG. 5.11

information about oneself and decoration, all serving as impression manipulation. Thus what is defined as private or public, which activities and symbols are deemed appropriate for each set of regions, the barriers and rules used and the symbolic treatment of the areas are all culturally variable and related to front and back regions, the latter being places where behavior can become less self-conscious, where roles can be prepared, where the mask can be taken off (Goffman 1957, 1963).

This has been confirmed empirically in housing studies in several countries, with the distinction between display (lawn, front garden, flowers, birdbaths and the like) and privacy (laundry, sheds, barbecue and so on) — front and back (Raymond *et al.* 1966; Shankland, Cox 1967; Rapoport 1971(c)); Pètonnet 1972(a)).

It also appears that differing definitions of front and back, and the appropriate behavior for them, may generate conflict, as in the case of working/lower and middle-upper class areas. In the former much social behavior occurs on the street or the stoop, i.e., the front, whereas the same behavior is meant to occur in the private and back domain in the middle class areas. This means also that the importance attached to front display in the latter is not present in the former, where the presence of badly maintained lawns, old furniture, junk and stripped cars in front areas is completely at odds with the middle class image of front. There is thus a complete contrast between appropriate behavior and symbolic treatment of the two regions in the two groups with almost inevitable conflict. These differences and conflicts have been found between blacks and whites in outdoor urban spaces in Baltimore, in the U.S., (Brower and Williamson 1974) and between traditional and westernized groups in India in terms of upkeep of houses (Duncan, in press, Duncan 1976).

There is thus a scale from self-display to extreme privacy with corresponding treatment, decorations and barriers admitting people, depending on their relationships and status to various parts of this system — i.e., with penetration gradients. This is also related to rules about whether the street, for example, is seen as a front or back region and whether its use for sitting, eating, working on cars and the like is appropriate or not. It is also related to social organization and definition of groups so that if a whole quarter is composed of kin it may be seen as a backstage region with a small front stage region for the reception of strangers (as in a Yoruba compound), whereas in the case of an area with many nuclear families there are many front and back regions (one per house) and the treatment of the fronts defines the group front region. Also the preference for the individual house is at least partly due to the ability of distinguishing between and manipulating front and back (Madge 1950; Raymond *et al.* 1966) and thus has major implications for the success of any attempts to change housing preference and hence urban form.

While the distinction of front and back at the urban scale is more difficult to demonstrate we have already seen that it exists. One can clearly distinguish streets and service lanes, common in many areas, eras and places; the front of cities along waterfront, stressed in the promenade or corniche in Mediterranean countries which is an important image element in planning there (e.g., Rapoport 1969(c)). There are also areas in cities — dumps, industry and poor areas which are clearly seen as back areas, ignored or avoided so that visitors are never shown those. For example, the American city has been contrasted with the European in terms of what the visitor sees on arriving — back regions in the U.S. city, front areas in the European (Jackson 1957). In the case of certain canal towns in Britain, there were two front areas — for those arriving by land and those arriving by water. Since the former were upper class people and the latter working class (bargees) the two front areas were very different (Porteous 1970). Generally, then, relationship between public and private domains, front and back regions and penetration gradients offers a useful typology of domains for urban analysis.*

Private and public, front and back domains — like privacy itself — can only be understood as part of a system of interaction and withdrawal. As we have seen, the same environments can be seen as too isolated by the elderly and too interactive by young families with children — i.e., one group seeking stimuli, the other seeking withdrawal from excessive interaction. This may also be used to interpret the front stoop and street behavior of working class people and the backyard behavior of the middle class, since the former tend not to find stimulus and interaction in their jobs while the latter do — sometimes excessively. In cultures with high physical densities, like India and Britain, one often finds clear separation of private and public domains, and also self-control and suppression of emotion although other mechanisms may be used. In India, for example, there is clear separation of groups, private and public domains and clear rules about behavior: Indian settlements can be analyzed in terms of private vs. communal areas at a number of scales — the dwelling, village, neighborhood and city (Rapoport 1969(a), p. 167; Kohn 1971; Fonseca 1969(a), (b); Vickery 1972).

---

* A student of mine at the University of Wisconsin — Milwaukee, Mrs. Donna Wade, in a graduate seminar based on this book, in Fall 1974, began an analysis of part of Milwaukee in terms of front and back regions which showed it to be a useful analytical device. Her paper is in the Architecture library.

In Japan, where high density and crowding have long existed, one finds behavioral rules, such as formalized, highly ritualized and hierarchical behavior, looking past each other when talking and smiling — all in the private domain: in public (streets, shops or public transport) rules and manners are dropped. Corresponding to this separation of private and public in terms of rules and behavior is a corresponding separation in terms of domains and environments: there is "private beauty and public squalor" (Meyerson 1963) and also strong separation of the dwelling and garden from the street, but little separation *within* the dwelling, i.e., the major separation is public/private (Rapoport 1969(a), p. 68; cf. Canter and Canter 1971; Smith 1971). Thus the Japanese city has an internal (private) and external (public) order which are strongly differentiated (e.g., Ashihara 1970). Simplicity and traditional values can be preserved inside the house/garden complex which is very different to the streets and shopping lanes. Taking off one's shoes stresses the boundaries between the two orders (a form of rites of passage). By understanding the nature of the rules in the two domains and the location and nature of barriers and transitions the two orders can be organized; in fact both are essential parts of the whole system. The private realm is, therefore, separated from the public both physically and socially — by walls, rules and behavior. It is inward looking, highly elaborated, cared for and personalized while the outside, public realm is often untidy and not maintained. Recall also that the city is separated into self contained, fairly homogeneous areas small enough to operate like villages with informal controls. Finally (and this relates to the house-settlement system) there are stress reduction mechanisms, both physical — large entertainment areas, geisha houses, baths, inns and the like, and social, e.g., drunkenness.

This basic seemingly simple notion, then, provides a most useful tool for analyzing a wide variety of urban forms, house-settlement systems and behaviors in many periods and places. It helps explain differential responses of different groups to the same environments, their different ways of using these environments. It may be possible, given the different definitions of privacy and mechanisms for achieving it, to relate particular forms, physical densities and systems in terms of interaction and withdrawal corresponding to a system of private and public, front and back domains and penetration gradients.

The classification of urban domains in such terms, and using a range of barriers from open to impenetrable, has in fact been used in the design of a "temporary" urban environment (Wiebenson 1969). This was done in terms of private/public only (not front and back) but is a most striking example, usefully compared to my previous analyses of Indian, North African and Aboriginal squatter settlements (Figs. 2.11—2.14).

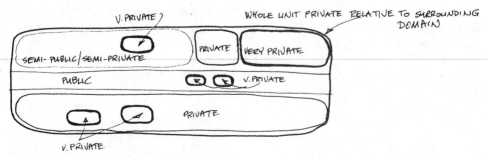

FIG. 5.12. "Soul City" designed in terms of privacy domains (after Wiebenson 1969).

This corresponds to the idea that in the same way that built environments can be seen as selective climatic filters allowing light, heat and the like to pass, one can see various physical elements of the environment, and socio-cultural devices, as selective information and communication filters, allowing more or less information to be communicated or transmitted; such filters can range from impermeable to open and inviting. Where to locate domains and boundaries, what boundaries to use and how to arrange them demands an understanding of the socio-cultural system, and its behavioral, spatial and symbolic components.

The variability of domains, of privacy and wanted vs. unwanted interaction, the barriers and rules used, can all be understood as preferences about the control of access of others, what one wants them to know, variations in cognitive categories, different mechanisms used, the definition of backstage regions and so on. They are also related to the organization of communication in terms of age, sex, race, class, caste, lifestyle or kin — the city as a set of places, of realms of privacy and commonality. This corresponds to earlier suggestions that urban form can be considered, at least partly, in terms of linkages and barriers (e.g., Maki 1964) although it is the specifics of which elements are linked and which separated, what barriers or rules separate them, which groups are defined as needing separation, selective admission or close linkage that are significant.

The dwelling and some of its surroundings (which vary with culture) are then the private region *par excellence* (with internal variations which do not concern us here) contrasting with the public nature of the city as a whole. The potential mediating function of "neighborhood" (depending largely on its homogeneity) provides an intermediate level of semiprivate, semipublic, group private of whatever. In given cases, if these are lacking, the system may be incomplete. Any given city can then be seen as a selected set of subsystems of varying degrees of publicness/privacy and frontness/backness, linked and separated in various ways by different barriers and mechanisms, and with variable numbers of steps or gradations among them. This reflects the value systems, lifestyle and ultimately the culture of the various groups who make up the city.

Even those parts of the city which are open and belong to the public at large, such as the center, may be selectively closed to some groups as a function of preference (Lamy 1967; Heinemeyer 1967). Thus the relative publicness and openness of various urban areas depends partly on cognitive definition and mental maps, so that high crime areas, those belonging to particular groups or with particular characteristics, may never be seen as being available and used. The private domain belongs to the family (of whatever type) and, in some cases, individuals within it; but the relation of this domain to work will

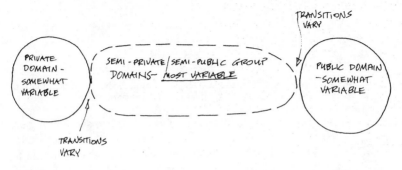

FIG. 5.13. Domains present in all cities.

differ among cultures. The most variable, however, are the shared, group, semiprivate/ semipublic domains which have, in fact, given planners and designers most trouble.

We thus have a general concept useful for analyzing social and urban change (e.g., Roggemans 1971) and also the meaning of urban space organization, while allowing for cultural differences at all levels of definition, choice of devices and rules. Thus, for example, one can compare the Moslem and Christian city in Spain (Violich 1962) or the inside-out city generally, with the internal domain of greatest importance and the street as left-over space, as well as other types of cities and parts of cities (see Fig. 1.2, 2.8, etc.)

Thus all cities and their parts can be seen in terms of public/private, front/back, show/hide and display/non-display areas at all scales and using different forms of defenses, associated rules and penetration gradients; it is the specifics which vary in different cultures. (See Fig. 5.14).

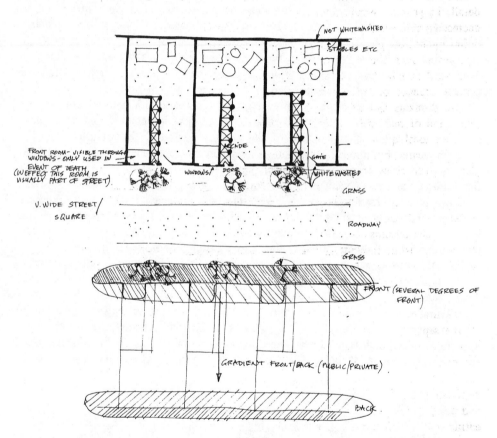

FIG. 5.14. Front/back domains in Magyapolany (N. W. Hungary) (based on information given by Prof. Corbez, School of Architecture, University of Montreal).

The differences in evaluation, use and success of various urban and housing designs for working and lower class families can be understood in terms of the former group seeing a group territory as a positive domain and the latter as a threatening one (Rainwater 1966; Yancey 1971 Hall 1971; Rothblatt 1971). Similarly the different evaluation of urban space for children's play by different groups, with some seeing the street as a place for children to play and the others as not (e.g., Schak 1972) depends on domain definition. Also cities which appear to have no order and appear chaotic can often be understood in terms of different domain definitions. At a smaller scale, much of our discussion on clustering of groups perceived as homogeneous can be seen in terms of *a mutual and shared understanding of what is private and what is public, what is front and what is back – and what are appropriate behaviors in each and the unwritten rules that go with them.*

The relationship of these ideas to the notion of defenses and hence the problems of environments with inadequate defenses for the levels of front/back separation desired are clear (e.g., Harrington 1965) as are the implications for density and crowding in situations where streets and stoops are used for living (e.g., Hartman 1963) compared to those where they are not. Both these cases can be conceptualized in terms of sets of defenses which use different devices and cues, and are also placed and arranged differently in detail. In general terms, however, they can all be seen as a series of boundaries of decreasing permeability as one approaches the dwelling: there is the same type of domain definition but the placement and rules differ (see Fig. 4.3).

·In some cities the whole structure is clearly based on a division into private and public as in Moslem and other traditional cities generally. In the case of Herat, Afghanistan, the system depends on a clear and strong separation and distinction between public and private domains and life and the enclosure and security of the private domain. The separation of residential quarters from other activities, the regular urban plan and the complex local quarters (which only insiders know – are *supposed* to know) (English 1973) is clearer, but not so different, from the purely residential areas of U.S., Australian and English cities, the use of curved streets and culs-de-sac to prevent excessive penetration, the use of walled and guarded estates and the like.

There is a difference, though. In the West the neighborhood has a small number of primary relationships and large public areas while in the Moslem city, such as Cairo, most primary relationships occur within the neighborhood where there is very little privacy and anonymity. While individuals have to move from one community to another, these are unimportant and not allowed to become "real" so that the overall system is very different (Abu-Lughod 1969, 1971). The success or failure of any specific environment can be understood in terms of the congruence of the public/private and front/back domains with ·the cultural norms.

The separation and distinction between public and private, and front and back, may also occur in terms of time. Although people seem to spend similar amounts of time in the dwelling (Pappas 1967) they spend different periods in the street and other places, such as pubs, coffee shops, cinemas and so on. The numbers and distribution of people in different places, in different cities and parts of cities at different times, is both variable and enlightening: such counts could be useful tools. Also whether places of congregation, eating and socializing are visible and public – stoops, streets, door-steps; visible and private – cafes, stores or shops or not visible and more private (pubs, clubs, restaurants, churches) and whether people meet mainly in their dwellings – and whether inside or outside (and then whether front or backyard), all provide important information about the relative importance of private and public places.

The definition of such domains may also be symbolic and periodic. In the case of the Jewish *Shtetl* of pre-World War II Eastern Europe, for example, the religious prohibition against carrying things on the Sabbath was solved in an ingenious manner. When a "fence" encloses a group of houses the area enclosed is seen as private, as part of one's home and the carrying of things is no longer prohibited. Hence a symbolic fence (*eyruv*), a cord or wire, was stretched around the whole town every Friday under the supervision of the Rabbi who then declared at the end of the ritual that the town was no longer a public domain but the domain of the individual (Zborowski and Herzog 1950, p. 50). If there was a break in the fence this no longer applied and I would argue that, since conceptual and cognitive domains precede physical, this is an intermediate stage between a permanent barrier and the purely symbolic domain definition of the Australian Aborigines. This also supports the view that the traditional city was, in itself, the definition of a sacred, group domain from the formless, chaotic and profane "public" domain (e.g., Eliade 1961; Rykwert (n.d.); Davis 1969; Wheatley 1971) and that within the city there are often similar, although subtle and unappreciated, definitions of various domains.

The differential use of streets which follows, the mix of housing and other facilities and hence the proximity of various services are all related to definitions of private and public and this affects meeting places, recreation, shopping — in fact, all aspect of urban organization and activity. They are best understood through an analysis of the behavior setting system and the house-settlement system, to which I now return.

Behavior Setting System

We have already seen that the extent of the home range varies greatly and defines the extent of people's behavioral space. These, as well as the division of the environment into private and public and other domains, are also related to the number and location of core areas, territories and other locales and their linking pathways — i.e., the home range is made up of *behavior settings* and their linking pathways. This affects the knowledge of the city and its subjective morphology. In all cases people's behavioral space is different to the physical size of places. Recall that children's behavioral space in small towns is greater than in large cities (e.g., Wright 1970) and also varies with culture, being larger in American than in English towns (Barker and Barker 1961; Barker and Schoggen 1973) and also varies with age and, finally, that home range and behavioral space vary for individuals and groups.

The behavior setting has been defined as a stable combination of one or more extra-individual patterns of behavior surrounded by non-psychological milieu; or as a combination of "standing patterns of behavior" and its surrounding milieu, i.e., a setting and a program (Barker 1968; Barker and Schoggen 1973). While this concept redresses the neglect of the environment in psychology, it still rather neglects the actual physical environment. This it seems useful to combine this definition with others stressing the role setting as a "stage" and using the dramatic analogy (Goffman 1957; 1963; Blumer 1969(a)). Thus when I use the concept "behavior setting" here, it is to be understood as a combination of these, with the stress being on the stage analogy. Behavior settings are then places where particular activities occur, and they have boundaries which inform people that they are entering a different place. Once inside, the setting provides cues for appropriate behavior which depends on these cues being noticed, read and obeyed — i.e., on cultural agreement about the nature of cues and appropriate behavior. It is significant that the same people behave very differently in different settings (Barker 1968), i.e., environmental cues guide and channel responses and reduce the variety of potential responses — if those cues are congruent with the rule system.

The setting for a particular activity, as a physical entity, must then supply it with the necessary props and facilities. While it does not determine behavior it is inhibiting, facilitating or neutral, and also suggests which activities are appropriate. There are differences in the nature, richness and facilities needed by different behavior settings although, in urban analysis, the behavior setting *system* is more important. In the urban context, while differences in the nature of settings exist — physical, social, in terms of overmanning and penetration, it is the differences in the system which are important: the number, arrangement, relationships, linkages and barriers among them.

One of the important things about behavior settings is that they must be discovered and not defined *a priori*. From our perspective this definition depends on cognitive schemata and is culturally variable; it is also related to latent as well as manifest functions, so that settings apparently congruent with specific activities are either not used, or used differently than expected.

Most environments consist of very many settings. For example, in a hospital 122 were found (Le Compte 1972; Willems 1972), in urban areas there are many hundreds or even thousands (Barker and Barker 1961; Barker and Schoggen 1973; Bechtel 1970; Bechtel *et al.* 1970). Different groups, and groups in different cultures, spend different amounts of time in different settings; different groups also have different amounts of access, of range (number of settings entered — always less than available) and penetration (how much active or leadership role one has in a given setting) depending on status, age, culture and so on. This relates behavior settings to urban activity systems, home range and many of the other topics already discussed. Settings can be described in terms of the amount of control which people have over them, whether there are more roles than performers (overmanning vs. undermanning) and the fact that, since people of similar background tend to spend most of their time in the same or similar settings, one finds grouping and clustering.

Also, since the time spent in various places is variable, while the total time available is constant, the differences or changes in home range can be interpreted in terms of time spent in a small number of settings or a large number of settings — which also relates it to work on time budgets. My suggestion is that the nature of networks and activity systems is best understood in terms of the relationships among various behavior settings — the behavior setting system. For all people, various buildings and urban places are behavior settings. It is, then, their nature and the spatial and temporal relationships among them which distinguish systems from one another. One can thus relate lifestyles, activities and behaviors to behavior setting systems and also distinguish lifestyles through their behavior setting systems. Such systems are also related to the cognitive domains, since behavior settings are domains and are also related to language: among the cues for behavior given by settings, one is what the setting is called, or identified as. Although such names may be disregarded, in a given group the name for a place gives cues for expected behavior, as do other cues within the setting.

Rather than becoming too deeply involved in the large literature on behavior settings, I wish to show that this concept, when combined with others discussed, improves the understanding of the city as a human system.

An important question is how, when and by whom a particular setting is used and how it relates to other settings. Playground use will be affected by what is available nearby, the nature of play and the people who are involved (e.g., Brolin and Zeisel 1968). The use of parks will be affected by the use of other kinds of places — such as streets; as we have already seen, neglecting the use of some football grounds in Lima distorts knowledge of the recreational system. Similarly the use of housing depends on what happens in the streets and other places. In the case of the elderly, for example, the use of lobbies is affected by the availability of the boardwalk — which can be a design aspect, or a climatic one (cf. Michelson 1971(a)); the use of the setting will also depend on the facilities it provides for the desired activities (Lawton 1970(b), (c)) as well as lifestyle and the like. Such use also depends on how well they match the requirements either in terms of isomorphic fit (i.e., fitting specific activities) or complementary fit (fitting activities which are missing elsewhere). This type of analysis enables one to specify the characteristics of behavior setting systems for various purposes and groups. It is necessary to discover the rules whereby settings and appropriate behaviors are defined, the activities which occur in various settings and how they are connected by paths, as well as their relation to home range, networks and behavior space — and hence urban knowledge and mental maps.

For some groups the neighborhood *per se* is, in effect, defined as a setting, for others it is a place containing other settings; for others yet it has no existence and life occurs in settings distributed throughout the urban milieu. This then, is another way of seeing the difference between "place-bound" and "non-place bound" groups. The neighborhood itself can be seen in terms of the coincidence of local behavior setting and core area behavior of homogeneous group (say on a daily basis). Since people seem to spend 70–75% of their time in the dwelling (Pappas 1967), it is the allocation of the remaining time among neighborhood, adjoining areas, the center of the city and elsewhere which will define the behavior setting system for different groups — and will affect design. Thus the definition of behavior settings also affects the definition of neighborhood and other urban areas leading to the distinction between "potential" and "effective" environments (Gans 1968, p. 5–6). Thus the potential environment (which is the designed one) only becomes effective when accepted by people and used by them and this is a function of their evaluation of its subjective appropriateness as a behavior setting system. The appropriate definition of boundaries, of cues in the setting, of supportive facilities within it, and congruence with appropriate rules for behavior, consideration of latent aspects of activities and relation to other settings should lead to greater use and acceptance of settings and thus greater certainty that potential environments will become actual.

Many designs have not worked because they have ignored such factors and been incongruent with the lifestyle of potential users. For example, people may choose autonomy rather than neighborliness and may opt for a community centered or family centered way of life (e.g., Willis 1969), in which case the behavior setting called "neighborhood" will not develop. In a case such as this the use of physical elements which will, in fact, encourage neighboring may be evaluated negatively by people who do not desire neighboring on the basis of geographical proximity and do not use urban space as a behavior setting in this way. The same feature will then be seen either positively and negatively and the effects will be very different in the two cases — all other things being equal.

For example, it seems that culs-de-sac, courts and narrow, short streets have more of a sense of community than wider, longer or busier roads (Wilmott and Cooney 1963; Appleyard and Lintell 1972). Whether this is seen as good or bad would vary and, as a result, the effects may be weaker or stronger — or, through habitat selection, there may be a population shift. Thus if some people prefer reserve and anonymity, and define their settings accordingly, an environment encouraging sociability will be seen as inhibiting while if they prefer sociability it will be seen as facilitating. The different life-styles will lead to different behavior setting systems, different uses, different evaluations and effects. The large literature on different types of neighborhoods, networks, varying evaluations of suburbia and the like can all be understood partly in terms of their congruence with people's images of appropriate behavior settings and their place in the system. Different neighborhoods are, therefore, not mutually exclusive types but represent a continuum.

The same argument also applies to the use of streets. It can be suggested that such use is partly a matter of culture and unwritten rules and partly a matter of physical design. Designing the "best" Italian or Greek Island street will have no effect if people do not regard streets as behavior settings for certain activities. If, however, streets form settings for activities — such as promenading, sitting, socializing, eating and drinking — then certain appropriate physical configurations are more likely to achieve this than others and some may be so inhibiting as to stop such behavior (Rapoport 1969(b). The distinction between two types of cities — those where the whole urban space is used for various activities and those where urban space is "waste" space to be traversed *en route* to other places (Rapoport 1969(a), p. 72), illustrated in Fig. 2.9, is clearly a distinction between two types of behavior setting systems; it is also one of ideal types rather than reality, although it distinguishes between middle-class and working/lower class neighborhoods. This proposed distinction has recently received empirical support: a pedestrian mall was seen by middle-class Americans as a space to be traversed while shopping while working class and "hippies" saw it as a place to sit, socialize, eat and play music (Becker 1973). The conflict between these views and behaviors was quite apparent and reinforces the importance of homogeneity and agreement about rules, norms and appropriate settings for behavior.

Similar differences are also found in other cases. Thus in "Midwest" the behavior setting "streets" were used for 77,544 hours per year while in "Yoredale" they were used 300,000 hours a year (Barker and Barker 1961; Barker and Schoggen 1973). If similar analyses were done in England and France, the U.S. and Italy, Greece and Australia, or even France and Brazil (Lévi-Strauss 1957) or used in comparing working class and middle class areas in the U.S. and Britain, even greater differences might be found; such differences are obvious from observation to any visitor, as are the differences in the *types* of activities occurring in streets. These differences become even more striking if one includes Moslem, South and Southeast Asian and African cities. All these are differences in the street as a behavior setting which influence the rest of the urban behavior setting system.

In Greece, for example, streets and squares act as settings for different activities and are also distinguished by time and sex. The square in a typical Greek island village is used by boys for soccer in the evening, for men to meet at the cafe during the day, for village youth to meet during the summer months and Sunday promenades, as a marketplace for women when a vendor passes through, a center for business transactions when crops are sold and a recreation center for men on Sundays where they play cards, drink and dance (e.g., Thakudersai 1972).* In fact the village lives in relationship to the square which is the most important behavior setting, or rather a set of settings separated in time. But even the house is used in relation to its immediate surroundings and the street, and streets

---

* Also based on personal óbservations during a number of trips to Greece.

generally form settings for many activities which occur in very different setting.
elsewhere.

These different street uses have major implications for planning. Thus in some
contexts open space means *green* open space, while in others it means also, or even more,
streets and squares. The differences in provision of space, in standards and evaluation of
adequacy, in the evaluation of density and crowding are clearly very great. Even when
streets are used as a major setting, the specific way of use and the various activities
allowed vary (e.g., Meyerson 1963; *The Australian* 1972(b)). These also vary with time in
a periodic manner as for the "dining" streets in Singapore, the periodic street markets still
found many places or the Mediterranean institution of the *Passagiata* where not only does
the street change uses on Sunday, but it is subdivided into a whole set of places (e.g.,
Allen 1969).

Different parts of parks are used by different groups, and different populations use
various types of parks. Thus parks themselves become systems of behavior settings (e.g.,
de Jonge 1967–68) quite apart from their relation to other settings in the city. Design in
terms of behavior setting systems would probably overcome the problem of non-use,
underuse or overuse of such facilities. Behavior setting systems, such as street use, have
clear effects on housing (e.g., Hartman 1963; Harrington 1965; Young and Wilmott 1962;
Rapoport 1969(a), 1975(b)) and on play and children's behavior. For example, children
often refuse to use playgrounds and play in parking lots, streets and other like places. In
some cases this is because such places provide more activity and danger, in others because
there may be important latent aspects of play such as impressing others or interacting
with the opposite sex (Brolin and Zeisel 1968) which depends on the relation of play
settings to the behavior-setting system and the consequences are not only for the activity
itself but the larger urban system.

The example, already discussed, of children's play in China is a question of the
behavior setting system, related to values, rules about behavior, appropriate loads of
supervision and influence on learning, enculturation and delinquency (Schak 1972;
Mitchell 1971; Anderson 1971); this also applies to certain black areas of the U.S.
(Yancey 1971; Hall 1971). Differences among behavior setting systems may also explain
cultural differences. In France and Britain children rarely use playgrounds and facilities,
and tend to play in streets and parking lots (Rapoport 1969(b), DOE 1973) whereas in
the U.S. there seems to be more use of such places (Coates and Sanoff 1972) possibly
related to the greater use of streets among European children. Subcultural differences are
also probably involved since there are cases where American children also favor parking
lots and roads (Saile *et al*. 1972); this difference may also be due to the design of the
playgrounds and their relationship to the larger system.

The appropriateness of particular settings may also be in terms of their perceptual
character (e.g., complexity for walking or playing) or the rules in it (e.g., the amount of
freedom and control people have). The latter, which is often a function of management
rather than design may greatly affect the success of designs. In the case of a housing
project, control prevented penetration of settings, there was low control and, at the same
time, the relationship of settings was inappropriate (Bechtel 1972), i.e., the behavior
setting system was inappropriate. Appropriateness may also be social – which affects the
penetration of settings – as a function of settlement size and the degree of overmanning/
undermanning (i.e., roles available per inhabitant). We have already seen that in smaller
settings people are more deeply involved and play a larger role (Bechtel 1970; Bechtel *et*

al. 1970; Barker and Gump 1964; Wright 1969, 1970) and the success of neighborhoods as intermediate between the individual and the city may be relevant in this connection.

Comparing a small town and *part* of a large city using behavior setting analysis, it appears that the amount of time spent in the dwelling is more or less constant (cf. Pappas 1967). However, there were three times as many behavior settings in a block (i.e., *ignoring the rest of the city*) as in a small town but, because city settings are overmanned, residents have less control and penetration than in the small town and are more passive (Bechtel 1970; Bechtel *et al.* 1970). This means that many more types of behavior were possible in the city, which would increase even more if the whole city were considered, i.e., the whole behavior setting system, since various blocks in the city differ. If the whole behavior setting system were considered, the differences between the city and small town would be even greater, as would the differences among groups and areas in the city. Recall the three population groups in Paris (Lamy 1967) and consider their behavior not only in terms of networks and home range but also in terms of the behavior setting system. Clearly, the three populations have quite different patterns of what they do where and when and the distribution of these settings in the city. (See Fig. 5.15).

More generally, the distribution of different settings results in a range of larger setting systems, from the urban village to the non-place urban realm. Both of these are ideal types and probably have no existence: it is a matter of different settings for different roles, at different times and for different populations, and the behavior setting system/home range/house-settlement system can be plotted.

Not only do behavior setting systems differ spatially — they also differ in time: different groups use such systems differently in terms of frequency, periodicity, etc. and the amount of time spent in different parts of the system. It is, therefore, essential to consider home and out-of-home activities together (Hitchcock 1972). The nature, extent and linkages of the behavior setting system have implications not only for an understanding how the city works and for the design of appropriate milieus for various groups, but also for the evaluation of the effect of various planning decisions. For example, the effect of a freeway through a particular area will be very different in the case of a group with an extensive behavior setting system than in the case of a highly localized group (Warrall *et al.* 1969) although if the latter group's networks are cut the consequences are apt to be more serious since the system is likely to be less flexible and adaptable.

All this discussion stresses the need to be specific and not deal with averages or generalized, unitary urban environments. Clearly different groups have different behavior setting systems. For some groups the house may be important, for others the street and neighborhood, while many others use the whole city and its settings. The relative importance of the house is not determining, so that in Los Angeles, where the house is a major setting (house, pool, barbecue and so on), people still use a wide range of urban settings, possibly no fewer than people in France for whom traditionally the house has been a much less central setting. What does vary in the two cases are the types of out-of-house settings used, the behaviors associated with them, and their spatial and temporal relationships. In effect, the various distinct urban areas are behavior setting systems or subsystems with differences in the appropriate behavior and rules and the facilities which support them, and the cues which make them known. Environmental preference can then be seen as being partly for particular behavior setting systems. This is reflected in the proximities among various facilities and groups, street use, shopping,

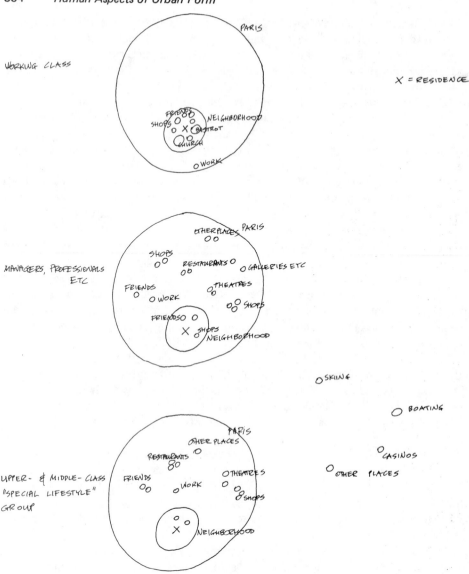

FIG. 5.15. Behavior setting systems of three groups in Paris (based on Lamy 1967).

visiting and socializing, barriers, linkages and boundaries, as well as the differences in the latent and manifest aspects of activities.

This offers one way of tackling the constancy, change and importance of place arguments. One could suggest that while many behavior settings remain constant, their proximity, extent and number used has changed greatly with urbanization, technology and so on. The fact that children have larger behavioral and cognitive spaces in small towns suggests that the growth of the extent of behavior setting systems is group specific, so that it may, in fact shrink for children, those without cars, the elderly, and the handicapped, and may be larger in traditional than in modern cities for such groups

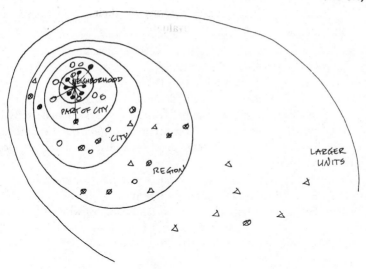

FIG. 5.16. Behavior setting system/home range/house-settlement system plotted diagrammatically for several populations.

(Rapoport 1973(c)). This also means that travel patterns can be related to the behavior setting system — the system of paths linking different settings — so that home range, movement space, behavior space, action space and similar concepts are all interrelated. Clearly, someone whose behavior settings are clustered, and where he spends much time, will have a very different movement pattern and amount of travel than someone whose behavior settings are widely separated and who spends relatively little time in each.

Behavior setting analysis in buildings has been extensively used and there has been some in urban settings. By using such analyses one can discover the nature and number of settings, the extent of the system, the intensity of links, the strength of barriers, and how frequently and for how long, settings are used. In effect, any location in the built environment possesses a behavioral character which can be described and mapped. At the same time the number of behavior setting systems in the city, and even parts of cities, are so vast that their study is rather difficult.

The House-Settlement System

In order to study behavior in environment it is clearly important to know where people go, what they do with whom and when. Given the importance of the dwelling, the question of the behavior setting system becomes, in any given urban situation, what other settings are primarily related to the dwelling. For example, if behavior is observed only within residential areas, critical behaviors which take place elsewhere may well be missed (e.g., Coates and Bussard 1974). Just looking at playgrounds (e.g., Hayward *et al.* 1974) is not enough — as we have seen one must consider *all* the places where play occurs.

In all such cases people may move in space to various places and activities, or activities may move in time to people, i.e., one place can become a setting for many activities, successively a market, fair, playground, restaurant and so on. Space and time can, thus, mutually replace each other. The greater the number of settings used for a set of activities, the larger the behavioral space. The dwelling and other elements of the system cannot be separated — nomads' dwellings and camps cannot be separated from their home range, either in terms of activities, privacy mechanisms or density and crowding calculations (e.g., Rapoport 1974). While it is particularly striking in that case, as a model it is of general applicability (e.g., Rapoport 1975(b)).

When related to the two kinds of cities and the use of streets, private and public and front and back domains home ranges, the behavior setting system and activity systems, and related to the dwelling, this leads to the concept of the *house-settlement system*. In a way this concept links much of the discussion in this chapter and a number of ideas discussed in earlier chapters.

I first proposed this notion a number of years ago arguing, in considering the *house*, that it cannot be separated from the settlement but must be seen as part of a total spatial and social system. People live in settlements and landscapes of which the house is only a part, and the way in which the larger settlement is used affects the use and hence the form of the house (Rapoport 1969(a), pp. 69–73).

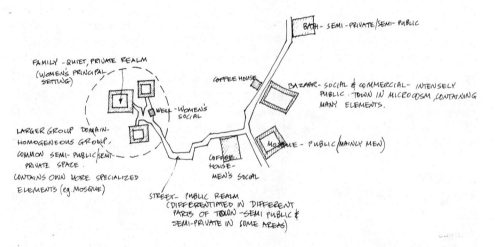

FIG. 5.17. House settlement system in Moslem town (modified, from Rapoport 1969(a)).

It can also be shown using our home range example before (see Fig., 5.8), that the use of dormitories is impossible to understand without considering where other activities take place. In this section I will concentrate on the city rather than the dwelling.

While the house-settlement system is always present, the specific elements and how they are related and used vary, i.e., different behavior settings form the house settlement system. This corresponds both to the different rule systems for public behavior and to the different domain definitions. Thus while the system itself is constant, and must always be considered, the specific nature of the elements and their relative importance are extremely variable. Different elements make up the system, different groups are involved who have different relations; the house-settlement system is influenced by kinship, social networks, sex roles, work patterns and the like — and, in turn, influences them. In the case of villages or medieval towns one worked in the house; in other cities there were guild quarters, in others yet work is strictly separated and distant: this greatly changes the specifics of the system. Life style generally influences the use of the system, one example being the four rush hours in Greece due to the siesta, the late evenings and hence use of out-of house settings and so on. The increase in leisure, if any (cf. Young and Wilmott 1973), also influences activity systems and has major implications for the house-settlement system, depending on whether the increased leisure occurs in the private or public domains and which particular settings are used.

The elements may also be far from obvious, particularly since they are related to latent functions: for example the recreational role of Japanese shopping and amusement areas which are structurally equivalent to parks in our cities (e.g., Ishikawa 1953; Nagashima 1970; Maki 1973). In fact, as we saw in Chapter 3, the definition of equivalent urban units is rather complex once simple morphological likeness is not the only criterion used. For example, a street is usually defined as "space between buildings"; it may more usefully be defined in terms of use and public/private domains — i.e., in behavior setting terms. In that case a court or compound may become an analogue, or activities may occur in restaurants, pubs, coffee shops, bazaars — or even houses; this variability both affects the definition of "street" and the description of a specific house-settlement system (Rapoport 1973(b)).

For example, in the Chinese or Punjabi village people meet in the wide part of the main street, in North Africa it is the well for women and the coffee house for men. In the Bantu village the space between the animal pens and the walls of the living compound. In Chan Kom, Yucatan, the meeting place is the steps of the little village store. In the Puerto Rican New York neighborhood the *bodega*, in South Chicago the stoop of the house for women and the elderly, the street for girls, the corners and taverns for men. In France it used to be the bistro and cafe, in Italy the piazza, galleria and cafe. In England it is the pub and street for the working class, the house and club for middle class. In Ancient Greece, it was the Agora, in Rome — the baths. Some areas have periodic promenades such as the *Passagiata* and there are many other places where social encounters in settlements take place.

It is not just the place where the meetings take place but its relationship to other places which is important: we are dealing with a system, so that a change in any one part changes all the others. In the case of housing for the elderly the use of space and the dwelling depend on adjoining areas — the boardwalk, health center, social center and the lake (Lawton 1970(b)). The use of student dormitories similarly depends on the other elements used. In effect, depending on the elements used, different groups have different behavior spaces. (See Fig. 5.18).

The specific use is related to the distinction among domains, the relevant rules and the latent aspects of activities which often determine whether they occur in front or back regions. The relationship of outdoor to indoor space is also critical: whether it is the use of the backyard-pool-barbecue-beach complex of southern California, the Anglo-Indian bungalow, club and sports grounds or the apartment where urban space must be used and which may be chosen because such use is desired. In all these cases the reliance on outdoor space increases the impact of climate *vis-à-vis* groups for whom outdoor urban space is less important, but the specific type of outdoor settings has differential effects. In any case the use of such settings has major implications for the design for specific groups. Thus the Maori of New Zealand traditionally use ten times as much space outside the dwelling as inside, and the communal open space (the *Marae*) is most important: clearly the design for them must be very different within an urban context than for

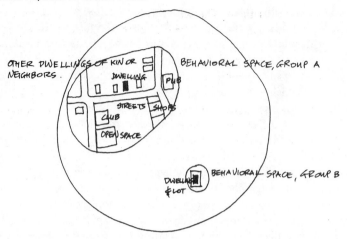

FIG. 5.18. Behavior spaces of two groups, immediate surroundings
of dwelling.

white New Zealanders (Austin 1973; in press; Austin and Rosenberg 1973; Challis and Rosenberg 1971). In that case there are also differences in dwelling requirements which would have effects on the urban system through density and height constraints.

One can also look at specific age and sex groups in terms of the house-settlement system. In the case of working-class people in London, and lower-class Chicago areas, men do not regard the dwelling as a major part of the system (Young and Wilmott 1962; Suttles 1968): their use of the city is very different to women's.

We have seen the lack of group space as part of the system may lead to juvenile delinquency because of lack of group control over children. In some cases children regard the house as a place to use and live, in others they only use it to eat and sleep but not to linger: they hence need other places in the urban system (Sprott 1958, pp. 70–71) and if these are not provided the social system may be affected. For example in New Towns it is often the lack of out-of-house places for teenagers which are a most serious problem (Australian Frontier 1971). When such places are provided they may be either the wrong ones in terms of preferences (as we saw in Chapter 2) or may be incorrectly related to other elements in the system (e.g., Brolin and Zeisel 1968): the correct relationships can only be derived from an understanding of the system.

Similarly the evaluation of various schemes can often be done in terms of the house-settlement system. For example in the case of East Liberty, Pittsburgh, the porch, as intermediate between the house and the street, between the private and public realms, was an essential link in the system. Its lack had serious consequences for socializing behavior. In this case as in others, different age groups have different systems (Bell and Kennedy *et al.* 1972). Since different groups have different systems, this concept can be used to differentiate among them and offers a theoretical schema which is both general and specific: the model applies universally, but the elements vary, may be unlikely from an ethnocentric perspective and need to be discovered rather than defined *a priori*.

In any city there is what has been called an internal and external order (Ashihara 1970). The house-settlement system links these orders, the private and public domains and, in a way, determines them. The way the external order is developed depends on what happens in the internal and vice versa. For example, as we have seen in the Japanese city, the external order is little developed. The private domain is most important and there are no public places in the Western sense of the word. The opposite extreme is provided by Ancient Athens where the house was largely for women and it was the public order which was central: a city was judged in terms of its public parts and most life took place there. Thus the parts themselves are incomprehensible without some knowledge of the whole system. It is necessary to know what happens in the house, what intermediate areas exist, where one works, meets, socializes, where public life occurs and so on. The internal and external orders are only meaningful in terms of each other. The different house-settlement systems reflect different values (the public valued highly in Athens, little in Japan), social networks of various groups, unwritten rules, public and private domains, the settings where various activities occur and so on.

Differences in these, and their spatial organization, can have major effects on planning and design at all scales. For example, community can be defined anthropologically as a "minimal unit of organization and transmission of culture" (Klass 1972). Such communities may be spatially clustered and correspond to, say, villages (or neighborhoods in the urban context). They may also be aspatial or transcend spatial clusters. Thus in India the village coexists with a caste network which extends far from it. In fact, a community in these terms, although often and importantly spatial, may also be aspatial and, in the case of West Bengal, there are five structural elements – family circle, neighborhood circle, village, circle of caste-mates and circle of villages (Klass 1972).

Knowing this helps planning and design, but may still present a problem in the case where there is no clustering; where the networks and house-settlement system lack clear spatial expression planning notions developed for such situations may not be applicable and may fail. Thus in the case of Indian tribesmen Community Development Schemes designed for villages, worked for those living in clustered villages (Doshi 1969) but not for those living in non-clustered villages; this also helps explain some of the opposition to nomads (Rapoport 1974). The relevance of this to my argument is that one can conceive, at the urban scale, the reverse situation – designers whose house-settlement system is extensive and non-clustered, designing for people who are clustered – and doing as badly. Or, more generally, planning and designing for systems which they neither know nor understand.

At the larger scale such systems can become very complicated. Consider rural China where the marketing system had great *social* significance and there was a marketing community which was a cultural unit which had a territorial identity reestablished annually through religious ritual. Once again, one cannot focus exclusively on the village and needs to consider eighteen or so villages related to a town, spread over 50 sq. kilometers and comprising 1,500 households (Skinner 1972). The operation of this marketing community can be understood in terms of the house-settlement system – more specifically the house-village-group of villages-town system, i.e., a macroscale example of the species. Movement among villages is important in the development of social networks and the *teahouse* plays an important role in meeting people. When going to market, at least an hour is spent in one or two teahouses. The peasant gradually develops links within his marketing community and knows little outside it, shopping, services and marriage are all related by the networks within the community but outside the village, as is recreation, offering a clear analogue with the city. At the same time villages in this situation are kin-based, i.e., homogeneous along those dimensions important in China; villages of the same lineage have additional links within the marketing community.

While this analysis is of the village as unit related to the larger system, and the household or individual only indirectly, it is significant that the house-settlement system seems applicable at regional as well as urban and sub-urban scales: the concept seems to be of great generality and power.

At the urban scale it enables us to examine critically various sweeping and unsupported generalizations about this or that group. For example, the fact that American middle class people use the house as the major setting for social interaction and neglect other parts of the system (such as restaurants or cafes) is deplored by some and compared to their disadvantage with Paris (Sennett 1970, pp. 76—78). Not only are these part of different systems, with different salience of the dwelling, but the French system is changing rapidly; it would appear to be more useful to understand the system operating and design for it. One also needs to be much more specific. For one thing we have seen that different groups in France have very different house-settlement systems intimately linked to lifestyle, values, images and the whole complex of profoundly felt notions about what is proper where. Even more importantly, it would be useful to study the rather extensive house-settlement system and home range of suburbanites, which may well exceed those of Parisians. It is thus important to understand and consider such variations rather than ignore, and possibly destroy, such systems because of ignorance or prejudice. For example, because the importance of the well in women's house-settlement systems in Moslem cities was not recognized, the introduction of running water had unforeseen, and serious, social consequences (Rapoport 1969(c)).

This concept can also apply to children's play. In China, working class children play in the street and have localized neighborhood-bound networks, while middle class children play in the yard and have extensive networks. This is not merely a matter of amount of space in the dwelling but also of values and lifestyle. The middle class stress the importance of good manners, being with good people and avoiding bad ones, so that there must be control of children which can be achieved in the backyard with invited playmates, but is difficult in the street (Schak 1972). The differences, within the context of Chinese culture, are very much like those between different Western sub-cultures and thus related to lifestyle in a more general way. It also, in the case of the middle class Chinese families, leads to other effects on the urban system: their children do not use parks which, therefore, attract different populations. In the case of Paris, on the other hand, while working class children also play in the street, middle and upper-class ones are taken to parks — another cultural difference.

Similarly the separation of the nuclear family from relatives and other kin, and larger social networks, will greatly affect the use of space and is one of the variables affecting the house-settlement system as are sex roles and, generally, rules about separation of groups and the use of domains. The specific house-settlement system will also affect the knowledge of the city and hence mental maps, and be influenced by preferences. These are expressed through hierarchies so that certain activities cannot occur in certain places because they are important, and hence front or public regions incongruent with the activities. The house-settlement system, thus reflects images of importance and appropriateness.

Consider one specific function — the socializing of males and as an example of the broader concept see how differently the house-settlement system operates in different cultures. The first thing that varies, of course, is that in some cases adult males socialize among themselves, in others male or other children may be included, in others male teenagers, while in others yet men and women socialize together, i.e., it is important to specify who is included and who excluded (see Fig. 5.9).

Different groups vary in the way they raise children and the extent to which children are included or excluded from the house and male company. We have seen that teenagers may or may not see the house as theirs. In Liverpool, boys above the age of twelve do not spend much time in the house unless they are ill and male solidarity is the conspicuous feature of social life (Sprott 1958). In Britain, as in the U.S., slum boys hang around with the gang and the street is important for them. In some cases, also, of course, the relationship of the street to adults is important for control, and hence crime and delinquency. In many lower class areas, in Britain and the U.S., males do not feel at home in the dwelling: there is a clear separation of groups by age and sex, with males using street corners and taverns or pubs for socializing (Suttles 1968).

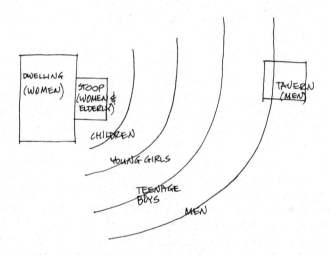

FIG. 5.19. Group separation, south side of Chicago (based on verbal description, Suttles 1968).

In Bethnal Green the pub was almost a part of the man's living room, an extension of his house and possibly more important than the dwelling, greatly influencing his use of the dwelling and urban space. Similarly her use of the house and street affects the women's use of urban space (Young and Wilmott 1962). (See Fig. 5.20).

With a move to Dagenham, the location and character of pubs change, as does the relationship between the house and the urban setting — streets, shops, other people and density. The rules also change (housing authority rules for one). All values are affected: a very different pattern prevails and the house takes on the dominant character of the middle class (Wilmott 1963) — i.e., *the house-settlement system changes*.

In the original diagram of the house-settlement system for Isphahan (see Fig. 5.17) I suggested that the coffeehouse, bazaar and mosque for men may be the equivalents of the pub for men in East London. In Turkey the function of the coffeehouse corresponds to that suggested for Isphahan on the basis of observation. Traditionally men met in guest rooms maintained by influential men, but the custom is waning and, in villages, the

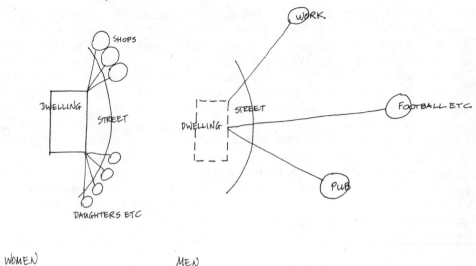

FIG. 5.20. House-settlement systems at Bethnal Green (based on verbal descriptions, Young and Willmott 1962).

coffeehouse begins to replace it — as it has already done in the city. In the latter case it has been well established since the 16th century and has survived many attempts to suppress it. It is an essential informal meeting place where men can socialize, engage in intellectual discussion, exchange gossip, do business, and where official information by the government can be got to men quickly; women never go there (Beeley 1970). Significantly, Turkish immigrant areas in Australia are distinguished by many coffee-houses as social centers.

This role of the coffeehouse is filled by all-male pub in Australia and the cafe in France which is used by both sexes. In France informal business, intellectual discussion and entertaining all tended to occur in the cafe, and there were cafes for various groups quite clearly, if informally, separated. The importance of the cafe in the French house-settlement system is clear to anyone who has lived there for any length of time, and is amusingly reflected in one of Simenon's novels where Maigret wonders how police in New York work since they have no cafes in which to stop, rest and pass the time. The cafe affects the use of the dwelling, street use and many other activities: it is a central link in the house-settlement system.

In some traditional African (and many other) settlements the men's house was the key element — without considering it the functioning of the house-settlement system cannot be understood (e.g., Fernandez 1970). In modern African cities the beer bar plays a similarly important role. These are used by both men and women and not only do people drink there but it is the main setting for recreation and games, for conversation, for joking and for the transmission of information (Gutkind 1969, p. 394): they are critically important social nodes which must be considered in analyzing the use of both dwellings and urban spaces.

In Austrian villages drinking plays a central role in the social system and is closely and intricately linked with the culture. While alcohol can be bought *anywhere*, socially the important location is the tavern or *gasthaus*. In one village with 800 inhabitants there were four such taverns (although no cafe) and within each tavern there are different rooms for different groups, and different taverns had partially different clienteles. Although drinking there is more expensive than in the house, and there are other locales for drinking at various social and ceremonial occasions, the complex web of drinking and the regular, nightly use of the tavern is of critical social importance and central to an understanding of the house-settlement system (Honigman 1963). The urban equivalent of this is the cafe in Vienna the role of which in the urban system has often been described, and the current decline of which both reflects and will clearly totally change the house-settlement system, and the use of dwellings, streets, parks and other urban elements, and people's spatial and temporal use of the city.

The Korean equivalent is the tearoom. This was important fairly recently, modified to suit Korean needs, and has become most important in the Korean city. While in Thailand the Buddhist temple became a hotel, restaurant, recreational center and bazaar, in Korea the tearoom changed in analogous ways. In 1968 there were 5,000 tearooms in Korea — 1,200 in Seoul, and 500 in Pusan: the average accommodation was 35–50. The tearoom provides rest and relaxation, is used as a place for conversation, messages and is mainly used by better educated, middle aged males. Patrons tend to use one tearoom, and visit it frequently — sometimes as often as twice a day. Its importance in the house-settlement system is due to its use as an office for business, its role as a setting for sociability and a place for local and world news to be obtained and exchanged; it is even used by academics and students — i.e., it plays an economic, social, informational and educational role (Lewis 1970) and is consequently a crucial element in the house-settlement system and must be considered in planning.*

A striking example of the often unexpected nature of such settings in the system is provided by the traditional Hungarian village. There the important male gatherings, at which most of the important decisions were made, took place in the *stables* of various important men. Without going into details, one could say that the social system of the village was crucially linked with the presence and location of these stables which were distributed throughout the village in a systematic way (Fel and Hofer 1973). If this important link was not known the relation of social organization and the house-settlement system could not be understood — and *a priori* it is unlikely that the socially critical roles of stables would be considered.

Other elements which have played similar roles are the corner drugstore and other shops in the U.S., baths in Iran and Moslem cities generally (English 1966, p. 167 for 3a). More recently regional shopping centers have become important elements: in Sydney many working class women spent most of their day there, drastically changing their use of the house-settlement system.

In the case of a city like Cairo, divided into urban villages, one finds that the coffeehouse is the meeting place for males, and serves particular groups resembling clubs more than shops (as is the case with many pubs and taverns). Women meet and socialize in streets, where children also play, and in house courtyards where laundry is done (Abu-Lughod 1969).

This role of the laundry has revived in modern cities where their latent function as social meeting places, particularly for young singles, is becoming a new and important element in the house-settlement system. This change which had occurred in the U.S. a

---

* An interesting architectural case is the role of the corridor in courthouses, described by Rapoport (1969(c)).

while ago, only reached Australia in the early 70's and therefore received notice (e.g., *Sunday Telegraph* 1972(a)). Laundromats act as meeting and pickup places, social arenas and even "psychiatric" clinics, and it has been reported that many single people visit them daily, with single pieces of laundry, so as to have a chance to socialize.

Clubs can also be an important element in the system. In the definition of neighborhood as socio-spatial schema clubs were important in defining the extent of the network and the social space. In New South Wales and Sydney, due to some law changes, many clubs developed in recent years. This has had major effects on the house-settlement systems and people's activities, with the clubs acting as drinking, dining, recreational and social centers, mainly for working class people, introducing them to lifestyles, standards and activities which they had not previously known (Vinson and Robinson 1970) and also changing their use of dwellings, pubs, beaches, football grounds and other places in the urban system.

This brief review of just one activity suggests that many other groups and activities could usefully be analyzed in detail and would help better to understand, plan and design urban areas. Some of the examples already given – of dining streets in Singapore, the use of shops in Puerto Rican areas of New York, shopping lanes in Japan, the role of mobile shops in India (e.g., Prakash 1972) and other areas, which have been neglected in urban analysis and design, all gain clarity through the use of this concept.

Similarly the effects of particular housing forms on different groups is also partly due to differences in their house-settlement systems. An understanding of this would help prevent the indiscriminate transfer of forms and solutions among countries and cultures. Consider the use of high-rise apartments. With all the problems for children, they may well be more successful in Continental Europe (where they seem less liked than commonly assumed, (e.g., Raymond *et al.* 1966)) than in England, Australia and the U.S. This would be due to the greater use of the city and lesser salience of the dwelling in the former; the difference is, in effect, between the two kinds of city. However, in examining the house-settlement system of the high rise dwelling in English-speaking countries, there is another group which should be considered – in addition to children, and whose needs are not met by high rise. These are men, who are affected because their masculine roles depend not on sitting around the coffeeshop, tavern or square but on household maintenance and gardening – which high rise flats do not provide (Social Council of Metrop. Toronto 1966). This can also be partly understood in terms of certain symbolic and latent functions of parts of the house-settlement system. The effects of high rises on juvenile delinquency at densities no higher than of other forms is also related to such factors – the role of group supervision in semi-public spaces.

The preferences for "slum" areas, such as the West End of Boston, are also related to the house-settlement system: the use of the dwelling, which seemed inadequate to planners was adequate, and the density and crowding quite low, when the whole neighborhood, streets, stoops, shops and other parts of the house-settlement system were considered (e.g., Hartman 1963) although there were, of course, also differences in definitions of environmental quality, privacy, desired interaction levels, modalities used and many other variables already discussed.

The concept of the house-settlement system thus links many of the ideas and concepts discussed in this and other chapters: for example that mental maps, as a representation of places and paths, are a reflection of the home range and, ultimately, of the nature of the house-settlement system.

In order to use the house-settlement system in analysis and design, it is necessary to be specific and do a profile which includes, among others (cf. Rapoport 1974):

Which places are used and their physical and symbolic characteristics.
By whom they are used (ethnic, class, age, sex, lifestyle groups) and where groups congregate or separate.
When places are used (weekend, weekday, time of day).
How long is spent in which places.
What is allowed or prohibited in various settings (the rules).
The latent aspects of activities.
The spatial and temporal relationships among the various places and their relationship to the dwelling.

In any place, and for any group, such an analysis is likely to prove extremely useful and offer a possible entry point into many aspects of man-city interaction.

CHAPTER 6

The Distinction Between Associational and Perceptual Worlds

I have already briefly argued for the usefulness of distinguishing between the perceptual and associational aspects of the environment. This distinction is partly based on the existence of a hierarchy of levels of meaning associated with any object in the physical environment which range from the concrete, through use and value to symbolic meanings. The distinction is clearly one of degree rather than kind and the perceptual and associational worlds are linked — the latter cannot exist without the former: the perceptual world is a necessary but not sufficient condition for the associational world. A setting can only be seen as suitable for a specific activity and as having some meaning after it is perceived as a setting. Although all human cognitive processes are an "effort after meaning" (Bartlett 1967), the suggestion is that the symbolic meanings may be more important than concrete or even use meaning. This has already proved useful in the study of landscape preferences (Sonnenfeld 1966); the way the English, for example, respond to landscapes is a function of such symbolic (historical and antiquarian) meanings (Lowenthal and Prince 1965, 1969) which, in the present context, can be equated with associational ones.

I have already suggested that higher levels of meaning are more culturally determined since appropriate associations need to be elicited and the object needs to be "read". We have also discussed the variability of associational aspects of the environment as compared to perceptual ones: the same forms in the perceptual world can elicit very different associational meanings for different groups and in different periods. Thus ancient ruins were clearly visible in Rome throughout medieval times. They formed part of the perceptual world and their use meaning was related to providing stone for building. Any associations were negative — they symbolized the devil's work. With the Renaissance a new set of associational meanings took over, symbolizing a golden age. Similarly, Amsterdam has many houses of a particular type along the canals, all of them forming an important part of the perceptual world. They have some associational aspects linked to their form — Amsterdam, Holland, 17th or 18th century. Their associations may be more variable at higher levels — charming, dull, desirable or undesirable. The Anna Frank house has very powerful associations for some people which do not *at all* depend on the form of the house (Rapoport 1970(c)); the separation of perceptual and associational worlds is almost complete.

As the value and symbolic end of the scale is approached, fewer people share meanings and it becomes difficult to design for associations. This was easier in the past, particularly in the case of traditional societies where there was better congruence between conceptual and physical environments: there was wide agreement about symbols. Today, while there is more agreement among members of a homogeneous group about such associations than among heterogeneous groups (an important reason for clustering) such meanings are still diverse and difficult to handle, although their role is crucial. For one thing, through such associations elements become important and meaningful, resulting in noticeable differences and complexity; for another they play a central role in environmental preference. By understanding their importance, and by encouraging clustering, some possibility exists for the use and manipulation of associational and symbolic aspects of environments.

The distinction between perceptual and associational worlds may thus help explain why nature scenes seem to be greatly preferred to urban scenes in the U.S., although within each group complexity does predict preference (Kaplan and Wendt 1972). The preference for natural over man-made is due, in this view, to a set of associational values attached to nature, at least in our culture, so that perceptual characteristics, such as complexity, are not used to discriminate between the two sets: associational criteria are used. Within each domain perceptual characteristics become more dominant. Also, given the relative strength of associational and perceptual elements, one may prefer simple natural settings to complex urban ones.

It is extremely likely that in other cultures, and at other times, there might have been different associations regarding the relative value of nature and cities so that the preferences may have been reversed. Alternatively, one could suggest that for evolutionary reasons nature will always be preferred, so that it is a matter of constant rather than variable associations: cross-cultural and historical analysis would help decide between these two positions.

The differences between known and used environments, and those seen in slides, may also be due to the inevitable associations which develop in the former — although all environmental preferences are partly associational and symbolic. Much of our discussion in Chapter 2 can be interpreted in these terms — the value of views, vegetation, maintenance, altitude or city center are all associational. Recall that central location still carries positive associational values and fringes negative ones in some countries. Thus in Paris the number of high status people in the center actually increased between 1954 and 1962 (Lamy 1967, p. 364) very unlike the U.S.: in France high status and positive associations relate to the center, whereas in the U.S. they relate to the periphery. The different positive or negative associations of proximity to center in various cultures mean that the relative position of groups to each other, to the center and the nature of the environmental characteristics associated with them tell those who can read the code a great deal about relative status expressed in environmental quality. It is well known that one of the principal expressed reasons for preferring suburban environments is that it is "good for children"; combined with notions of status and values attached to greenery, privacy and open space, these associational meanings play a role in environmental preferences and habitat selection. As associations change so do settlement patterns.

I am not suggesting that this is the only reason. The presence of large trees has positive effects on temperature, sound, dust and other environmental characteristics, as the disappearance of elms due to the Dutch Elm disease in Midwestern towns in the U.S. well shows (see Fig. 2.5). But associational preferences for trees are present. They may be general, because trees are part of human associations, or culture-specific and due to experience, so that "good" areas tend to be associated with many large trees and bad ones with their absence. Thus people's responses to environments partly depend on where they grew up or come from (e.g., Pyron 1971; Wohlwill and Kohn 1973): this may not only be a matter of adaptation levels but also of certain positive or negative associations attached to these environments.

In fact children's attitudes and evaluative standards are developed partly through where they live. Such experience leads to the learning of certain meanings and associations which go with particular environmental elements; they can be "profoundly important in shaping the individual's conception of standards of living, richness, comfort" and so on (e.g., Sherif and Sherif 1963). These associations are reinforced by media, reading, school and observation leading to certain environmental responses.

Such experiences affect standards of density and interaction, symbols of status and also shape associations which lead to environmental attitudes comparable to social attitudes. The perceptual world in which one lives and develops leads through direct and taught associations to an associational world, embodied in images, which is then used to evaluate and judge environments. For example, it is claimed that the freestanding house, no matter how close to another, enhances feelings of ownership, territory, privacy and self esteem (Pyron 1971, pp. 408–410; Cowburn 1966). The spacing and type of house may then have associational values particularly since it relates to children's ability to play freely, not be constrained and provides various subtle experiences which other dwellings do not (e.g., Bachelard 1969). Since such houses tend to stand in more natural landscapes than others, those preferences are also reinforced.

The congruence between form and activities depends on three aspects of environmental knowledge – type, intensity and significance (Steinitz 1968). All are part of the perceptual world, but while type congruence is mainly cognitive and the assessment of intensity is partly associational, significance is almost entirely a matter of associations and extremely variable, as the relative significance of the city center to different groups and in different countries, or the relative salience of urban elements, would suggest (e.g., Lamy 1967; Heinemeyer 1967; Doughty 1970). Significance depends on associations, and the elements selected from a given set will also vary greatly and influence noticeable differences.

Generally meaning, which is largely associational, seems to play an important, indeed central, role in the development of urban imagery (Harrison and Sarre 1971). This relates to the fact that perceptual, memory and meaning aspects of urban images use different aspects of the urban environment. Meaning, for example, seems more related to social aspects of the city than does perception (Rozelle and Baxter 1972). At the same time social aspects of the city are often judged through the meaning of physical elements, which are associational and symbolic.

Clearly, in the case of urban design, group associations are more important than individual ones as are the relationships between form characteristics, noticeable differences and association formation. Differences in behavior setting and house-settlement systems, activity systems and networks, knowledge of the city and mental maps are influenced by, and influence, the significance and associations which are also variable. This also follows from the very different urban hierarchies which have existed, with different elements ranked in different orders as in our comparison of Japan and Greece, or traditional cities (cf. de Lauwe 1965(a); Wheatley 1971; Krapf-Askari 1969; Rapoport 1969(c)). The inability to comprehend other hierarchies and the misunderstanding of such hierarchies is not just a matter of associational aspects but of environmental codes not being legible; but at this point it is significant that urban hierarchy depends on shared associations and one needs to examine urban hierarchies for subgroups in cities; to my knowledge they never have been.

This approach also throws additional light on the difference in urban cognition between U.S. and Arab cities: in the latter social and behavioral significance, associated with particular urban elements, was most important for imageability (Gulick 1963). These are clearly associational values and, while variable between, say, Tripoli and

Boston, should also be variable for various groups in each of these cities although probably less so in Tripoli than Boston. The difficulty which visitors had in identifying the Tell in Tripoli, and in learning what goes on there, can also be understood in terms of developing associations with specific elements and activities, and their congruence. The general conclusion that urban cognition is the product of both visual form (perceptual world) and social significance (associational world) suggests that the distinction between the perceptual and associational worlds is useful both generally and specifically in determining operationally the meaning of Lynch's elements (Lynch 1960) for any given group, which will partly depend on associations.

For example the selection of landmarks, or even the definition of elements as landmarks, may well vary with their significance, i.e., associational values; the definition of elements as paths or edges is associational, so that a freeway may be a path for some and an impenetrable barrier for others; the definition of a district and whether it is seen as a place which can be entered, or is to be avoided, are all matters of associations. Since they influence knowledge, mental maps, and behavior setting and activity systems, they are important.

The distinction between associational and perceptual worlds may also partly explain the differences and agreements in environmental preferences of various groups. Whatever the reasons for them, planners and designers lack the specific associations which users of areas have. Users' associations affect the emotional significance of elements and places, and the relative importance attached to various parts of the environment (e.g., lawns, plants and objects as opposed to spatial organization). They also play an important role in the "filters" which influence the perceived environment and help explain the variability of standards, and the fact that the stimulus properties of the environment are essentially symbolic. While the distinction proposed is abstract, related in the first instance to symbolism, not really operational, and difficult to use in design consciously at present, it still is most useful as an analytical tool. It helps understand many aspects of man–environment interaction not otherwise clear and suggests many areas needing research. It can also lead into important criteria for design: in the short range it is possible that, through the consistent use of particular forms and activities, associations may gradually be developed (as in the case of traffic systems); also, even today, there seem to be some culturally shared associations.

Symbolism and the Urban Environment

In the discussion so far the concept of symbolism has often been introduced. There have been many attempts to define symbols, but there seems to be agreement about certain features. They embody abstractions; they are distinct from signs which draw attention to the object or situation which they bespeak whereas symbols are understood when the idea which they present is understood. The function of symbols is thus communication and there may well be a relationship with environments which can communicate appropriate behavior and expectations. Behavior, artefacts and the environment can be understood as communicative and symbol systems giving concrete expression to concepts of values, meanings and the like (cf. Rapoport 1970(c)).

Clearly there is a relation here to our discussion about the nature of images and ideas embodied in environments, environmental quality, symbolic landscapes; the relationship between behavior settings and their non-verbal cues and appropriate behavior. Generally people respond actively, and often creatively, to stimuli; they shut out some, and modify others in various ways (DuBos 1965, 1966; Lee 1966; Kates 1966): they symbolize environmental stimuli and respond to these symbols. Therefore, in order to understand the effects of these stimuli, the stimulus properties of the environment must be related to their symbolic properties. People's responses effectively depend on the meaning which they attach to stimuli, which is associational and, in turn, depends on past experience, and culture influencing standards and environmental evaluation (Rapoport and Watson 1972).

It is this which makes it so difficult to use symbols in design today. In the past the meanings and associations were more fixed, and hence shared, whereas today we have shifting, multiple and varied meanings. There may still be shared meanings in one culture or even for all human beings, but most responses have become increasingly variable and unpredictable — i.e., idiosyncratic rather than discursive (Rapoport 1970(c)). In traditional cultures particularly, vernacular design being based on shared symbols was largely symbolic. It is interesting to note that in totalitarian countries — Nazi Germany in the past and Communist countries today — it was, and is, possible to speak of cities as "monumental propaganda" and "an important political problem".* This is because a single symbolic system can be imposed, and is assumed to communicate. The essence of design, therefore, is the act of symbolization which is only later given physical expression although, for example, place definition can occur without building as among the Australian Aborigines (Rapoport 1972(e)). In fact Aborigines' symbolic boundary definitions are very similar to those preceding the founding of a Roman City (Rykwert (n.d.)) except that the building never takes place.

The symbolism of landscape and forms clarifies many aspects of planning and design otherwise unclear: the relationship of Greek temples to the land (Scully 1962), the significance of Roman, Chinese, Indian, African and other cities (Wheatley 1969, 1971; Müller 1961) and buildings (Wittkower 1962). Not only were whole cities symbolic structures, within them there were also clear symbolic structures, such as the height symbolism of traditional Bangkok or the color symbolism of ancient Peking, where different physical devices were used to indicate status. In all these cases the symbolism was not only shared rather than idiosyncratic but, because the symbols were explicit, they could be clearly embodied in schemata. Today not only are symbols idiosyncratic, and hence variable, but they are largely implicit — hence difficult to express and to embody in schemata. The elements which are used for symbolic purposes vary accordingly and may be hair and clothing styles, cars, boats, drink, awnings — or car license plates (*Sunday Telegraph* 1972(b)). Thus, while many aspects of the modern city can still be explained in symbolic terms, this is neither clear nor evident to the users themselves.

The historical evidence is quite clear. The very fact that cities can be discussed as ideals and symbols suggests that they have these special qualities (Botero 1606; Lang 1952). Whole landscapes in primitive cultures can be so understood (Rapoport 1969(a), 1969(f)) so that in some cases, such as India, whole countries and their cities can be shown to reflect a single symbolic system (Sopher 1964). The distinctions between the American and English landscapes can also be best understood in terms of the images and symbols which they embody (Lowenthal and Prince 1964, 1965, 1969; Lowenthal 1968). Since

---

* See *Khudozhnik i Gorod* (The artist and the city), Moscow, Soviet Artist 1973.

landscapes are not "designed" but embody the activities, decisions and choices of many individuals and institutions, this demonstrates the pervasive nature of these symbols. This also applies to urban landscapes: the differences among cities in different places are due to the different symbols embodied in them.*

Even if one accepts this as applying in the past, and the evidence is overwhelming, the question is still posed, given the difficulties in using symbols today, whether there is any value in using this concept in the contemporary city, and whether such use will help designers either in understanding or designing urban environments. I will argue that such concepts are still most significant, particularly if approached through the *variations* in symbolism of different groups in different areas.

At present the overall shape of cities, which were the carriers of cosmological symbolism in the past, no longer play that role since modern cities have no shape in that sense of the word. One must, therefore, consider the symbolism of parts of cities, artefacts and eikonic systems such as signs; it may be something as "insignificant" as lawns or as major as the symbolism of city centers — both already discussed. The evidence is much clearer for buildings. For example the preference for individual houses has a large symbolic component (Rapoport 1969(a); Cooper 1971). Most people in many countries, of whatever income and background, indicate their ideal house as freestanding with space around (Raymond *et al.* 1966). Even those children raised in flats tend to draw houses in this way (Cowburn 1966; Rand 1972; King 1973) although their proportion is lower than for children in houses (Michelson 1968). Whether this is due to children's books and teachers, or whether it is a matter of archetypes, defined as the most likely schemata (e.g., McCully 1971) is difficult to say. In any case, this seems to be a very powerful image which is basically symbolic; flats are not seen as "home" in the same way (cf. Bachelard 1969).

This also applies to gardens; for example, in China it is possible to distinguish between Confucian and Taoist gardens (Moss 1965), i.e., philosophical systems are embodied in them. In fact one of the reasons for the importance of gardens, which influences the preference for individual houses, is that they can easily be used to symbolize various attitudes: the important distinctions between front and back, for example, are generally indicated through garden symbol manipulation. When these are related to the appropriate activities (and here the symbolism of their latent aspects may be the most important) it would seem that one of the symbolic systems in the city is in terms of front/back and other domain definitions, which are an important aspect of the organization of meaning. Similarly other cognitive categories and symbolic structures are embodied in environments generally.

Even when the evidence relates more to the dwelling, one can derive indications of urban significance from the house-settlement system. For example, whether the relationships between dwelling and street are positive or negative, which activities occur in the street, the nature of the dwelling and the separation and linking of people, will all have major effects on the urban setting and its use (Zeisel 1969; Brolin and Zeisel 1968). Since the preferred form of housing is a most important influence on the form of cities, it follows that the symbolic values which lead to particular housing forms, their spatial arrangements and location will have major effects on cities. It also follows that if we want to change housing forms in any given way, the symbolism of the dwelling must be

* Since this was written, a book which discusses this very well has appeared — Tuan (1974).

understood. For example, it will not help much to argue for the importance of clustered housing, flats or whatever unless the symbolic meanings of the preferred and disliked forms are understood; they can only easily be changed through manipulating the appropriate symbols.

The symbolism of dwellings and residential areas is central to habitat selection and the meaning attached to planning. Thus the presence of certain people is judged through houses of a certain price range and type (not too different and not too much alike) fine lawns, good maintenance, appropriate separation of front and back activities (Eichler and Kaplan 1967; Werthman 1968); these are all symbolic. Thus address and area are often used to indicate status and position. Dominant groups try to mark their differences through environment and location — as they have always done (Schnapper 1971, pp. 90, 126). Different groups use different symbols to indicate this — and there are groups which do not use dwellings and environment to indicate status; we have seen that when two such groups are close conflict is inevitable.

The cues used by any group can be very subtle and, unless understood, very misleading. Thus in Westchester County, near New York, in an area of very expensive houses, two very separate and distinct landscapes symbolize two groups. The higher status group relies on less well-maintained grounds and houses, less exposure, the absence of certain symbols such as elaborate mailboxes, and colonial eagles, and the very nature of streets — lack of sidewalks and streetlighting. Newcomers are evaluated in terms of their manipulation of such symbols (and also behavior and clothing) and the correlation between landscape and status (as indicated by other variables) is very high indeed (Duncan 1973). This is a particularly striking example of the symbols used by groups to assert their identity in modern urban areas, but many other examples exist demonstrating the subtle cues used — materials, planting, location of garbage cans, presence of certain people, perceived density and so on; all are used by people to read the status and nature of urban areas and the people living in them (e.g., Royse 1969) — if the environmental symbols can be read. Frequently new urban areas lack such legible cues, e.g., distinctions between front and back may not be present and social identity cannot be established through the environment. Since people cannot be judged through environmental cues, one plays safe and does not interact. An important function of environment is thus to express culture, values, activities, and relative status — inhabited space in an image of oneself (Petonnet 1972(a), p. 115; Lofland 1973). The symbolism of areas is also used to establish group territoriality, so that symbols indicate which group "owns" an area, what behavior is expected and whether one is welcome or not (Suttles 1968). This helps explain why originally identical areas in Los Angeles were transformed into different places, mainly through planting, by Japanese and Mexican-Americans (Rapoport 1969(a)).

Significantly, as in the case of other landscapes, this occurs through numerous individual decisions — i.e., it is based on shared symbols. The differences among designers and non-designers, and other group differences in environmental preferences discussed in Chapter 2, can all be attributed, in large measure, to symbolism: environmental quality is largely symbolic and expresses the images held by people, often unconsciously and beyond awareness. Thus the choices made, and the way houses are fixed, painted and remodelled, reflect symbolic values becoming indicators of culture. In Sydney, where there are many ethnic groups, one can distinguish among them through the types of houses, their colors and modifications, the relative importance of house and garden, of house and neighborhood (Stanley 1972). Clearly, if there is clustering, areas of variable character will develop, expressing the symbol systems of various groups. Under these conditions particular locations within the city, and their physical and social characteristics, all take on symbolic meaning and indicate much about individuals and groups; they become symbols of social, ethnic and other identity and play a role in the survival of such groups (e.g., Siegel 1970).

Consider clustering. The differentiation of functions, meanings and values in the city, which is hierarchic since social structure is rarely homogeneous, is related to, and reinforced by, symbolism. A space which is suitable for one group may well be most unsuitable for another — and hence the clustering process. In effect groups cluster according to symbols which express preferred lifestyles and behaviors — and communicate them. Since symbols are the largest elements for grouping information, it follows that shared and intelligible symbols are an efficient way of providing and handling large amounts of information.

Normative integration and acceptance of standards of behavior — i.e., membership in the group residing in an area — is helped by the symbolism of that area. We have seen that children absorb these partly through the environment; certain elements become accepted by groups as indicating their social identity, they become obligatory and exercise constraint on the individual and his behavior. While these symbols are not, of course, exclusively environmental, these latter play a role in this process and have been rather neglected and ignored — compared to more purely social and cultural symbols. Material elements and areas then become symbolic identification and are representative of meaning, values and identity, in turn, determining people's attitudes to them (Paulsson 1950, p. 90; Sawicky 1971, pp. 91 ff.). When there is congruence between conceptual environments with all they embody, and physical environments, they reinforce each other and there is a possibility of shared symbol systems — achieved partly through consistent use and associations. Thus the city can be analyzed as a system of symbol systems with different levels of generality — which, in fact, follows from our earlier discussion of images. There are hence central and standard areas known to most (although preference and use vary), down to areas of specific, local and idiosyncratic *group* symbolism. This ignores idiosyncracy at the individual level; one cannot design for these symbols, meanings and associations; for homogeneous groups, however, their variability is reduced and one can also allow for them through open-ended design.

Symbols, then, have the ability to keep values before individuals in daily life and thus heighten group consensus. From our perspective the question is whether it is the area itself which has this symbolic meaning or the artefacts within it. This question, however, is moot: the character of the area depends on the artefacts within it, is subjectively defined as an area of specific character through being noticeably different from other areas in terms of such artefacts and people and its definition and naming further reinforce this role. Thus, through the subjective definition of areas (and social homogeneity) people are, in effect, attaching symbolic values to areas. These symbolic representations are associated with the use and avoidance of space; the city can be seen as a complex set of symbolized areas. Any given group will only know some — most will be unknown, will be avoided. Thus when boundaries are defined as cognitive constructs they become barriers leading to avoidance, special use and so on — all indicated through symbols.

Thus even the nature of networks, kinship relations and home ranges are partly symbolic, as are the rule systems and non-verbal cues for behavior in specific settings.

Symbolism is thus linked to the communicative function of the environment generally — but only where this has not broken down. The difference between groups which are space- and neighborhood-bound are those which are less so may be seen in terms of strong or weak symbolic attachment to local areas as opposed to other symbol systems. The symbolism of old vs. new may have major implications for redevelopment, planning and rebuilding as in the effects of certain areas in Boston which prevented the typical U.S. disregard of older areas (Firey 1947, 1961) or when West German cities were rebuilt along traditional lines unlike the rest of Europe (Holzner 1970). Generally, the reconstruction of cities damaged by floods or wars on the same site, time after time, which has frequently been remarked, can also be seen in terms of symbolism of site and place.

Some of the problems of urban renewal can also be seen in terms of the importance of urban symbols. The destruction of urban areas by renewal not only disrupts social networks but also leads to a loss of symbolic identification — in terms of space, artefacts and with the past. For example, when Warsaw was rebuilt after World War Two, the old city (*Stare Miasto*) was the first place rebuilt, indicating the importance of this named place with critical symbolic value as a focus which transcended "practical" use. The rest of reconstruction could then follow — Warsaw was once more a place (Cox 1968). This is an urban analogue of the Barriadas in Lima where the front door takes precedence over a roof as a symbol of house and the facade and parlor are finished before the dwelling is complete (Mangin 1963; Turner 1967). It is also comparable with the fact that front lawns are the first things finished in new suburban areas even if one has to do without furniture (Werthman 1968).

This suggests that by manipulating the appropriate symbols, images of places can be changed and particular populations attracted. This has been demonstrated at least in one case in Denmark, where the decline of the town of Hostelbro was reversed through image manipulation using the appropriate symbols (Manus 1972). More generally, it could be suggested that new towns could attract middle class people by manipulating the appropriate images and symbols (Rapoport 1972(a)).

The symbolism of space in the city relative to status includes its amount, its quality and its location. Higher status groups have more space, of better quality and located better. While "amount" is relatively objective (although the actual standards may vary), the definition of better quality and location are variable and need to be understood, as do the symbols used to indicate them. Cities can be seen as symbolic message systems, although there may be disagreement about the messages, and the medium used: the messages may also not be understood. In addition to indicating status, group membership and social identity such systems can also be seen in terms of the organization of information, movement or eikonics (e.g., Kepes 1961; Scott-Brown 1965; Carr 1973). Cities in different eras and places and different groups within cities in a given context can be compared in terms of their symbolic systems.

We have seen that because of the multiplicity of groups in modern cities it is difficult to use symbols as compared to cities where people shared symbols, or where the symbolism of a single dominant group or individual could be imposed; also cities where heterogeneous populations are able to cluster and use appropriate symbols can more successfully handle heterogeneity symbolically.

There are symbols in modern cities: these may be for whole cities (e.g., Brasilia or Chandigarh) or at the smaller scale of projects and urban renewal. But these are designers', and tend to be idiosyncratic and lacking any common base with users. Where

such a base exists, or can be provided, the system has better chances of working —
· hether this base is agreement about the meaning of certain elements (Rapoport
1973(a)), movement systems or other ordering systems which filled that role in the past
(Bacon 1967). Examples, already discussed, include Moslem and Chinese cities which
relied on the quarter system within a formal framework with symbolic meaning, but each
quarter developed its own group identity. While these larger structures are important, the
major role of symbolism in the city is in terms of smaller settings for group behavior.
Cities have social structure, people are aware of one another and expect and exhibit
regular behavior. This social structure is given expression through objects symbolizing this
structure, its values, beliefs and knowledge. Legible symbolic information in the city enables people to perceive this structure and act accordingly (e.g., Beshers 1962, pp. 21, 55);
this is an important function of the built environment; since there is frequently no face-
to-face contact in the city, such environmental cues replace it through symbolic contact.

Thus, in the final analysis, the role of symbols is to communicate the socio-cultural
system and to give cues for appropriate behavior. As we have seen, environmental
symbols are increasingly important even though not used as consistently as in the past. If
one cannot communicate, one cannot relate and when differences among people become
so great that symbols no longer have common meaning then people search for new
symbols; generally the absence of symbols and symbolic integration may lead to
breakdown and social pathology (e.g., Duncan 1972). The search for an understanding of
how symbols work in the city, and how and what they communicate seems critical.

Environment as Communication

The built environment is partly the organization of meaning and communication. This
concerns the structuring of communication among people — facilitating, blocking,
separating and linking varying individuals and groups. It also concerns the organization of
the communication from the environment itself — i.e., the meaning it has for people.
Clearly, since people behave differently in different behavior settings, these settings are
able to elicit appropriate behavior; this implies that the settings contain cues for behavior
which the users are able to read and understand — and are willing to obey. But it also
·means that the environment can be conceptualized as a form of communication and, if
that is so, that this communication can be organized and structured.

This structuring, the establishment of environments and settings, are ways of eliciting
appropriate images, definitions of situations and behavior. Since subjective and
"objective" definitions are often incongruent, the settings, while permitting a variety of
responses, constrain them. Once defined culturally, environments limit behavior if the
cues are read, understood and one is ready to obey them. Put another way, an environment communicates the most likely choices to be made; settings are meant to elicit
congruent emotions and actions. Settings are meant to set up appropriate situations,
interaction or transactions (e.g., Blumer 1969(a)) and they can only do so if they
communicate; clothing, manners and other elements play a similar role (Rapoport, in
press(b)).*

This is also implicit in the notion of the indirect affects of environment on behavior. If
people read environmental cues, make judgements about the occupants of settings, and

---

* After writing this I came across a useful discussion of some of these notions from a somewhat
different perspective in Perinbanayagam (1974).

then act accordingly, it follows that the environment communicates social and ethnic identity, status and so on. In fact much of the discussion about symbolism, the associational world and the difficulty of manipulating it consciously, can be related to the notion of the environment as a form of communication.

In geography the notion of cultural landscapes as an active medium of communication, which not only embody values and ideals but influence human behavior, is to be found. The landscape becomes a system of behavior settings developed to elicit appropriate behavior. In this context, and also in that of what has been called the "new archaeology" (e.g., Chang 1968; Clark 1968; Ucko *et al.* 1972), the physical environment can be seen as congealed information, since it can be "read". This also follows from the choice model (Fig. 1.7) since sets of consistent choices are encoded in the built environment and relate to other systems (cf. Wagner 1972(a); Rapoport, in press(a)). The built environment thus contains symbolic information, is a major form of cultural information, and transmits many non-verbal messages which, if read, understood and obeyed (i.e., they can be rejected), and if congruent with shared rules, elicit appropriate behavior (cf. Wagner 1972(b).

In this view the environment is a form of non-verbal communication and the physical setting is not only an expression of a culture but also as a link with its unwritten rules and other forms of non-verbal communication.

To what extent can urban environments be used to communicate given messages in a situation where there are many different groups who might not be able to read, understand or be unwilling to obey the cues communicated? The willingness to obey cues once read and understood is implicit in the appropriateness of the messages; the important questions are then legibility and comprehension. If design is a form of encoding, and assuming the information is appropriate, the question is, then, whether users can read, i.e., decode, the cues (see Fig. 3.1). The problems of various groups in the environment, among them designers and users, can then be conceptualized as non-communication: of one group encoding information which others cannot decode. Social interaction can also be seen as a form of communication: the preference for clustering with like people is then a way of ensuring that social communication occurs, and also that the rules, cues and codes — behavioral and environmental — are shared and can be decoded and understood. Social networks thus express social communication and are affected by the physical environment which is itself also a form of communication.

Since much of non-verbal communication is culturally variable one needs to identify the cues which influence particular groups to define places and situations and act accordingly. This may well be in the form of cultural "stereotypes" embodied in schemata and images. In any case, one would then be able to provide the form-activity congruence which is necessary and indicate it through environmental cues, reinforced by properly placed verbal and graphic message systems; all these need to be highly redundant — involving all types of cues and sensory modalities. The problem for the designer is to indicate the appropriateness of settings, i.e., give cues for appropriate behavior by making the setting congruent with behavior rules.

Our discussion of noticeable differences is related to this: if certain characteristics indicate that a setting, such as a street, is commercial, industrial or tourist, and thus influences, guides and directs behavior, it is a form of communication (e.g., Ruesch and Kees 1956, pp. 89 ff.). Interestingly, the physical environment seems to have a similar communicative function among animals — it indicates status and reminds them about their unfinished plans (Miller, Gallanter and Pribram 1960, pp. 78–79); it clearly functions in this way for people.

The way urban landscapes indicate group identity is a prime example of this form of communication whereby the physical environment transmits certain cues about the social system and thus elicits appropriate behavior (cf. Sanoff 1973). The eliciting of appropriate behavior directly, as in front or back, private or public settings is also part of this process, as is the effect of even more specific areas, buildings and even rooms of particular character. The types of domains, the cues which mark them and the expected behavior all vary with culture but the process itself is common. In the colonial city in India different areas were clearly differentiated, elicited appropriate behavior and admitted and excluded various groups. In modern Indian cities housing is still carefully classified into a number of grades related to income and status and grouped so that, if the codes and standards are known the house type, size and garden indicates who lives there and what behavior is expected (Grenell 1972).

We have already seen that in middle class U.S. and Australian suburbs certain cues are used in such a way: well-maintained lawns are symbols of status and good behavior. Front lawns in new areas are done first even if one has to go without furniture, and the front yard is done before the back yard. Another important cue is the presence of a variety of house styles, although these must not be too different or depart from the norm – i.e., they should be words in a common language, not a different language. The relative importance of these cues may differ in various areas, or different cues (e.g., special recreational facilities) may be used, but all communicate status and an ideal lifestyle. For example lagoons or lakes with boats, horse riding paths or golf courses indicate certain images and communicate an identity, even though very few people would actually use them (16% for lagoons and 7% for golf courses (Eichler and Kaplan 1967, p. 114)). All these physical elements – shops, houses, landscaping, boulevards and recreational facilities communicate a high-status group image and maximize the symbolic status of the area. The proximity or distance of services and non-residential uses play a similar role; while there is an element of economic motive in this (protecting one's investment) this is done through symbolic and communicative elements which are the more important: they provide one of the few ways of indicating position and identity without face-to-face communication. Since such cues alone may not communicate, the tendency to cluster of like people, with similar forms of communication, can be seen as reinforcing the messages, if only through redundancy, and also to be able to use areas (address). In the case of a heterogeneous city, this is most useful since some cues, at least, are likely to be understood and tell people what to expect and how to act.

Thus the notion of multichannel redundancy, important in perception and orientation, also seems to be applicable to non-verbal communication (Birdwhistell 1968). While it has been investigated only for linguistic and paralinguistic behavior, comparing what is communicated verbally, through gestures, facial expressions, body posture, and so on (e.g., Birdwhistell 1968; Mehrabian 1972) it seems equally applicable to the physical environment. One could then argue that not only should urban environments try to achieve multichannel redundancy through all senses, through the congruence of activity and form, and through the coincidence of physical environment with verbal, graphic and eikonic symbols, but also through redundancy relative to social aspects. This means the clustering of people of like character with their common environmental preferences and symbols, and their varied, but internally consistent, linguistic and paralinguistic behaviors.

In that case the environment will reinforce, and be reinforced by, non-verbal behavior — gestures, facial expressions, proxemic behavior, voice loudness, manners, dress, appropriate front and back behavior and all the other unwritten rules.

The communicative function of the physical environment, both its organization and use, needs to be seen as part of the continuum of non-verbal communication ranging from fixed-feature, semi-fixed feature and non-fixed feature; (comprising the traditional subject matter of non-verbal communication studies, among them spacing, eye-contact, clothing, gesture and body posture). It is likely that the elements in these various classes vary systematically and there is at least some evidence of this at the microscale: at a conference the non-fixed and semi-fixed features varied consistently and systematically together (Collier 1967, p. 40) — clearly, given the time scale involved, fixed-feature elements could hardly vary.

Redundancy would also be introduced through consistent house and garden treatment, curtains and whatnots, house furnishings, street use, shops, restaurants and so on. This redundancy would make it more likely that messages and meanings would get through to their intended receivers than if there were none. Also by knowing through experience that given areas "belong" to specific groups, the types of cues to be expected would soon be learned; through consistent associations there would be additional likelihood of appropriate reading as well as willingness to "obey" — in view of the way strangers act in others' territories.

Since there are cultural differences in the stress on various senses, the use of different codes, and variability in channel sensitivity among individuals, the likelihood of communication among individuals and groups improves with increasing redundancy. This is also helped by systematic and regular relationships among behavior, environmental settings, symbols, form and manners, rules and so on; the communicative function of the physical and social environments improve as they become more predictable, as the culture "standardizes" them. Clearly the more complex and varied a culture the more complex must be the communicative systems — yet *in our cities the opposite has happened — as the system has become more complex, the communicative function of the environment has been reduced, not least because of the deliberate and forcible elimination of homogeneous areas with the possibility of multichannel redundancy.**

It seems that the problems of intercultural communication are due to non-verbal communicative elements, which one must be able to read and interpret. These surround the more formal communication channels, and can be spatial and environmental, as well as of the more commonly considered kind. The "adumbrations" (Hall 1964) account for a large proportion of the message in the case of linguistic and paralinguistic behavior (Mehrabian 1972). While there are no clear data on the specific role of environmental adumbration, it is likely to be rather important.

Since language is the main symbol system used by people, one can consider linguistic analogues. Linguistic models, while rather abstract, provide useful insights into the processes of non-verbal communication of this type (Gumperz and Hymes 1964). In these models there are notions of the integral relation between communicative form and function and the role of context. There is the notion of participants — senders and

---

* It is interesting to note that among animals there is a similar relationship between the complexity of a social system and the communication system (e.g., Brereton 1972). Given the species specific needs, there would appear to be interesting analogues among different groups of people and the link to redundancy is intriguing.

receivers – who use certain channels to send messages based on shared codes, which are thus related to social and cultural variables. The form of the messages plays a role in comprehension, as do the settings and whether messages are encouraged, permitted or prohibited. In some such models communication is studied in terms of the relation among setting, participants, functions of interaction, form and values held by the participants. The setting is seen as involving the locale (time and place, and the situation) which is very similar to the definition of the behavior setting. While, generally, little of this has been applied to the environment it seems applicable and the analogies and insights clear and useful.*

People can identify the nature of areas, judge their quality and status, identify settings and know how to behave. In the same way that restaurants and hotels are judged as being of particular types, with predictable behavior (Rapoport 1973(a)) urban areas can be evaluated in terms of status, whether public or private, front or back and, if the rules (or codes) are known, one can then act appropriately with regard to the environment itself or the people in it – i.e., there is the same relation among setting, participants, functions, forms, codes and values as in the linguistic model.

When one says that traditional cities had clear hierarchies and distinctions between important and unimportant, sacred and profane, city and country, primary and secondary streets, areas of group A or B, one is, in effect, saying that the city provided a clear system of communication where all messages were clear and, since symbols were shared, elicited predictable and appropriate behavior. In modern cities the message systems are disordered at various levels. Some systems serve the whole city in which many populations live; there is little provision for specific systems; there is the idiosyncratic nature of symbols and codes and, consequently, variability among legibility of cues, noticeable differences and associations, and the definition of domains and categories (which also vary with culture).

Proposals have been made for designing modern cities as message systems, such as the need to rely more on heraldic – verbal and eikonic – signs than on spatial cues (Scott-Brown 1965; Venturi *et al.* 1969, 1972; Carr 1973). Given proper attention to noticeable differences and other variables discussed this would help, particularly if general components of the system were standardized and thus generated consistent associations. But one needs to go beyond these and organize the urban environment itself: there the problems are greater because of the cognitive and definitional aspects, noticeable differences and the highly variable nature of environmental symbols.

Consider the suggestion for the use of clear distinctions between primary or secondary roads or streets. This depends on both noticeable differences and legibility of cues: in Chandigarh the seven types of roads are unclear, and even the major distinction between green strips and bazaar streets is unclear because they are not noticeably different. The use of cues to indicate other distinctions among roads is even less likely. In the traditional Indian city the clear distinction between bazaar streets and others, and among domains generally, makes the appropriate behaviors much more likely. It seems useful to accept that there is a wide vocabulary of noticeable differences and cues and that these can be organized. In the case of common areas, the city at large, including common facilities and

---

* There is a body of work which applies semiology and semiotic analysis to the environment – e.g., Barthes 1970–71, Choay 1970–71; Jencks and Baird 1969; Jencks 1972; among many others. This takes a rather different approach and is even more abstract. The work of René Parenteau and his group at the Université de Montreal is a good example of application.

movement channels, they are best considered in terms of noticeable differences, the perceptual world and simple, generally accepted, symbols and associations. Complex and affective meanings, and symbols, are best confined to smaller scale elements, even if that would make some areas unintelligible to outsiders. It suggests a city based on a hierarchy of meanings, symbols and levels of communication.

It is significant that most discussions of the city as a communicative environment deal with the large, designed systems (e.g., Crane 1960). For heterogeneous populations with variable symbols and codes a minimal, simple overall system which can be "imposed" and learned, partly through consistency, and stereotypes (i.e., noticeable differences uniformly linked to character) seems more useful. Within this overall framework understood by all and designed in terms of noticeable differences, legibility and consistent character, would be the more variable, rich, significant and more detailed areas and subareas with more complex meanings communicated to more homogeneous populations.*

The greater and more predictable communicative effectiveness of traditional settlements is due to the greater uniformity and sharing of symbols and a greater coincidence of conceptual and physical environment, helped by the greater consistency of the urban system itself. Recall the consistent relation of urban form and kinship in Ancient Mexico, of form and group membership in the Moslem city, the uniformity of spatial organization at all levels in Las Casas (see Fig. 1.4).

The Japanese city, which we have already discussed several times from different points of view, also well illustrates these points. For example the Japanese city has never had major public places: shopping and entertainment areas and religious buildings are used for activities partly occurring in parks, squares and other such spaces in Western cities. This means that the settings corresponding to these activities elicit different behaviors and appropriately so, although this could be misleading and disorienting to those not in the know who could not understand the cues.

Spatial domains are also organized very differently: this can be very confusing in terms of orientation; it also allows small, local areas (*chome*) to play a major role in coping with density. This latter is also aided by the difference in handling the separation of private and public domains, and the extreme variability of behavior rules in the two domains which are also confusing to outsiders. We have seen how special institutions — such as the inn, bath, and drinking — are used for stress reduction, and how the house-settlement system differs from other places. One can also trace major consequences for house and garden design, behavior, dress and the like due to sitting on the floor within the dwelling (e.g., Fitzgerald 1965, pp. 2–4) which plays a part in the total system.

Since most time is spent in the dwelling and immediate neighborhood, then the very different nature of these elements will greatly influence what is being communicated. The blank walls of the Japanese house, and the clear and "brutal" separation of public and private, can be extremely disturbing to Westerners who misread the city and its meanings. It has been suggested that the recreational elements are important in communicating the relationship of people to cities (Nagashima 1970). The major differences in the two sets of such spaces in the Japanese and Western city would be very critical in communicating attitudes about people–city relations. (This could also apply to Italians in the U.S.

---

* In effect this distinction is proposed by Bacon (1967) although his discussion is more in terms of spatial organization than communication — and he tends to attach a high symbolic meaning to the overall frameworks rather than make them simple.

lacking the appropriate public places for certain activities (cf. Gruen 1966, pp. 173–174)). Similarly non-Japanese would not understand how stress and overload are to be handled and how environmental cues relate to these functions. Without extending the argument, it follows that visitors and outsiders would be confused at all these levels because of misreading, and non-reading, of cues and not knowing the rules – i.e., non-communication – and behavior would become difficult.

The more familiar example of front/back behavior already discussed can also be interpreted in these terms. In an area where private socializing and interaction are a front activity and the environment is structured for it to occur in the back, the codes are inappropriate, the environment does not communicate what is expected, behavior will be at odds with the form of the environment, areas will be evaluated wrongly and conflict will occur.

Similarly we have already seen that the types of elements used to indicate status vary. While generally status and good maintenance go hand in hand, there are situations where this is not the case. There are also situations where high status demands absence of ostentation, so that space becomes meaner and smaller than for certain lower status groups. Thus, as with language, while there are certain general characteristics, specific symbols have meanings which are sometimes arbitrary and have to be learned.

This suggests two points. The first has already been raised – the question of constancy and change, of the interplay of species specific and culturally variable. The second concerns the distinction between emic and etic as applied to non-verbal communication in the environment. The emic approach deals with behavior inside a culture-specific system and the criteria and distinctions used within that system. The etic, on the other hand, looks at such a system using criteria external to it. In order to understand any one code, it is necessary to study the emic aspects. In order to compare it with others and to understand constancy and change – the etic. It is also necessary to consider tactic elements – how emic elements can be combined with others of the same order; these three, derived from anthropology and linguistics, provide a rather abstract schema for the study of communication in the environment. The point already made that people's reactions and evaluation of the environment are, in the first instance, affective needs to be stressed. Non-verbal messages from the environment are mainly affective, dealing with feelings and setting the mood for other aspects of communication.

Through enculturation, by learning from such non-verbal environmental cues, people learn certain ways of reacting to the environment. If the messages are then inappropriate, the solution may be to try and avoid them, thus avoiding inappropriate feelings: an appropriate environment is then one which makes visible, or concrete, culturally appropriate emotions and feelings (Langer 1953, pp. 92–100; 1966).

This suggests that people are sensitive and respond to environmental cues which indicate the purpose of a setting, the people in it and appropriate behavior. While most work has been done on architectural settings (e.g., Kasmar 1970) the process seems applicable to urban settings understood as being of high or low status, public or private, back or front, or belonging to group A or group B. At the architectural scale the communicative function of physical elements can easily be shown, as in the classic study of the courtroom and how it communicates the essence of the legal philosophy involved through the relationships among the five principal actors and their settings (Hazard 1962). However, various cues including architectural elements within the urban settings often establish character and group identity, either directly or through ritual.

We have already discussed the role of ritual in urban settings in general terms and seen that, as it becomes weaker, environmental symbols may become more critical. Thus certain architectural elements may become symbols which reinforce group cohesion and communicate expectations about behavior: they help to communicate group boundaries to members and non-members alike. For example, among the Mayo Indians of Sonora, Mexico, the house cross (and, to a lesser extent, some other types of crosses) are the major symbolic element in asserting and maintaining ethnic identity. In this case, as in others, the orientation of houses, their relation to the settlement and to group membership is linked to a principal architectural symbol which identifies the group. In fact the houses seem haphazardly arranged until the system is understood (Crumrine 1964) – i.e., until the code can be read. In this, and other cases, ritual and processions are important; for some groups such rhythmic ceremonial movements, using certain features in the environment, play an essential role in the integration of the group: these essential environmental elements only communicate to those who know the code (Vogt 1968).

It can be argued that as TV, newspapers, films and various other forms of communication have developed, the environment as communication becomes less important. For example, the close link between culture and environment among the Bororo Indians, where the destruction of the settlement form led to the destruction of the group (Lévi-Strauss 1955), is unlikely in a modern situation. But we have already seen repeatedly that communication from the environment is critical for some groups. For all there should be congruence between the cues in other systems and the environment thus increasing.

People in particular groups make sets of more or less consistent choices. This is what we call style, whether in the built environment or of life. Ideally the system is then consistent with regard to fixed, semi-fixed and non-fixed feature elements, i.e., there is congruence between the environment and lifestyle, and the environment communicates. If there is no congruence the environment may become meaningless.

Consider some examples at the large-scale. One concerns a European misreading of the American city, which is said to have no hierarchy, no heart or center, no quarters, no specialized functions, in a word – no order (Michel 1965). Clearly U.S. cities have all these – but they are very different than European cities. What is significant, however, is that a European observer feels that way and is unable to read the cues and rules encoded in the American urban environment and feels lost and disoriented. The environment, in effect, fails to communicate. We have already seen that hierarchies in various cities and cultures vary greatly and are difficult to read when the codes are not known. Hence the misreading of Moslem, Chinese and other non-Western cities by Western observers discussed before. Finally consider a French view of time and space in the American city (Lévi-Strauss 1955, pp. 78–79): New World cities are felt to lack a time dimension which would make them comprehensible. European cities are made attractive and beautiful by age – in America age makes cities ugly and they need to renew themselves as fast as they are built. This can be interpreted as a misreading of certain temporal codes and resulting disorientation which also applies between the English and American environments (Lowenthal and Prince 1964, 1965, 1969; Lowenthal 1968).

At smaller scales this happens in cities where there are long siestas, or people eat late, or rhythms and tempos of different groups are not properly synchronized. For example in Switzerland there are currently conflicts between Italian workers who, at 2 AM, have lights on, radios blaring, are singing and dancing and the Swiss, whose areas are silent and dark at that time (*New York Times* 1974); there are also conflicts due to jostling in supermarkets (i.e., personal distance and space) and hordes of children — all interpretable in terms of cultural codes.

The relationship between behavior and meaning can be analyzed through the latent and symbolic aspects of activities, and by analyzing specific environmental elements which may indicate status, appropriate behavior or whatever. One can then decode what has been encoded, and the environment becomes legible. This is far less sophisticated than linguistic or semiotic analysis (which may well be needed in the long run) but may be more immediately useful. Specific examples of such cues have already been discussed (particularly in Chapters 2, 4 and 5). Whatever the specific system, one can speak of hierarchies among urban residential areas, for example, which are communicated through many cues, thus increasing redundancy. In each case, various physical elements are used and can be understood without resorting to complex simiotic or linguistic categories and systems.

It is relatively easy to conclude that in the U.S. generally the physical elements identified with status are shady trees, large lawns, houses of a certain age, size and style, cozy backyards, swimming pools, certain recreational facilities and so on. One must always be specific, though. Thus there may be differences in the degree of maintenance, "manicured" and clipped vs. wild planting, and subtle variations due to the presence of certain apparently minor things in the landscape, materials, people, or types of shops (e.g., Duncan 1973; Royse 1969); other forms of environments also instantly communicate their identity — e.g., public housing. For some groups the differences are larger and clearer than for others. Yet in all cases the environment communicates and symbolizes group identity. The physical and social cues used in such cases are not difficult to discover once this communicative function of the environment is understood.

This function is only partly due to designers. What they do is critical, but it is the effect of many small changes and decisions of individuals and groups, creating a certain character — or the inability of certain groups to imprint such character — which plays a major communicative function, and has been neglected. It is the specific messages people wish to communicate, as individuals and members of groups, which work through individual and group personalization. Design and planning must allow for that.

To conclude: the environment can be viewed as a form of non-verbal communication, users need to read it so that the coding/decoding process must be considered. This seems to provide an analytical tool of potentially great power for decoding environments otherwise likely to be misunderstood, and also an approach to encoding which may make the designer's role and task easier, and also enable him to consider the limits of what he can do, the importance of open-endedness and an additional reason for looking at the city a set of more or less distinct areas with different codes and meanings.

Culture, Symbols and Form as Ways of Coping with Overload

Recall that in addition to seeing the environment itself as a form of communication, it can also be seen as a medium for facilitating or controlling communication among individuals and groups. In this connection the built environment can usefully be considered as embodying cultural ways of patterning, and providing cues to them. Patterning is a way of reducing social and environmental information overload. Some residential choices, such as suburbia in modern cities, can be seen as ways of reducing overload to manageable levels. Other forms of cities — Moslem, African, Chinese or Japanese — achieve the same objectives, but use very different means: all are ways of coping with overload — cognitive, cultural, social or physical. The similar, and related, mechanisms used for privacy can be understood in terms of controlling unwanted interaction and social communication. This may be either because the amount is excessive, or because one wants to avoid particular types of interactions, or interactions at particular times and circumstances. They also enable unavoidable unwanted interaction to be structured.

Whether dealing with environmental information or social interaction, one is dealing with a form of communication, one in the physical the other in the social environment. Hence one is dealing with mechanisms for the control and structuring of communication. We have seen that overload can be reduced in a number of ways, among them structuring the environment cognitively into chunks and symbols, using various social, psychological and physical defenses, and clustering in more or less homogeneous areas. These can be related to each other and to notions of coding and environment as communication. In other words, these various ways of patterning and structuring the physical and social environment are structurally equivalent, all being ways of reducing overload. It is useful to show the structural equivalence of apparently different forms such as suburbia and the "inside-out city", since both are among the more effective mechanisms for reducing stress and overload. It is also useful to show the equivalence of physical, cognitive, social and other mechanisms. In fact many images of suburban houses and areas reflect this and are implicit in environmental preferences. Many of the things liked about environments are stress reducing — physically, socially, psychologically, or through associations and symbols. House advertisements make this clear: some implicitly, such as those considered in Chapter 2 which stress environmental quality aspects symbolizing this — space, greenery, leisure activities, quiet, people like oneself and generally images associated with low stress. Others explicitly refer to the pressures and strains on people, the ordeal of driving to work and shops and add that "people have to find somewhere to go and retreat and relax, recover their energy to carry on the struggle . . . the only real, private retreat is the family home" (*Lynton Homes* 1972).

Clustering by perceived homogeneity, considered from this point of view provides an area analogue. The non-fixed feature aspects of non-verbal behavior mean that people react strongly to facial expressions, body motions, personal behavior, manners, gestures, clothing, smiles, speech, the smells of food and many other aspects. What is appropriate in one place is not appropriate in another and will be seen as an intrusion, as "kinky" or threatening. Since in cities people have visual, olfactory and acoustic contact with many people with whom they do not speak, they have many non-verbal contacts. These occur primarily in central and shopping areas and public transport. In addition to trying to reduce them even under those conditions (e.g., using particular group-specific shopping areas, avoiding central areas and using private cars) people try to live in areas which are havens of like people: this reduces stress and enables people to relax and get ready for the more stressful encounters in inevitably heterogeneous areas. In effect the whole residential area then becomes a backstage region communicated through physical and social cues.

Clustering with like people can, therefore, be seen as a stress-reducing mechanism, as can the preference for private cars (as opposed to public transport). In addition to being a territory and allowing seclusion, the private car assures that one does not have to be exposed to the non-verbal messages of unlike people at very close range and in ways difficult to avoid. The success of special buses from homogeneous areas, such as Reston, Va. to Washington, D.C. can also be understood in such terms. In the city at large and in residential areas, there are also artefacts which communicate. Thus homogeneous areas with their implicit agreement about standards, ways of treating physical elements, and the meaning of particular artefacts again helps reinforce the predictability of the communicative environment. This follows from the notion that the meaning of material objects and behavior is largely arbitrary and learned, even if there are some species-specific regularities.* Objects and behaviors only communicate within the framework of a shaded code and not only do meanings have to be known, but rules for their combination; the context and length of a "text" helps reduce uncertainty in non-verbal meanings (e.g., Greimas *et al.* 1970). Thus the more redundancy in the system, the more channels are used — buildings, spaces, fences, lawns, plants, colors, noise levels, dress, behavior, privacy rules, domain definition, temporal rhythms and so on, the more likely that the system will communicate and that the information processing load will be reduced.

Recall that defensive structuring helps to cope with long-term stress. In this, the presence of a few key cultural values is important and these are expressed through symbols which give people an easy way of identifying with the group and asserting group identity (Siegel 1970). This is helped by clustering, as is easy communication among group members, strong control at the group and family levels, dress and manners — all of which aid defensive structuring. These can most easily be combined with environmental symbols to form appropriate environments when clustering occurs. All these devices reduce social distance within the group and increase it to other groups, i.e., this is equivalent to setting up boundaries.

This also relates to subjective distance, desired proximities in the environment and the symbolic ease of transitions and contacts. Thus the environment communicates the preferred separation of people from people, people from objects and objects from objects.

The selective control of human contacts by cues in the social and physical environments corresponds to the definition of behavior settings with appropriate rules — which must be known and understood. Thus rather than calling for environments which facilitate human contact, it would be more useful to consider the variability of the amount and nature of contacts and the mechanisms used for their control.

This approach then relates to the relationship between design and the control of crime. Without either accepting or rejecting the validity of such arguments, it seems clear that perceived crime is now a major source of urban stress, and all these analyses are concerned with those forms of spatial organization which will prevent, or control, one form of unwanted interaction — between criminals and the public. It is also implicit in this work that certain forms of spatial organization fail, and crime generally is on the rise, because the rule systems and informal control mechanisms no longer work (e.g., Rainwater 1966; Yancey 1971; Newman 1971; Angel 1968). Clearly informal rule enforcement works better in homogeneous areas — because the rules and the cues are understood and shared. However, more common, and more general, problems relate to

---

* Note that there is a major argument in non-verbal behavior studies between proponents of culture specific codes (e.g., Birdwhistell) and those stressing the interplay of pan-human and culture specific elements (e.g., Ekman (1972)).

crowding, the presence of unlike people and overload due to the physical environment itself — as we have already seen, and are related to privacy, defined as the control of unwanted interaction.

Urban form, then, has an effect on the degree of control which one has over one's private life and involvement in public life. Using the idea of selective filters, one can conceptualize environments as allowing people to decide which mechanisms to use, how much to filter and what messages to let through and when. Note that one way of controlling what messages and information are being broadcast is through personalization and environmental cues such as lawns, maintenance, colors, fences and walls, front and back divisions and the rules about private and public behavior. When these messages, from and to individuals, are appropriate and fully and unambiguously understood, they can, in effect, be filtered, people can relax and be themselves and, in effect, interact less involuntarily (and hence more voluntarily). Front and back regions and various forms and layouts of environments, and the appropriate behavioral rules, can all be understood in terms of non-verbal messages. They all work more simply and with less stress when they are understood and the physical and social environments communicate. To use a simple example, propinquity in the U.S. tends to give certain neighborly rights which it does not in Britain (Bracey 1964). The same environmental cues, spatial organization, placement of boundaries and so on, are then misread by the other group and confusion and stress result. Americans complain that the English are cold; the English that Americans are pushy.

Homogeneous areas effectively extend backstage regions so that there is less need to be alert, conscious of what one does and what others do. They provide additional control by providing intermediate, protective filters; they also make much easier the communication of a permanent, public image through the environment. In effect there is a need for choice, and forcing interaction, whether direct or indirect, through non-verbal means, is an invasion of privacy. Choice and control are important because perceived control and choice seem to reduce stress (Glass and Singer 1972; Rapoport, in press(b)). One form of choice is of the form of the urban environment — homogeneous or heterogeneous, suburb or high-rise as well as choices within those environments. I would hypothesize that in modern, Western cities most people would choose homogeneous areas of "suburban" character since these offer least stress and most control. In other cultural contexts other, and for them more appropriate, forms exist.

Thus clustering, space organization, rules, solid and soundproof walls, doors and curtains, private gardens and backyards, courtyards and so on are all ways of controlling unwanted interaction. Of course the design conclusions at the programmatic level, let alone the actual designs, may still be very different. For example, I have been arguing for the desirability of clustering at certain scales, for a number of reasons. Implicitly using a similar model others draw exactly contrary conclusions, advocating information overload as a way of breaking down social patterns seen as undesirable and hence achieving radical change (e.g., Sennett 1970).

One can see the physical structure of the city, which ideally reflects conceptual and cognitive structuring, as a set of devices for avoiding overload and reducing stress in two senses: it communicates social and cultural rules which, if followed, reduce overload. The spatial organization of the urban fabric in itself is also one of the mechanisms which controls the amount of information processing needed. Furthermore conceptually similar spatial organizations may differ in detail, i.e., they may be transformations of certain larger patterns.* Thus small, homogeneous, self-contained areas in the city, suburbs, and the inside-out city are structurally equivalent ways of coping with stress and overload.

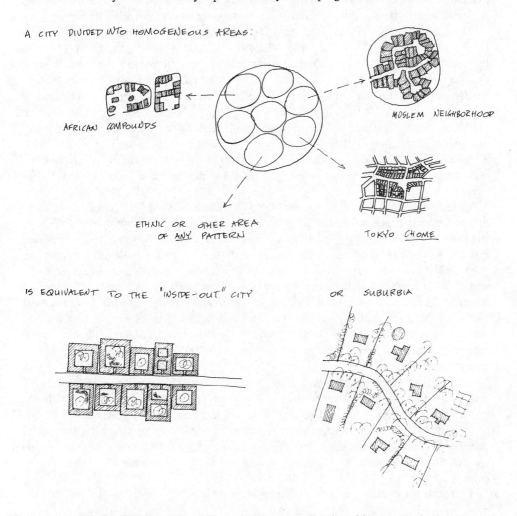

FIG. 6.1. Different, structurally equivalent, ways of coping with urban overload.

'These apparently very different urban forms are not only diagrammatically similar — they have the same objectives: to separate perceived incompatibilities and thus reduce unwanted interaction and overload, while allowing for voluntary interaction at specified places. The principal way in which the environment does this is through what it communicates to those who understand it. This is clear in colonial situations, since such cities were, almost by definition, culturally pluralistic. Their pattern was one of separation, stressing the physical and social distance among the various groups involved and using culture specific devices in the various areas. An example are the Indian cities of

* An analogue would be d'Arcy Thompson (1942) who demonstrated that apparently very different spatial organizations are transforms of similar patterns.

the British colonial period (e.g., King 1970, 1974(a), (b)) where, as we have seen, environmental differences were used quite clearly to stress and ensure social and ethnic segregation and where culture specific urban forms were used in the different areas.

These cities were built removed from the indigenous city, and frequently there were three separate settlements which strike visitors to India even today — the native city, civil lines and cantonment. In the colonial settlement generally, ample space expressing social distance was the principal device used. Within the traditional Indian city there were similar internal groupings, although more subtle, expressing equally great social distances among groups. In addition to location, and grouping by caste and occupation, the devices used were very different — courtyards and walls rather than space. These two ways of controlling interaction — distance or barriers, the suburb or inside-out city — seem basic. As a result the indigenous settlements were denser, with tight spaces, in contrast to the very distinctive and generous use of space and distance in the colonial settlement (see Fig. 5.11).

Within the colonial areas people lived in compounds which controlled social interaction and hence unwanted interaction. In these compounds within the civil lines, for example, life was private, relations with outsiders confined to those of a formal and secondary nature. Indians were excluded from those areas and compounds by unwritten rules and laws: codified rules were "merely the formal expression of social distances which had already been ingrained in people" (King 1970, p. 12) and well expressed spatially. There were thus sets of boundaries — around the English area, the compound and the dwelling providing cues for the rules and laws which helped assure control of interaction. The systems of social, work, and recreation facilities and the spatial character, were different enough in the colonial and indigenous areas to ensure separation.

This works two ways. Firstly through what it communicates stressing differences in form and hence establishing very strong boundaries (accompanied by rules and sanctions) and creating environments incongruent with culture, lifestyle and behavior. Secondly, using physical space in relation to movement, so that the largely pedestrian native population would find the open, low density spaces difficult to traverse, uncomfortable climatically, and very monotonous, as well as becoming very visible and hence easy to control.

From our perspective the details of the system are less important than the fact that the description of the English residential area reflects the English rural ideal, and could also describe the ideal suburb of today — freestanding houses in large grounds, lots of space, self-contained areas, keeping out "undesirable" people, and good transport to work, sports, leisure and club facilities which are kept distinct from housing. If we compare this to the indigeneous cities, we can go beyond superficial differences, the specific context and even high vs. low density. Considered in terms of the control of unwanted interaction, these differences are merely examples of the basic distinction between the inside-out city, the city of courts and barriers and one where comparable results are achieved through space, a specific example of some of the privacy mechanisms. Moreover both show clustering, rigid hierarchies and clear rule systems.

Thus apparently very different forms of physical environment use different cues to give similar messages, and use different mechanisms to achieve similar ends — all keep unwanted, and hence stressful, information and interaction at a minimum and thus reduce overload.

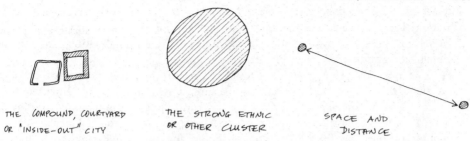

THE COMPOUND, COURTYARD   THE STRONG ETHNIC   SPACE AND
OR "INSIDE-OUT" CITY   OR OTHER CLUSTER   DISTANCE

FIG. 6.2. Three comparable and equivalent ways of controlling unwanted interation.

In other colonial situations group differences and perceived unwanted interaction are also very clear and reflected in the environment. These differences also reflect major differences in ideas of environmental quality of unlike groups and the spatial organizations and symbols they use to indicate behavioral rules. Since they also frequently have very different technological, cultural, social, economic and institutional systems, it is little wonder that colonial cities — whether Delhi, Marrakesch, Fez, Batavia (Jakarta) or whatever — provide striking examples of very clear differences in urban character. More generally, though, this is found wherever different cultural groups coexist in close proximity, although there the differences in character, and the symbols and cues used, are less dramatically different if filling a similar role. Thus all these different forms of separation, spatial organization and symbolic meaning are structurally identical — merely different ways of achieving the same objectives of establishing group identity, and information and stress reduction.

This latter point would also tend to follow from the more general idea about the importance of urban relationships (Rapoport 1969(e)). Since urban structure often consists of similar elements (the number of physical and socio-cultural devices is limited), what varies is their organization, the rules for their combination, and their meanings. Spatial organization is the designer's basic tool but it relates to cues, messages, rules and behavior; spatial organization can be seen as a form of coding and defense against unwanted interaction. Urban form can be understood as a way of eliminating undesired behavior and events (or those regarded as irrelevant) and hence as a way of controlling events and communication. This is achieved primarily through the organization of elements.

Thus different forms of urban organization, in the physical and social environments, are ways of structuring interaction, information and communication. They vary in the groups included or excluded, the temporal rhythms, the sensory modalities stressed, the cues used to indicate appropriate behaviors, the rules about what *is* appropriate behavior, and where and when it should occur; hence the definition of domains such as private and public, front and back, behavior settings generally and the way they are organized into systems such as the house-settlement system and networks and hence how the city is used. In fact most of what we have discussed so far becomes comprehensible if we consider the city ideally as a mechanism for controlling information and interaction.

Clearly, as possibilities for communication, interaction and information increase in modern cities and people have greater mobility and more potential contacts, and as the social and cultural rules become vaguer and less definite, ways of controlling such interaction are needed so that the city should become an instrument of selective filtration. The environment should help people make choices, separate private and public relationships, selecting some and rejecting others. This it can do itself and also by communicating appropriate behavior to homogeneous groups.

As one gets areas which provide security and retreat, interaction elsewhere becomes more likely, since they form two elements of a single system. It is thus not a matter either of encouraging or discouraging interaction, but controlling it appropriately for specific groups. It is, for example, not a matter of replacing spatial by non-spatial mechanisms, of accepting or rejecting the validity of clustering and geographic proximity, but of accepting various combinations, or coexistence, of different systems, of providing the degree and kinds of interaction and communication which meets the needs of various groups and individuals.

Most people limit themselves to spatial neighbors for some forms of interaction; having neighbors whose images and schemata they understand, whose rules and symbols are clear and unambiguous helps greatly. Rather than constant uncertainty and innovation there is certainty and security, and hence more efficient communication and interaction and less stress. The lack of such defenses can be serious: adequate and appropriate defenses are necessary — as we have repeatedly seen.

Much of the discussion has been about social overload and the role of the physical environment in helping people to cope with it. As we have seen, the direct effects of the physical environment as an information and communication medium, and as a surrogate for people, is similar. We have also seen that complex environments may reduce stress, while both chaotic and monotonous environments may increase it. This may be related to people's "openness" to complexity (e.g., Pyron 1971, p. 409) and if one accepts the view that inappropriate environments will lead to "turning off", and people are then "closed" rather than open to diversity, this may also lead to stress. Chaotic environments probably lead to more turning off than monotonous, which may lead to a search for stimulation and hence more openness, although this is highly speculative. We have seen that too numerous and insistent sensory messages demand excessive information processing and the result is overload and stress. This may also happen if the *meanings* communicated are too numerous and varied, if they are contradictory or inappropriate, if there is insufficient multichannel redundancy for them to be read, or if the codes are not legible.

Clearly, if the environment itself is a system of non-verbal communication, then if the cues and symbolic messages are clear, and legible, and the codes shared and understood, there is less need to read and interpret them, i.e., they can operate more automatically: as a result one needs to interact less with the environment itself. In effect the environment is more redundant, one can use it semi-automatically and there is less stress and more time and channel capacity for other activities and interactions. The results of culture shock, of having to use a strange environment, where the codes and messages are not clear, are well known: it is stressful, takes energy to learn and demands much attention, reducing the ability to deal with other aspects of life. As the environment becomes more legible through appropriate codes and meanings it frees people for other interactions and behaviors.

The concept of roles can also be seen in similar terms. Roles mean that people interact with fewer people and this interaction ends when the specific activity ends. In large cities (as in the case of large flocks of animals) individuals only develop affiliations with a small proportion of their neighbors and remain anonymous inbetween specific interactions.

Similarly, crowding is handled, by both people and animals, by controlling interaction (e.g., McBride 1970, pp. 149–150) and this control (privacy) occurs through several major mechanisms. All ways of controlling interaction and information flows reduce stress. Recall that, within limits, the choice of mechanisms is arbitrary so that in one case things are hidden by walls and courts, in others they are opened up, so that there is no need to wonder about what is being hidden. Social hierarchies and rules may substitute for the environments which do not provide protection, as in the case of the Yagua Indians where, with urbanization and weakening of rules, walls begin to substitute (Rapoport 1969(a)). In Samoa, for example, open dwellings do not provide protection and rules, do not allow retreat, i.e. they are not appropriate; control is obtained by retreating into one's own mind ("inner space") and going into a trance.* Whether or not this works in Samoa, it is doubtful whether this would work in more complex societies although it is implicitly suggested by some (Calhoun 1970).

The suggestion that control of space helps control interaction is, of course, related to territoriality and the rules which go with it. Territoriality, by controlling unwanted interaction may have direct physiological effects (e.g., Pontius 1967). Thus while some observers see territorial behavior as a primitive way of controlling information and interaction, it does so effectively through establishing an order, i.e., a consistent spatial patterning among individuals and groups (e.g., Paluck and Esser 1971). Some people are able to use social and cognitive forms of ordering, although the territorial and spatial order helps. For others, however, the territorial order may be critical and, as information overload grows, may become a more important element in the system, helping other methods of coping. It also appears from studies at the architectural scale that lower status individuals and groups need more territorial and spatial structuring (Sundstrom and Altman 1972); such variations may also be due to cultural traditions and rule systems.

All forms of controlling information levels have the purpose of making them congruent with the information needs and abilities of particular groups. These levels, and the mechanisms used to reach them, need to be understood in order to understand and organize, structure and design urban forms. Changes in variables such as culture and lifestyle are related to changes in desired interaction rates and lead to different forms and mechanisms. They also influence the environmental preferences of these groups and generally help clarify many of the topics discussed.

Thus environmental preference not only reflects specific characteristics of the environment, and specific solutions and devices used, but also differing levels of inter-action and input desired, and the meanings and associations of the elements. In the most general case, therefore, the environment can be seen as a mechanism to help achieve desired levels of information. It is not just a matter of reduction; in some cases it may be a matter of increasing rates. In fact, the different evaluation of areas by different observers can be understood in these terms. One of the major elements in this variability is the clarity and relative impermeability of barriers and defenses, and the rules which are associated with various domains defined as public or private, front or back. Thus the view that the city is partly a mechanism for controlling communication — with the environment and among people — leads to conclusions about its design and spatial organization which are at odds with the views of those theorists who argue that communication technology makes the physical design of the city and the spatial

---

* Personal communication, Professor Derek Freeman, Australian National University.

organization of people less important (e.g., Meier 1962; Webber 1963). In fact, the specific organization of the city, especially at the sub-area scale where most people actually live, and the organization of the meanings of such areas, become important devices for controlling, structuring and modulating information flows, from the environment itself or from other people. If overload is a major problem of the modern metropolis, the conclusion may be that design, as here discussed, becomes more rather than less important.

It seems inevitable that the environment be conceptualized as a way of manipulating channels of communication, barriers, linkages and separations between people and people and people and things. Although people can learn to handle increased information, there are limits which we may be reaching, and there are costs in learning to handle larger amounts of information, particularly at higher levels of meaning. Recall that there are different ways of reducing information. Some are cognitive, depending on grouping information into chunks and symbols and using images and schemata. Some depend on the development of habits, whether personal or group (i.e., cultural): through routinizing behavior one can ignore much and thus reduce the amount of information to be handled; i.e., efficiency is increased by habit. Another way, related to the last, is through clustering of like people which reduces the need to interpret behavior, dress, non-verbal communication or environmental symbols and cues; it also becomes easier to reduce interaction through implicit, unwritten rules and the physical elements which indicate them — in effect they can become "habitual" and information processing is reduced. Spatial and physical separation offer another set of devices for controlling information. Thus urban form and social patterning are all potential devices for structuring and modulating information.

Clearly this discussion relates the notion of environment as communication and the process of coding and decoding of information to that of the environment as a way of helping to control social interaction. Information processing in relation to culture depends on redundancy and predictability. This is achieved through learning the codes, i.e., the cultural rules and expectations of people and how environment expresses these. In effect learning the proper environmental cues assures that the restrictions imposed by the environment on social interaction, as well as the ways in which the environmental messages themselves are structured, are known, predictable and hence more manageable.

The continuum which is the sensory environment is structured in different ways into discrete units. An environment which is legible, i.e., properly encoded, does this for people, i.e., elicits the proper schemata, reducing the need for the individual to do so. The process of making the world meaningful is, of course, the cognitive taxonomic process discussed in Chapter 3, the encoding process at the largest levels consists of giving physical expression to, and making explicit, cognitive domains. At smaller scales the encoding relates to the symbols and cues which indicate appropriate behavior within domains and settings, the clarity with which they are understood as such and related to appropriate behavior, and indicate how they combine into comprehensible, and appropriate, systems. At these scales we then get congruence of form and activity, the meaning of environmental elements and so on. If properly coded, and hence capable of being decoded, these restrict the meanings and combinations possible, and thus increase predictability and redundancy. Even at the perceptual level the distinction between chaos and complexity depends on understanding, or reading, an order so that departures from it can be noticed.

To conclude this section I will consider the principal devices used to structure, code and control information in urban contexts. They will be discussed in order of a sequence from the least to the most design oriented.

Psychological devices. These are of two major kinds. One involves the use of chunks and symbols to "compact" information, the use of taxonomies and categories and also schemata of various sorts. The second, which in our context can be regarded as pathological, is internal withdrawal, "turning off", drugs or whatever.

Cultural devices. These are extremely numerous and varied. Some of them are important enough to be discussed separately. However, habits and routines in behavior and expectations are useful since activities, rules and manners can be made automatic. Manners and all the behavioral non-verbal aspects relate to this: they can be taken for granted (i.e., routinized) when shared and hence simplify behavior and are systematically related to form.

Rules. These are a specific cultural device and control the appropriate amounts of information, habits and ways of controlling, reducing or increasing interaction and information; if understood and shared, they make mutual behavior smoother and simpler, if not shared or understood, conflict, overload and stress may result. Examples would be unwritten rules about the relationship of proximity and neighboring rights and obligations, use of streets for various activities, the purpose of a backyard or stoop, acceptable noise levels, decorum, dress and undress, ways of storing garbage and working on cars, children's play and upbringing, sex roles and behaviors, proxemic rules, language and many others: some of these have environmental equivalents or indicators. Territorial and domain divisions, and behavior setting systems, are accompanied by various rules.

Such rules apply to suburban houses and high flats alike — in the latter, because of closer proximity and fewer defenses, they become more important and rigid, often made explicit and codified. This may create problems for adults and children alike (e.g., Blumhorst 1971; Bitter *et al.* 1967).

Such rules also apply to time. Different groups have different rhythms and tempos and their synchronization may be a problem: in the case of heterogeneous housing, this can lead to conflict. Given the extreme variability of time concepts and structuring, the sharing of temporal rules can play a major role in reducing the need to process information and make behavior and reaction to the environment easier and more automatic. Moreover, time rules and time allocation also relate to space use and activities through jurisdiction, so that activity systems in urban areas are intimately related to temporal rules. Such rules can sometimes substitute for spatial and physical defences but can also cause problems. With extensive urban networks and contacts, and the relative transitoriness of such contacts, it becomes important to live in areas where rule systems are shared and hence one understands when and where to do what, who "owns" space, and how spaces, activities and times are organized.

Clustering. This discussion clearly leads to that of clustering since one obvious way of assuring sharing of rules in a pluralistic context is to have areas of people who are homogeneous — i.e., share rules. This is a most efficient way of handling — or *avoiding* — overload since one can take rules and people for granted. Rules for private and public and front and back behavior are known, roles and norms are understood and the symbolic and non-verbal expression of all these in physical terms is clear. We have seen that the creation of enclaves reflects various perceived homogeneities, boundaries and discontinuities. In fact, one can argue that a major role of culture is to distinguish between "us" and "them", and cultural survival may often depend on setting up such group territories. In all these cases group identity is affirmed and reinforced, and social space established, through shared networks, behavior setting and house-settlement systems and through environmental symbols. If dominance and territoriality are linked, then one could argue that in large groups and complex societies it is impossible to have a single or workable hierarchy: group territories help greatly and are essential to prevent and reduce stress and conflict; they may, in fact, actually eliminate the need for absolute and rigid hierarchies.

Symbolic devices. A major reason why clustered areas work and rules are shared is that people in them understand the symbols which indicate status and group membership and indicate the various rules which apply in environments, the various degrees of control and their congruence with behavior. Within such areas not only are the personal symbols more likely to be understood, since the range of variability is more limited within the group than among groups, but the shared, group symbols of the overall environment add up, are understood and do not give contradictory information. This prevents the conflicts which arise when such cues are not understood, environmental elements are treated and maintained inappropriately, and inappropriate behavior occurs in various settings and domains. If one of the main kind of overload is in terms of "attractive" information (e.g., Lipowski 1971), i.e., the messages the city offers about attractive things to do, buy and achieve, then it is easier to overcome its effects, and reduce the impact, by having areas where homogeneous values, goals and symbolic meanings of asserting status and achievement are used.

Design devices. Some of the devices described above can be used, manipulated and provided by planners and designers. Many, however, cannot. If they are understood they can be encoded in various forms of physical design and space organization which are, from the designers' point of view, those over which he has most potential control.

These are of different kinds. One set is composed of the symbols, meanings and associations which indicate appropriate behavior through the rules which are associated with them. While these are difficult to manipulate today there is some possibility of doing so for people with shared symbol systems.

At the less symbolic level the design devices are of various kinds — separation by distance, separation by time, separation by mass or physical elements such as walls and barriers. As an example let us briefly consider two. These are space organization and mass, and space organization and distance. Both of these are ways of handling linkages and separations. They vary in their characteristics as well as in their location. The differences between Mexican, Moslem and Japanese urban areas on the one hand, and American/Australian suburbia on the other, can be understood in these terms.

Space organization and mass. The "inside-out city", the use of walls, courtyards, and clear and strong transitions is one way of expressing domains. In this case distance, as such, is of limited importance, and applies to location within the city. At the smaller scale it is the use of impermeable barriers (mass) which is critical to separate groups, areas and uses.

Space organization and distance. In this case the separation is principally through space and distance, among houses and groups, different areas and uses, although walls and fences may be used to complement it. In modern cities this is represented by the suburban order, in the sense of a particular spatial organization rather than the political or locational sense often used.

These two categories — space organization and barriers and space organization and distance are thus superficially different but structurally analogous, both to each other and to all the other devices discussed. Thus such apparently totally different environments as Brookline, Mass. and San Cristobal de las Casas or Isphahan are actually two ways of achieving the same objective. More generally they represent two views regarding the meaning and importance of space and hence environmental quality. This is extremely useful, and also helps distinguish among cultures where space is used for separation, those where barriers clearly define domains, and those where other mechanisms are used.

Two points follow. The first is that given the difficulty, if not impossibility, of adequate spatial separation in large cities other ways may suggest themselves. Secondly, it suggests that the major obstacle in using other devices may be in the communicative function of the various devices, their mutual unintelligibility even though they are structurally equivalent.

To illustrate this last point let me quote from a famous novelist. He is walking through a Central Asian city in the Soviet Union. He walks down narrow streets with no windows, high mud walls rise baldly from the streets. Gates are tunnels in these walls and one has to stoop to enter. Once inside one is in a court where there are benches, trees and walls all around with windows. This court was like a room — people lived in it. "It was completely un-Russian. In Russian villages and towns all the living room windows looked straight on to the street so that the housewives could peer through the curtains, and the windowbox flowers, like soldiers waiting in a forest ambush to see the stranger walking in the street and who was visiting whom and why. Yet Oleg immediately understood and accepted the oriental way: 'I don't want to know how you live, and don't you peep in on me'." (Solzhenitsin 1968, pp. 226–227).

I doubt that this alternate way would be so easily accepted in practice. One might also add that in Russia there is an additional spatial mechanism for those who can afford it — the *dacha*. This is a way of getting away in space by having a small country house (*Time* 1972(c)). More generally, the development and growth of country houses and second houses fits into this model as an additional device for coping with overload and information, not least by excluding those who cannot afford them.

The difference between the Central Asian city and Russian city is, as we have seen, found in many different places, for example in Spain where Moslem cities were inward facing and Christian ones were outward facing oriented to the street (Violich 1962). One can also understand the English landscape as a system of enclaves marked by facades as symbolic indicators of "front" (Lowenthal and Prince 1965, 1969). But this gets us into the subject of cultural landscapes which I will consider in the next section.

Cross-cultural View of the City — Differences in Form and Cultural Landscapes

One underlying theme of much of my discussion has been the interplay of constant and variable elements, although I have stressed cultural variability since this has been rather neglected. But the need to consider the interplay of constant and variable factors means that generalizations must be based on a broad sample and that history, as well as all the other approaches, is inextricably linked with design. Only in this way can one get an insight into the meaning of forms, their persistence and changes and their relationship to culture. I have also suggested that much urban theory, and most of the examples of planning and urban design, have been based on the Western tradition neglecting the non-Western. Yet the purposes of cities in social terms vary and, for example, in China and Iran the city has been a center of stability rather than of change as in the Western tradition (Murphy 1954; English 1966). Even the elements which define whether a place is a city — markets, baths, agoras or whatever, vary greatly in different places and cultures — what a city is depends on definition, and is essentially a cognitive and taxonomic process.

I have also suggested that much urban theory and most examples of planning and urban design have been based on the high-design tradition neglecting the vernacular tradition. Yet most of what man has built has been in the vernacular tradition so that by neglecting it, most of what has been built has been ignored and generalizations tend to be invalid. I suggested that design involves any decisions which modify the physical environment and most of these are taken by non-designers. Urban form and landscapes are the result of many decisions by very many people, yet they add up to a totality. Such landscapes reflect ideals, i.e., in most cases there is some underlying image or schema and we discussed the case of migrants and the choice and transformation of landscapes.

These images and schemata change from time to time and often there are corresponding changes in the resulting landscape (Heathcote 1972). In this connection the concept of cultural landscape is useful — particularly when applied to cities which are almost totally man-made. In its simplest terms a cultural landscape is the appearance of a specific culture area, which may be large or small but assumes a specific visible character as a result of the many decisions taken in the operation of the choice model. It may apply to whole countries, so that on either side of the U.S.—Mexican border totally different cultural landscapes developed in just over 100 years, or on either side of the boundary drawn by a Pope in Rome led to the very different character of Brazil and the rest of Latin America (Jackson 1966(c); Morse 1969). This may happen even in more homogeneous areas as witness the different cultural landscape on either side of the Victoria—South Australia border (A. J. Rose 1968). At a smaller scale different cultural landscapes may develop in an area as relatively small as Door County, Wisconsin (Henderson 1968). Not all cultural geographers agree on the nature or importance of cultural landscapes. Some argue that the study of cultural landscapes (the study of objects) should be contrasted with the study of the perceptual—behavioral approach (the study of people) (e.g., English and Mayfield 1972, pp. 212—213). Yet these two approaches can be linked — cultural landscapes are the physical expression of images and schemata underlying many decisions, choices and preferences, i.e., they are linked to human behavior. Cultural landscapes are, first of all, the visible physical result of human activity. It is then also, as one would expect from the view of the built environment as communication, a reflection of people's value systems, environmental attitudes and preferences: it is congealed information. The cultural landscape is thus a symbolic creation reflecting a set of attitudes. Different groups, often living side by side, no less than those living in different places, create varying physical environments and cultural landscapes, reflecting idealized images, visual and behavioral specifics and symbol systems of groups and can be understood as a series of relationships among physical and cultural elements providing cues for appropriate behavior for those who can read it.

This concept is extremely useful when applied to cities and parts of cities. We have already seen how major differences in landscaping, spatial organization and materials express different meanings. For example, the materials which for one group may be a desirable way of improving houses, and express concern and status, may be regarded by another as most undesirable so that the use of artificial stone to improve houses led architects to evaluate the area as a slum!!! (Sauer 1972). Similarly, on the South side of

Milwaukee aluminium awnings are extensively used — they are never seen on the East Side.

Two things follow. Firstly, that the appearance of areas is a most important communicator of various urban and social characteristics; secondly that such cultural landscapes and their meanings are extremely variable and cannot be assumed *a priori* by designers or imposed on users.

The change of initially identical areas into two very different areas — Japanese and Mexican-American (Rapoport 1969(a), p. 131 fn. 15) is one example of this process, the two areas of Westchester discussed before are another (Duncan 1973). An example which illustrates the process in action is provided by Le Corbusier's project at Pessac where so much individual change and personalization took place that the area was transformer (Boudon 1969). The generality of this process seems clear (Rapoport 1968).

Since one can conceptualize any man-made environment as resulting from a series of choices among alternatives, the cultural landscape reflects the specific choices made; when this is done by a diverse group of people there are random changes and the result is chaos. If consistent, however, they are equivalent to style, i.e., they reflect the decisions of a group sharing certain values, behaviors and symbols: the changes add up and produce a distinctive cultural landscape which communicates, helps interaction, indicates rules for behavior and acts as a symbol of group identity. It then becomes of great interest to urban designers, particularly since it relates appearance to meaning and, through the variability of urban areas and noticeable differences, it makes complexity possible; it also helps in the definition of areas and the construction of mental maps.

The urban cultural landscape, therefore, comprising spatial organization, vegetation and landscaping, materials, forms, colors, activities, people and the relationships among all the elements, can be understood as an expression of culture based images and ideals, different cognitive rules and systems of coding — i.e., the cultural landscape is a form of communication. This follows from the examples already discussed: the Moslem and Christian city in Spain, colonial cities, the meaning of the plaza in Indian and Spanish cities in Michoacan, the different uses of streets, recreational settings and house-settlement systems in various cultures among many others. It can also be shown that changes in urban form occur when culture changes, so that one is an expression of the other. For example consider the distinction between the Baroque, romantic and contemporary urban cultural landscapes in terms of privacy vs. communality, where the Baroque city plan is mainly communal, the romantic is mainly private (Jackson 1966(a)) whereas the modern may well be confused. American urban landscapes — from the New England town, through the settlements of the Virginia Colonies to those in the Midwest and elsewhere can also be seen and understood in these terms — as cultural landscapes reflecting particular values (Arensberg and Kimball 1965). (See Fig. 6.3).

An even more striking example, at a smaller scale, is provided by the cultural landscapes in a Mexican Municipio where two populations, Indians and Ladinos, live — different in language, dress, houses and household possessions, activities and values; they have produced totally different cultural landscapes which are clearly a result of choice rather than constraint. Not only are they a good indicator of culture, but they are changing with culture change in the area so that there is now an intermediate, mixed zone. One of the differences between the two groups is that for Indians the physical environment has a powerful mystical quality lacking among Ladinos for whom, unlike for Indians, it has objective reality and a merely physical nature. This means that Indians are

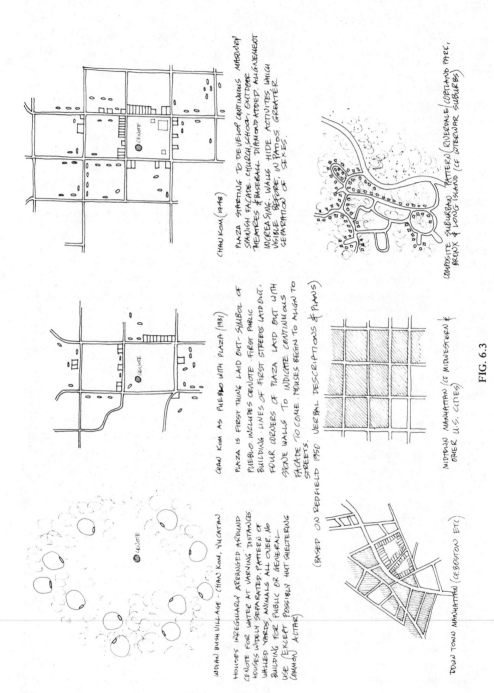

INDIAN BUSH VILLAGE - CHAN KOM, YUCATAN

HOUSES IRREGULARLY ARRANGED AROUND CENOTE FOR WATER AT VARYING DISTANCES. HOUSES WIDELY SEPARATED. PATTERN OF WALLED YARDS, ANIMALS ALL OVER. NO BUILDING FOR PUBLIC OR GENERAL USE (EXCEPT POSSIBLY HUT SHELTERING COMMON ALTAR)

CHAN KOM AS PUEBLO WITH PLAZA (1931)

PLAZA IS FIRST THING LAID OUT - SYMBOL OF PUEBLO. INCLUDES CENOTE. FIRST PUBLIC BUILDINGS. LINES OF FIRST STREETS LAID OUT. FOUR CORNERS OF PLAZA LAID OUT WITH STONE WALLS TO INDICATE CONTINUOUS FACADE TO COME. HOUSES BEGIN TO ALIGN TO STREETS.

CHAN KOM (1948)

PLAZA STARTING TO DEVELOP CONTINUOUS MASONRY SPANISH FACADE. CHURCH, SCHOOL, OUTDOOR THEATRES & BASEBALL DIAMOND ADDED. ALIGNEMENT INCREASING. WALLS HIDE ACTIVITIES WHICH VISIBLE BEFORE IN PATIOS. GREATER SEPARATION OF SEXES.

(BASED ON REDFIELD 1950 VERBAL DESCRIPTIONS & PLANS)

DOWN TOWN MANHATTAN (cf BOSTON ETC)

MIDTOWN MANHATTAN (cf MIDWESTERN & OTHER U.S. CITIES)

COMPOSITE SUBURBAN PATTERN (RIVERDALE/CORTLAND PARK, BRONX & LONG ISLAND (cf INTERWAR SUBURBS)

FIG. 6.3

less ready to change, modify and create artificial environments, resulting in landscapes which, among other things, differ along the natural — man-made dimension. The Indian area is on the periphery and is bucolic in character — quiet, green, with small thatch-roofed houses nestled among vegetation, whereas the Ladinos live in the center, around the Plaza, and the landscape is of greater density, with whitewashed abode and red tile roofs, unshaded, with markets and shops (Hill 1964).

This approach, when focussed on the specific and subtle differences within modern cities makes questionable the view that all cities, and particularly modern industrial cities, are the same. We have already seen that many areas in the U.S. are quite different, although Europeans have difficulty noticing them. Clearly, also, modern Japanese cities are quite different to modern American and English cities; at the same time within the Japanese city, there are differences in the character of the small areas into which it is divided, although Westerners cannot easily read them. In Tokyo it also appears that different areas have clearly different chromatic character, so that color can be used to distinguish among traditional, mixed, modern and industrial quarters (Lenclos 1972). Since cultural landscapes result from the interaction of groups and the areas which they occupy, cities and parts of cities are very different. Admittedly there is some blurring of such differences, not least as a result of the increasing difficulty of groups to cluster and be able to develop cultural landscapes, but differences still exist at a subtle level; with proper design and planning, these could be reinforced and stressed with consequent social, cultural, communicative, behavioral, perceptual and cognitive benefits.

It is, after all, still often relatively easy to tell where an urban scene is, or that it is somewhere else. In fact, such differences can be used as indicators of culture as we have already seen in several contexts such as Moslem and Christian cities in Spain in terms of spatial organization, or different groups in the Caribbean in terms of landscaping. Urban landscapes can be used for the same purpose. Thus in Pennsylvania two different forms of urban square — medieval and classical — are found and are associated with English and non-English settlement respectively. At the same time, in the first case, the square is seen as being a space separated from the street while in the latter it is seen as an extension, or widening, of the street (Pillsbury 1967). Similarly, also in Pennsylvania, the urban street pattern can be used as a culture indicator so that one of four types — irregular, linear, rectilinear and "Linear-R" are both determined by culture and are indicators of four culture areas of the state (Pillsbury 1970).

Similarly, Spanish and Portuguese (Brazilian) city plans in South America differ. The Spanish city uses the gri, and the Plaza Mayor is so important that the city can be conceptualized as a plaza surrounded by houses and streets rather than as a set of houses and streets around a plaza. The Plaza Mayor is missing in Portuguese cities and the nearest equivalents are either an open space in the center without embellishment which is gradually absorbed as the city grows, or a widening in the street (Morse 1969). In Argentina, village and field plan forms can be used to identify various ethnic groups which settled there — if they were able to develop their own forms (Eidt 1971). In Nova Scotia settlement form can also be used as an indicator of culture; in English areas there are no villages, and the community is scattered in farmsteads, whereas in French areas there is an attempt to retain a village form even though the main street may be five miles long!! (Collier 1967, p. 20).

In all these examples and studies the concern is with the original plats rather than with how the city actually grew and developed, in which process the individual decisions of many people are important and it is the personalization of individuals and groups, and their distribution and concentration which are important. This also becomes much more a matter of perception and meaning. I have already pointed out that apparently identical plans may be different in reality and in detail, as with the plaza in Michoacan (Stanislawski 1950) so that the meaning encoded in the forms is quite different. In that case it is the relationship of the central plaza and status. In the case of the use of axes in the Chinese and Baroque cities it is the different meaning encoded in these — in the one

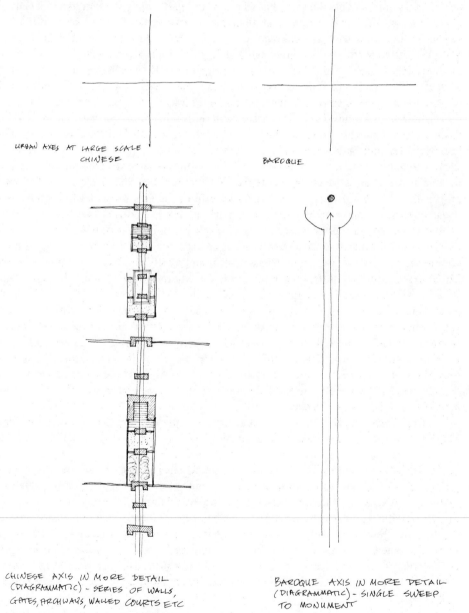

URBAN AXES AT LARGE SCALE
CHINESE

BAROQUE

CHINESE AXIS IN MORE DETAIL
(DIAGRAMMATIC) - SERIES OF WALLS,
GATES, ARCHWAYS, WALLED COURTS ETC

BAROQUE AXIS IN MORE DETAIL
(DIAGRAMMATIC) - SINGLE SWEEP
TO MONUMENT

FIG. 6.4. Two urban axes with different meanings.

case the axes had symbolic importance, in the other — visual importance: at a more detailed level the two spatial organizations indicate this. In the Baroque city the axis is a single sweep leading to the architectural feature which it reveals, while in the Chinese city, where symbolic significance is important, the axis is not a vista but a succession of varied spaces, separated by gates, towers and walls integrated into an axial whole (Wheatley 1971, p. 425). (See Fig 6.4).

I have already compared and contrasted the Moslem and Chinese city with its courtyard houses and the Western city — a difference one finds in Malaya to this day, where Chinese urban houses use courts and Malay ones do not. In China itself there were major differences in the character of the areas of cities at different periods depending on cultural attitudes, so that the quarters of T'ang cities were totally different — in use, layout and character — to those of the Sung period (Tuan 1969, pp. 134–135). This reinforces the point that it is necessary to understand the underlying social, cultural, and philosophical systems in order to understand cultural landscapes at whatever scale.

Since the clustering of groups varies greatly in the criteria used and the ways in which they cluster, there are corresponding differences in the spatial expressions and detailed character of buildings, landscaping and materials and their meanings. In Africa the differences among cities and parts of cities are very striking. In colonial cities in sub-Saharan Africa the physical layout reflected the separation of African and White, very much like in India in principle but different in the specifics. European residential areas were close to administrative offices, hotels, shops, and the like and tended to run into them, while African areas were strictly demarcated and well removed from the town center. At the same time the various African groups were also separated leading to the development of different cultural landscapes. The European areas also often reflected their native architecture — the Bavarian character of Dar-es-Salaam, The Belgian of Elizabethville, the English character of the Zambian copper belt towns (Epstein 1971) or the sidewalk cafes, inlaid sidewalks and Portuguese buildings of Lorenço Marques. In Portuguese colonies there is close continuity among areas as in Portuguese towns, while in English African towns there is the separation of various zones (de Blij 1968) as was the case in England — and British India. Belgian colonial towns also express their own traditions in the center and are divided into ethnic areas with different cultural landscapes. In the European residential areas the cultural landscapes reflected national character. The English looked for a cottage fronted by a superb lawn and if some roses could be acclimatized their happiness was complete; Belgians looked for large *comfortable* villas; the French tried to recreate fantasy and "bohemia", while the Portuguese recreated their traditional styles (Denis 1958).

Consider a city like Bamako. The European section had high-rise buildings, the African were one storey, built of cheap materials. In some African areas square courts were used with one-room-wide buildings opening into them, while in newer areas there is a change to more European forms with a cross between the old style and the bungalow. In traditional areas the courts are common to all tenants: women wash, cook, pound food in them, and animals are kept there. Streets are wide and of dirt, forming part of the house — children play there, women work there, peddlers and craftsmen work and sell, dances occur and so on. Such areas are also thickly overgrown and changes occur in the form and associations at different periods (Meillassoux 1968).

Thus, if we compare Bamako with an Indian colonial city, we find that the elements are very different producing very different cultural landscapes but, in both cases, distinguishing among groups. The number of these groups is greater in the African than the Indian colonial city. In a Ugandan town, for example, four groups could be identified — African, Indian, Arab and European. Africans in Uganda were dispersed, the other three groups clustered. Thus at the regional scale Africans lived in dispersed rural units, the other three groups in urban areas; within cities Europeans lived in the area with the administrative and European business functions, Indians were more dispersed in small clusters of trading centers. The Arabs had a different pattern again. The result was one of several distinct cultural landscapes, and each group had its characteristic way of organizing space within the city which existed side by side. In fact, as the various immigrant groups derived they developed spatial patterns which reflected their traditional spatial organizations, which formed a coherent system and was used to stress the differences from the indigenous culture (Larimore 1958). While it is possible that with time acculturation and homogenization would have occurred, it is also likely that, if this is not forced and group survival is made possible, differences would survive — if only in modified form.

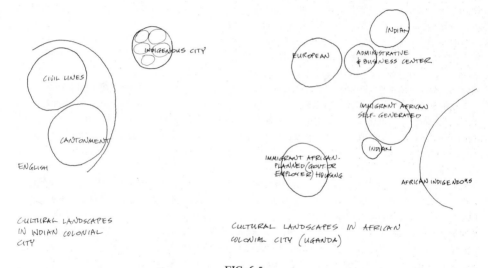

CULTURAL LANDSCAPES IN INDIAN COLONIAL CITY

CULTURAL LANDSCAPES IN AFRICAN COLONIAL CITY (UGANDA)

FIG. 6.5

Indigenous Africans. Dispersed pattern of households separated by fields. Groups of households, often on ridges, organized into villages with hereditary headmen. In 1958 very few had given up homesteads for urban dwellings provided by employers. Even when they did, they tried to grow some food and also preserve peasant holdings. Traditional houses were beehive shaped; with European influence they became rectangular or square, but preserved the dispersed pattern,,with 2—3 acre garden compound.

Immigrant Africans. These tend to be from different tribes: hence there is a lack of a common culture — a transient, fragmented group, neither tribal nor urban. In the towns two patterns are found (a) government or employer housing, i.e., planned housing (b) shacks on the outskirts. These latter are squatter settlements along unsurveyed streets, with bars, foodshops, other shops around open markets with stalls. There are also wandering craftsmen, sellers and repairmen who cluster and work under shade trees. There is relatively little clustering of the population into social or political units.

British Europeans. They recreate their own culture with modifications to suit local conditions. Since colonials moved frequently, there was no attachment to place. The standard everywhere was English suburbia where one could always feel at home. Houses were large, well built bungalows, with screened porches and hipped galvanized iron or tile roofs. (Some flats were provided). Houses were well set back, in spacious lots with large lawns, shade trees, flowers and hedges. Streets were paved and urban services provided. There were some foci with European shops, schools, churches and clubs.

Indians. These were mainly Gujarati, belonging to different castes. They lived in extended families and large households, with business, kinship and caste ties all over East Africa. They were highly clustered, both in the country and towns, centered around businesses. In fact most shops in East Africa were Indian. The pattern is of shops with residences behind, so that residential units are closely linked with livelihood and clustered in Bazaar areas. The pattern was imported from India, with buildings to the permissible limits of the site, close together, at high density with shops across the front shaded by verandahs and living behind in common living rooms, with open, walled, paved backyards, where most household work occurred. There were attempts to provide separate kitchen compounds for women and separate boys' quarters. Building had high walls and used stucco, filigree and roof ornaments. There was a lack of shade trees, plants or lawns. At the periphery of this intensive compound bazaar areas were clubs for different castes and sects, religious buildings and schools. (See Fig. 6.6).

Arabs. These were a marginal population who often intermarried with Africans. Little data is provided (in Larimore 1958) but the pattern was apparently imported and is described elsewhere. Thus in Mombassa, also, various groups built patterns like "back home". The Arabs and Persians built narrow alley-like streets, solid stone and cement houses, with courtyards, ornamental doors and small, shuttered windows and, in urban areas, markets and Mosques. Other groups built varying patterns in the old town but when the English came they built outside — and reproduced English suburbia. In Mombassa there are also areas like African villages, with the same houses, and gardens for cultivation; there is an attempt to recreate village layouts and groupings, reflecting the tribal backgrounds of the occupants. These various subareas have their own shops and churches, helping the adjustment and integration of the immigrants and producing very different cultural landscapes which also contrast with the old town, central business district and Arab and English residential areas (de Blij 1968).

Basically, then, African colonial cities (which I am using as an example) show varied cultural landscapes — European suburbs and central areas, workers' camps, Indian and Arab areas, African elements of great variety, depending on origin and culture and using different materials, but all somewhat village-like, dispersed, animated, noisy and colorful, with commerce everywhere: a profusion of shops, markets, stalls, stands and workshops, so that no street or lane is without them. At the same time activity shifts among areas — at dawn it is the central market, in the afternoon the small local outdoor markets in each quarter, then shifting markets as itinerant merchants stop on any piece of open land. In old Moslem cities like Kano, there are quarters organized by trades but in central Africa trades are everywhere (Denis 1958). Thus the cultural landscapes differ not only in terms of the space organization of streets and houses, form, materials and colors, but family structure, networks and behavior, in animation, activity systems and temporal rhythms, in smells, sounds and all the other non-visual characteristics we have already discussed.

Sub-Saharan African colonial cities thus provide different specific landscapes than

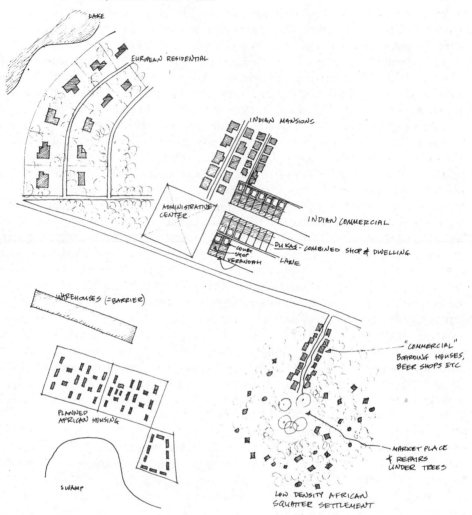

FIG. 6.6. Different cultural landscapes in Ugandan town (based on Larimore 1958).

Indian, South, East or North African ones, but the process is similar, illustrating the relationship of culture and group identity to cultural landscapes. In turn, these colonial cities are merely a clearer, and more striking, case of a more general principle that whenever different groups exist, settle and define areas and are able to express their own patterns and use their own symbols to express and control their own lifestyles, different and varied cultural landscapes will be produced — even in the case of squatter settlements where material means are minimal. These differences may be striking and dramatic, or they may be subtle, they may be at very large-scales or very small, but in all cases they express a cultural pattern, assert social identity and communicate appropriate behavior to those who can decode the cues.

Of course one cannot expect perfect correspondence between actual physical form, or behavior, and the ideal — between the image and its physical expression. Firstly, the ideal or image, while shared up to a point, is not clear or explicit and is represented by a range of interpretations. Then there are constraints — material, physical, economic, political and the like, on behavior. Also, there are always differences between ideal behavior and norms and actual behavior (e.g., Tuan 1968(a)).*

But even when the correspondence is imperfect there are insights to be gained, so that a knowledge of ideals, imagery and values is necessary better to understand existing cultural landscapes, as well as to design appropriate settings for various groups, and create the varied urban landscapes which so many people feel are necessary but so few know how to create without arbitrary variations which then have no meaning.

It is by considering all the elements which contribute to the formation of cultural landscapes that cities can become varied and complex systems. Only by understanding places as systems of cultural and subcultural landscapes can they be preserved, enhanced and strengthened through design. This would lead to increased satisfaction for various groups, and also increased richness, diversity and complexity for the total urban realm.

Cultural landscapes not only reflect values, ideals and images; these latter also affect how the landscapes are perceived and evaluated, since it is the perceived and cognized cultural landscape which affects human behavior, mood and satisfaction. By knowing the features which a given group regards and values highly, it should be possible to predict how the corresponding cultural landscape will be perceived in terms of noticeable differences, how it will be cognized and organized into schemata and hence used.

In effect, this pulls together our discussion of environmental evaluation and preference, cognition, perception, ethological and socio-cultural aspects, symbolism, environment as communication — in fact all that we have so far discussed. If cities consist of a variety of cultural landscapes — places which distinguish between here and there — then these represent cultural differences manifest in urban form, i.e., cultural landscapes give expression to schemata, images and ideals, they are the conceptual environment made visible. Ideally design tries to express images and make visible an ideal world. This applies whether we are dealing with high style or vernacular design: in all cases the choices made result in specific places. When physical environments are congruent with conceptual ones, they communicate, are meaningful and perceived and construed into schemata as intended — and used accordingly.

Designing for Cultural Pluralism

If urban form is indeed an expression of culture, an urban cultural landscape, and the city is ideally a series of areas of varied cultural and subcultural character, then a number of design consequences follow.

The first is that it is necessary to understand the cultures of the various groups involved and the influences on form of their values, lifestyle, activity systems, symbols and all the other variables which we have discussed. This will lead to major changes in planning and urban design, since these factors have not really been considered.

Secondly, if the city is composed of a series of areas of different character, this will influence the way in which it is perceived — in terms of noticeable differences and complexity, and also the way areas are defined subjectively and mental maps constructed. On the one hand such a city would lend itself more easily to a clear cognitive morphology while, on the other, if negative connotations attach to various clearly defined areas, rather large blanks in people's mental maps may result. A problem this may cause is that core

---

* This is a topic of great importance in anthropology generally, which I will not elaborate here.

areas for one group are spheres or domains for others, so that the system becomes rather complex or even unworkable, since the relationships of core areas and "neutral" areas for meeting may well become rather ambiguous. At the same time it would appear that even if core areas can exist there may be problems at the edges where conflict may occur. For example particular groups, say the elderly, may have certain environmental needs such as a higher degree of redundancy of environmental information and hence lower complexity, which are at odds with those of other groups. While some interaction, meeting and common use should occur, areas closely suited for the one group may be very unsuitable for others; at the same time, the transition at the edges may become very acute (Rapoport 1973(d)).

The third major point is that the design of a city for different groups with varied needs and values expressed in different environments as forms of code and communication; different symbols and use of space; different activity systems and time rhythms; different house-settlement systems and underlying images and rules becomes extremely difficult. The same elements may be seen in completely contradictory ways by different groups and their preferences and cognitions may be quite different.

Clearly the goal is conflict resolution at the urban scale; at the same time this seems to imply homogeneity at one scale and heterogeneity at another which "neutral" areas elsewhere. The questions which need answering, and for which there are yet no clear answers, deal with the scale of each of these, the degree of localization, the clarity of borders and the degree of interweaving. Thus it appears that between the extremes of rigid homogeneity on the one hand and random heterogeneity on the other there may be a balanced position of homogeneity interacting with heterogeneity – a form of system which seems easy enough to describe abstractly but very difficult indeed to express in practice.

Another problem in terms of design is that we are dealing with dynamic rather than static processes. On the one hand there is population change in the city, so that areas may be occupied by different groups and too tight a fit would not work and could be counterproductive; on the other hand given groups themselves change in their culture, values and way of life. These two factors, as well as the lack of clear relationship to physical environment in our existing theory, makes the design process under those conditions very difficult.

An approach suggests itself: to use open-ended design with some frameworks which link and relate them.

Open-ended design is a form of design which determines certain parts of the system allowing other parts, including unforeseen ones, to happen spontaneously (Rapoport 1968). This allows for some level of ambiguity, for giving meaning through personalization, for the expression of different values, needs and lifestyles in the environment. It also gets over the problem of tight fit: environments can be used by different groups and individuals. In cities, successive groups can more easily restructure the organization of space, time, meaning and communication.

With few exceptions, however, the consensus among architects, planners and those interested in planning is opposed to this view: everything needs to be controlled and planned and personal expression, by individuals or groups, is messy and ugly, so that "we must get away from our haphazard way of doing things and make sure that everything is planned down to the last detail" (Lunn 1971; cf. Rapoport 1968).

Not only is it impossible to plan "down to the last detail" – it is undesirable. The unexpected needs to be able to happen and change: improvisation and expression — the humanization of the environment — need to take place and specific cultural landscapes need to develop. The question is rather — what is the *least* that needs to be planned, designed and fixed so as to lead to some specified results. This conclusion seems inescapable. For example, if environments do not determine human behavior or feelings but act as an inhibiting or facilitating setting providing cues for appropriate behavior, then an overdesigned setting is effectively inhibiting either because it offers the wrong facilities or cues — and the more designed and planned it is the more likely it is to do that since the range of cues or facilities becomes narrower; or because, as the number of cues, constraints or rules increases, behavior is restricted unduly. While some channelling is essential for communication it results from group-specific, rather than general, constraints.

Open-ended design ideally creates environments which allow more degrees of freedom. Even though modification in the environment can be evaluated positively or negatively, and although forcing people to modify or become involved is as bad as the inability to do so, one might be able to evaluate cities and buildings in terms of the extent to which they do, or do not, permit freedom of action, involvement, active-creative adaptation and modification.

The distinction between the two types of urban space, and its implications for street use, offer an example. In an area where the street is seen as a transitional space it would be an imposition, and inhibiting, to design it as an activity space. But the reverse situation is also true — and is the norm. Most planners conceive of the street as a transitional space and do not allow for it to act as an open space, activity space or social space, yet such use can play an immensely important role in the design and planning of many cities, as we have seen in Mexico, Africa and elsewhere. Recall the important role of vendors in Mexico. In Asian cities also a consideration of the important role of mobile vendors and street stalls can totally change the approach to urban design and planning (e.g., Prakash 1972). The role of the street as recreational and open space can do so even more, yet because of notions about the designer's control of form and "quality" these are not given appropriate consideration and, in effect, such urban areas are overdesigned and not open-ended enough. For example, in a city such as Hong Kong there is a vast mixture of uses in streets and other areas which, in designed areas, do not find a place and these areas are consequently often inadequate.

In the small squatter colony of Aplichau, in Hong Kong, there were 145 shops and 196 hawkers (Wong 1971) and both types of shops fitted into an open-ended environment, whereas they would have been eliminated and constrained in a more highly planned setting. The importance of the open-endedness of squatter areas in the development of industries, commerce, and workshops, and of people being able to keep pets or food animals and to build up their equity through their own efforts explains some of their successes, it is also important in maintaining certain critical social groupings. All of these uses are made impossible in the tighter and less open-ended context of planned development. In fact whenever new development in the third world has been examined, in terms of recreation, housing, privacy or industry, the major weaknesses (whatever their specifics) can always be partly understood in terms of the absence of open-endedness (Laporte 1969; Joerges 1969; Turner and Fichter 1972). Similarly our discussion on the variability of standards and their inhibiting effects can be understood in this conceptual framework.

These rather "exotic" examples are merely more striking or clearer than the more subtle problems in more familiar areas. Here it is not merely a matter of cultural specifics which designers do not understand and for which their over-determined designs do not allow — although that is certainly part of it. There is a more general problem: planners and designers operate within the high-style tradition of design with a high degree of control. Such designs do not lend themselves to change, addition or subtraction. This is one of the primary differences between high-style and vernacular environments (e.g., Rapoport 1969(a); 1969(e)). An urban vernacular example can best be shown through an illustration.

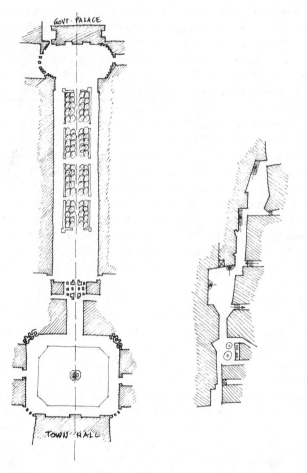

GRAND DESIGN: PLACE DE LA CARRIÈRE &
PLACE STANISLAS, NANCY
(FRANCE)

VERNACULAR DESIGN : LA ROQUETTE,
(ALPES MARITIMES, FRANCE)

FIG. 6.7. Linked urban spaces — vernacular and grand design (from Rapoport 1969(e)).

Even the typical "Main Street" or roadside architecture has this quality to a degree which high-style design does not. Shops, gas stations, apartments can all change their character, uses and space organization within the limits of the basic form. If one examined a typical main street over 40 or 50 years one would find a tremendous number of changes in the use of shops and places, facades, signs, trim and the like within the relatively flexible form, although at the urban scale the street is not very open-ended.

Given the importance of relationships among elements in urban design (Rapoport 1969(e)), then in the open-ended, vernacular situations relationships exist which allow for many different things to happen: they are dynamic rather than static, and clearly express culture. The elements themselves can also more easily be altered to reflect shifting needs and meanings (see Fig. 4.14).

Open-endedness is also intimately linked to territoriality since it allows personalization, which is an important way of defining individual and group domains. By allowing group signs to develop this also helps define the rules of occupancy, which are then not only noticed and understood, but willingly obeyed. Since these rules are subtle and frequently unstated, and also change subtly, the designer cannot provide for them — they are best allowed to develop within an open-ended framework and they can then also respond to changes in the population of the various areas. It is a principal way of giving meaning to the environment.

All the evidence seems to point in the same direction — designed environments must be able to absorb those variations which can never be designed or planned; they must encourage them without insisting on them. Furthermore it is not a matter of a single variation, or a small set, but the potential of many changes over time and for different people: given this evidence it seems clear that designers tend to overdesign.

While the scale of projects, and the difficulty of flexible planning, are some reasons for this, it also reflects a certain ideology, an *image*, which planners and designers hold. In fact, considering the role of images provides another reason for open-ended design. We have already seen repeatedly in the course of this exploration that designers and users differ markedly in their values and images of desirable environments; in effect they have different "universes of discourse" (Rapoport 1970(a)). Hence the assumptions which planners and designers make are frequently wrong. Part of the solution to these two sets of problems is open-ended design.* An open-ended environment, then, not only allows for disparate images and values, for involvement and varied expressions, for intensified meaning, increased complexity and clearer schemata and for accommodating change. It also gives the maximum number of options at any one time and over time. Thus open-endedness, process, change and involvement are all congruent.

The same conclusions about the need for open-ended design follow from a consideration of the differing lifestyles of different groups in the city, their varied activity systems, house-settlement systems and preferences. A pluralistic view implies that simple generalizations, standards norms and deterministic approaches are not valid. Since complete understanding of the system is impossible, open-ended planning and design become essential, although the starting point must be a maximum possible understanding of that system. While such requirements may be of varying criticality in different places, depending on their heterogeneity, all places are sufficiently heterogeneous to benefit, since preferred and meaningful urban landscapes reflect images and values belonging to the many groups of which even the most homogeneous place is composed.

Open-endedness is difficult to define at the urban scale, other than in terms of choice, rules and regulations. After all many urban elements at the large-scale must be determined

---

* An open-ended design *process*, i.e., one involving the public, is also an important topic which I will not discuss.

— the urban infrastructure must be fixed and this is an important role of planning; this also applies to the general and shared urban systems. Open-endedness becomes more comprehensible in terms of physical design as the scale goes down. At these smaller scales — subareas, projects or individual elements — there are certain things in common among most proposals for open-endedness. The stress is on physical elements which can be fixed so that others can be changeable and flexible. But this can also be conceived in terms of rules, and understood in social terms, behaviorally, economically and it is also important symbolically.* Open-endedness also corresponds with the desiderata of "functional" flexibility. This is a potential advantage, and if they can be made congruent, so much the better. Thus if meanings and home ranges (and house-settlement systems) are congruent very clear schemata should result. Yet they are not necessarily congruent, particularly if we relate function to latent aspects of activities, since then symbolic and communicative flexibility may be more important than use or instrumental flexibility.

In fact the desire to modify and influence is primarily symbolic, a way of communicating personal and social identity and defensive structuring, and of stressing lifestyle and activity differences — which are mostly at the latent and symbolic end of the scale. In considering open-endedness the stress should probably be on latent rather than manifest functions, on value and symbolic objects rather than concrete and use objects: it is more important to leave the former open. Yet designers tend to take the opposite view — they allow changes and openness in activities and use at the manifest level as long as they can control the symbolic and expressive aspects. All this suggest, however, that open-endedness is not just a matter of physical elements and also that it is important, in any given case, to determine which are the important domains which people feel they need to control and which are the elements which they are willing, or even anxious, to have determined. This will be variable for various groups (Rapoport 1968). If this could be discovered, and also the nature of those elements which change and need to be open, and those which do not, or change slowly and can be fixed, one would begin to address this important question.

The design problem, then, becomes one of creating a framework of common, neutral and shared areas and designing ever more specific and open-ended areas at ever smaller scales. The need for community-wide decisions, determining infrastructure, together with the concept of open-endedness implies the concept of some form of framework and infil. Seen most generally frameworks are guidelines which impose some form of limitation. These limitations, as well as the direction in which change is guided, and those areas left open or fixed must all be based on the types of criteria with which this book deals. All cities need structuring and guiding elements around and within which change can occur. These frameworks must not be thought of merely as physical infrastructure, although they must have a physical meaning. Rather they should be thought of in terms of domains of significance or symbolic elements — those elements in the city known by all, or by large numbers, as opposed to those only of local, or individual, concern.

It is at these smaller scales that much of the discussion about cultural specificity — in symbols, privacy domains, house-settlement systems and so on becomes particularly relevant. There is a possible parallel here with our discussion of cognition and perception. I suggested that the conflict between imageability and complexity is illusory because legibility is needed at one scale in order for complexity to exist at another. Similarly one

* An Example is the work of Habraken in Holland(now at MIT).

needs an overall structure at one scale for specific areas to be able to exist at other scales. Frameworks must have physical expression — even rule systems have physical consequences. It is one thing to say that we are not dealing merely with physical frameworks and "plug-in" cities (e.g., Cook 1970) and another to say that frameworks, in order to be understood and used, must have a physical identity.

Any environment is the result of many decisions; it must, therefore, be guided and constrained in some way. It is important to guide and constrain various decisions so that they are congruent with each other and with other sets of requirements. Physical frameworks are major urban design elements strong enough to accommodate and guide change and a great number of variations while retaining a unifying system. Such frameworks are major morphological elements, mainly of the high-style, which reflect guiding ideas and remain while change occurs all around. Until recently these changes were part of the vernacular tradition guided by the most unified and agreed-upon rule system which often worked so well that no other was needed. In fact formal framework rules, such as the Laws of the Indies, were introduced just at the time when the vernacular, shared unwritten rule frameworks no longer worked — or were absent (Rapoport 1969(a)).

There are many historical examples of various such frameworks. It is rather significant that the grid pattern has so frequently been seen as a major example of open-endedness. Thus the grid of the U.S. West, starting with Philadelphia, has been interpreted as an endless, open-ended framework for expansion, made even more striking by the numbering systems (Jackson 1966(b)).* The urban grid has also been compared with the invention of the skeleton frame (Kouwenhoeven 1961). Other examples of the grid are often found; axes, walls, gates and ceremonial ways were major elements within which changes occurred and which could be filled in variably and differently: the ceremonial parts were the framework, the rest was infil, although it was not haphazard and reflected rules of space organization, clustering and so on. (See Fig. 6.8).

An example of another type is the inside-out city, where the rule system provides a guide for the aggregating of courtyards or compounds: they are added in terms of a guiding principle expressing a hierarchy and system of more or less self-contained areas. These guiding rules were culture — specific and variable. At the smaller scale such frameworks may present the particular spatial organization of courtyards or compounds, the street pattern, the use of arcades or of residential squares.

It is relatively easy to see physical framework elements and rule systems acting in historical examples. It is more difficult to decide what frameworks and infrastructures might be valid today in various contexts. Here there are no clear answers; those frameworks which have been proposed ignore the variables which we have been discussing. In planning theory recently the grid has been advocated, not least for its open-ended qualities. This has also been the argument of those who have seen Los Angeles as a positive urban manifestation (e.g., Temko 1966; Banham 1971). All of these can be understood as advocating a framework and infil system and the specific form is not essential to this argument. A wide variety of urban forms can be evaluated as successful in terms of possessing certain framework elements, which have lasted and provided continuity and within and around which changes, infil and variability have occurred, allowing people to influence the environment and express themselves without loss of the larger organizing schema (e.g., Bacon 1967). Conceptually this is an instance of

* Recall World War II cartoons about Los Angeles city limits in the foxholes of New Guinea or North Africa.

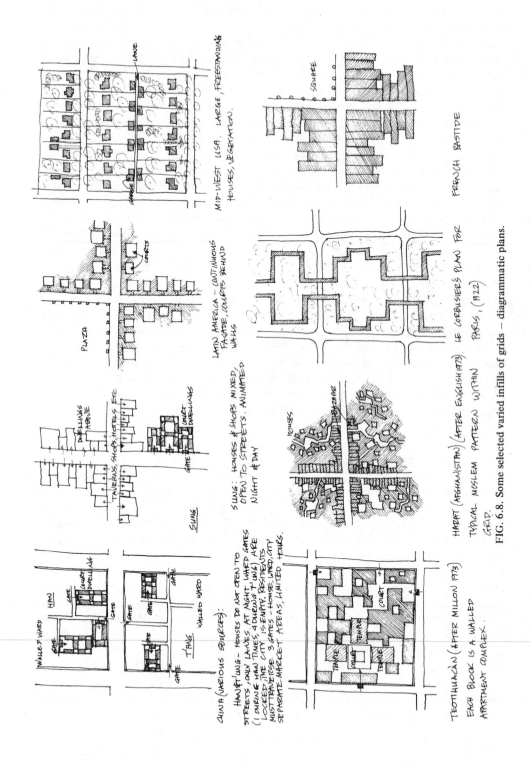

FIG. 6.8. Some selected varied infills of grids – diagrammatic plans.

continuity and change, and variations within an order, which we have already discussed in other contexts.

The major frameworks currently proposed, whatever their form, are based on movement systems: whether the highway strip (Venturi *et al.* 1972), some generalized movement system with places linked to it (Smithson and Smithson 1967), freeway systems (Banham 1971) or road systems generally.* Others have proposed linear elements linked, once again, to the movement system. It is rather significant that most, if not all, the current proposals take the *movement system* (meaning *mechanical* movement) as the structuring element. This tells us more about the values of planners, possibly reflecting those of part of the population, than about the values of other groups. Even more significantly it neglects the needs and responses of people and ignores the relationship of such frameworks to the way people use, value, perceive and cognize the city. While, in our culture, movement elements will inevitably play an important role, the question is their supremacy, and also whether they themselves should not respond to perceptual, cognitive and other considerations.

Other than movement systems and the grid there is relatively little in the literature on human aspects of urban form and hence on other possible kinds of frameworks. The desiderata of frameworks can be listed: they should allow the expression of the characteristics of various groups and their preferences, they should allow people to construct valid cognitive schemata, provide the proper perceptual information and meanings. Thus the evaluative, cognitive, perceptual, socio-cultural and symbolic aspects of the environment and characteristics of people should be the basis for designing areas and frameworks. Since the concern of this book is with the smaller scale, the stress on the variable and specific elements follows. It is also clear that in most places there is a dominant, majority culture — places where many equal cultures coexist are few. Thus the overall structure is related to that larger culture, with rather smaller and subtle variations in the areas of the various groups. That, of course, has the advantage of making communication and use of cities easier. One can argue that the success of many chain enterprises is due to the fact that, wherever one goes, they provide predictability, through clearly comprehensible and legible symbols which communicate expected behavior. The use of such consistent symbolic and spatial systems at the larger scale, so that the general, shared elements could be reinforced and learned, and associations could develop, would thus allow for the variability at other scales to exist (Rapoport 1973(a)).

These general systems need a high degree of redundancy — eikonic, symbolic, physical and social cues should all be congruent and consistent, and reinforce each other. They should also overlap, so that different people, using different routes and having different activity systems and home ranges should all know what the city has to offer. These important overall elements, which help orientation and cognitive structuring, should be easily physically accessible to most people (i.e., related to major movement systems) and related to the most widely shared images and symbols (i.e., symbolically and associationally accessible). This would facilitate the formation of associations and reading of cues and meanings. Such elements should also change slowly, and any change needs to be strictly controlled so as to preserve character, consistency, recognizability and the like. The systems and elements used by all should be so structured as to be simple and clear — at least to most. Clusters of areas and specific areas and subareas of ever greater

---

* E.g., Le Corbusier's plan for Chandigarh and, more recently, the work of C. A. Doxiadis, or the Llewellyn-Davies firm's plan for Milton Keynes in England.

specificity, and responding to specific groups, would be much more varied. Thus the commonality and consistency of general and common elements needs to be stressed — and also the uniqueness and specificity of specialized settings: i.e., one needs to stress the noticeable differences among them.

As areas move from the general and "universal" to the specific and local, their open-endedness should also go up, to increase the impact and influence of groups of ever greater homogeneity. Also, the general frameworks should be "closed" so as to retain their character and recognizability. In the case of dwellings there is, of course, the influence of individuals and families, the groups at the scale of the block, neighborhood, district and so on. The definition of these levels, the degree of open-endedness and what it means for various groups are still open questions, but this would be a most useful approach complementing the others discussed.

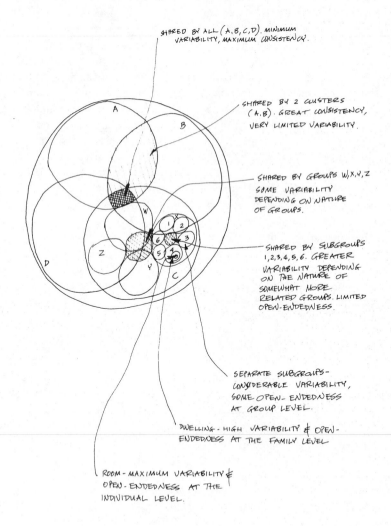

FIG. 6.9. Domains of generality/specificity and related
variability/open-endedness.

Any city contains heterogeneous populations. Clearly some cities (and countries) are more homogeneous than others, but all have more heterogeneity than is realized — particularly if subjectively defined, rather than *a priori*, criteria are used. This heterogeneity actually seems to be increasing as ethnic, lifestyle and other forms of identity are being reemphasized. In theory at least, every group has its own set of requirements and interpretations. It is necessary to identify the unique features of whatever groups exist and the corresponding variety of environments. To provide them it is further necessary to understand why they are different, in what ways they differ and which are the critical differences — and which differences are secondary; one should also know which important differences have been eliminated or blocked by extraneous factors. Ideally one would then be able to match the variety of groups with their corresponding environments. At the same time the commonalities must also be studied. In fact, in any one area, it is extremely likely that this type of study will reveal a large measure of overlap with some degree, greater or lesser, of uniqueness, the extent of which is difficult to predict, or know, given the lack of experience with this type of approach: it needs to be discovered.

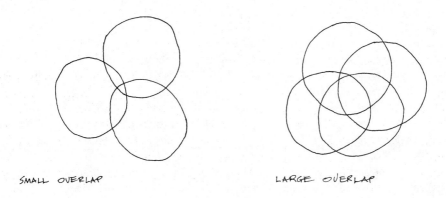

FIG. 6.10. Variations in degree of overlap.

Clearly the common, overlapping characteristics provide the overall urban structures and common elements, partial overlaps provide commonalities for clusters, while the uniquenesses provide the specific variability. This should provide overall imageability and structure, while allowing for characteristics of uniqueness to be expressed and also to change as population and culture both change. It should also be clear that in any specific case the physical elements which are used to stress and express group identity, lifestyle and uniqueness will vary — and in some cases may be relatively small. Of course the relative criticality of various elements for the well-being and survival of any group will also vary depending on the cultural competence and degree of environmental docility of the group and their reliance on environmental symbols (Rapoport 1968, 1972(d)).

The problem is not easy. If the images of different groups vary and so do their use of space, meaning of space and ways of indicating domains, the symbols used to indicate appropriate behavior, the use of time, the relative hierarchies of the urban fabric and so on, then the problem is clearly complex. Yet it is also difficult for groups to live in inappropriate environments — for groups with very different space, time and symbol uses to live together without conflict. It is clear that the variation of environment which would result not only present fascinating problems but also great environmental promise. In all cases the design process should seek congruence between the psychological, socio-cultural and symbolic schemas of the inhabitants and the environments in which they live.

Again suggestions about how to proceed are possible. Clearly, in most cities there are common time rhythms and tempos, as well as idiosyncratic ones. It may be possible to analyze time in this way and plan and design environments appropriately, with the common areas and systems being related to the common time use. We have seen that in most cities there are symbols and images pertaining to the whole city, which symbolize the city as such. It may be possible to match these with the generalized systems and the particular ones with the specific systems. Similarly for meanings, activity systems in space, networks, elements of the house-settlement system which overlap and are common and those which are not and so on.

Clearly, the more varied and heterogeneous a society the more difficult the problem — particularly if its values include equality for all and maximizing interaction, precluding separate and parallel development (which is easy to design). I would argue that the recognition of differences among groups and clustering, the city as a mosaic of different places, makes the task easier since one only needs to reconcile conflicts at the level of shared facilities. This separation of the common, major urban systems based on shared meanings, symbols, uses, activities, and so on with the ability to withdraw, live and maintain primary relationships in areas of homogeneity, would enable designers to achieve many goals which they talk about, and also make people's lives and use of the city better and more effective.

Of course the contrast is not binary and clear as described here. There is, as we have seen, a whole range from elements shared by all to those shared by large groups and then ever smaller groups leading, finally, to those specific to individuals which are not the province of urban design.

Consider recreation space. Among middle-class groups in the U.S. residential and urban areas have recently come to be organized around recreation. We saw that these facilities are not so much for use as for status and indicating certain values. As such they are shared. At the same time, among areas and within them, there are variations in the *type* of recreation stressed — swimming, sailing, tennis, riding, golf or whatever. These variations are regional, climatic and subcultural; in some places various neighborhoods are organized around a particular recreation type. This rather trivial example shows the interplay of a larger system — the presence of recreational emphasis in housing indicating status — and the possibility of stressing very different elements in subareas. The result are differences not only in the recreation type and the facilities required but, if developed further, could lead to varied housing types, spatial organization, landscaping and so on.

At the same time we have already seen that, among other groups, the amount of recreation space available and the forms vary greatly and may include streets, parks, shopping areas or "waste" land used for soccer. It may also include cemeteries — yet for some cultural groups this would not be acceptable. Thus the making available of cemeteries for certain forms of recreation (*Time* 1972(b), p. 46) would change the recreational system and availability of land for recreation for one group and not for another, which rejects this use and the accompanying cognitive change in categorization of use. For other groups street space should be made available, or front/back domains reversed, or parks, tennis courts or whatever provided — with obvious differences in the design and organization of various areas. Individual differences would clearly exist at the level of yards and dwellings.

It thus appears that at large, metropolitan or urban scales, it is necessary to get a large measure of agreement about uses, symbols and meanings. Then, through investigating the range of ways in which groups in any situation structure, comprehend and use various subsystems it may become possible to aggregate and to orchestrate the degree and extent of sharing of specificity, the size of groups involved and so on. Finally, there will be still smaller areas where the uniqueness will dominate, where the specifics of the groups will be expressed resulting in a wide range of different areas. Finally at the scale of the dwelling there will be family variability (within the limits of the group) and then individual variability. At every scale there will be no universal agreement but there will be a range — with less variability within and more outside — the group in question.

An additional factor is that some elements may be regarded by some groups as important to control and by others as relatively unimportant, so that there are likely to be individual and group variations to which the frameworks themselves should respond. It should also be reiterated that less is known about group variations than about individual ones, and they are less likely unless we are dealing with homogeneous groups. This, of course, brings us back to the subject of frameworks.

Their role is critical. Without them there is chaos and lack of continuity. Without the limitations imposed by frameworks and rules there can be no communication, since communication presupposes and implies some limitation on the number of elements and rules for their combination, while allowing for all the combinations necessary to express the range of meanings desired and considered important. This may mean defining categories and domains of significance for various groups, areas of generality and specificity, areas of fast and slow change — it may also mean defining and resolving domains of conflict while leaving areas of non-conflict more open. In all these cases the city needs to be analyzed in terms of general criteria, the specifics of which will be different in each case.

Different rules operate for different groups and that these may be contradictory in some cases. The relative priorities assigned to various elements and meanings need to be discovered. In addition to specifying the characteristics for particular areas, each with its requisite degrees of freedom at various scales, the specification of frameworks also implies a need to resolve conflicts among them in the least stressful way. The most difficult questions are about the most generalized urban elements: here less choice and less variability are possible, and they need to be designed so as to minimize conflict and signify equally for many people.

Given the size and extent of modern cities, it can be argued that open-ended local areas, related to the specifics of groups, are most important, from an urban design perspective, than the larger frameworks. The variability of local areas, the ability of people to personalize at the group and individual level, will help establish group identity, express preferences, proper domain definitions, proper activity, temporal, behaviors setting and house-settlement systems. This will create noticeable differences and complexity, will provide proper cues for schemata, help orientation and so on. It will also prevent the sterility of planned cities and more rapidly approximate the richness of "unplanned" ones.

In a system composed of frameworks and open-ended, variable infil there is a need to relate both fixed and open elements to human characteristics. In order to organize rules adequately the rules of designers and the various publics, unwritten as well as written rules, latent and symbolic objects and functions as well as concrete and manifest must all be considered. I have already suggested that variability goes up as scale goes down. Similarly the clarity of cognition and perception, the strength of images and meanings also goes up as scale goes down — and so does the degree and importance of active involvement. If this view is correct the infrastructure-framework can also be defined in terms of more widely shared, weaker images with the open-ended infil in terms of less widely shared, stronger images.

The fact that these concepts are still so uncertain does not detract from their potential utility. It allows for change over time and variability at a moment in time among groups. It leads to complexity, to noticeable differences and to congruence of form and activity. It leads to heightened meaning, communication and personalization. It leads to cities which are rich and more pleasing with a sense of human involvement and history shown by change. It allows the balance overall cognitive clarity with complexity of perceptual character and multiplicity of environments. It may generate clear orientational systems at large-scales and pleasing "lostness" at smaller scales. It may allow us to relate form and proximity to temporal rhythms. More generally it seems to offer one way of using the type of information which I have been reviewing, aiming for extreme congruence without overdesigning or producing counterproductive settings.

The Involvement of People in their Environment and its Consequences

Open-endedness and cultural landscapes imply an active role of people in their environment. Yet, in much of the environmental literature the public are seen as passive consumers. It has been assumed, if only implicitly, that users are, as it were placed in an environment which then acts on them. We have seen that, given an opportunity, people will select their habitat — i.e., choose an appropriate environment, and that this is the most important way in which the environment affects behavior. It is also, however, an important way in which people assert a sense of mastery and control over their environment and that is an important factor in their well-being.

The need for this sense of control is so basic that even animals show it, both through habitat selection and actual manipulation of the physical environment: it is both these which clearly differentiate between animals in the wild and in captivity. Among animals, modification of the environment is almost as important as habitat selection and part of the unnaturalness of zoos and laboratories lies in this very fact (Hediger 1955; Willems and Rausch 1969). Animals in the wild exercise a large measure of control over the environment and captive environments distort behavior through blocking most of this potential control. Animals in captivity eagerly take advantage of any possibility offered them to modify and manipulate their environment (e.g., Kavanau 1969). There is no need for extreme points of view (e.g., Morris 1970) to conclude that this need may be important for people also.

The ability to manipulate environments may also affect social relationships among people. Thus one finds that friendship is facilitated by cooperative activities involved in completing unfinished projects so that these result in more social organization and involvement than finished ones. (Festinger *et al.* 1950; Whyte 1956). A sense of control, or even the belief that one has it, modifies the effects of stress and crowding. For example, in the case of small groups in isolation, the development of social relationships, and behavior generally, were greatly affected by the ability actively to structure the environment. People rearranged chairs and beds, and restructured their use of space, in order to help structure their social relationships (Altman and Haythorn 1970). If people cannot act on the environment, and cannot rearrange it to suit, the environment may act more *on* them — and possibly in wrong ways. By increasing choice the effects of the environment on behavior are reduced (Proshansky *et al.* 1971(a)).

But the main impact is affective. When people feel that they can control and influence the environment, and have a visible imprint on it, they feel rather differently about it than if they cannot. In discussing territoriality, it was suggested that in humans an important way of territorializing and taking possession, is through personalization, i.e., impressing one's character and personality on a portion of the environment. The effects of small vs. large, and undermanned vs. overmanned, behavior settings can also be interpreted in these terms. Smaller, and undermanned, settings allow more control by occupants; while much of this control is social, it has physical equivalents. The congruence between designers and users is never perfect, and some conflicts are inevitable. These conflicts can be unconscious or conscious, passive or active. People adapt to environment in analogous ways — consciously or unconsciously, actively or passively. The preferred pattern of resolving conflicts and adapting seems to be through the participation of the inhabitants — conscious and active, i.e., creative (de Lauwe 1965(b), p. 164). This seems to apply not only to housing but also, although to a lesser extent, to planning and design.

In planning the interest has been in participation at the political level; in terms of the built environment what little work there has been, has been at the architectural scale. It seems clear that the ability to change, add, and decorate makes certain forms of environment, and ownership, desirable. I have implied that the ability to personalize may be an important reason for the strongly held preference for the detached dwelling compared to flats and higher density housing generally, because it allows for personalization and the definition of specific domains through the use of appropriate symbols. Generally, such environments can express individual or group identity in ways impossible in other settings. While there are clearly many other variables involved, a major advantage of the detached house is that it can be molded and shaped by the owners. It can be personalized by adding, subtracting, changing and reorganizing; the symbols used can also vary. This enables the house to be endowed with *meaning* by establishing identity through changing the outside and garden in appropriate ways (Raymond *et al.* 1966; Rapoport 1967(a), 1968).

Personalization provides a way of being creative for people whose work may be totally uncreative, as is the case among the English working class (Wilmott 1963). The importance of personalization and home improvement is also found in comparable groups in the U.S. Since working class people do not achieve status in work or community activities, the control over the environment becomes essential for a feeling of pride and self-esteem. One finds statements such as "my blood and tears are in this house" or "my body and soul", and many people not only spend most of their free time working on their houses but they even document the before and after conditions in albums (Fellman and Brandt 1970).

In addition to symbolic aspects there are also advantages of being able to convert dwellings for larger or smaller families and older people, (which may sometimes eliminate the need to move); or for new hobbies and activities. There are examples from a number of countries where moving people from squatter settlements or slums has had negative effects. One reason is that they were open-ended: one could build sheds for animals, keep pets, have a workshop whereas the new housing was "closed" and these things were impossible. This was frequently compounded by the inability, in the new areas, of maintaining certain family and larger social groupings such as homogeneous clustering which, as we have seen, helps defensive structuring: the use of appropriate symbols helps preserve the group and its identity, and maintain norms and informal controls and mechanisms (e.g., Laporte 1969). In comparing various groups in an area of Chicago, that group living in public housing was worst off, due partly to their inability to control the environment, express their identity socially, have shops and so on (Suttles 1968).

It seems clear that people desire to make changes and impress their personality on the environment, and that this is one of the criteria for evaluating environmental quality (e.g., Boudon 1969). While most of the changes and discussion have been at the architectural scale, they have clear areal implications – particularly where there is any degree of group homogeneity: then the many individual changes produce cultural landscapes expressing group identity with individual variability within that. Clearly it is easier to get group cooperation if the group is homogeneous. There is less conflict about individual modifications – which also add up to a larger whole. This relates choice, habitat selection and the ability to change and modify environments to clustering.

There are two possible views about the meaning of changes to the environment. One is that the more adaptations made, the more appropriate the environment (e.g., Perin 1970). The other, that too many changes may indicate an unsatisfactory environment (Brolin and Zeisel 1968). The question seems to be one of degree of change and its character. While there may be costs involved in having to make too many decisions, and too many changes, (and some of the arguments for this have gone too far, almost forcing people to make changes and become involved), it does seem that environments which can be modified and over which one has some measure of mastery impose less stress on people – even if that belief is "illusory" (Glass *et al.* 1969). The context, the degree of control and, more generally, the degree of predictability tend to affect greatly the effects of stressors – physical and social (Glass and Singer 1972, 1973; Wohlwill 1971). While there are other ways than open-endedness of reducing stress – for example habitat selection and clustering – they all involve *choice* – and hence a measure of involvement and open-endedness. They also operate in similar ways: thus we saw in Chapter 5 that homogeneity reduces social stress by increasing predictability, i.e., giving a sense of control (cf. Rapoport, in press(b)).

If activity and involvement are taken to mean the use of the urban environment, then we have already seen that this is related to the way people learn the city and construct mental maps. In one sense, therefore, our discussion of activity, behavior setting and house-settlement systems and home ranges is concerned with the extent of people's involvement. This is so particularly if one considers latent and symbolic aspects of activities. The additional element is that certain activities need to have *visible* effects on the environment.

This last point relates to perception and cognition, particularly given the evidence that in order to learn the environment, and become able to use it, animals must be actively involved and move through it: just seeing it passively is not enough (Held and Heim 1968). In the development of children, also, motor activity is crucially important (Piaget 1954, 1962, 1963(a), (b); G. Moore 1972). For adults also, it seems important to move through the environment and use it actively in order to learn about it and to map it cognitively. A static view gives much less information than is given through movement, partly because other sensory modalities can play a role, partly due to the interaction of motor experience and sensory data. Generally there is a relation between perception and locomotion, and urban knowledge varies with active exploration or more active modes of travel. In fact the effects of various modes of travel discussed in Chapter 3 can be interpreted in this way: the more active modes lead to better and fuller knowledge of the environment.

It is also clear that the home ranges of both children and adults are greatly affected by the possibilities for active involvement occurring through the development of mental maps. This, in fact, seems to be the meaning of the finding already discussed that children's cognitive maps are larger in small towns than large cities: it is clearly a function of the greater freedom they have to move independently through the former and be more actively involved in the various settings. The increasing difficulty children have of walking through the city, of using all of it, and actively and freely feeling in control of it, has likely effects on their sensory and mental development and for the function of the city as a field of learning (Parr 1965, 1967, 1968, 1969(a); Rapoport 1973(c)). A city in which one cannot walk, run and play, and be sensorily involved with the environment, is impoverishing. This view would find support from the large literature, from both animals and children, on the importance of exploratory and ludic behavior so that the ability of the environment to provide for such behavior is a critical requirement, and one which the present environment denies children and others.

This is well illustrated by the effects of long journeys to school by young schoolchildren. Using measures such as anxiety,· aggressiveness, depression, popularity with other children, intelligence and so on, bus journeys were more damaging than walking (Lee 1971(b)). Neither time nor fatigue seemed to be involved: the key seemed to be separation from the mother. Anything which maintains a line of communication with the mother helps alleviate separation symptoms. In this case it was perceived accessibility which was involved. Children who walked did so under their own power, knew the route and space traversed and *felt they were in control* – they could get back at any time. The barrier was one which the child could cross at will. Bus travel not only interferes with the construction of a connecting schema, but there is neither decision-making nor action. The child knows that once the bus disappears he cannot get back until it reappears. The key variable is clearly direct activity leading to a sense of mastery or competence.

Competence has been defined as a directed, selective and persistent behavior pattern directed toward mastery of the environment, an "intrinsic need to deal with the environment", producing effects on the environment is reinforcing and mastery of the environment produces a strong and positive self-image (White 1959; Perin 1970; Poole 1972). In dealing with the importance of involvement, activity and competence, one frequently finds oneself discussing the elderly, certain cultural groups or children. This is a result of the notion that reduced competence, or heightened environmental docility, increases criticality and heightens the effects of the environment on behavior (Lawton 1970(a), 1972(d); Rapoport 1972(d); in press(a)): those who are most dependent on the environment are most affected by it. In the case of such groups the effects are clearer, they also affect other groups. The need for control is general, but its criticality varies.

Thus the effects of high flats on children are more extreme than on adults since they affect their ability to act normally and be active, exploratory and play as they wish, due to fears of affecting neighbors. More generally one might argue that environments which block people's ability to act and be involved in ways appropriate with their needs are inhibiting and potentially harmful. Since appropriate behaviors vary greatly, the argument about homogeneity seems relevant to the topic of involvement and would also follow from the previous discussion of the differential effects of the same environment on different groups and the differential adaptation of various groups to certain environments.

Choice and active involvement seem to play a role in the finding that putting people into government housing has little effect on the lifestyle and "culture of poverty" while major changes occur if people move on their own — and even more if they build their own houses and communities (Mangin 1970, p. xxxii). Similarly the differential effects of moving to suburbs on people who choose to do so and those who are forced to move there are due partly to the fact that in the one case the environment is congruent with the lifestyle and values of the people whereas in the other it is not, and partly to the element of choice and active control both regarding the move itself and the control of the environment once moved. It thus appears that people define environments in terms of active involvement, what they do with things and to them. At the same time, what they want to do, what they need to do, where and when they do it, and so on are subjectively defined, so that there needs to be a more behavioral and socio-cultural definition of activity in planning with latent functions stressed.

Active control relates not only to habitat selection and physical modifications; it also includes the definition of domains such as private and public, front and back, the house-settlement system, use of streets, and other settings. Many of these are defined through particular involvement and use by various individuals and groups. The cultural differences in the extent of home range, and hence behavioral or life space, and many of the other aspects described before, receive their definition through the ability of people actively and freely to choose and act.

For example, the perceptual, cognitive, symbolic and behavioral definitions of urban open space are all linked through involvement and activity. One can then see open space as such if it allows people to act freely rather than when it is green — a change in approach with vast planning implications. Open space for particular groups might then be seen as providing freedom to enter and move through, lack of restriction and obstruction — whether physical or through rules, of "ownership" or occupancy, not being too determined, being responsive and not overdesigned, and allowing people to act freely in it. It might be described and loose rather than dense space (Skolimowski 1969). Open space can then be described by contrasting it to closed, or built, space. It is only open space if people can use it in ways which are congruent with their images and definitions of appropriate open-space behavior. These purposes must not be antisocial; moreover, to avoid conflict, they must also be congruent with each other which leads, once again, to the need for homogeneous areas.

I have already referred several times to the idea that the legibility of the physical environment and its ability to communicate, depends partly on the congruence among many perceptual, social and other aspects, for example form and activity. This is a specific example of the broader notion of congruence and a central concept in man–environment interaction. It is also important in how the city is understood and how it communicates — i.e., the efficiency of the city as a symbolic system. I have also suggested that this aspect of the city is not working too well as a result of the lack of a common language and codes, and the consequent inability to read cues for appropriate behavior. But it is also related to the congruence of form and social activity.

Activities can be seen from many points of view; many different disciplines consider activities, from their perspective, central in the understanding of the city as a system. I have stressed the subjective meaning of activities, their latent and symbolic aspects and also the possibility of experiencing vicariously others' activities through signs of modification and change. We are thus interested in noticeable differences in the urban environment due to activities, and congruence is then significant not only between activity and physical form but also between activities and those signs of them which can be grasped. For example a place may be centrally located and prominent, and in fact have a correspondingly important level of activity; that level, however, may not be noticeable from the nature of the place, or the signs of change may not be congruent with the activities taking place within it. There may then well be a lack of congruence between the location, form and signs of activity and conflict and uncertainty about the setting. Thus while for a given individual it is the congruence between his activities, the setting, its image and symbolic expression and location, for others it is with their judgement of the activities through noticeable cues.

Clearly this also relates to the multisensory nature of perception and experience, and the use of a wide variety of cues in orienting, structuring and construing the city. Recall that not only children use such cues: in orienting in large areas of new and rather uniform housing apparently minor signs of change and personalization become important elements de Jonge 1962). These not only become perceptually important noticeable differences, giving identity to otherwise uniform areas, but they also gain special significance, meaning and prominence through the associational values of being a sign of activity and human involvement.

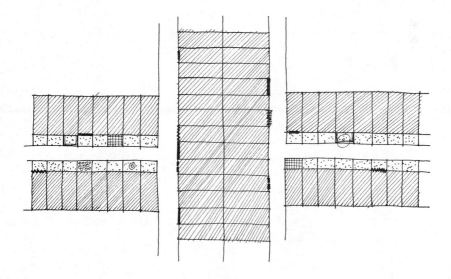

FIG. 6.11. In a uniform environment minor details become very important, i.e. noticeable.

Similarly, since different people use different orientational systems — some using layout, others landmarks and others yet associational values (Baers 1966), it is likely that for many people clear signs of human activity would become important cues and, if congruent with other elements and indicators, would greatly help orientation.

Thus in designing cities it seems essential to encourage the use of as many cues and signs of human activity as possible. For one thing, the use of multichannel capacity and redundancy makes possible many more expressions of the higher levels of congruence. The dominance of single modalities and systems — particularly the extraordinary dominance of car movement as the principal activity receiving expression in the city, and the effect of rules and regulations for this purpose blocking all other forms of expression (as well as the role in blocking most sensory modalities), is a serious hindrance to achieving congruence among forms, activities and their visible expression. Other constraints are technology with new materials and methods which block possible change; increasing density and lack of expressive elements such as gardens and plants; legal limitation on tenants being able to modify their environment, safety and insurance regulations and, finally, the policy of government and planners to create heterogeneous rather than homogeneous areas which inhibits changes, and also makes such changes as do occur less congruent with activites, since there are neither systematic changes or activities present.

While tourist and resident perceptions and preferences differ, the tourist preference for certain types of cities and countries is illuminating. It seems partly due to the fact that such environments more clearly show congruent signs of human activity and provide opportunities to be aware of people going about their daily tasks. This is made easier by pedestrian movement, by the ability of people to modify their environment, and by the fact that these changes, often being part of a clear cultural system, are congruent with all other aspects of life and the urban environment. While many people who enjoy this as tourists would detest it in their own environment, or would not like it as residents, it provides clues. These aspects seem important with regard to the congruence between form and activity, and the significance of people's involvement in the environment.

Firstly, people should be able to make visible changes and modifications to the environment at a number of different scales, as individuals and members of various groups. Secondly, they should be able to perceive, experience and be aware of others' activities and relate these to physical form in some consistent way — not least through their own involvement. Thirdly, in addition to experiencing activities directly, people should be able to read signs of present and past activity through various modifications to the environment which, by being congruent with activities, forms and other aspects, communicate appropriate information and also provide evidence of human involvement and mastery over the environment.

Clearly people's knowledge of the city is due to movement through it, action and behavior in it and involvement with it. Areas which are not seen and, even more importantly, not used or experienced actively, are neither known nor understood. Complexity is also closely related to the visible expression of people's active involvement in the environment. Apart from the effects of personalization on variety and meaning which leads to noticeable differences and complexity at a moment in time, complexity over time is also enhanced, because of the periodic changes which occur as a result of human activity. These are an essential element in reducing the dulling effects of adaptation. We have also seen that the richness of the environment depends on many unarticulated and impossible to note variations which increase its emotional impact (cf.

Without signs of human activity
1. Middle class apartments, Forest Hills, Queens, NY

With signs of human activity
2. Street, Lower East Side, NY (1956)

FIG. 6.12.   (*Photographs by author*)

Without signs of human activity
3. Wah Fu housing project, Hong Kong

With signs of human activity
4. Street, Hong Kong

(Photographs by Prof. R. N. Johnson, University of Sydney, by permission)

Without signs of human activity
5. Wah Fu housing project Hong Kong

With signs of human activity
6. Street, Hong Kong

(Photographs by Prof. R. N. Johnson, University of Sydney, by permission)

Without signs of human activity
7. Public housing, Singapore

With signs of human activity
8. Street, Singapore

(Photographs by author)

Ehrenzweig 1970, pp. 43–44). These elements cannot be designed, they must be allowed to happen – and they involve all senses. (See Fig. 6.12, pp. 375–378).

Complexity and active involvement in the environment are related in two more ways. The first is that incomplete figures tend to be seen as more complex than finished ones, because of the need for active completion (Bartlett 1967, p. 25). The second is that living things are the most interesting and noticeable to people (Bartlett 1967, p. 37; Weiss and Boutourline 1962). Recall also that activities and the social significance of urban elements are important in urban cognition and perception. Their main indicators, in addition to the activities themselves, are the visible signs of human activity; overdesign blocks this visible expression of human action, which is highly noticeable and hence contributes to complexity and becomes important in constructing schemata.

The question can be raised whether personal, direct involvement by all is essential or whether signs of others' involvement might be enough. We have seen that direct, motor activity is considered essential by some in order to understand the environment and construct schemata. There is another point of view which suggests that such activity is not really essential, that its purpose is only to bring the organism in contact with the cues which it needs for learning and that, if these cues can be made available in other ways, learning can occur (e.g., Kilpatrick 1971). Much of the evidence contrary to this latter view is based in children's development. It seems clear that for children direct, active motor involvement does seem important and that the more interaction with the environment there is, the more detailed and veridical are the mental maps. If there are places where things can be done, the environment is used and known; if not – it tends to be impoverished, less used and known (Anderson and Tindall 1972). In the case of adults this process also seems to play a part, although adults' behavior is less exploratory, there are more constraints on it and the role of signs of involvement may become more important. In the case of both adults and children inappropriate environments may lead to less activity and less knowledge. One of the environmental characteristics which encourages activity, because it is more complex and suggests that activity is possible, and also is more memorable and meaningful because it expresses human activity, is an environment showing signs of human action and personalization.

We have already seen that areas showing signs of human activity and modification are most important elements in children's and teenagers' urban perception and cognition. Architectural features, with the exception of a few well known monuments tend not to be very memorable or important in themselves but only if connected with some "vital activity" (Sieverts 1967), so that shops are more memorable than tall buildings. Similarly unfinished elements which allowed involvement to occur and to be visibly expressed, as well as all other elements indicating human presence and involvement were much more memorable than major buildings: in fact apparently minor elements which showed signs of human action – shop windows, signs, balcony window boxes, small allotment gardens and the like were of extraordinary importance (Sieverts 1969).

This is, of course, an example of meaning – i.e., signs of human modification, activity and involvement increase and intensify the meaning of elements which on the basis of size, prominence or location one would not expect to be highly significant. Signs of human activity thus have an important semantic function – they are an important aspect of the environment as the organization of meaning and offer a partial solution to the problems of designing for cultural pluralism. By employing open-ended design which allows such changes to occur, homogeneous groups could create meaningful environments. Even the larger systems would benefit — imageability and clear schemata are related to noticeable differences, and visible signs of change and activity are helpful, particularly if they are not random but systematic.

The success of areas generally, whether residential or center city, depends on the meaning they have for residents; meaning is the result of action, use and movement, i.e., of involvement (Prokop 1967; Buttimer 1972) and this is signified and signalled by visible signs of action. Preference is then partly affected by action and involvement, and this preference may well be linked in some way with the concept of competence. How one understands environments, their meaning and affective impact, may all be related to action and the ability to make an impress on the environment. Particularly in residential areas this gives a sense of competence, understanding, meaning and leads to a sense of satisfaction with both the environment and oneself. It has been suggested that vandalism — graffiti, breaking, spray painting and so on — are attempts to make an impress on environments which do not allow it. There are many other elements involved, but this may play a role.

This then becomes important in understanding the effect of the environment on people. The image people have of themselves, i.e., their self-image, is based on a sense of competence and influences the image they have of the environment, hence their evaluation of it and how they interact with it. This relates involvement, the role of images in man—environment interaction, human behavior and activity systems, the symbolic function of the physical environment in establishing group identity and urban perception and cognition.

A major complaint about new towns, and new developments generally, is that they are "dead" and "sterile". Designers have made strenuous efforts to liven these by changes in form and variations in plans and spaces — some of which have not been noticeable differences. They have not considered the importance of signs of human activity and involvement, and hence the possibility of allowing people to modify and alter the environment and thus generate richness and complexity. The distinction between planned and "natural" towns has also been of this type; what has been forgotten is the time element. Many so-called natural towns were initially planned. Time has made the difference; it has changed the character of these towns in some way. In fact it is the result of many small changes and variations introduced by people into much of the fabric of the city with the exception of the major symbolic and structuring elements.

In most new towns the impact of human activity and occupancy has not yet had a chance to occur and design often prevents its expression. With time, assuming design and management policy are appropriate, such changes will begin to accumulate and hence the city and its areas will be seen and evaluated differently, since they will be humanized, i.e., show signs of active human involvement and personalization. Personalization is thus not only something which occurs at the level of the individual but also through the activity of many individuals and groups. For this to happen, and to work at this group level, there must be areas of more or less homogeneous group character already discussed — a basic planning decision. There are also a set of other planning and design decisions which are essential. They must allow the possibilities of personalization, involvement and humanization that older urban environments provided and these variations must occur within some noticeable structuring frameworks so that they do not become chaos. Most recent designs do not provide the possibilities whereby cities can become humanized and acquire meaning.

What such devices might be at the urban scale is not easy to suggest. At smaller scales they are easier to describe. For example individual dwellings provide more such possibilities than flats, yet those also can be designed so as to make personalization possible. The role of gardens and landscaping is also important: they have not been considered or used consciously to help provide identity, meaning and symbolic identification to urban areas although, as we have seen they can easily do so. I have already referred to graffiti and the like. The use of billboards and hoardings for these purposes is interesting in this connection – they are often the only areas in cities which allow for the personalization and active involvement of people; they could be designed to further this. Older shops often allow owners to develop forms of personalization, such as advertising and display, which are much richer than more controlled forms and also more liable to be read as examples of personal action and be more variable in different areas and places. (See Fig. 6.13, p. 381, 382).

There has been little work on this subject at the urban scale and what there has been, while encouraging, often neglects important aspects. Thus in considering the function of walls, fences and other surfaces for people to express themselves and become involved, attempts have been made to distinguish between "passive structuring" as a function of fashion or peer-group acceptability (seen as "bad") and "active structuring" seen as "self-expression" (and hence "good") (Elmer and Sutherland 1971). This distinction would not seem to be valid. Firstly, they are two cultural expressions of a single process; secondly, if anything, the achievement of group identity may be more important than personal expression which dwellings and gardens often provide. This is because the approach is aesthetic and does not deal with the symbolic and communicative function of this process as an essential part of man–environment interaction.

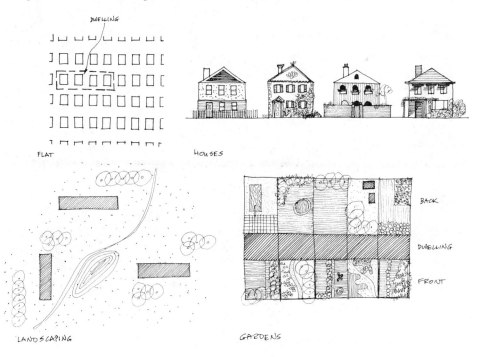

FIG. 6.13. Small elements of personalization in the city.

Hoarding, University of California. Berkeley, 1966.

Newsagent's Shop, Bendigo, Vic. (Australia)

FIG. 6.13. *(cont.).* Small elements of personalization in the city.

(Photographs by author)

More than painting on walls is involved. Activity, including its latent and symbolic aspects, is particularly important for meaning in the urban environment through the assertion of group identity by many individual efforts; human identity is communicated through the identity of areas in the city which express group meaning. Elements which, although used, do not *appear* to be used, i.e., do not express perceived use through changes in the physical fabric of the city, and which thus do not become identifiably those of members of particular groups, because less significant and hence less important in people's cognitive schemata (although the expressions of particular groups may be actively rejected). In turn, this leads to less use, less knowledge and so on in a vicious spiral of growing indifference and deterioration of many urban environments.

Conclusion

A set of urban design requirements from a sophisticated study (e.g., *Regional Plan Ass'n* 1969, pp. 31, 96) may include the following:

* An access system stressing *consistency*, *orientation* and *visual contrast*
* An *imageable* and *coherent* whole with elements *sharply differentiated* from surrounding areas
* Highly *visible* and *expressive* entry points on all major movement paths
* A *consistent* visual vocabulary
* Spaces *responsive to human density requirements*
* *Continuity* with local urban design and architectural style

All of these, and other comparable requirements, clearly depend on the meaning of these terms, the definition of the requirements and their relation to a knowledge of human characteristics.

The purpose of this book has been to review some of the evidence and findings bearing on these and other aspects of man—environment interaction as it applies to urban design, and to use these in new forms of analysis. It seems clear from the argument that this has utility — it raises new questions, introduces new insights, helps to redefine and reinterpret many concepts and shows the mutual relevance of apparently unrelated concepts, theories and studies.

The approach is not yet operational in a "formula" sense — if it will ever be. The basic argument has been that any findings about human preferences, preception, cognition, behavior, socio-cultural variables and so on will, in principle, have an impact on our understanding of urban form and through that will influence the way cities are organized and the criteria used in planning and design to supplement those now used. While a number of specific findings have been discussed, they are not complete although I believe them to be representative. The gaps become less significant in the light of the rapid growth in the field. In any case the basic approach is more significant — even if some of the specific findings were to change, to prove wrong or be greatly modified (as we can fully expect) the approach would remain valid.

In urban design the considerations relating to people and the way in which they interact with the city have tended to be neglected; when they have been considered it has rarely been based on the data and theory of man—environment studies. In addition there has been much overgeneralization about "human needs" and a neglect of the specifics which must be understood in order to design. Consequently the variability of concepts must be considered; through those, the constancies which are found *can* be understood, and become even more important. Underlying this variability there are much more invariant processual principles of the ways in which people interact with their urban environment. The absence of theory has also meant a lack of a consistent approach arising from the way people and urban environments interact rather than being based on *a priori* assumptions. Within the approach proposed, specific data and characteristics can be used. Given this approach design becomes a matter of providing a variety of environments, the qualities and characteristics of which need to be specified, as do the means for the achievement of these objectives; this also implies a need to evaluate the success of the hypotheses underlying design: in fact any design can be seen as a hypothesis needing to be evaluated.

Most of the conclusions seem to be congruent. Repeatedly, although I have tried to keep topics as separate as possible, cross-references have had to be made. The various aspects discussed seem to interact, to reinforce one another, and also suggest many interesting interrelationships, and certain examples can be used to illustrate many apparently different points.

There is no attempt to suggest that this approach is "better". Rather, the intention is that different approaches together, and the variety of "answers" obtained, will give a fuller understanding of the city, a more effective specification of requirements and lead to better environmental designs by enabling the designed elements to coincide to the greatest extent possible with how they are perceived, understood, evaluated and used. The question is basically how to obtain the highest degree of congruence possible (or the least degree of incongruence) between physical setting and human requirements as best understood at a given time, the model being traditional environments where congruence was at a maximum. In this enterprise new methods and insights as well as old should be used – the more we "triangulate" the more will be revealed. Thus much of what is said here is supplementary to other methods rather than a replacement for them.

References

Abercrombie, M. L. Johnson (1969) *The Anatomy of Judgement*, Harmondsworth, Penguin.

Abler, R., J. D. Adams and P. Gould (1971) *Spatial Organization* (the geographer's view of the world) Englewood Cliffs, NJ, Prentice-Hall.

Ablon, Joan (1971) "The social organization of an urban Samoan community", *SW J of Anthropology* vol. 27, No. 1 (Spring) pp. 75–96.

Abrahamson, Mark (1966) *Interpersonal Accommodation* Princeton, NJ, Van Nostrand (paperback).

Abrams, Charles (1969) "Housing policy 1937–1967" in B. J. Frieden and W. W. Nash (ed.) *Shaping an Urban Future*, Cambridge MIT Press.

Abu-Lughod, Janet (1969) "Migrant adjustment to city life: the Egyptian case" in G. Breese (ed.) *The City in Newly Developing Countries*, Princeton, Princeton University Press, pp. 376–388.

_____ (1971) *Cairo: 1001 Years of the City Victorious*, Princeton, Princeton University Press

Acking, Carl-Axel and R. Küller (1973) "Presentation and judgement of planned environments and the hypothesis of arousal" in W. Preiser (ed.) *EDRA 4* Stroudsburg, Pa., Dowden, Hutchinson and Ross, vol. 1, pp. 72–83.

Acking, Carl-Axel and G. Iarle Sorte (1973) "How do we verbalize what we see?" *Landscape Architecture* vol. 64, No. 1 (Oct.) pp. 470–475.

Adams, John S. (1969) "Directional bias in intraurban migration", *Economic Geography*, vol. 45 (Nov.) pp. 302–323.

Adams, Marie Jeanne (1973) "Structural bases of village art", *American Anthropologist*, vol. 75, No. 1 (Feb.), pp. 265–279.

Adjei-Barwuah, Barfour and H. M. Rose (1972) "Some comparative aspects of the West African Zongo and the black American ghetto" in Harold M. Rose (ed.) *The Geography of the Ghetto* DeKalb, Ill., Northern Illinois University Press.

Adler, B. F. (1911) "Maps of primitive people" (transl. and abridged by H. D. Hutorowitz), *Bulletin, Am. Geog. Soc.* vol. 43.

Agron, George (1972) "Some observations on behavior in institutional settings" in J. F. Wohlwill and D. H. Carson (ed.) *Environment and the Social Sciences: Perspectives and Applications*, Washington D.C., American Psychological Association, pp. 87–94.

Alexander, Christopher *et al.* (1969) *Houses Generated by Patterns*, Berkeley, Center for Environmental Structures.

Allen, D. Elliston (1968) *British Tastes* (an enquiry into the likes and dislikes of the regional consumer) London, Hutchinson.

Allen, Edward B. (1969) "The Passagiata," *Landscape*, vol. 18, No. 1 (Winter), pp. 29–32.

Alonso, William (1971) "The historic and the structural theories of urban form: their implications for urban renewal" in Larry S. Bourne (ed.) *Internal Structure of the City*, New York, Oxford University Press, pp. 437–441.

Altman, Irwin (1970) "Territorial behavior in humans – an analysis of the concept" in L. A. Pastalan and D. H. Carson (ed.) *Spatial Behavior of Older People*, Ann Arbor, University of Michigan, pp. 1–24.

Altman, Irwin and William W. Haythorn (1970) "The ecology of isolated groups" in Harold M. Proshansky *et al.* (ed.) *Environmental Psychology: Man and His Physical Setting*, New York, Holt, Rinehart and Winston, pp. 226–239.

Amato, Peter W. (1969) "Residential amenities and neighborhood quality," *Ekistics*, vol. 28, No. 116 (Sept.) pp. 180–184.

_____ (1970) "Elitism and settlement patterns in the Latin American city", *AIP Journal*, vol. 36, No. 2 (March), pp. 96–105.

Anderson, E. N. Jr. (1972) "Some Chinese methods of dealing with crowding," *Urban Anthropology*, vol. 1, No. 2 (Fall), pp. 141–150.

Anderson, J. (1971) "Space-time budgets and activity studies in urban geography and planning", *Environment and Planning*, vol. 3 (Aug.), pp. 353–368.

Anderson, Jeremy and Margaret Tindall (1972) "The concept of home range: new data for the study of territorial behavior" in W. Mitchell (ed.) *EDRA 3*, Los Angeles, University of California, vol. 1 pp. 1-1-1–1-1-7.

Anderson, N. and K. Ishwaran (1965) *Urban Sociology*, New York, Asia Publishing House.

Andrews, Frank M. and George W. Phillips (1971) "The squatters of Lima: who they are and what they want," *Ekistics*, vol. 31, No. 183 (Feb.), pp. 132–136.

Angel, Shlomo (1968) *Discouraging Crime Through City Planning*, Berkeley, University of California, Center for Planning and Development Research, working paper No. 75 (Feb.)

Antrobus, John S. (ed.) (1970) *Cognition and Affect*, Boston, Little Brown.

Appleyard, Donald (1968) in *Dot Zero 5* (Fall).

———— (1969) "Why buildings are known," *Environment and Behavior*, vol. 1, No. 3 (Dec.), pp. 131–156.

———— (1970(a)) "Styles and methods of structuring a city," *Environment and Behavior*, vol. 2, No. 1 (June), pp. 100–117.

———— (1970(b)) "Notes on urban perception and knowledge," in J. Archea and C. Eastman (ed.), *EDRA 2* pp. 97–101.

———— (n.d.) "Communicating the functional and social city" and "The plural environment and its design" (mimeo).

Appleyard, Donald and Mark Lintell (1972) "The environmental quality of city streets: the residents' viewpoint," *AIP Journal*, vol. 38, No. 2 (March), pp. 84–101.

Appleyard, Donald, K. Lynch and J. Meyer (1964) *The View from the Road*, Cambridge, Mass. MIT Press.

Appleyard, Donald and Rai Y. Okamoto (1968) *Environmental Criteria for Ideal Transportation Systems,* Inst. of Urban and Regional Development, University of California, Berkeley, reprint No. 56.

Architects Journal (1973) "High density housing" (Jan.), pp. 23–42.

Architectural Review (1971) (Special issue on India), vol. CL, No. 898.

———— (1972) "Covent garden," vol. CL11, No. 905 (July) p. 28.

Architecture Research Unit (1966) *Courtyard Houses, Inchview, Prestonpans*, University of Edinburgh, Dept. of Architecture.

Arensberg, C. M. and S. T. Kimball (1965) *Culture and Community*, New York, Harcourt Brace and World.

Arnheim, Rudolf (1969) *Visual Thinking*, Berkeley and Los Angeles, University of California.

Artinian, V. A. (1970) "The elementary school classroom" in J. Archea and C. Eastman (ed.), *EDRA 2*, pp. 13–21.

Ashihara, Y. (1970) *Exterior Design in Architecture*, New York, Van Nostrand/Reinhold.

Ashton, Guy T. (1972) "The differential adaptation of two slum subcultures to a Columbian [*sic*] housing project," *Urban Anthropology*, vol. 1, No. 2 (Fall), pp. 176–194.

Athanasiou, Robert and Gary A. Yoshioka (1973) "The spatial character of friendship formation", *Environment and Behavior*, vol. 5, No. 1 (March), pp. 43–66.

Auld, Elizabeth (1972) "Plum slice of Toorak goes for $301,250", *The Australian* (April 24).

Austin, M. R. (1973) "The Pakeha architect and the Polynesian problems," *Ekistics*, vol. 36, No. 213 (Aug.), pp. 143–144.

———— (in press) "A description of the Maori Marae" in Amos Rapoport (ed.) *The Mutual Interaction of People and Their Built Environment: a Cross-Cultural Perspective*, the Hague, Mouton.

Austin, M. R. and G. Rosenberg (1971) "Living in town," paper given at second South Pacific Seminar, Lancala, Suva (mimeo).

Australian Frontier (1971) *Help* (a short report on the Elizabeth youth study) Adelaide.

The Australian (1972(a)) (March 3).

———— (1972(b)) (July 18), p. 9.

Awad, Hassan (1970) "Morocco's expanding towns" in William Mangin (ed.), *Peasants in Cities*, Boston, Houghton Mifflin.

Axelrad, Sidney (1969) "Comments on anthropology and the study of complex cultures" in W. Muensterberger (ed.), *Man and his Culture*, London, Rapp and Whiting, pp. 273–293.

Bachelard, Gaston (1969) *The Poetics of Space*, Boston, Beacon Press.

Bacon, Edmund N. (1967) *Design of Cities*, New York, Viking Press.

Baers, Ronald L. (1966) "A study of orientation", B. Arch. thesis, Berkeley (June) (unpublished).

Bailey, Anthony (1970) "The little room", I and II, *The New Yorker* (Aug. 8 & 15).

Baird, John C. *et al.* (1972) "Student planning of town configurations", *Environment and Behavior*, vol. 4, No. 2 (June) pp. 159–188.

Baker, S. (1961) *Visual Persuasion*, New York, McGraw Hill.

Banerjee, Tridib and Kevin Lynch (1971) "Research guide for an international study of the effects of economic development on the spatial environment of children" (mimeo) (Sept.)

Banham, Reyner (1971) *Los Angeles*, (the architecture of the four ecologies), London, Penguin.

Barker, M. L. (1968) "The perception of water quality as a factor in consumer attitudes and space preferences in outdoor recreation" (paper presented at the Annual Meeting, Ass'n Am Geog, Washington, D.C.) (mimeo).

Barker, Roger G. (1968) *Ecological Psychology*, Stanford, University Press.

Barker, Roger G. and Louise S. Barker (1961) "Behavior units for the comparative study of culture" in B. Kaplan (ed.), *Studying Personality Cross-Culturally*, New York, Harper and Row, pp. 457–476.

Barker, Roger G. and Paul V. Gump (1964) *Big School, Small School*, Stanford, University Press.

Barker, Roger G. and P. Schoggen (1973) *Qualities of Community Life*, San Francisco, Jossey-Bass.

Barnes, J. A. (1971) "Networks and political processes" in J. Clyde Mitchell (ed.) *Social Networks in Urban Situations*, Manchester, University Press.

Barnlund, Dean S. and C. Harland (1963) "Propinquity and prestige as determinants of communication networks," *Sociometry*, vol. 26, pp. 467–479.

Barrett, B. (1971) *The Inner Suburbs* (The evolution of an industrial area), Melbourne, University Press.

Barth, Fredrik (1969) *Ethnic Groups and Social Boundaries*, Boston, Little Brown.

Barthes, Roland (1970–71) "Semiologie et Urbanisme," *Architecture d'Aujourd'hui*, vol. 42, No. 153 (Dec. 1970–Jan. 1971), pp. 11–13.

Bartlett, Sir Frederick (1967) *Remembering*, Cambridge Press (paperback) (originally published 1932).

Bartlett, S. (1971) "Perceived environment: the commuter" in Ross King (ed.), *Perception of Residential Quality: Sydney case Studies*, Ian Buchan Fell Research Project on Housing, Collected papers No. 2, University of Sydney (Aug.), pp. 111–116.

Barwick, Ruth (1971) "Perception of the environment of adjoining suburbs: Killarney Heights and Forrestville" in Ross King (ed.), *Perception of Residential Quality: Sydney Case Studies*, Ian Buchan Fell Research Project on Housing, Collected papers No. 2, University of Sydney (Aug.), pp. 96–104.

Baum, Andrew *et al.* (1974) "Architectural variants of reaction to spatial invasion," *Environment and Behavior* vol. 6, No. 1 (March), pp. 91–100.

Bechtel, Robert B. (1970) "A behavioral comparison of urban and small town environments" in J. Archea and C. Eastman (ed.), *EDRA 2*, pp. 347–353.

————— (1972) "The public housing environment: a few surprises" in W. Mitchell (ed.) *EDRA 3*, Los Angeles, University of California, vol. 1, pp. 13-1-1–13-1-9.

————— *et al.* (1970) *East Side, West Side and Midwest* (a behavioral comparison of three environments) Kansas City, Mo., Greater Kansas City Mental Health Foundation, Epidemiological Field Station.

Becker, Franklin D. (1973) "A class-conscious evaluation" (going back to Sacramento's mall) *Landscape Architecture*, vol. 64, No. 1 (Oct.), pp. 448–457.

Beeley, Brian W. (1970) "The Turkish village coffee house as a social institution," *The Geog. Review*, vol. LX, No. 4 (Oct.), pp. 475–493.

Beer, Stafford (1966) *Decision and Control*, London, Wiley.

Bell, Gwen, Margrit Kennedy *et al.* (1972) "Age group needs and their satisfaction: a case study of the East Liberty renewal area, Pittsburgh" in W. Mitchell (ed.) *EDRA 3*, Los Angeles, University of California, vol. 1, pp. 15-1-1–15-1-8.

Berenson, Bertram (1967–68) "Sensory architecture," *Landscape*, vol. 17, No. 2 (Winter), pp. 19–21.

Berger, B. M. (1960) *Working Class Suburb*, Berkeley and Los Angeles, University of California Press.

————— (1966) "Suburbs, subcultures and the urban future" in S. B. Warner (ed.) *Planning for a Nation of Cities*, Cambridge, MIT Press.

————— (1968) "Suburbia and the American dream" in S. F. Fava (ed.) *Urbanism in World Perspective: a reader*, New York, Crowell.

Berlin, Brent and Paul Kay (1969) *Basic Color Terms*, Berkeley and Los Angeles, University of California Press.

Bernstein, B. *et al.* (1966) "Ritual in education" in J. Huxley (ed.) *Ritualization of Behavior in Animals and Man*, Philosophical Transactions of the Royal Society of London, Series B, vol. 251 (Biological Sciences), pp. 429–436.

Berry, J. W. (1969) "The stereotypes of Australian states." *Aust. J. of Psych.* vol. 21, No. 3 (Dec.), pp. 227–233.

Beshers, J. M. (1962) *Urban Social Structure*, New York, the Free Press.

Best, Gordon (1970) "Direction finding in large buildings" in David Canter (ed.) *Architectural Psychology* London RIBA.

Best, J. B. (1963) "Protopsychology," *Scientific American*, vol. 32, No. 208 (Feb.), pp. 54–62.

Birdwhistel, Ray L. (1968) "Communication without words", *Ekistics*, vol. 25 (June).

Bishop, R. L., G. L. Peterson and R. M. Michaels (1972) "Measurement of children's preference for the play environment" in W. Mitchell (ed.) *EDRA 3*, Los Angeles, University of California, vol. 1, pp. 6-2-1—6 2-9.

Bitter, C. *et al.* (1967) "Development and well being of little children in modern flats," *The Social Environment and its Effect on the Design of the Dwelling and its Immediate Surroundings*, CIB Report 5/68, Stockholm (Oct.), pp. 69—80.

Blaut, James M. *et al.* (1970) "Environmental mapping in young children," *Environment and Behavior*, vol. 2, No. 3 (Dec.).

Blaut, James M. and David Stea (1970) "Notes towards a developmental theory of spatial learning," paper given at *EDRA 2* (not published in proceedings) (mimeo).

——————— (1971) 'Studies of geographic learning," *Annals Ass'n. of Am. Geog.* vol. 61, No. 2 (June), pp. 387—393.

Bleiker, Annemarie H. (1972) "The proximity model of urban social relations," *Urban Anthropology*, vol. 1, No. 2 (Fall), pp. 151—175.

Blumer, Herbert (1969(a)) *Symbolic Interactionism*, Englewood Cliffs, NJ, Prentice Hall.

——————— (1969(b)) "Fashion: from class differentiation to collective selection," *The Sociological Quarterly* (Summer), pp. 275—291.

Blumhorst Roy (1971) "Welcome to Marina City — the shape of the new style" in Walter McQuade (ed.), *Cities Fit to Live In*, New York, Macmillan, pp. 26—29.

Boeschenstein, Warren (1971) "Design of socially mixed housing," *AIP Journal*, vol. 37, No. 5 (Sept.), pp. 311—318.

Bonnett, Alvin (1965) "A study of path selection," unpublished B. Arch. thesis, Berkeley (June).

Borhek, J. T. (1970) "Ethnic group cohesion," *Am. J. of Sociology*, vol. 76, pp. 33—46.

Borroughs, Patricia and Margaret Sim (1971) "Wahroonga and Vaucluse: the perceived environment in two high status suburbs of Sydney" in Ross King (ed.), *Perception of Residential Quality: Sydney Case Studies*, Ian Buchan Fell Research Project on Housing, Collected papers No. 2, University of Sydney (Aug.), pp. 53- 60.

Bose, M. K. (1965) "Calcutta: a premature metropolis," *Scientific American*, vol. 213, No. 3 (Sept.), pp. 90—105.

Botero, Giovani (1606) *A Treatise Concerning the Greatness and Magnificence of Cities*, Ann Arbor, University Microfilms.

Boudon, Philippe (1969) *Pessac de Le Corbusier*, Paris, Dunod.

Boulding, Kenneth (1956) *The Image*, Ann Arbor, University of Michigan Press (paperback edition 1961).

Bourne, Larry S. (ed.) (1971) *Internal Structure of the City*, New York, Oxford University Press.

Bower, T. G. R. (1966) "The visual world of infants," *Scientific American* (Dec.), pp. 80—92.

——————— (1971) "The object in the world of the infant," *Scientific American*, vol. 225, No. 4 (Oct.) pp. 30—38.

Boyce, Ronald R. (1969) "Residential mobility and its implications for urban spatial change," *Proceedings, Ass'n of Am. Geog.* vol. 1, pp. 22—26.

Boyden, S. V. (ed.) (1970) *The Impact of Civilization on the Biology of Man*, Canberra ANU Press.

——————— (1974) Conceptual Basis of Proposed International Ecological Studies in Large Metropolitan Areas (mimeo).

Bracey, H. E. (1964) *Neighbours*, London, Routledge and Kegan Paul.

Brail, Richard K. and F. S. Chapin Jr. (1973) "Activity patterns of urban residents," *Environment and Behavior*, vol. 5, No. 2 (June) pp. 163—190.

Bratfisch, O. (1969) "A further study of the relation between subjective distance and emotional involvement," *Acta Psychologica*, vol. 29.

Brereton, John L. (1972) "Inter-animal control of space" in A. H. Esser (ed.) *Behavior and Environment*, New York, Plenum Press, pp. 69—91.

Briggs, Ronald (1972) *Cognitive Distance in Urban Space*, Columbus, Ohio, Ohio State University, Ph.D. Dissertation in Geography (unpublished).

——————— (1973) "On the relationship between cognitive and objective distance" in W. Preiser (ed.) *EDRA 4*, Stroudsburg, Pa., Dowden, Hutchinson and Ross, vol. 2, pp. 186—192.

Brigham, Eugene F. (1971) "The determinants of residential land values" in Larry S. Bourne (ed.) *Internal Structure of the City*, New York, Oxford University Press, pp. 160—169.

Broadbent, D. E. (1958) *Perception and Communication*, Oxford, Pergamon.

Brolin, Brent C. and John Zeisel (1968) "Mass housing: social research and design," *Arch. Forum*, vol. 129, No. 1 (July/Aug.).

Brookfield, H. C. (1969) "On the environment as perceived" in C. Board *et al.* (ed.) *Progress in Geography* (Int. views of current research), vol. 1, London, Edward Arnold.

Broom, L. and P. Selznick (1957) *Sociology*, New York, Harper and Row.

Brower, Sidney M. (1965) "The signs we learn to read," *Landscape*, vol. 15, No. 1 (Autumn), pp. 9—12.

Brower, Sidney N. and P. Williamson (1974) "Outdoor recreation as a function of the urban housing environment," *Environment and Behavior*, vol. 6, No. 3 (Sept.), pp. 295–345.

Brown, H. J. (1975) "Changes in work place and residential location," *AIP Journal*, vol. 41, No. 1 (Jan.), pp. 32–39.

Brown, L. Carl (ed.) (1973) *From Madina to Metropolis*, Princeton, Darwin Press.

Brown, Lawrence A. *et al.* (1970) "Urban activity systems in a planning context," in J. Archea and C. Eastman (ed.) *EDRA 2*, pp. 102–110.

Brown, Lawrence A. and J. Holmes (1971) "Search behaviour in an intra-urban migration context: a spatial perspective," *Environment and Planning*, vol. 3, pp. 307–326.

Brown, Lawrence A. and Eric G. Moore (1971) "The intra-urban migration process: a perspective" in L. A. Bourne (ed.) *Internal Structure of the City*, New York, Oxford, pp. 200–210.

Browne, G. (1970) "Environmental measurement: the appearance of flat buildings" in Ross King (ed.) *Collected Papers: Architecture Research Seminars*, Ian Buchan Fell Research Project on Housing, Collected Papers No. 1, Sydney, University of Sydney (Dec.), pp. 109–130.

Bruner, Edward M. (1972) "Batak ethnic associations in three Indonesian cities," *SW J. of Anthropology*, vol. 28, No. 3 (Autumn), pp. 207–229.

Bruner, Jerome (1951) "Personality dynamics and the process of perceiving" in R. R. Blake and G. V. Ramsey (ed.) *Perception: an Approach to Personality*, New York, Ronald Press.

————— *et al.* (1956) *A Study of Thinking*, New York, Wiley.

————— (1968) "On perceptual readiness" in R. N. Haber (ed.), *Contemporary Theory and Research in Visual Perception*, New York, Holt, Rinehart and Winston.

Bryson, L. and F. Thompson (1972) *An Australian Newtown* (life and leadership in a new housing suburb), Harmondsworth, Penguin.

Buehler, R. E. *et al.* (1966) "The reinforcement of behavior in institutional settings," *Behavior Research and Therapy*, vol. 5.

Bunker, Raymond (1970) "What is Sydney", *Arch. in Australia* (June), pp. 474–476.

————— (1971) *Town and Country or City and Region*, Melbourne, University Press.

Burby, R. J. III (1974) "Environmental amenities and new community governance: results of a nationwide survey" in D. H. Carson (ed.) *EDRA 5*, vol. 1, pp. 101–124.

Burch, Ernest S. Jr. (1971) "The non-empirical environment of the Arctic Alaskan Eskimo," *SW J. of Anthropology*, vol. 27, No. 2, pp. 148–165.

Burnett, Jacquetta Hill (1969) "Ceremony, rites and economy in the student system of an American high school," *Human Organization*, vol. 28, No. 1 (Spring), pp. 1–10.

Burnette, Charles H. (1972) "Designing to reinforce the mental image: an infant learning environment" in W. Mitchell (ed.) *EDRA 3*, Los Angeles, University of California, vol. 2, pp. 29-1-1–29-1-7.

Burnley, I. H. (1972) "European immigration settlement patterns in Metropolitan Sydney 1947–1966," *Aust. Geog. Studies*, vol. X, No. 1 (April), pp. 61–78.

Burns, Tom (1968) "Urban styles of life" in Centre for Environmental Studies SSRC/CES Joint Conference, *The Future of the City Region* (working paper No. 6), London (July).

Burton, Ian (1972) "Cultural and personality variables in the perception of natural hazards" in J. F. Wohlwill and D. H. Carson (ed.) *Environment and Social Sciences: Perspectives and Applications*, Washington, D.C. American Psychological Association, pp. 184–197.

Burton, Ian and Robert W. Kates (1972) "The perception of natural hazards in resources management" in P. W. English and R. C. Mayfield (ed.) *Man. Space and Environment*, New York, Oxford University Press, pp. 282–304.

Butterworth, Douglas S. (1970) "A study of the urbanization process among Mixtec migrants from Tilantongo in Mexico City" in W. Mangin (ed.) *Peasants in Cities*, Boston, Houghton, Mifflin, pp. 98–113.

Buttimer, Anne (1969) "Social space in inter-disciplinary perspective," *Geog. Review*, vol. 59, No. 3 (July), pp. 417–426.

————— (1971) "Sociology and Planning," *Town Planning Review*, vol. 42, No. 2 (April), pp. 145–180.

————— (1972) "Social space and planning of residential areas," *Environment and Behavior*, vol. 4, No. 3 (Sept.), pp. 279–318.

Cadwallader, Martin T. (1973) "A methodological examination of cognitive distance" in W. Preiser (ed.) *EDRA 4*, Stroudsburg, Pa., Dowden, Hutchinson and Ross, vol. 2, pp. 193–199.

Calhoun, John B. (1970) "Space and the strategy of life" in A. H. Esser (ed.) *Behavior and Environment*, New York, Plenum Press, pp. 329–387.

Calvin, James. S. *et al.* (1972) "An attempt at assessing preferences for natural landscapes," *Environment and Behavior*, vol. 4, No. 4 (Dec.), pp. 447–469.

Campbell, Donald T. (1961) "The mutual methodological relevance of anthropology and psychology" in L. K. Hsu (ed.) *Psychological Anthropology*, Homewood, Ill., The Dorsey Press.

Canter, David and Sandra Canter (1971) "Close together in Tokyo," *Design and Environment*, vol. 2, No. 2 (Summer), pp. 60–63.

Canter, David and S. K. Tagg (1975) "Distance estimation in cities," *Environment and Behavior*, vol. 7, No. 1 (March), pp. 59–80.

Caplow, Theodore (1961(a)) "The social ecology of Guatemala City" in G. A. Theodorson (ed.) *Studies in Human Ecology*, Evanston, Ill., Row, Peterson, pp. 331–348.

————(1961(b)) "Urban structure in France" in G. A. Theodorson (ed.) *Studies in Human Ecology*, Evanston, Ill., Row, Peterson, pp. 384–389.

Carpenter, C. R. (1958) "Territoriality: a review of concepts and problems: in A. Roe and G. G. Simpson (ed.) *Behavior and Evolution*, New Haven, Yale.

Carpenter, Edmund (1973) *Eskimo Realities*, New York, Holt, Rinehart and Winston.

———— *et al.* (1959) *Eskimo*, Toronto, University of Toronto Press.

Carpenter, Edmund and Marshall McLuhan (1960) "Acoustic space" in Edmund Carpenter and Marshall McLuhan (ed.) *Explorations in Communication*, Boston, Beacon Press.

Carr, Stephen (1970) "The city of the mind" in H. M. Proshansky *et al.* (ed.) *Environmental Psychology*, New York, Holt, Rinehart and Winston, pp. 518–533.

———— (1973) *City Signs and Lights: A Policy Study*, Cambridge, MIT Press (done with Ashley, Meyer, Smith).

Carr, Stephen and D. Schissler (1969) "The city as trip: perceptual selection and memory in the view from the road," *Environment and Behavior*, vol. 1, No. 1 (June), pp. 7–36.

Carrington, R. Allen (1970) "Analysis of mobility and change in a longitudinal sample," *Ekistics*, vol. 30, No. 178 (Sept.), pp. 183–186.

Carson, D. H. (1972) "Residential descriptions and urban threats" in Joachim F. Wohlwill and D. H. Carson (ed.) *Environment and the Social Sciences: Perspectives and Applications*, Washington, D.C. Am. Psych Ass'n, pp. 154–168.

Cassirer, Ernst (1957) *The Philosophy of Symbolic Forms*, vol. 3 (The phenomenology of knowledge), New Haven.

Challis, E. C. and G. Rosenberg (1973) "Pacific islanders in New Zealand," *Ekistics*, vol. 31, No. 213 (Aug.), pp. 139–143.

Chang, Amos (1956) *The Existence of Intangible Content in Architectonic Form*, Princeton, Princeton University Press (and University Microfilms, Ann Arbor, Mich.).

Chang, K. C. (ed.) (1968) *Settlement Archaeology*, Palo Alto, National Press.

Chapin, F. Stuart Jr. (1968) "Activity systems and urban structure: a working schema," *AIP Journal*, vol. 34, No. 1 (Jan.), pp. 11–18.

———— (1971) "Free time activities and quality of urban life," *AIP Journal*, vol. 37, No. 6 (Nov.), pp. 411–417.

Chapin, F. Stuart Jr. and H. C. Hightower (1966) *Household Activity Systems – A Pilot Investigation*, Chapel Hill Center for Urban and Regional Studies.

Chartres, John (1968) "Where souls are built in," *The Times* (London) (March 4).

Chermayeff, Serge and Christopher Alexander (1965) *Community and Privacy*, Garden City, NY, Anchor Books.

Chermayeff, Serge and Alexander Tzonis (1971) *Shape of Community*, Harmondsworth, Penguin.

Cherry, Colin (1957) *On Human Communication*, New York, Wiley.

Choay, Françoise (1970–71) "Remarques a propos de semiologie urbaine," *Arch. d'Aujourd'hui*, vol. 42, No. 153 (Dec.–Jan.), pp. 9–10.

Choldin, Harvey M. (1972) "Population density and social interaction," paper presented at the Population Ass'n of America, Toronto (April 14) (mimeo).

Choldin, Harvey M. and Michael J. McGinty (1972) "Population density and social relations," Urbana, University of Illinois, Dept of Sociology (mimeo).

Christy, Francis T. Jr. (1971) "Human needs and human values for environmental resources" in Robert M. Irving and George B. Priddle (ed.) *Crisis* (readings in environmental issues and strategies) New York, St. Martin's Press, pp. 211–221.

Chudacoff, Howard P. (1971) *Urban History Newsletter*, No. 16, University of Leicester (Summer), p. 9 (Report of Meeting).

Clark, David L. (1968) *Analytical Archaeology*, London, Methuen.

Clark, W. A. V. (1971) "Measurement and explanation in intra-urban residential mobility," *Ekistics*, vol. 31, No. 183 (Feb.), pp. 143–147.

Clarke, W. T. (1971) "Present environment and future residential preferences of school children" (2) in Ross King (ed.) *Perception of Residential Quality: Sydney Case Studies*, Ian Buchan Fell Research Project on Housing, Collected papers No. 2 (Aug.), University of Sydney, pp. 67–77.

Clayton, Christopher (1968) *Human Perception of Urban and Rural Environments*, unpublished masters thesis (geography) University of Cincinatti (cited in Saarinen 1969).

Cleary, Jon (1970) *Helga's Web*, London, Collins.

Coates, Gary and E. Bussard (1974) "Patterns of children's spatial behavior in a moderate-density housing development" in Robin C. Moore (ed.) Childhood City (*EDRA 5*, vol. 12), pp. 131–142.

Coates, Gary and Henry Sanoff (1972) "Behavioral mapping: the ecology of child behavior in a planned residential setting" in W. Mitchell (ed.) *EDRA 3*, Los Angeles, University of California, vol. 1, pp. 13-2-1–13-2-11.

Cohen, Abner (ed.) (1974) *Urban Ethnicity*, London, Tavistock.

Cohen, John (1964) "Psychological Time," *Scientific American* (Nov.), pp. 116–124.

_____ (1967) *Psychological Time in Health and Disease*, Springfield, Ill. Charles C. Thomas.

Coing, Henri (1966) *Renovation Urbaine et Changement Social*, Paris, Editions Ouvrières.

Collier, John (1967) *Visual Anthropology*, New York, Holt, Rinehart and Winston.

Congalton, A. A. (1969) *Status and Prestige in Australia*, Melbourne, Cheshire.

Cook, J. A. (1969) *Gardens on Housing Estates: A Survey of User Attitudes and Behaviour on Seven Layouts* BRS, Current Paper 42/69 (Oct.).

Cook, Peter (1970) *Experimental Architecture*, London, Studio Vista.

Cooper, Clare (1965) "Some social implications of house and site plan design at Easter Hill Village: a case study," Berkeley, University of California, Center for Planning and Development Research (Sept.).

_____ (1970(a)) "The adventure background: creative play in an urban setting as a potential focus for community involvement," Berkeley Institute of Urban and Regional Development, Working Paper No. 118 (May).

_____ (1970(b)) "Resident attitudes towards the environment at St. Francis Square, San Francisco: a summary of the initial findings," Berkeley, University of California, Center for Planning and Development Research, Working Paper No. 126 (July).

_____ (1971) *House as Symbol of Self*, Working Paper No. 120, Institute of Regional and Urban Development, University of California, Berkeley (May).

_____ (1972) "Resident dissatisfaction in multifamily housing" in William M. Smith (ed.) *Behavior, Design and Policy Aspects of Human Habitats*, Green Bay University of Wisconsin, pp. 119–146.

Cooper, Robert (1968) "The psychology of boredom," *Ekistics*, vol. 25 (June).

Coss, Richard (1973) "The cut-off hypothesis: its relevance to the design of public places," *Man–Environment Systems* (Nov.).

Coughlin, Robert E. and Karen A. Goldstein (1971) "The extent of agreement among observers of environmental attractiveness," *Man–Environment Systems* (May).

Coulter, John (1972) "What the Flinders Ranges mean to me" in D. Whitelock and D. Corbett (ed.), *The Future of the Flinders Ranges*, Department of Adult Education/Town and Planning Association, University of Adelaide (Australia) Publication No. 28.

Cowburn, William (1966) "Popular housing," *Arena: Journal of the AA* (London) (Sept.–Oct.).

Cox, Harvey (1966) *The Secular City*, Harmondsworth, Penguin Books.

_____ (1968) "The restoration of a sense of place: a theological reflection on the visual environment," *Ekistics*, vol. 25 (June).

Cox, Kevin and Georgia Zannaras, "Designative perception of macro-spaces: concepts, a methodology and applications" in J. Archea and C. Eastman (ed.) *EDRA 2*, pp. 118–130.

Craik, Kenneth H. (1968) "The comprehension of the everyday physical environment," *AIP Journal*, vol. 34, No. 1 (Jan.), pp. 29 37.

_____ (1970) "Environmental psychology" in Theodore M. Newcomb (ed.) *New Directions in Psychology*, 4, New York, Holt, Rinehart and Winston, pp. 3–121.

Crane, David A. (1960) "The city symbolic," *AIP Journal*, vol. 26, No. 4 (Nov.).

_____ (1961) review of *Image of the City AIP Journal*, vol. 27 (May).

_____ (1964) "The public art of city building," *Annals. Am. Academy of Political and Social Science* (March).

Crone, G. R. (1962) *Maps and their Makers: an Introduction to the History of Cartography*, London, Hutchinson.

Crumrine, N. Ross (1964) *The House cross of the Mayo Indians of Sonora, Mexico* (a symbol of ethnic identity) Tucson, University of Arizona Press, Anthropology Paper No. 8.

Csikszentmihalyi, M. and S. Bennett (1971) "An exploratory model of play," *American Anthropologist*, vol. 73, No. 1 (Feb.), pp. 42–58.

Cullen, Gordon (1961) *Townscape*, London, Architectural Press.

_____ (1964) *A Town Called Alcan*, London, Alcan Industries.

_____ (1968) *Notation*, London, Alcan Industries.

Culpan, Maurice (1968) *The Vasiliko Affair*, London, Collins (Crime Club).

Daish, J. R. and P. J. Melser (1969) "A case study of twenty state houses and families" (preliminary findings) Housing Division, Ministry of Works, Wellington, NZ (Feb.) (mimeo).

Daly, M. T. (1968) "Residential location decisions: Newcastle, NSW," *Aust. and NZ Journal of Sociology*, vol. 14, pp. 18–35.

Daniel, Terry C., Lawrence Wheeler, Ron S. Boster and Paul R. Best (n.d.) "Quantitative evaluation of landscapes: an application of signal detection analysis to forest management alternatives" (mimeo).

Davis, Gerald (1972) "Using interviews of present office workers in planning new offices" in W. Mitchell (ed.) *EDRA 3*, Los Angeles, University of California, vol. 1, pp. 14-2-1–12-2-9.

Davis, Gerald and Ron Roizen (1970) "Architectural determinants of student satisfaction in college residence halls" in J. Archea and C. Eastman (ed.) *EDRA 2*, pp. 28–44.

Davis, John (1969) "Town and country," *Anthrop. Quarterly*, vol. 42, No. 3 (July) pp. 171–185.

Davis, K. (1965) "The urbanization of the human population," *Scientific American*, vol. 213, No. 3 (Sept.), pp. 40–53.

Davis, Shane (1972) "The reverse commuter transit problem in Indianapolis" in H. M. Rose (ed.) *Geography of the Chetto* DeKalb, Ill., Northern Illinois University Press.

Daws, L. F. and A. J. Bruce (1971) *Shopping at Watford*, Building Research Station.

DeBlij, Harm J. (1968) *Mombassa—an African City*, Evanston, Ill., Northwestern University Press.

Deetz, James (1968) "Cultural patterning of behavior as reflected by archaeological materials" in K. C. Chang (ed.) *Settlement Archaeology*, Palo Alto, California National Press, pp. 31–42.

de Jonge, Derk (1962) "Images of urban areas: their structure and psychological foundations," *AIP Journal*, vol. 28 (Nov.) pp. 266–276.

————— (1967–68) "Applied Hodology," *Landscape*, vol. 17, No. 2 (Winter), pp. 10–11.

de Lauwe, P. H. Chombart (1960) *Paris: essai d'observation Experimentale*, Paris CNRS.

————— (1965(a)) *Paris: essais de Sociologie 1952–1964*, Paris Editions Ouvrières.

————— (1965(b)) *Des Hommes et des Villes*, Paris, Payot.

————— (1967) *Famille et Habitation*, Paris CNRS.

Delaval, B. (1974) "Urban communities of the Algerian Sahara," *Ekistics*, vol. 38, No. 227, (Oct.), pp. 252–258.

DeLong, Alton J. (1967) "A preliminary analysis of the structure points of interpersonal and environmental transactions among the mentally impaired elderly," Philadelphia Geriatric Centre (Aug.) (mimeo).

————— (1970) "Coding behavior and levels of cultural integration" in J. Archea and C. Eastman (ed.), *EDRA 2*, pp. 254–265.

————— (1971(a)) "Dominance territorial criteria and small group structure," *Comparative Group Studies*, vol. 2 (Aug.), pp. 235–266.

————— (1971(b)) "A context for the concept of culture" (mimeo draft paper) (June).

————— (1971(c)) "Content vs. structure: the transformation of the continuous into the discrete," *Man–Environment Systems* (Jan.).

Denis, J. (1958) *Le phenomène urbain en Afrique centrale*, Brussels, Academie Royale des sciences coloniales, classe des sciences morales et politiques.

Department of the Environment (DOE) (1972) *The Estate Outside the Dwelling*, London, HMSO.

————— (1973) Children at Play (Design Bulletin 27) London, HMSO.

Department of Social Work (University of Sydney) (n.d.) "An areal analysis of social differentation in Sydney" (mimeo) (using 1961 census data).

Densor, J. A. (1972) "Towards a psychological theory of crowding," *J. of Personality and Soc. Psych.* vol. 21, No. 1, pp. 79–83.

Deutsch, Karl W. (1971) "On social communication and the metropolis" in Larry S. Bourne (ed.) *Internal Structure of the City*, New York, Oxford University Press, pp. 222–230.

de Vise, Pierre (1973) work presented at the 9th ICAES and reported in *Chicago Daily News* (Aug. 31) and *Chicago Tribune* (Sept. 1).

Dewey, Alice G. (1970) "Ritual as a mechanism for urban adaptation," *Man*, vol. 5, No. 3 (Sept.), pp. 438–448.

de Wofle, Ivor (1971) *Civilia*, London Architectural Press.

Dixon, N. F. (1971) *Subliminal Perception: the Nature of a Controversy*, New York, McGraw Hill.

Doeppers, D. F. (1974) "Ethnic urbanism and Philippine Cities," *Annals. Ass'n Am. Geog.* vol. 64, No. 4 (Dec.) pp. 549–559.

Doherty, J. M. (1968) *Residential Preference for Urban Environments in the United States*, London, LSE Graduate School of Geography, Discussion Paper No. 29.

Donaldson, Scott (1969) *The Suburban Myth*, New York, Columbia University Press.

Doob, Leonard W. (1971) *Patterning of Time*, New Haven, Yale University Press.

Dornic, S. (1967) "Subjective distance and emotional involvement: a verification of the exponent invariance," University of Stockholm (mimeo).

Doshi, S. L. (1969) "Nonclustered tribal villages and community development," *Human Organization*, vol. 28, No. 4 (Winter), pp. 297–302.

Doughty, Paul L. (1970) "Behind the back of the city: 'provincial' life in Lima, Peru" in William Mangin (ed.) *Peasants in Cities*, Boston, Houghton Mifflin, pp. 30–46.

Downing, Margaret (1968(a)) "What it's like to live in Tower Hamlets," *Evening Standard* (London) (May 28).

_____ (1968(b)) Reply to letter by Mr. Longstaff, *Evening Standard* (London), (June 11).

Downs, Roger M. (1967) Approaches to, and problems in, the measurement of geographical space perception, *Seminar Paper* Series A, No. 9 (Dept. of Geography, Bristol University) (mimeo).

_____ (1968) *The Role of Perception in Modern Geography*, Dept. of Geography, University of Bristol, Seminar Paper Series A, No. 11 (Feb.).

_____ (1970) "The cognitive structure of an urban shopping center," *Environment and Behavior*, vol. 2, No. 1 (June), pp. 13–39.

Downs, Roger M. and David Stea (ed.) (1973) *Image and Environment* (cognitive mapping and spatial behavior), Chicago, Aldine.

Doxiadis, Constantinos (1968(a)) "A city for human development," *Ekistics*, vol. 25 (June), pp. 374–394.

_____ (1968(b)) *Ekistics*, London, Hutchinson.

Dubos, Rene (1965) "Humanistic biology," *American Scientist*, vol. 53.

_____ (1966) *Man Adapting*, New Haven, Yale University Press.

_____ (1972) "Is man overadapting to the environment?" *Sydney University Union Recorder*, vol. 52, No. 6 (April 13).

Duncan, H. D. (1972) *Symbols in Society*, New York, Oxford.

Duncan, James S. Jr. (1973) "Landscape taste as a symbol of group identity," *Geog. Review*, vol. 63 (July), pp. 334–355.

_____ (in press) "Landscape and the communication of social identity" in Amos Rapoport (ed.) *The Mutual Interaction of People and their Built Environment: A Cross-Cultural Perspective*, the Hague, Mouton.

Duncan, James S. and N. G. Duncan 1976 "Social worlds, status passage and environmental perspectives: a case study of Hyderabad, India" in G. T. Moore and R. G. Golledge (ed.) *Environmental Knowing*, Stroudsburg, Pa., Dowden, Hutchinson and Ross.

Duncan, Otis and Beverly Duncan (1955) "Residential distribution and occupational stratification," *Am. J. Sociol.* vol. 60 (March).

Dunham, H. W. (1961) "Social structures and mental disorders: competing hypotheses of explanation," *Milbank Mem. Fund Q.* vol. 31.

Eastman, Charles M. and Joel Harper (1971) "A study of proxemic behavior-toward a predictive model," *Environment and Behavior*, vol. 3, No. 4 (Dec.), pp. 418–437.

Eberts, E. H. "Social and personality correlates of personal space" in W. Mitchell (ed.) *EDRA 3*, Los Angeles, University of California, vol. 1, pp. 2-1-1–2-1-9.

Eckman, Judith *et al.* (1969) "Gregariousness in rats as a function of familiarity of environment," *J. of Personality and Soc. Psych.* vol. 11, No. 2, pp. 107–114.

Ehrenzweig, Anton (1970) *The Hidden Order of Art*, London, Paladin Books.

Ehrlich, Allen S. (1971) "History, ecology and demography in the British Caribbean: an analysis of East Indian ethnicity," *SW J. of Anthropology*, vol. 27, No. 2, pp. 166–180.

Eibl-Eibesfeld, I. (1970) *Ethology: the Biology of Behavior*, New York, Holt, Rinehart and Winston.

Eichler, Edward P. and Marshall Kaplan (1967) *The Community Builders*, Berkeley and Los Angeles, University of California Press.

Eidt, Robert C. (1971) *Pioneer Settlement in Northeast Argentina*, Madison, University of Wisconsin Press.

Eisenberg, J. F. and W. S. Dillon (ed.) (1971) *Man and Beast* (comparative social behavior) (Smithsonian Annual III) Washington D.C., Smithsonian.

Ekambi-Schmidt, Jezebelle (1972) *La Perception de L'Habitat*, Paris, Editions Universitaires.

Ekman, G. and B. Bratfisch (1965) "Subjective distance and emotional involvement: a psychological mechanism," *Acta Psychologica*, vol. 24.

Ekman, Paul (1972) "Universals and cultural differences in facial expressions of emotion" in J. Cole (ed.) *Nebraska Symposium on Motivation*, Lincoln, University of Nebraska Press.

Eliade, Mircea (1961) *The Sacred and the Profane*, New York, Harper and Row.

Elisséeff, Nikita (1970) "Damas à la Lumière des Théories de Jean Sauvaget" in A. H. Hourani and S. M. Stern (ed.) The Islamic City Oxford, Cassirer, pp. 157–177.

Ellis, Michael (1972) "Play: theory and research" in W. Mitchell (ed.) *EDRA 3*, Los Angeles, University of California, vol. 1, pp. 5-4-1–5-4-5.

Ellis, William R. (1972) "Planning, design and black community style: the problem of occasion-adequate space" in W. Mitchell (ed.) *EDRA 3*, Los Angeles, University of California, vol. 1, pp. 6-12-1–6-12-10.

Elmer, Frank L. and Duncan B. Sutherland (1971) "Urban design and environmental structuring," *AIP Journal*, vol. 37, No. 1 (Jan.), pp. 38–41.

Elon, Y. and Y. Tzamir (1971) "The perception of the built environment of public housing," Haifa, Israel, Faculty of Architecture and Town Planning, Center for Urban and Regional Studies, Technion, Project No. 020–019 (July) (English abstract).

English, Paul W. (1966) *City and Village in Iran*, Madison, University of Wisconsin Press.

———— (1973) "The traditional city of Herat, Afghanistan" in L. Carl Brown (ed.) *From Medina to Metropolis*, Princeton, Princeton University Press, pp. 73–90.

English, Paul Ward and R. C. Mayfield (ed.) (1972) *Man, Space and Environment* (part 3), New York, Oxford University Press.

Epstein, A. L. (1969) "Urbanization and social change in Africa" in Gerald Breese (ed.) *The City in Newly Developing Countries*, Englewood Cliffs, NJ, Prentice-Hall, pp. 246–287.

Esser, A. H. (1970(a)) "Interactional hierarchy and power structure on a psychiatric ward-ethological studies of dominance behavior in a total institution" in S. J. Hutt and C. Hutt (ed.) *Behavior Studies in Psychiatry*, Oxford, Pergamon, pp. 25–59.

———— (1970(b)) "The psychopathology of crowding (human pollution)" Am. Psychiatric Ass'n Meeting (Sept. 4) (mimeo).

———— (ed.) (1971(a)) *Behavior and Environment*, New York, Plenum Press.

———— (1971(b)) "Towards a definition of crowding," *The Sciences* (NY Academy of Sciences) (Oct.).

———— (1972) "A biosocial perspective on crowding" in J. F. Wohlwill and D. H. Carson (ed.) *Environment and the Social Sciences: Perspectives and Applications*, Washington, D.C. Am. Psych. Ass'n., pp. 15–28.

———— (1973) "Experience of crowding: illustration of a paridigm for man–environment relations," *Repr. Research in Soc. Psych.* vol. 4, No. 1 (Jan.), pp. 207–218.

Everitt, John and Martin Cadwallader (1972) "The home area concept in urban analysis: the use of cognitive mapping and computer procedures" in W. Mitchell (ed.) *EDRA 3*, Los Angeles, University of California, vol. 1, pp. 1-2-1–1-2-10.

Eyles, J. D. (1969) *Inhabitants' Images of Highgate Village, London – an Example of a Perception Measurement Technique*, London, LSE, Dept of Geography, Discussion Paper No. 15.

Fel, Edit and Tamas Hofer (1973) "Atany patronage and factions" (tanyakert-s patron-client relations and political factions in Atany) *American Anthropologist*, vol. 75, No. 3 (June), pp. 787–801.

Feldman, A. S. and C. Tilly (1960) "The interaction of social and physical space," *Am. Sociological Review*, vol. 25, No. 6 (Dec.), pp. 877–884.

Feldt, Allan G. *et al.* (n.d.) *Residential Environment and Social Behavior* (a study of selected neighborhoods in San Juan, Puerto Rico) Ithaca, NY, Dept of City Planning, Cornell University (mimeo).

Fellman, Gordon and Barbara Brandt (1970) "A neighborhood a highway would destroy," *Environment and Behavior*, vol. 2, No. 3 (Dec.), pp. 281–302.

Fernandez, James W. (1970 "Fang architectonics," paper given at conference on traditional African architecture (Sept. 1) (Mimeo).

Festinger, L. *et al.* (1950) Social Pressures in Informal Groups, Stanford, Stanford University Press.

———— (1957) *The Theory of Cognitive Dissonance*, New York, Harper and Row.

Festinger, Leon and Harold H. Kelly (1951) *Changing Attitudes Through Social Contact* (an experimental study of a housing project) Ann Arbor University of Michigan Research Center for Group Dynamics, Institute for Social Research (Sept.).

Firey, Walter (1947) *Land Use in Central Boston*, Cambridge, Harvard University Press.

———— (1961) "Sentiment and symbolism as ecological variables" in George A. Theodorson (ed.) *Studies in Human Ecology*, Evanston, Row Peterson, pp. 253–261.

Fisher, Gerald H. (1968) *The Frameworks for Perceptual Localization*, Dept. of Psychology, University of Newcastle upon Tyne.

Fitzgerald, C. P. (1965) *Barbarian Beds*, London, Cressett Press.

Flachsbart, Peter G. and George L. Peterson (1973) "Dynamics of preference for visual attributes of residential environments" in W. Preiser (ed.) *EDRA 4*, Stroudsburg, Pa., Dowden, Hutchinson and Ross, vol. 1, pp. 98–106.

Fonseca, Rory (1969(a)) "The walled city of New Delhi" in P. Oliver (ed.) *Shelter and Society*, London, Barrie and Rockliffe, pp. 103–115.

———— (1969(b)) "The walled city of Old Delhi," *Landscape*, vol. 18, No. 3 (Fall), pp. 12–25.

Forgus, R. H. (1966) *Perception: the Basic Process in Cognitive Development*, New York, McGraw Hill.

Foster, Donald W. (1972) "Housing in low income barrios in Latin America: some cultural considerations", paper presented at the 71st annual meeting of the American Anthropologists Ass'n, Toronto (Dec.) (mimeo).

Fox, Robin (1970) "The cultural animal," *Encounter*, vol. XXXV, No. 1 (July), pp. 31–42.

Frank, Lawrence K. (1966(a)) "Tactile communication" in E. Carpenter and M. McLuhan (ed.) *Explorations in Communication*, Boston, Beacon paperback, pp. 4–11.

———— (1966(b) "The world as a communication network" in G. Kepes (ed.) *Sign, Image, Symbol*, New York Braziller, pp. 1–14.

Frankenberg, Ronald (1967) *Communities in Britain*, Harmondsworth, Penguin.

Franks, Lucinda (1974) "Yorkville fighting loss of old flavor," *New York Times* (April 12).

Fraser, Douglas (1968) *Village Planning in the Primitive World*, New York, Braziller.

Fraser, J. T., F. C. Haber and G. H. Muller (ed.) (1972) *The Study of Time*, New York, Springer Verlag.

Fraser, Thomas M. (1969) "Relative habitability of dwellings – a conceptual view," *Ekistics*, vol. 27, No. 158 (Jan.), pp. 15–18.

Freides, David (1974) "Human information processing and sensory modality: cross-model functions, information complexity, memory and deficit," *Psych. Bulletin*, vol. 81, No. 5 (May), pp. 284–310.

Fried, Marc (1963) "Grieving for a lost home" in Leonard J. Duhl (ed.) *The Urban Condition*, New York Basic Books, pp. 151–171.

———— (1973) *The World of the Urban Working Class*, Cambridge, Harvard University Press.

Fried, Marc and Peggy Gleicher (1961) "Some sources of residential satisfaction in an urban slum," *AIP Journal*, vol. 27, No. 4 (Nov.) (reprinted in H. M. Proshansky *et al.* (ed.) *Environmental Psychology*, New York, Holt, Rinehart and Winston (1970), pp. 333–346).

Friedberg, M. Paul (1970) *Play and Interplay*, New York, Macmillan.

Frolic, B. Michael (1971) "Soviet urban sociology," *Int. J. of Comp. Sociol.*, vol. 12, No. 4 (Dec.), pp. 234–251.

Gans, Herbert J. (1961(a)) "Planning and social life" (Friendship and neighbour relations in suburban communities), *AIP Journal*, vol. 27, No. 2 (May), pp. 134–140.

———— (1961(b)) "The balanced community" (homogeneity or heterogeneity in residential areas), *AIP Journal*, vol. 27, No. 3 (Aug.), pp. 176–184.

———— (1968) *People and Plans*, New York, Basic Books (English edition 1972, Harmondsworth, Penguin).

———— (1969) *The Levittowners*, New York, Random House, Vintage Books Edition.

———— (1971) "The West end: an urban village" in Larry S. Bourne (ed.) *Internal Structure of the City*, New York, Oxford University Press, pp. 300–308.

Garbrecht, Dietrich (1971) "Pedestrian paths through a uniform environment," *Town Planning Review*, vol. 42, No. 1 (Jan.), pp. 71–84.

Gardiner, Stephen (1973) "How can it happen in France?" *RIBA Journal*, vol. 80, No. 11 (Nov.), pp. 555–560.

Ghaidan, U. (1974) "Lamu: a case study of the Swahili town," *Town Planning Review*, vol. 45, No. 1 (Jan.), pp. 84–90.

Gibson, J. J. (1950) *The Perception of the Visual World*, Boston, Houghton Mifflin.

———— (1968) *The Senses Considered as Perceptual Systems*, London, Allen and Unwin.

Giedion, Siegfried (1962) *The Eternal Present* (the beginnings of art) New York, Pantheon Books.

———— (1964) *The Eternal Present* (the beginnings of architecture) New York, Pantheon Books.

Gittins, J. S. (1969) "Forming impressions of an unfamiliar city: a comparative study of aesthetic and scientific knowing," MA thesis, Clark University (unpublished).

Glass, D. C. *et al.* (1969) "Psychic cost of adaptation to an environmental stressor," *J. of Personality and Soc. Psych.* vol. 12, No. 3 (July), pp. 200–210.

Glass, David C. and Jerome E. Singer (1972) *Urban Stress*, New York, Academic Press.

———— (1973) "Experimental studies of uncontrollable and unpredictable noise," *Repr. Research in Social Psych.* vol. 4, No. 1 (Jan.), pp. 165–184.

Glass, Ruth (1955) "Urban sociology," *Current Sociology*, vol. 4, No. 4.

Goffman, Erving (1957) "The presentation of self in everyday life," Garden City, NY, Doubleday.

———— (1963) *Behavior in Public Places*, New York, Free Press.

Goheen, Peter G. (1971) "Metropolitan area definition: a re-evaluation of concepts and statistical practice" in Larry S. Bourne (ed.) *Internal Structure of the City*, New York, Oxford University Press, pp. 47–58.

Gold, Seymour (1972) "Non-use of neighborhood parks," *AIP Journal*, vol. 38, No. 6 (Nov.), pp. 369–378.

Goldfinger, Erno (1941(a)) "The sensation of space," *Arch. Review* (Nov.).

———— (1941(b)) "Urbanism and spatial order," *Arch. Review* (Dec.).

———— (1942) "The elements of enclosed space," *Arch. Review* (Jan.).

Golledge, R. G. (1969) "The geographical relevance of some learning theories" in K. R. Cox and R. G. Golledge (ed.) *Behavioral Problems in Geography*, Evanston, Ill., Northwestern University, Dept. of Geography, Studies in Geography No. 17, pp. 101–145.

_____ (1970) Seminar at the University of Sydney (May).

Golledge, R. G., R. Briggs and D. Demko (1969) "The configuration of distance in intra-urban space," *Proceedings. Ass'n Am. Geog.* vol. 1, pp. 60–65.

Golledge, R. G., L. A. Brown and F. Williamson (n.d.) "Behavioral approaches in geography: an overview," Columbus, Ohio, Dept. of Geography, Ohio State University (mimeo).

Golledge, R. G. and Georgia Zannaras (n.d.) "Cognitive approaches to the analysis of human spatial behavior," Columbus, Ohio, Dept. of Geography, Ohio State University (mimeo).

Gombrich, E. H. (1961) *Art and Illusion*, New York, Pantheon Books.

Gonzales, Nancie L. (1970) "Social functions of carnival in a Dominican city," *SW J. of Anthropology*, vol. 26, No. 4 (Winter), pp. 328–342.

Goodey, Brian (1969) "Messages in space: some observations on geography and communication," *North Dakota Quarterly*, vol. 37, No. 2 (Spring), pp. 34–49.

_____ *et al.* (1971) *City Scene* (an exploration into the image of central Birmingham as seen by area residents) University of Birmingham, Centre for urban and regional studies, Research Memorandum No. 10 (Oct.).

Goodey, Brian and Sue Ann Lee (n.d.) *City Scope: Image Mapping in Hull* (mimeo).

Gordon, Cyrus H. (1962) *Before the Bible*, London, Collins.

Gordon, Milton (1964) *Assimilation in American Life*, New York, Oxford.

Gottmann, Jean, P. M. Hauser, Kenzo Tange and J. R. James (1968) "Images of the future urban environment," *Ekistics*, vol. 125, No. 150 (May).

Gould, P. R. (1972(a)) "Location in information space," paper at Cognitive Seminar following *EDRA 3* Conference, Los Angeles (Jan. 29) (mimeo).

_____ (1972(b)) "On mental maps" in Paul W. English and Robert C. Mayfield (ed.) *Man, Space and Environment*, New York, Oxford, pp. 260–281.

Gould, P. R. and P. R. White (1968) "Mental maps of British school leavers," *Regional Studies*, vol. 2 (Nov.), pp. 161–182.

_____ (1974) *Mental Maps*, Harmondsworth, Penguin.

Gould, Richard A. (1969) *Yiwara*, New York, Charles Schribners Sons.

Green, Helen B. (1972) "Temporal attitudes in four Negro subcultures" in J. T. Fraser *et al.* (ed.) *The Study of Time*, New York, Springer Verlag, pp. 402–417.

Greenbie, Barrie B. (1973) "An ethological approach to community design" in W. F. Preiser (ed.) *EDRA 4*, Stroudsburg, Pa., Dowden, Hutchinson and Ross, vol. 1, pp. 14–23.

Greer, Scott (1960) "The social structure and political process of suburbia," *Am. Sociol. Review,* vol. 25, No. 4, pp. 514–526.

Gregory, R. L. (1969) *The Intelligent Eye*, London, Weidenfeld and Nicolson.

Greimas, A. J. *et al.* (1970) *Sign, Language, Culture*, The Hague, Mouton.

Grenell, Peter (1972) "Planning for invisible people: some consequences of bureaucratic values and practices" in John F. C. Turner and R. Fichter (ed.) *Freedom to Build*, New York, Macmillan, pp. 95–121.

Grey, Arthur L. *et al.* (1970) *People and Downtown* (urban renewal demonstration grant project No. Wash D-1) College of Architecture and Urban Planning, University of Washington, Seattle.

Gruen, Victor (1964) *The Heart of our Cities*, New York, Simon and Schuster.

_____ (1966) "New forms of community" in L. B. Holland (ed.) *Who Designs America?*, Garden City, NY, Doubleday, pp. 172–213.

Gubrium, Jaber F. (1970) "Environmental effects on morale in old age and the resources of health and solvency," *Gerontologist*, vol. 10, No. 4 (Winter), Part 1.

Guildford, Michael *et al.* (1957) "Description of spatial visualization ability," *Educational and Psychological Measurement*, vol. 17.

Gulick, John (1963) "Images of an Arab city," *AIP Journal*, vol. 29, No. 3 (Aug.), pp. 179–198.

Gump, Paul V. (1972) "Linkages between the 'ecological environment' and behavior and experience of persons" in William M. Smith (ed.) *Behavior, Design and Policy Aspects of Human Habitats*, University of Wisconsin, Green Bay, pp. 75–84.

Gumperz, J. J. and Dell Hymes (ed.) (1964) *The Ethnography of Communication (American Anthropologist* special publication No. 3 (vol. 66, No. 6, part 2)).

Gutkind, Peter C. W. (1969) "African urbanism, mobility and the social network" in G. Breese (ed.) *The City in Newly Developing Countries*, Englewood Cliffs, NJ, Prentice-Hall, pp. 389–400.

Gutman, Robert (1966) "Site planning and social interaction," *J. of Social Issues,* vol. 22, No. 4 (Oct.), pp. 103–115.

Gutmann, David (1969) "Psychological naturalism in cross-cultural studies" in Edwin P. Willems and Harold L. Rausch, *Naturalistic Viewpoints in Psychology*, New York, Holt, Rinehart and Winston, pp. 162–176.

Guttentag, Marcia (1970) "Group cohesiveness, ethnic organization and poverty," *J. of Social Issues*, vol. 26, No. 2, pp. 105–132.

Haber, Ralph N. (ed.) (1968) *Contemporary Theory and Research in Visual Perception*, New York, Holt, Rinehart and Winston.

Hall, Edward T. (1961) *The Silent Language*, Greenwich, Conn., Faucett.

———— (1963) "Proxemics – the study of man's spatial relations" in I. Galdston (ed.) *Man's Image in Medicine and Anthropology*, New York, International Universities Press, pp. 422–445.

———— (1964) "Adumbration as a feature of inter-cultural communication" in J. J. Gumperz and Dell Hymes (ed.) *The Ethnography of Communication* (*American Anthropologist* special publication No. 3, vol. 66; No. 6, part 2), pp. 154–163.

———— (1966) *The Hidden Dimension*, Garden City, NY, Doubleday.

———— (1971) "Environmental communication" in A. H. Esser (ed.), *Behavior and Environment*, New York, Plenum Press, pp. 247–256.

Hallowell, A. Irving (1955) *Culture and Experience*, Philadelphia, University of Pennsylvania Press.

Hamilton, Peter (1972) "Aspects of interdependence between aboriginal social behavior and spatial and physical environment" in Royal Australian Institute of Architects Seminar on low-cost self-help housing for Aborigines in remote areas, Canberra (Feb. 10–11).

Hammond, B. E. (1970) "Environmental perception and mental maps," Dept. of Geography, University of Sydney (unpublished).

Hampton, William (1970) *Democracy and Community* (a study of politics in Sheffield), New York, Oxford University Press.

Hardin, G. (ed.) (1969) *Science, Conflict and Society*, San Francisco, W. H. Freeman.

Hardy, R. and D. Legge (1968) "Cross-modal induction of changes in sensory thresholds," *Quarterly J. of Exp. Psych.* vol. 20, part 1 (Feb.).

Harrington, Molly (1965) "Resettlement and self image," *Human Relations*, vol. 18, No. 2 (May), pp. 115–137.

Harris, Evelyn G. and R. J. Paluck (1971) "The effects of crowding in an educational setting," *Man–Environment Systems* (May).

Harrison, James D. and William A. Howard (1972) "The role of meaning in the urban image," *Environment and Behavior*, vol. 4, No. 4 (Dec.), pp. 389–411.

Harrison, John and Philip Sarre (1971) "Personal construct theory in the measurement of environmental images," *Environment and Behavior*, vol. 3, No. 4 (Dec.), pp. 351–374.

Harrison, Paul (1972) "Piccadilly participation," *New Society* (Dec. 14).

Hart, R. and G. T. Moore (1971) *The Development of Spatial Cognition: a Review*, Worcester, Mass., Graduate School of Geography/Dept. of Psychology, Clark University, Place Perception Reports No. 7 (July).

Hartman, Chester W. (1963) "Social values and housing orientations," *J. of Social Issues*, vol. 19, No. 2 (April), pp. 113–131.

Hass, Hans (1970) *The Human Animal*, London, Hodder and Staughton.

Haugen, Einar (1969) "The semantics of Icelandic orientation" in S. Tyler (ed.) *Cognitive Anthropology*, New York, Holt, Rinehart and Winston, pp. 330–342.

Havinghurst, R. J. (1957) "Leisure activities of the middle aged," *Am. J. Sociology*, vol. 63, No. 2.

Haynes, Robin M. (1969) "Behavior space and perception space: a reconnaissance," *Papers in Geography* No. 3, Dept. of Geography, Pennsylvania State University (June) (mimeo).

Hayter, Stanley W. (1965) "Orientation, direction cheirality, velocity and rhythm" in G. Kepes (ed.) *The Nature and Art of Motion*, New York, Braziller, pp. 71–80.

Hayward, D. G. *et al.* (1974) "Children's play and urban playground environments," *Environment and Behavior*, vol. 6, No. 2 (June), pp. 131–168.

Hayward, Scott C. and S. S. Franklin (1974) "Perceived openness-enclosure of architectural space," *Environment and Behavior*, vol. 6, No. 1 (March), pp. 37–52.

Hazard, J. N. (1962) "Furniture arrangement as a symbol of judicial roles," *ETC: a Review of General Semantics*, vol. 19 (reprinted in R. Gutman (ed.) *People and Buildings*, New York, Basic Books, 1972, pp. 291–298).

Heath, T. F. (1971) "The aesthetics of tall buildings," *Architectural Science Review*, vol. 14, No. 4 (Dec.), pp. 93–94.

Heathcote, L. R. (1965) *Back of Burke* (a study of land appraisal and settlement in semi-arid Australia) Carlton Melbourne University Press.

———— (1972) "The visions of Australia 1770–1970" in Amos Rapoport (ed.) *Australia as Human Setting*, Sydney, Angus and Robertson, 1972, pp. 77–98.

Heckhausen, H. (1964) "Complexity in perception: phenomenal criteria and information theoretic calculus – a note on Berlyne's 'complexity effects' " *Canadian J. of Psych.* vol. 18, No. 2 (June), pp. 168–173.

Hediger, H. (1955) *Studies of Psychology and Behaviour of Animals in Zoos and Circuses*, London, Butterworth.

Heinemeyer, William F. (1967) "The urban core as a centre of attraction: a preliminary report" in *Urban Core and Inner City*, Leiden, Brill.

Heiskannen, Veronica S. (1969) "Community structure and kinship ties: extended family relations in three Finnish communities," *Int. J. of Comp. Sociol.* vol. 10, No. 3–4 (Sept./Dec.), pp. 251–262.

Held, Richard and Alan Heim (1968) "Movement-produced stimulation in the development of visually guided behavior" in Ralph N. Haber (ed.) *Contemporary Theory and Research in Visual Perception*, New York, Holt, Rinehart and Winston, pp. 607–612.

Held, Richard and Whitman Richards (ed.) (1972) *Perception: Mechanisms and Models*, San Francisco, W. H. Freeman.

Helson, H. (1964) *Adaptation-Level Theory*, New York, Harper and Row.

Henderson, D. B. (1968) *Impacts of Ethnic Homogeneity and Diversity on the Cultural Landscape of Door County, Wisconsin* (M.A. thesis in Geography, University of Wisconsin-Milwaukee).

Henry, L. and P. A. I. Cox (1970) "The neighbourhood concept in new town planning: a perception study in East Kilbride," *Horizon*, No. 19.

Herpin, Isabelle and Serge Santelli (1970–71) "Le Bidonville, phenomène urbain direct," *Arch. d'Aujourd'hui* No. 153 (Dec.–Jan.), pp. XXI–XXIV.

Hewitt, Kenneth and F. Kenneth Hare (1973) *Man and Environment* (conceptual frameworks) Commission on College Geography, resource paper No. 20, Washington, DC Ass'n. American Geog.

Hill, A. David (1964) *The Changing Landscape of a Mexican Municipio* (Villa LaRosas, Chiapas) Chicago, University of Chicago, Dept. of Geography Research Paper No. 91.

Hinshaw, Mark and Kathryn Allott (1972) "Environmental preferences of future housing consumers," *AIP Journal*, vol. 38, No. 2 (March), pp. 102–107.

Hipsley, E. H. in S. V. Boyden (ed.) (1970) *The Impact of Civilization on the Biology of Man*, Canberra, ANU Press.

Hirschon, Renee and Thakudersai (1970) "Society, culture and spatial organization: an Athens community," *Ekistics*, vol. 30, No. 178 (Sept.), pp. 187–196.

Hitchcock, John R. (1972) "Daily activity patterns: an exploratory study," *Ekistics*, vol. 34, No. 204 (Nov.).

Hochberg, Julian (1964) *Perception*, Englewood Cliffs, NJ, Prentice-Hall.

————— (1968) "In the mind's eye" in R. N. Haber (ed.) *Contemporary Theory and Research in Visual Perception*, New York, Holt, Rinehart and Winston, pp. 309–331.

Hochschild, Arlie Russell (1973) *The Unexpected Community*, Englewood Cliffs, NJ, Prentice-Hall.

Hoffman, Gerald and Joshua A. Fishman (1971) "Life in the neighborhood" (a factor-analytic study of Puerto Rican males in the New York City area), *Int. J. of Comp. Sociol.* vol. 12, No. 2 (June), pp. 85–100.

Hoinville, G. (1971) "Evaluating community preference," *Environment and Planning*, vol. 3, pp. 33–50.

Holmes, Thomas H. (1956) "Multidiscipline studies of tuberculosis" in P. J. Sparer (ed.) *Personality, Stress and Tuberculosis*, New York, International Universities Press.

Holubař, J. (1969) *The Sense of Time*, Cambridge, Mass., MIT Press.

Holzner, Lutz (1970(a)) "The role of history and tradition in the urban geography of West Germany," *Annals. Ass'n. Am. Geog.* vol. 60, No. 2 (June) pp. 315–339.

————— (1970(b)) "Urbanism in South Africa," *Geoforum*, vol. 4, pp. 75–90.

Honigman, John J. (1963) "Dynamics of drinking in an Austrian village," *Ethnology*, vol. 2, pp. 157–169.

Hooper, D. (1970) cited in Stanley Milgram, "The experience of living in cities," *Science*, vol. 167 (March 13).

Horton, Frank E. and David R. Reynolds (1971) "Effects of urban spatial structure on individual behavior," *Economic Geography*, vol. 47, No. 1 (Jan.), pp. 36–48.

Hosken, F. P. (1968) *The Language of Cities*, New York, Macmillan.

Hourani, A. H. and S. M. Stern (ed.) (1970) *The Islamic City*, Oxford, Cassirer.

Howard, I. P. and W. B. Templeton (1966) *Human Spatial Orientation*, London, Wiley.

Howe, Irving (1971) "The city in literature," *Commentary*, vol. 51, No. 5 (May), pp. 61–68.

Howell, Sandra C. (1972) "Environment and vulnerability" (mimeo).

Howland, Bette (1972) "Public facilities – a memoir," *Commentary*, vol. 53, No. 2 (Feb.).

H.U.D. (1969) *Urban Land Policy-Selected Aspects of European Experience*, Washington, D.C. HUD 94-SF (March).

Hurst, M. E. Eliot (1971) "The structure of movement and household travel behavior" in Larry S. Bourne (ed.) *Internal Structure of the City*, New York, Oxford University Press, pp. 248–255.

Huxley, J. (ed.) (1966) *Ritualization of Behaviour in Animals and Man*, Philosophical transactions of the Royal Society of London, Series B, vol. 251, Biological Sciences.

Hymes, Dell (1964) "Towards ethnographies of communication," *American Anthropologist* special publication, vol. 66, No. 6, part 2 (Dec.).

Ingham, John M. (1971) "Time and space in ancient Mexico: the symbolic dimensions of clanship," *Man*, vol. 6, No. 4, pp. 615–629.

Isaacs, Harold R. (1972) "The new pluralists," *Commentary*, vol. 53, No. 3 (March).

Ishikawa, Enjo (1953) *The Study of Shopping Centers in Japanese Cities and Treatment of Reconstructing*, Memoirs of the faculty of Science and Engineering No. 17, Tokyo: Waseda University.

Issawi, Charles (1970) in Ira Lapidus (ed.) *The Middle Eastern City*, Berkeley and Los Angeles, University of California Press.

Ittelson, William H. (1960) "Some factors influencing the design and function of psychiatric facilities," Brooklyn, Dept. of Psychology, Brooklyn College (Nov.).

———— (1970) "The perception of the large scale environment," paper presented to the New York Academy of Sciences (April) (mimeo).

———— *et al.* (1970) "The use of behavioral maps in envifonmental psychology" in H. M. Proshansky *et al.* (ed.) *Environmental Psychology*, New York, Holt, Rinehart and Winston, pp. 658–668.

———— (ed.) (1973) *Environment and Cognition*, New York, Seminar Press.

Ittelson, William and H. Proshansky (n.d.) "The use of bedrooms by patients on a psychiatric ward," Env. Psych. Program CUNY (mimeo).

Jackson, J. B. (1951) "Chihuahua – as we might have been," *Landscape*, vol. 1, No. 1 (Spring).

———— (1957) "The stranger's path," *Landscape*, vol. 7, No. 1.

———— (1964) "Limited access" (review of Peter Blake's *God's Own Junkyard*) *Landscape*, vol. 14, No. 1 (Autumn), pp. 18–23.

———— (1966(a)) "The purpose of a city-changing city landscapes as manifestations of cultural values" in Marcus Whiffen (ed.) *The Architect and the City*, Cambridge, MIT Press.

———— (1966(b)) Seminar, Dept. of Landscape Architecture, University of California, Berkeley.

———— (1966(c)) "Boundaries" Seminar lecture, University of California, Berkeley (Feb.) (mimeo).

———— (1972) *American Space*, New York, Norton.

Jackson, L. E. and R. J. Johnston (1974) "Underlying regularities to mental maps: an investigation of relationships among age, experience and spatial preference," *Geographical Analysis*, vol. 6, No. 1 (Jan.), pp. 69–84.

Jacobs, Jane (1961) *The Death and Life of Great American Cities*, New York, Random House.

Jakle, John A. and James O. Wheeler (1969) "The changing residential structure of the Dutch population of Kalamazoo, Michigan," *Annals. Ass'n. Am. Geog.* vol. 59.

James, L. D. and D. R. Brogan (1974) "The impact of open urban land on community well being" in C. P. Wolf (ed.) *Social Impact Assessment – EDRA 5*, vol. 2, pp. 151–167.

Jeanpierre, C. (1968) "La perception de l'espace et les dimensions des loceaux d'habitation," *Cahiers du Centre Scientifique et Technique du Batiment*, No. 90 (No. 779) (Feb.).

Jencks, Charles (1972) "Rhetoric and architecture," *AAQ*, vol. 4, No. 3 (Summer), pp. 4–17.

Jencks, Charles and George Baird (ed.) (1969) *Meaning in Architecture*, New York, Braziller.

Joerges, B. (1969) "Communication and change at the local level," *Ekistics*, vol. 27, No. 158 (Jan.), pp. 60–64.

Johnson, Ann (1971) "An investigation of the mental maps of well travelled routes of some residents of Killarney Heights" in Ross King (ed.) *Perception of Residential Quality: Sydney Case Studies*, Ian Buchan Fell Research Project on Housing, Collected Papers No. 2, University of Sydney (Aug.) pp. 117–122.

Johnson, Philip (1965) "Whence and whither: the processional element in architecture," *Perspecta 9/10* (The Yale Architectural Journal), pp. 167–178.

Johnson, Sheila K. (1971) *Idle Haven* (community building among the working class retired) Berkeley and Los Angeles, University of California Press.

Johnston, R. J. (1971(a)) *Urban Residential Patterns*, London, George Bell.

———— (1971(b)) "Mental maps of the city: suburban preference patterns," *Environment and Planning*, vol. 3, pp. 63–69.

Jonassen, C. T. (1961) "Cultural variables in the ecology of an ethnic group" in G. A. Theodorson (ed.) *Studies in Human Ecology*, Evanston, Ill., Row Peterson, pp. 264–273.

Jones, A. (1966) "Information deprivation in humans" in B. A. Maher (ed.) *Progress in Experimental Personality Research*, vol. 3, New York, Academic Press.

Jones, Emrys (1960) *The Social Geography of Belfast*, Oxford, University Press.

Jones, F. Lancaster (1968) "Social area analysis: some theoretical and methodological comments illustrated with Australian data," *British J. of Sociology*, vol. XIX, No. 4 (Dec.).

Jones, Mark M. (1972) "Urban path-choosing behavior: a study of environmental clues" in W. Mitchell (ed.) *EDRA 3*, Los Angeles, University of California, vol. 1, pp. 11-4-1–11-4-10.

Jones, Philip N. (1970) "Some aspects of the changing distribution of coloured immigrants in Birmingham 1961–1966," *Transactions. Inst. of British Geographers*, No. 50 (July), pp. 199–219.

Jones, W. T. (1972) "World views: their nature and their function," *Current Anthropology*, vol. 13, No. 1 (Feb.), pp. 79–109.

Jung, Carl (1964) *Man and His Symbols*, Garden City, NY, Doubleday.

Juppenlatz, M. (1970) *Cities in Transformation* (The urban squatter problem in the developing world) St. Lucia, University of Queensland Press.

Kaës, R. (1963) *Vivre dans les grands ensembles*, Paris, Editions Ouvrières.

Kaiser, E. J. and S. F. Weiss (1969) "Decision agent models of the residential development process: a review of recent research," *Traffic Quarterly*, vol. 23, pp. 597–630.

Kaplan, S. (1970) "The role of location processing in the perception of the environment" in J. Archea and C. Eastman (ed.) *EDRA 2*, pp. 131–134.

————— (1971) "A psychological approach to ecology," Am. Psych. Ass'n. Meeting, Washington, D.C. (Sept. 4) (mimeo).

Kaplan, Stephen and J. S. Wendt (1972) "Preference and the visual environment: complexity and some alternatives" in W. Mitchell (ed.) *EDRA 3*, Los Angeles, University of California, vol. 1, pp. 6-8-1–6-8-5.

Kasl, Stanislav and Ernest Harburg (1972) "Perceptions of the neighborhood and the desire to move out," *AIP Journal*, vol. 38, No. 5 (Sept.), pp. 318–324.

Kasmar, Joyce V. (1970) "The development of a usable lexicon of environmental descriptors," *Environment and Behavior*, vol. 2, No. 2 (Sept.), pp. 153–169.

Kates, R. W. (1962) *Hazard and Choice Perception in Flood Plain Management*. Chicago, Dept. of Geography, University of Chicago, Research Paper No. 78.

————— (1966) "Stimulus and symbol: the view from the bridge," *J. of Social Issues*, vol. 22, No. 4 (Oct.), pp. 21–28.

Kates, R. W. Ian Burton *et al.* (ongoing) Research on Natural Hazard Perception.

Kavanau, J. L. (1969) "Behavior of captive white-footed mice" in E. P. Willems and H. L. Rausch (ed.) *Naturalistic Viewpoints in Psychological Research*. New York, Holt, Rinehart and Winston, pp. 221–270.

Keats, John (1956) *The Crack in the Picture Window*, Boston.

Keller, Suzanne (1968) *The Urban Neighborhood* (a sociological perspective) New York, Random House.

Kelly, G. A. (1955) *The Psychology of Personal Constructs*, New York, Norton.

Kepes, Gyorgy (1961) "Notes on expression and communication in the city-scape," *Daedalus*, vol. 90, No. 1 (Winter), pp. 147–165.

Khudozhnik I Gorod (1973) (The Artist and the City) Moscow, Soviet Artist.

Kilpatrick, F. P. (1971) "Two processes in perceptual learning" in H. M. Proshansky *et al.* (ed.) *Environmental Psychology*, New York, Holt, Rinehart and Winston, pp. 104–112.

Kimber, Clarissa (1966) "Dooryard gardens of Martinique," *Yearbook, Ass'n. Pacific Coast Geographers*, vol. 28, pp. 97–118.

————— (1971) "Interpreting the use of space in dooryard gardens: a Puerto Rican example" (mimeo).

————— (1973) "Spatial patterning in the dooryard gardens of Puerto Rico," *Geog. Review* (Jan.), pp. 6–26.

King, A. D. (1970) "Colonial urbanization: a cross-culture inquiry into the social use of space," 7th World Congress of Sociology, Varna (Bulgaria) (Sept.) (mimeo).

————— (1974(a)) "The language of colonial urbanization," *Sociology*, vol. 8, No. 1 (Jan.), pp. 81–110.

————— (1974(b)) "The colonial bungalow-compound complex: a study in the cultural use of space," *J. of Architectural Research*, vol. 3, No. 2, pp. 30–43.

King, Ross (1971(a)) "Perception, evaluation and use of residential space," *Circa* 70 (Sydney University School of Architecture) (Feb.).

————— (ed.) (1971(b)) *Perception of Environmental Quality: Sydney Case Studies*, University of Sydney Faculty of Architecture, Ian Buchan Fell Research Project, Collected Papers No. 2 (Aug.).

————— (1973) "Some children and houses," *Arch. in Australia*, vol. 62, No. 5 (Oct.), pp. 83–94.

Kittler, Richard (1968) "Some spatial and environmental considerations of the [sic] architectural design based on the perceptual phenomena under daylight conditions," paper given at the Bartlett School of Architecture, London (mimeo).

Klass, Morton (1972) "Community structure in West Bengal," *American Anthropologist*, vol. 74, No. 3 (June), pp. 601–610.

Klein, Hans-Joachim (1967) "The delimitation of the town centre in the image of its citizens" in *Urban Core and Inner City*, Leiden, Brill, pp. 286–306.

Knapp, E. K. (1969) *Heterogeneity of the Micro-Neighborhood as it relates to Social Interaction*, PhD Dissertation, Michigan State University (unpublished).

Knittel, Robert E. (1973) "New town knowledge, experience and theory: an overview," *Human Organization*, vol. 32, No. 1 (Spring), pp. 37–48.

Knowles, Eric S. (1972) "Boundaries around social space: dyadic responses to an invader," *Environment and Behavior*, vol. 4, No. 4 (Dec.), pp. 437–445.

Koestler, Arthur (1964) *The Act of Creation*, New York, Macmillan.

Kohn, Bernard (1971) "A new deal for the village," *Arch. Review*, vol. CL, No. 898 (Dec.).

Kouwenhoeven, A. (1961) *The Beer Can by the Highway*, Garden City, NY, Doubleday.

Krapf-Askari, Eva (1969) *Yoruba Towns and Cities*, Oxford, Clarendon Press.

Kroeber, A. L. and Clyde Kluckhohn (1952) *Culture (a Critical Review of Concepts and Definitions)* New York, Vintage Books (Reprinted from Harvard University, Papers of the Peabody Museum, vol. XLVII, No. 1).

Kuhn, Thomas (1965) *The Structure of Scientific Revolutions*, Chicago, University of Chicago Press.

Kummer, Hans (1971) "Spacing mechanisms in social behavior" in J. F. Eisenberg and W. S. Dillon (ed.) *Man and Beast* (Comparative Social Behavior) (Smithsonian Annual III) Washington, D.C., Smithsonian.

Kuper, Leo (1970) "Neighbor on the hearth" in H. M. Proshansky *et al.* (ed.), *Environmental Psychology*, New York, Holt, Rinehart and Winston, pp. 246–255.

Ladd, Florence C. (1970) "Black youths view their environment: neighbourhood maps," *Environment and Behavior*, vol. 2, No. 1 (June), pp. 74–99.

———— (1972) "Black youths view their environments: some views on housing," *AIP Journal*, vol. 38, No. 2 (March), pp. 108–116.

Lamy, Bernard (1967) "The use of the inner city of Paris and social stratification" in *Urban Core and Inner City*, Leiden, Brill, pp. 356–367.

Lancaster, O. *Classical Landscape With Figures*, cited in P. Kriesis (1963) *Three Essays on Town Planning*, St. Louis, Mo., Washington University, School of Architecture, Special Publication No. 1 (May).

Lang, S. (1952) "The ideal city from Plato to Howard," *Arch. Review*, vol. 112 (Aug.), pp. 91–101.

Langer, Suzanne (1953) *Feeling and Form*, New York, Schribner.

———— (1966) "The social influence of design" in L. B. Holland (ed.) *Who Designs America?* Garden City, NY, Anchor Books, pp. 35–50.

Lansing, John B. and Robert W. Marans (1969) "Evaluation of neighborhood quality," *AIP Journal*, vol. 35, No. 3 (May), pp. 195–199.

Lansing, John B. Robert W. Marans and Robert B. Zehner (1970) *Planned Residential Environments*, Ann Arbor, Institute for Social Research, University of Michigan.

Lapidus, Ira (ed.) (1969) *Middle Eastern Cities*, Berkeley, University of California Press.

Laporte, Roy S. B. (1969) "Family adaptation of relocated slum dwellers in Puerto Rico," *Ekistics*, vol. 27, No. 158 (Jan.), pp. 56–59.

Largey, G. P. and D. R. Watson (1972) "The sociology of odors," *Am. J. of Sociology*, vol. 77, No. 6, pp. 1021–1034.

Larimore, Ann E. (1958) *The Alien Town* (patterns of settlement in Busoga, Uganda) Chicago, University of Chicago, Dept. of Geography, Research Paper No. 55.

Lawton, M. Powell (1970(a)) "Ecology and aging" in L. A. Pastalan and D. H. Carson (ed.) *Spatial Behavior of Older People*, Ann Arbor, University of Michigan, pp. 40–67.

———— (1970(b)) "Public behavior of older people in congregate housing" in J. Archea and C. Eastman (ed.), *EDRA 2*, pp. 372–380.

———— (1970(c)) "Planning environments for older people," *AIP Journal*, vol. 36, pp. 124–129.

Layton, R. (1972(a)) "Defining psychographics," *The Australian* (Marketing) (March 30).

———— (1972(b)) "Life styles and how to use them," *The Australian* (Marketing) (April 6).

Leach, Edmund (1970) *Lévi-Strauss*, London, Fontanna.

LeCompte, William F. (1972) "Behavior settings: the structure of the treatment environment" in W. Mitchell (ed.) *EDRA 3*, Los Angeles, University of California, vol. 1, pp. 4-2-1–4-2-5.

LeCompte, William F. and Edwin P. Willems (1970) "Ecological analysis of a hospital: location dependencies in the behavior of staff and patients" in J. Archea and C. Eastman (ed.) *EDRA 2*, pp. 236–247.

Ledrut, Raymond (1968) *L'espace social de la ville*, Paris, Editions Anthropos.

Lee, Douglas F. K. (1966) "The role of attitude in response to environmental stress," *J. of Social Issues*, vol. 22, No. 4 (Oct.), pp. 83–91.

Lee, Hahn-Been (1968) "From ecology to time: a time orientation approach to the study of public administration," *Ekistics*, vol. 25, No. 151 (June), pp. 432–438.

Lee, Maurice (1968) "Islamabad—the image," *Ekistics*, vol. 25, No. 150 (May), pp. 334–335.

Lee, Terence R. (1962) "Brannan's law of shopping behaviour," *Psych. Report* No. 11, p. 662.

———— (1968) "Urban neighborhood as socio-spatial schema," *Human Relations*, vol. 21, No. 3 (Aug.), pp. 53–61.

———— (1969) "The psychology of spatial orientation," *Architectural Association Quarterly*, vol. 1, No. 3 (July), pp. 11–15.

———— (1970) "Perceived distance as a function of direction in the city," *Environment and Behavior*, vol. 2, No. 1 (June), pp. 40–51.

———— (1971(a)) "Psychology and architectural determinism" (Part 2) *Architects Journal* (Sept. 1), pp. 475–483.

———— (1971(b)) "Architecture and environmental determinism" (Part 3) *Architects Journal* (Sept. 22), pp. 651–659.

Leibman, Miriam (1970) "The effects of sex and race norms on personal space," *Environment and Behavior*, vol. 2, No. 2 (Sept.), pp. 206–246.

Lenclos, Jean Philippe (1972) "Couleurs et paysages," *Architecture d'Aujourd'hui* No. 164 (Oct.–Nov.), pp. 41–44.

Lenneberg, F. H. (1972) "Cognition in ethnolinguistics" in P. Adams (ed.) *Language in Thinking*, Harmondsworth, Penguin, pp. 157–169.

Lévi-Strauss, Claude (1955) *Tristes Tropiques*, Paris, Plon.

Levine, C. (1974) "La Habana Chica: Miami's lively Latin Quarter," *Pastimes* (Eastern Airlines Magazine) (Jan./Feb.), pp. 11–20.

LeVine, Robert A. (1973) *Culture, Behavior and Personality*, Chicago, Aldine.

Lewin, Kurt (1936) *Principles of Topological Psychology*, New York, McGraw-Hill.

———— (1951) *Field Theory in Social Science*, New York, Harper Torchbooks.

Lewis, Oscar (1965) "The folk-urban ideal types" in P. M. Hauser and L. F. Schnore (ed.) *The Study of urbanization*, New York, Wiley, pp. 491–517.

Lewis, Ralph (1970) "The Korean tearoom: its function in Korean society," *Sociology and Social Research*, vol. 55, No. 1 (Oct.), pp. 53–62.

Leyhausen, P. (1970) "The communal organization of solitary mammals" in H. M. Proshansky *et al.* (ed.) *Environmental Psychology*, New York, Holt, Rinehart and Winston, pp. 183–195.

———— (1971) "Dominance and territoriality as complemented in mammalian social structure" in A. H. Esser (ed.) *Behavior and Environment*, New York, Plenum Press, pp. 22–23.

Lime, David W. (1972) "Behavioral research in outdoor recreation management — an example of how visitors select campgrounds" in J. F. Wohlwill and D. H. Carson (ed.) *Environment and the Social Sciences: Perspectives and Application*, Washington, D.C., Am. Psych. Ass'n., pp. 198–206.

Linge, G. J. R. (1971) "Government and spatial behaviour" in G. J. R. Linge and P. J. Rimmer (ed.) *Government Influence and the Location of Economic Activity*, Canberra, Australian National University Research School of Pacific Studies, Dept. of Human Geography, Publication HG/5.

Lipman, Alan (1968) "Building design and social interaction in a preliminary study of three old people's homes," *Architects Journal* (Jan. 3).

Lipowski, Z. J. (1971) "Surfeit of attractive information inputs: a hallmark of our environment," *Behavioral Science*, vol. 16, No. 5.

Littlejohn, James (1967) "The Temne house" in J. Middleton (ed.) *Myth and Cosmos*, Garden City, NY, Natural History Press, pp. 331–347.

Lloyd, Barbara (1972) *Perception and Cognition: a Cross-Cultural Perspective*, Harmondsworth, Penguin.

Lofland, Lyn H. (1973) *A World of Strangers* (order and action in urban public space), New York, Basic Books.

Longstaff, Owen (1968) Letter to the Editor, *Evening Standard* (London) (June 6).

Loo, Chalsa (1973) "Important issues in researching the effects of crowding in humans," *Repr. Research in Social Psych.*, vol. 4, No. 1 (Jan.).

Love, Ruth (1973) "The fountains of urban life," *Urban Life and Culture*, vol. 2, No. 2 (July), pp. 161–210.

Loveless, N. E. *et al.* (1973) "Bisensory presentation of information," *Psych. Bulletin*, vol. 73, No. 3 (March).

Lowenthal, David (1961) "Geography, experience and imagination: towards a geographical epistemology," *Annals. Ass'n. of Am. Geog.* vol. 51, No. 3 (Sept.), pp. 241–260.

———— (1967) "An analysis of environmental perception," 2nd interim report to Resources for the Future, Inc. No. 2 (mimeo).

———— (1968) "The American Scene," *Geog. Review*, vol. 58, No. 1, pp. 61–88.

———— (1971) "Not every prospect pleases" in Robert M. Irving and George B. Priddle (ed.) *Crisis*, New York St. Martin's Press.

Lowenthal, David and Hugh C. Prince (1964) "The English landscape," *Geog. Review*, vol. 54, No. 3, pp. 309–346.

———— (1965) "English landscape tastes," *Geog. Review*, vol. 55, No. 2, pp. 186–222.

———— (1969) "English Facades," *AAQ*, vol. 1, No. 3 (July), pp. 50–64.

Lowenthal, David and M. Riel (1972) "The nature of perceived and imagined environments," *Environment and Behavior*, vol. 4, No. 2 (June), pp. 189–207.

Lowrey, Robert A. (1970) "Distance concepts of urban residents," *Environment and Behavior*, vol. 2, No. 1 (June), pp. 52–73.

Lucas, John (1972) "Lae – a town in transition," *Oceania*, vol. 17, No. 4 (June), pp. 260–275.

Lucas, Robert C. (1970) "User concepts of wilderness and their implications for resource management" in H. M. Proshansky *et al.* (ed.) *Environmental Psychology*, New York, Holt, Rinehart and Winston, pp. 297–303.

Lundberg, G. *et al.* (1934) *Leisure: a Suburban Study*, New York, Agathon Press (Reprinted).

Lunn, Hugh (1971) "Brisbane boom could become a nightmare," *Sunday Australian* (Dec. 26) (quoting Professor Gareth Roberts, then professor of Architecture at the University of Queensland).

Lurie, Ellen (1963) "Community action in East Harlem" in L. J. Duhl (ed.) *The Urban Condition*, New York, Basic Books, pp. 246–258.

Lyman, S. M. and M. B. Scott (1970) *A Sociology of the Absurd*, New York, Appleton, Century Crofts.

Lynch, Kevin (1960) *Image of the City*, Cambridge, MIT Press.

———— (1962) *Site Planning*, Cambridge, MIT Press.

———— (1965) "The city as environment", *Scientific American*, vol. 213, No. 3 (Sept.), pp. 209–219.

———— (1972) *What Time is this Place?* Cambridge, MIT Press.

Lynch, Kevin and Malcolm Rivkin (1970) "A walk around the block" in H. M. Proshansky *et al.* (ed.) *Environmental Psychology*, New York, Holt, Rinehart and Winston, pp. 631–642.

Lynton Homes (1972) "Paul Nelson, homes and my favourite topic," Advertisement in *Sydney Morning Herald* (June 10).

Mabogunje, Akin L. (1968) *Urbanization in Nigeria*, London, University of London Press.

MacCormack, Richard and Peter Wilmott (1964) "A Radburn estate revisited," *Architects Journal* (March 25).

MacEwen, Alison (1972) "Stability and change in a shanty town: a summary of some research results," *Sociology*, vol. 6, No. 1, pp. 41–57.

MacKay, D. B., R. W. Olshavsky and G. Sentell (1975) "Cognitive maps and spatial behavior of consumers," *Geographical Analysis*, vol. 7, No. 1 (Jan.), pp. 19–34.

Mackworth, N. H. (1968) "Visual noise causes tunnel vision" in Ralph N. Haber (ed.) *Contemporary Theory and Research in Visual Perception*, New York, Holt, Rinehart and Winston.

MacMurray, Trevor (1971) "Aspects of time and the study of activity patterns," *TP Review*, vol. 42, No. 2 (April), pp. 195–209.

Madge, Charles (1950) "Private and public spaces," *Human Relations*, vol. 3, No. 2 (June), pp. 187–199.

Maki, Fumihiko (1964) *Investigations in Collective Form*, St. Louis, School of Architecture, Washington University Special Publication No. 2 (June).

———— (1973) "Some observations on urbanization and communication in the Japanese metropolis." Paper given at Conference on Urbanization and Communication, East-West Center, Honolulu (Jan.) (mimeo).

Mangin, William (1963) "Urbanization case history in Peru," *Architectural Design,* vol. 33 (Aug.).

———— (1967) "Latin American squatter settlements: a problem and a solution," *Latin Am. Research Review,* vol. 2, No. 3 (Summer).

———— (ed.) (1970) *Peasants in Cities*, Boston, Houghton Mifflin.

Mann, L. (1969) *Social Psychology*, Sydney, John Wiley (Australasia).

Manus, Willard (1972) "Hostelbro," *Ekistics*, vol. 34, No. 204 (Nov.), pp. 379–376.

Marans, Robert W. (1969) "Planning the experimental neighborhood at Kiryat Gat, Israel," *Ekistics*, vol. 27, No. 158 (Jan.), pp. 70–75.

Marans, R. W. and W. Rodgers (1973) "Evaluating resident satisfaction in established and new communities" in R. W. Burchell (ed.) *Frontiers of Planned Unit Development: a Synthesis of Expert Opinion,* New Brunswick, NJ, Center for Urban Policy Research, Rutgers University, pp. 197–227.

Markman, Robert (1970) "Sensation seeking and environmental preference" in J. Archea and C. Eastman (ed.) *EDRA 2*, pp. 311–315.

Marks, J. (1973) "The SoHo phenomenon," *American Airlines Magazine* (July).

Marris, Peter (1967) "Reflections on a study in Lagos" in H. Miner (ed.) *The City in Modern Africa*, London, Pall Mall Press, pp. 40–46.

Marsh, Alan (1973) "Race, community and anxiety," *Ekistics*, vol. 36, No. 213 (Aug.), pp. 111–114.

Marshall, Nancy J. (1970) "Environmental components of orientations towards privacy" in J. Archea and C. Eastman (ed.) *EDRA 2*, pp. 246–251.

Marston, Wilfred G. (1969) "Social class segregation within ethnic groups in Toronto," *Canadian Review of Sociology and Anthropology*, vol. 6, No. 2 (May), pp. 65–79.

Martin, Jean I. (1967) "Extended kinship ties: an Adelaide study," *Aust. and NZ J of Sociology*, vol. 3, No. 1, pp. 44–63.

Martin, Jean I. (1967) "Extended kinship ties: an Adelaide study," *Aust. and NZJ. of Sociology*, vol. 213–214.

Maurer, Robert and James C. Baxter (1972) "Images of the neighborhood and city among black-, anglo-, and Mexican-Americans," *Environment and Behavior*, vol. 4, No. 4 (Dec.), pp. 351–388.

Mavros, Anastasia (1971) "Residential quality perceived by Greek migrants in Sydney" in Ross King (ed.) *Perception of Residential Quality: Sydney Case Studies*, Ian Buchan Fell Research Project on Housing, Collected Papers No. 2, University of Sydney (Aug.), pp. 32–40.

McBride, Glen (1964) "A general theory of social organization and behavior," St. Lucia, University of Queensland, Faculty of Veterinary Science Paper, vol. 1, No. 2.

———— (1970) "Social adaptation to crowding in animals and man" in S. V. Boyden (ed.) *The Impact of Civilization on the Biology of Man*, Canberra, ANU, pp. 142–166.

McCully, R. S. (1971) *Rorschach Theory and Symbolism*, Baltimore, Williams and Wilkins.

McKechnie, G. E. (1970) "Measuring environmental dispositions with the environmental response directory" in J. Archea and C. Eastman (ed.) *EDRA 2*, pp. 320–326.

McKenzie, R. D. (1921–1922) "The neighborhood: a study of local life in Columbus, Ohio," *Am. J. of Sociology*, vol. 27.

Meenegan, Thomas M. (1972) "Community delineation: alternative methods and problems," *Sociology and Social Research*, vol. 56, No. 3 (April), pp. 345–355.

Meggitt, M. J. (1965) *Desert People* (A study of the Walbiri Aborigines of Central Australia), Chicago, University of Chicago Press.

Mehrabian, Albert (1972) *Nonverbal Communication*, Chicago, Aldine.

Mehrabian, Albert and James A. Russell (1973) "A measure of arousal seeking tendency," *Environment and Behavior*, vol. 5, No. 3 (Sept.), pp. 315–333.

———— (1974) *An Approach to Environmental Psychology*, Cambridge, Mass., MIT Press.

Meier, Richard (1962) *A Communications Theory of Urban Growth*, Cambridge, MIT Press.

———— (1966) *Studies on the Future of Cities in Asia*, Center for Planning and Ev Research, University of California, Berkeley (July).

Meillassoux, Claude (1968) *Urbanization of an African Community* (Voluntary associations in Bamako), Seattle, University of Washington Press.

Meining, Donald (1965) "The Mormon culture region: strategies and patterns in the American West 1847–1964," *Annals. Ass'n. Am. Geog.* vol. 55, No. 2 (June), pp. 191–220.

Melser, Peter J. (1969) "A study of medium density housing," Housing Division Ministry of Works, Wellington, NZ (Nov.) (mimeo).

Mercer, David (1971(a)) "The role of perception in the recreation experience: a review and discussion," *J. of Leisure Research*, vol. 3, No. 4 (Fall), pp. 261–276.

———— (1971(b)) "Discretionary travel behaviour and the urban mental map," *Aust. Geog. Studies*, vol. 9, pp. 133–143.

———— (1972) "Beach usage in the Melbourne region," *The Australian Geographer*, vol. 12, No. 2, pp. 123–137.

Metton, Alain (1969) "Le Quartier: étude géographique et psycho-sociologique," *Canadian Geographer*, vol. 13, No. 4 (Winter), pp. 299–315.

Meyerson, Martin (1963) "National character and urban development," *Public Policy* (Harvard), vol. XII, pp. 78–96.

Michel, Jacques (1965) "Second renaissance à Chicago," *Le Monde* (Sept. 1).

Michelson, William (1966) "An empirical analysis of urban space preferences," *AIP Journal*, vol. 32, No. 6 (Nov.), pp. 355–360.

———— (1968) "Most people do not want what architects want," *Transaction* (July/Aug.).

———— (1969 "Analytic sampling for design information: a survey of housing experiences" in H. Sanoff and S. Cohn (ed.) *EDRA 1*, pp. 183–197.

———— (1970(a)) *Man and His Urban Environment*, Reading, Mass., Addison-Wesley.

———— (1970(b)) "Selected aspects of environmental research in Scandinavia," *Man–Environment Systems* (July), p. 2 ff.

———— (1971(a)) "Some like it hot: social participation and environmental use as functions of the season," *Am. J. of Sociology*, vol. 76, No. 6 (May), pp. 1072–1083.

_____ (1971(b)) "Environment, social adjustment to," *Encyclopedia of Social Work*, vol. 1, pp. 290–304.

Michelson, William and Paul Reed (1970) *The Theoretical Status and Operational Usage of Lifestyle in Environmental Research,* Research Paper No. 36, Center for Urban and Community Studies, University of Toronto (Sept.).

Milgram, Stanley (1970) "The experience of living in cities," *Science*, vol. 167 (March 13), pp. 1461–1468.

_____ et al. (1972) "A psychological map of New York City," *American Scientist*, vol. 60, No. 2 (March–April), pp. 194–200.

Miller, D. C. (1971) *Sydney Morning Herald* (Dec. 28) (letter).

Miller, G. A. (1956) "The magical number seven plus or minus two: some limits on our capacity for processing information," *Psych. Review*, vol. 63, pp. 81–97.

Miller, G. A., E. Gallanter and K. H. Pribram (1960) *Plans and the Structure of Behaviour*, New York, Holt, Rinehart and Winston.

Millon, René (ed.) (1973) *Urbanization at Teotihuacan, Mexico* (vol. 1, parts 1 & 2), Austin, University of Texas.

Mills, Robert (1972) "Melbourne experts look east for price growth: (business and investment)" *The Australian* (March 27).

Milwaukee Journal (1973) "Home owner wants a different view" (Sept. 26).

Miscler, E. G. and N. A. Scotch (1963) "Socio-cultural factors in schizophrenia: a review," *Psychiatry*, vol. 26.

Mitchell, J. Clyde (1970) "Africans in industrial towns in Northern Rhodesia" in W. Mangin (ed.) *Peasants in Cities*, Boston, Houghton, Mifflin, pp. 160–169.

_____ (ed.) (1971) *Social Networks in Urban Situations*, Manchester, University Press.

Mitchell, Robert E. (1971) "Some social implications of high density housing," *Am. Social Review*, vol. 36, No. 1 (Feb.), pp. 18–29.

Mittelstaedt, Robert et al. (1974) "Psychophysical and evaluative dimensions of cognized distance in an urban shopping environment" (Paper given at the Fall Conference, Am. Marketing Ass'n., Portland, Oregon) (Aug.) (mimeo).

Moles, Abraham (1966) *Information Theory and Esthetic Perception*, Urbana, University of Illinois Press.

Moore, Eric G. (1972) *Residential Mobility in the City*, Commission on College Geography Resource Paper No. 13, Ass'n. of Am. Geog., Washington, D.C.

Moore, Gary T. (1972) "Elements of a genetic-structural theory of the development of urban cognition," Cognitive Seminar following *EDRA 3* (mimeo).

_____ (1973) "Developmental differences in environmental cognition," in W. Preiser (ed.) *EDRA 4*, Stroudsburg, Pa., Dowden, Hutchinson and Ross, vol. 2, pp. 232–239.

Moore, G. T. and R. G. Golledge (ed.) (1976) *Environmental Knowing,* Stroudsburg, Pa., Dowden, Hutchinson and Ross.

Moore, Robin (1966) "An experiment in playground design," MCRP Thesis MIT (Nov.) (unpublished).

Moriarty, Barry W. (1974) "Socio-economic status and residential locational choice," *Environment and Behavior*, vol. 6, No. 4 (Dec.), pp. 448–469.

Morris, Desmond (ed.) (1967) *Primate Ethology*, Chicago, Aldine.

_____ (1970) *The Human Zoo*, New York, McGraw-Hill.

Morse, Richard M. (1969) "Recent research on Latin America: a selective survey with commentary" in G. Breese (ed.) *The City in Newly Developing Countries*, Englewood Cliffs, NJ, Prentice-Hall, pp. 474–506.

Moss, Lawrence (1965) "Space and direction in the Chinese garden," *Landscape*, vol. 14, No. 3 (Spring), pp. 29–33.

Mukerjee, R. (1961) "Ways of dwelling in the communities of India" in G. A. Theodorson (ed.) *Studies in Human Ecology*, Evanston, Ill., Row, Peterson, pp. 390–401.

Müller, Werner (1961) *Die Heilige Stadt*, Stuttgart, Kohlhammer Verl.

Murch, Gerald M. (1973) *Visual and Auditory Perception*, Indianapolis, Bobbs Merrill.

Murdie, Robert A. (1965) "Cultural differences in consumer travel," *Economic Geography*, vol. 41.

_____ (1971) "The social geography of the city: theoretical and empirical implications" in L. S. Bourne (ed.) *Internal Structure of the City*, New York, Oxford University Press, pp. 279–290.

Murphy, Peter E. (1969) *A Study of the Influence of Attitude as a Behavioral Parameter on the Spatial Choice Patterns of Consumers*, unpublished PhD Dissertation in Geography, Ohio State University.

Murphy, Peter E. and Reginald G. Golledge (n.d.) "Comments on the use of attitude as a variable in urban geography," Columbus, Ohio, Dept. of Geography, Ohio State University (mimeo).

Murphy, Rhoads (1954) "The city as a center of change: Western Europe and China," *Annals. Ass'n. Am. Geog.* vol. 44.

Nagashima, Koichi (1970) "Future urban environment: evolution of social and leisure space with reference to Japan," *Ekistics*, vol. 30, No. 178 (Sept.), pp. 218–222.

Nahemow, Lucille (1971) "Research in a novel environment," *Environment and Behavior*, vol. 3, No. 1, pp. 81 ff.

Nahemow, Lucille and M. Powell Lawton (1973) "Toward an ecological theory of adaptation and aging" in W. Preiser (ed.) *EDRA 4*, Stroudsburg, Pa., Dowden, Hutchinson and Ross, vol. 1, pp. 24–32.

Nairn, Ian (1955) *Outrage*, London, Architectural Press.

————— (1956) *Counterattack*, London, Architectural Press.

————— (1965) *The American Landscape* (a critical view), New York, Random House.

Neisser, Ulric (1967) *Cognitive Psychology*, New York, Appleton-Centure-Crofts.

————— (1968) "Cultural and cognitive discontinuity" in R. A. Manners and D. Kaplan (ed.) *Theory in Anthropology*, Chicago, Aldine, pp. 354–364.

Nelson, Howard J. (1971) "The form and structure of cities: urban growth patterns" in L. S. Bourne (ed.) *Internal Structure of the City*, New York, Oxford University Press, pp. 75–83.

Neumann, E. S. and G. L. Peterson (1970) "Perception and the use of urban beaches" in J. Archea and C. Eastman (ed.) *EDRA 2*, pp. 327–333.

N. J. County and Municipal Government Study Commission (1974) *Housing and Suburbs*.

Newman, Oscar (1971) *Architectural Design for Crime Prevention*, US Dept. of Justice, Law Enforcement Assistance Administration, Washington, D.C.

New York Times (1971) (Jan. 24).

————— (1972) (Jan. 24), p. 1.

————— (1974) "Swiss voters defeat plan to oust half of foreigners" (Oct. 21).

New Yorker (1969 (July 19).

Nicolson, Marjorie Hope (1959) *Mountain Gloom and Mountain Glory*, Ithaca, NY, Cornell University Press.

Nielson, Helen (1971) *Shot on Location*, London, Golancz.

Nilsson, S. A. *et al.* (n.d.) *Tanzania: Zanzibar – Present Conditions and Future Plans*, Lund, Dept. of Architecture, University of Lund.

Nimtz, Maxine (1971) Zanzibar in the 1930's (unpublished paper).

Norberg-Schulz, C. (1971) *Existence, Space and Architecture*, New York, Praeger.

Noton, David and L. Stark (1971) "Eye movements and visual perception," *Scientific American*, vol. 224, No. 6 (June), pp. 34–43.

Ohnuki-Tierney, Emiko (1972) "Spatial concepts of the Ainu of the Northwest coast of Southern Sakhalin," *American Anthropologist*, vol. 74, No. 3 (June), pp. 426–457.

Ojo, G. J. Afolabi (1969) "Development of Yoruba towns in Nigeria," *Ekistics*, vol. 27, No. 161 (April), pp. 243–247.

Olver, R. and J. Hornsby (1972) "On equivalence" in P. Adams (ed.) *Language and Thought*, Harmondsworth, Penguin Books, pp. 306–320.

Ommaney, Francis P. (1955) *Isle of Cloves*, London, Longmans Green.

Onibokun, Gabriel O. (1970) "Socio-cultural constraints on urban renewal policies in emerging nations: the Ibadan case," *Human Organization*, vol. 29, No. 2 (Summer), pp. 133–139.

Oram, Nigel (1966) "Health, housing and urban development," *Architecture in Australia* (Nov.), pp. 98–107.

————— (1970) "The development of Port Moresby – what and who are the problems?" paper given at 42nd ANZAAS Congress, Port Moresby TPNG, published in *Search*, vol. 1, No. 5 (Nov.), pp. 282–288.

Orleans, Peter (1971) "Differential cognition of urban residents: effects of social scale on mapping," School of Architecture and Urban Planning, UCLA (Nov.) (mimeo).

Orleans, Peter and Sophie Schmidt (1972) "Mapping the city: environmental cognition of urban residents" in W. Mitchell (ed.) *EDRA 3*, Los Angeles, University of California, vol. 1, pp. 1-4-1–1-4-9.

Orme, J. E. (1969) *Time, Experience and Behavior*, London, Iliffe.

Ornstein, R. E. (1969) *On the Experience of Time*, Harmondsworth, Penguin.

Ortiz, Alfonso (1972) "Ritual drama and the Pueblo world view" in A. Ortiz (ed.) *New Perspectives on the Pueblos*, Albuquerque, University of New Mexico.

Osgood, Charles E. (1971) "Exploration in semantic space: a personal diary," *J. of Social Issues*, vol. 27, No. 4, pp. 5–64.

Pahl, R. E. (1968) *Spatial Structure and Social Structure*, London Centre for Environmental Studies, Working Paper No. 10 (Aug.).

————— (1971) *Pattern of Urban Life*, London, Longmans.

Pailhous, Jean (1970) *La Représentation de L'Espace Urbain* (L'exemple du chauffeur de taxi), Paris, Presses Universitaires de France.

Pallier, M. (1971) "The perception of a boundary to a residential area" in Ross King (ed.) *Perception of Residential Quality: Sydney Case Studies*, Ian Buchan Fell, Research Project on Housing, Collected Papers No. 2, University of Sydney (Aug.), pp. 87–95.

Paluck, Robert J. and A. H. Esser (1971) "Controlled experimental modification of aggressive behavior in territories of severely retarded boys," *Am. J. of Mental Deficiency*, vol. 76, No. 1, pp. 23–29.

Pande, Shashi K. (1970) "From hurried habitability to heightened habitability," *Ekistics*, vol. 30, No. 178 (Sept.), pp. 213–217.

Panoff, M. (1969) "The notion of time among the Maenge people of New Britain," *Ethnology*, vol. 8, No. 2 (April), pp. 153–166.

Papageorgiou, A. (1971) *Continuity and Change*, London, Pall Mall.

Pappas, P. (1967) "Time allocation in eighteen Athens communities," *Ekistics*, vol. 24, No. 140 (July), pp. 110–127.

Parducci, A. (1968) "The relativism of absolute judgements," *Scientific American*, vol. 219, No. 6 (Dec.), pp. 84–90.

Parkes, Don (1972) "Some elements of time and urban social space," Paper given at ANZAAS Congress, Sydney (Aug.) (mimeo).

–––––––– (1973) "Timing the city: a theme for urban environment planning," *Royal Aust. Planning Inst. J.*, vol. 11, No. 5 (Oct.), pp. 130–135.

Parr, A. E. (1965) "City and Psyche," *The Yale Review*, vol. LV, No. 1 (Autumn), pp. 71–85.

–––––––– (1967) "Urbanity and the urban scene," *Landscape*, vol. 16, No. 3 (Spring), pp. 3–5.

–––––––– (1968) "The five ages of urbanity," *Landscape*, vol. 17, No. 3 (Spring), pp. 7–10.

–––––––– (1969(a)) "Lessons of an urban childhood," *The American Montessori Society Bulletin*, vol. 7, No. 4.

–––––––– (1969(b)) "Problems of reason, feeling and habitat," *AAQ*, vol. 1, No. 3 (July), pp. 5–10.

–––––––– (1969(c)) "Speed and community," *The High Speed Ground Transportation Journal*, vol. 3, No. 1 (Jan.).

Passini, R. (1971) "Response to an urban environment and the formation of mental images: experiments based on the varying of sensory modalities" (in French, English abstract) Montreal, School of Architecture, University of Montreal (mimeo).

Pastalan, L. A. and D. H. Carson (ed.) (1970) *Spatial Behavior of Older People*, Ann Arbor, University of Michigan.

Paulsson, Gregor (1952) *The Study of Cities* (notes about hermeneutics of urban space), Copenhagen, Munksgaard.

Pavlou, Kandia and Christine Kelly (1971) "Movement of Greek migrants within Sydney: the effect of the perceived environment" in Ross King (ed.) *Perception of Environmental Quality: Sydney Case Studies*, Ian Buchan Fell Research Project on Housing, Collected Papers No. 2, University of Sydney (Aug.), pp. 41–45.

Pawley, Martin (1971) *Architecture vs. Housing*, New York, Praeger.

Payne, Geoffrey K. (1971) "A squatter colony," *Architectural Review*, vol. CL, No. 898 (Dec.), pp. 370–371.

–––––––– (1973) "Functions of informality: a case study of squatter settlements in India," *Architectural Design*, vol. 43, No. 8, pp. 494–503.

Peattie, Lisa R. (1969) "Social issues in housing" in B. J. Frieden and W. W. Nash (ed.) *Shaping an Urban Future*, Cambridge, Mass., MIT Press, pp. 15–34.

–––––––– (1972) *The View from the Barrio*, Ann Arbor, University of Michigan Press.

Perin, Constance (1970) *With Man in Mind*, Cambridge, MIT Press.

Perinbanayagam, R. S. (1974) "The definition of the situation: an analysis of the ethnomethodological and dramaturgical view," *Sociological Quarterly*, vol. 15, No. 4 (Autumn), pp. 521–541.

Peters, Roger (1973) "Cognitive maps in wolves and men" in W. Preiser (ed.) *EDRA 4*, Stroudsburg, Pa., Dowden, Hutchinson and Ross, vol. 2, pp. 247–253.

Peterson, George L. (1967(a)) "A model of preference: quantitative analysis of the perception of the visual appearance of residential neighborhoods," *J. of Regional Science*, vol. 7, No. 1, pp. 19–31.

–––––––– (1967(b)) "Measuring visual preferences of residential neighborhoods," *Ekistics*, vol. 25, No. 136 (March), pp. 169–173.

–––––––– (1969) "Toward a metric for evaluating the impact of urban highway construction on neighborhood structure," paper at Joint Meeting Am. Astronautical Society/Operations Research Society (June) (mimeo).

Peterson, G. L. and R. D. Worrall (1969) "On a theory of accessibility preference for selected neighborhood services," Joint National Meeting Operations Research Society (35th Annual Meeting) Am. Astronautical Society (15th Nat. Meeting) (June).

Peterson, George L., R. L. Bishop and E. S. Neumann, "The quality of visual residential environments" in H. Sanoff and S. Cohn (ed.), *EDRA 1*, pp. 101–114.

Petonnet, Collette (1972(a)) "Reflexions au sujet de la ville vue par en dessous," *L'Année Sociologique*, vol. 21, pp. 151–185.

———— (1972(b)) "Espace, distance et dimension dans une société musulmane" (A propos du bidonville Marocain de Douar Doum à Rabat) *L'Homme,* vol. 12, No. 2 (April/June), pp. 47–84.

Phelan, Joseph G. (1970) "Relationship of judged complexity to changes in mode of presentation of object shapes," *J. of Psych.* vol. 74 (1st half) (Jan.), pp. 21–27.

Piaget, Jean (1954) *The Child's Construction of Reality*, New York, Basic Books.

———— (1963(a)) *The Origins of Intelligence in Children*, New York, Norton.

———— (1963(b)) *The Psychology of Intelligence*, Totoya, NJ, Littlefield Adams.

Piaget, Jean and B. Inhelder (1962) *The Child's Conception of Space*, New York, Norton.

Pick, Herbert L. Jr. *et al.* (1967) "Perceptual integration in children" in Lewis P. Lipsitt and Charles C. Spiker (ed.), *Advances in Child Development and Behavior*, vol. 3, New York, Academic Press, pp. 192–223.

Pillsbury, Richard (1967) "The market or public square in Pennsylvania 1682–1820," *Proceedings. Pa. Academy of Science*, vol. 41.

———— (1970) "The urban street pattern as culture indicator: Pennsylvania 1682–1815," *Annals. Ass'n. Am. Geog.* vol. 60, No. 3 (Sept.), pp. 428–446.

Plant, J. (1930) "Some psychiatric aspects of crowded living conditions," *Am. J. of Psychiatry*, vol. 9, No. 5, pp. 849–860.

Plotnicov, Leonard (1972) "Who owns Jos? Ethnic ideology in Nigerian urban politics," *Urban Anthropology*, vol. 1, No. 1 (Spring), pp. 1–13.

Pollock, Leslie S. "Relating urban design to the motorist: an empirical viewpoint" in W. Mitchell (ed.) *EDRA 3*, Los Angeles, University of California, vol. 1, pp. 11-1-1–11-1-10.

Pontius, A. A. (1967) "Neuro-psychiatric hypotheses about territorial behavior," *Perceptual and Motor Skills*, vol. 24 (June), pp. 1232–1234.

Poole, M. E. *et al.* (1972) "A rationale for teaching communication skills to the culturally deprived," *Aust. J. of Soc. Issues*, vol. 7, No. 1 (Feb.).

Porteous, J. Douglas (1970) "The nature of the company town," *Transactions Inst. British Geog.* vol. 51, pp. 127–142.

———— (1971) "Design with people (the quality of the urban environment," *Environment and Behavior*, vol. 3, No. 2 (June), pp. 155–178.

Porter, Tyrus (1964) "A study of pathtaking behavior," unpublished B. Arch. thesis, Department of Architecture, University of California, Berkeley.

Prakash, Aditya (1972) "Rehri: the mobile shop of India," *Ekistics*, vol. 34, No. 204 (Nov.), pp. 328–333.

Pred, Allan (1964) "The esthetic slum," *Landscape*, vol. 14, No. 1 (Autumn), pp. 16–18.

Price-Williams, D. R. (ed.) (1969) *Cross-Cultural Studies*, Harmondsworth, Penguin.

Prince, Hugh C. (1971) "Real, imagined and abstract worlds of the past" in C. Board *et al.* (ed.) *Progress in Geography* (International reviews of current research), vol. 3, London Edward Arnold, pp. 4–86.

Prokop, Dieter (1967) "Image and functions of the city" in *Urban Core and Inner City*, Leiden, Brill, pp. 22–34.

Proshansky, Harold M. *et al.* (1970(a)) "Freedom of choice and behavior in a physical setting" in H. M. Proshansky *et al.* (ed.) *Environmental Psychology*, New York, Holt, Rinehart and Winston, pp. 173–183.

———— *et al.* (ed.) (1970(b)) *Environmental Psychology*, New York, Holt, Rinehart and Winston.

Pryor, E. G. (1971) "The delineation of blighted areas in urban Hong Kong" in D. J. Dwyer (ed.) *Asian urbanization* (a Hong Kong casebook), Hong Kong, University Press, pp. 70–88.

Pryor, R. J. (1971) "Defining the rural-urban fringe" in L. S. Bourne (ed.) *Internal Structure of the City*, New York, Oxford University Press, pp. 59–68.

Pyron, Bernard (1971) "Form and space diversity in human habitats" (perceptual responses) *Environment and Behavior*, vol. 3, No. 2 (Dec.), pp. 382–411.

———— (1972) "Form and diversity in human habitats (judgemental and attitude responses)" *Environment and Behavior*, vol. 4, No. 1 (March), pp. 87–120.

Quick, Stephen L. (1966) "The influence of the peer group on city planning," unpublished paper done for course (Rapoport, Arch 249A, Social and Cultural Factors in Design) Berkeley, California, Dept. of Architecture (Fall).

Rainwater, Lee (1966) "Fear and house-as-haven in the lower class," *AIP Journal*, vol. 32, No. 1 (Jan.), pp. 23–31.

Raison, Timothy (1968) "Touching, smelling, feeling, looking – the desire for increased sensuality," *Evening Standard* (London) (Nov. 26).

Rand, G. (1972) "Children's images of houses: a prolegomena to the study of why people still want pitched roofs" in W. Mitchell (ed.) *EDRA 3*, Los Angeles, University of California, vol. 1, pp. 6-9-1–6-9-10.

Rapoport, Amos (1957) "An approach to urban design," M. Arch. Thesis, Rice University (May) (unpublished).

_____ (1964–65) "The architecture of Isphahan," *Landscape,* vol. 14, No. 2 (Winter), pp. 4–11.

_____ (1965) "A note on shopping lanes," *Landscape,* vol. 14, No. 3 (Spring), p. 28.

_____ (1966) "Some aspects of urban renewal in France," *Town Planning Review*, vol. 37 (Oct.), pp. 217–227.

_____ (1967(a)) "Whose meaning in architecture," *Interbuild/Arena* (Oct.), pp. 44–46.

_____ (1967(b)) "Yagua or the Amazon dwelling," *Landscape,* vol. 16, No. 3 (Spring), pp. 27–30.

_____ (1968) "The personal element in housing: an approach to open-ended design," *RIBA Journal* (July), pp. 300–307.

_____ (1968–69) "The design professions and the behavioural sciences," *AA Quarterly*, vol. 1, No. 1 (Winter), pp. 20–24.

_____ (1969(a)) *House Form and Culture*, Englewood Cliffs, NJ, Prentice-Hall.

_____ (1969(b)) "Housing and housing densities in France," *Town Planning Review*, vol. 39, No. 4 (Jan.), pp. 341–354.

_____ (1969(c)) "Facts and models" in G. Broadbent and A. Ward, *Design Methods in Architecture*, London, Lund Humphries, pp. 136–146.

_____ (1969(d)) "The Pueblo and the Hogan: a cross-cultural study of two responses to an environment" in P. Oliver (ed.) *Shelter and Society*, London, Barrie and Rockliffe, pp. 66–79.

_____ (1969(e)) "The notion of urban relationships," *Area* (J. of Inst. of British Geog.), vol. 1, No. 3, pp. 17–26.

_____ (1969(f)) "Some aspects of the organization of urban space" in Gary J. Coates and Kenneth M. Moffett (ed.) *Response to Environment*, student publication, School of Design, NC State University No. 18, Raleigh, NC, pp. 121–140.

_____ (1969(g)) "An approach to the study of environmental quality" in H. Sanoff and S. Cohn (ed.) *EDRA 1*, pp. 1–13.

_____ (1970(a)) "Observations regarding man–environment studies," *Man–Environment Systems* (Jan.) reprinted in *Arch. Research and Teaching*, vol. 2, No. 1 (Nov. 1971).

_____ (1970(b)) "The study of spatial quality," *J. of Aesthetic Education*, vol. 4, No. 4 (Oct.), pp. 81–96.

_____ (1970(c)) "Symbolism and environmental design," *Int. J. of Symbology*, vol. 1, No. 3 (April), pp. 1–10.

_____ (1971(a)) "Designing for complexity," *AA Quarterly*, vol. 3, No. 1 (Winter), pp. 29–33.

_____ (1971(b)) "Environmental quality: guidelines for decisionmakers" in G. J. R. Linge and P. J. Rimmer (ed.) *Government Influence and the Location of Economic Activity,* Research School of Pacific Studies, Dept. of Human Geography, Publication HG/5, Canberra, Australian National University.

_____ (1971(c)) "Observations regarding man–environment studies," *Man–Environment Systems* (Jan. 1971); *Arch. Research and Teaching*, vol. 2, No. 1 (Nov. 1971).

_____ (1971(d)) "Programming the housing environment," *Tomorrow's Housing*, Dept. of Adult Education, University of Adelaide, Publication No. 22.

_____ (1971(e)) "Human and psychological reactions" in *Australian Report on Environmental Aspects of the Design of Tall Buildings*, ASCE–IABSE Committee; also in *Architectural Science Review*, vol. 14, No. 4 (Dec.), pp. 95–97.

_____ (1972(a)) "Environmental quality in the design of a new town" in D. Whitelock and D. Corbett (ed.) *City of the Future* (The Murray New Town Proposal) Publication No. 33, Dept. of Adult Education, University of Adelaide, reprinted (with some material left out) in *Royal Australian Planning Journal*, vol. 10, No. 4 (October).

_____ (1972(b)) "Some perspectives on the human use and organization of space," paper given at Symposium of Space and Territory, Australasian Ass'n. of Soc. Anthrop., Melbourne (May), published in *AA Quarterly*, vol. 5, No. 3 (Autumn 1973) (References in *AA Quarterly*, vol. 6, No. 2, 1974).

_____ (1972(c)) "Environment and people" in Amos Rapoport (ed.) *Australia as Human Setting*, Sydney, Angus and Robertson.

_____ (1972(d)) "Cultural variables in housing design," *Architecture in Australia*, vol. 61, No. 3 (June), reprinted as "The ecology of housing" in *The Ecologist* (London), vol. 3, No. 1 (January 1973) abstracted in *Ekistics*, vol. 36, No. 213 (Aug. 1973).

_____ (1972(e)) "Australian Aborigines and the definition of place" in William J. Mitchell (ed.) *EDRA 3*, Los Angeles, University of California, vol. 1, pp. 3-3-1–3-3-14.

————— (1973(a)) "Images, symbols and popular design," *Int. J. of Symbology*, vol. 4, No. 3 (Nov.), pp. 1–12.

————— (1973(b)) "Some thought on the methodology of man–environment studies," *Inter. J. of Env. Studies*, vol. 4, pp. 135–140.

————— (1973(c)) "The problems of today, the city of tomorrow, and the lessons of the past," paper given at the Symposium on Urbanization AAAS Meetings, Mexico City (July) and published in *DMG/DRS Journal*, vol. 7, No. 3 (July/Sept.).

————— (1973(d)) "Urban design for the elderly: some preliminary considerations," paper given at a conference on *Environmental Research and Aging*, St. Louis (May 13–15), published in Thomas O. Byerts (ed.) *Environmental Research and Aging*, Washington, D.C., Gerontological Society, 1974.

————— (1973(e)) "An approach to the construction of man–environment theory" in W. Preiser (ed.) *EDRA 4*, Stroudsburg, Pa., Dowden, Hutchinson and Ross, vol. 2, pp. 124–135.

————— (1974) "Nomadism as a man–environment system," paper given at conference on Psychosocial Consequences of Sedentarization, UCLA (Dec.) (mimeo).

————— (1975(a)) "An 'anthropological' approach to environmental design research" in Basil Honikman (ed.) *Responding to Social Change*, Stroudsburg, Pa., Dowden, Hutchinson and Ross, pp. 145–151.

————— (1975(b)) "Towards a redefinition of density," *Environment and Behavior*, vol. 7, No. 2 (June), pp. 133–158.

————— (1976) "Environmental cognition in cross-cultural perspective" in G. T. Moore and R. G. Golledge (ed.) *Environmental Knowing*, Stroudsburg, Pa., Dowden, Hutchinson and Ross.

————— (in press(a)) "Socio-cultural aspects of man–environment studies" in Amos Rapoport (ed.) *The Mutual Interaction of People and the Built Environment: a Cross-Cultural Perspective*, The Hague, Mouton.

————— (in press(c)) "Culture and the subjective perception of stress."

Rapoport, Amos and Robert E. Kantor (1967) "Complexity and ambiguity in environmental design," *AIP Journal*, vol. 33, No. 4 (July), pp.210–221.

Rapoport, Amos and Ron Hawkes (1970) "The perception of urban complexity," *AIP Journal*, vol. 6, No. 2 (March), pp. 106–111.

Rapoport, Amos and Newton Watson (1972) "Cultural variability in physical standards" in R. Gutman (ed.) *People and Buildings*, New York, Basic Books, pp. 33–53 (originally in *Transactions of the Bartlett Society*, vol. 6, 1967–68).

Rapoport, Anatol and H. Horowitz (1960) "The Sapir–Whorf–Korzybski hypothesis – a report and a reply," *ETC: Journal of General Semantics*, vol. 17.

Ravetz, Alison (1971) "The use of surveys in the assessment of residential design," *Arch. Research and Teaching*, vol. 1, No. 3 (April), pp. 23–31.

Ray, Talton F. (1969) *The Politics of the Barrios of Venezuela*, Berkeley and Los Angeles, University of California Press.

Raymond, H. *et al.* (1966) *L'Habitat Pavillonnaire*, Paris, Centre de Recherche d'Urbanisme.

Redfield, Robert (1950) *The Village that Chose Progress* (Chan Kom revisited) Chicago, University of Chicago Press.

Reed, Roy (1973) "A different kind of inner-city community," *NY Times* (Aug. 3).

Regional Plan Association (1969) *Urban Design Manhattan*, London, Studio Vista.

Reid, John (1973) "Community conflict in N Ireland: analysis of a new town plan," *Ekistics*, vol. 36, No. 213 (Aug.), pp. 115–119.

Rent, George S. (1968) "Changing homogeneity of occupational prestige in urban residential areas," unpublished PhD Dissertation, Florida State University.

Reynolds, Ingrid *et al.* (1974) "The quality of local authority housing schemes," *Architects Journal* (Feb. 27), pp. 1–10.

Rhodes, A. Lewis (1969) "Residential stratification and occupational stratification in Paris and Chicago," *The Sociol. Quarterly* (Winter), pp. 106–112.

Riley, P. J. (1971) "The image of the city in aboriginal primary school children living in inner Sydney," 1st year essay in my MES course, Sydney University.

Ritter, Paul (1964) *Planning for Man and Motor*, New York, Macmillan.

Rivizzigno, V. and R. G. Golledge (1974) "A method for recoverying cognitive information about a city" in B. Honikman (ed.) *EDRA 5*, vol. 11, pp. 9–18.

Robinson, G. W. S. (1973) "The recreation geography of South Asia," *Ekistics*, vol. 35, No. 208 (March), pp. 139–144.

Robinson, John P. and Robert Hefner (1968) "Perceptual maps of the world," *Public Opinion Quarterly*, vol. 32, No. 2 (Summer), pp. 273–280.

Rock, I. and C. S. Harris (1967) "Vision and touch," *Scientific American* (May), pp. 96–104.

Rogers, David S. (1970) *The Role of Search and Learning in Consumer Space Behavior: the Case of Urban In-Migrants* MSc Thesis in Geography, University of Wisconsin (unpublished).

Roggemans, M. L. (1971) *La Ville Est Un Système Social*, Institut de Sociologie, Université Libre de Bruxelles.

Rokeach, Milton and Seymour Parker (1970) "Values as social indicators of poverty and race relations in America," *Annals. Am. Ass'n. of Political and Social Science*, vol. 388 (March), pp. 97–111.

Romanos, Aristides, G. (1969) "Illegal settlements in Athens" in P. Oliver (ed.), *Shelter and Society*, London, Barrie and Rockliff, pp. 137–155.

————— (1970) "Squatter housing," *AA Quarterly*, vol. 2, No. 2, pp. 14–26.

Roos, Philip D. (1968) "Jurisdiction: an ecological concept," *Human Relations*, vol. 21, No. 1, pp. 75–84.

Rose, A. James (1968) "Some boundaries and building materials in Southeastern Australia" in *Land and Livelihood* (Geographical Essays in honor of George Jobberns), pp. 255–276.

Rose, Daniel M. (1968) "Culture and cognition: some problems and a suggestion," *Anthrop. Quarterly*, vol. 41, No. 1 (Jan.), pp. 9–28.

Rose, Harold M. (1969) *Social Processes in the City: Race and Urban Residential Choice*, Commission on College Geography Resource Paper No. 6, Washington, D.C., Ass'n. Am. Geog.

————— (1970) "The development of an urban subsystem: the case of the Negro ghetto," *Annals, Ass'n. Am. Geog.* vol. 60, No. 1 (March), pp. 1–17.

Rosenberg, Gerhard (1968) "High population densities in relation to social behavior," *Ekistics*, vol. 25 (June), pp. 425–427.

Rosenberg, M. J. (1970) "The experimental parable of inauthenticity: consequences of counter-attitudinal performance" in J. S. Antrobus (ed.) *Cognition and Affect*, Boston, Little Brown.

Rosser, C. and C. Harris (1965) *The Family and Social Change: a study of Family and Kinship in a South Wales Town*, London, Routledge and Kegan Paul.

Rossi, Peter H. (1955) *Why Families Move*, Glencoe, The Free Press.

Rothblatt, Donald N. (1971) "Housing and human needs," *Town Planning Review*, vol. 42, No. 2 (April), pp. 130–144.

Royal Commission on Local Government (1969) *Community Attitudes Survey* (Research Study No. 9), London, HMSO.

Royse, Donald C. (1969) *Social Inferences Via Environmental Cues*, Cambridge, Mass., MIT Planning, PhD Dissertation (unpublished).

Rozelle, Richard M. and James C. Baxter (1972) "Meaning and value in conceptualizing the city," *AIP Journal*, vol. 38, No. 2 (March), pp. 116–122.

Rudofsky, Bernard (1969) *Streets for People*, Garden City, NY, Doubleday.

Ruesch, J. and W. Kees (1956) *Non-verbal communication*, Berkeley, University of California Press.

Rushton, Gerald (1969) "Analysis of spatial behavior by revealed space preference," *Annals. Ass'n. of Am. Geog.* vol. 59, No. 2 (June), pp. 391–400.

Ryan, T. A. and M. S. Ryan (1940) "Geographical orientation," *Am. J. of Psych.* vol. 53, No. 2 (April), pp. 204–215.

Rykwert, Joseph (n.d.) *The Idea of a Town*, Hilversum, G. Van Saane.

Saarinen, Thomas F. (1966) *Perception of Drought Hazard in the Great Plains*, Chicago, Dept. of Geography, University of Chicago, Research Paper No. 106.

————— (1969) *Perception of Environment*, Commission on College Geography Resource Paper No. 5, Washington, D.C., Ass'n. of Am. Geog.

Saegert, Susan (1973) "Crowding: cognitive overload and behavioral constraint" in W. Preiser (ed.) *EDRA 4*, Stroudsburg, Pa., Dowden, Hutchinson and Ross, vol. 2, pp. 252–260.

Saile, David G. *et al.* (1972) "Families in Public housing: a study of three localities in Rockford, Illinois" in W. Mitchell (ed.) *EDRA 3*, Los Angeles, University of California, pp. 13-7-1–13-7-9.

Salapatek, Philip and William Kessen (1968) "Visual scanning of triangles by the human newborn" in Ralph N. Haber (ed.) *Contemporary Theory and Research in Visual Perception*, New York, Holt, Rinehart and Winston.

Sandström, Carl-Ivar (1972) "What do we perceive in perceiving?" *Ekistics*, vol. 34, No. 204 (Nov.), pp. 370–371.

Sanoff, Henry (1969) "Visual attributes of the physical environment" in G. J. Coates and K. M. Moffat (ed.) *Response to Environment*, Student Publication, School of Design No. 18, Raleigh, NC, North Carolina State University, pp. 37–62.

————— (1970) "Social perception of the ecological neighborhood," *Ekistics*, No. 177 (Aug.), pp. 130–132.

————— (1973) "Youth's perception and categorization of residential cues" in W. Preiser (ed.) *EDRA 4*, Stroudsburg, Pa., Dowden, Hutchinson and Ross, vol. 1, pp. 84–97.

Sanoff, Henry and Man Sawhney (1972) "Residential liveability: a study of user attitudes towards their residential environment" in W. Mitchell (ed.) *EDRA 3*, Los Angeles, University of California, vol 1, pp. 13-8-1–13-8-10.

Sapir, E. (1958) "Language and environment" in D. G. Mandelbaum (ed.) *Selected Writings of Edward Sapir in Language, Culture and Personality*, Berkeley, University of California Press.

Sauer, Louis (1972) "The architect and user needs" in William M. Smith (ed.) *Behavior, Design and Policy Aspects of Human Habitats*, Green Bay, University of Wisconsin, pp. 147–170.

Savarton, S. and K. R. George (1971) "A study of historic, economic and socio-cultural factors which influence aboriginal settlements at Wicannia and Weilmeringle NSW," unpublished B. Arch. Thesis, University of Sydney.

Sawicky, David S. (1971) *A Definition of Urban Sub-Areas Using Social Disorganization as a Conceptual Framework*, Cornell Dissertations in Planning, Dept. of City and Regional Planning, Ithaca, NY (Jan.).

Schachtel, Ernest G. (1959) *Metamorphosis* (on the development of affect, perception, attention and memory) New York, Basic Books.

Schak, David C. (1972) "Determinants of children's play patterns in a Chinese city: an interplay of space and values," *Urban Anthropology*, vol. 1, No. 2 (Fall), pp. 195–204.

Schmidt, R. C. (1966) "Density, health and social disorganization," *AIP Journal*, vol. 32 (Jan.), pp. 38–40.

Schnapper, Dominique (1971) *L'Italie Rouge et Noire* (Les modèles culturels de la vie quotidienne à Bologne), Paris, Gallimard.

Schoder, R. V. (1963) "Ancient Cumae," *Scientific American* (Dec.), pp. 109–121.

Schorr, Alvin L. (1966) *Slums and Social Insecurity*, US. Dept. of HEW, Social Security Administration, Division of Research and Statistics, Research Report 1; partly reprinted in H. M. Proshansky *et al.* (ed.) *Environmental Psychology*, New York, Holt, Rinehart and Winston (1970) pp. 319–333.

Schwartz, Barry (1968) "The social psychology of privacy," *Am. J. Sociology*, vol. 73, No. 6 (May), pp. 541–542.

Schweitzer, Eric *et al.* (1973) "A bi-racial comparison of density preferences in housing in two cities" in W. Preiser (ed.) *EDRA 4*, Stroudsburg, Pa., Dowden, Hutchinson and Ross, vol. 1, pp. 312–323.

Scott-Brown, Denise (1965) "The meaningful city," *AIA Journal*, vol. 43, No. 1 (Jan.).

Scully, Vincent (1962) *The Earth, the Temple and the Gods*, New Haven, Yale University Press.

Seagrim, G. N. (1967–68) "Representation and communication," *Transactions of the Bartlett Society*, vol. 6, pp. 9–24.

Seamon, David (1972) "Environmental imagery: an overview and tentative ordering" in W. Mitchell (ed.) *EDRA 3*, Los Angeles, University of California, vol. 1, pp. 7-1-1–7-1-7.

Seddon, George (1970) *Swan River Landscape*, Nedlands, University of Western Australia Press.

Segal, S. J. (ed.) (1971) *Imagery: Current Cognitive Approaches*, New York, Academic Press.

Segal, S. J. and V. Fusella (1971) "Effect of images in six sense modalities on detection of visual signal from noise," *Psychonomic Science*, vol. 24, No. 2 (July), pp. 55–56.

Segall, Marshall H., D. T. Campbell and M. J. Herskovits (1966) *The Influence of Culture on Visual Perception*, Indianapolis, Bobbs Merrill.

Sennett, Richard (1970) *The Uses of Disorder*, New York, Alfred Knopf.

Sewell, W. R. Derrick (1971) "Crisis, conventional wisdom and commitment: a study of perceptions and attitudes of engineers and public health officials," *Environment and Behavior*, vol. 3, No. 1 (March).

Shafer, Elwood, L. Jr. *et al.* (1969(a)) "Natural landscape preferences: a predictive model," *J. of Leisure Research*, vol. 1, No. 1 (Winter), pp. 1–19.

———— (1969(b)) "Perception of natural environments," *Environment and Behavior*, vol. 1, No. 1 (June), pp. 71–82.

Shafer, Elwood L. Jr. and H. D. Burke (1965) "Preferences for outdoor recreation facilities in four state parks," *J. of Forestry* (July).

Shafer, Elwood L. Jr. and James Mietz (1972) "Aesthetic and emotional experiences are high with Northeast wilderness hikers" in Joachim F. Wohlwill and D. H. Carson (ed.) *Environment and the Social Sciences: Perspectives and Applications*, Washington, D.C., Am. Psych. Ass'n, pp. 207–216.

Shankland, Cox and Associates Social Survey (1967) *Childwall Valley Estate*, Liverpool, London (Aug.) (mimeo).

Sharp, Thomas (1968) *Town and Townscape*, London, John Murray.

Sharply, Anne (1969) "This . . er . . . rush to the . . er . . . Hayward," *Evening Standard* (London) (May 8).

Shepard, Paul (1969) *English Reaction to the New Zealand Landscape before 1850* (Pacific viewpoint Monograph No. 4) Wellington, Victoria, University of Wellington, Dept. of Geography.

Sherif, Muzafer and C. W. Sherif (1963) "Varieties of social stimulus situations" in S. B. Sells (ed.) *Stimulus Determinants of Behavior*, New York, Ronald Press, pp. 82–106.

Siegel, B. J. (1970) "Defensive structuring and environmental stress," *Am. J. of Sociology*, vol. 76, pp. 11–46.

Sieverts, Thomas (1967) "Perceptual images of the city of Berlin" in *Urban Core and Inner City*, Leiden Brill.

———— (1969) "Spontaneous architecture," *AA Quarterly*, vol. 1, No. 3 (July), pp. 36–43.

Simmons, J. W. (1968) "Changing residence in the city: a review of intraurban mobility," *Geog. Review*, vol. 58, No. 4 (Oct.), pp. 622–651.

Sinclair, Robert (n.d.) *Town Spotter*, Take Home Books.

Sitté, Camillo (1965) *City Planning According to Artistic Principles*, New York, Random House.

Skinner, G. William (1972) "Marketing and social structure in rural China" in Paul W. English and Robert C. Mayfield (ed.) *Man, Space, and Environment*, New York, Oxford, pp. 561–600.

Sklare, Marshall (1972) "Jews, ethnics and the American city," *Commentary*, vol. 53, No. 4 (April), pp. 70–77.

Skolimowski, Henry K. (1969) "Human space in the technological age," *AA Quarterly*, vol. 1, No. 3 (July), pp. 80–83.

Smailes, A. E. (1955) "Some reflections on the geographical description and analysis of townscapes," *Trans. Inst. of British Geog.* vol. 21, pp. 99–115.

Smets, G. (1971) "Pleasingness vs. interestingness of visual stimuli with controlled complexity: their relationship to looking time as a function of exposure time," *Perceptual and Motor Skills*, vol. 40, No. 1 (Feb.), pp. 3–10.

Smith, B. J. (1960) *European Vision and the South Pacific 1768–1850*, Oxford, Clarendon Press.

Smith, Peter F. (1972) "The pros and cons of subliminal perception," *Ekistics*, vol. 34, No. 204 (Nov.), pp. 367–369.

———— (1973) "Symbolic meaning in contemporary cities," *RIBA J.* vol. 80, No. 9 (Sept.), pp. 436–441.

Smith, Richard A. (1971) "Crowding in the city: the Japanese solution," *Landscape*, vol. 19, No. 1, pp. 3–10.

Smith, Suzanne *et al.* (1971) "Interaction of sociological and ecological variables affecting women's satisfaction in Brasilia," *Int. J. of Comp. Sociol.* vol. 12, No. 2 (June), pp. 114–127.

Smithson, Alison and Peter (1967) *Urban Structuring*, London, Studio Vista (New York, Reinhold).

Social Council of Metropolitan Toronto (1966) "A preliminary study of the social implications of high density living conditions" (April 4) (mimeo).

Soen, Dan (1970) "Neighborly relations and ethnic problems in Israel," *Ekistics*, vol. 30, No. 177 (Aug.), pp. 133–138.

Soja, Edward W. (1971) *The Political Organization of Space*, Commission on College Geog, Resource Paper No. 8, Washington, D.C. Ass'n. Am. Geog.

Solzhenitsin, Alexander (1969) *Cancer Ward* (part 2), London, The Bodley Head.

Sommer, Robert (1968) "Hawthorn Dogma," *Psych. Bulletin*, vol. 70, No. 6, pp. 592–595.

Sonnenfeld, Joseph (1966) "Variable values in space and landscape: an inquiry into the nature of environmental necessity," *J. of Social Issues*, vol. 22, No. 4 (Oct.), pp. 71–82.

———— (1969) "Equivalence and distortion of the perceptual environment," *Environment and Behavior*, vol. 1, No. 1 (June), pp. 83–99.

———— (1972) "Geography, perception and the behavioral environment" in Paul W. English and Robert C. Mayfield (ed.) *Man, Space, and Environment*, New York, Oxford, pp. 244–250.

Sopher, David (1964) "Landscapes and seasons: man and nature in India," *Landscape*, vol. 13, No. 3 (Spring), pp. 14–19.

———— (1969) "Pilgrim circulation in Gujarat," *Ekistics*, vol. 27, no. 161 (April), pp. 251–260.

Southworth, Michael (1969) "The sonic environment of cities," *Environment and Behavior*, vol. 1, No. 1 (June), pp. 49–70.

Spencer, Paul (1971) "Towards a measure of social investment in communities," *Arch. Research and Teaching*, vol. 1, No. 3 (April), pp. 32–38.

Spoehr, Alexander (1956) "Cultural differences in the interpretation of natural resources" in W. L. Thomas Jr. (ed.) *Man's Role in Changing the Face of the Earth*, Chicago, University of Chicago Press, pp. 93–102.

Spradley, James P. (ed.) (1972) *Culture and Cognition: Rules, Maps and Plans*, San Francisco, Chandler.

Spreiregen, Paul D. (1965) *Urban Design: the Architecture of Towns and Cities*, New York, McGraw-Hill.

Sprott, W. J. H. (1958) *Human Groups*, Harmondsworth, Penguin.

Sprout, Harold and Margaret Sproud (1956) *Man–Milieu Relationship Hypotheses in the Context of International Politics*, Princeton University, Center of International Studies.

Stacey, G. (1969) "Cultural basis of perception," *Science Journal* (Dec.), pp. 48–52.

Stagner, Ross (1970) "Perceptions, aspirations, frustrations and satisfactions: an approach to urban indicators," *Annals, Am. Academy of Political and Social Science*, vol. 388 (March), pp. 59–68.

Stanislawski, Dan (1950) *The Anatomy of Eleven Towns in Michoacan,* Austin, University of Texas, Institute of Latin American Studies, No. X (Austin, Texas).

———— (1961) "The origin and spread of the grid-pattern town," in G. A. Theodorson (ed.), *Studies in Human Ecology*, Evanston, Ill., pp. 294–303.

Stanley, Jane (1972) *Migrant Housing* unpublished MSc (Arch.) Thesis, School of Architecture, University of Sydney.

Starr, Roger (1972) "The lesson of Forest Hills," *Commentary*, vol. 53, No. 6 (June).

Stea, David (1965) "Space, territory and human movement," *Landscape*, vol. 15, No. 1 (Autumn), pp. 13–16.

———— (1967) "The reasons for our moving," *Landscape*, vol. 17, pp. 27–28.

———— (1969(a)) "Environmental perception and cognition: toward a model for 'mental maps'," *Student Publication of the School of Design*, vol. 18, Raleigh, North Carolina State University, pp. 63–76.

———— (1969(b)) "The measurement of mental maps: an experimental model for studying conceptual spaces" in Kevin Cox and Reginald Golledge (ed.) *Behavioral Problems in Geography*, Evanston, Ill., Northwestern University, pp. 228–253.

———— (1969(c)) "On the metrics of conceptual spaces: distance and boundedness in psychological geography," paper presented at Congress of Sociedad Interamericana de Psicologia, Montevideo, Uruguay (April) (mimeo).

———— (1970) "Home range and use of space" in L. A. Pastalan and D. H. Carson (ed.), *Spatial Behavior of Older People*, Ann Arbor, University of Michigan.

Stea, David and J. M. Blaut (1970) "Notes towards a developmental theory of spatial learning" (mimeo).

———— (1971) "Some preliminary observations on spatial learning in Puerto Rican school children" (mimeo).

———— (1972) "Notes toward a developmental theory of spatial learning" in Cognitive Seminar following the *EDRA 3* Conference, UCLA (Jan.) (mimeo).

Stea, David and Daniel H. Carson (n.d.) "Navajo color categories and color discrimination: an experiment in the relation between language and perception" (mimeo).

Stea, David and Roger M. Downs (1970) "From the outside looking in at the inside looking out," *Environment and Behavior*, vol. 2, No. 1 (June), pp. 3–12.

Stea, David and S. Taphanel (n.d.), "Theory and experiment in the relation between environmental modeling ('toy play') and environmental cognition," UCLA, School of Architecture and Urban Planning, Discussion Paper No. 33 (mimeo).

Stea, David and D. Wood (1971) *A Cognitive Atlas: Explorations into the Psychological Geography of Four Mexican Cities*, Chicago, Environment Research Group, Place Perception Research Report No. 10.

Steinberg, S. (1969) Cartoon in the *New Yorker* (April 12), p. 43.

Steinitz, Carl (1968) "Meaning and congruence of urban form and activity," *AIP Journal*, vol. 34, No. 4 (July), pp. 233–248.

Stephens, William N. (1963) *The Family in Cross-Cultural Perspective*, New York, Holt, Rinehart and Winston.

Stewart, Norman R. (1965) "The mark of the pioneer," *Landscape*, vol. 15, No. 1 (Autumn), pp. 26–28.

Stilitz, I. B. (1969) *Behaviour in Circulation Areas*, University College Environmental Research Group, London (June).

Stokols, Daniel (1972) "A social-psychological theory of human crowding phenomena," *AIP Journal*, vol. 38, No. 2 (March), pp. 72–83.

Stone, G. P. (1954) "City shoppers and urban identification: observations on the social psychology of city life," *Am. J. Sociology*, vol. 60.

Strauss, Anselm (1961) *Images of the American City*, New York, Free Press.

Stringer, Peter (1971) "The role of spatial ability in a first year architecture course," *Arch. Research and Teaching*, vol. 2, No. 1 (Nov.).

Strodbeck, Fred L. and L. H. Hook (1961) "The social dimensions of a twelve man jury table," *Sociometry*, vol. 24, pp. 397–415.

Suchman, R. G. (1966) "Cultural differences in children's color and form preferences," *J. Soc. Psych.* vol. 70, pp. 3–10.

Sud, K. N. (1973) "The unwanted tenant," *Sunday World* (India), (Oct. 14).

Sun, The (1971) (Sydney, Australia), "Remember when you were a little boy" (Dec. 29).

Sunday Australian (1972) "Clontarf attracts the individualist to help keep its strictly private peninsular air" (Real Estate Section) (April 16).

Sunday Telegraph (1972(a)) (Sydney, Australia) "Where they hang out the big hang-ups" (Aug. 20).

————— (1972(b)) (Sydney, Australia) "Rare car numbers fetch up to $5000 (Sept. 3).

Sundstrom, Eric and Irwin Altman (1972) *Relationship between Dominance and Territorial Behavior* (field study in a youth rehabilitation setting) US Dept. of Justice, Law Enforcement Assistance Admin, Technical Report.

Sutcliffe, J. P. and B. D. Crabbe (1963) "Incidence and degrees of friendship in urban and rural areas," *J. of Social Forces*, vol. 42, No. 1 (Oct.), pp. 60—67.

Suttles, Gerald D. (1968) *The Social Order of the Slum* (Ethnicity and territory in the inner city), Chicago, University of Chicago Press.

————— (1972) *The Social Construction of Communities*, Chicago, University of Chicago Press.

Swan, James (1970) "Response to air pollution: a study of attitudes and coping strategies of high school students," *Environment and Behavior*, vol. 2, No. 2 (Sept.), pp. 127—152.

Swedner, Harald (1960) *Ecological Differentiation of Habits and Attitudes* (Lund studies in Sociology), Lund, CWK Glerup.

Sydney Morning Herald (1972) Issues of August 29, Oct. 13, Nov. 21.

Szalay, Lorand B. and Jean A. Bryson (1973) "Measurement of psychocultural distance: a comparison of American blacks and whites" in *J. of Personality and Soc. Psych.* vol. 26, No. 2, pp. 166—177.

Szalay, Lorand B. and Bela C. Maday (1973) "Verbal associations in the analysis of subjective culture," *Current Anthropology*, vol. 14, No. 1—2 (Feb.—April), pp. 33—50.

Taeuber, Karl E. (1965) "Residential segregation," *Scientific American*, vol. 213, No. 2 (Aug.).

Tagore, Rabindranath (1928) *City and Village*, Calcutta, Visva-Bharati, Bulletin No. 10 (Dec.).

Taut, Bruno (1958) *Houses and People of Japan*, Tokyo, Sanseido Co.

Taylor, Nicholas (1973) *The Village in the City*, London, John Teple Smith.

Temko, Alan (1966) "Reshaping super-city: the problem of Los Angeles," *Cry California*, vol. 1, No. 2 (Spring), pp. 4—10.

Thakudersai, S. G. (1972) "Sense of place in Greek anonymous architecture," *Ekistics*, vol. 34, No. 204 (Nov.), pp. 334—340.

Theodorson, George A. (ed.) (1961) *Studies in Human Ecology*, Evanston, Ill., Row Peterson.

Thibaut, J. and H. H. Kelley (1959) *The Social Psychology of Groups*, New York, Wiley.

Thiel, Philip (1961) "A sequence: experience notation for architectural and urban spaces," *Town Planning Review*, vol. 32, No. 2 (April), pp. 33—52.

————— (1970) "Notes on the description, scaling, notation and scoring of some perceptual and cognitive attributes of the physical environment" in H. M. Proshansky *et al.* (ed.) *Environmental Psychology*, New York, Holt, Reinehart and Winston, pp. 593—619.

Thomas, W. L. Jr. (ed.) (1956) *Man's Role in Changing the Face of the Earth*, Chicago, University of Chicago.

Thompson, Donald L. (1969) "New concept subjective distance" (Store impressions affect estimates of travel time) in P. J. Ambrose (ed.) *Analytical Human Geography*, London, Longmans, pp. 197—203.

Thompson, Kenneth (1969) "Insalubrious California: perception and reality," *Annals, Ass'n. Am. Geog.* vol. 59, No. 1 (March), pp. 50—64.

Thompson, W. d'Arcy (1942) *On Growth and Form*, Cambridge, University Press.

Thorne, Ross and David Canter (1970) "Attitudes to housing: a cross-cultural comparison," *Arch Research Foundation*, University of Sydney, Research Paper No. 1 (also in *Environment and Behavior*, vol. 4, No. 1 (March 1972) pp. 3—32).

Tibbett, Paul (1971) "A philosopher examines the organism-environment relation in modern ecology and ethology," *Man—Environment Systems* (May).

Tiger, Lionel (1969) *Men in Groups*, New York, Random House.

Tiger, Lionel and Robin Fox (1966) "The zoological perspective in social science," *Man*, vol. 1, No. 1.

————— (1971) *The Imperial Animal,* New York, Delta Books.

Tilly, Charles (1971) "Anthropology on the town" in L. S. Bourne (ed.) *Internal Structure of the City*, New York, Oxford University Press, pp. 40—46.

Time (1972(a)) Reviewing D. and H. Franke, *Safe Places* (March 6).

————— (1972(b)) (June 26).

————— (1972(c)) "La dacha vita" (July 10).

Timms, Duncan (1971) *The Urban Mosaic (Towards a Theory of Residential Differentiation)*, Cambridge, University Press.

Tolman, Edward C. (1948) "Cognitive maps in rats and men," *Psych. Review*, vol. 55, pp. 189—208.

Toon, John (1966) "Housing densities and standards," *Architectural Science Review*, vol. 9, No. 1 (March), pp. 6—15.

Townsend, Peter (1957) *The Family Life of Old People*, London, Routledge and Kegan Paul.

Treisman, Anne (1966) "Human attention" in B. M. Foss (ed.), *New Horizons in Psychology*, Harmondsworth, Penguin Books.

Trowbridge, C. C. (1913) "On fundamental methods of orientation and mental maps," *Science*, vol. 38, No. 990 (Dec. 19), pp. 888–897.

Troy, P. N. (1970) "The quality of the residential environment," Seminar Paper, Urban Research Unit, Australian National University, Canberra (Oct.) (mimeo).

Tuan, Yi-Fu (1968(a)) "Discrepancies between environmental attitude and behavior: examples from Europe and China," *Canadian Geographer*, vol. 12.

———— (1968(b)) "A preface to Chinese cities" in R. P. Beckinsale and I. M. Houston (ed.) *Urbanization and its Problems*, Oxford, Blackwell, pp. 218–253.

———— (1969) *China*, Chicago, Aldine.

———— (1971) *Man and Nature* Commission on College Geography, Resource Paper No. 10, Washington, D.C., Ass'n. of Am. Geog.

———— (1974) *Topophilia* (The study of environmental perception, attitudes and values), Englewood Cliffs, NJ, Prentice-Hall.

Tunnard, Christopher and Boris Pushkarev (1963) *Manmade America: Chaos or Control*, New Haven, Yale University Press.

Turner, John F. C. (1967) "Barriers and channels for housing development in modernizing countries," *AIP Journal*, vol. 33, No. 3 (May).

Turner, John F. C. and R. Fichter (ed.) (1972) *Freedom to Build* (Dweller control of the housing process), New York, Macmillan.

Tyler, Stephen A. (ed.) (1969) *Cognitive Anthropology*, New York, Holt, Rinehart, and Winston.

Ucko, Peter *et al.* (ed.) (1972) *Man, Settlement and Urbanism*, London, Duckworth.

UCLA, School of Architecture and Planning (1972) *Facing the Future* (Five alternatives for Mammoth Lake, Calif.) (Los Angeles).

Urban Core and Inner City (1967) Leiden, Brill.

Valentine, C. W. (1962) *The Experimental Psychology of Beauty*, London, Methuen.

Vance, J. E. Jr. (1971) "Focus on downtown" in L. S. Bourne (ed.), *Inner Structure of the City*, New York, Oxford University Press, pp. 112–120.

Van der Ryn, Sim and C. Alexander (1964) "Special study of urban amenities" (Progress report to Arthur D. Little) (Jan.) (mimeo).

Van der Ryn, Sim and W. R. Boie (1963) "Measurement and visual factors in the urban environment," Berkeley, College of Environmental Design, Design Research Laboratory (Jan.) (mimeo).

Van der Ryn, Sim and M. Silverstein (1967) *Dorms at Berkeley*, Berkeley, University of California, Center for Planning and Development Research.

Van Lawyck-Goodall, Jane and H. Van Lawyck-Goodall (1971) *Innocent Killers*, Boston, Houghton Mifflin.

Vatuk, Sylvia (1971) "Trends in North Indian urban kinship: the matrilateral asymmetry hypothesis," *SW. J. of Anthropology*, vol. 27, No. 3 (Autumn), pp. 287–307.

———— (1972) *Kinship and Urbanization* (White collar migrants in North India), Berkeley, University of California Press.

Venturi, R. (1966) *Complexity and Contradiction in Architecture*, New York, Museum of Modern Art.

———— *et al.* (1969) "Mass communication on the people freeway," *Perspecta, 12* (Yale Arch Journal), pp. 49–56.

———— *et al.* (1972) *Learning from Las Vegas*, Cambridge, MIT Press.

Vernon, M. D. (1955) "The functions of schemata in perceiving," *Psych. Review*, vol. 62, pp. 180–192.

Vernon, Raymond (1962) *The Myth and Realities of our Urban Problems*, Cambridge, MIT-Harvard Joint Center.

Vickery, R. L. Jr. (1972) *Anthropophysical Form*, Charlottesville, University of Virginia.

Vielle, A. (1970) "Relations with neighbours and relations in working class families in the Department de la Seine," in C. C. Harris (ed.) *Readings in Kinship in Urban Society*, Oxford, Pergamon Press, pp. 99–117.

Vigier, François (1965) "An experimental approach to urban design," *AIP Journal*, vol. 31, No. 1 (Feb.), pp. 21–31.

Vinson, A. and A. Robinson (1970) "Metropolitan clubs: spatial and social factors," *RAIA News* (June), pp. 63–66.

Violich, Francis (1962) "Evolution of the Spanish city," *AIP Journal*, vol. 28, No. 3 (Aug.), pp. 170–179.

Vogt, Evon Z. (1968) "Some aspects of Zanacantan settlement patterns and ceremonial organization" in K. C. Chang (ed.) *Settlement Archaeology*, Palo Alto, California National Press, pp. 154–173.

_____ (1970) "Lévi-Strauss among the Maya," *Man*, vol. 5, No. 3 (Sept.), pp. 379–392.

Vogt, Evon Z. and E. M. Albert (ed.) (1966) *People of Rimrock: a Study of Value in Five Cultures*, Cambridge, Mass., Harvard University.

von Gruenebaum, G. E. (1958) "The Moslem town," *Landscape*, vol. 1, No. 3 (Spring).

Von Hoffman, N. (1965) "L. A. man: noble savage in a plastic jungle," *S. F. Sunday Examiner and Chronicle* ("World," pp. 16–20), (Oct. 3).

von Uexküll, J. J. (1957) *Umwelt und Innerwelt der Tiere*, Berlin 1909 translated as "A stroll through the world of animals and men" in Claire H. Scholler (ed.) *Instinctive Behavior*, New York, International Universities Press.

Voorhees, Alan M. (1968) "Land use/transportation studies," *J. of the TPI*, vol. 54, No. 7 (July/August), pp. 331–337.

Wagner, Philip L. (1972(a)) "Cultural landscapes and regions: aspects of communication" in Paul W. English and Robert C. Mayfield (ed.) *Man, Space and Environment*, New York, Oxford, pp. 55–68.

_____ (1972(b)) *Environments and Peoples*, Englewood Cliffs, Prentice-Hall.

Walker, Edward L. (1970) "Complexity and preference in animals and men," *Annals of the NY Academy of Sciences*, vol. 169, Article 3 (June 23), pp. 619–653.

_____ (1972) "Psychological complexity and preference: a hedgehog theory of behavior," Paper given at NATO Symposium, Kersor, Denmark (June).

Wall Street Journal (1973) "A sense of identity – small ethnic groups enjoy revived interest in cultural heritages" (July 11).

Wallace, Anthony F. C. (1965) "Driving to work" in M. E. Spiro (ed.) *Context and Meaning in Cultural Anthropology*, New York, Free Press, pp. 277–292.

Ward, David (1971) "The emergence of central immigrant ghettoes in American cities" in L. S. Bourne (ed.) *Internal Structure of the City*, New York, Oxford, pp. 291–299.

Warr, Peter B. and C. Knapper (1968) *The Perception of People and Events*, London, Wiley.

Warrall, R. D. *et al.* (1969) "Toward a metric for evaluating urban highway construction on neighborhood structure," Am. Astronautical Society (15th annual)/Operations Research Society (35th national) Joint Meeting (June), (mimeo).

Waterman, T. T. (1920) *Yurok Geography*, Berkeley, University of California Press.

Watson, J. Wreford (1969) "The role of illusion in North American geography: a note on the geography of North American settlement," *Canadian Geographer*, vol. 13, No. 1, pp. 10–27.

Webber, Melvin M. "Culture, territoriality and the elastic mile" in H. Wentworth Eldredge (ed.) *Taming Megalopolis*, Garden City, NY, Anchor Books, vol. 1.

_____ (1963) "The urban place and the non-place urban realm" in M. M. Webber (ed.) *Explorations into Urban Structure*, Philadelphia, University of Pennsylvania Press.

Wecker, Stanley C. (1964) "Habitat selection," *Scientific American*, vol. 32, No. 211 (Oct.), pp. 109–116.

Weiss, Robert S. and Serge Boutourline (1962) *Fairs, Exhibits, Pavilions and their Audiences* (mimeo report).

Weiss, S. F., K. B. Kenney and P. C. Steffens (1966) "Consumer preferences in residential location: a preliminary investigation of the home purchase decision," Research Previews (University of North Carolina) (mimeo).

Werner, Heinz and Seymour Wapner (1952) "Toward a general theory of perception," *Psych. Review*, vol. 59, No. 4 (July), pp. 324–338.

Werthman, Carl (1968) *The Social Meaning of the Physical Environment*, Berkeley, University of California, Dept. of Sociology, PhD Dissertation (unpublished).

Weulersse, J. (1934) "Antioche-essai de géographie urbaine" *Bulletin d'Etudes Orientales* (Institut Français de Damas), vol. IV, pp. 27–79.

Wheatley, Paul (1963) "What the greatness of a city is said to be," *Pacific Viewpoint*, vol. 4, No. 2 (Sept.), pp. 163–188.

_____ (1969) *City as Symbol*, London, Lewis.

_____ (1971) *The Pivot of the Four Quarters*, Chicago, Aldine.

Wheeler, J. O. (1971) "Residential location by occupational status" in L. S. Bourne (ed.) *Internal Structure of the City*, New York, Oxford University Press, pp. 309–315.

Wheeler, Lawrence (1972) "Student reactions to campus planning: a regional comparison" in W. Mitchell (ed.) *EDRA 3*, Los Angeles, University of California Press, vol. 1, pp. 12-8-1–12-8-9.

White, L. E. (1970) "The outdoor play of children living in flats: an inquiry into the use of courtyards as playgrounds" in H. M. Proshansky *et al.* (ed.) *Environmental Psychology*, New York, Holt, Rinehart and Winston, pp. 370–382.

White, Morton and Lucia White (1962) *The Intellectual vs. the City*, Cambridge, Mass., Harvard University Press.

White, R. W. (1959) "Motivation reconsidered: the concept of competence," *Psych. Review*, vol. 66, pp. 313–324.

White, W. P. D. (1967) "Meaning of character in architectural space" (unpublished B. Arch Thesis) Raleigh, N. C., School of Design, N. C. State University (May).

Whorf, Benjamin Lee (1956) *Language, Thought and Reality* (Selected writings of Benjamin Lee Whorf, Edited by John B. Carrol), Cambridge, MIT Press.

———— (1972) "The relation of habitual thought and behavior to language" in P. Adams (ed.) *Language in Thinking*, Harmondsworth, Penguin, pp. 123–149.

Whyte, William H. Jr. (1956) *The Organization Man*, New York, Simon and Schuster.

———— (1968) *The Last Landscape*, Garden City, NY, Doubleday.

Wicker, Allan W. (1973) "Undermanning theory and research: implications for the study of psychological and behavioral effects of excess populations," *Repr Research in Social Psych.* vol. 4, No. 1 (Jan.), pp. 185–206.

Wiebenson, John (1969) "Planning and using resurrection city," *AIP Journal*, vol. 35, No. 6 (Nov.).

Wiggins, L. L. (1973) "Use of statistical methods to measure people's subjective responses to urban spaces," *DMG-DRS Journal*, vol. 7, No. 1 (Jan.–March), pp. 1–10.

Wilkinson, Robert (1969) "Some factors influencing the effect of environmental stressors upon performance," *Psych. Bulletin*, vol. 72, No. 4.

Willems, Edwin P. (1972) "Place and motivation: independence and complexity in patient behavior" in W. Mitchell (ed.) *EDRA 3*, Los Angeles, University of California, vol. 1, pp. 4-3-1–4-3-8.

Willems, Edwin P. and Harold L. Raush (ed.) (1969) *Naturalistic Viewpoints in Psychological Research*, New York, Holt, Rinehart and Winston.

Williams, Anthony V. and Wilbur Zelinski (1971) "On some patterns in international tourist flows," *Ekistics*, vol. 31, No. 184 (March), pp. 205–212.

Willis, Margaret (1969) "Sociological aspects of urban structure," *Ekistics*, vol. 28, No. 166 (Sept.), pp. 185–190.

Willis, Richard H. (1968) "Ethnic and national images: people vs. nations," *Public Opinion Quarterly*, vol. 32, No. 2 (Summer).

Wilmott, Peter (1962) "Housing density and town design in a new town," *Town Planning Review*, vol. 33 (July), pp. 115–127.

———— (1963) *The Evolution of a Community*, London, Routledge and Kegan Paul.

———— (1964) "Housing in Cumbernauld: Some Residents' Opinions," *TPI Journal*, vol. 50, No. 5 (May), pp. 195–200.

———— (1967) "Social research and new communities," *AIP Journal*, vol. 33, No. 6 (Nov.), pp. 387–398.

Wilmott, Peter and Edmund Cooney (1963) "Community planning and sociological research: a problem of collaboration," *AIP Journal*, vol. 29, No. 2 (May), pp. 123–126.

Wilson, James Q. (1967) "A guide to Reagan country," *Commentary* (May).

Wilson, Robert L. (1962) "Liveability of the city: attitudes and urban development," in F. Stuart Chapin Jr. and Shirley F. Weiss (ed.) *Urban Growth Dynamics*, New York, Wiley, pp. 359–399.

Wilson, Roger (1963) "Difficult housing estates," *Human Relations*, vol. 16, No. 1 (Feb.), pp. 3–43.

Winkel, Gary, R. Malek and P. Thiel (1969) "A study of human response to selected roadside environments" in H. Sanoff and S. Cohn (ed.) *EDRA 1*, pp. 224–240.

Wirth, Louis (1938) "Urbanism as a way of life," *Am. J. of Sociology*, vol. 44, pp. 1–24.

Wittkower, Rudolf (1962) *Architectural Principles in the Age of Humanism*, London, Tiranti.

Wober, M. (1966) "Sensotypes," *J. of Soc. Psych.* vol. 70, pp. 181–189.

Wohlwill, Joachim F. "The concept of sensory overload" in J. Archea and C. Eastman (ed.) *EDRA 2*, pp. 340–344.

———— (1971) "Behavioral response and adaptation to environmental stimulation" in A. Damon (ed.) *Physiological Anthropology*, Cambridge, Havard University Press.

Wohlwill, Joachim F. and Imre Kohn (1973) "The environment as experienced by the migrant: an adaptation-level view" *Repr. Research in Social Psych.* vol. 4, No. 1 (Jan.), pp. 135–164.

Wolfe, Alvin W. (1970) "On structural comparison of networks," *The Canadian Review of Sociol. and Anthrop.*, vol. 7, No. 4 (Nov.).

Wolffe, A. (1972) Letter about Gloucester Township, Camden County, NJ in *Design and Environment*, vol. 3, No. 1 (Spring), p. 6.

Wolforth, John (1971) "The journey to work" in L. S. Bourne (ed.) *Internal Structure of the City*, New York, Oxford University Press, pp. 240–247.

Wolpert, Julian (1964) "The decision-making process in spatial context," *Annals, Ass'n. Am. Geog.* vol. 54, pp. 537–558.

———— (1966) "Migrations an adjustment to environmental stress," *J. of Social Issues*, vol. 22, No. 4 (Oct.), pp. 92–102.

Wong, S. K. Luke (1971) "The Aplichau squatter area: a case study" in D. J. Dwyer (ed.) *Asian Urbanization* (A Hong Kong casebook) Hong Kong University Press, pp. 89–110.

Wood, Dennis (1969) "The image of San Cristobal," *Monandnock*, vol. 43, pp. 29–45.

Wood, L. J. (1970) "Perception studies in geography," *Trans. Inst. British Geog.* No. 50 (July), pp. 129–142.

World Federation of Mental Health (1957) *Mental Health Aspects of Urbanization* (UN discussion) (March).

Worskett, Roy (1969) *The Character of Towns*, London, Arch Press.

Wright, H. F. (1969) *Children's Behavior in Communities Differing in Size*, Lawrence, University of Kansas.

———— (1970) "Children in smalltown and largetown USA," Lawrence, Kansas, Dept. of Psychology, University of Kansas.

Wülf, F. (1938) "Tendencies in figural variation" in W. D. Ellis (ed.) *A Source-book of Gestalt Psychology*, London, Routledge and Kegan Paul, pp. 136–148.

Wynne-Edwards, V. C. (1962) *Animal Dispersion in Relation to Social Behavior*, Edinburgh, Oliver & Boyd.

Yaker, H. M. *et al.* (ed.) (1971) *The Future of Time*, Garden City, NY, Doubleday.

Yancey, William L. (1971) "Architecture, interaction and social control" (The case of a large-scale public housing project), *Environment and Behavior*, vol. 3, No. 1 (March), pp. 3–21.

Young, M. and P. Wilmott (1962) *Family and Kinship in East London*, Harmondsworth, Penguin.

———— (1973) *The Symmetrical Family*, New York, Pantheon.

Zborowski, M. and E. Herzog (1955) *Life is with People* (The Jewish littletown of Eastern Europe), New York, International Universities Press.

Zehner, Robert B. (1970) "Satisfaction with neighborhoods: the effects of social compatibility, residential density and site planning," unpublished PhD Dissertation, University of Michigan.

Zeisel, John (1969) "Symbolic meaning of space and the physical dimensions of social relations," Paper, Am. Sociological Ass'n Annual Meeting (Sept. 1) (mimeo).

Zubrzycki, Jerzy (1960) *Immigrants in Australia*, Melbourne, University Press.

Index of Names

Index of Places

Subject Index

Urban and Regional Planning Series

Other Titles in the Series

Urban and Regional Planning Series